Within the Plantation Household

Black
and White
Women
of the
Old South

Within the
Plantation
Household

Elizabeth Fox-Genovese

The University of North Carolina Press

Chapel Hill & London

Printed in the United
States of America

92 91 90 89

5 4

Library of Congress Cataloging-in-Publication Data

Fox-Genovese, Elizabeth, 1941–
    Within the plantation household: Black and white
women of the Old South / Elizabeth Fox-Genovese.
        p. cm.—(Gender & American culture)
    Bibliography: p.
    Includes index.
    ISBN 0-8078-1808-9 (alk. paper)
    ISBN 0-8078-4232-X (pbk.: alk. paper)
    1. Women—Southern States—History. 2. Plantation
life—Southern States—History. 3. Slavery—Southern
States—History. I. Title. II. Series.
HQ1438.A13F69   1988   88-40139
305.4'0975—dc19   CIP

FOR NAN

Contents

Illustrations

Acknowledgments

While preparing to write this book, I published several essays in which I explored dimensions of the experience of southern women. I remain grateful to David Ammerman and Lewis Bateman for their confidence in the possibilities suggested by these essays and for having encouraged me to send them to Iris Tillman Hill, who has proved the most supportive of editors, the most acute of readers, and, more important, a valued friend. Iris sent the manuscript to Linda Kerber and Nell Painter, both of whom gave me insightful readings and invited me to publish it in their series, Gender and American Culture. Pam Upton has my heartfelt thanks for the care, patience, and sensitivity with which she copyedited the manuscript.

It is a pleasure to acknowledge my debts to those who have supported and assisted me through the years of research. A fellowship from the American Council of Learned Societies and the Ford Foundation supported a semester's leave in 1984. In 1984–85 I held a fellowship from the National Humanities Center that permitted a luxurious year at the center and in the rich collections of the Southern Historical Collection at the University of North Carolina, Chapel Hill, and the Perkins Library at Duke University. In 1987 I received a generous research grant from the National Endowment for the Humanities in support of my project with Eugene Genovese, *The Mind of the Master Class*, and that grant also assisted me in completing this book. The State University of New York at Binghamton provided financial assistance during my leaves and administered the first six months of the NEH grant, a task that was then assumed by Emory University.

My work has depended heavily on the knowledge, interest, and extraordinary helpfulness of innumerable librarians and archivists. It is an honor and a pleasure to acknowledge the very special debt that I owe to Carolyn Wallace and Richard Shrader of the Southern Historical Collection, who cheerfully put up with my requests and questions for the better part of a year and who have continued generously to offer assistance. Allen Tuttle and his staff at the National Humanities Center tirelessly sought and found materials at libraries in the Re-

search Triangle and around the country. Innumerable others throughout the South have given proof of the proverbial southern hospitality
by sharing both their knowledge and their resources, in person or
through correspondence: Mattie Russell and Ellen Gartrell at the Perkins Library; Alan Stokes at the South Caroliniana Library; David
Moltke-Hansen at the South Carolina Historical Society; Mimi Jones
at the Alabama Department of Archives and History; and the many
others at the North Carolina Department of Cultural Resources, the
Louisiana State University Archives, the Baptist Collection at Wake
Forest University, the Archives of Salem College, the Archives of Auburn University, the Hoole Special Collections at the University of
Alabama, the Mississippi Department of Archives and History, and the
University Libraries at Austin. Since my move to Atlanta, I have especially benefited from the generosity of our local community. The staff
of the Emory University Library, including Emory Special Collections,
has facilitated my work at every turn, but so have those of the Georgia
Department of Archives and History, the Atlanta Historical Society,
and the Archives of the University of Georgia. I owe a very special
debt to the Emory interlibrary loan personnel, who have handled
countless requests with wonderful patience and good humor.

Throughout the years, I have also been spoiled by the comradely
assistance of friends and students who, while conducting their own
research, have kept their eyes open for items that would interest me. I
am particularly beholden to Louis Ferleger, Stephanie McCurry, Robert Paquette, and Craig Simpson. During the early years of this project, I enjoyed wonderful assistance from Douglas Ambrose, Beth Ma-
lasky, and Jennifer Murphy. Especially during the past year, when the
demands of establishing a new Women's Studies Program at Emory
University have been considerable, nothing would have been possible without the devoted efforts of an extraordinary group of research
assistants. Doug Ambrose, Russell Andalcio, and John Rodrigue have
proved indefatigable in tracking down last-minute citations. John
Merriman has given the ultimate compliment and support that a student can offer by developing a generous personal interest in the work
that he has seen grow through successive drafts and by doggedly tracking down precise citations and new documents from Texas to Alabama
to Georgia to London. His heart-warming interest in my chapter on
households can be explained by his own research in southern political
economy and slave society; his yet more touching commitment to
Sarah Gayle can be explained only by his selfless dedication to the
project as a whole. Rosemary Hynes has taken time from her own

work on the American Revolution in Georgia to live intimately with antebellum women, black and white, checking and double-checking all references to them; to learn Microsoft Word so that she could enter last-minute additions to the notes; to read draft upon draft; and in general to keep me on course during the final harried months. Beyond indispensable assistance, she has offered an extraordinary companionship and support, all the more valued for having withstood the test of seeing me at my most exposed.

While this book gradually took shape, it benefited directly and indirectly from the probing criticism of countless friends and colleagues. The prologue was first delivered as a lecture at the Newcomb Women's Center of Tulane University, then during Women's History Month at Brandeis University, and finally as a public lecture for the Humanities Council at Auburn University. Stephanie McCurry delivered a version of chapter 1 for me to the Social History Conference at Irvine University. An earlier version of chapter 2 appeared in *Review* as "Antebellum Households: A New Perspective on Familiar Questions." An earlier version of chapter 6 was presented at the conference to honor the fortieth anniversary of Herbert Aptheker's *American Negro Slave Revolts* and appeared, as "Strategies and Forms of Resistance: Focus on Slave Women," in *In Resistance: Studies in African, Caribbean, and Afro-American History*, edited by Gary Okihiro (Amherst, Mass., 1986). A preliminary version of chapter 4 was delivered at the Smith/Smithsonian Conference on Gender Conventions in February 1984. A version of chapter 5 was delivered at the annual meeting of the Organization of American Historians in April 1987 and benefited from the thoughtful criticisms of Carol Bleser, John Boles, Armstead Robinson, and Carolyn Wallace. A version of chapter 7 was delivered at the annual meeting of the Social Science History Association in October 1987, and benefited from the skeptical but friendly comments of Catherine Clinton.

There are few pleasures that compare with learning from one's students. I am especially grateful to the graduate students in women's and southern history at SUNY-Binghamton, who for years endured my developing views of southern women and who have continued to challenge and support my work while pursuing their own. Doug Ambrose, Betsy Colwill, Stephanie McCurry, and Deborah Symonds have now suffered my idiosyncrasies and pushed my thinking for years and have, to my pride and joy, become friends and colleagues. Nancy Barr, Virginia Gould, and Barbara McCaskill of Emory similarly are stretching me as they embark upon their own research.

During the press of the past few months, I have been especially mindful of the generosity of colleagues who have taken time from their own projects to read and criticize mine. No, I do not intend to hold them accountable for my errors, but I am happy to record my deep gratitude for their interest and suggestions. John Hope Franklin deserves my very special thanks for having found time to read the manuscript during a particularly awkward moment in his always busy life, and for offering frank and constructive criticism. Stanley Engerman, Louis Ferleger, Barbara Fields, Steven Hahn, Robert Paquette, Jonathan Prude, James Roark, and Harold Woodman have all read the entire manuscript with the care, learning, and acumen for which I value and respect them. And most of them have read at least parts more than once, pressing me to clarify my thinking on one or another point. Allan Kulikoff has read the entire manuscript twice with a rare combination of enthusiastic support and attention to every detail that I had no right to expect but feel myself fortunate to have received. They have, above all, made me feel welcome among the company of rural and southern historians. Carol Bleser, Drew Faust, Linda Kerber, and Nell Painter, with their extraordinary and diverse qualifications, have challenged me on my readings of southern women and my view of women's history. With friends such as these, I can reasonably claim that we are developing a scholarly sisterhood that encourages respect for various points of view within a common enterprise. And, with all historians of southern women, I owe an inestimable debt to the pioneering work of Anne Firor Scott, notwithstanding serious differences in interpretation and conclusion.

Fabienne McPhail has made it all possible and, in defiance of all reasonable expectations, remained cheerful throughout. She has loyally protected my time to write, duplicated countless copies, kept track of me and them, and never lost her sense of humor. Her interest, dedication, and, above all, enthusiasm have done much to keep me going and have provided a welcome confirmation that scholarship can address questions that have implications for women's sense of themselves.

Living so long with these southern women has constantly reminded me of the importance of families and confirmed my sense of how blessed I am in my own. My mother, Elizabeth Fox, and my sister, Rebecca Fox, proved, as usual, the best and most appreciative of readers. My father, Edward Fox, and my brother-in-law, William Scott Green, proved, as usual, the best of intellectual companions—even if southern women lay somewhat off their beaten tracks. My brother,

Edward Fox, responded with calm and good cheer to panicky phone calls about crashing computers or the fine points of word processing programs at all hours of day or night. Cleopatra, Georgia, and Carolina rolled in mountains of computer paper and did their best to keep off the keys. Josef endured, pondered the weightier questions, accompanied me on research trips, and looked forward to the day when it would all be over.

Gene there is no thanking. No, to paraphrase him, he does not deserve to be coauthor, although this book is an integral part of our joint work on the slaveholders and builds upon his and our previous work. No, he did not darn my socks or type my manuscript, although he did take over the cooking. But without what he did do, I should never have been able to complete this book this summer, and whatever book I eventually completed would have been sorely impoverished. He read every draft, twice and thrice over, catching me on inconsistencies and infelicities, honing my prose, pressing me to say what I wanted to say. He endured and, more important, enjoyed. But the real debts lie elsewhere. He came to appreciate my readings of his beloved southern ladies, even when they did not always conform to his own. He shared his own incomparable knowledge of southern history, never being sure of precisely the uses to which I would put it. Most important, he paved the way. Writing a book that is at once so deeply a part of our work together and so much my own, I have come to appreciate more than ever the force of his vision of southern history and his commitment to encouraging the independent work of others.

This book is dedicated to my friend, Nancy Wilson. One of the many joys of a friendship that has stood the test of time and distance has been the shared sense of work as central to who each of us is—of each other's work as something that matters and that grows as we grow. My account of Sarah Gayle originated as a letter to Nan, an attempt to explain what moved me about the sources I was reading. It seemed only fitting to dedicate a book that has so much to do with women's sense of themselves in relation to their communities to its first imagined reader.

WEST VIRGINIA

VIRGINIA

Orange Co.
Cecil Co.

Amelia Co.

Richmond

● Broadway

KENTUCKY

Bertie Co. ● Halifax Co.

Rockingham Co.

Franklin Co.

Greensboro ●
Burlington
Raleigh

ashville ●
Murfreesboro ●
NORTH CAROLINA

ENNESSEE

Camden ●
Wilmington

SOUTH CAROLINA

● Florence

Abbeville ●
● Columbia

Atlanta
Calhoun Co.

Athens
Augusta
Redcliffe

Tuscaloosa
Colleton
District
Charleston

Greene Co.
Macon ●
GEORGIA
Savannah

Montgomery
● Liberty Co.

ALABAMA
● St. Simon's Island

Conecuh
Glynn Co. ●

ile ●

FLORIDA

Within the Plantation Household

Prologue

Sarah Haynsworth married John Gayle when she was still a girl—by her own lights a wild one—not quite sixteen. Her journal and letters offer glimpses of what the twenty-eight-year-old man must have seen in her. At the time that he proposed, the young Miss Sarah did not even suspect his intentions. She thought he had been courting another. They were riding near her parents' farm, with her mother following closely, when suddenly he spoke to her of poetry. She cantered to his side and pushed back her sunbonnet. Immediately, "the change in his countenance struck me dumb, almost senseless—he was without a shade of color . . . spoke in a quick earnest and unsteady voice." Reminding her that she had known him all her life, he asked her to place her happiness in his keeping. Struck dumb once again, she felt that on pain of death she could not have spoken. He pushed back the bonnet that had fallen over her face. She did not know "what he read there" or how she replied, "but his features were quivering & beaming and said he was the happiest of men." She looked back at her mother. But when Mr. Gayle took his leave, she "gazed after him," scarcely daring to ask "is *that my plighted husband?*" Knowing him to be the "darling of my parents," she "never had seen a fault in him," had called him brother in childhood, friend in youth, and now whispered "in the depths of my bosom—*lover*."[1]

Sarah Gayle was not the most polished, cultured, or pious of slaveholding women, nor the most accomplished of diarists. But her many special qualities included an immediacy of voice, a charm of style, and a poignancy of narrative. Her self-representation differs from those of most of her peers by an extraordinary, if gentle and muted, perspective on herself. Those qualities set her apart as a personality even as the contours of her life and beliefs linked her to the other women of her class.

In 1828, when Sarah Gayle was twenty-four, she recorded in her journal—and for its especially intended readers, her daughters—her vision of herself as the child she had been and the young wife and mother she had become. She imagined herself at age twelve, sitting upon the bank of the Alabama River, catching a glimpse of a young girl, "not more than *fourteen*," who was gliding by in a bark. On first impression, she fancied the girl to be in danger, on second, she admired her skill in navigating and "the novelty of her appearance." For across the boat, the young girl had a fowling piece and a fishing line, and in its bottom she had scattered wild flowers.

> The young voyager had dropped her bonnet upon her shoulders and a profusion of black glossy hair sometimes fell over her face obscuring a pair of dark laughing eyes. . . . Exercise had given a fine glow to her somewhat sun-burnt countenance, and an arch smile lurk'd around her mouth, with an expression frank, artless, and one would say bold, had her appearance not evidently told that the customs of cultivated life had not yet taught her to veil the feelings of nature.[2]

The boat of Sarah Gayle's fantasy drifted away and left her hoping that the young girl might find a life as gentle and quiet as the waters over which she floated. In the same passage, she wrote that years later she found herself in the same spot and was startled to have her recollection of the previous encounter interrupted by the reappearance of the bark. This time, "the sounds of childish glee now came upon the air, mix'd with accents I knew to be maternal." The bark now contained a woman "with a blooming girl at her feet—one still younger sleeping in the nurse's arms, and a boy . . . dipping his hand in the current." The woman's "cheek was pale and thin—her hair braided and simply confined around her head—her eye was dark and in the place of its joyous wildness a calm tenderness, a touching indescribable something shone out." In a moment of mutual recognition, the girl-turned-woman breathed to Sarah Gayle: "My cargo is now a treasure." And Sarah Gayle noted for her future readers: "Daughters of my heart that girl was thy parent, those precious children, thee my Sarah & Amelia."

Sarah Gayle's girlhood, like her motherhood and her daughters' girlhood, weaves through her unfolding picture of herself. She embraced the threads of memory that brought her back to the places, relations, and pleasures of her youth, even if she believed that it "would not answer, to whisper to the more refined of this day, what composed my pleasures." But her daughters, her dears, may find it "amusing to know what made your mother's spring time happy, while so many aids are call'd in to render yours so."[3]

A contemporary biographer described Sarah Gayle, in the rhetoric appropriate to the day, as "very beautiful," with features of "classic regularity." Of "noble bearing" and "fascinating manners," she won "universal admiration." A "highly cultured" and "graceful writer," she had written some lovely poems and "left a Journal of charming pictures of her home life." Her picture of herself in the journal broke through the stereotypes of those formulaic phrases. She depicted her adult self with pitiless realism, even as she cherished memories of herself as "a wild and happy being, whose dreams of the world were awakened by the reading of novels and poetry." Her minimal schooling never disciplined that early, untutored reading: "I was left to select books for myself and no wonder I lost myself in delicious mazes, romances spread around me. My taste has never been reclaimed—it is impossible to apply myself now to useful reading."[4]

The adult life that Sarah Gayle depicted in her journal consisted primarily in the normal round of childbearing and childrearing, household responsibilities, supervision of slaves, worries about money, visits to friends, concerns with religion, and fears of death. As she wrote to John in July 1832, he would find in her letter:

> all news of a publick nature, and as for that which belongs peculiarly to me, you know when there is the usual health, that one day is but the double of the other—a chance visit, the going to Church, shopping, an odd volume read, an odd page written—and when the long list of seams and hems and gatherings added, my life is given, at least the mode of spending it.[5]

Traces of the impetuous girl lingered in the woman who importunately concluded a letter to her husband: "oysters! oysters! oysters!" But her intermittent journal for the late 1820s and early 1830s shows her as maturing. Near her thirtieth birthday she noted that she who had married as a child now looked older than her husband. Her youthful looks had survived her marriage by only a few years: "A woman, no matter how much younger she looks, at her marriage, soon fades except in rare instances." When Sarah Gayle was only twenty-four, she had been startled to note dramatic changes in her sister-in-law, Ann. "Her complexion has quite lost its whiteness and polish—her teeth are much gone—her beautiful black hair, which used to curl over her shoulders when she threw it down, is now thin, and can no longer be call'd an ornament." The marks that time had etched on Ann offered Sarah Gayle a mirror on herself: The "gay lovely, sparkling creature whom I can almost *see*—she tells me I would scarcely know." The enchanting girl Sarah Gayle knew herself to have been had given way to one who is "large, roughened almost toothless, *smoking* and *chewing*!—the scolding manager of the family of four children."[6]

Her teeth especially worried her. By the time she was twenty-four, the dentist had already filled the front ones and was proposing to extract the rear ones. "This loss of my teeth has been the severest mortification to which my vanity has ever been subjected." She grieved at their loss because she shrank from "the idea of appearing to so much disadvantage in the eyes of that *one* for whose dear sake I would still, if possible, preserve some trace of youth." What she could so plainly recognize, her husband could not fail to see. She wrote to him that she had been "silly enough" to go to the dentist, but his efforts only revealed their decay "to an appalling extent." She predicted the impending ruin of her physical charms: "Good Heavens, what a sight I shall be in a little time! I *will* not write sentimentally, or I would tell you, *charge you, beseech you*, to let the affection, my pride and joy, and all upon earth endure even after this wreck of all that belonged to youth."[7]

During the years covered by her journals, 1827 to 1835, Sarah Gayle divided her time between Greensboro and Tuscaloosa in Alabama, and at the end of that period, she was preparing to move to Mobile with her husband. During these years John Gayle practiced law, served as a judge, and embarked on the political career that would earn him a seat in the state legislature, then the governorship, and, eventually, a seat in the U.S. House of Representatives. John Gayle's career typified those of other transplanted South Carolinians who were playing such an important role in Alabama, as did his wife's.[8]

The Gayles cast their lot with Alabama when it was still a territory. Sarah Gayle was never among those who bemoaned the material aspects of westward migration and "frontier" life. Indeed, her cherished recollections included the westward journey in 1810 and a stay at Fort Stoddert, Alabama, where she lived with her parents. If she valued a new bonnet or a new carpet or books for her children as highly as any other woman, she could also recall with delight the pleasures of riding astride, camping out along the way, and being pampered by soldiers; she could even recall without undue alarm the shadowy presence of Indians, although she knew that her father "slept with arms under his head, and any stir amongst the horses at night roused all and put them on their guard." Her picture of herself on this trip conforms to the fantasy of the girl on the bark depicted for her daughters. She recollected herself as having, by turn, run "with the negroes" and perched herself on a packhorse, as having felt her greatest glee "when mounted on one to myself, allowed to follow my humor in keeping to the path (road there was none in many places) or wandering off, at short distances, amongst the undisturbed shades of trees that encroached on the trace we travelled." The soldiers, who entertained her by placing her on the wheel of a canon and encouraging her to "stand the report without shrinking," delighted her no less. She was, she recalls, "frankly lively—fearless they endeavored to make me, and partly succeeded for the time." Nor did she especially protest against living conditions on the frontier, as did Juliana Margaret Conner when describing her visit to Tennessee in 1827. But then, where the young Sarah Gayle found coffee in a tin cup and food cooked over an open fire delicious, Juliana Conner found even settled conditions in Mecklenburg County, North Carolina, rather primitive by her lowcountry standards.[9]

Sarah Gayle's parents, like John Gayle's, had migrated from Sumter County in the South Carolina upcountry and, although they ranked as bona fide slaveholders, they hardly ranked among the "Chivalry," as the lowcountry elite liked to style itself. Sarah and John Gayle's lives resembled those of many other second- or indeed first-generation transplanted South Carolinians. Both came from slaveholding families and identified completely with the slaveholding class but, unlike their parents, did not live as planters in the strict sense. During the early years of their marriage, they owned perhaps twenty to thirty slaves, most inherited from Sarah Gayle's parents, but financial constraints forced them to sell some, and by the early 1830s they probably owned no more than ten or fifteen. Throughout her journal, as John's political and legal activities forced them to reside in various towns, Sarah Gayle returned time and again to her dream of buying a "farm" that would give them a sense of permanence—would permit them to settle the slaves they retained and to repurchase at least some of those they had sold.[10]

Sarah Gayle spent most of her married life in one of those ubiquitous villages with resident populations of little more than one hundred that constituted the focus of the lives of so many slaveholders, including planters. Greensboro, Alabama, in Greene County, had been founded in 1816. When, in 1826, John Gayle purchased a house there for his wife and their two small children, it was already a thriving community that boasted a hotel, a tailor's shop, five stores, and a law office and had benefited from mail service since 1818. Sarah Gayle variously attended the churches of the Methodists, the Baptists, and most frequently the Presbyterians. She also enjoyed the company of female friends and neighbors, notably her husband's sister and sister-in-law, who lived in the village and with whom she shared her life of children, errands, sewing, and churchgoing.[11]

Village life, even in a rising town like Greensboro, retained a rural cast. Indeed, for decades Greensboro retained a reputation as turbulent and disreputable. At each of the houses in which she lived there, Sarah Gayle had a garden. But if she found it less turbulent than neighboring Erie, not to mention Tuscaloosa, she nonetheless deplored its class of undesirables, with whom even her own brother-in-law, Levein, was wont to associate in periods of idleness. And she bitterly protested having to purchase food, rather than grow their own, although she also noted that they were cultivating a field of corn about two miles distant. She regretted not wanting to urge a Mrs. Matheson, who was visiting in town because of her poor health, to come to her for a protracted stay: "I find it so awkward and difficult to procure comforts for the table. . . . It would be vastly convenient to have a little farm, where we could obtain necessaries more readily, and cheaper than we do now."[12]

Village life gave rise to its special pettinesses. Sarah Gayle frequently complained of real or imagined slights from villagers, notably one of the storekeepers whose establishment she was loath even to enter. Just before her husband's election for his first term as governor, she complained that he had been designated the *"would be Governor,"* she the *"novel reader."* Yet the fellowship of the village and county could, on occasion, evoke her deepest feelings. So long as she lived, she vowed never to forget "the *first Monday in August*" 1831, never to forget "the confidence, friendship and enthusiasm" with which Greene County had borne her husband's name to the ballot box.[13]

The quality of Sarah Gayle's life rested upon the labor of servants. The time she spent reading and playing with her children, or visiting with her friends, depended upon the slaves' performing all of her basic housework and helping her with childcare. When she mentioned household tasks in her journal, she referred to "having" them done or to supervising their being done. At first glance, her words frequently suggest that she was caring for the children herself, but close attention reveals that care to have been amply seconded by servants. When, during church service, the child with her cried violently and was unable to sit still, Sarah Gayle did not pick up the child herself; she followed the nurse from the church. And she wrote a friend from Tuscaloosa of her pleasure in moving from the second to the first floor so that her children, Mary and Haynsworth, could more easily go outside to play and "Rose can draw them in the fine little basket carriage their pah bought for them."[4]

In March 1833, when Sarah Gayle moved to Tuscaloosa, the state capital, to join her husband, she embarked upon the strange new life of boarding houses, which, she duly noted, offered her company and maximum relief from household responsibilities. Since the Gayles brought their own furniture to their rented rooms, boarding house life also provided some familiarity. And Sarah Gayle enjoyed many aspects of real town life: the wide selection of churches and high quality of the preaching; her friendship with Mr. and Mrs. Alva Woods; the freedom from household responsibilities; and some of the many social gatherings to which she, as the governor's wife, was invited. Together with other ladies, she also attended the sessions at the state house. On a previous visit to Tuscaloosa, she had attended the legislature to hear "what is call'd the Lady's bill discussed."[5]

She was less pleased with the potentially unsavory influences on her son, Matt, of the students at the new university, which Mr. Woods, a leading Baptist, had come to direct, and with the visibly deleterious influences of town blacks on her own servants. Whatever her complaints about Greensboro, its dangers paled beside those of Tuscaloosa. She appears to have experienced Tuscaloosa, which numbered no more than a thousand inhabitants, as the public sphere incarnate. Its muddy streets, although probably no muddier than those of Greensboro, symbolized the mire in which any of her charges might run amuck. She never dwelt obsessively on the dangers of town life, never emphasized pastoral harmony in contrast to urban corruption. She knew too well that even smaller towns harbored social dangers. Tuscaloosa may have been larger and more turbulent than Greensboro, but it was a nonstarter among the candidates for urban jungle. From Sarah Gayle's perspective, Tuscaloosa, like Greensboro, consisted primarily of a network of slaveholding families—albeit primarily political and professional, rather than planting, slaveholding families. But in Tuscaloosa, unlike Greensboro, that natural elite had to contend with more disorderly folks, black and white, who did not fall under their immediate, personal control. And Sarah Gayle took seriously the threat that such beings posed to her world.[16]

Sarah Gayle may have felt especially vulnerable to the lurking dangers of her life because she so deeply regretted her lack of immediate family and kin. An only child, she felt that her parents' death when she had already become an adult had left her an orphan. Perhaps especially because of her sense of having been cut loose in the world, she invested her deepest yearnings for love, unquestioning acceptance, and connection in her husband. It would be hard to imagine a wife who loved her husband more or, not to mince judgments, loved her husband better. She brought to her courtship, and developed in her marriage, respect, companionship, intimacy, shared values, humor, and all the elements of that deep love which stands the test of time, proximity, and separation. She also recognized the difficulties of holding a husband's interest and affection. In 1828 she noted with unaccustomed anxiety that, for the first time in their married life, "Mr. G. stayed from me 'till long past midnight." The circumstance was too novel to permit complacency, or even sleep. She did not blame him, could not be so disingenuous or such a fool "as not to know unless home is lit up by cheerfulness and good humor, it will lose its attraction to the kindest and best—that he has always been *that* to me my inmost heart freely acknowledges." But she could not refrain from contrasting her need of him with his engagement in a larger world. She had no one but him to talk to, and "little, unmeaning talk too, so senseless to a man whose thoughts have been accustomed to follow higher matters." How could she wonder that "he desires to relieve himself from what must be uninteresting?" How could she wonder that he had no interest in what she viewed as women's chatter. Nor was the boredom engendered by her domestic concerns all. She recognized full well "my own perplexing quarulesness—my want of command over my temper—the carelessness with which I betray whatever gives me either uneasiness or displeasure." Add to her temper that she allowed her naturally plain face to "express the utmost sourness, and whatever else is disagreeable dare I murmur that this forbidding countenance should be left for something more pleasing?"[17]

These fears invariably resurfaced as the anniversary of their wedding approached, especially when John Gayle was away from home for the day itself. In December 1827, she wrote of it to him, with a prescience that their lives would confirm:

Do not let the 12th of this month pass by, without giving a smile and a sigh to "auld lang syne." It was our *wedding day*, and they are talismanic words, to wake up all that is precious and hallowed in memory. Dear, dear period—if I had been asked to single out from the whole earth, a being exempt from care, and in possession of perfect happiness, I would have laid my hand on my own bounding heart, and said, "she is here." And am I not yet? There is but one only drawback, a single shadow, the path before me, and that is that it *must end*,—that it may be in a few years, perhaps months, the *survivor* will ask the question, "have I *ever* been happy?"[18]

Sarah Gayle's knowledge of her small world lent an edge to her nagging anxieties about her ability to hold the love and attention of her husband. Here and there throughout her diary, she noted the woes that beset other married women. Mrs. Buchanan's daughter, "the idol of her parents," seemed to have an ideal marriage. "Yet has this unfortunate wife a grief preying on her heart, from which no charm of this life can win her." In pity and benevolence, she welcomed an unfortunate woman into her home only to see her guest, with "an awful want of woman's virtue," alienate from her "the affection of the man upon whose bosom her head has rested for perhaps seventeen years." Other men of her acquaintance had proved themselves brutal as well as faithless husbands. One man drove his wife to hide in terror in a swamp. Drink caused serious problems for women, but so did profligate sexuality. Of one man, Sarah Gayle reported: "His children and his son's children are their slaves, and probably, nay I think I heard, that his *child* and his *grand-child* have one mother?" Of such men in general, she wrote with horror and disgust: "And those fathers whose beastly passions hurry to the bed of the slave do they feel no compunction when they see their blood sold, basely bartered like their horses? This sin is the leprosy of the earth nothing save the blood of the cross cleanses from it." If for no other reason, she loved the Christian man more for being free of it—if, indeed, all southern Christian men were.[19]

In marriage, as in the world, the relations between men and women remained unequal. For the woman, in "her circumscribed sphere, fewer objects present themselves, by which her feelings may be momentarily won away, from the channel in which they naturally flow. She is scarcely placed in any situation that her weakness does not require his presence as her safeguard, or her tenderness yearn for it, to complete some pleasure, that is but half enjoyed, if he be not there to participate in it."[20]

Sarah Gayle apparently transferred to her love for John her feelings for her beloved family of origin that had so nearly evaporated. The diary suggests that she especially associated her husband with her revered mother, whose loss haunted her adulthood. In times of trouble or unspeakable fear, she could always turn to her mother. "Before my marriage she was friend, sister, parent all in one." She was also model and teacher and everything that Sarah Gayle aspired to be for her own daughters: "I never think of woman's character as it should be but, my mother my dear mother, rises up in all her excellence, all her native purity. It did not need the precepts of men to make her all she should be her heart was the handy work 'of the Creator, and he planted in it the seeds of good.'" And she was quick to note similar devotion to a departed mother among her friends. Mrs. Woods's "soft black eyes filled with tears" as she ridiculed her own fondness for a particular chair in which Sarah Gayle had been blissfully ensconced, and she whispered "that the secret of her love consisted in her having so *often seen* her *mother seated in* it."[21]

In the absence of parents and siblings, she longed for some member of her family to fill the gap she "always felt to exist, caused by the absence of such as are called 'our brethren'—such as would be bound to love and cherish us, because we were of one household." She tried to keep up with her uncle, William Haynsworth, who, like her father's mother, had remained in South Carolina, and she perked up at any hint that he was thinking of moving to Alabama. She also worried and confessed to "foolish apprehensions that he may possibly not suit Mr. Gayle." She could not bear to think that her husband "should not entertain sentiments at once of esteem and affection and even admiration for my kin folks." She knew her apprehensions to be misplaced: "I do not pretend to reason with myself about anything so silly, but it is so." She cherished the family names that reminded her of her own kin nearly as much as she cherished the husband who had become the repository of so many of her memories and the custodian of her happiness. Right after the birth of their third (and second surviving) son, she noted that he had not as yet been named. She earnestly wished to call him John, "but I believe it will not be *that*." Her husband told her "to name him for my father, and it would be difficult for me to give a reason for hesitating, when my very heart would bestow it." More than two months later, she recorded that the babe had finally "received the name of Richard Haynsworth, the last being the one by which he is called, as it is prettiest and more peculiarly my own—my blessing on it, for I never hear it with indifference."[22]

Memories and memorials anchored Sarah Gayle's sense of herself as the member of interlocking families. In 1833 she celebrated her proposed removal to Tuscaloosa to join her husband. "My pleasure is great that we will at last be settled, be at *home*, for I cannot call that place home, which I anticipate leaving every year." She longed for a house in which each room was peopled with memories. Her desire for settling included the desire to collect the graves of her loved ones in one place. She had found her mother's grave leveled and she agonized, unable to bear that it "should be effaced from the earth, the plough, and the foot of the brute and the slave pressing on the bosom, once the seat of all that was good and noble, 'tho that bosom be dust." She determined to rebuild it with her own hands, if no one else would. That memory required the most substantial memorial possible. More, she sought to gather together the graves, "the sacred dust," of both parents and the two infants she had lost. Did she but know "where my final home would be," she would bring them all together in that place.[23]

Sarah Gayle was not alone among the women of her class in investing kin and the signs of family with deep emotional significance. She did, however, place more than the common explicit emphasis on the importance of kinship to her sense of her own identity, in the double sense of who she was—who we can see her to have been—and whom she perceived herself to be. Those feelings intertwined with her relations to her husband and her own children; they constituted at once the wellspring and the prolongation of her mature identity as wife and mother. Her journals and letters forcefully suggest that, as an adult, she settled into who she had been or was intended to be. Her relation to her own womanhood conveys an aura of realization—of fulfilling a destiny more than of creating one. Time and again, her progress through life brought her back to her origins. She believed that no one ever would or could know her better than those who had known her as a child. No spot, she wrote, "possesses more attractions than another, except it be the *grave yard*, where some I loved lie, already forgotten, except it be indeed, by me." Especially in moments of melancholy, she longed only to be reunited with those who had gone. The class of affections for a father or a mother—"in fact anyone with whom I may claim a tie of blood"— "are like isolated creeping plants—ever throwing out tendrils with nothing to cling to."[24] She also believed that

John Gayle was her best friend, her greatest comfort, and the anchor not merely for her life but for her self. Somewhere between her consciousness of her own distinct origins and of her love for him lay her sense of her own considerable independence and force of character.

The dentist, perhaps especially because of the limitations of his craft, loomed large in Sarah Gayle's story. He confirmed her awareness of her rapid aging, and, in his futile attempts to arrest her tooth decay, he inflicted a pain that surpassed bearing. In July 1835, when she was thirty-one and with Mr. Gayle away from home, she braved an operation on her teeth. Had she foreseen its horror, she would never have consented. "The torment of filling the tooth is unspeakable." Yet she was glad that Mr. Gayle was "from hence,—my little courage always leaves me when he is hear, for I really feel as if his presence could lessen the pain, or do away the necessity of enduring it." His absence permitted her to muster her own courage and, with one brief lapse, she came through with stoic endurance. The lapse, as she described it, was poignant and revealing:

> I only was *once* weak enough to shed tears, and that was, when he had filed some time, and I suddenly relaxed the state of tension in which I had held myself, and leaned back on the chair, while the perspiration stood thickly on limb and face. He laid his hand over my eyes and forehead, and pressed it there for a minute, to still the throbbing. Then that hand made me think of Mr. Gayle, and I gave way, just one moment, to the delicious weakness.

Normally, she preferred to have John Gayle at her side during her moments of pain and danger, even at the risk of giving way. She especially dreaded the unavoidable circumstances that took him from home near the time of her confinements. In 1829, toward the end of a pregnancy, she contemplated the possibility that he would be away when she delivered, as frequently happened with other women's husbands, no matter how sensitive and loving. Politicians, judges, ministers, doctors, and planters with several holdings and elaborate business connections had vast spaces, often connected by poor roads, to cover. Their wives had to understand. The Sarah Gayles did. She also understood that it was doubtless trying for a man "to witness the sufferings of his wife then, but I own I am too selfish not to covet the comfort and support of his presence during the trial." For none could tell that "it may not be the termination of all others, and I would not leave the world divided from him whom I have loved above all in it."[25]

Beyond the immediate context of family, friends figured prominently in Sarah Gayle's sense of her self in the world. She recorded her
comings and goings from her friends' houses, their sharing of skills,
resources, and amusements. "Friend" and "neighbor" rank as the highest accolades she could bestow on the women of her acquaintance. In
her village, from which the men were frequently absent on politics
or business, women relied heavily on each others' skills and companionship, even sharing their milk with a friend's child. "Dear Mrs.
Draughan," for example, "was the patient nurse of me and my feeble
boy, when illness had rendered me unable to nurse him myself—that
delicate as she was, dampness nor indisposition (when slight) nor
family cares could prevent her coming to share her milk with my
helpless one." On many occasions she had reason to appreciate her
friends' devotion as nurses. In 1828, John Gayle was returning from
hearing a case of great importance at the supreme court in Tuscaloosa
when Sarah Gayle delivered and lost an infant. An "uncontrollable
yearning for the consolation my husband could have bestowed" had
prevented her from seeking the help of friends. Yet they had lovingly
seen her through, with Catherine Hunter at the head of the list. "Had
my own mother stood by me I could not have call'd her with greater
confidence." And she never felt safer than when her dying infant lay on
Mrs. Hunter's knees or on Mrs. Hall's. "To the latter I am more
indebted than I can ever repay, or make her understand but I believe in
ministering to the sufferer she did what has no northern ice about it."
And there were many others. Whenever "I opened my eyes some frank
and friendly countenance met them," and her hand could not fall on
the bed but that it "was rubb'd or kindly held by some silent but
assiduous nurse." The full measure of what Sarah Gayle's Greensboro
friends meant to her came home when John Gayle wrote to tell her of
the new law that required her residence, as the governor's wife, in
Tuscaloosa. She wrote of having known that as "a Community these
were benevolent, friendly, industrious, very hospitable, the best of
nurses in sickness, as I have fully proved," and that she gave her love to
them "as soon as I knew I had been received amongst them,—stranger
as I was,—in all faith and friendship." Now that she had to say farewell, her memories and her friends' worth pressed almost unbearably
upon her.[26]

Girlhood friends who had moved away also remained important.
Sarah Gayle dotted her journal with references to her "*friend* of
friends," Swep. "Others I esteem, approve, may love, but there is for

her deep in the bottom of my heart that to which no other may lay claim." That friendship was founded on their having been "children together," and to it she imputed "much of the happiness of my life." She saw Swep, like herself, as having been a gay, wild creature whom "the formalities of the world had never fettered." In 1827, Swep had been married for two years to a Dr. Houstis of Catawba, Alabama. By 1830, Sarah Gayle and Swep had had some kind of falling-out. Yet Sarah Gayle continued to write of Swep's possible visits, to hope for a true reconciliation, and to reassure herself that Swep's impossible be-havior and persisting stubbornness accounted for the quarrel. She named at least two of her daughters, Maria and Amelia Ross, after especially valued friends. Her oldest, Sarah, had been named for her, as she had been named for her own mother, and her mother before her for hers.[27]

Memories of friends peopled Sarah Gayle's journal and her imagina-tion. Distant and departed friends, like distant and departed kin, jos-tled the living in her pages and constituted the human ties through which she defined her identity. Fiction, on her own accounting, played a similar role, creating a haze of romance through which to view imperfect human relations, physical decay, and frontier conditions. Yet the journal never suggests that she turned to the characters of fiction for companionship or models. On balance, her world provided her with both. Rather, the fiction to which she was addicted seems to have offered her a rhetoric, a language from which to make sense of her world. Her wide reading ranged from Walter Scott to Wilberforce on religion, to Mrs. Hamilton on education, to Mrs. Montagu's letters, to Washington Irving's *Sketchbook* (which she especially liked), to what she herself considered little more than trash. Her own inability to become immersed in ponderous and uplifting treatises bothered her, but never enough to wean her from the other type of writing. At most she wanted reading that was "not so light as romance, nor very grave, or which requires too much thought."[28] Yet for all her self-depreca-tion, she expected literature to embody decent values. The theater appalled her, as it did the increasingly militant evangelical preachers. After seeing *Adeline or Seduction*, she vowed never to go again. She knew that her reasons were understood only by herself and were not shared by others, but she could not abandon them. "I wish I could see the world as other people do. They tell me I cannot reform it, which I know, and if I do not like its ways, I ought to let them pass and not think of them."[29]

The rhetoric of Sarah Gayle's journal, like many of her attitudes, derived from her extensive reading. Musing on the location of her father's grave, she bemoaned the 130-mile distance at which it lay and the roughness of the terrain that surrounded it. The spot was "so lonely, rugged and neglected, that I cannot visit, because it fills me with feelings of entire gloom—a scene to which nature gave no interest, and art never improved."[30] Her vocabulary and formulations inadvertently betrayed her tentative interest in writing for publication, even as they betrayed her immersion in a broadly disseminated Romantic discourse. Throughout her journal, she interspersed her own poems. At the end of the volume, she grouped a number of them and noted that she had made a copy of some lines and given them to Mrs. McGuire, telling her to tell her husband that "if he had a corner in his paper, for which he could find nothing better, he was welcome to them, for it." But after recording her initiative, she thought better of it and determined to send for them that very night. "It seems like arrogance in one like me to offer anything of my own, for publication."[31] It was one thing to write, quite another to claim the public and unfeminine mantle of authorship.

Yet her journal, for all its frequently rushed and breathless quality, reveals Sarah Gayle's natural talent and a concern for craft, however hesitant she was to dignify her jottings by an official title. Picking it up again after many days' neglect, she noted that it "offers itself to me now in my solitude like some unassuming quiet but amusing friend who steals the tediousness from Time, as he flies by, but who is laid aside when superseded by others better loved." Mr. Gayle, as she herself referred to him, had just left upon an eleven-week circuit. So the pages that she sometimes dignified "with the title of *journal*" provided a link to her absent husband and, perhaps, beyond him to her departed mother—to those whose love grounded her sense of self. And the human network embodied in those pages also extended to the next generation. For if she wrote to reaffirm her bonds to those on whom she depended for emotional sustenance, and for the pleasure and satisfaction of craft, she also wrote for the daughters from whom death would one day snatch her. Yet even during her life, her journal probably had readers, in particular John Gayle, for in December 1830 she noted:

I have laid aside my Journal, if, indeed these unconnected sheets deserve the name. Mr. Gayle pressed me to let him take them to

Tuscaloosa to have them bound; but they do not deserve that honor, and, besides, I would hesitate to have them laid open to the curiosity of a book-binder, for my heart is revealed in these loose sheets.[32]

The author who sketched Sarah Gayle's life for the *Encyclopedia of Alabama Biography* also knew of the journal's existence. Something more than a personal confession, something less than an autobiography or novel, the pages embodied the self-representation of a woman who trusted her heart to the scrutiny of the immediate circle that constituted her identity, and whose sense of self included the ability to represent personal experience in a crafted idiom.

Preoccupation with her performance as a mother also troubled Sarah Gayle. She made much, but not too much, of her love for her children and her determination to care for them as her mother had cared for her. She also dared to hope that they might provide the support to her in her old age that she provided them in their childhood. She enjoyed them. And she was capable of stepping back and seeing them as others might see them. One evening, when her eldest son, Matt, came in from hunting, she imagined to herself how the right painter could capture the rumpled hair and ruddy cheek. She also recognized Matt's interest in hunting as the sign of his entrance into the male sphere and of the demise of her own empire. She addressed her diary to her daughters. Her feelings for her male and female children shed a special light on her sense of herself. On one terrifying occasion, a horse ran away with Matt, and she could do nothing to control it. Matt called to her as the horse dashed past,

> and if he had been kill'd happiness would not have visited my heart again. I love my daughters very dearly do I love them, and all that is amiable & good, intelligent & lovely would I have them, but all I possess of ambition, pride & the hope that steps over the threshold of home all such is centered in him, and if Death had crushed them, I should have mourned as Rachel.[33]

Religion figured centrally in Sarah Gayle's sense of herself. She lived intimately with the fear of death—her own and that of those she held most dear. Sickness, epidemics, childbirth, the dentist, all evoked the "Angel of Death." Violence perpetrated by slaves against whites, or by whites against each other, reinforced the terror. The news of Nat Turner's revolt, followed by rumors of slave risings in other states, alarmed her: she dreaded the winter "without protection, or any friend to keep me company." Like most slaveholders, she rarely noticed, or at least rarely commented on, white violence against blacks. Sarah Gayle was not given to panic. The fear of death flickers through her journal, never reaching fever pitch, never paralyzing her, but always latent and ready to flare up. Religion provided the most promising antidote to those fears, the most satisfying consolation against loss. But for Sarah Gayle, the struggle for faith remained precisely a struggle. If she understood God as the guarantor of the human spirit, and if she accepted the role of the church in mediating between God and his people, she never fully committed herself to a single church or theology. Withal, her fiercest hopes concerned her future reunion with all her family in heaven: musing on the position of her father's grave between those of his son and his grandson, she wrote of her hope that "the trio have formed a band of *angel spirits*, gather'd into the household above." And when the present weighed heavily upon her, she allowed that it might not be "well for me to know now, that I was to have my husband, my children & my parents with me thro' an eternity of felicity" lest, "Mighty God, I should be tempted to rush into thy presence unbidden, to draw to me those who I love, and madly seek all I have lost—all to which I was idolator."[34]

Sarah Gayle proved as uncommonly intelligent and self-critical in her reflections on religion as in other matters. Musing on John Gayle's prospects of success on a trip to acquire Indian lands, she assured herself that his having been unlucky in early speculations did not prove that he would be in subsequent ones: "Fortune will smile, at last, on honest perseverance." Immediately she caught herself, asking why she had used the words "*Fortune, good luck*, etc., instead of Providence. I never do without reproaching myself for it afterwards. The habit is Heathenish." Normally she did not have to remind herself of God's power and mercy, but she did frequently remind herself that faith must run deep and cannot be reduced to mere lip service. As she told John Gayle when they were discussing which church to attend, she cared nothing about one denomination or another, but "I would give worlds to possess that faith which triumphed over the fear of death, and looked with hope and confidence beyond the grave." Mr. Gayle agreed that such faith was to be desired.[35]

The related themes of motherhood and death recurred frequently in Sarah Gayle's thoughts on religion. Occasionally she felt especially burdened by her own ill health and attendant melancholy, not to mention the woes of the world at large, and was tempted to view "the residue of life" as "worthless." A glance at her children restored her: "I humbly pray to be spared, that I may train them as well as I am able in the way they should go." The week before this entry she had been overcome by the spectacle of thirteen children's being Christened at once. "I felt as if I should suffocate, absolutely choke with my feelings." No ceremony was better calculated to "touch a woman's, a mother's heart." Never had her two daughters, who stood on either side of her, been dearer. "The solemn responsibilities of my station as a parent, pressed heavily on me, and I felt as if I would have given all things else for that faith which led their fathers and mothers to the sanctuary with their flocks."[36]

That faith eluded Sarah Gayle. As she watched two of her friends take the sacrament, "in its sacred awfulness," her feelings choked her and she wept freely: "I wished to see the fitness of the ceremony, to feel its propriety, and more than all, I wanted the pride and vanity, rioting at my heart to be destroyed, and humility and faith and hope to be implanted in their place." Even when most overwhelmed by the prospect of death she admitted to feeling "none of the humility, the adoration of a Christian." She wished she did, but did not: "Bewildering questions of the necessity of atonement perplex me. If I could satisfy myself at all, why man should have fallen at the first, then the atonement would have been a splendid instance of love and gracious compassion, calling for gratitude from every creature." She would not follow these ideas, for they led to "what seems little better than impiety."[37]

The ubiquitous threat of death also intensified her determination to secure the strongest possible influence over her children, to shape their characters decisively. For, if she should die, they would lack those "*maternal* connexions, who, in general, guard and comfort the orphan with double kindness." She never doubted that their material welfare would be attended to, but she worried about the spiritual, worried that they would be subject to "that false kindness which spares the body, but ruins the soul." They must grow up honest, upright, decent. For any of her children to become, in any way, double-dealers would be "more bitter than the pangs of dissolution." She hoped for the best, but, above all, she would "try, while I am with them, to acquire an influence over which the grave will have no power."[38]

Whatever her hesitations, Sarah Gayle viewed religion as an essential frame of reference for human affairs. When John Gayle took the oath

John Gayle as governor of Alabama, ca. 1835.
Courtesy of Alabama Department of Archives and History

Gayle House, Greensboro, Alabama, built ca. 1828. Home of Sarah Ann
Haynsworth Gayle and John Gayle in the late 1820s.
Courtesy of Historic American Buildings Survey, Library of Congress

as governor of Alabama, she regretted that he swore only on the constitution and not on the Bible. In complex ways, religion guaranteed
and properly ordered for Sarah Gayle the relations in her world that
most concerned her. The affairs of this world and the memories of
those who had died constituted the heart and pulse of her consciousness and purpose, but she never doubted that their justification would
have to be cast in reference to a religious discourse. It was a matter of
legitimation.

Sarah Gayle also never doubted that firm principles governed all
social relations. She had, for example, no illusions about the appropriate roles of men and women. She frequently coped with complex
household activities, including the management of occasionally difficult servants, but even during John Gayle's protracted absences she
never envisioned herself as the official head of the household. Writ-

Letter from Sarah Gayle to John Gayle, 19 May 1831.
Courtesy of Hoole Special Collections, University of Alabama

ing to him of her attempts to improve the appearance of their plot of land with "presents" of shrubs and flowers, she concluded: "Oh! come home, for mercy's sake, *what can a woman do without her husband?*" Her other social attitudes also bore the marks of her class and region. Generous and warm, she nonetheless mercilessly dismissed those whom her social position did not oblige her to know. The more she heard of Mrs.——, the more did she congratulate herself "on having no intercourse with her, since she came amongst us. There can be no doubt of her possessing intelligence, but I think evidently without principle." And, more ruthlessly, she wrote of another newcomer to her neighborhood: "Nothing renders a personal acquaintance necessary between us."[39]

Sarah Gayle's attitudes and beliefs were firmly rooted in a southern society that provided the texture of her life. She thought, spoke, and wrote in the common vocabulary of a discourse that had its roots in Western bourgeois culture as a whole. But her profound immersion in the specific social and physical topography of her own region—her "country" as she called it—informed all her words and influenced all her beliefs. Living in Alabama in the 1820s and 1830s, Sarah Gayle took slavery for granted, for it grounded her life and pervaded her sense of herself in the world. It concretely influenced her views of excellence for her children, achievement for her husband, and order for her society. Conversely, her most—and least—admirable characteristics permeated her relations with her slaves. She experienced slavery as simultaneously a set of human relations and a social system. It brought out her best and her worst and her everyday in-between.

Sarah Gayle did not find the supervision of slaves easy, especially when John was away from home. On one occasion she, like so many other slaveholding women, gave vent to her deepest impatience with that unending responsibility. "I despise myself," she wrote, "for suffering my temper to rise at the provocations offered by the servants. I would be willing to spend the rest of my life at the north, where I never should see the face of another negro." But, she added, acknowledging her identification with her own society, "perhaps it is my cross—as such I will try to bear it as well as I can, & that is bad enough." She had her share of "lazy" slaves who seized every opportunity to shirk their tasks. Mary Ann frequently evoked a flare of temper, as had to be expected or at least endured. Blake invariably got into squabbles when he had been drinking. "Ellick is really unendurable, too lazy to live." And then there was illness, real or feigned. Hetty looked as if she would never get well, had been of no service for three or four months. "I believe my servants are going to craze me." Such were the trials of human property, which especially taxed the skill and patience of a young mistress.[40]

Sarah Gayle shouldered her own responsibilities for what she perceived as her servants' ungovernability: "Indulgence has ruined them —they are idle yet full of complaints easy to take offense at the slightest admonition which they frequently merit and then attachment has weakened in proportion as their discipline has been slackened, so that I doubt if any of them would not believe a change of owners could benefit them." Her parents, she admitted, did better than she in this respect. They were "uniform and strict in their management of the servants." Nor did they allow her "to exercise tyranny or injustice of any sort towards them and on the other side the most implicit submission was exacted towards me." Should she use improper language, the servants would go to her mother for redress. Should she command what was proper and reasonable, "they dared not hesitate." Now all was different. She no longer had confidence that her orders were being obeyed and even obedience "is accompanied by murmuring, sour looks & often surly language, that almost put me beside myself."[41]

When Sarah Gayle's sister-in-law, Ann, was having recurring trouble with "that most perplexing of servants, Sarah," Sarah Gayle thought that Ann should exchange the slave for another. She sympathized deeply with Ann's tribulations, for she herself had "long had a severe trial with old Hampton, whose insolence and contrary disposition, I have for several years borne."[42]

Hampton featured a special order of insubordination. Sarah Gayle, in desperation, threatened to sell him, but Hampton treated the threat with contempt:

> I never saw such a negro in all my life before—he did not even pretend to regard a command of mine, and treated me, and what I said, with the utmost contempt. He has often laughed in my face and told me that I was the only mistress he ever failed to please, on my saying he should try another soon, he said he could not be worsted, and was willing to go.

But what, beyond Sarah Gayle's account, do we know of Hampton? Her account permits only speculation. Was he a manly man who was standing up to an imperious, insensitive, and morally illegitimate authority? Was he a punk who would have cowered before John Gayle, but was quick to take advantage of a young wife who had not learned to use the powers at her command? Would he have, as many male slaves did, resisted the master as stubbornly as he resisted his young mistress? Or one of the many human possibilities in between? Hampton did not record his side of the story, and we cannot tell enough from hers. We know only that he was married to Hetty; that like another slave, Mike, whom Sarah Gayle cherished, he had belonged to her father; and that, like Sarah Gayle herself, he longed to see the entire family settled on a farm.[43]

Mistresses, even the kindest, commonly resorted to the whip to maintain order among people who were always supposed to be on call; among people who inevitably disappointed expectations; among people whose constant presence not merely as servants but as individuals with wills and passions of their own provided constant irritation along with constant, if indifferent, service. Did Sarah Gayle go to her whip or encourage her husband to do it for her? She does not tell us, but, given her high spirits and impatience with perceived impertinence, we would do well to assume that she, like most others, had her bad moments. We can further assume that whatever authority she embodied in her class and race, her gender left her at a disadvantage. Mistresses did not necessarily take second place to masters in their violence toward slaves, but both they and the slaves knew that the master embodied the ultimate authority in the household. We shall never know exactly what transpired between Sarah Gayle and Hampton, but we have good evidence that the personal chemistry between mistress and man was bad, and some evidence that the consequent daily relations were trying.[44]

Beyond doubt, the intimacy of life with what she saw as lazy, indifferent, and above all, insubordinate slaves weighed heavily on Sarah Gayle. And yet they too were part of the household, for as David Brown, a northerner, observed, the word "household" was used in the South "in the Scripture sense, including slaves, but not *hirelings*." In 1831 she wrote to John that if they were to stay in Greensboro, they "must have negro houses. I think I could get along with them far better, if I were not obliged to see them every time I look out." Then she could effectively forbid offenders access to the kitchen. Sarah Gayle complained endlessly about recalcitrant servants and her problems in governing them, but she formed deep attachments to particular servants. Throughout the late twenties and early thirties, she wrote in her journal and to her husband of her longing to repurchase Mike and his family, whom the Gayles had apparently sold after Sarah Gayle's father's death. Especially during the early thirties, when their plans to relocate were particularly uncertain, she associated buying Mike and his family with her own desire for a permanent residence. Her only purpose was that of "buying back Mike and his family, and settling them with the few others we have on a farm." She had no pecuniary goal. "No ideas enter my head of cotton, or of corn, or of money—but simply the longing to say once more my father's old servants, are *mine* again." Never before had she pushed John Gayle in this way, nor would she now, "but that it does seem to me I *cannot* be happy unless it is done." Above all, she longed for Mr. Gayle to inform her that he had bought a rich piece of river land and "that on the way back he called at Mr. Hobson's and for a reasonable price, bought Mike and his family, who were with the other few to be sent to our home, there to live in comfort, and in the same time, in industry, engaged in making their own support, and assisting him to pay for them."[45]

By her account, Mike shared her desire to be reunited. She reported that he came to see her "on the old subject," and that he would have spoken to Mr. Gayle as well did he not fear offending him. Mike had heard rumors that they might be moving and begged that they not think "'of leaving me, for I should be a lost man,' and the poor fellow really was choked into silence." Only gradually did Sarah Gayle come to understand that John had opposed her in this matter not out of failure to respect her feelings, but from a lack of cash. When it finally dawned on her that he had been carrying much heavier expenses than she suspected, she was abashed. But her regrets about her own insensitivity to her husband's worries merely encouraged her to develop new strategies to meet her goal. She found no insurmountable difficulty for, as she had mentioned in an earlier letter, Mike and his family could contribute to their own upkeep and purchase: "It is strange if the negroes cannot pay for themselves, hiring at the rates they do in Mobile, and Mike a pretty good common carpenter, his wife so brisk, and three or four of his children able to bring in their share. Henry is about 12, Albert between 10 and 11, and Ellen more than 8—the size that I want for a nurse now that I have lost poor Rose."[46]

Sarah Gayle's attachment to Mike and his family sprang from her love for her own parents. Bereft of close relations, she turned to the slaves who had known her parents and had known her as a child. To repurchase them was to repossess some piece of that past she mourned, was to satisfy her own deepest psychological needs. During the years in which she did not own Mike, she knew where he was, who did own him, and the names and ages of his children as they came along. She would not likely have been better informed about distant relatives or friends. Yet it never crossed her mind that this family should be free. Her unquestioning acceptance of slavery emerged from her unquestioning assumption that even though Mike and his family could provide for their own support and even contribute to their purchase price they should remain slaves. She saw nothing contradictory between her deep affection for—and emotional dependence on—people whom she proposed to hold in perpetual slavery and her acknowledgment of their ability to take care of themselves as well as her.

Rose, the servant whose death left Sarah Gayle without a nurse, had also come from her father's family. "She was raised at my feet, and was my child's nurse, a most kind and excellent nurse, and the play fellow of all my children." Rose died in April 1834 of lockjaw, which she had contracted from a large splinter that ran up into her foot and remained a week. Sarah Gayle reproached herself for not having noticed Rose's limping sooner, but she had had no reason to expect serious effects from a wound of that sort. Suddenly Rose began to manifest spasms and other symptoms of lockjaw. She lay ill for three weeks, "during all which time, I thank God, I did not leave her day or night." Nor would Rose suffer her to leave, but called for her whenever she left the door. They "placed [her] in a neat, and every way comfortable room—nothing was spared which might add to her comfort." In her dreams, Rose always addressed Sarah's son, Haynsworth, and when awake attended to his voice. In the last motion Sarah Gayle recollected Rose's making, she stretched "out her arms to him, and when I placed my hands on them, she drew me to her, as if she had taken the child." Sarah Gayle closed Rose's eyes and "in tears and fervor prayed that God would cause us to meet in happiness in another world." At that moment, she knew "that color made no difference, but that her life would have been as precious, if I could have saved it, as if she had been white as snow." The entire family followed Rose to her grave. Thereafter, the children's countenances would sadden "when something occurs to remind them of poor Rose, and my own heart will swell as Haynsworth sings snatches of the songs his nurse taught him."[47]

Sarah Gayle's text shows how closely Rose's life was intertwined with that of her white family but offers no clue to Rose's own kin or attitudes. Possibly Rose, like her mistress, had intermingled black and white families beyond easy disentangling. If Sarah Gayle grasped the equality of souls before God, she accepted the inequality of ranks in this world. Within households, personal ties crossed class lines. Slave-holders and slaves participated in a shared imaginative universe that could shimmer with mutual affection or, as in the case of Hampton, shatter in mutual antagonism.

For her warmth, compassion, humor, intelligence, and love for her family, black and white, Sarah Gayle ranks among the most attractive women diarists of the early nineteenth century. But her finest qualities cannot be divorced from her willing complicity in a social system that permitted them to flourish through the enslavement of others—cannot be divorced from the iniquities that she accepted and perpetuated. Her experience and perceptions as a woman depended upon the social system in which she lived. Her ineffable charm cannot responsibly be severed from its social moorings.

Whatever Mike and Rose really thought of Sarah Gayle, John Gayle valued her as the treasure of his life. Responding to one of her letters, he admitted failing to put his true feelings into words. She had, he thought, some idea of the "ecstasy which apparently swells the bosom of the converted christian. I felt exactly the 'joy unspeakable and full of glory.'" Her letter brought him a happiness that drowned his concern for debts, property, and all such trash. "My wife is the great engrossing object of my affections. In comfort she is indispensable to my peace, and a consciousness of her love is essential to my existence."[48]

Sarah Gayle had been preparing for death at least since she began to bear children. During the early 1830s, when her health was poor and her spirits occasionally low, she returned to the prospect. In 1831, she actually sat down and drew up instructions for John Gayle to follow in the event of her death. He must, she insisted, do as she proposed: "No *stepmother* for my poor girls—she may be an Angel for you, but very different for them." In February 1835, Sarah Gayle safely gave birth to her last child, Ann Maria. Yet she had been right to concern herself with the fate of her girls should something befall her. The dentist proved her nemesis, Rose her precursor. Sarah Gayle, like Rose, contracted tetanus. Servant and mistress, equal in vulnerability before the deadly disease, were unequal only in the means of contracting it. Sarah Gayle would not have picked up a splinter in the yard; she would not have gone unshod. Rose would not have had complications from dental work; she would not have gone to the dentist—a doctor who occasionally pulled a tooth, maybe, but a town dentist, not likely.[49]

When Sarah Gayle fell ill, John Gayle was away in Indian Territory, trying to restore their fortunes through speculation in Indian lands. As she had so often feared at the time of her confinements, he did not hear of her illness in time to see her alive. That absence was hard to bear, although the absence of the man whose love and care permitted her to give way to her fears may, in the end, have helped her to face the death she had so dreaded with the courage she would have wanted. Just before dying, she mustered her strength to pen a final message: "I testify with my dying breath that since first I laid my young heart upon his manly bosom I have known only love and happiness."[50] She did not have to be the one to ask whether she had ever been happy. Her daughters did get a stepmother.

Were Sarah Ann Haynsworth Gayle's story written as a novel, the interlocking of themes would appear to defy real life. Sarah Gayle harbored a genuine literary talent. She especially developed an external perspective on her subjective experience. Her fragmented and discontinuous journal reflects narrative choices as surely as any fiction. But the choices that endow her narrative with such coherence were not entirely hers to make. The tetanus, the dentist, John Gayle's absences, lay beyond her choice. She chose, however unconsciously, to underscore her identification with her family of origin by representing her devotion to her parents' servants. She chose to identify her commitment to religion with her fear of death and her responsibilities as a mother. She chose to borrow from the prevailing romantic discourse to cast her literary aspirations. She chose all this and more. Her choices reflect the self-conscious and unconscious workings of the mind of a special woman. The conditions that governed her imaginative life and shaped her life lay beyond her choice. Those conditions also governed the lives of innumerable other slaveholding women, who would express their personalities discretely but who would, like Sarah Gayle, work with the materials that lay to hand.

Sarah Gayle cannot uncritically be presented as typical of slaveholding women. Women's lives varied according to region, generation, and the size of the slaveholdings to which they were born and into which they married. She lived as a girl, and for much of her womanhood, in what remained very close to frontier conditions. Yet her family connections and the number of slaves that her father owned and bequeathed to her established her as a member of the solid slaveholding class even if she did not live in the lap of lowcountry luxury. Her experience differed from that of other slaveholding women in innumerable particulars, but she shared with countless others, whose position entitled them to claim the status of lady, the structural constraints that governed the lives of privileged women in a slave society.

In this book, I have purposed to tell the story of black and white women of the southern plantation household—or at least some of its essentials—and, along the way, to make a modest contribution to southern and women's history. Black and white southern women differed from their northern and European sisters for a complex of reasons, first among which was the unfolding of their lives within a modern slave society. The experience of all women, those of the Old South included, varies according to class and race, in accordance with the communities and societies to which they belong and the historical periods in which they live. Hence I use the term *gender*, in contradistinction to *sex*, for gender is a social, not a biological, category and, therefore, fundamentally a historical category.

Throughout, I variously refer to *gender relations*, *gender roles*, and *gender identities*. By gender relations, I mean the relations between women and men within specific societies and communities. Gender relations constitute the foundation of any society and lie at the core of any individual's sense of self, for gender relations map the most fundamental relations between any individual and the other members of society. We do not experience our gender in the abstract, but in relation to others: To be a woman is to be a woman in relation to men. Just as societies have characteristic social relations, so they have characteristic gender relations. Societies have also tended to promote distinct roles for women and men. Those gender roles constitute the activities through which women and men are encouraged to contribute to the collectivity and in which they are encouraged to find their identities— their deepest sense of who they are. Under stable social conditions, gender relations, gender roles, and gender identities tend to merge into a natural continuum. Under unstable or oppressive conditions, the continuum may be shattered.

Slavery as a social system, and not merely as one institution among many, left an indelible mark on the lives—the relations, roles, and identities—of both slaveholding and slave women. Ownership of slaves relieved slaveholding women of many forms of domestic labor while it imposed upon them the responsibilities of slave management. Being owned deprived slave women of many forms of control over their own lives and especially deprived them of the protection of the law for their personal relations as daughters, wives, and mothers. This lack of control never crippled black people as a people, but it did cripple many thousands of individual men and women and did have heartrending consequences for the relations, roles, and identities of all.

I shall try to show that the distinct experiences of slave and slaveholding women, although radically different, derived directly from their membership in rural slaveholding households that contained within themselves much more basic economic production than was common in the North or in western Europe. Each of these households came under the direct authority of a single man, the master, who assumed accountability for its internal and external order.

The domination of the master weighed heavily on slaveholding and slave women alike, but with very different consequences. For slaveholding women, that domination merged with their personal relations as daughters, wives, and mothers in a way that encouraged them to see it not merely as legitimate but as natural. For slave women, it superseded their relations as daughters, wives, and mothers with the men and women of their slave community. In the end, relations with the master and life within the household over which he presided discouraged slaveholding women's opposition to the system as a system even as it spurred personal resistance to wrongs and abuses—to lapses from professed norms. Domination, especially the abuse of male prerogative, inflicted misery and frustration upon many slaveholding women but did not tempt them into feminism, much less abolitionism. They complained about their lives, but their complaints rarely amounted to opposition to the system that guaranteed their privileged position as ladies. The domination of the master and life within the household over which he presided led many slave women to counterpose their own wills directly to his. Their response, however different from that of slaveholding women, had little to do with the patterns of emerging feminism in the Northeast. For it had little to do with the slave woman's gender. It expressed a rejection of naked power.

Chapter 1 develops an interpretation of the distinctive experience of southern women, black and white, and of the nature of the southern household. I have tried to render the arguments simply and directly, with as few concessions as possible to the cumbersome apparatus and language of the social sciences. But those with no taste at all for theoretical arguments may choose to pass over it lightly and turn to chapters 2 and 3, which offer direct testimony of slaveholding and slave women about their own experiences. In chapter 4, I discuss the gender conventions that defined the roles and shaped the identities of slaveholding women, and in chapter 5, I turn directly to those identities— to their imaginative worlds. Chapter 6 presents the actions and feelings of the women who did oppose slavery: slave women themselves. In chapter 7, focusing on the celebrated Mary Boykin Chesnut, I take respectful exception to the attempt of learned friends and colleagues to find among the slaveholding women a significant measure of proto-feminism and protoabolitionism.

In this prologue, I have attempted to recreate the life and the dimensions of the identity of one slaveholding woman, Sarah Gayle of Alabama. I make no claim that Sarah Gayle was "typical," whatever that might mean. Rather, I suggest that the themes of her life recurred in the lives of innumerable other slaveholding women in different decades, different regions, and different kinds of slaveholding households. In the epilogue, I attempt one possible reading of the narrative of a slave woman, Harriet Jacobs, who achieved freedom, to illustrate how the ultimate resistance of slave women stripped away the trappings of gender. No more than Sarah Gayle should Harriet Jacobs be considered typical, but the themes of her narrative, including her polemical picture of the abuses of slavery, capture dimensions of the experience of innumerable other slave women who, remaining in slavery and being unlettered, could not easily tell their own stories.

There are many badly needed studies that I do not attempt in this book but that we may expect to have done by others in the coming years. I do not provide a narrative history of black or white southern women throughout the expansion of the slaveholding South, from the seventeenth century until the Civil War. The vast portion of my evidence derives from the antebellum period proper, 1820–61. I do not provide a history of town women, black or white, or of yeoman women. I have worked largely with the private papers—especially the diaries, journals, and correspondence—of slaveholding women and with the narratives of former slaves. I do believe that slavery, institutionalized in a network of rural households, also decisively influenced the lives of town, yeoman, free black, and poor white women, but I have not here explored these experiences. Knowing of work in progress—for example, that of Stephanie McCurry and Virginia Gould—has made it easier for me to live with the limitations imposed by circumstances.

The concept of *household* is central to my argument and may cause some misunderstanding. I am using household, in the sense increasingly used by anthropologists, sociologists, and some historians, to mean a basic social unit in which people, whether voluntarily or under compulsion, pool their income and resources. As such, it has no necessary relation to family, although members of households may be related and many households may be coterminous with family membership. Above all, it has no necessary relation to *home*, which is a modern and ideologically charged term. I have chosen to use the term household precisely because it is, or should be, an emotionally and ideologically neutral term—a way of identifying a unit of analysis. During the antebellum period the U.S. census described basic social units as families, not households, but I agree with those social historians who worry that *family* emphasizes personal rather than social bonds. Not for nothing did southern slaveholders refer to their households as "my family white and black."

In this spirit, I am using household as the basic term for all rural units that pooled income and resources; that is, I am using it to supersede previous distinctions between and debates about the nature of farms or plantations. The use of those terms varied considerably between the seventeenth and the mid-nineteenth centuries and has generated vigorous debate, but those debates confuse the issues that concern me here. I am, accordingly, using *farm* and *plantation* only as descriptive, not as analytic, terms and intend by their use no intervention in the larger debates. I use *plantation household* descriptively to evoke a slaveholding household that contained twenty or more slaves. *Slaveholding household*, in contrast, can refer to a household with upwards of three slaves, and *farm household* to a household with three or fewer slaves. Although *yeoman households* typically included no slaves, they could move in and out of slaveholding without altering their basic character. Scholars disagree on the precise number of slaves that transformed a yeoman household into a slaveholding household, although ownership of three or more slaves for a decade could be taken as a good indicator of a shift. Any farmer who owned nine slaves for a decade had become a small slaveholder, although he might still be described as a farmer. So much for precision. This book is primarily about the lives of the black and white women who, for better or worse, shared plantation households.

Any attempt to recreate the lives and feelings of black and white women of the plantation household depends upon the interpretation of sources that inevitably remain less full and more ambiguous than we should wish. The narratives of former slaves present serious but, I believe, not insurmountable problems, which have been exhaustively discussed by recent historians of slavery. Like the letters, diaries, and other writings of the slaveholding women, the narratives remain necessary and valuable tools, to be used with care. One way to use them carefully is to check them, so far as possible, against each other and against statistical and more traditional historical sources. Another is to read them in context—to learn as much as possible about the matters to which the texts refer and to subject the texts themselves to rigorous internal criticism. I have done my best and may as well confess that I have tried to recreate the inner world of the household in full knowledge that a large dose of subjective judgment is inescapable. But persisting problems trouble me.

When recording the words of former slaves, white interviewers ascribed to them not so much black dialect as bad English. Somehow, when whites are quoted in the sources they usually come out speaking impeccably. No one familiar with the poor spelling, shaky grammar, and other speech peculiarities of white country women and their men would credit this picture for a moment. I am prepared to believe that many black women spoke in dialect and that many, being uneducated, also spoke bad English. But when an interviewer records "'no'" for "know," you know that he or she is up to no good. Hence, the problem: Do you report the black women's speech as recorded, knowing that to some extent it is a racist fabrication, or do you censor it all out? If the latter, you lose their voices completely. Swallowing hard and filing this caveat, I have reported their words as recorded, changing spellings only in cases in which the interviewer exceeded all decency.

I, like others, have been forced back upon the narratives because of the paucity of other sources, especially first-person sources. Few slave women wrote journals, diaries, and letters. As a group, they did not enjoy even the precarious access to the world of published writings enjoyed by white women and former slave men. We cannot be sure of the extent to which they participated in the literate culture of others, although we know they heard sermons by white and black preachers and know also that they knew much more of politics and their people's history than the slaveholders would have imagined. But our reliable information about their personal responses is fragmentary at best. I have not felt it possible to write with certainty of their feelings and ideas about a variety of topics on which slaveholding women left personal responses. And I have feared it presumptuous to speculate, however great the temptation.

For me, slave women's voices emerged most clearly from their children's recollections of their work and from the records of their resistance. Slave women worked as many as eighteen hours a day. Their regular relations with the other women, the men, and the children of the slave community were grounded in that work—in the skill of performing it well, in the fellowship of performing it together, in the determination to establish and defend its limits, and, when the master's work was over, in the love of beginning all over again for the black family or members of the slave community. And slave women demonstrably resisted the worst effects of slavery, resisted them at the very core of their identities. By the end of my research, I had no doubt that they resisted slavery as members of a community, as well as in lonely defiance. Their multiple contributions to the culture and communities of their people constituted a web of resistance that sought, above all, to protect the identities and cohesiveness of members of succeeding generations. We are gradually learning to tease the evidence out of unpromising sources, and I can only hope that others will come to fill the gaps that I have left.

In attempting to understand the collective story of slaveholding women, I have read widely in their papers, especially their journals and correspondence. There can be no question of a scientific sample, but rather of a very special universe of introspective women whose papers have survived. In writing, I have had to choose between invoking the letters and diaries of as many women as possible or those of a few who seem to me representative of slaveholding women in general and of their many variations according to wealth, region, and age. I have supplemented these central stories with references to the writings of the others but have chosen to stress the few so that the reader might be able to follow the various threads of their stories. I see no particular advantage to one method over the other but do hope that the one I have chosen helps to bring at least some of these women alive.

Withal, this book has grown out of my best sense of who these women, black and white, felt themselves to be in time and place. I have tried to follow the cycles of their lives and their interests. Many topics have been treated less fully than some might wish, and others have barely been touched upon. Sexuality ranks high among the topics to which I have devoted little attention. Since I have had a number of years of psychoanalytic training, this might seem a strange omission, but I have made a conscious choice. I have read with interest and sometimes with genuine instruction the speculations of my colleagues on the sexual dimension of the women's lives. I cannot deny that at some future point I hope to be able to intervene in the discussion. But at the risk of giving unintended offense to my colleagues, I must at this point express my considered judgment that the available sources and methods do not permit responsible speculation beyond narrow limits. I have therefore tried hard to stay within those limits, however uneasy I remain about the potential significance of the long silence.

What of the relations among the women themselves? Sharing the domination of white men—of the master—did slave and slaveholding women share bonds? participate in a sisterhood? The simple and inescapable answer is no. The privileged roles and identities of slaveholding women depended upon the oppression of slave women, and the slave women knew it. Slaveholding and slave women shared a world of mutual antagonism and frayed tempers that frequently erupted in violence, cruelty, and even murder. They also shared a world of physical and emotional intimacy that is uncommon among women of antagonistic classes and different races. Slaveholding women were elitist and racist. With some pain I am compelled to express my considered opinion that, in some essential respects, they were more crudely racist than their men. Yet they could deeply mourn the death of a favorite slave, who might have nursed them or their children, or whose children they (less frequently) might have nursed. Life would be easier if we could dismiss them as oppressive tyrants or exonerate them as themselves victims of an oppressive system. We cannot. By class and race, they were highly privileged ladies who reveled in their privilege, but many were warm and attractive women and, by their own lights and the standards of their society, God-fearing, decent women. They were women who owned—whose husbands, fathers, and sons owned— slaves in a world that increasingly recognized slavery as a moral evil and a political danger. Many of them were also women who loved their families, tried to care for their slaves, attended to their own and their slaves' immortal souls, and wrote sometimes entrancing, sometimes moving diaries, journals, and letters. Slaveholding women, like all groups of women, ranged from loving to vicious, from charming to unlovable, with all the ordinary human in-between.

Slave women, who displayed the same variations in personality, lived on the opposing side of those antagonistic class and race relations and confronted the inescapable consequences of their condition. Some would like to see them as having enjoyed an autonomy that was denied to the white women of their day, but autonomy may be a misleading word. Slave women lived free of the legal constraints of marriage and lived with the necessity to work as hard as men, frequently at tasks considered inappropriate for white women. At the limits of resistance, they lived with a sense of isolation. Yet many of them loved their men and children, tried to meet their obligations to God and the other members of the slave community, and struggled to create the strongest possible legacy for the next generation. Their isolation resulted from the extreme consequences of the oppression against which they struggled. Beyond resistance itself, the goals of that struggle pointed toward the strengthening of a community in which they could be women among their own people.

1

Southern Women, Southern Households

Our whole fabric of society is based on slave institutions, and yet our conventional language is drawn from scenes totally at variance with those which lie about us.

—Frederick Porcher

Now it is the genius of slavery to make the family the slave's commonwealth. The master is his magistrate and legislator. . . . He is a member of a municipal society only through his master, who represents him. . . . The integers of which the commonwealth aggregate is made up, are . . . single families, authoritatively represented in the father and master. And this is the fundamental difference between the theory of the Bible, and that of radical democracy.

—Robert L. Dabney

The temptation is strong to write the history of southern women from the discrete stories of Sarah Gayle and of the thousands who were both very much like her and, simultaneously, very much like no other women. Women's diaries, journals, and correspondence reveal much of the fabric of their lives—especially their personal perceptions—and much about the dynamics of antebellum southern society. Yet southern women's history consists in something more than the sum of these stories. First, this subjective evidence reveals only part of the story, for it disproportionately favors the literate and introspective over the illiterate and circumspect, favors white women over black women, favors slaveholding women over yeoman and poor white women. Second, the value of any subjective evidence depends upon the questions put to it—depends heavily upon our assumptions about the nature of the society to which southern women belonged.[1] To understand the subjective evidence, we must locate it within the specific context of southern society, must identify not merely what southern women shared with other women across time and space, but what they shared with the men of their class and race and what differentiated them from other women.

Antebellum southern women, like all others, lived in a discrete social system and political economy within which gender, class, and race relations shaped their lives and identities. Thus, even a preliminary sketch of the history of south-

ern women must attend scrupulously both to their immediate conditions and to the larger social system in which the immediate conditions were embedded and by which they were informed. We have, in a
sense, two views: the view from within and the view from without—
the view of the participants and the view of the historians. Women do
not normally experience their lives as manifestations of the laws of
political economy, although they may register sharply the vicissitudes
of economic fortunes. The papers of southern women are accounts of
troubles with servants and children, of struggles for faith, of friendships, and of turning hems. These intimate personal details and perceptions constitute a valuable record in themselves and suggest patterns of a larger social experience. We inevitably abstract from historical evidence in order to construct a narrative or an analysis. The most
significant differences among historians occur at this stage of abstraction, which itself influences the ways in which we interpret and organize the specific evidence. Southern history abounds in these debates,
which afford some of the most lively and theoretically informed writing in American history. But the debates have not yet taken adequate
account of the history of southern women. Nor has the experience of
southern women significantly penetrated the "larger" debates, which
badly need closer attention to gender.

Southern women belonged to a slave society that differed decisively
from the northern bourgeois society to which it was politically bound.
Slavery as a social system shaped the experience of all its women, for
slavery influenced the nature of the whole society, not least its persisting rural character. Southern slave society consisted largely of a network of households that contained within themselves the decisive relations of production and reproduction. In the South, in contrast to the
North, the household retained a vigor that permitted southerners to
ascribe many matters—notably labor relations, but also important aspects of gender relations—to the private sphere, whereas northerners
would increasingly ascribe them to the public spheres of market and
state. The household structure and social relations of southern society
had multiple and far-reaching consequences for all spheres of southern
life, including law, political economy, politics, and slaveholders' relations with yeomen and other nonslaveholding whites. And it had special consequences for gender relations in general and women's experience in particular.[2]

The persistence in the South of the household as the dominant unit
of production and reproduction guaranteed the power of men in society, even as measured by nineteenth-century bourgeois standards.

During the period in which northern society was undergoing a reconversion of household into home and ideologically ascribing it to the female sphere, southern society was reinforcing the centrality of plantation and farm households that provided continuities and discontinuities in the experience of women of different classes and races. Variations in the wealth of households significantly differentiated women's experience, but the common structure as a unit of production and reproduction under men's dominance provided some basic similarity. Effectively, the practical and ideological importance of the household in southern society reinforced gender constraints by ascribing all women to the domination of the male heads of households and to the company of the women of their own households. In 1853 Mary Kendall, a transplanted New Englander, wrote to her sister of her special pleasure in receiving a letter from her, for "I seldom see any person aside from our own family, and those employed upon the plantation. For about three weeks I did not have the pleasure of seeing *one white female face*, there being no white family except our own upon the plantation." The experience of black slave women differed radically from that of all white women, for they belonged to households that were not governed by their own husbands, brothers, and fathers. But even black slave women shared with white women of different social classes some of the constraints of prevalent gender conventions.[3]

As members of a slave society, southern women differed in essential respects from other American women, although their experience has not figured prominently in the development of American women's history, much less influenced the theory that informs generalizations about the experience of American women.[4] Southern women's history should force us to think seriously about the relation between the experiences that unite women as members of a gender and those that divide them as members of specific communities, classes, and races. It should, in other words, challenge us to recognize class and race as central, rather than incidental, to women's identities and behavior—to their sense of themselves as women.

American women's history, notwithstanding its success in challenging the dominant interpretations of gender, has followed the road of the great American consensus with respect to race and class. Historians of the "American woman" have charted "her" experience and traced her blossoming consciousness from the farms and towns of New England through the abolitionist and women's rights movements of that New England diaspora traced by Frederick Jackson Turner, to the Sanitary Commission, the Women's Clubs, the Woman's Christian

Temperance Movement, and access to higher education. From there, the modal history has progressed to the emergence of professional careers in social work or related occupations; growing participation in government through the Consumers' League, the Women's Bureau of the Department of Labor, and the activities of the New Deal; and on to the National Organization for Women (NOW), the vice-presidential candidacy of Geraldine Ferraro, and the fight for women's right to abortion.[5]

The tendency to generalize the experience of the women of one region to cover that of all American women has obscured essential differences of class and race. The generalization might be defended if it could be shown that structural similarities transcended regional variations, which could then appropriately be dismissed as little more than accidents of local color. But "New Englandization" cannot be reduced to local color, for the original New England model derives directly from dominant American attitudes toward class relations in history, and beyond them toward the prevailing mythology of who Americans are as a people.

The New England women whose experience has provided the dominant models for women's history belonged overwhelmingly to the emerging bourgeoisie. To be sure, industrial capitalism developed slowly and unevenly in New England as elsewhere; nonetheless, the market governed the development of social and gender relations even among people whose lives it touched indirectly. Some women's historians, notably Christine Stansell and Carroll Smith-Rosenberg, have challenged the simplicity of the New England model by insisting on the variations in women's experience by class. Stansell, for example, cogently argues that during the antebellum period the working-class women of New York City, who were less than impressed by the purported sisterliness of upper- and middle-class women, developed a distinct subculture, including particular attitudes toward work, family, sexuality, and self-presentation. And Smith-Rosenberg develops a welcome picture of women's special roles in an emerging bourgeois culture. Despite these promising new directions, we still lack a revised picture of the complex roles of different groups of women in the development of American life and political culture, much less a reassessment of the roles and values of southern women.[6]

Smith-Rosenberg's evocation of bourgeois culture, like Stansell's insistence on class conflict among women, should begin to move us beyond the uncritical acceptance of the cultural and political predominance of the fabled middle classes. Yet ultimately, we must also explain the persistence of that predominance and its abiding sway over our vision of our own identity as a people, for Americans have clung tenaciously to the view of themselves as a democratic, middle-class society. The very term *middle class* derives from a literature that sought to describe social stratification as an analytical alternative to class relations. Many southern women, like women throughout the country, can be said to have been "middle-class," broadly construed, but to have belonged to the middle class in a society in which some people owned others carried fateful consequences. To be a "middle-class" employer of free labor or of no labor at all was one thing. To be a "middle-class" owner of human flesh was—materially, ideologically, psychologically— quite another. Most societies, most systems of social relations, have a large middle, if only because most sociological analyses structure data in a manner that guarantees it. The question remains: Middle of what?

The model of womanhood that emerged in the northeastern part of the country rested upon a view of class relations that sought to deny the significance of class divisions—that sought to promote the illusion that all men were truly equal. This view claimed to embody universal rather than specifically middle-class values and, in the name of universalism, sought to impose middle-class values on the rest of the nation. That attempt, which began with evangelicalism, nativism, and an emphasis on the work ethic, ended with antislavery, the Republican party, and the war for the Union. Any attempt to apply such a model to women who—whatever else may be said about them—ended up on the other side of that confrontation requires some fancy footwork. Yet most historians who have considered the history of southern women at all have absorbed large doses of that model, even if they have also protested against simple assimilation of the experience of southern women with that of their northern "sisters."[7]

Joan Jensen has argued that the northeastern model of separate spheres does not adequately explain the experience of the small group of mid-Atlantic farm women whom she has carefully studied. For these women, the initial impact of capitalism resulted in a refiguration of their work within farm households, and only gradually in a loosening of the bonds that tied them to those households. Their religious convictions as Hicksite Quakers and their special experiences gradually led a small fraction of the wealthiest among them to espouse the cause of women's rights. But by that time they had reason to view their destinies as, in essential respects, separate from those of their household kin. Jensen's work offers a microcosm of the possible variations within the experience of different groups of women throughout the mid-Atlantic states and possibly the midwestern ones as well. But it also confirms that the logic of northern development, broadly interpreted, led toward women's growing engagement with the market, first as members of households and gradually as individuals. The development of southern slave society did not promote the same result. In this respect the experience of northern women, despite innumerable variations according to subregion and class, differed fundamentally from that of southern women, black and white.[8] The history of southern women does not constitute another regional variation on the main story; it constitutes another story.

Women's history, in part as a natural attempt to establish its own claims, has tended to emphasize what women shared across class and racial lines. It has, in short, tended toward an essentialist interpretation of women's experience—indeed, of women's "being." By "essentialist," I mean a transhistorical view of women that emphasizes the core biological aspects of women's identity, independent of time and place, class, nation, and race. From the perspective of many women's historians, to emphasize the class and racial determinants of women's experience and, especially, women's consciousness is to compromise the integrity of women's perception and to mute the pervasiveness of sexism and male dominance. Women's history has paid attention to the experience of women of different classes and is, increasingly if still inadequately, paying attention to the experience of women of different races. The problem is not that we have no history of working-class or black women. It is that, with notable exceptions, the histories we do have are being written as if class and race did not shape women's experience and even their identities.[9]

Neither women's history nor women's identities can responsibly be abstracted from the social relations of class and race in the society and communities with which we are here concerned. The history of the women of the Old South illustrates what should be a general rule of women's history: The history of women cannot be written without attention to women's relations with men in general and with "their" men in particular, nor without attention to the other women of their society. If we try to work with a general, not to mention an essentialist, view of women's nature, we must end in banality. All women, like all men, are a product of social relations defined to include gender, class, nationality, and race. Their innermost identities, their ideals for themselves, and their views of the world all derive from their sense of themselves as a woman in relation to men and other women—their sense of themselves as the female members of specific societies.[10]

Class and race deeply divided southern women, notwithstanding their shared experience of life in rural households under the domination of men. There is almost no evidence to suggest that slaveholding women envisioned themselves as the "sisters" of yeoman women, although there may have been some blurring at the margins when kin relations crossed class lines. In contrast, there is reason to believe that some slaveholding women felt minimal kinship with their female slaves, with whom they might have intimate, if tension-fraught, relations in everyday life. In general, but for women in particular, class relations in southern society remained essentially hierarchical. If anything, relations among women of different classes strengthened and reaffirmed class distance among free white families and served as an antidote to the elements of egalitarianism—or at least formal political democracy—that characterized relations among free white men. The relations among women also reaffirmed the special race relations of slave society, for the more established slaveholding women viewed their female slaves as somehow part of their affective universe in a way that they did not view yeoman women or even arrivistes. But they unavoidably viewed those slaves as social and racial inferiors whose station in life was that of perpetual servants. Thus, the arrivistes could in time "arrive," whereas the slaves had no prospects and the nonslaveholders could be perceived as having none.[11]

Gender, race, and class relations constituted the grid that defined southern women's objective positions in their society, constituted the elements from which they fashioned their views of themselves and their world, constituted the relations of different groups of southern women to one another. The class relations that divided and interlocked southern women played a central role in their respective identities. Slaveholding, slave, yeoman, poor white, and middle-class town women, as members of a gender, shared the imposition of male dominance, but their experience of that dominance differed significantly according to class and race.

The forms of male prejudice and dominance differ among societies that assign specific purposes and forms to prejudice and domination. The distinctive forms of male dominance in the South developed in conjunction with the development of slavery as a social system and reflected the rural character that slavery reinforced in southern society. In the South, as in many other societies, church and state substantially reinforced the prevalent forms of male dominance, some of which were national and some regionally specific. Within the South, the forms varied considerably according to community. Like religion and the law, the rural character of southern slave society impinged upon women of all classes and races in innumerable, albeit different, ways. Above all, it circumscribed their mobility and the size of the communities to which they belonged or within which they developed their sense of themselves. For most women, male dominance appeared specifically as a direct manifestation of the social and gender relations of particular communities, however much accepted as a general law of life.[12]

Superficially, the experience of southern women paralleled that of their northern counterparts in many ways. Religious conviction lay at the heart of country women's struggle to know themselves and to apply their knowledge so as to live and die as Christian women. The language of the Bible and sermons shaped country women's models of female excellence. The church offered one of their few social encounters outside the household, as well as their most immediate court for the enforcement of social relations and behavior. Christianity as a system of belief and the church as network and institution functioned analogously for southern and northern town and country women. Jean Friedman has convincingly argued that religion contributed to, rather than alleviated, southern women's sense of living in an "enclosed garden" under the domination of men. Yet most southern women probably experienced that enclosure within their purportedly ordained station as a natural manifestation of human and divine order rather than as arbitrary imprisonment.[13]

Southern religious values imperceptibly merged with the high culture and high politics of the slaveholders, which in turn permeated southern society. Religion, politics, and culture were rooted in and continually transformed the slaveholders' daily lives and attitudes. Women contributed to the hegemony of the slaveholding class, even though men normally figured as its premier spokesmen, and no claim to understand them can ignore those contributions. Slaveholding women, who never figured as mere passive victims of male dominance, benefited from their membership in a ruling class. Slave, yeoman, and poor white women experienced their own subordination as, in some way, legitimated by women as well as by men. Thus, the behavior and attitudes of slaveholding women in their daily lives simultaneously reflected and contributed to the ideology of the slaveholders and strengthened their cultural and political influence over society. The

relations of slaveholding women with the other classes of society—
notably the slaves, yeomen, and poor whites—articulated attributes of
class and race as well as gender. As ladies, slaveholding women enacted
the differences between social groups at least as much as they did the
similarities among women. As ladies, they reinforced slaveholding ideology even as they reformulated it in feminine guise.

The slaveholders enunciated their ideology in a variety of published
discourses—political, economic, religious, social, literary—but only a
minority of those to whom they were directed, including women of
the slaveholding class, read them. And yet broad dissemination ensured that the messages of this formal intellectual work ultimately
touched the ordinary lives of slaveholding women and influenced their
relations with the men and women of other classes. The private papers
of slaveholding women reveal that many of them engaged with the
high culture of their society through a wide variety of printed texts.
Few followed Louisa McCord in her passion for political economy, but
many concerned themselves with religion, literature, and history. The
ways in which and the extent to which women shared in this literate
culture varied considerably, but many had access through participation
in the networks of institutions through which ideas were disseminated
and class relations consolidated. The slaveholders, women and men,
were bound together in a web of belief and behavior by schools,
churches, watering places or resorts, and villages, and by lecture halls
that supplemented the family gatherings around the fire, at which the
head of the household read aloud the Bible or a printed sermon or
some other elevating or suitable work.[14]

The schools and churches of southern society developed on the basis
of available resources and choices about whom to instruct and whom
to hold in church fellowship. The choices resulted, albeit unequally,
from the beliefs and goals of the members of different classes and
races. Thus, if a group of black slaves sought to establish a church or a
school, they would either have to do so in secrecy and under adverse
circumstances, or with white support and control. Even yeomen, not
to mention poor whites, did not, with their scarce resources, enjoy
wide choice in such matters. Within the various classes, the choices of
women always partly reflected their class's view of proper gender relations and roles, in tension with women's independent views and access
to resources. Some southern women of all classes and races found
access to schooling and especially to church membership. Southern
women may even have outnumbered southern men in church mem-

bership, although possibly not in church attendance. The figures here remain far from conclusive, and possibly one of the significant differences between northern and southern society lay precisely in the greater proportion of men to women in southern church attendance, if not membership.[15]

No southern woman shared equal access to schooling with the men of her own class, although by the 1850s increasing numbers of women were attending academies sponsored by the churches and the more reflective political leaders. And although slaveholders frequently expended considerable effort to provide their daughters with educations appropriate to their station, they firmly discouraged those daughters from becoming teachers. When the disruptions of the war finally made it possible for Elizabeth Grimball to take a position as a teacher, her mother, Meta Morris Grimball, reported that although "the old Mauma has acted throughout [defeat and emancipation] with perfect consideration, she was terribly mortified by Elizabeth being a teacher, & Gabriella, & Charlotte keeping a school." Teaching a Sunday-school class might be viewed as a social responsibility; teaching a favorite slave to read might even be tolerated; but earning a salary for regular teaching was viewed as an unfortunate necessity for widows or, even worse, wives who had fallen victim to their husbands' inadequacies. It was not a fit occupation for a lady.[16]

Education underscores the difference between southern women and women throughout the rest of the country. In the late eighteenth century, northern bourgeois and, in lesser measure, southern slaveholders discovered the virtues of educating women to meet their responsibilities as republican mothers. But whereas, in the South, that elite tradition long continued to dominate prevailing attitudes toward women's education, in the North it was rapidly supplemented by a practical commitment to educating young women for careers as teachers. Because the South lagged far behind the North in the development of common schools, it did not develop the same expanding demand for low-paid, female teachers and, accordingly, did not develop institutions to train them. The South had nothing that resembled Emma Willard's academy in Troy, New York, which especially trained teachers. When circumstances forced slaveholding women to turn to teaching as a means of supporting themselves, they invariably opened small, transitory private schools, not unlike the dame schools of late-colonial New England. In northern society, education emerged as an essential ingredient in training displaced rural children and immigrants to take their places in a capitalist economy. Young women who were marrying later, or perhaps not at all, and who were no longer essential to their parents' households, were ideal candidates for the task of basic instruction, especially since they could be paid less than men for the same work.[17]

The figure of the lady, especially the plantation mistress, dominated southern ideals of womanhood. That slaveholding ladies were massively outnumbered by nonslaveholding or small-slaveholding women challenges any easy assumptions about the relation between the ideal and reality but does not undermine the power of the ideal. The temptation to demystify the figure of the lady has proved almost irresistible. It has even been argued that the plantation mistress closely resembled slave women in being the victim of the double burden of patriarchy and slavery. According to this view, southern ladies, isolated on plantations and condemned to bear many children, endured husbands who whored in the slave quarters and slaves who combined sauciness with sloth and indifference. It has been, if anything, more seductive to reason that ladies, who themselves suffered male domination, were the primary, if secret, critics of their society—nothing less than closet feminists and abolitionists who saw slavery as a "monstrous system." "Poor women, poor slaves," in the widely quoted words of Mary Boykin Chesnut. But most ladies, like Mary Chesnut herself, were hardly prepared to do without slaves and enthusiastically supported secession. Above all, they did not advance an alternate model of womanhood. The North, too, had its ladies and fashionable women, but northern society preferred to celebrate the virtues of domesticity over those of privilege.[18]

This modern view of the southern woman as the leading opponent of southern institutions strikingly conforms to that espoused by northern abolitionist women, including those southern expatriates, the Grimké sisters, who loudly denounced the special toll that slavery exacted from white women: In their view, the condition of women in a slave society can only be compared to that of slaves; life in a slave society intensified both women's enslavement and their consciousness of it. These perceptions encourage the view that privileged southern women were alienated from their own society and were feminists in much the same sense as were the northern advocates of women's rights. Black slave women figure in this picture of southern women primarily as evidence of the society's sexual disarray and as burdens on already overburdened slaveholding women. Rather than living a life of ease and privilege, so this argument goes, the southern lady lived a life of ceaseless responsibility and toil, as "the slave of slaves."[19] In truth, she did neither.

Slave women did not see their mistresses as oppressed sisters. But recent work on Afro-American slave women has—notwithstanding its generally high quality and good intentions—also paid inadequate attention to the consequences of class and racial oppression for slave women's sense of themselves as women. Similarly, historians of the slave community have minimized the consequences of enslavement for the relations between slave women and men, and, in defending the strength and vitality of Afro-American culture, have too easily assumed that the slaves developed their own strong attachment to a "normal," nuclear family life—a remarkably egalitarian form of conjugal domesticity and companionship.[20] The skewing of this picture derived primarily from assumptions about slave men and women as couples; assumptions about the most likely foundations for the demonstrably strong attachment of slaves to their families; and assumptions about the necessary underpinnings for male strength. These assumptions were accompanied by respectful attention to slave women as workers and as members of the slave community. Indeed, most of the male historians of slavery delighted in celebrating the strength of slave women, but they also did their best to make those women fit into their own preconceptions of what a strong woman should be—a cross between middle-class domesticity and the virtuous woman of Proverbs.[21]

The history of slave women, like that of the women of other oppressed groups, races, nations, and classes, demonstrates how dangerous it can be to study women in isolation from the interlocking systems of class, gender, and race relations that constitute any society. By modern feminist standards, slave women did escape some of the fetters of privilege that imprisoned white northern women. But surely they did not escape the larger constraints imposed by life in a slave society. Nor is there any reason to believe that they, any more than their men, escaped a heavy dose of cultural domination, even though they might appropriate, reinterpret, and turn to their own advantage those distinct elements of white culture that they could assimilate into an Afro-American culture of their own making. What can be the political and cultural moral of the story of slave women's purported independence? Did that independence materially free them from their own enslavement? From the perspective of Afro-Americans as a people, should the independence of women be interpreted as a collective gain, or merely as the confirmation of slave men's weakness relative to white men? Nothing can be gained by pretending that these complexities do not exist. Even the recognition of black women's "double" oppression and their uniquely creative solutions to the problems that confront all women cannot explain away the consequences of the enslavement of black men for black women's identities.[22]

Gender constitutes an indispensable category of analysis because it imposes the recognition that to be a woman or a man is to participate in a set of social relations in a specific way. When white slaveholding women invoked their own sense of "honor," as many did, they were invoking an ideal of excellence that could not be divorced from their identification with their men and their reliance on their class position for a sense of who they were. The ideal of honor was related, however imprecisely, to the ability to command the bodies and labor of others, to a model of social hierarchy in which some were born and would die superior to others, whatever their personal failings and economic vicissitudes. The independence and strength of slave women were inscribed in a social system in which slaveholding women had the right to command the obedience and deference of slave men, in which slaveholding men had the right to exploit the bodies of slave women, and in which slave men did not have the right to resist either form of assault, although they often did at the risk of their lives. Obviously, there were limits to the deference slave men could extract from slave women under these conditions. But how do we evaluate a female strength that may have derived less from African traditions than from an enslavement that stripped men of all the normal attributes of male power: legal and social fatherhood, the control of property, the ability to dominate households?[23]

The ways in which various authors want the story to end impinges on every effort to write it. Either the power that some people exercise over others has consequences or it does not. If it does not, then the arguments for freedom and liberation lose much of their force. If it does, then those who have suffered the inescapable dependence of forcibly imposed power must face the consequences. Those who favor the essentialist view of women's history may find, in the abstraction of the effects of slavery on black men, an asset for the story they wish to tell. Others may find the perspective daunting. Stripping men of power may well encourage female autonomy, but black women, slave and free, lived in a world dominated by men, even if those men were not of their own race. Nothing can disguise the horrible economic and social consequences of slavery for black men and women, both separately and together.

Everyone agrees that slavery imposed special burdens upon women. W. E. B. Du Bois reserved his harshest indictment of the white South for the treatment suffered by black women, and feminists like Angela Davis have similarly insisted upon the "double burden" that afflicts Afro-American women. Even slavery itself, Du Bois wrote, he could forgive, "for slavery is a world-old habit." But one thing he could "never forgive, neither in this world nor the world to come: its wanton and continued and persistent insulting of the black womanhood to which it sought and seeks to prostitute its lust." Du Bois's moving and revealing remarks rest on an unquestioning acceptance of an ideal of womanhood and, in this respect, invite comparison with those of Sojourner Truth at the middle of the nineteenth century. For Sojourner Truth, speaking to a white, middle-class, women's rights audience, called into question the very notion of womanhood in the experience of slave women. Her frequently cited remarks bear reiteration:

> Dat man ober dar say dat woman need to be lifted ober ditches, and to have de best place every whar. Nobody eber helped me into carriages, or ober mud puddles, or gives me any best place and ar'n't I a woman? Look at me! Look at my arm! I have plowed, and planted, and gathered into barns, and no man could head me—and ar'n't I a woman? I could work as much and eat as much as a man (when I could get it), and bear de lash as well—and ar'n't I a woman? I have borne thirteen chilern and seen em mos' all sold off into slavery, and when I cried out with a mother's grief, none but Jesus heard—and ar'n't I a woman?[24]

Truth and Du Bois concur that slavery assaulted the womanhood of slave women, but tellingly they emphasize different aspects of that womanhood: Truth, work and motherhood; Du Bois, sexuality. Both implicitly acknowledge that slavery decisively shaped the experience of slave women—that masters in particular and whites in general enjoyed the power to use and abuse slave women. Both Truth and Du Bois also draw upon an ideal of womanhood, or the idea of being a woman, to provide a standard for that core identity of slave women which resisted the use and abuse. Slave women, both Truth and Du Bois asserted, remained women although they were denied the protections that the dominant white society claimed to offer women, remained women although they were denied the attributes assigned by the dominant white society to womanhood. Du Bois represents the culmination of the most generous version of an Afro-American cultural tradition extending back to the free black community of the antebellum period. For if Du Bois deeply appreciates the strengths and accomplishments of Afro-American women, he also implicitly supports the view that bourgeois domesticity offers the best model for the assimilation of Afro-Americans into their rightful place in American society. He assumes the desirability of stable nuclear families under the leadership of men while allowing plenty of space for women's strength.

The structures and conventions of the white world hedged in slave women almost as firmly as they did white women, albeit more erratically and violently. In this respect, the racist component of class oppression and the black-nationalist dimension of class consciousness and struggle emerge from the history of Afro-American slave women and dramatize problems inherent in all women's history. These racial and nationalist dimensions reinforce rather than negate the class dimension of women's experience. Afro-American slaves did not enjoy the freedom to preserve intact their African ancestors' view of the world. However determined their resistance and however resolute their spirit, forced transplantation to the New World deprived them of the material bases of West African culture, especially in the southern colonies, and later states, of North America, in which the ratio of white to black and the average size of plantations militated against their establishing potentially autonomous enclaves free of white influence. Afro-American culture owed more to the persistent struggle between slaves and masters than to passive acceptance, but recognition of the tenacity of the struggle should not obscure the inescapability of white influence. The interactions between slaveholders and slaves rested upon a prior history of a wide variety of informal interactions between slaveholding and nonslaveholding whites and slaves during the seventeenth and eighteenth centuries.[25]

The evidence from slavery and from Reconstruction strongly suggests that black men espoused their own version of "white" views of male dominance within and without the family, and that they actively encouraged the domestic subordination of women as a necessary contribution to the survival and progress of "the race." James Horton has suggested that, at least among the free blacks of the North, this attitude imposed a terrible burden on women. Should women seek, however modestly, to assert their own rights, they were seen as guilty not merely of personal rebellion against one man, but of political rebellion against the interests of their people. Evelyn Brooks has demonstrated how firmly the black men of the National Baptist Convention USA, Incorporated, insisted on the domestic subordination of women as an essential weapon in the struggle for respectability for black people. She has also demonstrated how fiercely the women resisted the men's demands while finding their own ways to struggle against the oppression of black people and promote opportunities for black women.[26]

Women's historians, including Pan-African feminists, question the prevalence of these attitudes, although the evidence strongly suggests that antebellum northern free blacks and many postbellum freed men and women espoused them. Suzanne Lebsock, for example, argues that antebellum free black women, given the opportunity, chose to live without husbands. Other work on the free black women of New Orleans, Louisiana, and Mobile, Alabama, confirms that there was a strikingly high proportion of free black female heads of households. But census data do not reveal the reasons that free black women chose to avoid marriage, although they do reveal that, because many more free black women than free black men lived in the cities, opportunities for marriage were limited. Lebsock sees their behavior as the manifestation of a commitment to women's networks, but she does not determine whether these women preferred to live without men altogether nor explore all the possible reasons for their avoidance of marriage. At least in New Orleans and Mobile, many free black female heads of households had liaisons with white men, who provided them with property and resources but who could not marry them. In Charleston, many free black women were "married" to slave men. Free black women may have chosen to avoid the control that a husband could legally exercise over their lives, but this reading also suggests that these women expected black men to embrace the dominant white model of gender relations. Alternatively, free black women may have chosen to avoid marriage out of a reasonable concern that the white community would be more likely to view property held by men—as a married woman's property would be—as a potential threat to white dominance. Whatever the explanation, it must be assessed against the powerful evidence that freed men and women enthusiastically sought marriage after emancipation.[27]

The relation between African and Afro-American patterns remains unclear. Let us assume that West African traditions allowed women greater independence from the dominance of one man within a nuclear family than British traditions allowed white women; let us also assume that many of the West African societies from which most slaves came featured distinct matrilineal or matrifocal practices, or both.

How should we assess the persistence of those traditions under slavery and their contribution to the slaves' struggles with their masters? And how do we assess the significance of West African practices of polygyny? West African societies did promote clear models of gender relations and, whatever the differences between those and Anglo-Saxon models, they rarely encouraged women's political and military leadership. Throughout the antebellum period, slave women resisted slavery in innumerable ways, but they did not figure among the leadership of the larger, organized revolts. This pattern suggests that the West African values favoring male political and military leadership received powerful support from Anglo-American social and gender relations. In other words, the amalgamation of West African and Anglo-Saxon customs imposed undeniable constraints on slave women, who, like other southern women, forged their lives and identities within the constraints of a specific slave society.[28]

Modern chattel slavery shaped a southern society that, from its inception, developed in response to a capitalist world market, to which it was indissolubly linked and yet deeply antagonistic in spirit. Slavery especially influenced the experience of southern women by consigning them overwhelmingly to households under the domination of men—in the case of black slave women, not even their own men. In the modern world, the impact of capitalism on women's position or status remains the central question in the comparative women's history of nations, classes, races, and communities. Debates about the nature and development of capitalism rank among the most hotly contested in historical studies. Many scholars use capitalism in a general, heuristic fashion to apply to concentrations of wealth, participation in commerce, the presence of banks, and the quest for income. Although such definitions, properly qualified, may serve some useful analytical purposes, they carry the debilitating tendency to conflate all historical experience by focusing on ubiquitous—and therefore ahistorical—attributes of all or most economic life. In this book I understand capitalism to consist in historically specific, if diverse, social relations of production. Capitalism as a social system depends upon the divorce of labor from the land, the transformation of labor-power (not labor) into a commodity, and the political recognition of both land and labor as entities of absolute property that can be freely exchanged on the market.[29]

Capitalism could nowhere appear as a pure, ideal type, if only because of its slow and uneven development. Restrictions upon the accumulation and disposition of wealth persisted, as did restrictions upon the free disposition of labor, but the logic of the system emerged from the earliest stages. By the sixteenth century, the elements of developing capitalism prevailed in England, consolidated by the abolition of feudal tenures during the English Revolution in the seventeenth century. Yet even in England capitalist development remained spotty and regional, with the north of England and Wales lagging behind the heartland. Following the civil war and the transformation of the state, however, capitalism developed on the principle of the absolute ownership of land and labor and the buying and selling of labor-power as a commodity like any other. The markets that embodied and fueled the rise and expansion of capitalism ranged from local to worldwide, but the most important element in the future development of capitalism lay in the national market, which itself depended upon the national state's guarantee of absolute property in land and labor.[30] Indeed, the consolidation and development of a national market made possible the creation or conquest of that world market which would become the hallmark of the modern industrial-capitalist era.

In the United States, as elsewhere, capitalism did not conquer everyday life, or even all sectors of the economy and society, in one fell swoop. From the English Revolution onward there was a bias in favor of absolute property and attendant bourgeois social relations. Thenceforth, the history of the northern and middle colonies consisted in large part in the growing intrusion of capitalism into northern households, and in the strengthening of its hold upon colonial and then national economic and social life. Slavery and various forms of tenancy nonetheless existed in the northern and especially in the mid-Atlantic colonies, as well as in the South. Not until the era of the American Revolution did the North repudiate slavery in particular and unfree labor in general, although both had long been declining in importance. The changes in property and labor relations—notably slavery—that occurred during the Revolutionary era created a social, economic, political, and cultural gulf between North and South that deepened with time. For the South did not repudiate slavery when it abandoned other forms of unfree labor. Rather, it embraced slavery as the foundation of its social relations and, in so doing, established massive barriers to the penetration of capitalism into southern life and institutions, even as it mortgaged its economy to the world market.[31]

By the mid-eighteenth century, and especially after the American Revolution, southern society had acquired a hybrid or bifurcated character that resulted from the tensions between its foundations in slave labor and its membership both in a democratic republic and a capitalist world market. Southern society was something new under the sun—different from the societies from which it grew, different from that northern bourgeois society into which it would, in time and with much bloodshed, be assimilated. To call it prebourgeois or precapitalist serves the limited, if useful, purpose of delineating the basic character of its social relations, but the terms are awkward at best and misleading at worst. And the South was in no sense seigneurial or feudal, as such conservative interpreters as Allen Tate and Richard Weaver have asserted. Nor was it based on some putative slave or plantation mode of production, for by the time southern society came to be dominated by the master-slave social relation it had become enmeshed in a transatlantic market within an unfolding and conquering worldwide capitalist mode of production.

The South had a slave system within a capitalist mode of production. Or, more simply put, the South was in but not of the bourgeois world. The tentacles of capitalism permeated southern society, but bourgeois social relations did not reign and did not dominate southern thought and feeling. Antebellum slave society can, as Eugene Genovese and I have argued at some length, most instructively be viewed as a discrete social formation that originated in the determination to provide labor for plantation agriculture; it emerged during the expansion of the capitalist world market, but before the triumph of the market in labor-power that would characterize the exponentially accelerating growth of industrial capitalism. In this perspective, its social relations of production developed as "modern" relative to European feudalism, and as "retrogressive" relative to emerging capitalism.[32]

As a distinct slave society, the antebellum South developed its fundamental social, cultural, intellectual, gender, and political relations under the aegis of the slave system. In this respect, the nature of its relation to the progress of transatlantic bourgeois society matters less than its significant deviation from the bourgeois society that was developing in the North and in western Europe on the basis of free labor. The slave South emerged as a brave, if deeply flawed, new world, not as a copy or recreation of the precapitalist European society out of which it, like the North, had grown. Its essential character derived from the master-slave relation—from slavery as a social system—which shaped the culture, intellectual life, and politics of the slaveholders in particular and the society in general. Sections of the Lower South and much of the Upper escaped the direct impact of slavery and even spawned alternate cultures. The South, even the plantation South, was not monolithic. But the basic social relations of slavery dominated the great southern heartland and determined its mind as well as it interests. Slavery as a social system thus engendered a distinctive southern *mentalité*, with its fateful political consequences.[33]

The plantation South would never have existed, much less expanded, had it not been for the capitalist world market. From its origins in the tobacco economy of the seventeenth-century Chesapeake until the development of the cotton belt of the nineteenth-century Deep South, the plantation system grew apace with the development of and demand for staple crops exchanged in the world market. The dimension of change over time is critical. Expansion of the South entailed the extension of slaveholding into newly opened territories. Yet some of the older areas, although they remained in the slaveholding sphere, remained out of or withdrew from the international staple market in favor of greater communal self-sufficiency. The profitability of slavery is not at issue. Although individual planters might withstand depressions in the market by virtue of credit extended by merchants or kin, the system as a whole required profits to survive and expand. At issue remains the nature of the social formation and the characteristic productive relations that produced the staples. The most telling characteristic of southern political economy may well have been that the decisive social relations of production were contained within the household rather than outside it, for the household constituted the dominant unit of production throughout the antebellum era. Not all southern households were plantations or even farms, not all southern households included slaves, and not all slaveholding southern households followed the same economic strategies, but the slave system and the household reinforced each other to discourage capitalist development.[34]

The Old South, in short, remained dependent on a capitalist world market, the principles of which were not embodied in its dominant labor system. Unlike northern farms, which can be understood as agricultural versions of petty commodity production, southern plantations depended on slavery, which was radically distinct from the capitalist wage relation. As M. I. Finley has insisted, human societies have manifested a range of partially unfree labor systems that form a continuum with respect to degrees and forms of unfreedom, but slavery constituted a radical break with them all. In the South, slavery's domination of the economy shaped even the development of nonslaveholding farms. Southern households took shape as specific manifestations of the merchant capital that presided over the birth of southern society.

Yet southern households, as the embodiment of a particular tendency within merchant capital, helped to endow southern society with its distinctive character as a specific social formation.[35]

By social formation, I mean the distinct crystallization of social relations, political economy, and culture that constitutes a subsidiary society within a dominant mode of production. In this sense the North, like the South, can be viewed as a social formation and, from this analytic perspective, as a comparable one. But the two differed in character. During the eighteenth century, their respective statuses as social formations spawned by merchant capital seemed clear, and they were especially similar in their structural difference from contemporary European social formations. They could be seen as enclaves of new patterns within the Western world. Even during the eighteenth century, both manifested a double indebtedness to Elizabethan and Jacobean legacies and to capitalist innovations. In both cases, the mixture of old and new took novel forms that still depended upon merchant capital, but by the late eighteenth century, capitalist innovation had begun to gain decisively on Elizabethan and Jacobean legacies in the North. And by the 1820s at the latest, capitalism had so progressed in the North as to subsume the vestiges of merchant capital to itself. Henceforth, capitalism constituted the internal as well as the external dynamic of northern development. In contrast, the South forestalled capitalism's penetration of its fundamental relations of production. It remained an enclave within the capitalist world market, albeit no more hermetically sealed than it had ever been. As a social formation, it assimilated elements of capitalist social relations and political economy as well as those of bourgeois culture. But these elements never predominated and, above all, did not provide the central dynamic of southern life. That central dynamic remained embedded in southern households and in the communities they engendered.

The choice of the term *social formation* unabashedly represents a compromise between the description of southern society as a regional variant of northern capitalist society and as a distinct slave mode of production. Although neither of these positions has proved adequate, each contributes an insight. The Old South developed as a unique form of modern society that no familiar theoretical categorization captures. It evolved in conjunction with the development of the capitalist world market of which it was a product, but in its emergence as a social system it extruded social and political barriers to the working-out of the capitalist market. Thus slavery and capitalist social relations coexisted in a kind of symbiosis, but without fully merging. Important features of the capitalist market penetrated the South—notably commercial entrepôts, banks and financial institutions, canals, railroads—and even generated pockets or enclaves of distinctively capitalist social relations. But they never characterized the determining productive relations of southern society. Whatever the risks of imprecision—of lack of rigor—in the alternative formulation employed here, it claims the merit of bringing a measure of order to the disorderly complexity of a southern society that has claim to uniqueness well beyond that which may be claimed for any other society.[36]

Part of the confusion stems from inadequate attention to the household in particular, and the network of households in general, both as an institutional barrier against the intrusion of the capitalist market into the daily relations of production and reproduction and as the institutional consolidation of a distinct set of social relations of production and reproduction. Because those relations were inscribed in a capitalist market and a bourgeois polity, they were never able to flower into a discrete mode of production. Yet because of their strength, they did forestall capitalist development and create enclaves in which they could develop a life of their own. This development, institutionally grounded in the household, can best be understood as a social formation—that is, as a system of social relations of production historically associated with the precapitalist era but nonetheless extruded by capitalism itself and therefore in essential respects congruent with capitalist forces of production.[37]

The debate over the impact of capitalism on American women in general remains inconclusive, and the subject has barely been raised for southern women in particular. The basic issue concerns the possible improvement or decline in women's position with the changes in social and economic relations engendered by the emergence of capitalism. Allowing for variations, historians basically are divided between those who argue that women's condition declined with the spread of capitalism—and especially industrialization—and those who argue that it improved. Those who argue for a decline contend that women in colonial society enjoyed positions of respect within the colonial household, because of the indispensability of their labor; some opportunities for autonomy within the economy at large; and also some legal protections, notably dower rights that insured their independence as widows. Those who argue for improvement point out that the colonial household subjected women to the unalleviated domination of men, barred them from literacy, and generally devalued them as a sex. The former group asserts that capitalism and especially industrialization confined women to the home, stripped them of productive labor, and generally reduced them to dependence upon men. The latter group claims that the American Revolution offered women unprecedented opportunities to run farms and plantations in their husbands' absences; to participate in the public sphere in conjunction with other women, if only in sewing to support the Revolutionary effort; and to acquire access to literacy and develop their distinct discourses.

As the subtle and nuanced work of Linda Kerber suggests, the debate does not admit of easy resolution. Middle-class women generally gained in prestige as women, but that prestige accompanied a narrowed definition of activities appropriate to their gender. Thus they made dramatic gains in literacy and in access to education, but they were expected to participate in both according to strict definitions of their appropriate social roles, notably motherhood. Their experience resembled, if we allow for national differences, that of western European women who, during the same period, were being encouraged to embrace new models of bourgeois womanhood.[38]

At best, we can say that the combined impact of the American Revolution, developing capitalism, and incipient industrialization resulted in a tendency—which would grow stronger—to confine women and their labor to the household, increasingly represented as a nurturing home rather than a productive unit, and to associate them explicitly with motherhood and domesticity, viewed as specialized responsibilities. Under these conditions, women were excluded from political life but did gain in literacy and embark on the development of a distinct female discourse. In the urban North, this constellation of conditions led directly to the development of women's voluntary associations and reentry into public life as the custodians of a distinct female perspective. Such developments decisively influenced women's self-perceptions as well as their social roles, for capitalism was accompanied and articulated by the development of a distinct culture of bourgeois individualism.

At issue is not the historical ubiquity of individual impulses and desires or self-representations. Just as the propensity to acquire wealth is as old as recorded history, so apparently is the propensity to self-centeredness. At issue, instead, are the historical structures through which these impulses have unfolded and have been acknowledged. Bourgeois individualism rested on the assumption that the individual rather than the collectivity or its divinely ordained leader—say, the absolute monarch—provided the locus of sovereignty and perception. Bourgeois individualism revolutionized all previous systems of thought by assuming that the individual constituted the locus of sovereignty and of consciousness and the only possible rationale for restrictions upon individual action. Although the full implications did not emerge full-blown with the bourgeois revolutions, they were inherent at the start. Bourgeois universalism flowed logically from bourgeois individualism in assuming that, theoretically, all individuals were interchangeable, even if each was unique.[39]

There is no need to rehearse the failures to deliver on those bright promises. Slaves, women, and working people all suffered exclusion from that privileged category of "individual." Their exclusion decisively contributed to men's ability to accept each other as individuals across class lines and regional and ethnic diversities. The inherent logic of the system nonetheless claimed, at an accelerating rate, vast territories of thought for its own sway. However much it depended upon the exclusion of some from its benefits, it offered even the excluded a hegemonic discourse that they would gradually claim for themselves. If bourgeois individualism aborning coexisted easily with—in fact, may be said to have depended upon—slavery and the domestic subordination of women, mature bourgeois individualism would, in opposition to its practical goals, generate the antislavery movement and the movement for women's rights. For bourgeois individualism was, at its core, universal rather than particular, egalitarian rather than hierarchical.[40]

The class and gender relations of antebellum slave society weighed heavily on white and black women alike, but weighed differently than their emerging bourgeois equivalents on northern women. Throughout history it has been common, indeed almost universal, for gender relations to emphasize the separation of male and female spheres. Yet women's history has frequently been written as if the separation by spheres emerged in the late eighteenth and early nineteenth centuries along with the separation of home and work that many take as the hallmark of modern women's oppression. The confusion arises when historians identify a common human tendency to divide the world by gender with a more specific form of division.[41]

Emerging bourgeois ideology promoted a strict division of labor and spheres by gender as the foundation of its own legitimacy. It did not invent either the notion of division of labor between men and women or that of separate spheres, both of which have characterized most human societies. Instead, it gave those notions new content, and, in so doing, it both drew upon inherited values and introduced innovations. The bourgeois ideology of domesticity propounded the radical separation of public and private spheres and the unswerving identification of men with the former and women with the latter. It further insisted upon women's primary identity as wives and mothers under the protection and domination of their husbands. At law, it embraced the Blackstonian version of coverture and shuddered at the possibility of women's independent property. In these essentials it could be said to differ only marginally from much previous theory and practice, but the principles that underlay the essentials differed significantly. For the bourgeois ideology of domesticity represented a concerted attempt to perpetuate a longstanding subordination of women to men within an emerging and potentially antagonistic ideology of individualism. The tensions would eventually tear to shreds the inherited values and the illusions of continuity and order they had fostered, but those tensions and their implications emerged only slowly.[42]

In western Europe and the urban northeastern United States, the ideology of bourgeois domesticity accompanied the triumph of capitalist social relations. From the perspective of bourgeois women, the gains and losses it signaled may have balanced each other. The losses have been taken to consist primarily in women's greater domestic confinement; their greater exclusion from the public worlds of exchange and manufacture; and, perhaps, their declining entitlement to such traditional rights as dower. The gains have been taken to consist primarily in an increasingly positive image of women, especially the view of them as "mothers of the republic"; their increased literacy and attendant increased access to education; their growing tendency to draw strength from their association with other women in their "bonds of womanhood"; and their acknowledged dominion in the home to which they were confined.[43]

The separation of home and work—the reduction of household to home—constituted the material embodiment of northeastern men's and women's separate spheres. What, from one perspective, looks like women's confinement to the home, from another looks like women's acquisition of their own dominion. From this experience, northern women frequently drew a strong sense of their rights and responsibilities as women. The apparent chasm between male and female experience became, in the hands of some women, the grounds for a moral imperative for women's distinct voice in the affairs of society as a whole. They represented half its members. The force of this social categorization by gender led many bourgeois women to the belief that women of all classes shared the same experiences and needs. Northeastern middle-class women's attitudes toward immigrant and other poor or laboring women, however, might not impress us as wholly sisterly. Articulate southern women, as well as southern men, mercilessly chastised northern men and women for their inhuman relations with their laboring population and celebrated the particularism they claimed for their own relations with their slaves. In contrast, middle-class northern women increasingly assumed that, by and large, all women wanted and needed the same things. They viewed women's common biological experience as the foundation for a common social experience and therefore rejected the proslavery appeals of southern women, who recognized a class solidarity with their fathers and husbands.

In time, many northern advocates of women's rights would argue that women must have expanded social and political rights precisely because of their differences from men. Other northern advocates rested their case on women's rights as individuals. That the two positions defy rigid separation reveals much about the true nature of "woman's sphere" in northern society, for both the expansion of capitalist social relations and the hegemony of bourgeois ideology rested upon the systematic and revolutionary theory and practice of individualism. The doctrine and practice of separate spheres simultaneously extended and masked the penetration of individualist principles into the fabric of bourgeois America. Even among westward-bound northern farm families, the elements of individualism and universalism remained important, although those families temporarily reverted to rural households under male dominance. But in those families there was also considerable struggle among the women and the men about appropriate expectations, notably what kind of work women who aspired to nineteenth-century domesticity should be expected to do.[44]

Many northeastern, as well as some mid-Atlantic and midwestern, women found the logic of the ideology of bourgeois individualism powerful and enthusiastically claimed it for themselves. From this perspective, their struggle for married women's property rights and greater equality for women within marriage, as well as women's political rights, constituted and was interpreted as a broadside attack on the last bastion of corporatism in a democratic society: marriage. Northern women's gradual assertion of their "rights" combined elements of individualism with elements of the doctrine of separate spheres. They believed that the evangelical and secular bourgeois values of work, thrift, and sobriety could be realized in their performance as female individuals. To be sure, as their writings reveal, the contradictions wracked them, and the assertion of their own authority remained the source of great anxieties. But they lived in a capitalist society that was undermining, at an accelerating pace, all the constraints and protections that mediated the relations between the individual and the market.[45]

The dominant values of southern society did not accord the same prestige to individualism in general and work in particular. The South did place high value on the "liberties" of its white men, and thus it advanced views and encouraged practices that bore superficial resemblance to those of the North. As a Christian society the South, like the North, celebrated the special relation of the individual to God, and, as a plantation-based slave society, it sought to protect the rights and power of the individual male head of household from undue influence by the state. But the southern notion of individual rights coexisted with corporatist values that legitimated white men's personal power over dependents. Market relations did not deeply penetrate the boundaries of the southern household, which, containing within itself both productive and reproductive relations, remained securely under the dominance of individual males. Southern women, however great their discrete powers, functioned as the deputies or lieutenants of their male kin, normally their husbands. The persistent force and multiple forms of male dominance in southern society have led many to describe it as "patriarchal," in a more restricted sense than the generalized use of the term, which describes all forms of male dominance, including that which persisted in bourgeois society. Southern society assuredly professed a strong commitment to male honor and domination, but that commitment alone does not define it as patriarchal.[46]

In ancient Roman society the male head of the household could, at his discretion, kill his wife and children, not to mention his slaves. That was a patriarchy. But the South was not ancient Rome. Those who invoke the theory of a southern patriarchy should recall that many prominent proslavery spokesmen simultaneously rooted their defense of slavery in the subordination of women and condemned explicitly, and even passionately, the patriarchal power of the Roman paterfamilias. Although some proslavery theorists invoked "patriarchy" as a positive description of their orderly society (and even they were usually careful to qualify the term beyond recognition), others, especially the influential proslavery divines, carefully criticized the injustices and barbarism of true patriarchy—its special form in ancient Israel—and hailed the advent of Christianity, which replaced the old system with a form of male authority that recognized the human rights of women, children, and slaves. In truth, invocations of Christianity notwithstanding, antebellum southern domestic relations owed much of their companionate tenor to the bourgeois rhetoric of domesticity, including companionate marriage and the modern ideologies of motherhood and childrearing. But even that rhetoric, which developed in Britain and then swept France and the American colonies during the eighteenth century, varied in its concrete referents from society to society.[47]

Southerners participated in the unfolding bourgeois culture, including the ideologies of spheres, motherhood, and domesticity, but they interpreted and applied those ideologies according to their own social and gender relations. Use of the term patriarchy, for the considerable number of southerners who, having been taught the classics, knew what it meant, was an offense against their sense of their own society's integrity. Bourgeois social relations offended their sense of human decency and the responsibilities of the upper to the laboring classes. Just as the division of society by gender permitted northerners to gloss over deep class divisions, so an ideology of male-dominated households permitted southerners to perpetuate the ideal of democratic political relations among free men in a society unmistakably grounded in hierarchical and corporatist relations of all kinds. Southerners were no more likely than northerners to favor independent rights and identities for women, but, unlike northerners, southerners espoused a worldview that celebrated the positive virtues of many forms of inequality. They thereby escaped, or at least held to a minimum, the ideological tensions that were wracking the North. Their peculiar combination of hierarchically sanctioned male dominance in the household and bourgeois egalitarianism among men in the public sphere can best be described as paternalism. For paternalism invokes a specific metaphor of legitimate domination: the protective domination of the father over his family. The invocation of the metaphor does not guarantee the benevolence of those who exercise the domination, but it does signal a distinction between the principles that govern domestic relations—including relations with unfree laborers—and those that govern the polity.[48]

There is little evidence that black slave women valued bourgeois domesticity as highly as some scholars have proposed. Some historians of black women have primarily intended to emphasize the independence of black slave women from their men and to show that slave women probably valued motherhood more highly than marriage; probably viewed menarche, rather than sexual initiation, as the more important rite of passage in a young slave woman's life; and probably drew upon the values and transmitted the support provided by a distinct community of female slaves. This work reveals, even in its reversals, the influence of the questions formed by the history of northern women. More important, it also reveals the ways in which the elements of the "universal" model of bourgeois womanhood can be disaggregated and recombined. Motherhood and marriage, rites of passage (if any), relations with other women—such are the elements of women's experience. But the referents of the words change from society to society. The contrast between New England and the antebellum South, being less sharp than that between West Africa and antebellum New England, is more difficult to analyze but is nonetheless significant.[49]

The household world of southern women evolved as part of the development of southern slave society. It crystallized during the period of the American Revolution and the Early Republic. Some scholars, notably Allan Kulikoff, insist, in fact, that by 1750 Chesapeake society had developed the models of social relations that would persist and influence all subsequent southern development. Others place the date later, variously from the 1780s to the 1820s. The differences in part reflect differences of opinion over the salient features of southern society. Those, for example, who emphasize culture in general and religion in particular are more likely to incline toward the later period. And those who see the Revolution itself as a watershed naturally emphasize its impact. The divergence among these various positions can be exaggerated. No one who reads the papers of slaveholding men and women can doubt the importance of the Revolutionary legacy to their interpretations of the emerging bourgeois discourse of domesticity and evangelical Protestantism. Nor could anyone reasonably deny the impact of the Revolution and its message of liberty and equality for all on the imagination of Afro-American slaves. Yet these developments were received and interpreted by black and white southerners who already recognized themselves as members of a distinct society.[50]

The results of the Revolution, especially the abolition of slavery in the northern states and the creation of a federal government, deeply affected the imaginations of southerners but did not significantly disrupt their established social relations. The Revolution's institutional and ideological impact did not, ultimately, change white southerners' sense of themselves in their world. As Edmund Morgan has argued, it may even have strengthened their conviction that the freedom of some depended upon the enslavement of others. Southerners, during the period of the Early Republic, appear to have assumed that the new bourgeois discourses of politics and domesticity properly expressed their own values. They could, with justification, see themselves as the premier custodians of such values, which had their roots in the pre-Revolutionary world. It is true that during the 1780s and 1790s a significant minority in the upper South interpreted republican values as a mandate for the manumission of slaves. They apparently sought to expel the blacks or to create a system similar to the sharecropping system that ultimately developed during and after Reconstruction. Most gentlemen and yeomen recoiled in horror before that vision, as the fervent proslavery petitions of the period testify. The road to an alternate path of development was firmly and rapidly closed. By the 1820s, the crisis over Missouri and the increasingly rapid growth of cities and manufactures in the North revealed the extent of sectional divergence and led southerners to strengthen their defense of their peculiar institution.[51]

Earlier, the potential conflicts between national culture and regional institutions were less evident, yet they were there. Southern experiences and values during the late eighteenth and early nineteenth centuries were not extensions of northern patterns. Between 1750 and 1820, southerners participated in national events and borrowed from the emerging national bourgeois culture, but on their own terms and in conformity with their own social relations. They did not understand the full implications of the ideas they were adopting, much less where they would lead. As the developments of those years strengthened the household as the fundamental unit of southern society and the primary locus of southern women's experience, they also engendered a growing disjuncture between the bourgeois vocabulary that southerners used and the social and gender relations to which they applied it. In time, southern forms of expression referred ever less precisely to southern values and behavior.

For all southern women, the relations of gender, class, and race, like the ideology that encoded them, were mediated through southern households that increasingly differed from the households of the North. The difference between southern and northern households did not concern their respective degrees of self-sufficiency at any given moment. At least during the early decades of the nineteenth century, significant numbers of northern rural households clearly retained more self-sufficiency than historians had previously assumed. Nor did the difference concern only some northern households' movement away from household production. The deep ideological differences between northern and southern households resulted primarily from the different social systems in which they were embedded. Northern farmers did not merely participate in capitalist market relations, on whatever scale—they were an essential part of the market. Historians of northern rural households have noted the tension between those households and the emerging towns and cities and have argued that the tension betrayed resistance to the market. Significantly, there may have been less tension of this kind in the South, primarily because southern cities were not the foci of an engulfing capitalist market.[52]

Northern and southern households gradually diverged in their total production—not merely in the special and variable case of subsistence—and in the social surplus that they generated, both within and without the household. Nevertheless, as households, they may usefully be viewed as units that pooled income or resources, albeit from different sources and of different kinds. Households should not be treated uncritically as harmonious units. In the North, as in the South, sons might differ with fathers or wives with husbands about the appropriate use of resources. Southern slaves strenuously differed with slaveholders about "household" decisions that affected the size of rations or, especially, the sale of family members.

Critics might plausibly counter that the distinction between nineteenth-century northern and southern rural households misses obvious similarities, and that the everyday lives of southern and northern households were more similar than different. In both northern and southern yeoman households the family—however grudgingly—pooled labor under the direction of the household head, or father, to produce primarily for its own subsistence and only secondarily for the market. Yet even southern yeoman households were profoundly affected by the slave society in which they were embedded. At issue, albeit in special form, is the debate between those who view the southern slaveholders as a distinct social class and those who would assimilate them to the transatlantic capitalist class.[53] Southern and northern rural households both resembled and differed from each other, but, without denying similarities, I insist upon that degree of difference which contributed to shaping the slaveholders as a historically distinct social class and to shaping the society that they dominated.

The network of southern, rural households contained a variety of different types. Yeoman and slaveholding households, to take the obvious examples, differed significantly in size and composition, and especially in numbers of slaves. For purposes of this discussion, however, I am assuming that, notwithstanding differences in degree, all southern households from yeoman farms to large plantations operated under similar structural constraints. These constraints coalesced in the historically distinct pattern of production and reproduction that is here called a social formation. The claim for structural similarity among different kinds of southern households refers precisely to structural constraints rather than internal dynamics. The differences between yeoman and large slaveholding households, as between slaveholding households of different sizes, remained significant. Not least, from the perspective of this book, the size of a household could have a decisive impact on the work assignments and living conditions of slave women, and on the kinds of work performed by the wives and daughters of household heads.

But when all the internal differences are taken into account, the external constraints remain. The nature of markets affected all households by encouraging a greater degree of household production than was common in the North. If wealthy slaveholding women did not spin or weave, their slave women did, and so did yeoman women and frequently the wives of very small slaveholders. Yeoman women were much more likely to engage in textile production within the home than in factories. Yeoman and slaveholding households were much less likely than their northern equivalents to participate in a labor market, either as sellers or buyers of labor-power. When a yeoman farmer could afford labor in addition to that of his own family, he was likely to buy a slave—to buy the laborer and not merely the labor-power. Northern women (and children), who participated directly in the work of the farm, had a larger voice in decisions about its management than did slaveholding wives (and children), who played far less important roles in production. In the end, the primary difference between southern and northern households remains that the northern household was free, the southern included slaves.[54]

Southern households intersected with each other through a variety of overlapping communities. The word "community," which carries a nostalgic aura of organic, noncontractual relations in the manner of Tönnies, admittedly lacks analytic precision. I am using it here, despite its imprecision, to refer to the primary groupings, beyond the immediate family, in which people lived and through which they defined their place in their world. In this respect, community does, in some measure, depend upon subjective perception: People, in a limited sense, create their own communities through their personal relations with others. But that subjective dimension operates within objective constraints. Thus, the "slave community" remained largely bound by individual plantations or groups of adjacent plantations and farms and the villages they spawned. Those who argue that those boundaries were reduced to little more than walkable distances miss the point. Walkable distances did not exist as an abstraction. Instead, workloads, plantation regulations, relations among masters, the social investment in roads, and much more determined the miles that would be walkable in a given amount of time and by whom. Similarly, the community or republic of letters extended, like a net, over broad distances, but its membership remained tightly circumscribed by literacy and education—in large measure by class, gender, and race. Between these two extremes, the antebellum South included a variety of communities, notably households, villages, and churches.[55]

The size and nature of the relevant communities differed for women of different classes and races. Among the slaveholders, communities could transcend the material limitations of a particular locality. Slaveholding women could attend schools that lay far from their homes and could visit resorts as well as friends in distant regions. They could reside in the state or even the national capital in conformity with the political careers of their male kin. Women as different as Sarah Gayle, Susan Davis Hutchinson, Julia Hammond, Mary Chesnut, and Mrs. Roger Pryor enjoyed an acquaintance with members of the political class of their region and even the nation. Visiting or living in Columbia, or Tuscaloosa, or Raleigh, or Washington, they developed friendships with other women that they might maintain for years through correspondence and renew when the opportunity for male escort permitted them to meet again. Women whose families were wealthy enough to send them away to school or to take them to spas or springs similarly had a chance to participate in the social networks that bound the members of that political class together. The famous Virginia Springs, for example, provided a meeting place for the elite women of the Carolinas, especially of the lowcountry, as well as of Virginia—and, indeed, attracted women and men from as far away as Louisiana and Texas. Yeoman, free black, poor white, and slave women rarely if ever enjoyed such opportunities, except for those slaves who went along as servants. They nonetheless shared with slaveholding women the difficulty of traveling without male escort and the sense of primary identification with their immediate community. Even the most mobile slaveholding women derived their primary identification and formed their principal ties with the women—and men—who belonged to their own immediate communities, the households or networks of neighboring households.

The small number of urban centers in the South closely restricted the experience of southern women of all races and classes. The predominantly rural character of southern society—defined here to include the small towns and villages integrated into the countryside— excluded southern women from many of the opportunities that were opening up for their northern sisters, notably to live and work independently by their own labor, to develop sustained female networks beyond the household, and to form voluntary associations of various kinds. As a result, southern women interpreted the emerging bourgeois discourse of separate spheres, which itself reflected the development of a capitalist city-system in the North, through the prism of a social context different from that of northern women.

With only occasional exceptions historians, especially women's historians, have treated the rural character of southern society as accidental rather than essential, as though the South just happened to remain rural and therefore differed from the Northeast, the old Northwest, or the Middle Atlantic region only by lagging behind in a common pattern of development. Suzanne Lebsock perhaps gives the impression that women of Petersburg, Virginia, typified the experience of southern women, but in 1810, in the middle of the period she considers, Petersburg ranked as the sixth-largest city in the South, exceeded only by Baltimore, Charleston, New Orleans, Norfolk, and Richmond, and was among the eight cities with a population of four thousand or more.[56] These arguments display the same logic as those that contend that southern society was inherently as capitalist as northern society. That logic virtually implies what only the rashest of economic historians from that school of thought would dare to state: that southern society was, in the classical French double sense, essentially "bourgeois." According to this view, southerners retained slavery only because it permitted them to maximize profits and because they lacked the imagination to envision a desired racial dictatorship on a nonslaveholding basis; in other words, the South remained rural because agriculture performed by slave labor remained profitable. The logic is flawed. Southern society remained rural primarily because of southerners' commitment to slavery, especially plantation slavery, as a social system; and, because of the persistence of slavery as a social system, the

South's rural character differed fundamentally from that of the North even on their respective frontiers.[57]

The rural character of southern society emerges clearly from the comparative figures for American urban development. We lack a systematic, modern, state-by-state comparison of the growth of cities during the antebellum period, but even a crude statistical analysis of the aggregate data in the published federal census for 1790 to 1860 reveals striking divergences. Throughout the antebellum period, only two of the states that eventually joined the Confederacy—which consisted of all the slaveholding states except Delaware, Kentucky, Maryland, and Missouri—boasted an urban population (cities of 2,500 or more inhabitants) of 10 percent or above. The urban population of Virginia grew from 8 to 10 percent between 1850 and 1860. The urban areas of Louisiana contained 22 percent of the state's total population as early as 1800, and the figure grew to 28 percent by 1860, although the presence of New Orleans, which served the whole Mississippi Valley, heavily skewed the figures.[58] These figures invite comparison with those for Connecticut, Massachusetts, New Hampshire, New Jersey, New York, Pennsylvania, and Rhode Island, all of which had passed the 10 percent urban population mark by 1840—four had passed it in 1790. But, as some urban historians and geographers have insisted, aggregate figures—especially when lifted in an unrefined form from the census—do not tell the whole, or even the most important, story.

Cities vary tremendously in character and function, notably in relation to their place in an entire urban system. Cities have anchored and articulated civilization for most of human history. Yet the cities of ancient Mesopotamia bear little relation to those of modern industrial-capitalist societies.[59] Even the cities of early modern Europe, the direct ancestors of modern cities, varied among themselves and differed significantly from their successors. Early modern Europe boasted three principal types of cities: administrative centers (Paris, Rome, Vienna, Moscow); great commercial centers, notably the burgeoning Atlantic ports (Bristol, Glasgow, Bordeaux, Nantes); and smaller market towns (Exeter, Pontoise).[60] Any city could combine two or more of these characteristics, just as any could contain a manufacturing sector, but the greatest of the predominantly manufacturing cities arose as products of a later industrial capitalism.[61] The case of Naples during the early modern period, like that of Mexico City today, demonstrates that the largest concentrations of population are not necessarily found in

TABLE I
Urban Population of Selected States, 1800–1860

	1800		1820	
	Total	% Urban	Total	% Urban
Maine	151,719	2.4	298,335	2.9
New Hampshire	183,858	2.9	244,161	3.0
Vermont	154,465	0	235,981	0
Massachusetts	422,845	15.4	523,287	22.8
Rhode Island	69,122	20.8	83,059	23.0
Connecticut	251,002	5.1	275,248	7.6
New York	589,051	12.7	1,372,812	11.7
New Jersey	211,149	0	277,575	2.7
Pennsylvania	602,365	11.3	1,049,458	13.0
Delaware	64,273	0	72,749	0
Maryland	341,548	7.8	407,350	16.3
Virginia	807,557	2.6	938,261	3.8
North Carolina	478,103	0	638,829	2.0
South Carolina	345,591	5.4	502,741	4.9
Kentucky	220,995	0	564,317	1.6
Tennessee	105,602	0	422,823	0
Georgia	162,686	3.2	340,989	2.2
Florida	NA	NA	NA	NA
Alabama	1,250	0	127,901	0
Mississippi	7,600	0	75,488	0

Source: U.S. Bureau of the Census, *1980 Census of Population*, vol. 1, *Characteristics of the Population*, pp. 1-51–1-56, table 13.

the most economically dynamic cities. The case of London nonetheless demonstrates that large cities which combined two or more of the major functions could set the pace for an entire economy. London, special case though it might be, charted the model of successful development for administrative cities with an important commercial sector that could adapt to the rise of manufacturing. It offers the prime example of a city that rode the wave of merchant capital and the transition from a precapitalist to a capitalist and then to an industrial-capitalist economy, finally to emerge as what urban historians and demographers are calling a "central place."[62]

1840		1860	
Total	% Urban	Total	% Urban
501,793	7.8	628,279	16.6
284,574	10.0	326,073	22.1
291,948	0	315,098	2.0
737,699	37.9	1,231,066	59.6
108,830	43.8	174,620	63.3
309,978	12.6	460,147	26.5
2,428,921	19.4	3,880,735	39.3
373,306	10.6	672,035	32.7
1,724,033	17.9	2,906,215	30.8
78,085	10.7	112,216	18.9
470,019	24.2	687,049	34.0
1,025,227	6.9	1,219,630	9.5
753,419	1.8	992,622	2.5
594,398	5.7	703,708	6.9
779,828	4.0	1,155,684	10.4
829,210	0.8	1,109,801	4.2
691,392	3.6	1,057,286	7.1
54,477	0	140,424	4.1
590,756	2.1	964,201	5.1
375,651	1.0	791,305	2.6

Presumably George Tucker, Virginia's outstanding political economist, had something like central places or city-systems in mind when he wrote that the "proportion between the rural and town population of a country is an important fact in its interior economy and condition." According to Tucker, this proportion largely determines the country's "capacity for manufactures, the extent of its commerce, and its amount of wealth." And Tucker's calculations from the censuses of 1830 and 1840 reveal that the southern and southwestern states trailed far behind those of New England and the Middle Atlantic region. Not satisfied to base his calculations only on the large cities of ten thousand or more residents, Tucker included towns of two thousand to give an accurate picture of urban development as it affected the general tenor of life in a region.[63]

On the basis of these figures Tucker found that, whereas the New England states had 35.3 percent urban population and the Middle Atlantic states 20.8 percent, the southern states had only 4.4 percent and the southwestern 6.6 percent. Furthermore, New Orleans totally overwhelmed the statistics for the southwestern states, which, without it, would have had a considerably smaller mean percentage of urban population (1.590 percent). Thus, despite Tucker's own hopeful attitude toward the possibilities for southern economic progress, his analysis clearly revealed the South as lacking precisely that network of growing towns which he identified as essential to anchor and multiply that development. In short, his sophistication as a political economist exposed the South's lack of an expanding network of dynamic cities. Even at that, Tucker seriously erred in assuming that southern towns could or did play the same role as northern ones in the regional economy and culture. To the contrary, southern towns primarily reflected the countryside. Most, especially the politically and culturally influential towns, were centers and extensions of the plantation region, not instruments of its gradual dissolution.[64]

Tucker foreshadowed the modern argument that, as central places, cities constitute the nodes of networks that articulate interlocking social and economic systems. In particular, cities develop in relation to their hinterlands, for which they provide concentrations of resources. The links that bind cities to hinterlands include transportation, communication, and markets. The heated debates over the respective roles of supply and demand in the growth of these links need not concern us here. Let it suffice that cities should be understood in the context of the societies and economies that they serve and off which they feed. As Allan Pred has convincingly argued, the system of cities that developed in the northeastern and Middle Atlantic regions, and gradually expanded with their frontiers, differed radically from the system of cities that developed in the South. The argument that southern cities belonged to a different system than northern cities inescapably impinges on the debates about whether the South had been integrally linked to a national market and whether or not it was embarking on industrial development before 1860. To emphasize the distinctive character of southern cities within southern society and in comparison with northern cities is, in effect, to emphasize the weakness of the ties that bound

FIGURE I
Urban Population of Selected States, 1820 and 1860

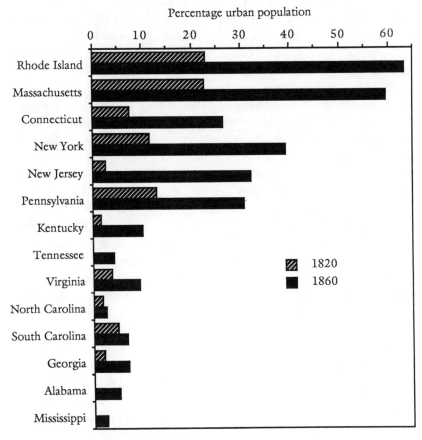

Source: See Table 1.

the South to the national market and the strong internal barriers to industrialization thrown up by slavery as a social system.[65]

Discussions of the political economy of southern cities and of the history of southern women have unfolded without reference to each other. Yet the numbers, size, and nature of southern cities profoundly affected the experience of southern women, just as that experience itself illuminates the development of southern society. From the perspective of those interested in the development of city-systems, the census classification of a city as an incorporated body of population that numbers 2,500 or more appears arbitrary and misleading. In New England and the greater New England diaspora of western New

York—to take the obvious contrast with the South—many towns crossed the population threshold in a particular decade, frequently between 1830 and 1840, but they had been behaving much like a city, or certainly like a part of an urban system, well before that time. Failure to incorporate, or lack of a few hundreds of population, could condemn a place to nonurban status even when its behavior was consistent with the urban standard.[66]

The same pattern obtained for the Middle Atlantic region. The great metropolises that dominated that region spread their tentacles throughout their hinterlands. Although, in different ways, Boston, New York, and Philadelphia all had roots in the patterns of merchant capital that had dominated the eighteenth century, by the early nineteenth century at the latest they were combining their commercial functions with the functions of a capitalist central place and were operating as the foci of rapidly expanding city-systems. They anchored interlocking local and regional markets, for which they served as hubs of transportation and communication. They developed the specialized services essential to the development of manufacture in their hinterlands as well as within their own boundaries. And, especially important for our purposes, they developed complex patterns of social relations that transformed older patterns of education, confinement, and charitable assistance.[67]

During the antebellum period, the South as a whole followed a different course. Among the states of the future Confederacy, Virginia most closely resembled the North in its urban development, but the differences in aggregate statistics remain striking. The presence of slaves—and indeed free blacks—in southern cities further complicates the issue. Virginia, the pacesetter, only reached an urban population level of 10 percent during the 1850s—the same period during which Connecticut had reached 27 percent; Massachusetts, 60 percent; New Hampshire, 22 percent; New Jersey, 33 percent; New York, 39 percent; Pennsylvania, 31 percent; and Rhode Island, 63 percent. The border states, with their lower percentages of slaves and their increasing ties to the northern economy, more closely resembled the northern urban pattern than the plantation states: By 1860, Delaware's population was 19 percent urban; Kentucky's, 10 percent; Maryland's, 34 percent; and Missouri's, 17 percent. At the same time, among the states of the old Northwest, Illinois and Ohio—with which Kentucky and Missouri appropriately should be compared—had attained urban populations of 14 percent and 17 percent, respectively.[68]

FIGURE 2

Urban Population by Region, 1800–1860

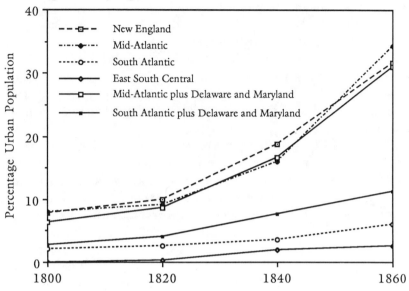

Source: See Table 1.

Key:
New England (Maine, New Hampshire, Vermont, Connecticut, Rhode Island, Massachusetts)
Mid-Atlantic (New York, New Jersey, Pennsylvania)
South Atlantic (Virginia, North Carolina, South Carolina, Georgia, Florida)
East South Central (Kentucky, Tennessee, Alabama, Mississippi)
Mid-Atlantic plus Delaware and Maryland
South Atlantic plus Delaware and Maryland

Note: The exact percentages for each region are: New England, 7.8 (1800), 9.9 (1820), 18.7 (1840), 31.7 (1860); Mid-Atlantic, 8 (1800), 9.1 (1820), 16 (1840), 34.3 (1860); South Atlantic, 2.2 (1800), 2.6 (1820), 3.6 (1840), 6 (1860); East South Central, o (1800), 0.4 (1820), 2 (1840), 5.6 (1860); Mid-Atlantic plus Delaware and Maryland, 6.4 (1800), 8.7 (1820), 16.6 (1840), 31.1 (1860); South Atlantic plus Delaware and Maryland, 2.7 (1800), 4.1 (1820), 7.6 (1840), 11.3 (1860).

The real significance of the development of the northeastern city-system and its frontier offshoot lies not in the existence of a few very large cities, but in the extension of the city-system in an exponentially growing network of smaller cities. In contrast, southern urban development continued to be concentrated in a small number of very large cities. In 1850, 92 percent of all urban southerners lived in one of nine cities; in 1860, 97 percent did.[69] By 1860, only fourteen southern cities (including Washington, D.C., and St. Louis) had populations of ten thousand or more. During most of the antebellum period, many of the largest cities within the South remained closely tied to their roots in the commercial world of merchant capital. In 1860, New Orleans, with its 168,675 inhabitants, accounted for more than 80 percent of Louisiana's urban population; Baltimore, with its 212,418 inhabitants, for more than 90 percent of Maryland's; even Charleston's 40,522 inhabitants assured it 75 percent of the urban population in a state in which only two other towns officially ranked as cities. Moreover, if Baltimore, by virtue of its slaves, ranked as a southern city, its economic relations marked it as integrally linked to the expansion of northern markets.[70]

The case of Charleston, if not typical, is instructive. For Charleston, unlike New York or Boston or Philadelphia, never developed beyond its heyday in the eighteenth century. By the opening of the nineteenth century, it was clearly showing signs of the stagnation that would lead it into a decline relative to other southern and northern cities and even, during the 1850s, into an absolute decline. Few, if any, southern cities outside Virginia and the border states developed significant manufacturing sectors. The links that bound southern cities to each other and to the national market for manufactured goods remained fragile. Maps of railroad and telegraph lines for the late antebellum period reveal that the South lagged far behind the North and the Midwest, and even the progress of the 1850s primarily linked staple-crop-producing regions to markets rather than binding industrializing towns and cities to each other.[71]

Southern society, as a whole, did not generate a city-system. Villages and small towns abounded but rarely crossed the threshold to urban status. In 1860, North Carolina contained only four cities of more than 2,500 inhabitants; South Carolina, three; Florida, two; Arkansas, one; Alabama, five, of which only Mobile exceeded 4,000; Georgia, ten, of which six included 4,000 or fewer residents; Louisiana, six; Maryland, three; Mississippi, five; Tennessee, three; and Texas, five.[72] Virginia, with its thirteen cities—including seven with more than 5,000 inhabitants and five with more than 10,000—looks positively modern in contrast to the others. But even Virginia did not begin to approach northern standards. The South as a whole did not include enough heavy concentrations of population to counterbalance its overwhelmingly rural character. Above all, from the perspective of women's history, its cities did not establish models for the transformation of women's experience.

The model of separate spheres, which has dominated the interpretation of women's experience during the first half of the nineteenth century, derived directly from the development of a complex capital-ist—and increasingly industrial and urban—society. The model unmis-takably reflects this particular urban experience. The tight link between the model of separate spheres and urban life is easy to miss, for many of the most devoted exponents of the model associated its virtues with rural life. Proponents of domesticity tended to deplore urban corrup-tion and the excesses of fashionable life, and indeed many of them may have been writing out of small-town rather than urban experience, as defined by the census. But they were writing out of incipient capitalist-urban social and gender relations. Their celebration of rural virtues, notably simplicity, suggests an ideological gambit rather than an accu-rate representation. Their incessant war against the dangers and cor-ruptions of urban life testifies to their sense of an immediate threat. The publications through which they propounded their views, like the associations through which they organized themselves and the evils they sought to redress, depended upon the facilities that only a na-scent, modern city-system could provide. To complicate matters fur-ther, the rural values of the model directly reflected its implicit class bias. Whereas middle-class women saw the city as a threat and, accord-ingly, saw working-class women as part of the problem to be ad-dressed, working-class women, who were developing their own urban culture and networks, disagreed. Also, the lives of northern rural women, who continued to contribute to household production, al-though frequently in new ways, did not unambiguously reflect the values of town domesticity.[73]

Living in an age of transformation, the proponents of rural values drew upon older ideas in order to interpret new conditions, but they inescapably transformed those ideas in applying them. Like so much else in antebellum American culture, the ideology of separate spheres and the attendant view of women's special nature contained enough of the old and general pieties to appeal to women—and men—who did not share in their development. But the original, specific referents derived from the world of capitalist cities and the towns in their orbits.

Specifically, the ideology of separate spheres rested upon the as-sumption that home and work constituted distinct domains that fell to women and men respectively. The very idea of the home represented a transformation of the older notion of household. The new image as-sumed that production occurred outside the walls of the home, which served to protect personal life from the intrusions of market relations. From this idea women, encouraged by men in general and clergymen in particular, rapidly developed the notion that they served as custodians of a special, private morality. Almost as rapidly, women themselves set about applying their moral standards to the larger world. They drew from the experience of conflicting moral standards an increased awareness of the values for which they, as women, stood. In organizing themselves to apply those values to the world outside the home, they availed themselves of the opportunities for meeting afforded by the city-system. And they especially addressed the problems that the city-system engendered: orphans, homeless women and children, prostitution. The special culture of northern women thus emerges as essentially urban and as the natural complement to the developing urban culture of northern men.[74]

The South also developed an urban culture, but of a different kind. As members of the national culture in particular and of the Western republic of letters in general, southerners drew upon the emerging bourgeois discourse to explain their own world to themselves. But they drew upon it selectively, and above all they never completely accepted the full implications of bourgeois individualism, much less the notion of the separation of home and work. The southerner's urban culture articulated the intersection between that bourgeois discourse and southern rural society. Cities did not dominate southerners' perceptions of proper relations between women and men, masters and servants, rich and poor. For the vast majority of southerners, including town and many city residents, the ideal of community remained grounded in the reality of southern society as preeminently a network of rural-rooted households that contained within themselves relations of production as well as those of reproduction.[75]

The class structure of southern society, with its rural character, perpetuated the view of charity as largely a private matter. Groups of women might join together to decorate a church for a holiday, or even to put on one of the South's noted "benevolent fairs." But these events remained exceptional and were closely linked to special occasions. The South as a whole lacked the groups, quickly becoming ubiquitous in the North, in which women came together to provide moral support for mothers who were rearing their children in a threatening urban environment, or to redeem prostitutes, or to provide for orphans, or to train fatherless working-class girls. Typically the southern ladies' societies were attached to the churches and were under male supervision. Occasionally they raised money to build, repair, or expand church facilities, but more often they raised money for domestic and, especially, foreign missions. In a few cities, well noted by travelers who placed what they saw in a European or northern context, southern ladies worked among the poor, but even in these cases they were usually acting as helpmeets to the ministers. For the most part, southern women did their charitable work individually, selectively, and close to home, if not within their own households.[76]

Because southern society discouraged women from developing many of the characteristics identified as typical of northeastern women—networks, bonds, voluntary associations, mothers' clubs, an ideology of domesticity—it powerfully discouraged them from developing such distinct northeastern attitudes and values as feminism and abolitionism. In many parts of the North there was a logical progression from women's networks to specific social and political attitudes, but that progression resulted from the capitalist and increasingly urban character of northern society rather than from some inherent property of women's networks. Southern women had, as all other rural women always have had, their own networks with neighbors and kin. But the ideological importance ascribed to northern women's networks obscures the recognition that women's networks have not always generated abolitionist and feminist attitudes.[77]

In these ways and many more the social relations of southern slave society crystallized for women in the household, which both contained and circumscribed their daily lives. The paucity of cities and even of large towns consigned the vast majority of southern women of different races and classes to rural lives. The distances between the houses of even modest farms obliged women to spend most of their time with the other members of their own households. Wealthy slaveholding women were more likely to live on large plantations with extensive boundaries, but they also had slaves to perform many of their gender-specific chores. Yeoman women lived on smaller farms, but they had few, if any, servants to perform their chores. Distance in the one instance may well have balanced labor obligations in the other. Black slave women suffered the double burden of distance and labor. But even if the specifics varied, the general rule obtained: Most rural southern women lived their lives within and interpreted their identities through the prism of specific households.

Northern women also suffered domestic confinement, but increasingly within homes rather than productive households. If, in the North, the self-revolutionizing potential of the capitalist market faced significant resistance from some households, even the most recalcitrant inevitably succumbed to the expanding tentacles of the market, albeit according to different timetables that depended upon location and nature of production. In other words, northern households increasingly functioned as more or less permeable extrusions of the market rather than as enclaves within it. Southern households proved more resilient. In this respect, southern society developed as a brave new world indeed. It yanked a society from the self-revolutionizing jaws of capitalist development and expended brains, brawn, heart, and ultimately blood to defend what it had wrought: a distinctive social formation composed of a network of rural households that, politically and economically, took their decisive character and relations from slavery as a social system.

The concept of "household" has enjoyed a growing popularity among American historians, especially among rural and colonial historians. In association with "*mentalité*" and "peasantry," it is used to undercut the stereotype of all Americans as incipient capitalist entrepreneurs since the beginnings of settlement. A "household mode of production" has even been proposed as an appropriate concept to elucidate the exceptionalism of early American society. Yet the theoretically and historically imprecise concept of household offers historians a valuable tool of analysis only on condition that they carefully define it as a unit, pay attention to its internal dynamics, and establish its relation to the dominant mode of production.[78] From African chiefdoms, to the Greek *oikos*, to the peasantry of medieval France, to the Italian city-states, to the early-modern English countryside and beyond, various productive systems, like various political relations, have been anchored in households. Thus, the early French attempts at systematic taxation assessed obligations by hearths or households (*feux*). One can sympathize with those harassed royal officials: The fledgling state they represented could not begin to keep track of family members, who had disconcerting tendencies to die or to migrate temporarily. But they, like others in their situation, could identify households as taxable units of residence and probably production. It was left to the members to determine the principles that governed each one's contribution to the common obligation.

The contemporary use of the term "household" by historians largely derives from anthropology, and especially from West Indian fieldwork. The anthropologists who elaborated the concept probably had much the same concerns as the early French tax collectors. They wanted to account for units or groups of people who did not seem to conform to what ethnocentric Western scholars regarded as normative or even normal organization—so-called coresident nuclear families.[79] The household offers one way of studying basic social units without becoming embroiled in the complexities of kin relations. And household frequently offers the seductive mirage of precision, for the element of coresidence suggests that households are simply objective categories—subunits of a territory or state. Unfortunately, life resists pigeonholes, and therefore so must scholars. Household members need not reside in households, although to be called members they probably must return occasionally, contribute income, or in some other way identify themselves with the unit. But the problems of membership do not exhaust the complexities of the household as a unit of analysis.

We cannot afford to postulate transhistorical households any more than we can afford to postulate transhistorical cities. We should not, that is, turn to households as to so many *dei ex machinae*, to distract from or to solve apparently intractable problems of class relations, modes of production, and forms of development. The very nature of the household depends upon its relations to the larger systems in which it is embedded. The household should more appropriately be seen as a symptom or manifestation of historically specific social relations than as their cause or essence. To argue that dominant political, social, and economic relations influence the formation, development, and persistence of households is not to deny that households also influence those relations. Obviously they do. But political and legal institutions, the complexity, nature, and availability of markets, and the social relations of production, among other factors, shape the ways in which households develop. Households may legitimately be viewed as the primary mediating units between the individual and society, as genuinely pivotal institutions, but they must be subjected to a scrupulous analysis of their specific character and activities in interaction with different social systems. Households may, to take a few examples, include more or less production, rely more or less heavily on kin relations for their self-definition, include more or fewer members, or be more or less permeated by the principles of commodity production and the wage relation. Households may, in short, incorporate more or less of the business of society within themselves. They may vary from a single room, to which a single individual returns to sleep, to a self-sufficient family farm, to—conceivably—a large noble compound in some West African society.

Southern historians have, by and large, paid less attention to the role of households than have historians of the northern colonies and states, notably those who study colonial and rural America, and some students of working people since that time.[80] Some southern historians, particularly Steven Hahn, have admirably discussed the distinctiveness of southern yeoman households but have paid less attention to the importance of slaveholding plantations as households. The lively and occasionally acrimonious debates over the nature of southern slave society have focused largely on aggregate characteristics. There have been numerous and sometimes excellent studies of individual plantations or farms, but even they have not normally devoted much attention to the relations between the social and productive dynamics of the plantation or farm as a household.

The existing studies of plantations and farms can, in some measure, be adapted to the study of the household, but they cannot be expected to correct the general analyses simply through an accumulation of case studies.[81] Scholars who interpret southern slave society as essentially capitalist, like those who interpret it as manifesting decisive noncapitalist features, converge in their descriptions of plantations or farms. They differ in their interpretation of the social and economic characteristics of relations among households, in their assessment of the principles that informed household organization, and, especially, in their estimates of the permeability of household boundaries. They do not disagree over the capitalist character of the world market within which southern households were embedded or over the importance of chattel slavery as compared to free wage labor in the larger units of production. They do disagree over the implications of chattel slavery for the political economy, the political culture, the developmental possibilities, and the worldview of southern society. Normally, they do not consider the implications of any of these factors for southern women, white or black.

At one extreme in the debate over the implications of chattel slavery for antebellum southern society, scholars such as Lewis C. Gray, Kenneth Stampp, Robert Fogel, and Stanley Engerman have emphasized the compatibility of chattel slavery and capitalist development. This tendency emphasizes the planters' similarity to all other rational capitalist entrepreneurs. More recently, James Oakes has attempted to assimilate southern and northern farmers into a single category of aggressive, middle-class men-on-the-make. Fogel and Engerman, acutely sensitive to the tie between labor relations and political economy as a whole, drive the capitalist interpretation to its logical conclusion and insist upon the similarities between slave labor and capitalist wage labor. Tellingly, despite their determined effort to pay attention to slave women's experience, their failure to consider gender in the context of household relations leads them to slight obvious significant differences between the experience of free and slave labor.[82]

At the other extreme, a group of primarily Marxist scholars, including Eugene D. Genovese, Steven Hahn, Harold Woodman, Mark Tushnet, Barbara Fields, and Armstead Robinson, insists upon the special character of slave labor and its implications for the general political economy of the society. The general conclusions of their work are compatible with those of a variety of other scholars such as Peter Kolchin and Drew Faust, and even with those of such conservatives as Lewis Simpson and M. E. Bradford, despite very different formulations. Others, from Ulrich B. Phillips onward, have remained ambiguous on the main theoretical point. Gavin Wright, who has made seminal contributions to the discussion of political economy and who emphasizes the duality of the southern economy, curiously avoids the interpretation that would logically seem to flow from his own work, namely that decisive political and ideological differences evolved from slaveholding or nonslaveholding. All adherents of the various general interpretations of slave society have turned to the plantation to illustrate and buttress their interpretations, but none has systematically examined plantations or farms as households that pooled incomes or resources, and none has placed the question of gender relations at the center of his or her picture of southern society.[83]

Scholars whose primary interests lie in small slaveholders and yeomen have naturally emphasized the farm rather than the plantation as the characteristic southern agricultural unit. Indeed, the growing attention to the ubiquity of small and medium-sized farms throughout the antebellum South has tempted some—most recently Oakes—to argue that the plain folk harbored the real lifeblood of southern society. The demographic predominance of the yeomanry and small planters has never been in doubt, but the most fruitful way to interpret their experience and impact remains subject to debate. Hahn has recently developed Wright's view of the dual economy within an explicitly Marxist context and has demonstrated that, despite superficial similarities, the character of the Georgia yeomanry differed dramatically from that of their northern farmer counterparts. Initially, Hahn did not explicitly evoke the household as a unit of analysis, even though his work suggested the rich potential of the household as a prism through which to view not merely the discrete units that constituted southern society, but also the nature and force of the ties that bound those units to each other. In his more recent work, however, the household has assumed a more important place.[84]

The household constitutes an indispensable unit of analysis for southern society, but southern households can hardly be taken as monolithic. In this book, I consider only agricultural households, for the primary wealth of southern society came overwhelmingly from agriculture throughout the antebellum period. The models of women's roles in particular and gender relations in general derived primarily from their prototypes within rural households. The salient distinctions among rural households remain problematic, but I provisionally accept the conventional classification of planters as those holding more than twenty slaves, small planters as those holding ten to nineteen slaves, and yeoman slaveholders as those holding nine slaves or fewer. Households that contained no slaves at all prove yet more difficult to classify, for they included everything from poor whites to prosperous yeomen to slaveholding offspring who would rapidly become slaveholders themselves. To complicate matters further, the nature, composition, and boundaries of various southern households cannot be assumed a priori, not least because the stark number of slaves does not correspond to the number of hands. A holding of twenty slaves normally included a family or two and some unattached men or women.[85]

The attempt to view southern society as a network of households thus requires not merely a preliminary understanding of the nature of the society, but also a working model of the household and its dynamics. Southern households challenge neat categorization, but they do conform to some of the general principles that have emerged from the comparative study of households. Donald Bender has suggested that any analysis of households must recognize the three theoretically distinct, if practically overlapping, categories of kin (consanguineal and affinal relations), propinquity (coresidence), and domestic functions. His proposal appropriately calls attention to the fallacies of reducing households only to family or coresidence, even if family or coresidence may, in any specific situation, constitute important principles of household membership and the salient features of household members' self-representation. The caution especially obtains for southern plantation society, in which master and slave households interlocked in a complex web of interdependency.[86]

A working definition of households as units that pool income or resources implicitly respects Bender's objection to equating them arbitrarily with families or coresidence but does not solve all problems. As a hypothesis, the formulation of a household as the pooling of income or resources emphasizes the material bases of any household. But that hypothesis must also take account of the changes in forms of income and resources and the changing social relations that generate them. It also requires precise reference to the ways in which the boundaries of the household should be drawn and the criteria for household membership established. Unmodified, concentration on the pooling of income and resources implicitly distracts attention from the relations of dependency and power between the members of genders, generations, and possible classes who have claims upon the income or resources of the unit. Households, whatever their boundaries, presumably share income and resources in the interests of consumption, reproduction, or possibly production. In each of these activities, household members differ in their contributions to and their control over the common fund. Differential contributions and rewards constitute a significant problem and a possible source of latent or manifest conflict in all households, but the nature and substance of those conflicts also differ according to the relations between specific households and the larger society in which they are inscribed.

Harriet Friedmann has argued provocatively that peasant households do not embody the principles that characterize the capitalist markets in which they sell their products. She sharply distinguishes between peasant households and households engaged in petty commodity production, for, in her view, petty commodity producers can move to full "commoditization" by a simple intensification of the relations and process in which they are engaged, whereas peasant households must undergo a thorough transformation in order to be assimilated fully into capitalist social formations. To embody the logic of the capitalist wage relation, peasant households must, in Friedmann's word, "decompose" before they can reconstitute themselves as units fully integrated into the logic of the capitalist mode of production.

Friedmann does not discuss the antebellum southern household per se, but she suggestively distinguishes between the hacienda and postbellum southern sharecropping units as respectively precapitalist and capitalist social formations. In her judgment the hacienda, in its various forms, remains logically tied to its roots in the *encomienda* ("which conferred the right to the labour of specific indigenous peoples") and the *mercedes de tierras* ("which granted lands to colonists for military service"). It thus remains closely bound to the manorial forms that predominated in medieval Europe. Sharecropping, by contrast, rests upon contractual relations, even though it may coexist with independent household production.[87] As Eugene D. Genovese and I have argued elsewhere, the specific social formations of antebellum southern plantations cannot be assimilated directly to the hacienda, in part because of their discrete origins, but they did rest upon unfree labor relations that distinguished them sharply from fully capitalist agricultural units.[88] Friedmann's argument proves compatible with the view that southern slave society developed as an offshoot of merchant capital and did not shed its hybrid character until the Civil War.

The debate over the character of the southern economy and its potential for growth has generated a massive investigation of the aggregate indicators of southern economic performance. Although the statistics permit a variety of interpretations, ultimately the most telling of them suggest that the main features of southern development were the role of world demand in establishing the level of profits; the low rate of urbanization and industrialization; the high level of regional self-sufficiency in conjunction with the low level of development of internal markets; the disinclination of planters to invest in industry despite its potentially high profits; and, especially, the underdeveloped market in free labor-power. Recent work on southern law, notably that of Mark Tushnet, has demonstrated the ways in which the legal implications of the master-slave relationship permeated southern legal institutions. Certainly chattel slavery decisively shaped the experience and possibilities of southern women. And the defense of slavery penetrated every element of southern ideology, reshaping national, political, economic, and religious discourses into characteristically southern patterns.[89]

It has become a commonplace that households—or families—reproduce the dominant social relations and ideologies of the social formations to which they belong. But aside from its heuristic, commonsensical value, the proposition leaves much to be desired. Like any tautology, it fails to account for change and, more important for our purposes, it fails to account for the wide variation in the material foundations of households and thus for the wide variation in the possible ways that households might ensure the compliance of their members. In this perspective the specific nature of specific types of households as units that pool income and resources becomes decisive, especially if one pays close attention to the sources of income as structural relations between the household and the larger economy and society.

The separation of labor from the land and the emergence of capitalist ground rent in Great Britain—the emergence of a market in labor-power and in land—exercised a decisive influence on the establishment of southern households. The southern colonies of North America rapidly manifested a demand for labor that was met, especially during the middle and late seventeenth century, by the surplus labor generated by the internal transformation of the British economy.[90] Initially, the migration of landless whites provided a pool of indentured servants as dependent laborers for early southern settlers, but at the end of their term of service these laborers actively sought to establish their own households based on the ownership and exploitation of land. Although the demographic characteristics of the first generations of settlers, at least through the middle of the seventeenth century, precluded rapid expansion—and even reproduction—of households, the independent household remained the dominant model despite the difficulty for many of ensuring its survival. With the consolidation of settlements and demographic adaptation, the opportunity for landownership seriously undermined the supply of wage labor, and by the third quarter of the seventeenth century the foundations for the development of a slaveholding society had been laid, although its specific form did not coalesce until the mid-eighteenth century. The difficulty of securing a long-term, stable agricultural wage-labor force led successful planters to the use of slaves. The introduction of slavery did not modify the structure of the settlements as a network of households, but rather reinforced it. The world market simultaneously strengthened the colonies' dependence on the metropolis and widened the divergence between southern and metropolitan social systems.[91]

From the seventeenth century until the collapse of southern slave society, southern household formation followed a variety of patterns according to crop, region, and level of income. But throughout the period, southern society grew as a proliferation of households. Although in this respect southern expansion did not necessarily differ from northern, the early introduction of slavery as the foundation for the cultivation of staple crops breathed a different content into the dominant form of southern households. In particular, it established distinct limits on the penetration of market relations into the interstices of southern households.

Students of antebellum southern economy and society have tended to regard the degree of self-sufficiency as a principal indicator of the character of southern slave society, but the debate remains confused with respect to both argument and evidence. In no instance should self-sufficiency be taken to mean autarchy. The extent of self-sufficiency varied according to region, stage of settlement, and level of income. Northern farm households—or communities of households—may have been more self-sufficient than previously assumed. Frontier households normally went through at least a brief period of imposed self-sufficiency. Preliminary investigations nonetheless suggest that many southern households engaged in more household manufacture and produced more of their own foodstuffs, and for a longer period of time, than did northern ones. Even so, the substantial outlay for equipment (cards, looms, spinning wheels) required by household production may have limited the extent to which poorer households could engage in it.[92]

Both those who view the antebellum South as essentially capitalist and those who view it as a distinct slave society have defended and attacked the position that antebellum southern households were largely self-sufficient. Those who contend that the antebellum South was essentially capitalist and that the slave plantations were essentially self-sufficient apparently wish to demonstrate the rationality of the planters as entrepreneurs, the flexibility of slave labor, and the existence of economies of scale in southern agriculture. Those who take the position that the antebellum South was a distinct slave society and that the slave plantations depended largely on food purchase apparently wish to demonstrate the irrationality of the planters, the limitations imposed by the use of slave labor, and the economic dependency of the region as a whole.[93] Samuel Hilliard has argued that the South as a whole was more self-sufficient—that is, less deeply engaged in market exchange—than were the Northeast or the old Northwest. He also argues that discrete areas within the South, notably those with the highest concentration of large plantations and slaves and those adjacent to large waterways and ports, were heavily engaged in market transactions for basic foodstuffs and other supplies.[94]

Because Hilliard's work relies on aggregate statistics, it cannot answer questions about the behavior of specific households—questions whose answers can only be determined through the study of individual records—and may even be misleading about the behavior of households of different sizes. In the light of more recent work, access to transportation appears to have been more important than size of household. But access to transportation primarily meant access to the national, world, and, in some measure, regional markets. Local markets remained small, scattered, and fragile. Above all, they did not supply the needs of the larger households, which frequently bought in bulk or ordered luxury goods from distant places, including the North and Europe. Their market behavior did not, accordingly, contribute significantly to the development of local marketplaces except in the cases of a few large and medium-sized cities—Charleston, Mobile, New Orleans, Memphis.[95]

The specific form of the debate over self-sufficiency has partially obscured the most serious consequences of southern slavery for southern economic development. The preference of individual planters for household production or for the purchase of food and basic goods may have had significant consequences for the economic success of the planter. A planter who speculated unwisely on the possible price of cotton, only to face a collapse in cotton prices at the moment he had committed his household to heavy dependence upon the purchase of food, could incur dangerous indebtedness and risk the forced sale of some of his slaves—in short, capital losses and social derangement.[96] But however portentous these choices in individual cases, they had little effect on the general structure of southern households or on the large planters who purchased food and other consumer goods in the aggregate.

As a general rule, southern households purchased their provisions from the same merchants or factors on whom they depended for the sale of their cotton or extension of their credit. Their demand reinforced the dependence of their region on merchant capital and external capitalist social formations; it did not contribute to the capitalist development of the region. Their behavior thus strengthened the tendency of smaller households to turn to cotton or some other staple as the first cash crop, and to turn to the purchase of slaves for any increase in their labor force. The aggregate statistics for household production fall into roughly the same pattern as those for food purchase. The per-capita value of household manufactures remained higher throughout much of the South than it did for the rest of the nation. The southern counties in which the per-capita value of household manufactures was negligible are the same as those in which the value of purchased food stuffs was highest. But this information only confirms that the regions surrounding New Orleans, Charleston, Mobile, and other ports constituted variants of the classic plantation economies that had been generated by merchant capital at least since the early colonization of the Azores.[97]

The debate over the self-sufficiency or market dependence of southern farms underscores the importance of southern households as a basic unit of analysis for southern society. Lewis C. Gray, in his indispensable study of southern agriculture, proposed differentiating yeoman farmers from small planters according to their choice of diversification or staple cultivation. In fact, his distinction between those who diversified and those who cultivated the staple probably applies to all categories of southern households as defined by numbers of slaves. In this respect, it could be said that the proportion of land that any farmer gave to diversification and staple cultivation reflected a choice by a farmer in any particular category of household, but was not the determining characteristic of the household. Yet the location of the household, its access to transportation, and the suitability of its soil and climate for staple cultivation all influenced the choices made by farmers. Regions such as northern Virginia early tended toward the diversification and self-sufficiency that characterized that region by the late eighteenth century and the Tidewater by the early nineteenth century. But even those regions most given over to general cultivation, in which the households most resembled units of petty commodity production, remained tied to the slave system as a whole—in part because of political connections and in part because the path to economic growth lay through the acquisition of slave labor rather than through the kinds of capital intensiveness that characterized industrial capitalist development and was increasingly coming to characterize the agricultural sector of northern capitalism.[98]

Multiple ties bound the yeomanry to the larger slave society. Much of the expansion of southern society occurred through the proliferation of yeoman households, which became numerically preponderant throughout much of the South, especially the Upper South. These households developed, not as discrete units in an atomized world, but within and subject to the vicissitudes of slave society. The nature of southern slave society encouraged regionally specific forms of production and reproduction, notably a sharp distinction between the internal dynamics of the household and the capitalist world market. Like the larger plantations that dominated the economy, yeoman households remained largely impermeable to the intrusion of the market, specifically to the wage relation, and thus heavily dependent upon family labor. Expansion of production led them toward the hire and purchase of slaves rather than the employment of free labor. Women's labor played an essential role in assuring the viability of yeoman households. Even yeoman production of cotton may be linked to the self-sufficiency of the farm and the role of women's labor. Many yeoman households produced cotton for internal consumption as well as, or even instead of, for the market. Yeoman women transformed cotton into clothing for household members or engaged in networks of local exchange—for example, trading wool for carding or cotton for weaving.

The plantation or farm constituted the essential unit within which masters and slaves pooled income and resources. Coresidence and division of domestic functions normally defined the unit. There were exceptions in the case of very large planters, who might own more than one plantation or who might divide a single plantation into two or more quarters. But throughout much of the South, the empirically self-evident unit of the contiguous farm or plantation was coterminous with the boundaries of the household. These households largely circumscribed the daily lives of women and slaves. The masters who presided over them constituted the principal, although never exclusive, mediators between the inhabitants of the household and the larger world. This view of households as units that pooled income and resources underscores the interdependence of slave and slaveowning households. Whether from the perspective of income or from that of power—understood as the minimal ability to make the important decisions that affect one's life—slaves belonged to the households of their masters. Such truncated households as slaves did manage to form existed at the pleasure or with the sufferance of the master. They had no independent economic bases worthy of the name, and they could not withstand the exercise of the master's will or the fluctuating economic fortunes of his household. This estimate of the respective abilities of masters and slaves to form viable households does not imply acceptance of the thesis of an infantilized or docile slave force. Slaves resisted the ramifications of their situation in innumerable ways, and their adjustment reflected, not passive acquiescence, but active struggles to shape their own lives as much as conditions would permit. In decisive ways, however, they could not control those conditions.[99]

The debates about North American slavery as political economy and as social system have not, on the whole, addressed the question of the household. Presumably, those who view southern society as capitalist and those who view it as precapitalist would be likely to differ about the problematical status of slave households. Yet it is striking that similar pictures of the large plantations emerge from the writings of those who differ sharply on other matters. Fogel and Engerman, for example, do not pose the question of the slave household. They insist upon the integrity of the slave family and its Victorian mores, on the work ethic of the slaves as laborers, and on the independent accomplishments of the slave community, but when they turn to describing the daily workings of the large plantation they emphasize, intentionally or not, the slaveholder's direction of a complex interrelated household. They supplement their picture of the master's leadership with emphasis upon slave cabins, supplemental activities, and strong family ties among slaves. But they never assess the nature of the slave household, much less its changing status and composition over time within a specific plantation. Their general description presents the master rather than the slaves as the one who determined the basic allocation of income and resources. Only on South Carolina rice plantations did the slaves, who worked according to the task system, develop greater control over their own resources.[100]

How far can we stretch the evidence? Even Fogel and Engerman, with their strong views on the capitalist nature of the system, do not describe the sustenance of the slave as a wage. There can be no doubt that the slave's sustenance could be categorized as income in the most general sense, but that description contributes little to an analysis that seeks to expose the specific character of slavery as a system of labor relations. In particular instances, individual slaves might generate bits of income for themselves, through their "rights" to retain a portion of their hire or through the sale of commodities that they had cultivated or produced on their own time. Some even saved enough to buy their freedom. But even in most of these cases, the hire of slaves—certainly of rural slaves—was negotiated by masters or with their approval, and the slaves' commodities were sold to masters who discouraged independent marketing or peddling. In short, in the vast majority of cases, masters mediated the slaves' income-yielding labor.

When we consider the various categories of income—wages, household subsistence activities, marketing, rent, and transfer payments—it becomes clear that slaves, with the possible exception of those of the South Carolina rice coast, rarely if ever determined their own relation to income and, as a rule, assuredly did not do so as members of independent households. Those who worked by the task rather than the gang system may have enjoyed better opportunities to work for themselves, but not enough to undermine significantly the prevailing system. Studies of individual plantations suggest that masters actively sought the maximum control of their slaves' lives. And, although masters might emerge less than victorious from struggles with individual slaves or with their slave force as a whole, they were reasonably successful in their attempts to forestall the formation of independent slave households. Such households did exist, but they existed on the sufferance of the master, even when, as Herbert Gutman forcefully argues, they did not conform to white models.[101]

Slave households, in other words, cannot profitably be considered without reference to the condition of chattel slavery, no matter how much African and other influences are taken into account. Slaves— even more than serfs, peasants, or proletarians—lacked the margin of autonomy or choice that would permit them to constitute anything but fragmentary or truncated households. If the pooling of income and resources was problematical among slaves who lived on the same plantations, it was next to impossible for slaves who lived on different plantations. Slaves regularly and even heroically struggled with their masters to shape their own lives, relations, and culture, but their residence within those masters' households inescapably confronted them with long odds.[102]

Slaves can more appropriately be regarded as members of the household of their master—defined as the plantation or farm—than as primarily members of distinct slave households. Defined as property, slaves could not legally own property. Although they could, within limits, shape the composition of the subhouseholds to which they belonged, they had no legal right to do so. Only at the margin could they affect the nature of the income they received or even its disposition. It is possible to consider the basic support allocated to slaves as the maintenance of working capital from the perspective of the masters, rather than as wages from the perspective of the slaves, but neither description is satisfactory.

Slaves normally received their basic support in kind: rations, clothing, lodging. Frequently they contributed to the production of these goods through their own subsistence activities, because many farms and plantations produced their own basic food supply. Most slaveholders were likely to buy shoes and some clothing for their slaves, although many bought cloth and made clothing from it, and some even produced cloth. Slave cabins were usually—there were many exceptions—constructed by slaves, normally from logs cleared from the plantation land. But all goods belonged to the master, and to the extent that the slaves participated in their production, they did so under the master's direction. The master even oversaw the cleaning of slave cabins. Many masters required a thorough cleaning one to four times a year. The cleaning, and sometimes the whitewashing of cabins and the resetting or reliming of floors, would be undertaken by all members of the plantation household on the same day. The master also assumed primary responsibility for the health care for his slaves.

Slaves could contest their master's control in innumerable ways, and most masters, even the most authoritarian, learned to be more flexible than they might have preferred in their management of their "troublesome property." A wise master might well tolerate a range of behavior, from malingering in the infirmary for a few extra days, to running away for short periods, to pilfering. Never the "total institution" that some have claimed it to be, southern slavery always permitted considerable give-and-take. On many plantations, slaves cultivated their own garden plots to supplement their diets or even raised a few chickens for the eggs or for sale. Slave men often hunted small game to add variety to the basic rations and sometimes even sold it to their mistresses. These additional forms of income, like pork stolen from the master's storehouse, would be shared with other members of the slave community, especially the members of one family or cabin. But, to the extent that the slave—and the slave's time—belonged to the master, these forms can best be understood as redistributions of the income of the plantation household as a whole. And indeed, the slaves rationalized their stealing as "taking"—as a mere transmutation of the master's property from one form to another—and explicitly asserted their own sense of redistribution within a household of which they were a part. The success of the plantation as a whole thus governed the basic income and resources of all its members. And most slaves recognized the importance of the master's prosperity to their own well-being, even if they did not accept his view of them as perpetual dependents.

Southern slaveholding women accepted their position of dependence within the household more readily than slave women. They even propounded the virtues of an ideology that, in its positive aspects, celebrated the benefits of corporatism, hierarchy, and the proper submission of some members of society to others. Their class position afforded them innumerable privileges relative to the other women in their society. They did not commonly bemoan this social and economic position, even if they occasionally complained about specific inconveniences. Their protests against the price extracted from them by the system rarely amounted to a systematic defense of the rights of women as women. The differences between their attitudes and those of northern defenders of women's rights can best be understood if, with no insult intended, we consider various defenses of women's interests and perceptions as a form of sibling rivalry.

Women who protest specific burdens normally seek for themselves what they perceive their brothers as enjoying. Southern slaveholding women were not, as a general rule, pining to become northern middle-class housewives, and they assuredly were not advocating equality among the women in their society. They would have been happy to have their husbands, brothers, and fathers cease trifling with slave women. They would have been happy to escape some of the trials of the supervision of human property, provided, of course, that they would neither have to do their own cooking and washing nor, heaven forbid, have to manage detested Irish servants. The voluminous papers of educated women display a clear and often militant defense of their class privileges and their distance from lower-class white as well as black women.

The complex class relations of southern society confronted slave-holding women with special problems. To take their own favorite example, plantation mistresses carried heavy responsibilities for overseeing the work of house slaves. The tensions between mistress and servant could run high, all the way from angry blows to companionship. The law—not to mention the social emphasis placed on male governance of the household and its members—discouraged women from managing slaves. The law never formally prohibited, and in fact the men's frequent absences encouraged, women's everyday management of plantations. But both the law and the tradition of male dominance sharply limited the practical and psychological effectiveness of their discipline. The master normally administered the heavy punishments, and the slaves knew it. Slave men often challenged masters and overseers, but usually not in the way that Hampton challenged Sarah Gayle. As slaves would have been the first to insist, and as both male and female slaveholders well knew, mistresses could be the very devil. A mean mistress stood second to no master in her cruelty, although her strength was less. Most mistresses managed slave women rather than slave men, for most of the house servants were female, and in the absence of the master most mistresses relied on overseers or drivers to discipline the field hands. Thus, although mistresses could and did brutally abuse their female slaves, on grounds of physical strength they were less likely than men to kill them. The plantation mistress's class and race enabled her to tell slaves what to do, to try to get them to do it, and to box or whip them if they did not. But her gender plainly informed them that she was no "massa."

If black and even white southern women were known to rail against "massa" and the system that empowered him, they did not do so in the language of bourgeois feminism or in the spirit of its content. In the case of black slave women, the objects of resistance and revolt increasingly focused on the violent repudiation of the system and on the assertion of their own wills and personal worth. Class and racial struggles assumed priority over the gender struggle, even though class and racial struggles might be experienced and expressed in gender-specific, and indeed sex-specific, ways. Black slave women's primary gender struggles concerned their relations with black men, although these struggles, too, were deeply affected by their common confrontation with white men and women. The gender struggles of white slaveholding women also primarily concerned their relations with the men of their own race and class. But those struggles did not assume the forms or use the language developed by the early northern feminists. The hard truth is that slave and slaveholding women occupied antagonistic positions, frequently mediated by complex and conflicted personal relations. The experience, consciousness, and goals of yeoman women complicate the picture further, for they had their own antagonisms to both slave and slaveholding women, and perhaps some bonds with both.[103]

Rural southern women of all classes and races shared a distaste for housework and an uneasy relation to the bourgeois and evangelical virtues of work, thrift, and cleanliness. Critical visitors to the South concurred that slavery was inimical to bourgeois domesticity. Northern bourgeois literature featured the kitchen as the heart of the household, the mother's empire. In the kitchen, housework became nurture and the woman's prescribed toil became a mission of love.[104] Southern literature, like southern architecture, honored the kitchen by expelling it from the house. Whereas New Englanders had developed their houses, including the kitchens, in conjunction with the development of capitalist agriculture, southerners, beginning in the seventeenth century, developed theirs by banishing the kitchen to a separate building. Slaveholding women visited the kitchen and supervised its denizens, but did not linger. Slave women primarily worked in the kitchens of others, preparing food for others, although at least some slave cooks took much more pride in the kitchen than their mistresses did. Slave women also cooked over open fires for their own families in the quarters, where they did not have kitchens at all. For both slave and slaveholding women, their positions as wives and mothers remained divorced from the labors of domesticity with which those positions were closely linked even in the rural sectors of the bourgeois North.[105]

Southern women, black and white, lived largely within the confines of the plantation households that embodied the fundamental relations of southern slave society. Their confinement, which should not be confused with the domestic confinement of middle-class northeastern women, bound them in the explosive intimacy of a shared world but not in a woman's sphere.

The special hybrid character of the South as a slave society in but not of the transatlantic capitalist world and the internal and external relations of the southern plantation household had distinct consequences for the character, culture, and politics of the southern slaveholding class and for those of the slaves and yeomen as well. The household determined the daily lives of southern women, and the network of households determined women's social context. The slave South, as a social formation, imposed special constraints on the lives of all southern women. It bound them together in webs of production and reproduction over which white men presided. The role of head of household formed the basis for the illusion of equality as citizens that informed the political culture of white men. The exclusion from that role, as in a distorted mirror image, established the constraints under which black slave men suffered. It especially constrained them by granting the jural-political control of black women to white male heads of households. The distinct southern form of male dominance was anchored in the household as the fundamental productive and reproductive unit of slave society. The experience of individual women, like the relations among women of different classes and races within and among households, had its roots in a web of familial and social relations anchored in individual farm and plantation households and in the households of the villages and towns they extruded.

2   *The View from the Big House*

. . . a chance visit, the going to Church, shopping, an odd volume read, an odd page written—and when the long list of seams and hems and gatherings added, my life is given, at least the mode of spending it.
—Sarah Ann
  Haynsworth Gayle

Southern women normally viewed the household from within rather than from without, as a web of relations and responsibilities, and especially as the social networks that anchored their daily lives—the living embodiment of their relations with and obligations to others. Immersed in the household, they responded to the specifics of everyday life in patterns of behavior and belief that had negative as well as positive overtones. When they stepped back from the press of immediate tasks and encounters they asked themselves what they were about in this world and what they could hope for in the next. For they were generally God-fearing women who interpreted everyday relations and responsibilities as manifestations of social and divine order.

For slaveholding women, and in some measure for slave women too, the most positive interpretation of the household lay in the metaphor "my family, white and black," which captured the important, if elusive, vision of an organic community. The white slaveholding women's sense of community rested upon a psychological sense of belonging to a proper order—upon an obliteration or softening of the boundaries between egos, rather than an accentuation of them. In this respect, the positive sense of household membership verged on an encompassing feeling of identification—of self as bound to others. Conversely, the negative sense of household membership derived primarily from the experiences of conflict with other household members, of abandonment, of responsibilities that exceeded a woman's patience and strength. Frustration, danger, and conflict exacerbated a sense of separation. In both senses, the metaphor of family obtained: The relations of the household defied neat sociological classification and remained relations among those who were bound together by ties deeper than mere interest. In this quality they resembled the relations among family members.

Relations among household members, like relations among family members, were not equal. Just as the family fell to the authority of the father, the household fell to that of the master, and father and master were one and the same. The man who exercised the two roles drew upon each to strengthen the other: The beneficent paternalism of the father was ever shadowed by the power of the master, just as the power of the master was tempered by the beneficent paternalism of the father. As Charles Colcock Jones, Jr., wrote to his parents upon the death of a neighbor: "The hopes of a family, the thousand social relations incident to the situation of father, master, citizen, neighbor, are thus in a moment sundered."[1]

The very phrase, "my family, white and black," expressed the abiding paternalistic male dominance of southern social relations. The "my" of the metaphor first and foremost embodied the perspective and preeminence of the white slaveholder, who dominated the household at home and represented it abroad. Whether viewed metaphorically as family or structurally as household, the unit was in the first instance the master's, although other members could also name it as their own. Indeed, they were encouraged to, but only according to their station. For if the master no doubt welcomed their heartfelt identification, he never intended the identifications of others to challenge the primacy of his own. Women members, black and white, surely understood and tended to comply with these implicit rules, but their very compliance colored their own identifications with the unit that simultaneously protected, verified, and confined them. Women's personal identification included all the tensions that resulted from subordinate and dependent status in southern society as well as in the households that anchored it.[2]

White and black women's complex and frequently conflicted relations with the premier custodian of their own specific and different subordinations lay at the core of their identities and informed their everyday lives in innumerable particulars. Women were bound to each other in the household, not in sisterhood, but by their specific and different relations to its master. White women rarely challenged the

legitimacy of paternal domination directly, even if they covertly resisted its abuses, especially its departures from their own definitions of
legitimacy. Black women challenged the master with far greater frequency and bitterness, but even they were more likely to protest his
failure to fulfill his responsibilities than to resist his pretensions to
authority. And when they did resist those pretensions, they were pro-
testing the system of social relations embodied by the master's authority. In other words, both black slave and white slaveholding
women contributed through both resistance and acquiescence to the
definition of the specific everyday practice of the male dominance that
informed southern society. In 1889, Emmaline Eve penned a recollection of her father before the war:

> He brought his children up in the fear of God and by precept and
> example taught the way of life. Himself the Patriarch of his house-
> hold. He conducted the church service at home when no other
> place of worship was in reach. . . . He was particularly faithful to
> his numerous slaves, having those around him at family worship
> every morning and evening. He built for his plantationers a
> church on Butler's Creek which he had dedicated, and is still in
> use by the negroes.[3]

Rural and village slaveholding households provided the structure
for the characteristic articulations of southern social relations. Those
households resembled each other in disposition of buildings, nature of
tasks, and mixed black and white membership. Distinctions of size and
wealth bore heavily upon both black and white women, but only at the
upper and lower limits did they recognizably affect the essentials of
everyday life. Even at the upper level of the lowcountry Chivalry and at
the lower level of the smallest slaveholders, these distinctions did not
transform women's experience so thoroughly as to render it qualitatively different from that of the women who belonged to middling
slaveholding households.

The typical slaveholding household, which differed significantly
from northern homes and midwestern farmsteads, invariably included
house, outbuildings, fields, gardens, and slave quarters. It could vary
in the size, complexity, and comfort of the buildings, as well as in the
size and variety of fields, gardens, pasture, orchard, and forest. Emily
Burke, writing home from Georgia to northern friends, described
what she considered a typical example. The main house lodged "the
father of the family and all the females." The other buildings provided
for other members and functions. The second most impressive build-

ing accommodated the steward [overseer] and the boys of the white family. The next in importance served as schoolhouse. "Then the cook, the washer-woman, and the milk-maid, had each their several houses, the children's nurses always sleeping upon the floor of their mistress' apartment." In addition, the household had separate buildings to serve as "the kitchen, the store-house, corn-house, stable, hen-coop, the hound's kennel, the shed for the corn mill." At considerable distance from the master's dwelling, "yet not beyond the sight of his watchful and jealous eye," clustered the field hands' huts, each of which included a small patch of ground cultivated by the slaves on their own time.[4]

Katherine DuPre Lumpkin, invoking the days of her father's youth, described another Georgia slaveholding household as "a community and business rolled into one," and her grandfather, who presided over it, as "a heavily burdened man." Her grandfather's household, like that described by Burke and many others, included not merely the big house, but "slave quarters, stables, and springhouse, and the work radiating out into the fields from this hub of activity." Grandfather Lumpkin, with his thousand-odd acres and his fifty-odd slaves, fig-ured—if only barely—as a large planter who, from the 1830s to the outbreak of the war, devoted most of his time to presiding over his household in Oglethorpe County, Georgia. As nearly as possible, Lumpkin wrote, "Grandfather made his plantation provide for all his needs. On a place of this size he had to do so if he were to have any net cash income." His stables housed horses and cattle when they were not in pasture; carriages and other conveyances; farm wagons and ox-carts; the harness and gear for all these vehicles; plows and farm imple-ments. Buildings included the smokehouse, the blacksmith's quarters, and the carpenter's shop. The plantation household grew and pro-cessed basic foodstuffs, including corn and wheat, vegetables, pork for the slaves, and beef, lamb, mutton, pork, hams, bacon, chickens, tur-key, and geese for the big house. Grandfather Lumpkin's charges in-cluded five children by his first wife and sixteen by his second, in addition to his slaves. Clothing the slaves alone required hauling in bolts of goods from Athens or Augusta. "The garments then had to be made for men, women and children. . . . There was the mending also. Altogether the sewing could probably keep a few women busy practi-cally all of every day." Large households would also include an infir-mary and a nursery for slaves.[5]

Katherine Lumpkin emphasized the convergence of the household as space, tasks, and personal relations in the person of the plantation master. His enormous responsibilities and ability to meet them determined the life and safety of his dependents and his own standing in his community: The life of the household and its economic efficiency could not be separated. The master looked on every natural and human-made feature of his property as part of himself, as familiar to him as "the palm of his hand." He expected to know every detail of every agricultural operation and every human problem within his household.

> Above all, he would know his slaves, each by name, and each for his good points and his foibles, most of them being inherited, or the children of those who had been handed down. He would expect constantly to guide and discipline and keep them contented by skillful handling. First and last, he would know that every plan, every decision, every quandary nagging his mind, save those of marketing his cotton and purchasing supplies from the outside, resolved itself into a human problem, if it could be so called: the problem of managing his black dependents. He would know he was master in all things on his plantation, everything, nothing excepted, including the life of his slaves. With it he would know that his station was secure as a southern gentleman.[6]

By the late antebellum period, the Lumpkin household constituted the primary residence and base of operations of a successful and respected planter. In many ways, it more resembled a prosperous farm than the great plantation mansion of myth. Yet in its structure, if not its lavishness, it also resembled the wealthy plantation that Emily Burke described as one of the largest in Georgia and "a township of itself." According to Burke, this plantation contained within its own borders "so many resources of convenience, that setting aside those things that can only be termed the luxuries of life, it could be quite independent of any foreign aid or article of merchandize." Its resources included "its own mills and shops of various kinds, its milliners and mantuamakers, tailors and barbers, and its cards, looms and spindles." Home industry, she insisted, supplied all the needs of the luxurious table except coffee, tea, and spices. The household also included teachers of languages, music, and the sciences, and the master was attempting to provide a plantation church and chaplain.[7]

Eliza Clitherall, in her recollections of her life as a young wife on a rice plantation near Wilmington, North Carolina, confirmed Burke's perception, at least with respect to planters' dependence on local resources for their lavish entertaining. In 1810, writing of her life in a manner reminiscent of William Byrd's memoirs of colonial Virginia, she recalled that she and her husband had pleasantly settled at Thornbury, their plantation, and "raising sufficient Poultry having a plentiful dairy, fine Garden a Barn yd & superfluous rice for fine Turkeys— The river abounding with fish & Wild Ducks in abundance, we could afford to entertain our friends at a trifling expense." In 1827, Juliana Conner described her father-in-law's plantation, Poplar Grove, near the Catawba River in North Carolina, in similar terms: "They live as it were independent, raise their own provisions and weave and wear their homespun, some of which is really handsome, the ladies feel considerable pride in displaying their domestic manufactures, knitting forms no small part of their employment and it appears merely an amusement."[8]

Elizabeth Meriwether offered a comparable description of Liberty Hall, the household of Mr. King of Crow Creek in the Cumberland Mountains, which she visited one summer in the 1840s as a young bride. King represented the link between planters and affluent yeomen in his style of life, which she fancied was very similar to "the life of the patriarchs of old." He was sixty years old, strong, and knew only enough writing to sign his name to a check. He ruled his family like a patriarch whose word was law to his sons and grandsons and all the womenfolk. "Many of his children were born out of wedlock, but the King made no distinction between them and the others." Laws other than those of household heads were disregarded in that country. The women smoked big, black cigars, or, failing cigars, pipes, and "drank whiskey freely." Thirty to forty people regularly gathered around King's table "and when travelers happened by, the number was even larger."[9]

The southern plantation house constituted only one part of a complex unit, for, as Burke noted, in the South "it required more than one building to make up a family residence." Whereas, in the North, all necessary apartments would come under one roof, in the South "there were nearly as many roofs as rooms." Only the very wealthiest slaveholding households remotely approximated the physical luxury and ease attributed to them in the romantic legend that was strong even then but would grow stronger in the days of "the Lost Cause." Burke counterposed a detailed and sobering description of what she apparently considered a typical plantation to make the point. A paling, she wrote, enclosed all the buildings "belonging to the family and all the house servants." In the middle of this enclosure stood the principal house, which she found less than impressive. In accordance with general custom, it stood atop four posts that permitted circulation both of air and, to her disgust, of animals. Like other southern houses, it was built low to forestall the worst effects of the heavy gales to which the South was prey. Boards, arranged like clapboards, covered the exterior to shield it from rain. They accounted for the "entire thickness of the walls, there being no ceiling, lathing, or plastering within." The floors, which manifested no greater concern with construction, "were all single and laid in so unworkman like manner, I could often see the ground beneath, when the carpets were not on the floor, and they are always taken up in the summer to make the apartments cooler." The roof was so shabbily laid, that "not only the wind, but the light and rain often finds free access into the upper apartments, through ten thousand holes among the shingles."[10] The windows did have the uncommon luxury of panes of glass, but they were rarely used for protection against the elements.

Numerous southern women confirmed Burke's impression without her sense of surprise. Eliza Clitherall described the house at Thornbury as having four rooms on the first floor and two above. Subsequently, her husband added another room to serve as a nursery. A few decades later, Anna Matilda Page King, a great lowcountry heiress and wife of a politician of some note, sustained Burke's verdict about the modest nature of even a prosperous household's big house when she complained about the rain coming through the cracks of her residence on St. Simon's Island. In the 1850s, the young Agnes Lee described the renovation of the big house on the Lee plantation in Arlington, recalling its previous condition: "the old brick walls thickly & most confusedly covered with dusky pictures half unframed, the thick rafters above fit harbingers for cobwebs & dust, the rusty brass bolts, unpolished floors and unpainted wood." Burke speculated that planters constructed no better dwellings for themselves because of "changing their places of residence so often, on account of the soil, which in a few years becomes barren, owing to the manner in which it is cultivated." Even those who were not moving on to fresh soils might change residences often. Many lowcountry planters—certainly the wealthier ones—normally spent some months at the plantation, some months at the town house in Charleston, and some months during the sickly season on Sullivan Island or upcountry or even at Newport, Rhode Island. Burke wrote: "They have but little property that is not moveable. Their possessions generally consist in slaves, herds of swine and cattle, horses, mules, flocks of goats, and numerous fowls of all kinds, fine carriages, furniture, plate, etc., which can be transported when occasion demands a removal from one old worn out plantation to another of newer and more fruitful soil."[11]

The planters of the southern heartland, from upcountry South Carolina or Georgia across the Cotton Belt to the Mississippi and beyond, did not often match the high style of the lowcountry Chivalry, but they, too, had more than one residence if finances permitted. A notable, if not easily measured, number of the wealthier planters of Alabama and Mississippi, for example, often preferred to have a permanent residence in a local village or town, if only to be near their preferred church, a good school for their children, and a cultural life that, however primitive it might appear to unsympathetic outsiders, had more to offer than is even now appreciated. These "local absentee" planters nonetheless rode out to their plantations often, drew regular supplies of foodstuffs and slaves from them, and lived on them with their families for parts of the year. They had to maintain at least two comfortable residences, and, if they also owned a second and more distant plantation, possibly more than two.

The widespread tendency to avoid constructing lavish, permanent residences colored most slaveholding women's specific forms of identification with the households of which they were members, even as it wove the realities of life in a slave society into the pattern of their sense of themselves in the world. They shared with other American women a concern for civilities and for the niceties of physical surroundings. Their correspondence with husbands and other traveling male kin especially testified to their interest in carpets.[12] Yet specific complaints, or even comments, about the houses in which they lived were rare, and the complaints that did surface normally expressed desires for a new carpet or for proper slave cabins. The complaints, in other words, focused upon the excesses of discomfort rather than on what were accepted as the normal conditions of life. It required an outsider—a visitor like Emily Burke, or a later descendant like Katherine DuPre Lumpkin—to describe as unusual the environment that antebellum southern women took for granted.

A woman's everyday life in the household depended in significant measure both on her own place and on that of the household in their respective life cycles. Most women, slave and slaveholding alike, grew up in established households, although during their mid- to late teens they might move to new, and newly established, households. Each generation was also likely to establish new households, some in the region in which their parents lived, others westward or southward in the expanding Cotton Belt. The life cycle of the plantation household began with the purchase or inheritance of the plantation itself. Its formation required a considerable initial capital outlay. A young man might inherit a plantation with slaves; he might inherit or be ceded land, to which his wife might add a dowry or inheritance of slaves; he might lack resources but—being a minister, lawyer, or physician, or for some other reason being perceived as having good prospects to match a good character—he might marry an heiress with land and slaves; or he might accumulate some capital to invest in land and slaves through one of those professions, especially the often lucrative practice of law. In some instances, he might even begin his landholding by renting a plantation or hiring slaves.[13] In the settled regions of the Upper South, the odds were great that the plantation, however acquired, would already be an operating unit, although it might well be slowly transformed into a "home place" for those with more viable investments in the plantations of the Cotton Belt. Throughout the antebellum period, slaveholders in the Lower South were more likely to participate actively in founding new plantations or in founding households that could move in and out of actual working plantations in accordance with the careers and interests of their male heads.

Even prosperous slaveholders could not normally provide land for all of their sons, and they rarely tried to do so for their daughters. Although some sons and even daughters inherited operating households at the time of their majority or marriage, many did not. But despite the diversity of individual histories, common patterns obtained. To put it differently, the structure established by rural and village slaveholding households dominated the experience of the members of the slaveholding class, as well as that of their slaves. Accordingly, women's experience of everyday life in the household conformed to patterns independent of the numbers of slaves or even of the degree of household market production and self-sufficiency at any given moment. Sarah Gayle in Greensboro, Alabama, had much in common with Anna Matilda King on St. Simon's Island off the Georgia coast; both shared experiences with Eliza Carmichael and Martha Jackson of Augusta, Georgia, or with Mary Moragne in the Abbeville District of South Carolina, or with Mary Bateman near Greenville, Mississippi, Mary Henderson and Eliza Clitherall in North Carolina, or Fannie Page Hume in Virginia, or with countless others.[14]

Regardless of their greatly varying degrees of self-sufficiency, slaveholding households produced more for the consumption of their members than did comparable households in the North, in part because southern society offered fewer opportunities for the purchase of basic foods, clothing, and other commodities. Personal papers and accounts abound with references to the purchase of luxury goods— shoes, carriages, sewing machines, cooking stoves, pianos, and gloves, to name the most obvious—from entrepôts such as Mobile, Charleston, and New Orleans and also from the North and from Europe. They even testify to the bulk purchase from the North of such ordinary items as shoes for slaves. Wives regularly wrote to their traveling husbands to request such simple items as books for their children and themselves. Notwithstanding this growing reliance on factors and others for important items, members of southern society lived their everyday lives on the assumption that most common needs would be met by the everyday efforts of household members.[15]

Women proved indispensable in the complex web of production and reproduction that defined the southern household. As a rule, their roles closely followed the prevailing norms of division of labor by gender, although departures from the norms abounded, with considerable variation according to class and race. The departures in the case of slave women merit close attention, but in the case of white slaveholding women they rarely represented challenges to the norm itself.[16] In some important respects, southern households remained bound by the realities of a rural society in which physical strength and the vulnerabilities of frequent childbearing made a decisive difference.

Women, like men, assumed the place dictated by their gender, as defined by their society and modified by their race and class. Since, in all essential respects, discrete households constituted a microcosm of rural southern society, women's roles within those households approximated the roles assigned by the ideology and culture of southern society, although not necessarily in all details. Prevailing southern ideology emphasized the ideal of the southern lady as gracious, fragile, and deferential to the men upon whose protection she depended. The myth passed lightly over such bourgeois and evangelical virtues as work, thrift, and duty. Southern divines, like northern ones, valued those qualities, and many of the southern women who attended to their words did their best to embody the ideal in their own lives. But their lives circumscribed the applicability of particular virtues, with the possible exception of duty, which itself meant something less and something more than its northern definition.

Depending in some measure upon the maturity, stability, and extent of the households to which southern women belonged, their everyday lives followed the routine of the farm day and the rhythms of the seasons, with some allowance for their own ages and stations in the plantation family. The mistress of the household—normally the wife of its master, but sometimes his daughter, widow, mother, or sister—assumed the mantle of ruling lady, whether she wore it gracefully or awkwardly. All other women of the household were subordinate to her. As symbol of her station, she carried the keys to the innumerable storerooms and domestic outbuildings. Should the master be permanently or temporarily absent, all members of the household would answer to her, but few such women enjoyed or successfully exercised that ultimate authority, and the vast majority of those who tried recognized themselves for what they were—delegates of the master, of male authority. Women's training for their household responsibilities rarely included training in the internal running or external representation of the plantation—the disciplining of field hands, especially male, or the marketing of crops, or any of the other responsibilities that linked the household to the market and the polity. Catherine Edmonston regretted her husband's absence, for "Master's eye and voice are much more potent than mistress."[17]

Girlhoods were protected. As Catherine Clinton has pointed out, most slaveholding women received little or no training to prepare them for the authority that would accrue to them as the mistress of a household. One young woman after another reported in her diary that she had failed (again) to rise in time for breakfast. "This morning," Gertrude Clanton noted, "I indulged in my old habit of lying in bed late so I did not take breakfast untill all the rest had partaken of theirs." Others reported their sense of inadequacy during the early years of marriage. Lucilla McCorkle felt that her mother had not trained her "for householders." But these young women's lack of preparation for the basic responsibilities of being mistresses should not be confused with a lack of specific training in many of the skills that would be required of them. With the possible exception of a few years away at an academy or "female institute," most young slaveholding women received all of their training, and much of their education, from their mothers, in whose daily routines they participated and whose skills they mastered. At marriage—their effective coming of age—they did not so much lack specific kinds of training as the general training necessary for the management of an entire household, and, however imperious in disposition, they frequently lacked the habit of command and the authoritative voice necessary to manage slaves, especially male slaves. Their unpreparedness testifies above all to the strength of women's identities first as daughters, then as mothers, and to the abruptness of the transition from the one to the other.[18]

The problem stemmed from the relation between identity and practice. Young women of the slaveholding class were trained from their earliest years to assume their responsibilities as females of that class and to perform specific skills. They were less well trained to assume the identity of mature women. The psychological dynamics, arresting if not crystal clear, cannot be understood apart from the internal relations of southern households, including relations with slaves. Gender and class identification intertwined to define women's place within the household.

In infancy and early childhood, the vast majority of slaveholders' daughters received much of their care from slaves, frequently in the company of their brothers. Although they often accompanied their mothers on visits to family, friends, or church, they normally did so with one or more slave nurses in tow. It is difficult to determine how much of the girls' actual training, in contrast to mere supervision, was provided by the nurses. Margaret Mitchell's picture of Mammy's instructing Scarlett in correct ladylike behavior may indeed take liberties with common practice. Elsewhere, as in Sarah Gayle's pictures of herself as a girl, hints abound that early girlhoods were permitted a measure of tomboyism. Mothers in any case appear to have supplanted nurses, if gradually, in the supervision of female children. Manners and literacy became the earliest claims of the slaveholding mother's empire, and often the two intertwined. Martha Jackson carefully supervised her daughters' earliest efforts at writing. The drafts of their letters to their father and their first journals testify to her corrections of grammar and tone. Under her watchful tutelage, the correctness of the prose became inseparable from the appropriateness of sentiment and the forms of address. Some mothers, it should be noted, performed this service for their young sons as well. Other mothers, having had little education themselves, worried about their ability to educate their daughters properly. And in the overwhelming majority of cases—so far as family records may lead us—fathers took charge of their daughters' formal education, usually assuming decisive control when it came time to provide a tutor or select an academy.[19]

Maternal training rapidly extended to the performance of simple and then more complicated tasks. Girls, in the company of their mothers, learned to behave, to read, to write, to sew, to supervise the garden, to put up preserves. Servants participated in many of these activities with the mistress and the young ladies, but as servants rather than as primary instructors, although in some cases they may well have been the latter. The servants' roles as supervisors normally extended no further than attending to the physical needs and keeping an eye on the physical safety of their charges. They influenced the young women's store of knowledge and association through songs, bits of folklore, and even religious precepts, but they did not normally impart skills. Masters and mistresses did not always regard their daughters' lessons in black folk culture as salutary and often expressed fear of the consequences.[20]

In this respect, young women's training for their future household responsibilities clearly embodied the basic assumptions of slavery as a social system: Slaves performed the labor that executed slaveholding women's skills. Thus Gov. Joseph Brown of Georgia and his wife, both from the hills of Georgia rather than the Cotton Belt, disliked having slaves around their children, not only because of their allegedly corrupting influence, but also because their very presence discouraged the white children from learning to work. As for the cultural influence of slaves, slaveholders expressed their worst fears with respect to the effects on their boys, for they were often willing to speak of sexual matters when discussing sons but not when discussing daughters. That they were, in fact, free of such fears about their daughters we have reason to doubt, but the silence was total. Rather, they worried about—or might be charmed by—the determination of the white girls on the Sea Islands to imitate the black women by trying to carry packages on their heads. They worried about—and were certainly not charmed by—their children's imitation of what was considered black speech. Above all, they worried about ghost stories and African tales, to which all sorts of ill effects on white girls could be attributed. The girls, often as strong-willed as their mothers were known to be, nonetheless slipped off to be entertained.[21]

Young women of the slaveholding class do not appear to have been taught much about slave management. They enjoyed the freedom to command slaves, but their commands were guaranteed by their mother's authority and, beyond hers, their father's. In obeying young Missy, the slave was obeying Missus or Massa, who remained the ultimate arbiters of what could appropriately be asked. Likewise, young southern women do not appear to have been taught much about the raising of children, even though they frequently had numerous younger siblings. Because the youngest children were left largely to the care of nurses, young women did not normally see their own mothers' taking care of children's basic needs. Julia Howe wrote to her friend, Louisa Lenoir, of how awkward she felt upon first assuming the "management" of her baby, but she was gradually "learning to wash, dress, and undress her without half as much anxiety." They might see their mothers breast-feed younger siblings but were less likely to see them washing them. Toddlers and younger children were commonly left to the care of nurses and other house servants while slightly older daughters accompanied their mothers. Since childrearing did not dominate slaveholding women's lives—notwithstanding the centrality of motherhood to their identity—the older daughters who shared more and more of their mothers' lives did not absorb childcare as a central responsibility.[22]

Slaveholding daughters grew up in their mothers' shadows and under their tutelage. They learned the fundamentals of adult responsibilities from their mothers rather than from teachers, even when they had governesses or went away to school. Their mothers afforded the primary models of how to conduct oneself in a world that merged a woman's most important responsibilities of doing and being. Whatever personal accomplishments daughters might acquire added grace notes, but not much substance, to the basic model. Under these conditions, many daughters appear to have developed extraordinarily close ties to their mothers, who, as Sarah Gayle suggests, frequently became friends as well as mentors and were, above all, objects of deep devotion. Because mothers and their daughters began bearing children very young, they were often close in age and could easily become friends.

The respective roles of mother and daughter nonetheless remained strongly pronounced. Women normally married too young to develop into young adults in their parents' households. They went to their marriages still firmly identified with the role of daughter. No wonder, then, that they found the new responsibilities of household mistress bewildering. However they coped with those responsibilities, their own motherhood would likely follow closely on the heels of marriage and force an abrupt transition to womanhood. Many daughters whose mothers survived into their own adulthood appear to have begun to identify more closely with their mothers as women and to share aspects of their lives as equals. But in most instances the identification as women across the discrete statuses of mother and daughter followed rather than preceded marriage and depended upon the daughter's acquisition of her own household and children.

The primary household responsibilities of slaveholding daughters included the care of their own rooms and clothing, the gathering and arrangement of flowers, and perhaps a contribution to the putting up of preserves. Gertrude Clanton's day normally consisted—beyond reading, visiting, and shopping—in dressing and fixing her hair for the evening, gathering flowers to dress flower pots, arranging her room, gathering roses and putting the leaves up to dry, and mending her kid gloves. Occasionally she passed a whole day in doing nothing at all. Occasionally she participated in household tasks by overseeing servants' work, for example, "seeing some meat which Pa brought, counted and placed in the smoke house." Once, when visiting Mrs. Berry, they actually weighed cotton "(By the by I had never done it before)." And on rare and carefully noted occasions, she stepped briefly into her mother's shoes. When her mother went to care for her grandmother, she took Gertrude's sister Anne and cousin Emily along to help her: "So Cousin Eliza and I will have to keep house." On another occasion, when they had guests: "Ma being busily engaged with company I officiated in the capacity of Housekeeper." Mary Moragne, from the Abbeville District of South Carolina, more analytically evoked a similar experience: "I am wielding the sceptre of household despotism since yesterday, Mother haveing abdicated for a few days the weight of empire— Well it is at best a crown of thorns. I do not sigh for it: 'uneasy lies the head that wears a crown'—."[23]

Then, during the summer of 1852, when Gertrude Clanton was twenty and had just returned from school, she assumed the "housekeeping duties" on her father's plantation near Augusta for the summer. Her first task was "giving out supper [to the slaves]." The next day she began the normal round of gathering squashes and beans for dinner and cucumbers for making pickles. She and some house servants arranged the parlor and got a start on other rooms. The next morning she and Mamie, a servant, gathered fruit and saw to the cucumbers, which were soaking in brine. "How very domestic I am!" she noted. "Quite a transformation really." Gertrude Clanton was unusual, although not unique, in making the transition from daughter to mistress within another's household rather than after acquiring her own.[24]

Not all brides immediately took up the full responsibilities of household mistress. Brides of lawyers, ministers, doctors, and younger planters began with modest establishments and only a few slaves. Among those who assumed the full load at once, some, whose husbands were already well established, entered households with smoothly functioning routines. Others, whose husbands were taking up new plantations, had to establish the routines as well as ensure their smooth functioning. The size and age of the household colored the young wife's sense of her role as mistress, but certain basic attributes obtained independent of those differences.[25]

Household responsibilities began with setting a tone for husband, children, and servants. Mary Henderson, echoing many, noted, "I arose earlier than usual, as I find nothing goes on properly if I lie abed, it is therefore not a privilege that I can indulge." Servants had to be supervised constantly, even in the regular preparation of meals. Lucy Rutherford wrote to her cousin Sarah Jackson: "You ask me if I have become better acquainted with the duties of my menage, I am afraid not, and fear that it will be some time before I shall become noted for my housewifery." She suspected that her blunders would amuse her cousin: "Once or twice leaving home without ordering my meals, and once when I expected company to dinner, I was mounted on my horse ready to start off, before it occurred to me, that I had not ordered anything for them to dine on." Mary Hamilton Campbell, another recent bride, wrote to her husband David that he was wrong to attribute her neglect in writing to him to the "trouble I have in managing my domestic affairs." Happily, she had never before in his absence had so little difficulty. For a change, "the servants have been very obedient, and the farmers have brought me all the necessary produce for living, without the least exertion on my part." Clearly, it had not always been so.[26]

Age and experience brought greater success in the general management of the household, but, like Sarah Gayle, many women never found it easy. Their specific skills, however useful, were never the main issue, for they do not seem to have placed a great stake in their practical competence as housewives. When they spoke of abilities in housewifery, they primarily meant their ability to order, persuade, or cajole servants to do assigned tasks properly and at the proper time—or better, and considerably more difficult, to train servants to keep the household running smoothly without minute supervision. Mary Boykin Chesnut's mother-in-law, Mary Cox Chesnut, embodied the role of plantation mistress at its most successful. Under her "capable and unquestioned generalship," the entire household ran like "a well-oiled clock which Mrs. Chesnut wound every morning by the apparently simple device of giving detailed daily orders to her head cook, pastry cook, maids, and seamstresses, who in turn oversaw the work of twenty-five house servants." In contrast to Mary Cox was her fellow South Carolinian, Floride Calhoun. Her loving husband, the great John C. Calhoun, proudly praised her character, virtue, and charm as a hostess, but lamented her utter inadequacy as slave mistress and household manager. Most women no doubt did better than Floride Calhoun, but few appear to have rivaled the performance of Mary Cox Chesnut. Relations with servants lay at the core of housewifery and ensured that success would require a good deal more than facility in specific domestic tasks. For a slaveholding woman would not normally perform many of those numerous and burdensome tasks herself, although she needed some knowledge of them.[27]

The Reverend Mr. Charles Colcock Jones described his wife's daily life to their son, for it kept her so busy she could not write herself. She rose early. Breakfast concluded and dinner ordered, she attended to the garden and then "takes a walk of observation and superintendence about the kitchen yard and through the orchard and lawn, accompanied by any friends she may have with her and who may be disposed to take a walk of a quiet domestic nature." Having completed her exercise, she returned to the house, refreshed herself, and then "disposes of her seamstress and looks that the house has been well put to rights and in point and in perfect order." Next she devoted "herself to cutting out, planning, fitting, or sewing, giving attention to the clothing department and to the condition of the furniture of chambers, curtains, towels, linens, etc." She also attended to the servants' wardrobes. She then might spend an hour or two with visitors before dinner, after which she retired for another hour or two. In mid-afternoon, she "makes her appearance dressed for the evening. Then she is full of her uniform cheerfulness, and attracts everybody to her—husband, children, servants, visitors, old and young." Finally, at the end of the day, with the guests departed and family worship concluded, she was able to retire to her room for reading, writing, and conversing. "She says this is the pleasantest part of the day to her." The Reverend Mr. Jones assured his son that he would "recognize all this as very natural—what you have seen many times."[28]

However varied, the responsibilities of a slaveholding woman normally reflected a deep sense of appropriate division of labor by gender. She oversaw the house and its natural extensions, notably flower and vegetable gardens and perhaps the dairy. She had primary responsibility for clothing the white and black families. She oversaw all food for the white family and sometimes basic rations for the blacks, although the master usually preferred to distribute the slaves' rations himself, thereby demonstrating his role as provider and source of all largesse. She presided over the infirmary if the household had one, and she helped in childbirth and illness if it did not. The nature of her responsibilities conformed to time-honored notions of women's work in rural communities, but the way in which she met them reflected her society's deepest sense of class and race relations. Whether or not she qualified, by wealth and bearing, as what the lowcountry blacks called "a ruling lady," she remained a lady nonetheless—a female counterpart to the men of her class and race, a being superior to poorer whites as well as to slaves.[29]

The divisions between men and women within the slaveholding class were clear. Nettie Alexander wrote of conditions in Forsythe County, Georgia, in 1859: "Ladies do not look after the farming interest of the country." By farming interests, she and others meant cultivation of the basic staple and subsistence crops in the fields. The garden and even the dairy and the poultry yards, depending upon the wealth and location of the plantation household, were another matter. As a grown and recently widowed woman, Sarah Adams spent some time on her mother's plantation, where she assisted in a wide variety of tasks. One morning, she "rose early to save our dear Mother the trouble of the dairy very busy this morning buttering." Martha Jackson, who was away on a visit, wrote to her husband, Henry, of her regret at hearing "of the loss of my Ducks but place it under the head of lessor evils." She then instructed him in how to cope should they continue to follow the hens, testifying, in her precision, to her intimate knowledge of the behavior of this particular group of fowls.[30]

Although women did not always participate in buttering or understand the quirky behavior of poultry—duties which the more affluent usually placed in the hands of a prestigious female slave—they almost invariably kept gardens, sometimes substantial ones. Martha Jackson "worked" hers with her young daughters. Anna Matilda Page King frequently wrote to her absent husband that her own and her children's greatest pleasure lay in the afternoons that they spent in the garden: "Every afternoon the dear children and myself go down to the garden. We walk and work until dark. This garden is indeed a very pleasant resort to us." The garden contributed to the household's stock. "We had very poor fruit this season and now but few vegetables—but the corn & potatoes look well also the arrow root & cane." The basic labor in the garden, however, was provided by a slave, to whom she gave permission to take a special trip in return for his effort. Mary Henderson regretted that the celery in her garden might not do well because, although "an abundance" was planted, "Tom seems not to understand the culture of it so I will not calculate upon any crop."

Mary Hamilton Campbell wrote to her husband that "poor old Leathy & myself made a little garden" in which they planted a square of peas.[31] Mary Jones gardened earnestly, with a host of assistants:

> Breakfast concluded . . . Little Jack gathers up his "*weepons*," as he calls them . . . and follows his mistress, with her sunbonnet on and her large India-rubber-cloth working gloves, into the flour and vegetable gardens. In these places she spends sometimes near two hours, hoeing, planting, pruning, etc., Little Jack and frequently Beck and several other little fellows and Gilbert in the bargain all kept as busy as bees about her—one sweeping, another watering, another weeding, another planting and trimming, and another carrying off the limbs and trash. Then she dismisses the forces.[32]

The garden apparently came as a respite from "the same dull roteen of ordering breakfast—dinner & supper looking after the servants & then darning stockings & *thinking*." The routine, which varied according to size and location of household, constituted the mistress's principal responsibility. In fact, slaveholding women wrote little about the preparation of meals, presumably because they more often ordered than prepared them. Their references to cooking concern the putting up of preserves or pickles and the making of special pies or cakes, and even those tasks were sometimes assigned to slaves. Mary Henderson reported having "had 4 lbs of blackberry jam made" and having "commenced some blackberry wine also, which I hope will be good as I followed the recipe strictly and used the best loaf sugar." Martha Jackson's daughters, Martha and Sarah, worked endlessly on preserves with the servants. Mary Bateman's servant, Aunt Cely, made catsup from tomatoes, while she herself put up corn "after a fancy of my own." Household mistresses might on occasion prepare a special delicacy for their servants, especially for a servant's wedding party. Much more commonly, they referred to the ordering, storing, or safeguarding of basic supplies.[33]

References to supplies serve as constant reminders of the basic character of plantation households. Supplies were purchased or produced in bulk both because of the difficulty in obtaining them on a daily basis and the numbers of people to be served. Flour and whiskey were purchased by the barrel, sugar by the barrel or the hogshead, fancy sugar by the loaf, and coffee by the sack; chickens, when raised in insufficient numbers to serve the needs of the household, were purchased and slaughtered by the dozens; hundreds of pounds of pork and hams were smoked and dispensed. Sarah Adams helped Eliza, a slave, make sausages from the hogs her mother had cut up and salted—twelve one day, twenty-two a month and a half later. Mary Hamilton Campbell complained to her husband of having to undertake "the unpleasant task of superintending the cutting and salting of our meat." Martha Ogle Forman's journal offers an endless list of beef, hams, and pork processed and stored. One day she had seventeen hogs, weighing a total of 2,077 pounds, killed and had the tallow rendered and the sausage made.[34]

The very bulk of supplies required the constant assistance of slaves; the presence of slaves required that the supplies be kept under lock and key. On a large or even a middle-sized plantation, the mistress did not normally labor in the kitchen or the smokehouse, but she did carefully dole out the ingredients for which she was personally responsible. In her diary, Kate Carney pouted that when she came late to breakfast, her mother "would not have any put up for me, but when I went down I made Mildred get me some from the kitchen, but Ma would not let me have the keys to get any sugar or butter, which vexed me not a little." Anna Matilda Page King, writing to her husband from the perspective of Kate Carney's mother, bemoaned the responsibility of the keeper of the keys: "Our house is a perfect country tavern or inn or what ever you may choose to call it. I am kept in a constant state of anxiety about . . . something to put on the table." And Mary Moragne, substituting for her mother, who had set off on a trip for the benefit of her health, noted that the "cares of house keeping hang like a leaden weight on my mind & I have struggled toilsomely through this day."[35]

Basic housekeeping did not figure prominently in the accounts of slaveholding women, although it ranked high among their responsibilities. Because so many of their houses were simple, many of those who lived on plantations may not have placed a premium on cleaning—which they did not do themselves in any case, except when they washed and polished precious glassware, china, and silver plate. Eliza Carmichael was unusual in her frequent references to housecleaning, and yet more unusual in her open acknowledgment of servants' active participation. Others noted general cleanings in spring or fall, the placing of carpets, or other special activities. Anna Matilda Page King planned, when her visitors had all left, to "have the house right-sided—count-over my stores put-up chickens to fatten." Those who began with small establishments—notably ministers' wives—wrestled more directly with housekeeping, although even they had the assistance of servants. Some occasionally mentioned washing, normally as a task assigned to appropriate slaves. Mary Henderson reminded herself: "I must really put Polly to washing tomorrow assisting Annette to get the clothes in. . . . She must starch my fine clothes tomorrow if the day is favorable." Some women made candles. Susan Davis Hutchinson even recorded one unfortunate occasion on which the illness of one female servant obliged her to accompany the other to the spring to bring back a bucket of water. Since peasant custom historically ascribed these activities, including carrying water, to women, slaveholding women, in effect, were participating with other women, black slaves as well as other white women, in a common pattern of the division of labor by gender, even if their class position normally relieved them of the labor itself.[36]

To a large extent, American and western European societies have assigned textile production to women, and slaveholding women proved no exception to this rule. In one way or another, the preparation and repair of clothing accounted for a significant portion of their time, and, in this case, they participated in the actual labor. Whereas slave women cleaned their mistresses' houses, prepared their food, nursed their children, and seconded their efforts in the care of gardens and the preservation of fruits and vegetables, mistresses frequently sewed for their slaves, or at least cut out their clothes. Slave women assisted and, when given the opportunity, sewed for themselves. On the largest plantations, they might well do most of their mistresses' sewing. On the Sea Islands in particular, but elsewhere as well, slave women wove the cloth from which their clothes were made. Slave women cultivated their own skills in quilting and thereby testified to their distinct Afro-American aesthetic sense and their own acute sense of fashion and elegance. Yet slaveholding women's accounts rarely depicted mistress and slave as sewing together, unless it be in the unending task of preparing the "negro clothes" or, occasionally, in the ordinary sewing for the household.[37]

Slaveholding women's private writings abounded with accounts of their own sewing. Of the mending of their own clothes and those of their white family there was no end. Socks had to be darned, gloves mended, collars turned, dresses refurbished, children's clothes sewed or repaired. Sometimes, a husband's shirt or pair of pants had to be made. Southern women tatted, embroidered, and knitted. They did not write much of quilting or of sewing other linens, although—especially in the early decades of the century—they occasionally wrote of making carpets. They wrote endlessly of cutting and sewing the clothes for the slaves. In all of these instances, their relation to cloth articulated dimensions of their lives and their relations with others—dimensions of their identities.[38]

Northern women also spent much of their lives needle in hand, but their households had, by the antebellum period, effectively shed most substantive textile production, unless the women were working for merchant outputters. In the South, the extent of textile production varied dramatically according to the size and location of the household, as well as according to decade. After the Napoleonic Wars, importation of English cloth resumed, and by the 1820s the North was joining England as a regular source of cheap manufactured cloth. From the 1820s through the 1860s, household manufactures declined overall in the South as they did in the North, albeit at a significantly slower rate. But even with that aggregate decline, a wide variety of households, from yeoman farms to large plantations, continued to produce a noteworthy portion of their own textiles. The masters, usually strapped for cash, understood the value of home manufactures and cheerfully assigned the task to slave women. "All the cotton clothing and part of the woolen," John Leigh of Yalobusha County, Mississippi, reported, "is spun and wove by women kept employed at that business on the plantation." Throughout the South, field women were sent indoors on rainy days, sometimes even when the men were not, to spin and weave. During the 1810s and 1820s, Martha Ogle Forman, at Rose Hill in Maryland, regularly recorded the preparation and storing of flax. By the 1850s, Frederick Law Olmsted, traveling in Mississippi, noted that "In Ohio the spinning-wheel and hand-loom are curiosities, and homespun would be a conspicuous and noticeable material of clothing, [but] half the white population of Mississippi still dress in homespun, and at every second house the wheel and the loom are found in operation."[39]

By the 1850s, women above the rank of the smallest slaveholders did not dress in homespun and did not commonly work at spinning wheels or looms, although many of their slaves did. As a rule, slave women paid much more attention to basic household textile production than their mistresses did, for they spent long hours in spinning and weaving. Mistresses presided over the production of homespun clothing for the slaves and occasionally over the basic preparation of wool and flax as well as cotton cloth. Mary Henderson, mistress of a particularly self-sufficient plantation in North Carolina, noted, for example, "Had over 16 lbs of wool washed." Sarah Cobb, near Augusta, Georgia, worried that they would not have enough cloth for their people's clothes, for the overseer "gave the wool out to be spun with-

Sand Hills Plantation, Richland County, South Carolina, built ca. 1830.
Home of Keziah Goodwyn Hopkins Brevard in the 1840s and 1850s.
Courtesy of South Caroliniana Library

Pond Bluff Plantation, Berkeley County, South Carolina, built ca. 1820.
Representative of an ordinary slaveholding house.
Courtesy of South Caroliniana Library

out weighing it, and I expect more than half was taken." Sarah Cobb
still had some fine wool that had been spun on their place. But on
most plantations, textile production consisted primarily in the cutting
and sewing of garments, which persisted as a principal activity at least
until the Civil War, when, at least for a few years, textile production
may have substantially increased to offset the effects of the Union
blockade of southern ports.[40]

Increasingly, home sewing intermingled with purchases of clothing,
but only the most elegant dresses did not require some additional
attention, customarily provided by the woman herself or perhaps a
seamstress. Even when, as was common, cloth was purchased, the
slaves' clothes still had to be made. During the 1850s a few households,
notably those of the lowcountry elite, took advantage of the new sewing machines, but even they could not rely on them for all of their
textile production. Thus the forms of textile production differed only
slightly between slaveholding and yeoman households. In both, textile
production remained women's preserve, and through it women contributed substantially to the household.[41]

Gippy Plantation, Berkeley County, South Carolina, built ca. 1852. Representative of a more substantial slaveholding house.
Courtesy of South Caroliniana Library

Retreat Plantation, St. Simon's Island, Georgia. Home of Anna Matilda Page King and Thomas Butler King in the 1840s and 1850s.
Courtesy of Museum of Coastal History

Anna Matilda Page King, 1870, portrait from an earlier likeness.
Courtesy of Dr. Alexander Heard

Even women who belonged to well-to-do town households sewed. Mahala Roach, in 1853 Vicksburg, was busy all day "cutting out the children's dresses in the morning, and fixing Nora's dress after dinner." Mary Henderson prided herself on finishing "one little night gown and almost another" and on planning to finish "my two little petticoats and that gown." In Virginia in 1861, Fannie Page Hume congratulated herself for her industry in "altering my silk dress" and making "me a beautiful little bonnet out & out." No accomplishment had ever made her prouder, "for I had no assistance & never saw one made." Fannie Hume spent much of her time sewing everything from dresses for herself to bed ticks and shirts for the men. Fannie Bumpas, the wife of a Methodist minister, made a gown and a pair of pants for her husband. Months later, she noted that she had completed "an Alpacca dress," which she had been busily making for herself, but she worried that her mind had been "too much occupied with my work, & too little with religion."[42]

Girls began to sew young. Few mentioned who had taught them to sew, but many wrote of sitting at their mothers' sides while working on this or that. Sarah Rootes Jackson noted in her first journal that she had been to see old Aunt Sarah, a slave, and had carried her a "handkerchief, which I had hemmed for her." From early adolescence, girls began to assume some responsibility for their own clothing, in which most of them acquired a consuming interest. Gertrude Clanton, who came from a wealthy family and lived much of the time in Augusta, wore mainly store-bought clothes and throughout her teens constantly mentioned the dresses she had seen in particular stores and the dresses her father had bought for her.[43]

Kate Carney of Murfreesboro, Tennessee, also in her teens, offered a running chronicle of her clothing and the sewing it entailed. Her mother, she reported, "had six Yokes for chemises stamped, for her to work for me, also two pairs of pantalets, and a night gown." The next day she made herself a night cap. Her parents, like Gertrude Clanton's, frequently purchased clothes for her: "Pa got me two beautiful merinoes." But she sewed at least some of her own everyday clothes. In February 1859, she reported her progress on a new calico dress, for which she had borrowed a friend's dress as pattern. By the end of the month she had nearly finished it. In April she wrote that she had been sewing some and had mended her hoop skirt. Meanwhile her mother had finished sewing another yoke and embroidering three sets of sleeves for chemises for her. And, considering the final product, she wrote that in "after years I should like to know how I was dressed sometimes, & how my dress was made, just to remark the change a few years will make. I have on a dark calico dress, yoke neck, a point in front & one behind, the sleeves are perfectly placed, with a little band and ruffle at the hand. Heel shoes are worn."[44]

Kate Carney did not, in fact, explain how all the parts were made, but she did reveal a precise knowledge of the parts of clothing that derived at once from her own growing expertise in sewing and the importance she attributed to dress as the external manifestation of herself. Her running account of her clothes also testified to her relations with her mother, from whom she had been learning and with whom she shared the techniques of sewing and the fine points of fashion. She had learned to put the flowers on her new bonnet: "It is only my common bonnet." Her mother put the lace on a new cape after it came home from the dressmaker: "She is such a good Mother."[45]

These women viewed their work on their own clothes as proof of their industry, but they also enjoyed doing it. Not least, they shared sewing with other women of their households, with kin, and with acquaintances. They took a less happy view of their work on their slaves' clothes. Each year, the slaves had to be provided with two sets of clothes. Normally, the cloth arrived in huge bolts and had to be cut and sewn with any assistance that could be marshalled. One woman after another, frequently with impatience, noted the time expended in this labor. And when the clothes were finally done, the master more often than not dispensed them, thereby confirming not only his authority but also his role as the slaves' Lord Bountiful. Withal, the burden of providing clothing for the slave force did not prevent individual women from taking pleasure in sewing something special for a particular slave. Kate Carney reported making clothes for a favorite slave's twin infants and "sewing on a calico, I gave the little darkie, Fannie."[46]

Production of clothing did not alone, or even primarily, account for the burdens that southern women felt were imposed by their duty to care for and manage their servants. But clothing manufacture offers a good example of the complex relations between mistress and slaves, for without the slaves' labor the mistress could not have produced the clothing, even if she did not "see" that labor. As in so many other instances, she saw herself as doing what was in fact done for her, albeit under her direction. Her attitude paralleled that of the typical planter, who would note that he had "ploughed my field." Historians have not commonly taken those assertions at face value and have recognized that a man with twenty or so slaves resorted to metaphor in claiming to perform his own labor. Those same historians have, however, been less quick to recognize the metaphor as invoked by southern women, although it bears heavily on any attempt to understand the relations between mistress and slaves in the household. Sometimes southern women noted the activities of slave women, sometimes not. Their papers abound with accounts of barrels of flour opened, gardens tended, clothes washed, candles made—all as if done on their own. The making of slave clothes is telling only because it offered the mistress an occasion to make explicit her sense of being burdened by the care of her slaves. Slaves' illnesses offered another such occasion. In both, the mistress did meet her special woman's responsibilities to those who depended on her, and she rarely let her efforts go unremarked.

Slaves' illnesses plagued the mistresses with nuisance, worry, and grief. The nuisance of having a slave absent from everyday tasks was hard to bear. Sarah Gayle waxed impatient. Anna Matilda Page King plaintively cried out to her husband of the consequences for her of an outbreak of dysentery among the servants. Sixteen years later, beset with worries about their debts, she wrote him that it was worth paying top prices for good bacon "in order to let the Negros keep well." Eliza Carmichael worried about the illness of one of her servants, whose services would be difficult to replace if the sickness persisted, and a week later noted that she had spent a busy day "with sick servants and their crying babys 3 in number." Jeremiah C. Harris, a teacher and small farmer who was determined to spare his wife as many household chores as possible, wrote of his slave cook in 1855, "Maria is laid up this morning with a bad cold, she is mightily missed in the house, no one can supply her place." Mahala Roach complained that she was obliged to stand in for sick servants herself: "Our little nurse still so sick that I am nurse"; and again, "Margery was taken sick in the night and has been quite sick all day—so I have had to work hard." Mistresses frequently railed at the inconvenience of replacing a valued house servant, even for a brief period, just as they frequently railed at the demands that nursing sick servants placed upon them. The nursing ranked as a double worry by reminding the mistress of her particular responsibilities to the prosperity of the plantation. The loss of a slave was a capital loss, as well as a human loss.[47]

Mistresses frequently expressed genuine personal concern and grief over the illness or death of their slaves. Susan Davis Hutchinson paid a condolence call on an acquaintance who had lost a favorite servant, who, she said, "had been more of a mother than a servant to her."

While visiting on another plantation, she was asked to visit a treasured family servant who was very feeble. "I went to see her and found her room furnished like a lady's, carpeted and curtained with all the needful furniture about her—but she was almost white—a beautiful woman." And again, she called on the very sick servant of a Mrs. Clarke, who "takes as much care of Cynthia's [the servant's] two children as if they were her own." Mary Jeffreys Bethell sadly reported the death of one of her own servants, Bill, after an illness of five months. "I felt very bad after he died, I could not sleep well for two nights."[48]

Eliza Clitherall similarly reported that one of her married daughters had, during a slave's last illness, stayed with him day and night, showing him "all that the kindest & most unremitting attention cou'd bestow." Eliza Clitherall stood by his bedside at the end "and watched the spirit gradually depart." But the greatest blow came with the loss of her own "faithful old Hagar" who had begun life's journey with her. Hagar's eyes were closed by Eliza Clitherall's oldest daughter, the first of the children Hagar had nursed. Eliza Clitherall nursed and then mourned Hagar as Sarah Gayle had nursed and mourned Rose. Yet that same Eliza Clitherall noted, at the death of her daughter's slave, Theodore, "My poor child loses by him his wages of $350 per anum." Anna Matilda Page King, slowly disintegrating under the loss of her own oldest son, Butler, devotedly nursed a favorite young slave, Annie. Her ceaseless care availed nothing. Annie died and her mistress faltered under the blow, which she clearly interpreted as a repetition of the death of her son. In a letter to her husband, she described herself as unmindful of God's mercies and blessings: "grieving—grieving for the death of a favorite servant girl—forgetful that we must all die—that not only must I die—but—I may have the misery of seeing those I love better than life—whose lives are dearer to me than my own soul—taken, & I left to mourn their loss."[49]

Death confronted mistresses with the humanity of their slaves and with the ties—often reaching back to previous generations—that bound them to those whom they held in bondage. It may be objected—and often is—that these were atypical reactions or atypical relations, but the objection misses the point. These heartfelt cries from the mistresses certainly do not prove that they would have reacted in a similar way to the death of a field hand whom they knew barely or perhaps not at all. But for the moment we are not concerned with the perceptions of slave women, who surely had their own stories to tell, but rather with the effects of one close relationship on the perceptions of the mistresses. For one single such sense of intimacy, affection, and love for a slave would be enough to confirm the mistress, psychologically and ideologically, in her own vision of herself as bound by ties of human fellowship to those whom she not only governed but owned—a confirmation achieved without necessarily betraying a trace of hypocrisy.

Even the extreme cases—Sarah Gayle's mourning for Rose or Anna King's for Annie—do not constitute evidence of the mistresses' everyday ability to live up to the ideal. More than likely, they above all demonstrate that the mistresses invested their slaves with their personal feelings for others—Sarah Gayle's for her dead parents, Anna King's for her dead son. Nor does recognition of the mistresses' grief belie the perception of the former slave from Tennessee, who described a mistress's crying like a baby over the death of a slave she had constantly whipped and who explained the grief: "Huh, crying because she didn't have nobody to whip no more."[50] Everyday life in the slave household and the metaphor of family in which it was draped permitted both interpretations—in combination as well as separately, for both touched part of a deeply conflicted reality.

Mistresses lived intimately with their female house slaves, especially their own and their children's nurses, and in an extended personal circle—a real if also metaphoric family—with many of the slaves of the larger household. The position of mistress wrapped the slaveholding woman in a symbolic mantle, which the tensions of everyday life often strained but rarely shredded. Fannie Kemble painted a searing picture of the aura with which the class and gender relations of the household shrouded the mistress. On each of her husband's plantations, the slaves—especially the women—greeted her with enthusiasm and inundated her with petitions. When they arrived at Pierce Butler's plantation on St. Simon's, one of the women "went down on her knees, and uttered in a loud voice a sort of extemporaneous prayer of thanksgiving at our advent." In Fannie Kemble's rendition, the woman cried: "tanks to de good Lord God Almighty that missus had come, what give de poor niggar sugar and flannel." Slave women on the other plantations betrayed similar attitudes toward their mistress's special relation to the master's power when they petitioned her to intervene with him to get their burdens lightened, or simply for "sugar, rice, and baby clothes." Their confidence in her powers of intervention overrode her own protestations of impotence: "Oh yes, missus, you will, you will speak to massa for we; God bless you, missus, we sure you will." Mr. Butler would have none of it and with rising impatience and brutality declined to receive those petitions through her.[51]

Fannie Kemble, with her literary gifts, her flare for the dramatic, and her antislavery passion, was capable of exaggeration, but she grasped a central truth about plantation households: Missus was not Massa. In Fannie Kemble's version, the slave women cast the mistress as the intercessor, as the softer, female counterpart to the head of household; the slaves attributed to the mistress feminine qualities of compassion and nurture; the slaves reminded the mistress that she, a woman like themselves, had also given birth to and lost children. More than likely, they were indulging in a bit of "puttin' on" the new mistress in the hope of encouraging in her a sense of obligation to them. The mistress of Fannie Kemble's slaves' construction unmistakably resembled the sainted mother Mary of centuries of Catholic tradition. And once we make allowance for a certain amount of elaboration, we can acknowledge the core of truth.

Whatever the specific virtues or failings of the particular mistress, tradition endowed her with a mantle that slaveholders and slaves alike conspired to embroider, albeit for different reasons. To the mistress accrued the feminine face of a paternalism that endowed the ownership of some people by others with whatever humanity it could muster. Just as the master, even if brutal or greedy, was a symbolic father, she as his helpmeet was mother. Mistresses could be demanding and quick with their whips in everyday life. They could also be brutal. The inherent injustice and inevitable atrocities need not be belabored: At issue are the ways in which human beings lived with and attempted to bring some order to what was indeed a "monstrous system." The slaves on whom the system weighed so heavily did their part to elaborate the metaphor of family and to hold their white folks accountable to their professed ideals. The mistresses, alternating between impatience with and compassion for—between chilling objectification of and complicated feelings for—their female slaves, were trapped at the center of a web of human relations in which both they and their slaves, however unequally, defined the responsibilities and imposed the burdens that constituted the role of mistress.[52]

By the mistresses' own accounts, female slaves did not normally have grounds for viewing them in a rosy glow. More than likely, Fannie Kemble's slaves did not unambiguously view her in the flattering terms they employed when they wanted her to do something for them. The favorable picture of Missus was designed to get her to effect the desired result or to produce the desired supplies, and to make sure that she felt she was betraying her ordained responsibilities if she did not. Slave women, especially when they worked in the house, had good reason to know their mistresses better than their mistresses knew them. Their knowledge pushed more than one mistress to the brink of distraction or despair. Sarah Gayle was not alone when she wailed that she feared her servants would craze her. Everyday relations within the household guaranteed a high level of struggle, but, however taxing and bitter on both sides, the struggle followed the lines established by the relations of gender, race, and class that crystallized within the household itself, and bound the women, black and white, into a network, if hardly a sisterhood.[53]

Anna Matilda Page King's daughter, Josey, underscored the intimacy when she wrote to her brother of her distress, which she knew he would share, at the death of "our poor little servant Annie." He would know "how attached we are to these house servants, these little girls have been brought up under our care and we love them, not as servants, but as something nearer." Eleanor J. W. Baker, commenting on Charleston house slaves, seconded her view, but with disapproval: "They are mostly well fed well dressed & well cared for & the house servants of the rich are often-times a lazy, pampered set. I look with perfect wonder at the indulgence & patience of southern housewives. The ladies take as much care of their slaves as if they were children & I am quite shocked to see the familiar way in which many of them are treated." She nonetheless admitted that "the reverse turnabout" was just as common.[54] The best and the worst of the relations between mistresses and slaves unfolded among people who, more often than not, recognized that they belonged to one household, and even one family, broadly construed.

For better or worse, mistresses remained most closely tied to their house servants, but they readily acknowledged their relations to all the slaves of the household, including the field hands, to whom they also had responsibilities and who embodied the larger meaning of "our family white and black." Juliana Margaret Conner, who, like Fannie Kemble, arrived as a newlywed mistress at one of her husband's plantations, described her presentation to the servants as an event equaled only by the arrival of Lafayette himself. The guests at her reception in a carpenter's shop "were all the negroes great and small belonging to the place." Raillery apart, "they were delighted to see their Master and welcomed *me* with pure sincerity and pleasure, as their new Mistress." At the end of their visit they rode out again "to bid farewell to the negroes—whom we found anxiously expecting us." Mary Hamilton Campbell captured the best of these feelings when she wrote to her husband of the pleasure she took from their servant Leathy's expressions of devotion to him: "How much I love to hear such sentiments from an old family servant. In them, when faithful, you meet with true affection. Indeed we sometimes find them more sincere than near relatives." Her picture did not differ markedly from those drawn, albeit in opposing ideological causes, by Fannie Kemble and Carolyn Lee Hentz.[55]

Indications of the mistresses' sense of their place in an extended black and white family also surfaced in ordinary responses to their own daily lives. When Eliza Quitman was finally able to come downstairs again after a protracted illness, she "was greeted with smiling faces all around, both white and black." Anna King wrote to her son, Lord, of her pleasure at receiving his letter, which she had already read aloud twice: "I expect to read it again & again—for every child & servant will want to hear all you have said." She in turn sent him detailed news about the servants on the place, assured him that the letter had delighted them all ("the servants *grin* at me whenever I meet them—so glad are we all to hear that you are well"), and concluded with the message that "all who are at home send *lots of love to you*—the servants all beg to be remembered." The servants similarly asked to be remembered to Thomas Butler King, to whom, if we are to believe his wife, they regularly sent their love. When leaving for school or a trip, Kate Carney warmly said goodbye to all the black family, and while away she regularly sent them her love. Fannie Page Hume noted that when her Aunt Sarah returned from a trip she "received a joyful welcome from the servants." Eliza Clitherall, who had been raised on a large plantation and lived the early years of her married life on another, wrote frequently of her and her servants' mutual devotion and recounted touching anecdotes of individual servants' particular acts of generosity toward her; in her later years, when, after considerable reversals of fortune, she had settled with her daughter, she devoted her best efforts to assembling "some of the servants together" in a "little congregation" to pray and hear the word of God. But Mary Hamilton Campbell's servant, Eliza, captured the mistress's ultimately subordinate place in the extended family when, in an attempt to console her mistress, who was in a particularly low frame of mind, she "came and caught hold of my hand and told me Mr. Lynch had gone to bring letters from our master."[56] The "our" was not lost on Mary Campbell.

Even the strongest expressions of human attachment never contradicted the inseparable assumptions about the white family's ownership of the black. Emmaline Eve, doubtless motivated by what she considered the warmest of feelings, chillingly demonstrated the underlying disregard for the slaves' independent feelings when she recalled her sister and brother-in-law's custom for welcoming a group of new slaves to their plantation. The new owners would:

> arrange the men in one row and the women in another and make signs to them to choose each man a wife and would read the marriage service to them and thus save time by settling their matrimonial affairs. The young people of the family would select names from novels they had read and other sources, and sew these names into the clothes of each. Sister Sarah chose two little maids and named them Martha and Fatima. The former was very good with the needle but with Fatima she had a great deal of trouble. Through patience and perseverance she succeeded in making her a beautiful seamstress. She embroidered handsome dresses for the sisters.[57]

The core of the mistress's identity remained firmly tied to her sphere—the complex of her particular responsibilities. As Massa's helpmeet and ruling lady, she was likely to know, help to clothe, and nurse slaves throughout the plantation, but in those extended relations she remained primarily his delegate, the implementer of his responsibilities. Even within her narrower sphere he held ultimate sway, although the specific responsibilities and relations fell more immediately to her. Within that sphere, above all, the tensions between mistress and slave percolated and sometimes exploded. There, the mistress directly disposed—or struggled to dispose—of the labor of her servants, who never could or would function as compliant extensions of her will and her hands. Slave women, in covert or overt defiance of their ascribed station, achieved in practice something like a perverse equality in their contributions to the tensions of everyday life.

Incompatible personalities, like the normal mood swings on both sides, accounted for many instances of bad chemistry between mistress and slaves, including the bad chemistry that plagued relations between mistresses and servants who normally got on well and even demonstrated unfeigned affection for each other. But that personal variation was mere gloss, for the foundation of the relations between mistress and slave lay in the nature, extent, and conditions of work. Slaves were expected to perform the major portion of the work for which the mistresses were responsible. Depending on the size of the household, female house slaves might find themselves pressed into service as maids of all work or, alternatively, might engage in highly specialized tasks. At either extreme, or anywhere in between, they invariably found themselves the butt of the mistress's impatience, dissatisfaction, and frequently of her unevenly applied standards. Who, after all, ever heard of a master or mistress who was wholly satisfied with the quality and quantity of the servants' performance?

Many mistresses had particular trouble in developing clear expectations. The evaluation of the quality and quantity of their servants' work depended upon the mistresses' fluctuating moods, upon what they noticed or cared about on a given day. Mrs. Isaac Hilliard was prompted to renewed vigilance by recent reports of neighboring houses having been burned to the ground. The catastrophes confirmed her view that "Negroes are nothing but a tax and an annoyance to their owners," who, "from fear, or mistaken indulgence," tolerated any degree of "impertinence and idleness." She especially deplored the idleness—"the devil's workshop"—and determined to combat it. "I believe it to be my duty, so long as I own slaves, to keep them in proper subjection and well employed. So come what may, I intend to make mine do 'service.'" Many other mistresses, who had no enthusiasm for idleness but who lacked Mrs. Hilliard's sense of grim determination, looked to their slaves for, above all, a feeling of confidence and harmony.[58]

Whereas some mature and practiced mistresses, like Meta Morris Grimball or Mary Cox Chesnut, had a definite conception of a smoothly run household and the proper allotment of tasks, others, especially young brides and mothers, simply desired that things run as smoothly as possible and that their own wills be implemented. Such expectations did not augur for success. Lucilla McCorkle noted with despair that domestic cares "engross my mind to the exclusion of all religious and social duties. Our servants are a source of discomfort. Their is a lack of confidence—so necessary to the comfort of that relation." A month later, she complained that the business of the house had been "negligently done & much altogether neglected." What she perceived as the servants' rudeness had driven her, for the first time, to use the rod on Lizzy. More likely than not, Lizzy had had enough of being shunted from one task to another and had her own ideas about how much work she should do and how well she could fairly be expected to do it.[59]

More poignantly, Mary Henderson reproached herself for having left her first beautiful little daughter, who had died, "to the care of my nurse, one old and experienced but selfish and lazy." She had frequently found the child wet. The nurse neglected her in that respect "and overfed her I fear with tea and bread *too much sweetened*." For months at a time, Mary Henderson's journal was given over to her heartfelt and bitter regrets about having confided her children too much to the care of servants. Several of them had died, and she constantly rehearsed the circumstances of their deaths, asking herself if she could have forestalled one or another by more direct personal attention. Most slaveholding women did not devote comparable attention to the specific treatment their children received from their nurses, but one after another continued to entrust them to nurses for hours and even days at a time. This reliance upon nurses proves nothing about slaveholding women's intense feelings about motherhood, which lay at the core of their own identities, but it does confirm that in motherhood, as in so much else, they delegated the most tiresome and routine tasks to slave women, who might, through covert rebellion or without the slightest hostile intent, disappoint them.[60]

As most slaveholding women knew, female house servants, notably cooks, were likely to know a great deal more about their craft than most mistresses—and frequently more about children, medicine, and life as well. Mary Bateman reported that one of the young ladies of the household refused to take the medicine that the doctor had prescribed for her but instead sent out for Big Lize to make her a prescription, which she took on the sly. Nurses, who commonly began their careers young, often received minimal training before embarking upon their responsibilities, although firsthand experience and the knowledge gleaned from other slave women eventually led them to equal or surpass the mistress in expertise. Although "mammies" may not have been surrounded with the romantic aura that the whites promoted during the political crises of the late antebellum, and especially of the postwar, periods, they indisputably existed and cut a wide swath. Meta Morris Grimball, for example, recounted how she found two of her sons, on leave from the war, dutifully visiting Maum Hanna in her room in the big house. Nurses, like other female house slaves, occasionally seconded by men, performed most of the labor that the mistress fancied she had done herself. Their specific tasks are rarely described: Mistresses saw only the result, or its absence, never the details of the work that produced it, and the slaves left only fragmented recollections.[61]

Slaves worked in the kitchens and smokehouses—which the mistresses rarely visited—to produce three meals a day, except perhaps on Sunday, and to hang and smoke innumerable pounds of pork. Slaves waited on table. Slaves washed and ironed; took up and put down carpets; carried the huge steaming pots for the preservation of fruits;

lifted the barrels in which cucumbers soaked in brine; pried open the barrels of flour; swept floors and dusted furniture; hoed and weeded gardens; collected eggs from the poultry. Slaves suckled, washed, and minded infants, freeing the mistress to shop, or visit, or read, or write. Slaves spun and wove and sewed household linens and "negro clothes." Slaves quilted. Slaves did whatever their mistresses needed or wanted done, and rarely, if ever, did those mistresses acknowledge their efforts as work, much less as skill or craft. For the mistresses, disinclined to do the work themselves, were no less disinclined to acknowledge it. In a moment of clear-sightedness, Anna Matilda Page King reassured her husband that things were not as bad as they might have been: "If my table is not so sumptuously supplied as formerly, if my attendants are fewer I have yet enough for real wants & have not been driven yet to the necessity of cooking or any such drudgery."[62]

House slaves worked in the big house in the same physical surroundings as their mistresses, but, unlike their mistresses, they also worked in the kitchens and smokehouses, of which the mistresses left few descriptions. Elizabeth Meriwether, however, retained a vivid recollection of the smokehouse into which she, as a child, had ventured against the strictest prohibitions. Her parents' smokehouse, like so many others, was "built of logs, with chinks between nailed up with 'clap boards' and daubed with mud to be air tight." Inside there was no floor, "only earth, and in the center a hole as big around but not as deep as a flour barrel." Above, "'scantlings' timbers" with spikes driven in them ran from wall to wall: "With the approach of Winter the hogs were killed and cut up into hams and shoulders and jowls, and these were hung from the spikes in the scantlings after they had been properly salted. Then a fire was kindled in the hole in the center of the floor and was smothered in such a way as to make a dense smoke. Never was the fire allowed to blaze." The smokehouse also served as storage house for "barrels of sugar, molasses, apples and lard . . . the barrels of lard buried in the earth almost to the tops of the barrel so as to keep it cool and prevent its becoming rancid." Her mother never visited the smokehouse, but customarily sent "the cook every morning to get what food stuff was needed for the day." Neither did her mother provide the labor for all the meat that was hung, the fires that were lit, or the barrels that were buried.[63]

Even Mary Henderson, more likely than most to record the specific work of her slaves, submerged it in a general account of her life in the household and worried about having so many idle servants who would be an expense. "Those who can sew I will employ immediately and put the rest to washing and field work." "Ann made a pair of drawers for me if she is industrious I can employ her all year." "Nancy hemmed an infant's skirt." "I had the ingredients prepared for my mince meat by Irene & finished after supper by herself & Sena." Earlier in the same month, Irene had been permitted to carry the baby to town for the day. "Ann hemmed 3 more shirts there are 8 cut off for Mr. H—— & 4 for Len." She did not say who cut them, but it may have been Sena, since Sena also cut out a pair of pants for Tom, which Sally was making while Rosa assisted with the washing, Tilda churned, and Henrietta made a new crib cloth. Meanwhile, Mary Henderson sent Tom to town to pick up her oil table cover, and when he returned she had him make a catch for the lock in Johnnie's room. The following day, Tom carried five bushels of wheat to the mill and then was set to varnishing her cradle, crib, and bureau. "Ann finished hemming the shirts & I gave her some edging to assist me in my work." Three years before, Tera had been "growing my citron" and then making it into "beautiful" preserves. Tera also dried figs, preserved mulberries and cherries, and, when her time was not taken with other tasks, quilted.[64] Ann, Irene, Tom, and Tera all had identifiable skills, but none of them was defined by his or her craft, and each was pressed into service for whatever needed to be done.

We cannot know if Ann, Irene, Tom, and Tera themselves took particular pride in their skills, any more than we can be sure how they learned them. Their relations with Mary Henderson appear to have been reasonably tranquil, and we know nothing about their relations with each other or with the other members of the black family. But even in this apparently harmonious situation, there were tensions and mutual dissatisfactions. Irene manifested an unmistakably resentful streak. When assigned to scour the back porch, she "as usual did not half do it," so that it had to be done over: "She is a smart servant but requires the strictest attention." Mary Henderson disliked having to "eye servants exceedingly—she is young however and I hope will improve." The next day, when sent to carry a bowl of soup to a neighbor, Irene, instead of hurrying back, stayed three hours, to her mistress's considerable annoyance. In other cases, also, relations between mistresses and servants had their bad moments. Mrs. McCollam recorded whipping her girl Priscilla and, six months later, whipping her again and sending her back to the fields. Another McCollam house servant,

Sally, had a chain put on her ankle to keep her from running about at night. Other servants were whipped for stealing, or for insolence, or because their mistress was out of sorts.[65]

In 1846, Eliza Magruder noted with discomfort in her diary that "Aunt Olivia whipped Annica for obstinacy" and, a month later, whipped her for obstinacy again. Less than a year after that incident, she recorded with even more discomfort that she herself had whipped Lavinia and begged for more governance of her own temper. During the succeeding years, Eliza Magruder developed a special affection for Annica, for whom she wrote letters to her mother on a faraway planta-tion. The growing intimacy did not prevent her from occasionally boxing Annica's ears for impertinence, and in 1855 she tersely noted "I whipt Annica." Meanwhile, mistress and servant exchanged extraordi-nary kindnesses, gifts, and other expressions of what appears to have been genuine affection.[66] In case after case, the offenses or perceived offenses and their punishments reflected the specific conditions of white and black women's roles in the domestic affairs of the house-hold. The intimacy of mistress and slave encouraged conflict as well as affection. The lines of class and race gave mistresses a license to inter-pret any sign of independence as impudence, impertinence, obstinacy. The slaves, we may be sure, saw it differently.

The shadow of the master brooded over all. The master did not normally intervene directly in the mistress's sphere unless requested to give assistance or advice, or unless things were going very badly in-deed. But he could. Many wives, not all of them young, wrote to absent husbands with news of and complaints about servants, often with requests for advice about how to handle the more recalcitrant ones. Their husbands' responses normally demonstrated extensive knowledge of the house servants and even of specific aspects of their wives' domestic responsibilities. Typically, however, they encouraged their wives to do as they saw fit, for they preferred not to interfere in the women's ascribed sphere. Thus, Fannie Page Hume noted with some surprise that her grandfather, the head of the household, "has been revolutionizing matters—put Rebecca in the kitchen in the place of Mary removed from some trivial cause—a domestic revolution."[67]

The repeated use of "revolution" may refer to the replacement of one slave by another, but it may also refer to intrusion into domestic affairs. Clement Claiborne Clay's son, for his part, viewed with disap-proval his Uncle Augustine's presumption in directing his grandmoth-er's servant on the serving of meals. Do you wish, he asked his father, "Uncle Augustine to curse and swear in our presence?" In the young

Clay's opinion, Uncle Augustine had done worse, but he sought his father's views. In one instance, his grandmother had stayed longer than usual at church, and Uncle Augustine "ordered Harriet to bring in dinner, and she did not do it as he wished, and he cursed her and promised that he would whip her for it." Uncle Augustine thereby showed a disrespect that the elder Clay had never been "guilty of, to your mother-in-law." But the crux of the matter lay in "whether must the servants mind Grandmama or him, as he struck Toney with a stick for not minding him in preference to her."[68] Young Clay expected his father to decide for Grandmama.

Male visitors, even near kin, were subject to the mistress within the household and could properly discipline the servants only through her. In well-run households, the servants were expected to attend punctiliously to the needs of guests as delegates of the mistress and implementers of her hospitality. Uncle Augustine was guilty not merely of bad manners but of usurpation. Above all, he failed in respect to Clement Claiborne Clay by failing to show respect for his domestic delegate, Grandmama. For the authority of the mistress ultimately derived from the authority of the master, who alone could override it. These niceties of station were not lost on the servants, who knew that the mistress they served was herself accountable to a higher authority.

Not for nothing did Eliza speak to Mary Hamilton Campbell of David Campbell as "our" master. And when Eliza's end came, David Campbell penned her epitaph. "She was a most dutiful and good servant to her mistress and master and although of a high temper naturally, yet for many years past most submissive to their commands." She repaid the mildness with which they treated her with "the most devoted attachment—They feel her loss and grieve for her as they would for a relation whom they loved." For years, she had been her mistress's waiting woman. "God has willed, and no doubt for good purposes, that she would be taken away—and we bow to his chastisement with humble resignation." David Campbell wrote as one concerned with the souls as well as the bodies in his care, and in terms similar to those with which innumerable slaveholders steeled themselves to accept as God's wisdom the deaths of those whom they held dear. Mistresses, too, frequently worried about the souls of their servants. Mistresses lived more intimately with their servants than masters did and more directly disposed of their everyday labor. But in all of these capacities, mistresses nevertheless exercised a delegated authority. In the words of one southern gentleman: "The patriarch possesses all power, juridical, legislative, and executive. He permits no one to settle disputes but himself, and the [slave] husbands are taught by sad experience to know that they shall not abuse their better halves."[69]

Slave women, well understanding the limits of the mistress's power, not surprisingly tested it. Gender ascribed white and black women to a common sphere within the household, even as class and race separated them. Female servants were always ready to press their mistresses on the point. The glorified image of the mistress as protector and intercessor rested on the assumption that slave and mistress were equal in their womanhood. The relations of race and class, in which the household was embedded and which it did so much to sustain, should have left no room for such illusions, but everyday life within the household invited constant probing. Slaves not only knew that the master had ultimate authority, they also knew that at least some mistresses chafed under it. Slave women, seeing themselves as rightful delegates of the order that the master guaranteed, also held their mistresses to correct behavior. Caroline Merrick claimed to have liked to go into the kitchen, but she frequently found herself denied access by her cook, who, having been twelve years in training, scorned her inexperienced youth and rebuked her: "'*Go* inter de *house*, Miss Carrie! Yer ain't no manner er use heah only ter git yer face red wid de heat. I'll have dinner like yer wants it. Jes' read yer book an' res' easy til I sen's it ter de dining room.'"[70] Like mistress, like maid: The argument always took the form of "It's all for your own good!" The chafing of the mistress and the testing of her servant remained a series of interminable struggles over this-and-that and were most unlikely to take the form of a frontal attack. Submerged in the flow of everyday life, they constituted a jockeying for position within a defined world more than a systematic opposition to it.

After marriage Elizabeth Meriwether, who came from a large slaveholding household, was convinced, over her own opposition to slavery, that a southern lady could not survive without at least one slave. She thoroughly agreed with her brother "that I did not wish to do domestic drudgery if there was a way to get it done by a slave." So she got fourteen-year-old Evelyn, who expressed the utmost delight at becoming Miss Betty's servant, because she could then go "trablin'" and "besides I wants ter git away from Mammy. She do beat me so." Evelyn proved willing, if opinionated. She never left the house without a calico sunbonnet. "'Laws a mussy, Miss Betty, you doan want my har to burn red, does yo'?" If Miss Betty attempted to do any work about the house, "Evelyn would run up, take the broom or duster out of my hand and say: 'Laws a mussy, Miss Betty, dat ain't no work fer a lady. Dats nigger's work. Gib dat broom ter me.'" Evelyn took great pride in her appearance and in her growing ability to sew herself fancy dresses. Then one day she set fire to the porch. Investigation revealed that before setting the fire Evelyn had packed her trunk with all her possessions, ready to flee. Under her master's questioning, she confessed but claimed that she had never intended to burn the porch down and begged that Mammy not be told. "'Mammy, she'd beat me plum ter death.'" Her intentions had been innocent, for she only wanted to provoke a move to town "to 'bode in a boden [boarding] house.'" She found the country "'powerful lonesum'" and much preferred town, for "'I lubs ter see de folks on de streets en I lubs ter walk 'long en see deir fine close and hab 'em see my close.'"[71]

We know Evelyn's story only through the memories of Elizabeth Meriwether, who may well have exaggerated for dramatic effect or simply distorted the facts, for despite her claims always to have disliked slavery, she committed the ultimate sin against the independent experience of the slaves: She trivialized it. In her narrative, Evelyn emerges as cute or curious—if potentially dangerous. Elizabeth Meriwether took the inferiority of blacks for granted. Yet there is scant reason to doubt the details of her account. She was not sufficiently interested in Evelyn, whom she saw primarily as an arresting facet of her own youthful life, consciously to distort it. Beneath the offensive tone, the details depict a young slave woman, barely more than a girl, whose slave mother had sought to beat into her the basic principles of decency and self-respect, including a respect for the proper ordering of the world. From this training, Evelyn had retained a clear grasp of what befitted a mistress and what befitted a slave. But, like other adolescents who react against strict parents, she had developed a love for fancy clothes and display. She also harbored a lurking streak of cruelty toward those less powerful than she. According to Elizabeth Meriwether, Evelyn was "incapable of telling the truth" and, worse, was wont to torture kittens and puppies and chickens and engage in other acts of cruelty, "not from anger or spite, but sheer love of seeing animal suffering." When questioned, Evelyn responded that she did no harm, for "chickens, 'and sich like,' had no feelings."[72]

The defensive blindness that led Elizabeth Meriwether to assert that Evelyn harbored no anger afflicted other slaveholding women as well. Living with the constant threat of serious retaliation from their slaves, they had to deny the certain dangers amidst which they lived. But on Elizabeth Meriwether's own evidence, Evelyn's resistance was no laughing matter, and the master, who held his wife's safety dear, saw no choice except to sell her. Evelyn's case remains arresting, and through its distorting source it suggests a picture of a young woman who displaced resentment of her condition from the desire for freedom in the abstract to the desire for the bustle of town life and the definition of self through fancy clothes. Notably, she also conflated proper behavior toward her mistress with the expectations of her own "Mammy," whose standards and retribution she resented and feared. Her mother apparently had raised her to conform as correctly as possible to the inescapable conditions of her life. Her beatings may well have been informed by a deeply ingrained sense of what her daughter could expect from the world, as well as by an anxious love that sought to arm her against a world that subjected blacks to the whims of whites. Elizabeth Meriwether could not match Mammy's seriousness, as Evelyn clearly sensed.

Mary and Lethe, as described by Solomon Northup, fully matched the seriousness, albeit in radically different ways. Mary "was one of those, and there are very many, who fear nothing but their master's lash, and know no further duty than to obey his voice." Lethe, who "was of an entirely different character," joined seriousness to a fierce opposition to her condition. "She had sharp and spiteful eyes, and continually gave utterance to the language of hatred and revenge." She had no attachment to the master who had sold her husband, and she was sure that, in an exchange of masters, she could not fare worse. "She cared not whither they might carry her. Pointing to the scars upon her face, the desperate creature wished that she might see the day when she could wipe them off in some white man's blood!"[73]

Evelyn took more extreme measures than most, although some, more sorely pressed than she, successfully executed their attempts at arson or even murder. But Evelyn's dramatic attempt to influence the conditions of her life doubtless had its unsung counterparts throughout slaveholding households.[74] Mistresses and slaves, bound together by their gender and the forms of labor that derived from it, nevertheless remained divided by class and race. Intimacy and distance, companionship and impatience, affection and hostility, all wove through their relations. Slavery as a social system afforded mistresses the possibility of implementing their own responsibilities through the labor of other human beings, who recognized the mistresses themselves as handmaidens of the system as a whole. Caroline Merrick acknowledged that her comfort "was greatly promoted" by the ownership of well-trained slaves, yet she complained that the "common idea of tyranny and ill-usage of slaves was often reversed." She claimed to have been "subject at times to exactions and dictations of the black people who belonged to me, which now seem almost too extraordinary to relate."[75]

Other women felt the same, but slaves of slaves they were not. For although themselves subjected to a male authority, to which they may have consented, but hardly with much genuine freedom of choice, they lived—and knew they lived—as privileged members of a ruling class.

3

Between Big House and Slave Community

Slave women lived between the two worlds of the plantation household and the slave community. Even those born in the South developed between two cultures: that of the African past and that of the Afro-American present. Their experience unfolded between two realities: the dominion of their white masters and their relations within the black slave community. Their lives and their identities as women combined these strands into a complex and distinctive pattern. From birth, the slave girl's dual membership in the plantation household and the slave community shaped her identity. For her, unlike the white girls of the big house, master and father, mistress and mother, were two, not one. The West African past of her people permeated her life and consciousness but could never entirely shape her world, for it largely lacked an independent institutional foothold in southern slave society. She participated in a cultural world fashioned by slave men and women from the traditions of various West African peoples. The texture of her life, from music to personal relations, from spiritual values to food, encoded memories of a vanished world, even as it proclaimed appropriation of a new one.[1]

Born to a mother who worked "from sunup to sundown" and beyond, the slave girl enjoyed considerable freedom during her childhood. Shortly after birth, when her mother returned to long hours in the fields or possibly in the house, she was entrusted to the supervision of an elderly slave woman or of slave girls only slightly older than herself. Adam Singleton remembered that, on his plantation, there "was an old woman by de name of Phylis, who keered fur de lil'l darkies," and who "lived in de cabin right back uf de kitchen." Barney Alford's mother was her mistress's cook, "en ennudder ole woman named 'Lit' lived in one corner uf de yard, en she tuk keer of all de black chilluns, en I played round her door steps till I was a big feller." On one South Carolina plantation, women who were "too old to do any work" would "take and study what to do fer ailments of grown folks and lil' chilluns. For de lil' chilluns and babies dey would take and chaw up pine needles and den spit it in de lil' chilluns mouths and make dem swallow. Den when dey was a teachin de babies to eat dey done de food de very same way."[2]

Like the white girls of the big house, the slave girl spent her earliest years in play, but the play gradually yielded to training for her future responsibilities. By the time she was seven, possibly even younger, she would have been put to small tasks, frequently minding other, younger children ("tending baby"). Mary Jane Simmons went to work for Mrs. Watson, "nursing the children by the time I was six years old." Molly Ammonds's only work on the plantation was "to nuss some little niggers whar dere mammy an' pappy wuz in de fiel's. Tw'arn't hard." Mattie Fannen started nursing for her master's second wife when she was five or a little older, and she nursed for a long time. "I didn't like children yet on that account I got so many whoopings on their blame. I'd drop 'em, leave 'em, pinch 'em, quit walking 'em and rocking 'em. I got tired of 'em all the time."[3]

Mattie Fannen may not have been the only small nurse who did not like babies—at least not white babies. A Marengo planter wrote in 1854, in the *American Cotton Planter*, of his plan to put slave children as young as five to work in the fields—something he knew was a disagreeable proposition for the overwhelming majority of slaveholders, who kept the slave children out of the fields before the age of ten and excoriated the use of child labor in British factories. Those who preferred to put young slaves to nursing until they were twelve might suppose this bad treatment, the planter admitted, but they should reconsider. He accepted the view, which the Jesuits had long promoted, that the impressions made on a child before the age of seven have a lasting impact and, accordingly, he argued that it made sense to expose young children to the work they would have to pursue in later life—field work. It had been his experience that "small nurses have been the cause of death and many cripples among infants, which would not have occurred if the old and invalid grown negroes on the plantation had been put to nursing, and the children required to take up their work."[4]

It is difficult to imagine Elizabeth Meriwether's servant, Evelyn, who tortured puppies and kittens, as a caring nurse. But why should she, or any other six- or seven-year-old, have been? Adult slave women demonstrated fierce love for their own children and frequently strong attachment to the white children whom they nursed as well. But while still children themselves, they could not be expected to dote on the white children. They had, after all, been wrenched from their own childhood play to care for them. If, like Evelyn, they had already been beaten by their own mamas, some must have relished the opportunity to pass on the punishments, much as many adult slaves developed a reputation for abusing horses and mules. But others welcomed their nursing responsibilities. Elizabeth Keckley wrote that when she was only four her mistress had given birth to a sweet baby, who became her "earliest and fondest pet." Her first duty consisted in caring for the baby. "True, I was but a child myself—only four years old—but then I had been raised in a hardy school—had been taught to rely upon myself and to prepare myself to render assistance to others."[5]

As infants, slave girls no more enjoyed the undivided attention of their mothers than did their mistresses' daughters. Normally, slave women received only a one—or at most two—month's release from work for childbirth and recovery, after which they returned to their responsibilities. They were then released from work four or five times a day to nurse their infants, who otherwise were tended by one woman. As soon as the infants had grown a bit, the old nurse who had charge of them during the day brought them to their mothers in the field for nursing. James Tait resolved to adopt the old Carolina rule for his suckling women. They must be allowed to carry their children to the field with them, he believed, for "they loze so much time going to the house & it is so hard on them to go so far." But not all slaveholders agreed. On the plantation where Martha Allen's mother lived, the "cook nussed de babies while she cooked, so dat de mammies could wuck in de fiel's." The mothers just "stick de babies in de kitchen do' on dere way ter de fiel's." Frederika Bremer had serious doubts about the ability of the older women to care for and discipline the children entrusted to them. She believed that slave children fared better on small plantations and farms, where they were more likely to be cared for by the white mistress because it would be hard to spare an adult slave woman from other kinds of labor.[6]

On large farms and plantations, the mothers whose daughters were sent to the big house could take charge of them during their free time at night and on Sundays and parts of Saturdays, but they rarely enjoyed the chance to indulge in full-time mothering. Even when they had their daughters with them in the quarters, they probably often shared the care of them with fathers and especially with female kin and friends. According to Susan McIntosh, "there ain't much to tell about what we done in the slave quarters, 'cause when we got big enough, we had to work: nussin' the babies, totin' water, and helpin' Gran'ma with the weaving and such like."[7]

The material embodiment of the slave community consisted primarily in the quarters, or cabins, which sometimes were clustered near the big house but usually were further removed. The size and quality of cabins varied by date, region, and, above all, the size and wealth of the plantation. In All Souls Parish of the Georgetown District on the South Carolina Rice Coast, the clusters of cabins, well removed from the big house, seemed to some visitors to resemble English villages. There, single and double cabins fronted on a "street," and the most comfortable were said to have boasted two stories and separate rooms for male and female children. Today no two-story cabins survive, and even on the Rice Coast in the 1850s such cabins may have been rare, as they surely were elsewhere. Yet one prosperous Mississippi planter wrote that, for the 150 slaves on his plantation, he had provided twenty-four houses "made of hewn post oak, covered with cypress, 16 by 18, with close plank floors and good chimneys, and elevated two feet from the ground." The houses were laid out in the village style, "in a double row from north to south, about 200 feet apart, the doors facing inward, and the houses being in a line, about 50 feet apart."[8]

Allowing for variation, slave cabins customarily consisted of a single room of about sixteen by eighteen feet, or two rooms of the same dimensions that were separated by a hallway or "dogtrot," and that housed separate families, who might share a central fireplace. In rare instances, planters provided their slaves with dormitories rather than individual cabins, but families normally had their own cabins. The cabins were almost invariably of makeshift construction, usually built by the slaves themselves but sometimes by hired laborers, who, in any case, might be called in for such specialized work as building chimneys and making door frames. Building materials varied according to region, but the typical slave cabin was set off the ground and would have a chimney, a door, and a fireplace, but probably no windows. Fannie Kemble described the cabins on her husband's plantation as "filthy and wretched in the extreme," but other travelers, including critics of slavery, were impressed by the cabins' construction and comfort.[9]

On smaller farms, especially those on the frontier at the beginning of the century, slaves might have no housing of their own and instead sleep in the kitchen or sheds about the place, but during the late antebellum period, plantation slaves were likely to enjoy at least a primitive shelter of their own for sleep, lacking in comfort though it were. Instead of windows to let in light and air, they had holes, which in winter could be filled in to keep out the cold. The cold nonetheless seeped through the cracks between the logs. And although some cabins were raised above the ground, others sat directly upon it, with nothing but dirt for floors. As a general rule, the tendency throughout the antebellum period was toward better-constructed cabins with real floors, occasionally timber siding for the walls, and more windows. The most comfortable of the cabins, with flowers in front and adjacent gardens, far surpassed the housing of Irish peasants, Russian serfs, or most British industrial workers of the same period, whereas the least comfortable still might compare favorably with the housing of the poorest whites, whose dwellings in truth resembled sheds for animals. The vast majority of slave cabins fell somewhere between these two extremes, although all remained extremely rudimentary. And, as often as not, their location and unsanitary conditions made them breeding grounds for disease.[10]

At least in the early antebellum period, slave cabins frequently betrayed the African origins of their builders and occupants in their sharply slanted and pointed thatched roofs, and in their characteristic room dimensions of ten by twelve feet. On the largest plantations, as the cabins became slightly more elaborate, they tended to lose their African attributes and become, if on a much-reduced scale, more similar architecturally to the houses of the masters. Julia Larken remembered them as log cabins, "a piece from de big house. Dem Cabins had rock chimblies, put together wid red mud. Dere wern't no glass in de windows and doors of dem cabins—jus' plain old home-made wooden shutters and doors." Cabin furnishings, always rudimentary, followed the same trend. By the 1850s, throughout the South, slaves normally had a crude bed made of straw-covered boards and a blanket, although some had only corn-shuck mattresses, which lay on the ground. Archaeological evidence suggests that cooking and eating utensils were also minimal, perhaps a single cast-iron pot per cabin, in which meat, vegetables, and grains were combined, perhaps also ceramic tableware such as bowls, plates, jugs, jars, and platters, but more commonly tin plates and eating utensils fashioned from shells and gourds. On a few of the wealthier plantations, such as John Couper's Cannon's Point on the Sea Islands, slaves occasionally enjoyed the luxuries of teacups and saucers and chamber pots.[11]

Even with improvements, slave cabins hardly offered a solid foundation for an independent domestic sphere over which the mother of the family could preside. Primarily places to sleep, take shelter, and eat the last meal of the day, they did not harbor the real life of slave families, much less of the slave community. Harrison Beckett's mother, for example, came in from the fields at nine or ten o'clock at night, often too tired to cook for her husband and children—although she had to if they were to eat. "But lots of times she's so tired she go to bed without eatin' nothin' herself."[12]

However crude and uncomfortable, the cabins bore the mark of their role as extensions of the big house. Like the kitchen, the smokehouse, and other outbuildings, they embodied the features of household life that slaveholders preferred to keep at some remove, if also under supervision. Care for her cabin did not normally figure at the core of a slave woman's identity. Especially in the villages of the larger plantations, the slaves could enjoy some sense of their own domestic space, but even there the nearby overseer's house reminded them of the master's observation and control. As often as not, cabins were built and maintained as a responsibility of the household rather than the individual. Many planters would have all the cabins whitewashed by the hands on one occasion and perhaps the floors limed on another. They issued thin cotton blankets that served as the slaves' standard bed coverings. Slaves frequently made an effort to add personal touches here and there. The women contributed quilts to cover the wood beds that slave men often made, and they accumulated small items to make life more comfortable. But there is no evidence that they placed a premium on cleaning or that they could have been especially successful at it if they had. Between the infestations of bugs and the ubiquitous poultry and small animals, not to mention the rigors of field labor, they faced overwhelming odds.[13]

The daughters of specialized nurses, cooks, or textile workers might spend the major part of their time with their own mothers. Mattie Logan's mother was much prized by her mistress, "Miss Jennie" (Mrs. John B. Lewis), all of whose children she nursed. Since Mattie and her siblings and Miss Jennie's children were all conveniently born at about the same time, Mattie's mother just raised "the whole kaboodle of them" together. Mattie Logan "was born about the same time as the baby Jennie. They say I nursed on one breast while that white child, Jennie, pulled away at the other!" Mattie wryly noted that the arrangement served the mistress well, "for it didn't keep her tied to the place and she could visit around with her friends most any time she wanted 'thout having to worry if the babies would be fed or not." Phyllis Petite "just played around" until, at about age six, she was sent to the big house to work with her mother. "She done all the cording and spinning and weaving, and I done a whole lot of sweeping and minding the baby," who was only about six months old. She "used to stand by the cradle and rock it all day, and when I quit I would go to sleep right by the cradle sometimes before mammy would come and get me." Slave mothers, nonetheless, left a strong impression on their daughters, who, after emancipation, variously recalled their mothers' love, discipline, cooking, and occupations. But if slave girls were assigned to general work in the big house, they might not begin their training under their own mothers' direction, and their early years of service might even, to their mothers' distress, remove them from immediate maternal influence.[14]

Slave girls between the ages of six and twelve were frequently enlisted for service in the big house. Nurses might easily be obliged to sleep in their charges' rooms or in the rooms of other white family members in order to be on call during the night and to make the morning fire. Mistresses liked to have a young servant sleep on the floor of their rooms, and even when the girl did not sleep in the room, she would be expected to appear early to make the fire. One slave woman recalled that during her childhood she slept in the bed of her widowed mistress. Another recalled that she slept with her mistress "till I was too big and used to kick her," and that she thereafter slept on the floor. Yet another slept at the foot of her master and mistress's bed. Some advantages, such as special food and pampering, may have accompanied the move, but they were frequently bought at the price of her everyday relations with her own mother. Sarah Debro, the daughter of a field hand, recalled that when her mistress took her to the big house for training, her own mother cried because she would no longer be living with her.[15]

Other slave girls simply had to be on hand in the big house, "pickin' up chips, sweepin' de yard an' such as dat." Alice Shaw's job as a child was "to fan the flies off the table while the white folks eat and to tote the dishes to the kitchen." Should she drop one, "Miss cracked me on the head." According to Harriet Benton, who had performed the same tasks, "de kitchen wuz way out from de big house," but when it rained "dey had a kin o' cover to put over de trays an' dey jes' come on in de house." The food stayed dry. "Cose, de slaves, dey always got drenched to de bone." When Joanne Draper was six she was taken into the big house "to learn to be a house woman, and they show me how to cook and clean up and take care of babies." Charity Anderson's first job "was lookin' atter de corner table whar nothin' but de desserts set." Initially, young slave girls did not have highly specialized tasks in the house, but, if their nursing sometimes escaped close supervision, their behavior around the mistress did not. Ida Adkins's mistress had snapping black eyes "an' dey seed everythin." "She could turn her head so quick dat she'd ketch you every time you tried to steal a lump of sugar." Ida Adkins preferred her master, whom all "us little chillun" called "Big Pappy. And every time he come back he brung us niggers back some candy."[16]

Convenience alone did not account for the slaveholders' propensity to absorb slave girls into the big house. It was widely believed that the best way to develop good house servants, who were notoriously difficult to come by, was to raise them. In effect the mistress, ably seconded if not outclassed by the cook or mammy, presided over a kind of primary school for servants. Not all of the slave girls who passed through this preliminary training went on to become house servants. Some proved so unpromising that they were assigned to field work as soon as they were considered strong enough to be useful, at about the age of twelve. Others were kept on for more specific training, but, especially in the older regions of labor surplus, they were sold once they had acquired the skills that would net their masters a good return. A few progressed through their apprenticeship to full status as regular house servants, at which point they might have spent their formative years in closer contact with the white family than with the black. At least, the whites hoped so, for the further these black women distanced themselves from the mass of the field slaves, the less likely they would be to spy in the big house. In the many cases in which planters and their families lived much of the year in villages, towns, or cities, the house girls, even if they were with their mothers, grew up well removed from the immediate influence of the slave community.[17]

Within the big house, slave girls received their first introduction to the conditions of their future lives. Even the youngest could become the object of the mistress's flash of anger. The odd piece of sugar was difficult to resist, and the mistress's eagle eye and quick hand did not serve as effective deterrents against repeated attempts. Yet odd tokens of kindness may have had a more lasting effect. As a child, Sally Brown was responsible for carrying food from the kitchen to the big house. The temptations were considerable, for even house slaves were not allowed to eat the delicacies prepared for the white family. One morning, she "wuz carryin' the breakfast to the big house" and there were waffles "that wuz a pretty golden brown and pipin' hot. They wuz a picture to look at and I jest couldn't keep from takin' one." Never was a waffle so hard to eat, especially because she had to get it down before arriving at the big house, but the real difficulty, she claimed years later, came from her own conscience. "I jest couldn't git that waffle down 'cause my conscience whipped me so." More commonly, the white folks rather than conscience administered the whippings. For the slave girl, the quick blows and occasional whippings rapidly became an expected feature of everyday life. If she could drop a baby without being observed, it is safe to assume that older white children could tease and hit her without adult intervention or even observation. Random cruelty and violence were part of what whites did—part of what they were. Even the kindnesses that singled out particular whites as good masters and mistresses were interpreted as the result of their own basic characters or passing whims, rather than as a response to the slave girl's good efforts.[18]

The early years in the big house could, as intended, frequently develop a slave girl's familiarity with the ways of the house and even a sense of attachment to the white family, but they did not readily foster the kind of systematic training that would have developed a firm sense of the relation between performance and reward. Cicely Cawthon started young in the big house, where her mother had been a house servant since childhood. She had no clearly defined tasks, but "just staid around the house with the Mistis. I was just, you might say, her little keeper." She waited on the mistress, "handed her water, fanned her, kept the flies off her, pulled up her pillow, and done anything she'd tell me to do." Her mother combed the mistress's hair and dressed her. Cicely Cawthon remembered that hair as being so long that her mistress could sit on it, light in color, and "so pretty! I'd call it silver." Fanny Smith Hodges recalled an early master and mistress as "good people." When she began working for them, she was "big enough to draw water, an' put it in a tub an' wash Miss Mary, Miss Annie, an Miss July." Her job was to keep them clean. "I had to comb dey hair an' dey would holler an' say I pulled. I was tol' not to let anything hurt dem chilluns." Fanny Smith Hodges had no mother to monitor her performance or to set an example, for she and her mother lived on different plantations. Just when she had become big enough to dress and wash little children in the household, the master had sold her.[19]

For some slave girls, early association with the white family in the big house provided lasting lessons in what they themselves came to see as "de quality," and occasionally with the roots of what developed into genuine attachment for the white family. If they occasionally bore the brunt of the white children's temper and impertinence, they also shared games and a feeling of childhood camaraderie. Queen Elizabeth Bunts, who owed her name to her young mistress's admiration for the intelligence of that monarch, had a first job of playing with the white children and keeping them entertained. She credited her close association with her master's family for many of her attitudes. "I was never very superstitious, as I was reared by white people and they were never as superstitious as the colored people." Other slave girls played with the white children for fun. Harriet Benton played "hide and seek" and "stealing bases" with the white children. "I looked up to my white folks, of course, but thought of us all, white and black as belonging to one family." As a girl, Mary Anderson visited other plantations with her mistress and looked after the baby girl, Carrie. As Carrie grew up, Mary Anderson remained her special attendant and companion. "She taught me how to talk low and how to act in company. My association with white folks and my training while I was a slave is why I talk like white folks." When Thomas Bayne removed his family from New Orleans to a cottage in Mississippi to avoid the summer heat, he took along four nurses. At the same ages at which the white and black girls were playing together, the white and black boys began to develop special ties through the hunting and fishing that they shared and from which the girls were largely excluded. But even young slaves exercised their own influence on the members of the white family. Virginia Clay-Clopton retained a vivid impression of the "ghastly ghost stories" that she had been told by a house servant, who threatened the white children that if they did not go to sleep immediately, "evil spirits would descend on them."[20]

For slave as for slaveholding girls, the mixed play of early childhood gave way, by early adolescence at the latest, to preparation for their adult roles, at least for those who remained in the big house. Those who were dispatched to the fields also felt the influence of white and black attitudes toward appropriate gender roles, but not so much in their work, which could include many of the tasks normally ascribed to men. Those who stayed on in the big house increasingly found their working lives, however physically demanding, defined by the same expectations about gender roles that governed the lives of slaveholding women.[21]

Slave codes rigorously prohibited teaching slaves to read and write, and well over 90 percent of the slaves remained illiterate. Slave girls' training rarely included the instruction in letters so important for slaveholders' daughters, although continued service in the big house slightly increased their chances of learning to read. As the white girls began to learn to read and write from their mothers, they in turn might try to teach their favorite slaves, who might—but might not—be interested in learning. Many mistresses as well as their daughters frequently avowed their commitment to teaching the female house slaves religious principles and read to them from the Bible or tried to draw them into family prayers. These well-meaning mistresses rarely recognized the slave mother's role in raising her daughter with religious principles. Eliza Clitherall purchased a young maid toward whom she hoped to do her religious duty only to learn, from a letter from the slave girl's mother, "that she has been religiously brought up."[22]

Many slaves passed their girlhoods in the big house, and many more had easy access to it. In any case, they enjoyed light work loads and an appreciable amount of time for play. Elsie Moreland was "a little gal, 'bout six or eight years old, when they put me ter sweepin' yards." When that was done, she would drive cows to pasture and, when she was somewhat older, she "toted water ter the field hands an when they's ginnin' cotton I driv' the gin with fo' mules hitched ter it." During the same period, her sister was a waitress in the big house. Boys as well as girls were regularly assigned to carry water to the field hands and fetch wood for the kitchen. Even girls who worked in the house could be called upon for farm labor. Lily Perry remembered having been a "house gal, pickin' up chips, mindin' de table an' feedin' de hogs." Feeding the hogs taxed her strength, because "de slop buckets wus heavy an' I had a heap of wuck dat wus hard ter do." She did her very best, "but often I got whipped jest de same." One woman, when very young, had accompanied her mother to the fields to tend the baby, her younger sibling. She "tote it down to de fiel' for her to nuss. Den de baby would go to sleep and we'd lay it down 'twixt de cotton rows and ma would make me help her." But working with her mother did not spare her the threat of discipline, for her mother, who had permission to leave the fields when she had completed a specified amount of work, expected her daughter to work at a rapid pace. Mother had a "long switch and iffen I didn't wuk fast enuf, she switch me." More often than not they would finish by noon and return to the quarters, where, if it was "fruit time," mother "put up some fruit for mistis."[23]

Between the ages of six and twelve, slave girls who did not go to the big house spent much of their time in the yard, where they would work with old slaves and other slave children in the trash gang. Caroline Ates "never did no house work 'till after freedom," although one of her aunts was a cook for the master, another his house maid, and her mother the cook for all of the slaves. "When I wuz 'bout leben, I began totin' water ter the field han's. Then, they started learnin' me ter chop cotton an' I soon began workin' there, too." Gradually the girls were eased into field work, where—at least initially, perhaps even more than in the big house—they might be introduced to their working lives by their own mothers, who could teach them such basic tasks as picking cotton and perhaps protect them from the impatience of the overseer. Fannie Moore's mother was whipped by the overseer for fighting him when he whipped her children. As their work in the fields became a regular responsibility, slave girls, like slave boys, were treated as half-hands and worked with other children at the lighter tasks. Jim Allen remembered that he and a girl worked in the field, "carrying one row" since it "took two chillens to make one hand." During the picking season on cotton plantations, children joined the women in picking. Nicholas Massenburg noted that in September, while the women were spinning, the "small hands" were pulling peas and doing other light tasks. By their mid-teens, young slave women would be assuming their adult work loads.[24]

Neither slaves nor mistresses provided clear accounts of how young slave women were trained for their adult responsibilities, although occasionally a mistress noted that she was training or would have to train a young maid. Such passing remarks do not clarify whether the mistress herself would do the training or whether, as in so many other instances, she would delegate the task to one of her house slaves. Masters showed even less interest in training the young female field hands, although their notations on the work of mature women demonstrate that the women who worked in the fields developed distinct skills from plowing to spinning. Young slave women learned primarily from older slave women, in some instances their own mothers. Picking cotton is the clearest example, but there are others. The slave girls who worked in the big house had more supervisors than they wanted, from the mistress and her daughters to the established house servants. When there was a meal to prepare, an experienced cook expected swift obedience from her helpers, especially from her own daughter, however easygoing she might be under more relaxed circumstances. Few had patience with dropped dishes or flies in the dessert.[25] But there remained a gap between the expectation of performance and the acquisition of skills.

Slave nurses, more commonly than other slaves, reported that they had been "trained up" for their occupation. Mistresses frequently wrote of nurses who, like Sarah Gayle's Rose, had been nursing since their earliest years. Among the many baby-minders, some showed an aptitude for their work and continued in it as more babies came. By the time they had nursed three, four, or more of their mistresses' children, they had reached womanhood with an established identity as a nurse, and by then the mistress's oldest daughter might be needing a nurse for her own firstborn. Amos Gadsden's grandmother had nursed all the children and grandchildren on the plantation, but her own daughter, instead of following in her mother's path, had become a laundress. Margaret Thornton had been brought up to nurse and believed that she had done her share. She reckoned that she had nursed "'bout two thousand babies." More modestly, Maggie Black, who was also raised to be a nurse, only claimed that she probably had more children than any sixty-year-old in the vicinity. No, she had no children of her own: "Aw my chillun white lak yuh." But Liza Strickland, who also began by tending her mistress's children, went on to become a "waiting maid," who did just about everything around the house. Amanda McDaniel, who also spent her early years nursing, went on to field work. During her early years in the fields she planted peas and corn and picked cotton, but "never had to hoe and do the heavy work like my mother and sisters did."[26]

Young slave women had to acquire a variety of skills, for although the cooks and other specialized house servants spent most of their lives in their craft, others were drawn into whatever tasks required pressing attention. On the largest plantations, especially the more pretentious ones, a woman was more likely to be sent from the house to help out in the fields than the reverse. Lucy McCullough was raised in the kitchen, where her mother was cook, and in the backyard. "Ah wuz tuh be uh maid fer de ladies in de big house. De house servants hold that dey is uh step better den de field niggers. House servants wuz hiyyah quality folks." Her mother had high standards for her daughter's "quality" behavior. When she was little more than four years old, Lucy McCullough listened to her mistress "scol my mammy 'bout de sorry way mammy done clean de chitlins." She had never heard anyone berate her mother before. In turn, she drew herself up and rebuked her mistress, "Doan you know Mammy is boss ef dis hyar kitchen. You can't come a fussin' in hyar." Lucy's mother grabbed a switch "en gin ticklin' my laigs." "Miss Millie" laughed. Only her intervention saved little Lucy from a serious whipping.[27]

Lucy McCullough and her mother both grasped an important feature of the status of the most experienced and responsible house servants. Even as a tot, Lucy McCullough had learned that her mother reigned supreme in the kitchen, into which Miss Millie would not normally venture. Doubtless her mother enjoyed wielding her authority, which the other servants had—at least up to a point—to respect. She had doubtless already told her daughter that Miss Millie did not know anything worth knowing about the secrets of cooking. But Lucy's mother knew that Miss Millie ranked higher than her accomplished and indispensable cook in the hierarchy that emanated from the master. No, Miss Millie did not know much about the cleaning of "chitlins," but in practice as well as in theory she had the right to meddle. If she, as mistress, was in one of those moods, the cook had to wait for a more appropriate moment to remind her that they both worked for a higher authority. The assertiveness of cooks and so many other skilled slaves suggests that, in their own scale of values, competence had its own hierarchy, as even the master himself should appreciate. In extreme cases, the reminders—as mistresses knew but did their best to repress—could take the form of poison. Lucy's mother could not afford to raise her daughter in the illusion that it was permissible to defy Miss Millie's position as mistress, even if she was already privately teaching her to mock Miss Millie's pretensions to culinary expertise. She could—as did more than a few others—instruct her in the most powerful weapons at her disposal.[28]

Men as well as women might be cooks, but Frederika Bremer, who mainly visited large plantations, mostly described the cooks as women who deservedly took great pride in their cooking. Frederick Law Olmsted, on a visit to a small plantation, observed that the cook did all the planning for meals, as well as the procuring and preparation of the food. The mistress visibly knew little about such matters, which she was happy to leave to her servant. Cooks might be highly—even professionally—trained, or they might have learned at the side of an older cook, possibly their own mother. Sophie Belle's mother, a professional pastry cook, enjoyed a secure position in a prosperous household. Mandy Morrow's mother and grandmother were "powerful good" cooks and "dey larnt me and dat how I come to be a cook." Whatever their training, cooks occupied positions of considerable prestige—and knew it.[29]

Cooks were respected by the black as well as by the white folks. Julia Glover said that her master regarded her mother as his "right hand bough," and that all of the five hundred slaves on his two plantations "looked up to her." The kitchen over which cooks presided, and which mistresses almost never described before the war, left a lasting impression on many younger slave women. Julia Larken's mother was one of the cooks in her household, and years later her daughter insisted that "I kin jus see dat kitchen now. It warn't built on to de big house, 'cept it was at de end of a big porch dat went from it to de big house." A "great big fire place" stretched "'most all de way 'cross one end of dat kitchen, and it had racks and cranes for de pots and pans and ovens." It even had a cookstove—"a real sho' 'nough iron cookstove." Most kitchens were less well equipped but were none the less impressive. Cicely Cawthon's mother had been a house girl, her grandmother a cook, and she herself had spent most of her time at the big house. "Our kitchen," she remembered, stood apart from the big house. "I never saw such a big one. The sticks of wood for the fireplace was twelve feet long." There were hooks all around, "two big hooks up in the chimney." She remembered seeing them "hang lambs' and calves' hind quarters up in that chimney to smoke." The white folks would kill more than they could eat, so to keep the food from spoiling they would smoke it. "The sweetest stuff you ever ate in your life!"[30]

Notoriously, cooks challenged their mistresses' greatest diplomacy in supervision. Commonly, cooks would be older, as well as more experienced, than the mistresses they "served" but who could not run a proper household without their compliance. Alcey, reputedly an unpleasant woman but a talented cook, got along with her mistress but had no use for the other members of the white family. After her mistress died, she resolved to get herself reassigned to field work and "systematically disobeyed orders and stole or destroyed the greater part of the provisions given to her for the table." She won, to the regret of the white family. She had been the best cook they had had in Mississippi, but what were they to do? There was no way to beat good cooking out of her.[31]

The talents deployed in the kitchens owed much to the slave women's special way with herbs and spices and to recipes developed and handed down among themselves. They brought similar skills and even greater ingenuity to the preparation of food for their own families and friends. Regularly resisting the masters' preference for communal kitchens, slaves pressed to receive raw rations they could prepare for themselves. On some plantations, one woman would cook for all the slaves in a kitchen built specially for the purpose, but even then, the last meal of the day usually was prepared individually in the family cabins. Basic rations were supplemented by slaves' hunting, fishing, and tending their own gardens, raising their own poultry, and "taking" from their masters' storehouses. With such ingredients, innumerable slave cooks produced highly acclaimed one-pot meals, notably coosh-coosh, and such special treats as the ash cakes that their children fondly remembered. Ash cakes, which embodied a special ingenuity, were made on the fireplace "outen meal, water and a little pinch of lard; on Sundays dey wuz made outen flour, buttermilk an' lard. Mammy would rake all de ashes out de fireplace den Kivver de cake wid de hot ashes an' let it cook till it was done." But however great the ingenuity of slave cooks, they suffered under the constraints of the implements and ingredients at their disposal. Their most impressive cooking was reserved for the kitchen of the big house, in which they had access to wonderful fireplaces, a wide variety of pans, and the sugar, white flour, preserves, and other items that the mistress did her best to seal away under lock and key. The slave cooks, who were so highly valued for their skills, produced the greatest delicacies of southern cuisine, but they did so in the master's kitchen and for his family and guests.[32]

Nursing, like cooking, ran a gamut from the least to the most specialized form of slave women's work and, at its most specialized, resulted in high status as a house servant. In Ellen Betts's household you had to "stoop to Aunt Rachel," who was both cook and mammy, "jes like dey curtsy to Missy." Aunt Rachel's husband, who apparently took exception to such deference, gave her a blow that left a visible lump on her head. She told her solicitous master that the blow resulted from an accident, for she did not want him to whip her husband. Susan Dabney Smedes recalled that no one would dare whip "Mammy," unless he wanted the biggest white men in Alabama to settle accounts with him. Her tale smacks of postbellum romance, but it is not far different from that of a former slave. The overseer in "Ma" Eppes's household once made the mistake of whipping her mother, the mammy. The mistress fired him. "I druther see dem marks on my own shoulders den to see 'em on Mammy's. Dey wouldn't hurt me no wuss." Sarah Louise Augustus's grandmother "was called black mammy because she wet nursed so many white children. In slavery times she nursed all the babies hatched on her master's plantation."[33]

Edward Pollard, visiting in Georgia in the 1850s, was very much impressed with Aunt Dolly, whom he described as "an aged colored female of the very highest respectability," who looked, in her white apron and colorful bandanna, "to use one of her own rather obscure similes, 'like a new pin.'" As an established mammy, Aunt Dolly had definite ideas about her own position in the household. She, like Maum Hanna in Meta Morris Grimball's house, slept upstairs in the big house. She called other blacks, who did not in her opinion match her in respectability, "de nigger" and did not hesitate to whip the kitchen servants when she thought it necessary. Should her mistress dispute her authority, "Aunt Dolly is sure to resume the reins when quiet ensues." Annie Laurie Broidrick was raised by Mammy Harriet, who had raised her mother and grandmother before her. Mammy Harriet took her responsibilities seriously. Once, when Annie Laurie Broidrick's mother was already married, Mammy Harriet corrected an impropriety with a slap. "My father said he used some pretty strong language to the old lady, and she never repeated the offense." But she renewed her campaign with the next generation. "She never allowed us to go into the kitchen. That was considered extremely low taste." Nobody, she lectured the young misses, "but niggers go in thar. Set en de parlor wid' en book in y'or hand like little white ladies."[34]

A mammy could enjoy the devotion of her charges and the confidence of her master and mistress. Laura S. Tibbetts wrote to her sister-in-law that she would not hesitate to visit if she could bring her servants, "but I could not bring my baby without assistance. She is a great deal fonder of her *Mammy* than she is of me. She nurses her and it would be a great trial to go without her." Lindsey Faucette's grandmother, Mammy Beckie, "toted de keys to de pantry, and her word [was law] with Marse John and Mis' Annie."[35]

Not all nurses rose to the position of mammy, not least because in all but the largest households even senior nurses were not relieved of other responsibilities. But senior nurses who became established house servants brought to their tasks an intimate knowledge of the white family that they rarely hesitated to use. When Thomas Bayne's father remarried, "the old family servants at home" opposed the marriage and "exerted an influence on me to keep me at a distance from my step-mother." House maids tended to be especially close to the young ladies of the household with whom they had played, whose beds or rooms they had shared, and whom they had nursed. They frequently became confidantes who, through contacts with servants in other households, provided a welcome fund of gossip about local affairs and especially the doings of possible suitors. In the wealthiest households, a favorite servant might be sent to New Orleans for professional training in hairdressing, embroidery, and "everything that would perfect her in being of use to her mistress." Upon her return, she would spend long hours dressing her mistress's hair and preparing her person and clothes for social appearances—and gossiping.[36]

The mistress's years as a belle were brief enough, and the images of confidences and clothes include a strong dose of romance but also a strong dose of fact. When Virginia Tunstall Clay, packing to go to Richmond during the war, told Emily, her maid, that there was no need to take any velvets or jewels, for they were going there to nurse the sick, Emily had a different view. "There's bound to be somethin' goin' on, Miss Ginnie an I ain't goin' to let my Mistis be outshined by Mis' ——— and dem other ladies." Many other house servants no doubt enjoyed the fuss about clothes and the talk of social occasions, but while their mistresses were enjoying the fleeting social whirl that preceded marriage and motherhood, they, however they yearned for a pampered adolescence of their own, were learning the practical management of the household. Simultaneously, they were learning the insurmountable distinctions between themselves and the young white women with whom they had played as children.[37]

The younger house servants came into their own when young miss finally assumed the position of mistress, for they were better prepared than she for the responsibilities at hand. Both young servants and young mistress also had to come to terms with the older servants who had presided over both of their girlhoods. However much affection the older servants might have for young Missus, they considered her much too young and inexperienced to know what she wanted. Had they not known her since her birth? Did she not "call them mammy or aunt in consideration of their superior age?" Even the servants close to her in age usually had had much more practical experience.

No servant, however senior or accomplished, could realistically pretend to assume the mistress's place, but many could realistically try to take the management of the house into their own hands, leaving their mistresses with the pretense of supervision. M. D. Cooper, tacitly acknowledging an experienced servant's capabilities, wrote to his son that "my house on the plantation can be left in charge of Old Charity under the supervision of the overseer." Liza Strickland, who lacked seniority but had been reared as a house maid, recalled that "I jest done everthing about a house in general, jest whet ever." "Jest whet ever" amounted to a host of skills that it would take a young mistress years to understand and that she might never master. Frequently, in the ensuing struggle between servants and mistress, only the intervention of a respected servant like a mammy or cook could reestablish order.[38]

The imbalance between the authority of many mistresses and the experience of many servants lay at the core of the relations between white and black women in the slaveholding household. Occasionally, that imbalance was, if not resolved, mediated by a de facto compromise. One former slave woman, whose young mistress had received her as a wedding present from her father, claimed hardly to have known that she was a slave, "'cause I was really only ole mis' housekeeper; kept house took care of her money and everything; she was one o' these kinds women that couldn't keep up with nothing, kinda helpless, you know, and I just handled her money like it was mine almost."[39]

Not many mistresses who could not keep up with things settled easily into the role of the "kinda helpless" lady who confided to a slave the ultimately sensitive and symbolic responsibility of handling money. Those who did not would most likely take out their frustrations in fits of temper and impatience directed at slaves whose work they did not fully understand and could not control, especially since they rarely understood or controlled those slaves' separate lives and identities in the slave community. Charles Wiltse's description of Floride Calhoun nicely fits that of innumerable others: "Even at her best she managed the domestic slaves not too skillfully. She was inclined to be lax and easygoing, and then when things threatened to get out of hand, imperious and slightly panicky." John C. Calhoun loved and admired his wife but worried about her emotional stability, which he knew to be sorely tried by the necessity of managing the servants. Even the feeblest mistress had inducements of food, clothing, and privileges to offer her house servants as lures to their identification with her, but only a wise mistress indeed would understand the limits of those bribes. For whatever the indisputable intimacies and even friendships between black and white women within the household, the realities of ownership overshadowed all.[40]

Accomplished mistresses backed up their authority with evidence of expertise, even when they did not perform the work themselves. Mary Jones wrote to her daughter, Mary Sharpe Jones, of her distress that Sue had ironed shirts so badly. She advised the younger woman to have Lucy teach Sue how to wash and iron shirts properly: "She must use grists for starch and put a little tallow or candle grease. She [Sue] ironed them with *dirty irons*. Tell her from me that *they must be properly done up*, and she must not depend upon Titus, but do the washing herself, making him help with the coarse things and his own and George's clothes. And when she breaks off buttons she must sew them on again. Even the new shirts are nearly ruined." Sue must not be allowed to forget that her senior mistress was still in charge. Young Mary must tell her that "I expect to come down and see after things, and your brother's clothes must look very much improved or I shall be very much displeased." It is reasonable to conjecture that Sue fully appreciated the senior Mary Jones's standards but had tried, in her absence, to cut some corners.[41]

Work in the big house offered slave women specific kinds of responsibilities, opportunities, and supervision. Working for the mistress did not necessarily have any more to recommend it than working for the master, much less his delegates. Hannah Plummer's mother was the washerwoman for Gov. Charles Manly and his family. "Missus Manly . . . did not take any particular interest in her servants," although she presided over a large establishment that included "servants for everything: a wash and ironer, a drawing room and parlor cleaner, a cook, waiting men, waitresses and a maid who did nothing but wait on her." Hannah Plummer's mother received no special perquisites. She received "meal and meat and had to cook. . . . They didn't allow her food from the great house."[42] In houses of all sizes, blows notoriously were meted out with or without provocation. If the staff of house servants was small, a black woman could find herself thrown much more closely into the company of slaveholding women than into the company of her own kind. But even in the largest households, a maid remained at her mistress's beck and call and risked suffering from her flares of temper. In smaller households, the slave woman worked in almost constant company with her mistress, and her work followed roughly the same division of labor by gender that applied to her mistress. Invariably, she worked harder and longer and at dirtier and hotter jobs, but she did women's work.

The work of house slaves on small farms sheds some light on the normal lives of yeoman women. Mary Lindsay was given by her master to "keep" his daughter, who had married a poor white blacksmith. "That sho' was hard living ther' I have to git up at three o'clock sometimes so I have time to water the hosses and slop the hogs and feed the chickens and milk the cows, and then git back to the house and git the breakfast." Conditions in some yeoman households might be more attractive but were unlikely to be any easier. Yeoman women worked hard, performing a vast array of household and barnyard chores as well as engaging in various forms of household production.

The evidence from the Civil War years confirms that they primarily engaged in tasks usually defined as women's labor, rather than laboring in the fields, but that women's work included long hours and heavy physical labor. Yeoman houses, which fell somewhere in the spectrum between the more modest plantation houses and slave cabins, normally had no windows and sometimes no floors. Even a semblance of cleanliness—given ubiquitous bugs and animals—required heroic efforts. The preparation of meals over open fires required the lifting of heavy cauldrons and exposure to intense heat. Yeoman women, assisted by their daughters or an occasional slave, assumed responsibility for all baking, including bread, and for the preservation of foods from meats to fruits, although they might get their men to help hang and smoke carcasses. And they nursed and supervised their children themselves. Although the responsibilities of the yeoman woman resembled those of the slaveholding woman, she, unlike her privileged sister, actually performed the labor to meet those responsibilities.

The actual extent of household production remains difficult to determine from the aggregate figures. Looms, spinning wheels, and other equipment for textile production remained expensive throughout the antebellum years, although the prices had dropped since the colonial period. Prosperous yeoman women might well spin, weave, and card cloth—or their husbands might hire a slave woman to do so for them. They certainly sewed most of the clothes for the household and were much more likely than slaveholding women to sew men's clothes. And, unlike slaveholding women, they quilted. They made candles and soap, and they also made curtains and carpets if they had them at all. Although statistical data is lacking, impressionistic evidence suggests that, in recognition of the weight of the yeoman woman's burdens, yeoman men were likely to purchase, as their first slave, a woman to assist their wives. But that first slave would not replace the yeoman woman's own labor—she would supplement it.[43]

Only the largest plantations could support a large staff of specialized house servants, and even these servants were required to perform enormous amounts of drudgery. But association with the big house on such a plantation brought status and, frequently, a measure of comfort unlike anything available to many white people. Class, not race, differentiated Mary Lindsay's mistress from a Mary Cox Chesnut or a Meta Morris Grimball. Even slave women who did not themselves experience the worst knew the difference. House servants were known to claim attributes of class for themselves as the associates and delegates of their mistress. Occasional evidence of angry bickering among house servants suggests a jockeying for position within the complex hierarchy of the larger houses. Occasional mistrust of house women by field women suggests that the field women did not always trust the discretion of someone who slept in the house. Yet all but the most specialized and pretentious house servants were more bound to than they were separated from the other women of the community of slaves.[44]

The distinction between house and field work broke down for many reasons. Most of the young slaves who began their working lives in the house were moved out to the fields when they became strong enough to be useful. Because most of the female house servants were probably recruited on an as-needed basis, whether they were chosen from among the daughters of other house servants or drivers, purchased, or simply brought in from the fields, they could, upon the whim of the mistress—or the master—be dispatched to from whence they had come. Martha Jackson's daughter, also named Martha, reported that her mother had made Silla and Betsy help her and her sister "string some of the grapes that had already been pressed to make some vinegar," until "it was time for them to return to the fields to pull fodder." Even those who remained in the house often married field hands, and, except on the very largest plantations, social life—for example, Saturday night parties—centered in the quarters. The distinction especially broke down in household production, which did not normally attract the special interest of the mistresses. Washing and spinning, like drying meat and making candles and soap, required regular attention, but they did not necessarily demand the same personal attributes that mistresses who could choose in these matters sought in their personal maids. Innumerable slave women knew how to spin, although their masters were more likely than their mistresses to note that they could do so. They probably learned from older slave women rather than from their mistresses, who might not know how to spin. The mistresses of farms and smaller plantations, like yeoman women, were more likely to know how to spin, wash, make soap and candles, and weave, and they might impart their skills to the few female slaves who worked alongside of them. Susan McIntosh, who grew up on a large plantation, learned to weave from her grandmother, "who made cloth for the white folks and slaves on the plantation," but her grandmother had learned to weave from a white mistress—"a foreigner," which meant someone not born in Georgia.[45]

Sally Brown, who "wuz give away when I wuz jest a baby" and never saw her mother again, offered a clear picture of the ways in

Kitchen and smokehouse on the Pond Bluff Plantation, Berkeley County, South Carolina, built ca. 1820.
Courtesy of South Caroliniana Library

which slave women trained the younger women of their community. Because the family to whom she was given offered her no kindness—"they done everything mean to me they could"—she entertained no illusions about their beneficent role in her development. At five, she "wuz put to work in the fields . . . pickin' cotton and hoein'." For nine years she slept on the floor; had nothing but a cotton dress, her shimmy, and drawers to wear; and regularly suffered cowhide lashings. Yet she had a deep, warm feeling for the "we" of the slave community from whom she learned everything, from how to ease pain by putting a rusty piece of tin or an axe under a straw tick, to cooking fresh vegetables in a pot placed over hot coals on an iron rack; to making yeast from hops; to baking light bread on a wood fire. The older slave women taught her how to work. "We all used battlin' blocks and battlin' sticks to help clean the clothes when we wuz washin'." First they placed the clothes in the suds, then took them out and soaped them, and then "put 'em on the block and beat em with a battlin' stick which was made like a paddle. On wash days you could hear them

Kitchen on the Bloomsbury Plantation, Camden, South Carolina, built ca. 1850 by Colonel James Chesnut.
Courtesy of South Caroliniana Library

battlin' sticks poundin' every which way." They made their own soap out of old meat and grease, "and poured water over wood ashes, which was kept in a rack-lak thing, and the water would drip through the ashes. This made a strong lye. We used a lotta sich lye, too, to bile with."[46]

From the slave women Sally Brown also learned the uses of herbs, which they trusted much more than a doctor's prescription. A tepid bath of leaves was good for dropsy, jimsonweed for rheumatism, chestnut-leaf tea for asthma. For colds they used "ho'hound"—"made candy out'n it with sorghum Molasses"—and also rock candy and whiskey. "They had a remedy that they used fur consumption—take cow manure, make a tea of this and flavor it with mint and give it to the sick pusson." They also used crushed peachtree leaves for upset stomachs. "I still believes in them ole ho'made medicines too and I don't believe in so many doctors." As a matter of fact, some whites, including substantial planters, agreed with her, for their own records confirm consultations with black "root doctors."[47]

Woman and child in rice field, Sapelo Island, Georgia, late nineteenth century.
Courtesy of Georgia Department of Archives and History

Woman at work, Ben Hill County, Georgia, late nineteenth century.
Courtesy of Georgia Department of Archives and History

The slaves concurred even more firmly in Sally Brown's preference for herbal remedies. Slave women nurtured, shared, and transmitted their medical skills. Solomon Caldwell's "ma would take fence grass and boil it to tea and have us drink it to keep de fever away." She also "used branch elder twigs and dogwood berries for chills." Another way to forestall chills was to "dip a string in turpentine, keep it tied around de waist and tie a knot in it every time you take a chill." R. S. Taylor's mother, who "looked after most of us when we were sick," depended upon "roots, herbs, and grease" as well as the medicine the overseer got in town. "When my mother got through rubbin' you, you would soon be well." Bob Mobley's household included a doctor "right there on the place" to look after the slaves when they got sick, but his "mother was a kind of doctor too." She would "ride horseback all over the place an' see how they was gettin' along. She'd make a tea out o' herbs for them who had fever an' sometimes she gave them water from slippery elms."[48]

Slave medicine reflected African as well as local folk beliefs. Sally Brown remembered that when they heard an owl "come to a house and start screechin'," they always knew that somebody was going to die. At the sound of that mournful screech, "we'd put the poker or the shovel in the fire and that always run him away; it burned his tongue out and he couldn't holler no more." Presumably, the women of the slave community were also responsible for the demanding conscience that plagued Sally Brown for snitching a waffle, since her white folks did not command the respect or affection that would have led her to internalize their wishes.[49]

Young slave women, in the house or in the field, matured into a distinct female sphere shaped by the assumptions of both slaveholders and slaves about gender relations (the proper relations between women and men) and gender roles (the proper occupations of women). But slave women viewed matters differently than their mistresses. Slaveholders were more likely to assign slave women to work considered appropriate for women in the house than in the fields, although even in the fields they normally preferred to have women work with other women rather than with men. Had slave women wanted to, they could not often have opposed their assignment to the heavy labor that whites sought to avoid for their own women. But many actually preferred some forms of labor normally viewed as reserved for men, notably plowing, and many others simply took pride in their physical strength and skill. Nonetheless, they never accepted their performance of men's work as a denial of their identity as women among their own people. Slave women who performed the most demanding work in the fields also engaged in various forms of women's work, through which they established lasting bonds with other women of the slave community and through which they inducted younger slave women into their ranks. The house servants' superficially closer identification with the slaveholders' views of femininity had more to do with class—"de quality"—than with gender. No more than the house servants can the field hands be credited with innate gifts for nursing, cooking, weaving, or other ostensibly feminine traits, but they, like the house servants, usually did develop those skills within their own slave communities.[50]

In the fields, slave women gradually moved from lighter to heavier tasks as they matured, and simultaneously they moved away from the direct supervision of their mothers. Although the slaveholders determined the timing of this shift, it also figured within the slave community as one sign of a young woman's coming of age. No slaveholder refrained, out of respect for female delicacy, from letting a slave woman exercise her full strength, and as "full hands" women participated in the most demanding labor of the planting cycle. Instinctively, masters tended to direct slave women toward hoeing and slave men toward plowing. In Alabama, as in other cotton-growing districts, this division was normally respected, but nonetheless a great many women did plow. Frederick Law Olmsted described the women of a Louisiana hoe gang as "forty of the largest and strongest women I ever saw together: they were all in a single uniform dress of a bluish check stuff, the skirts reaching little below the knee; their legs and feet were bare; they carried themselves loftily, each with a hoe sloping over the shoulder and walking with a free powerful swing, like Zouaves on the march." In their wake followed the "cavalry, thirty strong, mostly men, but some women, two of whom rode astride, on the plow mules."[51] Note the "astride," for white ladies more commonly rode their horses sidesaddle in deference to the delicate sensibilities of their gentlemen.

The number of women who plowed was noticeable. Olmsted noted that, on a large plantation in Louisiana, women generally performed the plowing with both single and double mule teams. "Very well performed, too." The former slave women who recalled plowing, or seeing their mothers plow, took pride in the excellence of the performance even as they also emphasized the difficulty of the work. Lila Nichols's mother plowed all year with a two-horse plow "when she warn't cleanin' new ground or diggin' ditches." Obviously, some women preferred to plow, perhaps because they enjoyed a difficult accomplishment, perhaps because they preferred riding or walking to stooping, or perhaps because plowing gave them a slightly greater measure of freedom in their work. Liddie Aiken's mother preferred plowing to chopping. "She was a big woman and they let her plough right along with her two little brothers." William Brown's mother "was one of the leading plow hands on Bill Nealy's farm. She had a old mule named Jane." Henry James Trentham noted that some of "de women plowed bare footed most all de time, an' had to carry dat row an' keep up wid de men, an' den do dere cookin' at night." Yet Henrietta McCullers, who "plowed an' dug ditches an' cleaned new groun'," claimed that "hard wuck ain't neber hurted me yit." Even accomplished house servants might prefer field work, for, in the words of one cook, "We could talk and do anything we wanted to, just so we picked the cotton; we used to have lots of fun."[52]

Most slave women engaged in a wide variety of farming tasks and, more often than not, worked at them in the company of other women. During January and February, during the slow season, they grubbed and hoed; mended old or put up new fences; shrubbed hedgerows and raked manure in the yard; cut down and picked up corn stalks; burned blown-down logs and brush; picked out cotton and thrashed out oats. The making and repairing of fences often fell to women. And always, during inclement weather or when nothing else was pressing, they spun. By late February and early March, even as the shrubbing, burning of logs, and cutting down of cornstalks continued, the planting

began. Peg, Nicholas Massenburg's plow woman, would be out with
the other plow hands, whom he referred to as "plows," bedding up
cotton lots and preparing beds for corn and potatoes. She may even
have been the lead plow, since it was she who rode the carriage horse.
Other women, along with the children, whom he referred to as "small
hands," planted cotton, corn, rye, peas, and Irish potatoes and began
weeding. Throughout the summer they continued to hoe and weed
the various fields one after the other. In August, with the beginning of
the wheat harvest, they spread and stacked hay and began to rake
leaves. Then came the cotton harvest. In 1838 the women and the small
hands began to pick cotton on 24 September and were still picking it
in Massenburg's Spring Field on 1 November. In 1836 they did not
finish picking the cotton in the Spring Field until 29 December. In
between picking cotton, they pulled up the "Bonna Bess" beans, beat
out the peas, gathered apples, made the fence to protect the corn when
it was hauled up to shuck, and began "picking out" the cotton—
removing the seeds to prepare it for spinning. When it was too wet to
harvest, they spun. As the fall wore on and the crops came in, they
devoted more and more time to spinning.[53]

On the Massenburg plantation, men did most, but not all, of the
plowing. They also mauled on roads, cut and collected wood, cut
hay, mended chimneys, dug ditches, worked the road, raked manure,
cut the ground, hilled corn, shelled corn, thrashed out oats, mended
shoes, and made baskets. Occasionally one man would work with one
or two women at a special task, and frequently the overseer accompanied the women. Massenburg apparently assumed that certain kinds of
heavy work were especially suited to men, for he never set women to
digging ditches, working on the roads, or cutting timber, although he
did regularly set them to making fences. The principles that governed
his assignment of tasks are not always clear, and perhaps were not to
him. He more frequently set men to raking manure than women, but
apparently he did so because the men could rake manure on a wet day
while the women were spinning. He showed a strong preference for
grouping his field hands by gender and assigning the children to the
women. His journal does not reveal the influence of the field hands'
preferences on his decisions, either those which concerned grouping
by gender or those which concerned his assignment of tasks to men
and women respectively, but perhaps the choice to set men to basket
making was not his but theirs. In Africa men made baskets.[54]

Massenburg, who practiced diversified agriculture as well as growing cotton for the market in Franklin County, North Carolina, noted

more carefully than most planters the tasks to which he assigned his female slaves. James Hervey Greenlee, who engaged in diversified farming on a smaller scale in Burke and McDowell counties, North Carolina, also paid close attention to men's and women's work, which he carefully noted. The women on his plantation cut stock and briars, planted pumpkin seed, shelled corn, pulled flax, cut briars, stripped clover seed out of the field, gathered clover seed, dug sweet potatoes, sprouted new ground, cut sprouts in the new ground, and hoed corn.[55]

Patterns differed in other regions and with the cultivation of other crops. Above all, they differed according to the size of the holding, for small slaveholders could not divide their few hands by gender. A slaveholder needed upwards of fourteen working hands before he could organize gangs at all. Farmers with only a few slaves had to send men and women into the fields to work side by side. Even on the larger holdings, planters differed in the way they organized work. Those of the South Carolina Rice Coast relied on the task system, which provided greater flexibility in labor assignments than did the gang labor system. In contrast, the hemp growers of Kentucky regarded women as physically unfit for the essential tasks.

Not everyone with a large slave force organized the gangs by gender, but most seem to have done so. Certainly, planters throughout the South, on plantations encompassing a variety of sizes and crops, reserved some tasks for women and others for men. Charles Joyner, in his microcosmic study of the lowcountry, has found that although, on the Rice Coast, both men and women worked in the fields, only the men worked at ditching, embanking, and preparing the fields for the crop. On Robert F. W. Allston's Chicora Wood rice plantation, while the men worked in the pinelands, the women hoed peas; while the men worked on the causeway at the farm, the women carried away the sand from the pits or picked "volunteer" rice; while the men picked peas, the women hoed the land for rye. In Florida, the overseers at El Destino plantation did not differentiate between men and women when they noted work in the fields, but they did note the special tasks performed by women, notably cooking for the whites, cooking for the hands, tying up fat, and spinning—mostly cooking and spinning. Bennet Barrow, a planter in Louisiana, regularly referred to the women as working at one or another task, frequently spinning. On the Belmead Plantation in Virginia, the women spun, cleaned the water furrows, opened the water furrows, and grubbed the land. Josephine Bacchus, from South Carolina, firmly insisted that women did not attend corn shuckings. "Dem kind of task was left to de men folks de most of de time cause it been so hot dey was force to strip to do dat sort of a job."[56]

Division of the field hands' labor by gender prevailed on the sugar as well as the cotton plantations of Louisiana. Franklin Hudson, a sugar planter in Iberville Parish, set the women to digging stubble and the men to working on the road. Once he noted that he allowed his overseer "to send 6 women in the place of 6 men." On the LeBlanc family cotton plantation in Iberville, the men rolled logs while the women cleaned up the grounds; the men chopped wood and plowed while the women hoed. Since women on the LeBlanc plantation also sawed wood, it appears that the division between women and men had more to do with the principle of division than with any particular respect for the tasks considered appropriate for women. On H. M. Seale's sugar plantation in Ascension Parish, Louisiana, the women cleaned up the land while the men ditched. On M. W. Philips's cotton plantation in Mississippi—among many throughout the South—the women worked as a group under a male foreman.[57]

Former slave women, recalling their or their mothers' days in the fields, were more likely to emphasize the difficulty and diversity of the tasks than whom they worked with. Gus Feaster, however, explicitly recalled seeing the "hoe-womens" setting off for the field as a group. Sarah Wilson hoed, chopped sprouts, sheared sheep, carried water, cut firewood, picked cotton, sewed, and was selected to "work Mistress' little garden where she raised things from seeds they get in Fort Sumter: Green peas and beans and radishes and little things like that." In the summer and spring, Mary Frances Webb's grandmother plowed and hoed the crops, and in the winter she "sawed and cut cord wood just like a man. She said it didn't hurt her as she was strong as an ox." She also spun and wove and sewed. "She helped make all the cloth for their clothes and in the spring one of the jobs for the women was to weave hats for the men." For the hats, they "used oat-straw, grass, and cane which had been split and dried and soaked in hot water until it was pliant, and they wove it into hats." As a field hand, Callie Donalson's mother also washed, ironed, carded, wove, and was "a good spinner." "She knitted mainly by night. All the stockings and gloves had to be knit." She taught her daughter to sew "with our fingers." But Sally Brown claimed to have had a very hard time. "I split rails like a man. . . . I used a huge glut made out's wood, and a iron wedge drove into the wood with a maul, and this would split the wood."[58]

Masters commonly assigned slave women to labor that they would have considered inappropriate for white women, but they also had differing expectations for the quantities of work that slave men and women should be expected to perform. James Bertrand, a former slave, recalled that "out in the field, the man had to pick three hundred pounds of cotton and the woman had to pick two hundred pounds," but he added that he remembered hearing his mother "talk about weaving the yarn and making the cloth and making clothes out of the cloth that had been woven." Because many masters and overseers permitted women to leave the fields before men in order to be able to attend to other matters, it is not clear if the women's lighter loads reflected concern for their physical frailty or simply the desire to free them for other kinds of labor. Yet on a noteworthy, if unmeasurable, number of plantations women matched or overmatched the productivity of the men. Plantation account books usually recorded with special care the amount of cotton picked, and women regularly figured among the top pickers. Some planters made pointed reference to a woman as their best picker or best general field hand.[59]

The overwhelming majority of adult slave women returned from their work in the fields to cook, wash, sew, knit, weave, or do other kinds of work, sometimes for the plantation household, more often for their own families—usually for direct consumption, but sometimes for sale. Occasionally, slave women returned from the fields too tired even to eat, much less cook for their families, but often they used the remainder of the day and much of the night for their second set of tasks. George Washington Browning's mother often returned from a hard day's plowing to card and spin clothes for her family. Fannie Moore's mother worked in the fields all day "and piece and quilt all night." She had "to spin enough thread to make four cuts for de white folks ebber night," and also had to piece quilts for them. Sometimes Fannie Moore, who "hab to hold the light for her to see by," never got to bed. Betty Brown's family "lived de ole-time way of livin', mammy done de cookin' an' we had plenty good things to eat." Her mother also "made all de clothes, spinnin', an' weavin' an sewin'. Ah learned to spin when ah wuz too little tuh reach de broach, an' ah could hep her thread de loom." Her mother was also "a shoe-maker, she'd make moccasins for all o' us." Hannah Plummer lived with her family in a plank house, "with three rooms and a shed porch." Her mother washed their clothes under the porch and at night she made their bed clothes. "She also made bonnets and dresses" at night and sometimes sold the bonnets. She would give sweets to the child who sat up with her, so Hannah "sat up with her a lot because I liked to eat." Billie Smith remembered that some of the spinners would "sit up at night and card and spin thread. They could sell the thread they spun at night."[60]

Slave women, whether in the big house or the fields, shared a common female experience that centered particularly around the preparation of food and cloth but also included such forms of basic household production as making candles and soap. Although mistresses sometimes taught their female slaves specific skills, slave women themselves normally transmitted those skills from one generation to the next. Some slave women specialized in household tasks, but, specialists or not, all slave women learned to contribute to general household labor and to provide for their own families. Large plantations had special houses for spinning and weaving; smaller ones might have a shed or a room. Bob Mobley recalled that on his plantation, where his aunt was a weaver, there was a house "built especially for spinnin' an' weavin'." Two or three of "the other nigger women made the clothes and they had to make 'em fit." The mistress kept a close watch on the fit and "made them be careful so the clothes would look nice." Other slaves "even learned to dye the wool so that we could have warm clothes in the winter." Washing, a central feature of household life, could be done in a wash house or at a creek or stream, normally on the plantation but, in the case of smaller holdings, outside. Soap and candles were made on the place, as were dyes and lye. Slave women sewed in the big house under the direction of their mistresses or a slave seamstress. They sewed in their own cabins with the assistance of their daughters, and they sewed and quilted with the other women of the quarters.[61]

Some slave girls began their working lives as apprentices and helpers in the production of cloth. Martha King had an easy time until she was about ten years old, when she started working in the field. At the same time she also began "to work in the weaving room." The slaves made all their own clothes, but the master bought their shoes. "I spun and wove cotton and wool." They also made fancy clothes. They could "stripe the cloth or check it or leave it plain." They also "wove coverlids and jean to make mens suits out of. I could still do that if I had to." Julia Stubbs also began with general work around the house and "wuz put at mos' anything dat come handy, jis' a doing fust one thing den another." Amidst her other tasks, she "learnt to spin, knit an' weave," and she "helped wid de washing an' toted to de long wash troughs loads o' water to be drawd an' toted to de long wash troughs." The troughs, made by hewing out big logs, were set on racks. "We had to rub de clothes by hand, some beat 'em on blocks wid hickory battling sticks." Washing took most of the day. "Deir wuz a heap o' ironing to be done. De white folks wore lots of white ruffled up, full things dat had to be starched and ironed."[62]

The extent and nature of these forms of household production differed from one plantation to the next, particularly with regard to specialization, and according to location and period. Annie Row's household included spinners and weavers who made all the cloth for the clothes "and thes what they raised me to do." The first step in her apprenticeship consisted in "teasin' de wool"—"pickin' de burrs and thrash and sich out od de wool for to git it ready for de cardin'." Betty Cofer belonged to a household that had a "crowd of hands," including two "sewin women" and "some who did all the weavin' an spinnin'." They "raised our own flax an' cotton an' wool, spun the thread, wove the cloth, made all the clothes. Yes'm, we made the men's shirts an' pants an' coats." In addition, they "wove the cotton and linen for sheets an' pillow-slips an' table covers" and "the wool blankets too." Such a quantity of textile production required specialization. "One woman knitted all the stockin's for the white folks an' colored folks too," and, as a result, "had one finger all twisted an' stiff from holdin' her knitten' needles." Angeline Smith, an accomplished seamstress, made all the clothes worn by the white family in her household. "She could card, spin, weave, and dye. She never used a pattern to cut by, but would take your measure and every dress had to fit snug and tight." Betty Cofer began by waiting "on the girl who did the weavin'. When she took the cloth off the loom she done give me the 'thrums [ends of threads left on the loom]. I tied 'em all together with teensy little knots an' got me some scraps from the sewin' room and I made me some quilt toys." Years later, she remembered her pride that the toys were so pretty.[63]

In smaller households, slave women had less opportunity to specialize, but textile work and other kinds of production figured prominently among their responsibilities. Like many slave women, Fannie Cawthon Coleman carded and spun: "Us used to spin and weave our clothes in them days—as well as work in the fields." She rose before the white family to get breakfast and to "milk and churn" before going to the fields. She left the field with the others "'bout sundown to get home and have time to feed and milk and do things for night." She had her bed in the kitchen, set off from the big house. Phoebe Banks belonged to a Creek Indian family, for whose slothfulness she had nothing but contempt. Her mother was their house girl, "cooking, waiting on the table, cleaning the house, spinning the yarn, knitting some of the winter clothes, taking care of the mistress girl, washing the clothes—yes she was always busy and worked mighty hard all the time," for the Indians "wouldn't hardly do nothing for themselves." Laura Caldwell's mother did not even work within her own household. A weaver, she went "to the white folks' houses" and wove "clothes for them for small pay." Those white families did all their carding and spinning at home.[64]

Slave women's work in textiles reveals far more clearly than the work of their mistresses the persistence of household production throughout the rural South. The largest and wealthiest plantations sustained a wide and diverse complex of textile production, even if they were also likely to be the heaviest purchasers of luxury textiles imported from elsewhere. The smaller the plantation or farm, the more likely it was to depend almost exclusively on the skills of its members for cloth and clothing. In this respect, these smaller units resembled yeoman households, with the difference that yeoman women did most of the work that slave women performed in plantation households. Even in yeoman households in which one female slave assisted the wife, the master might, as did the master of Laura Caldwell's mother, draw upon her skills or those of a hired slave for specialized tasks such as weaving. Up and down the social and economic ladder, the textile skills of slave women linked households in a common web and linked the slave women to one another.

Slave women were much more likely than their mistresses to comment on the household's self-sufficiency in textiles; their mistresses remained cognizant of a point that their slaves normally did not stress—the dependence of the white families on clothing produced off the plantation. Susan Snow remembered that "dey made all de niggers clothes on de place. Homespun, dey called it." The household included "spinnin' wheels an' cards an' looms. All de women spun in de winter time." On some plantations, older and pregnant women did the carding "wid hand-cards," and other women specialized in weaving, but "every woman had to learn to make clothes for the family, and they had to knit coarse socks and stockin's." Male as well as female slaves took pride in this production. Charlie Grant insisted that "de peoples bout dere have good clothes to wear in dat day en time. Dey was homemade clothes." His mother spun and then sent the thread to the loom house, where other women "dye dem wid persimmon juice en different things lak dat to make all kind of calicos." Even the shoes were made "right dere at home." The slaves would "clean de hair off de leather just as clean as anything en den de shoemaker cut en sew de shoes." Martha Everette allowed that the overseers' wives "learned some o' th' nigger women ter sew," but thereafter they "made most of 'em [the clothes]." Mistresses might supervise or even participate in making the slaves' clothing, but their efforts, which figure as such a burden in their accounts, seem diminished when viewed from the perspective of the slaves' work in spinning, carding, dying, and weaving. Betty Cofer credited her mistress with genuine skill, but not with much of the labor that went into the finished product: "Miss Julia cut out all the clothes herself for men and women too." Miss Julia must have wielded her sheers with panache, for Betty Cofer suspected that those "big sheers an' patterns an' old cuttin' table are over at the house now." She cut out all the clothes "an' then the colored girls sewed 'em up." After the sewing had been completed, she "looked 'em all over and they better be sewed right! Miss Julia bossed the whole plantation."[65]

As a rule, the slaves did not confuse bossing with skill. The slave women took great pride in their talent, and some of their men appreciated it, too. Ida Adkins proudly remembered her mother's work in the weaving room: "I can see her now settin' at de weavin' machine an' hear de pedals goin' plop, plop, as she treaded dem wid her feats. She was a good weaver." Maggie Black similarly cherished an image of her mother, who "set dere at dat ole spinning wheel en take one shettle en t'row it one way en den annuder de udder way en pull dat t'in en make it tighter en tighter. Sumptin say zum, zum, zum, zum en den yat haddar wuk yuh feet dere too. Dat wuz de way dey make dey cloth dat day en time." As a child, Josephine Bristow watched the grown women spinning and weaving on inclement days. "Man, you would hear dat thing windin en I remember I would stand dere en want to spin so bad." Before long she got so she "could use de shuttle en weave, too." But her grandmother was something else. When "she would get to dat wheel, she sho know what she been doin. . . . I mean she could do dat spinnin." According to Charles Anderson, "weaving was a thing the women prided in doing—being a fast weaver or a fine hand at weaving." Charity Anderson never worked in the fields, but "I could sho 'nuff wash, iron and knit and weave. Sometimes I weaved six or seven yahds of cloth, and do my house work too." Queen Elizabeth Bunts proudly remembered that her mother "was considered a very fine seamstress." Betty Abernathy, who grew up watching her mother and the other women weaving and sewing, learned from them how to spin and soon "could fill broaches and spin as good as any of 'en."[66]

The results testified to the skill that produced them. "Dey would make de prettiest cloth in dat day en time," and then they would dye it with indigo "en dey would color de cloth just as pretty as you ever did see." Willis Easter considered his mother not merely "de bes' cook in de county," but "a master hand at spinnin' and weavin'." She made her own dye: "Walnut and elm makes red dye and walnut brown color, shumake makes black color." Others dyed the thread they spun with maple bark and then made "all kinds of fancy cloth and dey made fancy counterpanes." The same women made jean cloth to make pants which, according to one of the young men who admired them, "never wore out." Another man recalled that the slave women of his household wove "pretty coverlets for the beds." Orelia Alexie Franks also insisted that they had had good clothes in slavery times: "Dey weave dey own cotton." The clothes, as Priscilla Gibson recalled, were "made of homespun what al nigger women weaved." Because her master raised sheep, they also had wool clothes for winter, "but he has no shoes." Anna Mitchel's mother, who as seamstress sewed the clothes, was known "ter wuck all night an' half de day ter make clothes fer de slaves."[67]

Some former slaves' fond memories of the quality of their clothes before emancipation must be weighed against the insistence of other former slaves and of many travelers that their clothing was sparse and inadequate, but they should not be dismissed out of hand as mere evidence of old people's romantic nostalgia for the days of their youth. The quality of slave clothing varied widely in accordance with the conscience and affluence of the master, but Charles Anderson, Barney Alford, Josephine Bristow, Willis Easter, Orelia Alexie Franks, and Priscilla Gibson were not focusing on the bounty or niggardliness of their masters. And when Priscilla Gibson did mention her master, she did so to contrast the absence of shoes, which he should have provided, with the quality of the cloth produced by the slave women. Accounts like Anna Mitchel's tale of her mother's staying up through the night to finish the slave clothes suggest that slave women viewed their labor for fellow slaves differently than they viewed their labor for the master. When the slaves viewed their clothes as the product of the talent and labor of their mothers, aunts, and grandmothers, they emphasized their quality. In the same spirit, a woman who shirked a task in the fields or the house might work overtime on the slaves' clothes, much as she worked at night for her immediate family. In part, the fond memories of slave clothes registered an appreciation for the slaves' efforts on each other's behalf. In part, as in the case of the young girls who looked with such admiration on the expertise of their elders, they reflected a recognition of skills handed down among each other from generation to generation.

Many slave women developed a fine eye for quality clothing and reveled in cast-off finery from the big house, but many also developed a sense of style in the clothes they made for themselves. When Sarah Graves was growing up and wanted "a nice wool dress, we would shear the sheep, wash the wool, card it, spin it, and weave it." When they wanted "it striped, we used two threads," which they would color "by using herbs or barks." Sometimes they had the wool carded at a mill, sometimes they carded it themselves. "But when we did it, the threads were short, which caused us to have to tie the threads often, makin' too many knots in the dress." Aunt Sarah Waggoner "jes had two dresses. De best one was made of plain, white muslin." To make it, she went out to the woods "and got walnut bark to color it brown." She "allus had to wash it on Saturday, 'cause we all had to go to church on Sunday." She also had another dress and a skirt, which she made "jes' like old Miss taught me." The dress was her walking dress and was "made with a cord 'round de bottom, a cord as big as my little finger, so's I couldn't tear it, cause I went over fences like a deer." Annie Mae Weathers had dresses "made out of cotton stripes and my chemise was made of flannelette and my underpants was made out of homespun." Alice Battle's mother wove the cloth for their clothes, while her mistress superintended the sewing. "Dresses were made very full, buttoned down the front, and with belts sewed in at the waist line."[68]

Textile work occupied a special place in the lives of slave women, as it did in the lives of their mistresses. Of the many kinds of labor that slave women performed in the house or the fields, in the cabins and gathering places of the slave community, textile work alone touched the lives of all. Some of their skills had African roots; others were learned from mistresses and overseers' wives. Lidia Jones's mistress, Miss Janie, herself "went to the wood ant got" the dye, which she said was indigo: "No Lord, she never bought *her* indigo—she *raised* it." By Lidia Jones's account, Miss Janie "could do most anything. Made the prettiest counterpanes I ever saw. Yes ma'am, she could do it and did do it." Miss Janie and her daughter, Miss Frances, "made all the clothes for the colored folks. They'd be sewin' for weeks and months." And they "woves such pretty cloth fer the colored. You know, they went and made themselves dresses and the white and colored had the same kind of dresses."[69]

Miss Janie and Miss Frances were exceptional and probably belonged to a small household in which slave and mistress worked side by side. Nor did their working with their slaves reflect much of a sense of sisterhood. The bride of a North Carolina planter noted snippily that the slave women "are not diffident, either. One of the field hands asked me to fix a dress for her the other day." Mary Childs worked alongside her mother, "the plantation weaver," and her mistress. "Mistis would cut out dresses out of the homespun. They was pretty. I had to sew seams." After her mistress had cut the cloth, Mary Childs would sit beside her while she made the pants, putting the raw seams (basting) around the pockets and down the legs. "She had a cowhide layin' side of her, 'bout as long as yo' arm, and if it warn't done right she'd whip me."[70]

However slave women learned their skills, once they had mastered them they imparted them to the younger women. Many aspects of their crafts exceeded their independent control. The mistress who insisted on cutting the cloth for the slave clothes, as many did, established a mold that the slave sewers had to follow. Their insistence may in part have reflected their concern to establish uniformity in slave clothing, but frequently, if Harriet Martineau's report can be credited, it also reflected their mistrust of their slaves' propensity to cut too generously and, accordingly, to "waste" cloth. Quilting was another matter. Frequently, slave women quilted together while the men enjoyed corn shuckings. As a man, Ed McCree knew little about the quilting sessions except that they were special occasions. "'Bout dem quiltin's! Now Lady, what would a old Nigger man know 'bout somepin' dat didn't nothin' but 'omans have nothin' to do wid?" Quilting offered slave women the chance to exercise their own imaginations. No white woman dictated their complex patterns, even if the pieces with which they worked were white women's scraps. No outsider interfered with the ceaseless flow of the gossip in which they delighted and through which they wove their own view of the world that usually impinged so heavily on their lives.[71]

Women's work in textiles provides a microcosm of the relations between mistresses and slaves in their shared sphere of women's labor. The white and black sources respectively offer strikingly different perspectives on women's textile production, but they describe the same world. Mistresses did not "see"—or at least did not bother to write about—most of their slaves' textile work, which accounted for most of the household's textile production. From the mistress's perspective, the "negro clothes" constituted a burden they frequently shouldered with something less than good grace. From the slaves' perspective, textile labor consisted in the spinning, carding, weaving, and dyeing—

the necessary prerequisite to the mistresses' sewing—in which they were specially skilled and in which they passed long hours in the company of other slave women. Had the mistresses considered this labor at all, they would probably have passed over it lightly as one of the many things that almost invisibly got done. Such work did not embody their sense of themselves as women. It did embody the slave women's sense of themselves as women, as did the sewing of the slaves' clothes, which became a labor of love for their people. The textile work of mistresses and slaves met in sewing, on which both prided themselves, yet neither mistresses nor slaves commonly emphasized their having sewed together. Mistresses and slaves shared their respective identifications with the textile labor that made an important contribution to the definition of women's roles within the household. Yet for both, that labor acquired its meaning in their relations to their distinct families and communities.

The slave women did not take pride and satisfaction in all aspects of household production, but they frequently did take pride in their own skills, even if those were exercised primarily for the benefit of the white folks. Like the men and women who worked in the fields, the house servants developed a sense of camaraderie in their work. According to Mary Frances Webb, on wash days slave women from different households met at the creek "to do the family wash [and] had a regular picnic of it as they would wash and spread the clothes in the bushes and low branches of the trees to dry. They would get to spend the day together." In the larger households, slave women did not often meet with women from other plantations to do the wash, but washing still required the participation of a number of them who could use the occasion to talk while they worked. Similarly, soap making on a large plantation required the concerted efforts of a number of slave women. Common soap "was made in a hopper" by hoisting a barrel "on a stand 'bove de ground a piece; wheat straw was then put into de barrell, hickory ashes was then emptied in, then water, and then it set 'bout ten days or more." To this mixture, the women added "fats and old grease, meat skins, and rancid grease." After it had stayed for a while, "de lye was drained out, put in a pot, and boiled wid grease. Dis was lye-soap, good to wash wid." Slave women also made candles "from tallow and beeswax," poured the wax into molds, and "wove our own candle wicks too." They worked on their mistress's preserves and cut and dried apples and peaches. They dried meat and made sausages. During the off season both house and field women often spent several days rendering and drying the lard from recently slaughtered hogs.

Taught by their mistress, some braided "shucks an' make foot mats, rugs and horse collars." Hammett Dell recalled that he, too, learned "to twist shucks and weave chair bottoms."[72]

The more routine aspects of household production offered slave women the maximum opportunity to work together under minimal supervision. Except in the smallest households, in which mistress and slaves worked side by side, the weaving room, the smokehouse, the kitchen, and the creek figured as their preserves. There they frequently kept their daughters with them as they worked. There they introduced younger women into the mysteries of their crafts or the gossip and chat that alleviated their boredom. There they defined themselves as women through their work and inducted the next generation into their sisterhood.

Field women, who rotated in and out of these female preserves according to age, weather, and the demands of the farming cycle, also worked primarily in the company of other women. But men usually presided over women's work in the fields and thus offered a constant reminder of the gender hierarchy of the larger society. Although women may have achieved the status of plow hand much more commonly than was once thought, they rarely, if ever, attained the status of driver, for southern men, black and white, defined command as a male attribute and responsibility. Women might, however, be charged with responsibility for the work of children or a group of other women. One South Carolina planter noted that, because in planting corn it was impossible "for master or overseer to be present at the dropping or covering of every hill," the best protection against sloppy work—"irregularity"—was "to select a trusty woman (men are usually engaged at heavier work at this season) who *covers*, and is responsible not only for her own but for the work of both corn droppers and coverers." He proposed, in his own words, "to make an overseer of her for the time," but only, as he made clear, an overseer of other women and possibly children. On another big plantation in Tennessee, "Aunty Darkens am overseer of de spinnin' and weavin'." There was one exception to this general rule: In fact if not in name, as young Lucy McCullough insisted to her mistress, cooks also functioned as de facto overseers of the kitchens, where men as well as boys might—although the evidence remains cloudy—work under their direction.[73] Julia Glover's mother attained her status as her master's "right hand bough" as a cook. The kitchen was, quintessentially, a central component of the female sphere, but white southerners did not endow it with the same prestige as northerners. Outside the kitchen, masters did not place women in command of men, and in this respect their prejudices accorded perfectly with those of their males slaves.

Women's exclusion from positions of command did not, as planters well knew, reflect women's innate docility or inclination to be bossed. Overseers found them, if anything, more independent and difficult than men. "H.C.," in writing "On the Management of Negroes" for the *Southern Agriculturalist*, laid down as a general rule that "the negro women are harder to manage than the men." In his opinion, only "kind words and flattery" made it possible to get along with them. "If you want to cure a sloven, give her something nice occasionally to wear, and praise her up to the skies whenever she has [done] anything decent." Slave women whom their masters and overseers found difficult to manage had something other than flattery in mind. Susan Snow's mother "was a black African an' she sho' was wild an' mean." Because she could not be whipped unless she was tied up, "sometimes my master would wait 'til de next day to git somebody to he'p tie her up, den dey'd fergit to whip 'er." Flattery would have been about as useful with Susan Snow's mother as with the cougar to which they compared her. "Dey was all scared of 'er." She was the cause "of my ol' masser firin' all de overseers." She was too valuable to lose, "an' she was so mean he was afraid dey'd kill her." All she wanted was to be left to her own oversight. "She'd work without no watchin' an' overseers wa'n't nothin' nohow."[74]

American-born women shared her feelings. Leonard Franklin's mother, Lucy, apparently worked just fine for her master, Mr. Pennington, but her attitude changed when he went off deer hunting for a few weeks, leaving an overseer in charge. In Pennington's absence the overseer tried to whip her. "She knocked him down and tore his face up so that the doctor had to tend to him." Upon Pennington's return, he queried the overseer about the patches all over his face. The overseer told him "that he went down in the field to whip the hands and that he just thought he would hit Lucy a few licks to show the slaves that he was impartial." The results were emblazoned on his face. Pennington offered scant comfort. "Well," he replied, "if that is the best you can do with her, damned if you won't just have to take it." Eventually, Pennington himself tired of taking it and sold Lucy to Jim Bernard. Bernard tried to reason with her. "Look out there," he told her, "and mind you do whet you told around here and step lively. If you don't, you'll get that bull whip." Lucy was unmoved: "Yes, and we'll both be gittin' it." Jim Bernard sold her to a man named Cleary, who was good to her, "so she wasn't sold no more after that." Cleary apparently decided that her skills warranted some accommodation. According to Lucy's son, not many men "could class up with her when it come to working. She could do more work than any two men." No one man would be well advised "to try to do nothin' wid her. No overseer ever downed her."[75]

Black women in undetermined numbers earned reputations as fighters. Josie Jordan's mother "just figured she would be better off dead and out of her misery as to be whipped all the time." One day the master found fault with her work and "started to raise his whip, but Mammy fought back and when the ruckus was over the master was laying still on the ground and folks thought he was dead, he got such a heavy beating." He was not, and Josie Jordan's mother was sold. Aunt Margaret Bryant proudly remembered that the white men "couldn't manage my ma." When one overseer threatened a whipping, her mother threatened, "I done my work! Fore I take a lick rather drowned myself." The doctor whose advice the overseer sought told her, "You too good labor for drown." She and her daughter were set to weaving. "Two womans fuh card; two spin. Ma wop 'em off. Sail duh sheckel [shuttle] through there." Knowing their worth and cherishing their pride, such women refused on principle to be mastered. Solomon Oliver's mother had special reason to resent her master and the discipline of his slave driver and overseer, but she also had reason to know that they could not lay a hand on her. She "was Massa's daughter," and he ordered the others to leave her alone. "High-tempered" to begin with, she "knew about the Master's orders not to whip her." She may even have taken advantage "and tried to do things that maybe wasn't right." But neither defiance nor special status did her any good: "One of the white men flogged her to death. She died with scars on her back."[76]

Most field women and probably all young girls could not resist whippings. Harman Pitman, the overseer for Robert F. W. Allston's Nightingale Hall Plantation, noted that "for howing corn bad" he had "flogged" slaves as follows: "Fanny 12 lashes, Sylvia 12, Monday 12, Phoebe 13, Susanna 12, Salina 12, Celia 12, Iris 12." Perhaps, this female gang had been working without male supervision and may well have devoted more time to gossip than to the task at hand. Or they may have had an overseer who wantonly went to his whip. Bad treatment required no provocation. A Mrs. Wilson was indicted "for not feeding and clothing her negroes," and a Mr. Hoover for the murder of his female slave:

> Through a period of four months, including the latter stages of pregnancy, delivery, and recent recovery therefrom, . . . he beat her with clubs, iron chains, and other deadly weapons, time after time; burnt her; inflicted stripes over and often with scourges, which literally excoriated her whole body; forced her to work in inclement seasons, without being duly clad; provided for her insufficient food; expected labour beyond her strength; and wantonly beat her because she could not comply with his requisitions. These enormities, besides others too disgusting to be particularly designated, the prisoner without his heart once relenting, preached . . . even up to the last hours of the victim's existence.[77]

Cruelty abounded, despite the widespread appeals for Christian decency, but it did not normally result in death. Masters—and especially overseers, who often lacked self-control or the personal motivation to value human property—may even have found women especially tempting objects for their random wrath. The white men were not saints, and slave women who worked in the fields were clothed scantily, with skirts hitched above their knees. The men's propensities to violence remained unchecked. Confronted with recalcitrance, could their reactions not have included a measure of sexual violence? Slave women knew what they were dealing with.

The women who resisted most fiercely appear to have been loners, for whom the problem was not the quality of their performance—which was, more often than not, exemplary—but the right of any man, especially a white man, to boss them. Some probably preferred to deal directly with the master rather than with his underlings. Others did not even want to deal with the master; they wanted to be left to determine the pace, quantity, and quality of their own work. Such women would prefer plowing to working in a women's gang. Women recently arrived from Africa and accustomed to independent agricultural labor must have found the chains of supervision intolerable. Women who knew themselves to be their master's children had special reasons to resent the orders of his overseers and drivers and to test the limits of their enslavement. But the vast majority of the field women, although by no means more accepting of their condition than their more overtly combative sisters, sought to recreate in the fields the camaraderie of the weaving room, even if without the same pride in craft. For the women who hoed casually, with their minds on the gossip of the day, were the same women who tossed the shuttle with zest and who worked late into the night for their families.[78]

Field women usually worked under a male foreman, white or black. When planters sent women off to a specific job, they frequently sent a male slave along, presumably as foreman. Black drivers exercised wide authority in the supervision of work, although less often in the administration of punishment. A driver might show considerably more concern and compassion for a slave woman than the white men, but then again he might not. Many drivers tried to protect their people, but others ranged from indifferent to brutal. Some acquired particularly nasty reputations for sexual exploitation of the women. Analiza Foster's mother told of one slave woman whom a driver "beat clean ter death." The woman was pregnant and fainted in the fields. "De driver said dat she wuz puttin' on an' dat she ort ter be beat. De master said dat she can be beat but don't ter hurt de baby." The driver then dug a hole in the ground into which he put the woman "'bout ter her arm pits, den he kivers her up an' straps her han's over her haid." He then took "de long bull whup an' he cuts long gashes all over her shoulders an' raised arms, den he walks off an' leaves her dar fer a hour in de hot sun." During the hour, "de flies an' de gnats day worry her, an' de sun hurts too an' she cries a little, den de driver comes out wid a pan full of vinegar, salt an' red pepper an' he washes de gashes. De 'oman faints an' he digs her up, but in a few minutes she am stone dead." Analiza Foster considered the case the worst she had heard of, but reckoned "dar wuz plenty more of dem."[79]

Even when slave women worked under a driver or in an all-female group under female supervision, the shadow of the master or the overseer hovered over them. On the larger plantations, overseers assigned and supervised their tasks and administered random whippings; on the smaller plantations, the master did. Ideally, the master sought to be viewed as something more than a mere taskmaster and above all to sustain the image of himself as a superior being—a true lord of the household. Few slave women appear to have been duped, even if most had their own reasons for preferring to view him as benevolent. For as owner, the master embodied the power literally to dispose of their lives through the sale of them, their children, their husbands, or others whom they held dear. Bitter resentment, fear, and the desire to placate combined in shifting and uneasy tension. The consequences of those complexities included the knowledge that power was no abstraction: It wore a white, male face.[80]

Love wore a black face, and it was as likely to be female as male, but like all loves, in all times and places, it remained hostage to the conditions and relations in which it was grounded. The "we" of the female community of slaves evoked a world of companionship that permeated work and leisure, delight and trouble. The "we" of the slave family grounded women's identities as wives and mothers, daughters and sisters. The "we" of church fellowship, like the "we" of music and dance and the birthing of babies, evoked membership in a culture poised between worlds, membership in a culture that, however proudly and lovingly transmitted, had to be reconquered in each generation. For like all predominantly oral cultures, the culture of Afro-American slave women could change without recording its own transformation. Grandmothers, mothers, and aunts, passing tales and songs and beliefs down to granddaughters, daughters, and nieces, modified and revised and at the same time believed that they were transmitting precisely what they themselves had received. African past thus gave way to Afro-American present without marking its own innovations. And Afro-American slave women's identities ever more firmly grounded themselves in a cultural world of their and their men's making, even as they struggled with the people and conditions that hedged it in.

4   *Gender Conventions*

Within the household, the everyday lives of slaveholding women, and in some measure those of slaves, conformed closely to prevailing notions of the appropriate division of labor by gender, following earlier British, European, and, to some extent, African conceptions of male and female spheres. Although some Euro-American and Afro-American views coincided, slaveholders and slaves did not contribute equally to the gradual crystallization of distinct southern patterns. With their power over slaves, slaveholders could set the terms of everyday life and could, if they chose, violate their slaves' notions of gender relations. Convention declared that the household responsibilities of slaveholding women were natural extensions of their personal relations as wives, mothers, and daughters, all of whom answered to a master who was husband or father. Slave women, in contrast, answered to a master who was not of their natural family, class, or race and who at any moment could exercise his power according to imperatives that had nothing to do with family feeling. They knew that he frequently exercised his power severely and might even make sexual demands that mocked the prevalent norms of gender relations to which he claimed to subscribe.

For slaveholding women, gender relations merged seamlessly with the sense of their own social roles and personal identities. Modern sensibilities may view them as the oppressed victims of male dominance, but few of them would have agreed, notwithstanding some bad moments. Their men's abuse of prerogatives, notably sexual philandering but also excessive drinking and the squandering of family resources, caused them untold distress. But their resentment of these abuses rarely passed into rejection of the system that established their sense of personal identity within a solid community.

For slave women, the power of masters over their lives and the lives of their men distorted their sense of the links between their relations with men and their roles and identities as women. For black women, social relations with black men did not necessarily mesh with work relations. They did not primarily devote themselves to the care of their own children and houses, and their gender roles did not necessarily emanate directly from their relations with black men or from African traditions. Within the big house, they performed the labor deemed appropriate to the gender roles of white women, but they worked as servants—the opposite of mistress. Even the exceptions—cook, mammy, and a few especially well-trained maids—did work that bore no necessary relation to their roles as mother or wife. Their field labor departed even further from Euro-American notions of women's gender roles, although it may have fit more comfortably with Afro-American traditions. From the perspective of the dominant culture, slave women were regularly assigned to men's work. White farm women, North and South, might work in the fields, but they were not expected to do the kind of heavy work routinely assigned to black women. The only concession to a notion of orderly gender roles for slave women lay in their being primarily assigned to work with other women rather than with men, and even that norm was frequently breached. Within the slave community women's activities were tied more directly to their personal relations with men, as, for example, when they cooked and sewed for their own families. But their roles as daughters, wives, and mothers depended upon the sufferance of a master who could always break up families. Under these conditions the slave's sense of herself as a woman—her gender identity—remained separable from the gender relations and roles that depended heavily on the vicissitudes of power in a slave society.

Both slave and slaveholding women lived in a world in which gender afforded a principle of the practical, political, and symbolic organization of society. Norms of appropriate gender conventions could be violated. Black women could be set to work considered unfit for white women. Slave women could be separated from their children and husbands and could be subject to a sexual violation that would have offended the honor and evoked the murderous retaliation of the husbands and fathers of white women. Violations of the norm painfully reminded slaves that they did not enjoy the full status of their gender, that they could not count on the "protection"—however constraining and sometimes hypocritical—that surrounded white women. Yet the norms also governed the opportunities available to slave women, for ruling men, like enslaved men, were unlikely to violate the norms in ways that would promote the independence of slave women. Slave women may not have had access to the privileges of slaveholding women, but they, too, remained excluded from a host of male prerogatives. In this respect, the gender conventions of slave society weighed equally on all women, regardless of race or class. Gender relations, in both their observance and their breach, constituted an essential aspect of the relations of power between classes and races.

The household worlds of slave and slaveholding women embodied and contributed to the dominant gender relations of southern society, forming a system of conventions that guided women's behavior and identities. Southern gender conventions simultaneously derived from and influenced social relations and operated like a language or discourse that helped individuals to make sense of their place in their world. The constant flux of relations between individual women and men, as with those among women of different classes and races, unfolded as discrete stories—the result of personality and circumstance—but gender conventions offered a way of interpreting those stories and linking them to society. The widespread acceptance of gender conventions limited a woman's freedom to write her life exactly as she might have chosen.

Gender conventions direct fundamental human impulses into socially acceptable and useful channels and thereby serve the needs of individuals as well as of society. They derive as much from custom and practice as from ideology. Influenced both by tradition and circumstances, they constitute compelling ideals disseminated through literate, visual, and oral cultures. They figure among society's most influential and binding elements, for, in telling people how to be men and women, they tell them how to relate to society. Modern cynicism about the observance of social rules has celebrated the breach rather than the observance of conventions in past societies. A healthy appreciation of people's determination to create their own lives and to resist the imprint of official values has led to doubts that official prescriptions had anything to do with life as it was actually lived.

Yet although the dominant gender conventions of the antebellum South reflected the values, aspirations, and anxieties of the dominant class, they also encoded a slave society's essential conditions of life for yeomen and slaves as well as for masters. The yeomen, not to mention the slaves, did not always share most of the slaveowners' concerns. They resisted many of their pretensions, not least because the slaveholders' conventions linked gender relations closely to attitudes toward class relations. But they could not readily forge alternate gender conventions, at least not in the great heartland dominated by the system of plantation households, whatever success they may have had in the yeoman-dominated upcountry. Slaveholders, slaves, and nonslaveholding whites—whatever their differences over specifics— shared an ideal of the universal division between women and men. They agreed that defined male and female spheres constituted the bedrock of society and community, even if they did not subscribe to emerging bourgeois notions about the nature of the spheres.

For southerners, gender spheres interlocked with networks of families and households; men represented those families and households in the larger worlds of politics and warfare, or, to reverse matters, women belonged within families and households under the governance and protection of their men. As Henry Wise wrote to his first wife, Anne: "My wife is not competent to advise the statesman or the politician— her knowledge, her advice, her ministry is in a kindlier sphere." Yet southerners, unlike northerners, did not view either families or households as primarily female preserves, but as terrain that contained woman's sphere. According to this view, women did not belong abroad alone; a woman alone on the public thoroughfares was a woman at risk. Women had no business to bear arms and no place in politics. They were not fit to meet men on equal terms in the combat of public life and, should they attempt to, they would open themselves to being bested by superior physical strength.[1]

Rural women lived within the constraints of these fundamental attitudes toward gender relations and spheres—within a set of firmly entrenched expectations about appropriate behavior for women and for men. Although rooted in the specific conditions of their everyday lives in rural households in a slave society, these expectations derived from longstanding Euro-American and Afro-American notions about the natural relations between women and men. At all levels, southern culture reflected and reinforced a view of the world in which women were subordinate to men. The view proved the more powerful because it conformed so closely to intuitive notions about "natural" differences between women and men.

Southern institutions contributed to the dissemination and reinforcement of gender conventions. The churches, in a class by themselves among southern institutions, preached a strong message of station and calling by gender in the household and larger community. Academically adequate schools and academies enrolled only a minority of southerners, but they also disseminated gender conventions, endowed the slaveholders with a sense of identity and mission, and established lifelong personal friendships that contributed to class coherence. The elite gathered during the sickly seasons at the Virginia Springs and the ubiquitous if lesser spas and resorts, and such gatherings provided occasions to form or strengthen ties across party divisions.[2] Many of the poorer whites, who never attended an academy or even one of the primitive "old field schools," were likely to learn their three Rs at a sabbath school, at least after 1830 or so. In old field schools and sabbath schools, as well as in academies, moral instruction ranked high. Moral instruction meant Christian instruction, and Christian instruction included the reigning gender conventions.[3]

The message of the churches reached all southern women, with varied effect. The message of high literate culture had a more limited impact, but, particularly in its attitudes toward gender, it remained closely bound to the teachings of the churches and to the fabric of everyday life in the household. Gender conventions reinforced the close ties between multiple aspects of everyday life and ideology— from the division of labor within the household to fashion, from theology to proslavery social thought, and everything in between. They permeated southern culture at all levels and constituted a system of signs that delineated models of the ways in which women and men lived as members of a gender. In their specific attributes, these models referred to the gender relations of southern society, while at the same time they invoked ideal types of womanhood and manhood as universal categories.

The most prestigious models promoted the ideals of the southern lady and gentleman or cavalier. The lady was expected to manifest in her character and bearing all that was best in her society. Gracious and delicate, she was to devote herself to charm and nurture within the circle of her own household. Meta Morris Grimball, emphasizing the culture she considered essential to any lady, wrote of her own daughter: "I know no one so cultivated and elegant in her manners as Elizabeth, or accomplished, she has a disciplined, and highly improved mind, and is the help to her parents & brothers and sisters, and the adorning attraction to the family circle." In Margaret Mitchell's captivating popular version, the southern lady was quintessentially milky-white of skin, slow of speech, and innocent of any hint of hunger, temper, or passion. Her male counterpart, the cavalier or gentleman, was strong, masterful, quick to anger, ready with his pistol, sometimes too fond of liquor, but, withal, chivalrous and protective of those who accepted the legitimacy of his claim to command. Above all, southern ladies and gentlemen represented their genders' specific contributions to civility and honor in society. These public roles carried serious responsibilities for the expression and reinforcement of social order.[4]

In innumerable subtle and overt ways, slavery as a social system marked southern gender conventions. In 1850, Mrs. Isaac Hilliard mockingly noted in her diary: "It is raining so furiously this morning that even the belle of the ball's wish ('Oh that I had a million slaves or more, To catch the raindrops as they pour') would . . . be of no avail." Mrs. Hilliard mocked but did not belie a fundamental premise of the southern ideal of womanhood: Women, to be ladies, had to have servants. If not a million servants to catch the raindrops, they had to have one or more to catch garments as they dropped or swat flies as they settled. Mary Jones, upon discovering a spider in her bath, "called loudly to my attendant, who came and soon dispatched it and two others. I *warned* her if she let one get on me I might have a fit in the water, and she would have to answer for it." The southern lady was not to be confused with northeastern or other bourgeois housewives.[5]

Euro-American culture in general valued a pale complexion, but to southerners paleness assumed special importance by implicitly distancing ladies from the dark skins of Africans. The emphasis on female delicacy and frailty implicitly recognized the positive value of male strength. In a dangerous world ladies required protection against unruly men, white as well as black. The emphasis on leisure and civility identified social classes freed from the labor afforded by slaves. Above all, as the religious and secular proslavery polemics tirelessly declared, the subordination of women to the men upon whom they acknowledged their dependence confirmed inequality among all members of society.

Southern theologians and proslavery ideologues insisted that the subordination of women was of a piece with all other legitimate forms of inequality and dependence, notably the relations between masters and slaves. In the view of Thomas Dew, who was heavily influenced by the Scottish Historical School, slavery moved humanity from barbarism to civility and in so doing markedly improved the lot of woman, which, among the savages, has everywhere been "painful and degrading." Dew approvingly cited Dr. Robertson's opinion that, among the aborigines of America, "servitude is a name too mild to describe their wretched state." The introduction of slavery, according to Dew, rescues woman from her misery by substituting "the labor of the slave . . . for that of the woman." From the first introduction of slavery, the woman appears "surrounded by her domestics"; she ceases to be a "mere *'beast of burthen'*" and becomes "the cheerful and animating center of the family circle." Class slavery, in short, replaces gender slavery and makes woman "no longer the slave but the equal and idol of man." By equal, Dew meant equal in freedom from degrading labor, and he expressed puzzlement that any woman could oppose the slavery to which she is "in a most peculiar and eminent degree indebted." He nonetheless also insisted that "equality" requires that she relinquish the very rights that man never relinquishes "without a struggle." For,

> her physical weakness incapacitates her for the combat; her sexual organization, and that part which she takes in bringing forth and nurturing the rising generations, render her necessarily domestic in her habits, and timid and patient in her sufferings. If man chooses to exercise his power against woman, she is sure to fall an easy prey to his oppression. Hence, we may always consider her progressing elevation in society as a mark of advancing civilization, and more particularly, of the augmentation of disinterested and generous *virtue*.[6]

For William Harper of South Carolina, Dew did not push the argument far enough. Slavery, Harper insisted, is not merely a principal cause of civilization, it is "the sole cause." Only "the coercion of Slavery" can "form man to habits of labor." Without slavery there can be no property, no provision for the future, no refinement. Surely those who condemn slavery as immoral or criminal do not mean "that man was not intended for civilization, but to roam the earth as a biped brute?" Surely they do not mean that "the Judge of all the earth has done wrong in ordaining the means by which alone that end can be obtained?" Equality is a chimera: It is "palpably nearer the truth to say that no man was ever born free, and that no two men were ever born equal." Who ever could have propounded such nonsense? Are not females "human and rational beings"? May not women be found who have "better faculties" and who are "better qualified to exercise political privileges, and to attain the distinctions of society, than many men"? Yet none would claim women to be men's equals. None, Harper insisted, would complain of an order of society that excludes women from political privileges and public distinctions. That exceptional women may possess talents equal to those of individual men changes nothing. Those exceptions do not justify the disruption of social order. Since society must, "of necessity . . . exclude from some civil and political privileges those who are unfitted to exercise them," there must, "of necessity . . . be some general rule on the subject," even if its operation entails hardship and injustice for some. Do they "not blaspheme the providence of God who denounce as wickedness and outrage, that which is rendered indispensable to his purposes in the government of the world?" The human condition is unequal. Every civilized society must have "an infinite variety of conditions and employments." The self-evident subordination of women to men confirms the legitimacy of slavery.[7]

George Fitzhugh pressed the case for slavery in the abstract to its logical conclusion in his uncompromising denunciation of individual freedom as the solvent of any society worthy of the name. "A state of dependence," he maintained, "is the only condition in which reciprocal affection can exist among human beings—the only situation in which the war of competition ceases and peace, amity and good will arise." Men love their wives because they are dependent. According to Fitzhugh, the agitation for women's rights in the North offered incontrovertible evidence of that society's dissolution. In the North, woman found herself in a false position. In the slave South, "be she white, or be she black, she is treated with kindness and humanity." Women, like children, have only one right—the right to protection. The right to protection involves the obligation to obey. "A husband, a lord and master, whom she should love, honor and obey, nature designed for every woman." If she accepts her obligation to obey, she runs little risk of ill treatment, but if she stands upon presumed rights, she will become "coarse and masculine." Man will loathe, despise, and in the end abuse her. Law can do nothing on her behalf, but "true womanly art will give her an empire and a sway far greater than she deserves."[8]

In effect, proslavery ideologues advised women to accept their natural position and to devote all their energies to charming men into protecting them and treating them with civility and respect. Few, if any, attempted to make a case for men's natural gentleness, which was assumed to be a fragile veneer at best and had to be encouraged by women's ability to please and cajole. Whatever their paeans to freedom from demeaning labor as the hallmark of the gentleman, the men knew that the exigencies of mastering that unfree labor force required a heavy dose of violence not far below the civilized surface. The gentleman might exercise a measure of self-control, might treat his dependents with kindness, might try to live up to the highest standards of paternalistic benevolence, but even at his closest approximation of the ideal, he badly needed the restraining influence of woman.

Bertram Wyatt-Brown has cogently argued that honor was the primary virtue that united white men across class lines. Although he minimizes the influence of slavery and households in the construction and dissemination of an ideal of honor, Wyatt-Brown forcefully underscores the importance of an ideal of male independence within a context of strong lineage networks. Kenneth Greenberg has deepened the discussion by grounding the code of honor in master-slave relations. Steven Stowe has also linked the defense of honor closely to the men of the slaveholding class, for whom it constituted a complex but precise system through which men identified themselves as men of respect in relation to other men. The defense of honor informed all relations, including written communications, among slaveholding men. Failure to observe the code of honor resulted in duels, which themselves followed—or were supposed to follow—a precise system of rules. Meta Morris Grimball casually noted that "Arnoldus Vanderhorst has had a duel with Alfred Rhett, neither of them hurt, the bench of honor managing the affair." At the core of the code lay a deep concern with the attributes and prerogatives of gentlemen and the equality among them. The ideal of honor thus assumed special force and meaning in slave society, in which the ability to command carried overwhelming importance.[9]

The southern code of honor wedded two sets of ideals in uneasy tension: the one concerned ideals of command and the ability to defend, or acquire, property and position by the force that had promoted male members of the gentry to their positions; the other concerned ideals of gentility that had been cultivated by the eighteenth-century Chesapeake and South Carolina gentry. Southern conventions of masculinity never abandoned the element of force or even brutality that northern conventions were submerging in the rational self-discipline appropriate to a commercial society. To be sure, those who sought to shape southern opinion preferred to celebrate a brutality veiled rather than naked. The iron fist in the velvet glove captured their notion of restrained lordship. But since the value placed on lordship far outweighed that placed on restraint, unchecked brutality surfaced frequently and escaped systematic reprobation. Southern conventions tolerated many manifestations of displaced brutality. Heavy drinking, gambling, and dueling were accepted, although hardly praised, examples of ritualized violence. Permitting its partial expression, they in effect held it on a loose rein—available in case of need—and scorned to repress it entirely.[10]

The presence of slaves accounted for much of this social need for disposable brutality. The planter ideal remained one of controlled, rational behavior, but paternalistic governance of the black family and black wills made the ideal difficult to attain. The master class always confronted a threat of violence. Mini-revolts, plots, arson and poisoning, and occasional murder fueled the masters' own propensity to violence as they engendered a realistic and by no means paranoid fear that mocked the hymns to allegedly happy and contented slaves. This dark current in southern society did not produce a celebration of brutality but did lead to its being taken for granted. Bennet Barrow wrote without misgivings of tracking and punishing a runaway: "Ran and trailed about a mile and treed him, made the dogs pull him out of the tree. Bit him madly, think he will stay home a while." And, a couple of months later, he wrote of catching another: "Dogs soon tore him naked, took him Home Before the Negro[es] at dark & made the dogs give him another overhauling."[11]

This toleration of male violence responded to the perceived exigencies of governing a troublesome people, but it acquired resonance and legitimacy as a convention for nonslaveholders as well as slaveholders. It assimilated to the mores of a modern slave society precapitalist notions of honor that had long privileged the idea of male dominance within the household and accountability for it without. The ideal of honor, which had a long history, acquired a new lease on life in southern society at precisely the moment at which it was declining elsewhere in the capitalist West. The political exigencies of a democratic society forced its extension to all free white male heads of households in the South. Chief Justice Pearson of North Carolina proclaimed in 1862: "The wife must be subject to the husband. . . . Every man must govern his household." The ethic that had originated as the special prerogative of class and birth, and that had since the seventeenth century been claimed by many southern yeomen, became the prerogative of all white men. As a result of the close association between slavery and the governance of the household, the democratization of the ideal of honor invited nonslaveholders to identify vicariously with slaveholders and to incorporate the governance of slaves into their model of masculinity. The generalized ritualization of brutality, dominance over women, formal political democracy, celebration of the unbridled independence of free white men, and especially racism reinforced the identification.[12]

The hegemony of the slaveholders did not go uncontested. Tensions riddled their relations with the yeomen, who had scant patience with pretensions to superiority, much less aristocracy. The conventions of masculinity, nonetheless, did much to mediate those tensions, especially since the yeomen did not rush to develop an alternative. The southern ethos succeeded in binding the American ideal of the independent head of household to the slaveholding ideal of the head of an extended household—a plantation family, white and black. It thereby perpetuated and even reinforced the acceptance of undisciplined male violence that bourgeois culture elsewhere was repudiating and containing. Throughout the United States each newly opened frontier invited a spirit of unrestrained adventurousness and lawlessness, but in the South those impulses became encoded in dominant conventions and even in institutions and laws.[13]

Southern gender conventions emphasized the radical differences between men and women but, unlike northeastern and European conventions, did not emphasize the similarities among all women and men within their respective genders. Southern gender conventions notoriously treated black women as special inferiors, but they also discriminated among white women of different classes. In this climate the radical difference between women and men figured explicitly as a central aspect of class and racial privilege and dominance. A lady was not a woman who happened to be more affluent than others. She was a white woman whose privileged position was essential to her identity and social role. J. S. Buckingham noted, in his account of his travels in the South, that "a female negro is called 'a wench,' or a 'woman'; and it is this, perhaps, which makes the term 'woman' so offensive to American ears, when applied to white females, who must all be called 'ladies.'"[14]

Withal, southern gender conventions could not develop in isolation from their emerging bourgeois counterparts, and southerners borrowed from the interlocking discourses of companionate marriage, motherhood, and domesticity. In their public and private utterances, they could wax as rhapsodic as any about women's special capacities for gentleness and nurture, about the sanctity of the family circle, and about the comforts of home. They, like others, were wont to view women as especially attuned to moral concerns and as especially suited for the early education of children. Above all, they emphasized women's obligation to manifest piety, purity, chastity, and obedience and to cultivate their special calling for motherhood. But for all the rhetorical similarities between southern and northern views of women's domestic mission, the two differed significantly on the practices they associated with the words and on the context in which the womanly ideal unfolded.[15]

The ideal of the lady constituted the highest condition to which women could aspire, but the lady, like other women, remained bound by a broad vision of appropriate gender relations. The activities of even the most prestigious lady remained carefully circumscribed by the conventions ordained for women in general, but southern culture placed a premium on her meeting her responsibilities in accordance with her station. The lady, like less privileged women, accepted the dominance of men but cultivated her own sense of honor, which depended heavily on her embodiment of the privileges of her class. In her case, the male dominance that weighed so heavily on black slave and many nonslaveholding white women was, in many respects, experienced as protection. Even as male prerogative hedged her in, it shielded her from direct contact with the disorderly folks who populated the world beyond her household.[16]

A concern with locking women firmly into coverture and domesticity prevailed throughout the United States during the first half of the nineteenth century. No region encouraged divorce or the ownership, much less the effective control, of property by married women, but southerners and their courts proved especially intransigent, the precocious married woman's property act of Mississippi (1839) notwithstanding. As Wyatt-Brown has insisted, southern women's legal standing affected "not only their livelihood but also their sense of themselves." In his judgment, "the effect of the law upon gender relations" has been so little considered that "the hard economic and legal reasons for women's passivity have been hidden from historical view. Too often advances in church life, opening new vistas for usefulness, have obscured the implications of restraints in law."[17]

In a world dominated by male strength, women could not aspire to be the head of a household. They might answer for the household as delegates of their families, but even then they required extensive support from male kin or friends. Slaveholding women might inherit households from their fathers or husbands, but they almost invariably turned the management over to men in practice, even if a will or marriage settlement had left them legally in the woman's control. In general, a widow's ability to assume command depended upon the age of her sons. Should they still be minors, she would have to make do, normally with the help of an overseer; should one son be an adult, he would probably try to assume control himself. Natalie de DeLage

Sumter of South Carolina ranked as one of the few women who, as a widow, genuinely managed a plantation, and even she had ample assistance from overseers. Keziah Brevard, who never married, did the same, relying upon male advice and the everyday assistance of her difficult driver, Jim.[18]

Whenever possible the male kin of heiresses assumed legal or de facto control. James Henry Hammond braved the wrath of the family of his bride, Catherine Fitzsimmons, to secure complete control of her large inheritance and made his "duties as plantation master . . . the focus of his existence." Anna Matilda King participated more actively than Catherine Fitzsimmons in the management of her extensive inheritance, for her husband, Thomas Butler King, was more often absent than present on the estate. Yet she always treated him as master of the household, consulting him on everything from the marketing of crops to the education of their children, and in everyday matters she relied heavily on the advice of male neighbors, factors, and kin. Eventually, to her delight and relief, her oldest son, Butler, took over completely. Margaret Campbell, who inherited Argyle Plantation in the Mississippi Delta from her husband, ran the place with the assistance of an overseer and neighbors and on the basis of constant consultation with her cousin, Robert Campbell.[19]

David Outlaw spent long periods fulfilling his obligations in the U.S. House of Representatives, leaving his wife, Emily, to preside over the household in Bertie County, North Carolina. He regularly wrote to her about the details of management but expected to provide her with male assistance for their execution. Emily Outlaw consulted him on everything, including the hiring of a governess and the appropriateness of letting their daughter give a party. "Really," he responded on the question of the governess, "I shall quarrel with you if you do not quit asking my advice and permission about matters of this kind." She was implying, whatever her intentions, "that I exact from you to do nothing without my permission." He did not deserve the reproach and had always considered theirs at least "a partnership of equals." He had the "most unlimited confidence in your prudence and discretion." Yet on the matter of the party, to which he had "no objection" and in which he could see no "impropriety," he admonished her "not to give your guest[s] liquor enough to get drunk and get Joe Cherry or some other gentleman to assist you."[20]

John Quitman did not take so tolerant a view. His wife, Eliza, reported that things were going badly on their Springfield Plantation, where the overseer "was in a constant state of intoxication," the "negroes were idle doing nothing whatever," the cotton had not been weighed, and the overseer had "shot some of the cattle for mere sport." She had requested Mr. Kent, who brought the news, to go up and discharge Rees, the delinquent overseer, at once. "I hope my dear John," she concluded, "that what I have done may meet your approbation. It appeared to me to be the only course to pursue in your absence." She hoped in vain. Quitman replied, "I fear you have done wrong in discharging Rees—These reports are generally exaggerated and at any rate no more harm could have been done before my return." He did not add that had he been present the harm might never have occurred at all.[21]

Like Sarah Gayle, many women cared deeply about having a plantation household—a farm—as a basis for family security, and some, like Floride Calhoun, preferred to remain at home while their husbands were off attending to politics or business. Yet few had the training or taste to oversee the management of farming or business activities themselves. Mrs. James Polk insisted on keeping the family plantation when her husband became president, but she had a competent overseer to run it. She apparently possessed uncommon business sense. The overseer consulted her on the timing of the marketing of the crop, but she consulted him on the specifics of managing the slaves. When John Grimball was away, he meticulously instructed his wife, Meta, on innumerable details, from the feeding of mulch cows to care of the horses to distributing molasses to sick slaves. As a widow, Hugh Legaré's mother retained the family plantation, but she always begged her son to assume responsibility for its management. Legaré, although devoted to his mother, did not respond to her pleas. Rachel O'Connor, a widow who presided over a cotton plantation in Feliciana Parish, Louisiana, had terrible trouble with her overseers and regularly wrote to her brother, David, for advice.[22]

A lack of business knowledge constituted only part of the problem for these southern women, for—romance aside—they could not exercise mastery of their own slaves, much less contribute to the control of the slaves in their communities. Women who managed plantations were, like all other planters, responsible for contributing to the patrols and to other community responsibilities such as building and repairing the levees on the delta, but women could not meet those obligations in person. Some women, in fact, relied heavily on slave drivers to manage the other slaves and even the basic farm operations of the household. During the Civil War, with many overseers as well as slaveholders away, the use of drivers to run plantations became even more common. When the driver was accomplished and loyal the results could be excellent; when he chafed under the direction of a mistress they could leave a good deal to be desired. Keziah Brevard was at her wits' end with Jim, her driver. Jim enjoyed the requisite authority over the other slaves: "Every servant knuckles to him. If they do not his family will put them down." But he was also "an impudent negro," whom Keziah Brevard mistrusted yet dared not punish. She believed him to be "a self willed negro" who "wants every servant on the place to look to him as a superior & he certainly has great influence over my negroes." She could only hope that he "begins to cave a little" and that "his power is on the wane." As Keziah Brevard, like Sarah Gayle and many others, knew, slaveholding women could not, in their own persons, embody the physical attributes of a master, who could, if circumstances demanded, whip his strongest male field hand himself.[23]

Thus, although some women owned plantations and more had to assume responsibility when their husbands were away, they "managed" them through men in all except the rarest of cases. Overseers exercised much wider authority when working for women than they would have dared to claim when working for men. Overseer or no, a woman planter almost always had a male relative or close friend in the neighborhood to look in on her plantation affairs. Not surprisingly, southern men assumed women's incapacity and discussed its consequences for the maintenance of community order. It will not do to dismiss their judgment as so much male prejudice, for the diaries and correspondence of these women with their husbands and others sustain it, and, more to the point, the evidence from the war years, when many women were put to the test, is overwhelming.[24]

The management of slaves remained inextricably intertwined with political power. Just as the citizen had to bear arms in defense of his country, so did the slaveholder have to deal personally with his servants, whose management constituted a political question of the highest order. Slaveholding women were not expected to embody the political attributes of the master, who carried and would draw a gun at the first sign of danger. Not many women learned how to shoot, and virtually none put their talent to work on human beings. Georgia King wrote with teasing pride to her father of her latest accomplishment: "I am sure you would never guess—*shooting*[.] Yes, indeed, dear Father I have killed *ten* robins." She hoped that upon his return he would "allow me to go out shooting *hawks* with you. Will you? I shall be very good & pull the trigger at the right time." The yeoman women, especially on the frontier, were more likely to know how to shoot, but they were no more—and possibly less—likely to be able to manage a farm, for bringing in a crop without slaves required a heavy dose of male labor, as their terrible travail during the war demonstrated. Thomas Butler King encountered a highly independent woman in Dangerfield, Texas, who, because her husband was blind, "had put on the breeches and was keeping a very comfortable house, *for Texas*." She told him that the previous year she had managed their farm "and was turned as black as a negro riding in the fields." But the experience convinced her "that she was more capable of managing a kitchen than a cornfield."[25]

In the absence of male protection, many slaveholding women felt themselves vulnerable even within their own households. Sarah Gayle, who was never especially timid, preferred to have a friend stay with her when John Gayle was away. Lucy Muse Fletcher worried that she was "alone tonight." She found it "a great trial to be left so entirely alone and unprotected," although she tried "to bear it as quietly & bravely as possible remembering that Our Friend is ever nigh." Women rarely ventured beyond the household without male escort. When Kate Carney's friend, Nannie, had been for a visit, "her Pa came . . . and carried her home." Kate Carney, like innumerable others, could not go away to school until her father could find enough free time to take her. Her father permitted her to take the carriage, horses, and driver to go to a party if she wished, "that is if Sister Mary and Dr. Wilson, would accompany me," for on that occasion he did not want to go himself. Kate Carney's father insisted that she travel in the company of her male relatives, and not just any man. In this spirit, Eliza Carmichael allowed that she was "much mortified at my Cathys coming home with a certain gentleman when she had two brothers that went with her— spoke to my boys about it, seems very sorry it happened so."[26]

Young, unmarried women like Kate Carney and Cathy Carmichael required special protection, although they enjoyed considerable freedom to attend parties and to mix with the young men of their own social set. Daughters exercised substantial freedom of choice in their selection of marriage partners. The condition of this freedom consisted in their being protected from meeting men who would not constitute acceptable marriage partners—who were not of their own class or, like a respectable young minister, an acceptable aspirant to that class. Mollie Mitchell wrote, a touch defensively, to her sister of the man whom she had just, quite unexpectedly, married. Mr. Mitchell was a Georgian and "a nephew of the Dr. Thomason that attended brother Andrew at the time of his death." Near her own age, he was an inch shorter than she but, upon the whole, "a handsome looking Gentleman." He was a farmer and "*not* rich," but not poor either—"and had he not one Dollar in the world, I should consider him a fortune within himself for he knows how to make it and have it made and then to take care of it after it is made." Although his education was not quite as good as she would have wished, "I would not be ashamed of him in any crowd."[27]

The real danger for a young lady lay in the possibility of her being, perhaps out of covert rebellion, drawn to the unsuitable male members of her own household. Mary Bateman worried when her cousin Margaret's daughter, Carrie, received another long letter from their former overseer, Mr. Wallis. "This affair to her, has been a very serious flirtation." Few even admitted to worrying about the possibility that a young woman might be drawn to slave men, but then, such things simply could not be made subjects for discussion. That some southern white women took black lovers could be freely acknowledged, for it was assumed that the women were lower class and disreputable. But ladies? Through the wall of silence seeped gossip and occasional hard facts. Liaisons between white ladies and black men may have occurred rarely, but they did occur, not only in cities like New Orleans, Charleston, and Washington but on the plantations. Some former slaves claimed that their mothers or grandmothers were white, not uncommonly northern or poor white women. But John C. Brown was told that his mother had been a lady who had visited his master and mistress, and Millie Markham's mother had fallen in love with the head coachman on her father's plantation. Periodically observers registered surprise at the measure of freedom young ladies enjoyed—as did, for example, the young Reverend Mr. Cornish, who encountered some entrancingly provocative girls on the beach at Jekyll's Island. But that freedom rested upon the conviction that they were encircled by a protective wall of class and race. During the war, the wall began to break down, but during the antebellum period young women were expected to move within a highly circumscribed world in which their fathers' and brothers' honor guaranteed their safety.[28]

Many young women reveled in their years as belles, which merged with their courtships and ended with their marriages. Lucy Muse Fletcher remembered Anne Hume, who married her cousin James Lewis, as a lovely, graceful young girl of "very sprightly, pleasing manners" and "a little given to flirting, but I believe sincerely attached to Cousin James." Lucy Muse Fletcher had set a rule for herself never to allow any gentleman "to comit himself by the *serious* expression of sentiment when it was possible to avoid it—having no ambition." Her friend, Cary Bryan, did have ambition and confided that "she meant to have as many declared lovers as she could bring to her feet to be a reputed belle." Cary Bryan was not unique in her delight in the brief moment of power that a young woman enjoyed as a belle. "H.," writing in the *Southern Literary Messenger*, roundly denounced "the hundreds and thousands of the gay, simple, fluttering insects dignified with the names of fashionable belles,—born and reared in the lap of luxury,—reposing in moral and intellectual sloth, and quaffing the delicious but fatal poison of adulation." Meta Morris Grimball's low-country sensibilities were shocked by the behavior of belles during the war, and she reported that the officers from New Orleans were scandalized as well. Throughout the winter, the Charleston belles "were dancing and flirting, balls lasting until day light, dancing the German waltze."²⁹

Lavinia Campbell wrote to her nephew, Henry, of a momentous change in her life—"one that I least expected would have ever been," for she had been "firm in the opinion that none other save those friends in whom I so much delighted would ever have a share in my affections." But what will Henry say when he learns that "*one* possesses a sufficient share in my affections to have obtained my consent to spend the balance of my life with him." Lavinia assured Henry that, although the man was not of their circle, he was in every way respectable—a Methodist preacher. Nor was she alone in her high opinion of him. An acquaintance of ten or eleven years had assured her "that he is a man of great piety, respectability, good talents, good family, tall slender person, black hair, hazle eyes, high forehead, &c &c——." Without such recommendations he probably would not have gotten near her in the first place. Similarly, Martha Foster, living in a boarding house while teaching in Clinton, Alabama, found her own husband, a Baptist minister. Her family was much distressed with her decision, not because of the Reverend Mr. Crawford's want of respectability, but because he intended to go abroad as a missionary and would remove her from the family circle.³⁰

Wartime conditions seriously undermined the invisible barriers that protected young ladies in their choice of marriage partners. Meta Morris Grimball learned from her gossipy acquaintance, Mrs. Irwin, that Mrs. Legg, who had been Miss Kennedy, had married "a man much beneath her in family and it came about in this way." The Kennedys moved to the upcountry from Charleston for the sake of Mr. Kennedy's health, "and Miss K[ennedy] was pleased with this Mr. Legg and engaged herself to him not knowing anything about him and after her marriage found he had very low relations." The incident, according to Meta Morris Grimball, "shows the imprudence of marrying among strangers." Miss Kennedy had been able to make her mistake because her parents, underestimating the dislocation of the times, assumed that she would be choosing only among people with respectable relations.[31]

Southern matrons could travel alone, although they rarely did so. At most, unlike younger women, they might travel in the company of other women and of trusted slaves, and they might chaperone younger women. Julia Gilmer promised her husband that, as soon as she could get household affairs in order, she would join him in Washington. "I will take Fanny, Chance, Mary, and Fanny Sloan with me and take Matilda for a nurse." When Mary Boykin Chesnut fled Camden in 1864 before the advancing Union troops, she found herself alone in Kingsville, South Carolina, awaiting her husband's arrival. She noted with dismay her torn dress and general disarray. The woman who kept the Kingsville hotel also noted them, with scorn. When Mary Chesnut announced herself as Mrs. James Chesnut of Camden, the woman retorted: "Not likely." She knew that "Mrs. Chesnut don't travel around by herself, no servants, no nothing."[32]

A woman who traveled alone violated the conventions of her class. Juliana Margaret Conner noted with surprise that on the road only twelve miles from Columbia, South Carolina, she and her husband met a woman "with an infant in her arms and a large bundle on her head." They inquired if she meant to walk all the way to Columbia. She replied that she did and that she had already come from Greene County, Tennessee, on foot. "I was perfectly amazed," Juliana Conner noted, "on hearing that a woman, alone, unprotected, and with an infant in her arms to perform such a journey and apparently with so little care." Only a few days later Juliana Conner, who clearly did not know much of the traveling habits of yeoman women, met another who was traveling alone on horseback with a child in each arm.[33]

The protection that surrounded unmarried slaveholding women established a barrier between them and men, reminding white men that the weapons of male relatives backed up a young woman's honor. It also reminded the world, black as well as white, of the honor, gentility, and social standing of the households and families to which such young women belonged. A young woman's purity merged with her racial and class status; her own honor merged with that of her kin, especially her male kin; and her behavior reflected upon the reputation of the other members of her family, household, and class. Kate Carney refused the pleasure of walking home from town with some friends of her own and a friend of her parents because her mother objected to her "walking out, & especially on Sundays." On another occasion, when she was invited to spend the evening with Mrs. David Wendles, her brother-in-law offered to attend her, and her parents' friend, Mr. Neilson, sent a card to offer his services, but her sister Mary answered it for her "by saying I would be pleased to accept, but would go in my own carriage." The Carney's carriage man, Uncle Peter, underscored her respectability. Mrs. Cain's daughter, Minerva Cain, deeply offended her sisters by failing to respect such rules. Mrs. Cain wrote to her that even she would "not offer my services to walk out with you to Mr. A's any more and indeed I do not expect *your old nurse* will be anxious to go with you again. She said she was very sorry you behaved as you did." Minerva Cain's sisters concurred with their nurse and sent Minerva word that she had better attend to their standards. "If you do not trust your brothers and sisters well you will never be respected by any one, either old or young, black or white."[34]

Brothers took a proprietary interest in the development and behavior of their sisters. Anna Matilda Page King, feeling herself to have been too long out of the world, counted on her sons to advise her daughters on their social lives. She wrote to her son Lord that she knew he would find pleasure in taking charge of her three dear daughters while they visited in the North. She prayed that she had done right to allow them to go at all, but she "had no one to advise with & was so anxious about their education." Her own dear boy was to give them all the advice he could. "Young men *of your character* can give perhaps better advice [to] young ladies how to avoid the shoals & quick sands which lead to destruction than a mother can who has so long been out of the world." His sisters "are pure in principles" and have "many beautiful qualities" but are "young & inexperienced—May God! protect them from all harm & restore them to me as pure & good as they left me." At age twenty-one William Osborne Gregory, requiring no maternal prompting, took those heavy responsibilities upon himself and reproved his sixteen-year-old sister for her social conduct. He was "so much displeased and mortified at your going to the wedding, which you were at, whilst I was in Mecklenburg." After all he had done for her, the least she could do was to show him proper deference. He enjoined her to examine her heart to discern the motives "which prompted the wish to go to the place alluded to, contrary to the advice, which I had given you and my evident wishes." He accused her of having been motivated solely by the desire to display finery and mingle with the elite. "Vanity is truly and emphatically the bane of the female heart." Now that she was a big girl, she must be mindful of the company she kept. She must look to her reputation—and his. He advised her to keep his letter for frequent rereading.[35]

William Gregory betrayed his own youth in his pomposity and his unfavorable view of female character. Fathers normally were more tolerant, and indeed so were most brothers, if we may judge by considerable if scattered correspondence. But fathers and mature brothers also feared the effects of an addiction to finery on a young woman's behavior and values. David Outlaw told his wife, Emily, that he had written to their daughter, Harriet, sending her ten dollars for herself and five for her sister, Betty, but also telling her that he and their mother worried about their extravagance. "I am anxious," he told his wife, "that she should have her pride and emulation awakened, for at one time I began to fear she would never care anything about books." A week later he wrote his wife that he regretted that their daughter had taken his letter on extravagance so hard. "My observations on her's and Betty's extravagance, were as kind as I knew how to make and were intended rather as advice and admonition than as a rebuke."[36]

A woman's extravagance could drain household resources, but it could also betray a growing fondness for inappropriate company. A lady had to recognize instinctively the fine lines between appropriate and inappropriate display. Typically, girls could demonstrate an exaggerated appetite for a self-display that verged on exhibitionism, even as they recklessly chafed under the restraints that insured their unquestioning identification with their class. Sarah Guignard complained to her father that he had done her adult cousin a great injustice, presumably in reproaching her for spending too much on his daughter's clothes. Sarah sent word that the cousin "is considered very economical and only wished me to look as respectible as other persons though not to be in the height of fashion and my dress is not as expensive as many others."[37]

The responsibilities of parents, and in some measure of brothers, included instructing young ladies in the nice distinctions. Slaveholders did not preach austerity to their daughters, who, from earliest girlhood, had been schooled in the qualities of fabric and the fine points of dress. A lady distinguished herself by her observation of fashion's conventions; lavish display for its own sake provided no substitute. Just as slaveholding mothers devoted infinite patience to perfecting their daughters' wardrobes, slaveholding fathers regularly indulged their daughters' desires for new frocks. Extravagance lay in an excess of display that exposed a young woman to the appearance of looseness, self-promotion, and limitless appetite. Fashion articulated class position; extravagance defied it. A lady had to know the difference, had to manifest in her person a restrained elegance that simultaneously betokened internalized self-control and solid male protection. Within those limits, fashion also provided her an outstanding opportunity for muted competition with other women. Emily Douglas, who had been born and reared in New Haven, Connecticut, before settling with her brother in Louisiana, described her sister-in-law as typical of Louisiana ladies. She was "always dignified" and, "whether in calico or silk," moved "about among her household in a manner which could not help command the love and respect of all."[38]

As an adolescent, Gertrude Clanton paid scrupulous attention to what she and others wore on their outings. On a visit to Mrs. Berry's, she wore her *"eternal tissue silk* & a black silk cape." For an ordinary morning at home, she donned her "pink calico dress black silk cape." To attend church on Sunday, she wore her "embroidered dress and black lace cape." For the same occasion, "Sis Anne wore her black silk dress. Cousin Emily wore white while Cousin Eliza wore her green barashe dress." She also attended to the proper dress for different occasions at home. Upon returning from church, Gertrude knew better than to change into a house dress, for she suspected that Mr. Merriwether and Mr. Griffin intended to call. Her sister Anne and cousin Eliza changed, and when the gentlemen called they had to dress again. By 1852 Gertrude Clanton was using two seamstresses in addition to her own sewing and purchases. She had one especially delicate dress washed in Charleston.[39] As a young woman, Gertrude Clanton in Augusta, like Kate Carney in Murfreesboro, took an inordinate interest in her own wardrobe as a sign of her emerging place in the world and an asset in her ability to attract the attention of a desirable man.

Mature married women also attended closely to their dress, especially if they moved in fashionable circles. On a given day, they could need "a morning dress, a dinner dress, an evening dress for teas, and a ball gown." Octavia LeVert, who affected elegant language, noted that for a quiet morning at home, she "threw on my robe de chambre." Years after the event, Lucy Muse Fletcher recalled that to attend the president's levee in Washington, her friend Charlotte "wore an embroidered blue satin robe, Sister, a rich brocade pattern silk (gold & silver, chageable, chiney) with blk velvet boddice," and she herself "a silk of the same description, with a rich French embroidered cape." A command of the niceties of fashion and the wherewithal to observe them articulated class differences. Juliana Conner found Hopewell,

North Carolina, sorely lacking in such discrimination. The appearance of the ladies who attended the country church disappointed her. "I had expected to see some attempt at Taste or Fashion, a few city airs and graces—but no such thing—I think I may venture to say there were not a bonnets [*sic*] which differed in shape and color in the whole congregation." They appeared to be following the dictate of the poet who held that beauty needs no help from "the foreign aid of Ornament." She hardly presumed to differ from that authority, yet "I humbly think—*they* needed it. They put to flight all my ideas of rural simplicity and neatness of a country church." Hopewell society as a whole she found utterly different in manners "from any which I have ever seen, they have none of the artificial distinctions which are kept up with such punctilious nicety in cities." They welcomed everyone with "the same hospitality, provided he is what Pope calls the noblest work of God 'An honest man' (I do not include the laboring class such as overseers etc)." Nor did they "indulge in the same luxuries and extravagances," although probably not from the lack of the "tastes or dispositions of the people I presume, but from the trouble and expense which would be incidental to their obtaining them."[40]

Juliana Conner, with her lowcountry background, held Charleston up as the standard for civility, which she associated with city life. But as she subsequently discovered, western territories could match the lowcountry in the essential aspects of class distinctions, if not in every detail of luxury. Her report of Hopewell reveals her own sense of the relation between fashion and class distinctions, and even she does not claim that the wives of the unpretentious substantial farmers of southern North Carolina invited the wives of ordinary honest men into their households. Had she visited such different towns and villages as Greenville or Holly Springs, Mississippi, Huntsville or Greensboro, Alabama, Camden or Columbia, South Carolina, Murfreesboro or Nashville, Tennessee, or Athens or Milledgeville, Georgia, she would have found the niceties of rank fully embodied in the dress of the ladies, which marked the class relations among white women. In contrast to her open celebration of fashion, many slaveholding women differentiated sharply between the exigencies of rank and "fashionable life," quietly supporting the former while deploring or regretting the excesses of the latter. Lucy Muse Fletcher was delighted with the visit of her friend, Charlotte Chapman, "who ever seemed happy while with us," although "fond of gaiety & accustomed to participate in many of those fashionable amusements, to which our situation as a ministers family & our principles as professing christians, alike excluded us." Sue Battle urged her sister to visit her in Tuscaloosa, Alabama, promising her all the comforts that "old friends & a *not very large* city can afford."[41]

Mary Campbell drew a sharp line between the external world of fashion and the internal world of the household. She wrote her husband that, for a few days after his departure, she had been "almost tempted to exclaim, why am I imprisoned when all the world is so free and gay. But after all, what has a woman of my age to do with the world of fashion?" She had experienced "its giddy round" and now in her retirement "have been able to examine its character and estimate its worth." She wondered what could be "more wretched than a woman of fashion obeying the every varying and yet monotonous dictates of her capricious fancy?" A fashionable woman spent the week "engaged in all sorts of frivolous dissipation, to the utter neglect of her children and her household, and on sunday endeavouring by the forms of religion to atone for all this neglect of duty—where any atonement is thought of at all." Looking clearly at the dichotomy, she allowed that she had "the happy disposition to make the best of my situation." However good her conscious intentions, Mary Campbell frequently used words like "prison" and "confinement" to describe her situation at home. Anna Matilda King bemoaned the dearth of society on St. Simon's. Others betrayed conflicts between contentment with the quiet of their lives in the household and desire for the fashionable whirl of the larger world—especially when their husbands were away on politics or business.[42]

The ladies especially gritted their teeth at the gay balls of White Sulphur Springs, where many vacationed, and indeed at local balls as well. For once married, no matter how young, they became superfluous. Fashion thus meant both dress and a way of life. As dress, it represented standing in the world. As a way of life it represented a continuation of those brief years as belles that they were expected to put behind them upon marriage. Not all women did. Mary Chesnut and Virginia Clay, both childless, relished their continuing ability to charm and attract male attention. Charleston, Natchez, Mobile, New Orleans, Richmond, and Washington all boasted their share of fashionable women who presided over an elegant and ornate social life. Susan Davis Hutchinson found "much to reprehend" at a brilliant wedding, complete with service "in the Episcopal manner," in Raleigh, North Carolina. "The vitiated style of dress, oh, surely, the ladies have forgotten that ever dress was necessary, or at least that they have anything to conceal. Their backs and bosoms were all uncovered." These "shameless women surrounded by their beaux" prompted her to turn abruptly away and hide her face in a handkerchief.[43]

Sarah Gayle was no more pleased by the society she encountered in Tuscaloosa, in which she sensed "an evil spirit of almost detraction, which needs correction." She was surprised to meet it "amongst our most fashionable and loveliest, the very persons who aspire to the character of amiability." In the end, she deplored the personal backbiting more than the dress and, when safe at home, tolerantly noted her sister-in-law Lucinda's "natural predeliction for whatever is gay, showy, fashionable." Yet she also expressed amazement "that Mrs. Hollinger's passion for dress and amusement receives no chill from an age which cannot be much short of 70 or 75. It is awful to see a woman so old, laced, curled, veiled, feathered and flowered and most surprisingly ridiculous." The exhibitionism of fashionable circles disquieted many slaveholders, who claimed to prefer the tranquility of the household. For women, the contradictions between the fashionable and the retired life had a special meaning, for they embodied the contradictions between personal glory and duty, between excitement and safety. The convention of the lady captured something of each without entirely resolving the tension between them. But whether in the world or in retirement, the lady relied upon fashion, upon dress, to demarcate her class position.[44]

Slave women, especially those who worked in the house, shared slaveholding women's appreciation of dress as the badge of class or quality. Their everyday clothes were crude homespun, although house servants in the larger households would frequently have neat checked or striped homespun, and, especially in the lowcountry, "a gaily colored head handkerchief which they arranged with much skill." Sunday preaching offered an occasion to dress up. The more favored had calico dresses and store-bought shoes. In Charleston, mammies wore white turbans to church. Amos Lincoln recalled that "the gals dress up on Sunday. All week they wear they hair all roll up with cotton. . . . Sunday come they com' the hair out fine. No grease on it. They want it naturally curly." Keziah Brevard complained that Dolly, one of her slaves, "would never go to church unless as fine and fashionable as possible." Masters and overseers, who acknowledged slave women's pleasure in finery, frequently rewarded good work with the present of a calico dress to wear to preaching, and to their Saturday night and holiday parties in the quarters.[45]

House servants, especially personal maids, had a proprietary interest in their mistresses' clothes. They took pride in having their mistress

Keziah Goodwyn Hopkins Brevard, ca. 1830.
Courtesy of Miss Jervey Hopkins and the South Caroliniana Library

Virginia Tunstall Clay (above and right), fashionable belle par excellence, 1850s.
Courtesy of William R. Perkins Library, Duke University

always look her best and outshine the other ladies. After her clothes had served that purpose, they were usually handed down to her maids and the other women of the quarters. Susan Dabney Smedes recalled that since her family knew "that the servants liked nothing so well as the well-made clothes that they laid aside, they wore their clothes but little. They justly considered that those who had labored for them had rights to them still fresh." Susan Dabney Smedes took a romantic view of plantation life and no doubt exaggerated the extent to which finery was relinquished out of respect for the labor that had produced it. She came closer to the general attitude in noting that the excuse of sending cast-off finery to the quarters made it seem less wasteful "for a daughter of the house to distribute, at the end of a season, as many as a dozen or more dresses that had been made up but a few months

before." Slave women who inherited those recently made dresses would be much more likely to be in fashion than yeoman women. Certainly, the house servants had a much better sense of the latest fashions than the yeoman women did. According to Gus Feaster, young white women could not eat much in public, for it was not stylish to display "any appetite to speak of. Culled gals tried to do jes like de young white missus would do."[46]

After emancipation, to the despair of many whites, the freedwomen enthusiastically took to carrying parasols and wearing veils. An officer of the Freedmen's Bureau reported to Sidney Andrews that "the wearing of black veils by young negro women had given great offense to the young white women and that there was a time earlier in the season when the latter would not wear them at all." The matter, Andrews

Octavia Walton LeVert, ca. 1840.
Courtesy of Georgia Department of Archives and History

Nancy Fort, ca. 1800. This is a rare portrait of a slave woman.
Courtesy of Georgia Department of Archives and History

noted, was of no small significance. As early as 1740, in the wake of the Stono Rebellion, South Carolina had passed legislation to restrict slaves to cheap clothing. The legislation proved unenforceable and, in the opinion of the great nineteenth-century jurist, John Belton O'Neall, should have been repealed. Charleston boasted an unusually large free black population, the independence of which made some whites uneasy. South Carolinians, like early modern Europeans before them, understandably viewed dress as a leading sign of class affiliation and saw in its regulation a privileged vehicle for reminding a lower class of its proper station.[47]

But the vast majority of southern blacks did not live free in towns. They lived within slaveholding households, in which their identification with the class standing of their owners could be interpreted as a source of stability rather than as a threat to social order. The case of Evelyn, who set the house on fire in the hopes of forcing a move to town and increasing her own access to fashionable life, warned of the slaveholders' blindness and self-deception in these matters, but other slave women explicitly expressed a preference for "de quality" and scorn for "de trash." With limited choices, they unhesitatingly identified with signs of the former over the latter. Mary Boykin Chesnut sympathetically noted her servant Polly's expression of disgust at the carryings-on of the "trash"—even monied trash. Polly extended her contempt from the white arrivistes to their servants. "They got no sense, niggers ain't," she exclaimed with disgust to Mary Chesnut. "When you got in that open carriage with that lady what does that impident man do? When he sees me up at the window, he begin to holler and bawl at me! And ladies in the carriage!" Worse, "his missis didn't say a word. I was that 'stonnished and outdone, if I could er found a rock handy I'd a liked to chunk him off that box. Him talking on his box, and his Missis in de carriage." Mary Chesnut shared Polly's astonishment. "'Wealth without civilization' I thought."[48]

Susan Cornwall had a less than favorable view of slave women's interest in clothing. "They rejoice," she wrote disparagingly, "over a new dress or a gay kerchief more than in a well ordered home." Susan Cornwall linked the love of finery to a pervasive insensitivity to the finer things of life. "Nature appeals to them in vain for an expression of admiration when unfolding to their dull senses her gayest or most sublime panoramas." She also linked it to a failure of true religious principles. "Their very religion seems to consist of feeling or impulses, more than principles." Their love of fashion, in her view, reduced them to the antithesis of personal and social order. "They have no law for the governance of their passions higher than the dread of punishment for an offense, or glimpses of a tangible reward for a correct course of conduct." Susan Cornwall's racist outburst sorely missed the main point of slave women's interest in fashion, for many slave women, like many slaveholding women, took seriously the discriminations that fashion encoded. Doubtless, many women of both groups were drawn to fashion as personal display, but many also valued it as a sign of the distance that separated superiors from inferiors in a hierarchical society.[49]

J. S. Buckingham found the women of Charleston "in general handsomer, more graceful, and more ladylike than those of the same classes in the north," and those of Savannah healthier than northern women, "in general dressed in better taste, less showily and expensively, but with more simple elegance in form, and more chasteness in colour." The women of Richmond he deemed no less ladies, but considerably more given to fashionable display. Although free of many of the habits of the Virginia gentlemen, Virginia ladies were known to share much of the gentlemen's

> aversion to labour, love of amusement and pleasure, and reckless-ness as to expense. A prudent manager of an estate, or a thrifty housewife, would hardly be esteemed in Virginia, and there are few who even aim at such distinction; but a desire for equipage and servants, love of dress, fondness for balls and parties, love of watering-places and gay assemblages, with rather more than a feminine share of taste for juleps, cordials and champagne—there being few who do not take one or the other of these more freely than is usual at the North—are prominent characteristics in the upper classes.

Allowances must be made. Buckingham was writing from Fauquier Springs, and his informant sought to "give as fashionable a character of both sexes as he could." The sobriety of the ladies of Charleston and Savannah and the display of their Virginia sisters nonetheless expressed a common commitment to the special forms of display of status in the person of the lady.[50]

Slaveholding women did not normally pay much attention to the dress of white women they considered inferior, although they remained conscious that their own dress set them apart. Kate Stone, traveling through Texas during the war and forced upon the hospitality of a poor yeoman family, praised their kindness and generosity but noted with horror that the two women and a girl had "nor a scrap of ribbon or lace or any kind of adornment in the house. I never saw a woman before without a ribbon." Certainly, she had never before been forced to notice a woman who did not have a ribbon. Travelers during the 1840s observed that, although yeoman women used homespun for their ordinary clothing, they bought some cloth for their fancy clothes in stores. Slaveholding women, especially during the war but also before, were known to wear the macon-muslin and calico that yeoman women used for their best dresses. Notwithstanding all such qualifications, the differences in dress remained unmistakable.[51]

Eliza Clitherall, during the early years of her marriage, took the daughter of a widowed yeoman woman into her household "to provide for, until she was large enough to assist her mother in earning a living." From Eliza Clitherall's perspective, the arrangement worked well. She taught the girl "to sew & to read" and "had her baptis'd, providential to her own name Susan." The yeoman mother was less pleased and took her daughter away, "grumbling that I drest her child in *Homespun*, & *my own* in callico." Eliza Clitherall remonstrated with her, pointing out that the child needed at least another year's instruction before she could be useful, but all the mother could say was "'that her child, was as good as mine.'" Eliza Clitherall had intended generosity, not insult, but it never crossed her mind that yeoman girls should be dressed the same as her girls. Nor did she reflect on the motives of the woman she had inadvertently insulted. The woman might have been expressing a commitment to equality among white women, and hence an aversion to the sartorial distinctions of class, or she might have merely been expressing a desire for her daughter to be treated as a young lady.[52]

Politics, not to mention the exigencies of self-preservation, required that slaveholders treat nonslaveholders with a modicum of respect, even if privately they did not consider them gentlemen. Eliza Clitherall and her husband, traveling on a stormy night along a dangerous road, had to ford a creek. "Providentially some voices were heard & torches seen, to cheer and assist." Their rescuers, wagoners who were also crossing the creek, led the Clitheralls' horses and carriages across. Mr. Clitherall tried to offer them money to compensate for the trouble and danger they had incurred. The wagoners refused, saying, "'twas no more than one man shou'd for another.'" Thomas Butler King, a politician who depended upon the votes of ordinary men, had to take the pretense of equality more seriously. When he was thinking of running for election to Congress in 1854 and feared that the voters might have forgotten him, his son, Butler King, wrote to reassure him. Butler

King could not go anywhere without someone's inquiring of his father's well-being. "I dont refir to the (so called) gentlemen of this part of the country—I speak of the second & third class." Only the other day, Butler said, he had met a fellow in Brunswick who told him that, although he had not seen Thomas Butler King since 1847, "all the poor people in Georgia remembered & loved you—for never did you think your self too good to sit down & talk to a poor man—& buy from him, if he had any thing to sell & that he & many others who had no shoos to their feet, had gone into your big house at Waynesville." For this reason alone, although there were others, the great planters increasingly preferred to leave the political jousting to trusted lesser or less socially squeamish slaveholders.[53]

Politics imposed no such caution on slaveholding women, who may, in fact, have contributed decisively to reminding nonslaveholders of the barriers that slaveholding men pretended to deny. Slaveholding women, including those who usually demonstrated graciousness, generosity, and compassion, proved ruthless in their demarcation of class lines. The code of honor, as applied to women, engendered a highly stratified ritual of knowing and not knowing. Ladies knew whom they should and should not greet in public places and observed punctilious rules in the matter of calls among themselves. Kate Carney, who as an adolescent was just learning the rules, explicitly distinguished between "fashionable calls" and "sociable calls" of friendship. Her friends, the Misses Nichol, called one morning but "only made a fashionable call, said they would come in Monday and stay some." On another evening, "Misses Sallie Nelson, Fannie Park, & Gertrude Bosily called on Sister Mary, & myself, but it was only a fashionable call."[54]

In towns and cities, from Natchez to Murfreesboro to Charleston, fashionable calls articulated a female society—a network of ladies who knew each other, even if not as close friends—that had to be maintained even among those who also shared the more informal relations of friendship. Mrs. Stevens sent word to Meta Morris Grimball that, because of the recent death of her mother, she was not visiting, but she would be glad to see her. So Meta Morris Grimball went by to make her acquaintance but did not pay a formal call. Joseph Jackson wrote to his sister-in-law, Martha Jackson, to introduce a female acquaintance, "Mrs. Charles Howard, a Lady of the City [Savannah]," who "goes to Athens to establish there her permanent residence." He vouched for Mrs. Howard's being not merely a lady "of the highest respectability and worth," but "a Lady of piety, and a member of the Presbyterian Church" and took "the liberty" by means of his letter "to make her acquainted with you." Being "satisfied that she merits the kindest attentions," he claimed "unqualified pleasure in being the instrument of affording her an introduction to the female society of Athens."[55]

The cycle of calls consumed a considerable portion of a lady's time. Anna Matilda King, on a visit to Savannah, wrote to her husband that they had been keeping "a list of the callers" and "up to this evening they amount to 112." She and her daughters, Georgia and Florence, had been returning them. "I have nearly got through—but they have yet a heavy debt on hand as more single than married ladies have called." Four days later she had "paid all my calls—but find new ones are made daily." Once established, the connections of calls and visits were difficult to break. Meta Morris Grimball's daughter, Charlotte, found herself receiving a visit from Mrs. Barlow and Mrs. Gummageon. Charlotte "did not altogether like them as visitors but she asked them last Spring & felt herself obliged to confirm it this April. They are very much talked about and therefore not desirable friends." Anna Matilda King, for all her desire to see an increase in the society on St. Simon's, shared Meta Morris Grimball's judgmental attitude toward new acquaintances. She bitterly regretted that all of the inhabitants of St. Simon's except her household and the Coupers were cultivating the Barrets with a view to encouraging them to settle there. The old man, she allowed, seemed amiable enough, if "*too polite*," but his wife and daughter and son "are so very common—We could never relish them as associates." If only a "respectable Christian family had purchas[ed] there would be some consolation—as it is the bitterness will never end." Unlike her neighbors, she could not accept wealth as a substitute for class, and she despaired of the outcome. "Oh! how wealth is worshipped but such is the world! —— Money before merit 99 times in 100. Toney [her small granddaughter] can speak the English language as well as Mr. Barret can. Oh what a bore to have such people as neighbors."[56]

Anna Matilda King and Meta Morris Grimball, who came out of the marrow of lowcountry society, never doubted the validity of the social standards that they embodied in their every gesture and response. Lucilla Agnes McCorkle, who, although very well connected, came from upcountry slaveholders and who had married a minister, lacked their training and self-confidence. Her worries about her own deficiencies offer a rare view of the feelings of those whose qualifications as ladies the Meta Morris Grimballs and Anna Matilda Kings questioned. Lucilla McCorkle candidly acknowledged that her "not having formed and established in early life a lady-like deportment & habits of dignity & self possession—will be a sore impediment to me in my intercourse with society." Yet she did not, on that account, reject the standards. "In mind and feeling my sympathies are with the refined—yet from early habits & associations—I feel my inferiority—and my feeling it will make it more perceptible to others." She had recently experienced the trials of not measuring up to refined social expectations. "During the past week—I have been thrown with some who place an undue estimate upon riches—dress &c yet from their superior bearing I could not dissent from their opinions—perhaps I fear (suspect) have left an impression on their minds of my imbecility—."[57]

The gradations of wealth and class background among the slaveholders in general and the conditions of life in the upcountry villages in particular ensured that innumerable slaveholding women like Lucilla McCorkle would face the kind of scrutiny that made her so uncomfortable. Anna Matilda King's oldest son, Butler, attended the University of Georgia in Athens rather than going north like his brothers. While there, he made the acquaintance of a young lady and her mother, who extended warm hospitality to him. Butler wrote to his mother that Miss Gus was to visit their region and requested that she and Georgia and Florence pay special attention to her. He did not want his mother to think that he was in love with her, "for I assure you I am far from it. But she & her Mother have been too kind to me for me not to wish you to make some return." Normally, Butler would have had every confidence in his mother's observance of the rules of reciprocity, but he worried about her reaction to Miss Gus who, he allowed, "has many faults owing to her upcountry education." Faults notwithstanding, however, "she has as good a heart & as proper feelings as any one I ever knew—and I wish G & F to know her."[58]

After the King ladies had complied with Butler's request and promptly invited Miss Gus to the island, he wrote to his mother that he could not "express my gratitude my kind mother" and "only hope you were pleased with her." He knew too well that "she has some peculiarities owing to this infurnal upcountry," for it had taken him a long time to overlook them. No doubt his mother was "somewhat astonished at the way she spoke of young gentlemen—that is when she likes them—confessing it so openly!" But he assured his mother that Miss Gus "is more reserved in that & every other respect tha[n a]ny of the other Athenan ladies." Butler also wrote to Georgia of his delight that she liked Miss Gus so well, for "she is indeed a very *'likeable'* young lady." He had only raised the question of upcountry manners "to prepare you on the only point any one can find fault with her upon."[59]

Butler King, in his own way, was trying to distinguish between appearance and substance. Miss Gus might indulge in unladylike expressions, but she had an irreproachable character. Martha Jackson, an unimpeachable lady who happened to live in upcountry Georgia, also noted the problem of upcountry manners but allowed for the possibility of improvement. Her cousin, John Flournoy, married a young lady from Jackson County who, "being a plain Countryman's daughter, did not appear to great advantage on this her first introduction to a large company, whose manners were altogether different from what she had been accustomed to." The bride was, nonetheless, "quite young, and should she and her husband get along pretty well she may improve." Like Butler King, Martha Jackson allowed that, however essential manners might be to the making of a lady, they did not in every instance have to be inculcated from birth and in particular circumstances might be learned. Juliana Margaret Conner had doubts. In Marion, Alabama, she stopped at a highly recommended hotel, the Mansion House, only to discover that several other ladies were also staying there, "at least such I would presume they were judging from their appearance," although "neither their manners or acquaintance with the common rules of politeness would justify such an opinion." She proposed no remedy but to "leave them to enjoy their state of blissfull ignorance—congratulating myself on not having ever before encountered similar persons and feeling well assured that we shall again."[60]

Many women found the distinction between appearance and substance—between manners and character—problematic, although not because they agreed with Juliana Conner on the overriding importance of manners per se. Rather, they believed that disorderly manners testified to disorderly character, with which they were loath to be associated. Sarah Gayle was made deeply uneasy by Mrs. Van Dyke's continuing overtures to her. She greatly feared that "there is no good understanding, no real peace, between her and her husband." Doubtless both partners were to blame, although "he most, for he is a *man*," but Mrs. Van Dyke's lesser culpability did not make her any more desirable as an acquaintance.[61] Sarah Gayle was even more shocked to learn from Mrs. Erwin that the brother of Mrs. —— and of Colonel Tucker "had been executed at Newbern, NC for killing a child! and that the mother of Mrs. —— herself (Mrs. ——'s grandmother) had lived with her Father until after the birth of several children, without being married to him." Sarah Gayle allowed that "we are fortunate, I believe, in not always knowing the private history of our associates. It was a long time before I called on them." Sarah Gayle was not moved by artificial notions of correct manners. Those upon whom she finally called included a Mrs. James, who "herself is a days wonder amongst the rustic folks, about one of whom I am proud to acknowledge myself." Mrs. James's flaws lay in "her short petticoats and coquettish drawers [which] deserve such criticism as Johnson or Addison could have bestowed." On the grounds of poor taste and immodesty, Sarah Gayle determined that Mrs. James would never "suit well" so that "nothing renders a personal acquaintance necessary between us."[62]

During the war, Meta Morris Grimball found herself abruptly transported into the midst of upcountry village society, which differed radically from the lowcountry society to which she was accustomed. The disruptions caused by the war compounded village laxity in the matter of ordered social relations. Mrs. Irwin, a longstanding village resident and an incorrigible gossip, provided her "with a perfect chronicle of parish events." Mrs. Wilson had left Mrs. Thompson's, where she was boarding, with half a month's rent unpaid yet told everyone who would listen that "no one was of any account except her family, the Gibbes." Dr. Boyd's wife, a Miss Thompson, drank "and was subject to fits brought on by the use of stimulants." The more Meta Morris Grimball heard, the more convinced she became that "this seems to be a district of low character in Morals. I do not hear of any one being more correct than another." When visiting Mrs. Irwin, she encountered Mrs. Lockwood, the village milliner, whose husband came to take his wife home, "walking in the chamber with out knocking." Mr. Lockwood was a tailor, "so we found ourselves in rather unusual company." "In a Village," she observed with uncharacteristic philosophy, "there is no distinction all meet on an equality, and consequently the manners of these people are more refined;—or rather more alike than is usually found."[63]

Meta Morris Grimball's friend, Dr. Smith, thought that the war "will be a great benefit to the country, enlargement of mind to very ignorant, contracted, country people." In order to follow the news, the families of soldiers started to take the newspapers, "and if they can't read themselves they get people to read to them, and some of them have learned to read themselves." Dr. Smith reported that one woman of his neighborhood "had learnt to write & read writing since her husband left her, and he had, too, learned to read & write that he might write to her, she could read his letter, but no other writing." Dr.

Smith delighted her even more with his charming talk of Bulwer-Lytton's novels and his intelligent discussion of Dickens. The society to which she was accustomed took literacy for granted and placed a premium on graceful conversation about topics of which country folk were completely ignorant.[64]

Meta Morris Grimball remarked upon Mrs. Irwin's lurid tales and even mingled with the people whose disorderly lives they described, but she did not identify with the comings and goings of village society. She found Mrs. Irwin herself, although from a family with a reputation for lying, a kind and hospitable woman and "quite a register of family events in the society which surrounds her." Mrs. Irwin had an undeniable gift for turning a tale and "narrates well and accurately and takes one through the lives of those she talks of from the cradle to the tomb," yet Meta Morris Grimball remained personally unmoved. "The perfect ignorance about these people, except from what she says makes one take no sort of interest in them, it is simply life & death." In sharp contrast, she noted her pleasure in listening to her own father's account of family news. An unbridgeable divide separated those one knew from those with whom one merely crossed paths. She could tolerate her daughter Charlotte's unkind manners, even though she disapproved. Charlotte was an "excellent, well principled woman, with a disagreeable temper & no manners: but in this world," Meta Morris Grimball tolerantly observed, "we must be thankful for the good we find in those who belong to us and not judge them too harshly."[65]

Belonging and not belonging lay at the heart of the matter. Slaveholding women differed slightly in their explicit criteria for belonging, with some emphasizing breeding, some manners, some character, but they essentially agreed on the fundamentals. To be welcomed into their circle, a woman must be a lady, and even the more generous among them agreed that yeoman and middling town women ("country girls") were not ladies. Their manners were too coarse, their voices too loud, and their culture sorely lacking. Lucy Muse Fletcher's pleasure in a Fourth of July celebration "was somewhat marred by the rudeness of some of the young girls from town throwing about torpedoes & Roman candles," one of which fell upon her dress, ruining a new lace muslin.[66]

Southern ladies implacably drew the social line between themselves and other white women whom they perceived as their inferiors. They were especially harsh toward arrivistes, who pretended to make their social way by a tasteless and exaggerated display of fashion, or toward women who proved incapable of keeping the disorder of their personal lives hidden from public view. Mary Henderson deplored the behavior of "poor Mrs. Barkin," who was "making herself the town talk" by seeking her "drunken and gambling husband" in the alley and "other places of dissipation." Mary Henderson could never have done the same, for she would have feared "some insult from the low degraded company assembled there—." She would also have feared the wicked tongue and prying eyes of gossip. She knew that she lived in "an awfully gossipping community," in which people slandered and picked each others' characters to pieces. "Such persons," she reminded herself, were "always to be dreaded—avoided[.] I really think a certain portion of them would contaminate a whole community." Slaveholding ladies were, however, capable of displaying a gracious condescension toward lower-class white women who cultivated a veneer of respectability and did not presume to claim equal social footing with their superiors.[67]

Slaveholding women were prepared to acknowledge the deference of nonslaveholding white women, provided that they could set the terms of contact. They were especially willing to pay charitable calls upon those who, in one way or another, depended upon their patronage. When Susan Davis Hutchinson's dear friend and former student, Catherine Alexander, was visiting her, they fulfilled a longstanding promise "to call and drink a cup of coffee" with her washerwoman, who "took much pains to provide liberally and really seemed to feel it a great privilege to have us eat under her roof." Susan Davis Hutchinson approvingly noted that she "lives very neatly—keeps a cow, a horse and garden & poultry—A large bible lay on her stand—." Susan Davis Hutchinson paid a similar call of condescension on Mrs. Card, who lived plainly with her husband "in a log house, but they keep an excellent garden and the old lady is pious." Kate Carney frequently paid such calls. Out on a walk with her friend, Nannie, they "stopped by a few minutes to see Mrs. Bumpass [the seamstress], who was out, at her door, & spoke to us." Normally, she stopped by Mrs. Bumpass's with her mother to see about having dresses made. She and her sister Mary went together "to see Mrs. Hall. A workman's wife." Kate Carney and Mary also went, at the request of a servant, to visit Mrs. Wheeler so that she could tell them the news that her old maid sister-in-law, Miss Lucy, was to marry the overseer. Miss Lucy was some ten or twelve years older than her prospective bridegroom, "though persons think she has done very well." Kate Carney and Miss Sarah Authurs were "to have the honor of putting the bride to bed." The Wheelers, although very small slaveholders, did not belong to the

il circle but were bound to it by reciprocal ties of defer-
...escension.[68]

...descension imperceptibly merged with charity calls. The
...zed their responsibility to assist the less affluent women
...iborhood, especially those with whom they had longstanding relations of patronage. In some instances, the primary purpose of the calls was to demonstrate their personal graciousness, in
others to provide material assistance, but normally the two reinforced
each other in defining an act of Christian charity.

Southern ladies took their religious responsibilities seriously, but
they were more likely to weave them into their ideals of rank than to
draw upon them for criticism of their society. In the South, as in the
North, piety figured among the attributes of woman's role. The evangelical tide that swept across the South during the first three decades
of the century attracted large numbers of women and offered them the
sense of individual purpose that the Second Great Awakening is said to
have offered the women of the Northeast.[69] The early evangelicals
promoted an ideal of womanhood that departed in significant respects
from the myth of the lady and that was apparently intended to attract
yeoman women, who might be assumed to share much with their
northern farm and urban middle-class sisters. This evangelical message
sharply criticized fashion and idleness, proclaimed the importance of
work, and in general evoked solid bourgeois values. The same evangelicals also condemned slavery. By the 1820s, the churches had made
their peace with slavery and with the more privileged classes. We have
no full study of the changes in their views of womanhood at that time,
but we may assume, at least provisionally, that when the evangelicals
determined to hold their southern constituencies by relinquishing any
serious pretensions to apply Christian standards to the affairs of the
world, they also relinquished any attempt to criticize the prevailing
conventions of womanhood.[70]

Mrs. Virginia Cary, writing in 1831 on the female character, with
special reference to "the peculiar difficulties of our southern housewives," expressed only modest hopes for the role of religion in wom-
en's lives:

> Religion, if not most manifest in feminine deportment, is at least
> most necessary to enable women to perform their allotted duties
> in life. The very nature of those duties demands the strength of
> Christian principle to ensure their correct and dignified perfor-
> mance; while the nature of female trials, requires all the meliorat-

ing power of faith, to induce a requisite measure of patience and fortitude.[71]

She seems to have been advocating religion as an aid for survival in slave society, rather than as a program for its reform. Jan Lewis has recently suggested that when Virginian ladies cautiously turned to the consolations of evangelicalism in the early nineteenth century, they were seeking escape from and comfort for the uncertainties of fortunes confided to male hands, rather than "a systematic program for reform."[72] Southern ladies who extended charity to less fortunate women, frequently in the company of their pastors, intended to strengthen their own sense of self-worth by their gestures of condescension, not to imply equality between themselves and those to whom they graciously ministered.

Above all, slaveholding benefactresses sought deference, gratitude, and some signs of neatness and piety in the recipients of their beneficence. Eliza Clitherall recalled that, when she and her husband were living in Smithville, North Carolina, she knew a Mrs. Betts, "a lame woman, whose husband has died . . . & her only resource was the sale of vegetables from a garden she was privileged to cultivate for a Sumner family." Eliza Clitherall's daughter, Harriet, visited Mrs. Betts regularly, "carrying her little comforts, such as soup, rolls &c &c & above all, by reading to her in the Bible." Through Harriet's efforts, Mrs. Betts was led "to seek the Lord." During the war, Mary Jeffreys Bethell tried to offer spiritual assistance to the women of her neighborhood and visited the poor and recently widowed Mrs. Watson to try to comfort her. She also went to see Sophia and Bettie De Jarnatte, "poor orphan girls, I pray that God may bless and take care of them." She promised herself to try to visit Mrs. Mitchell, another poor widow who had just lost her daughter. When she went, Mrs. Mitchell "seemed grateful for my visit." Of a deeply religious sensibility, Mary Jeffreys Bethell prayed that "the Lord help and bless all the poor of my neighborhood" and claimed that she herself felt "more resigned to God's will than I ever did, and I want to do his will."[73]

Mary Jeffreys Bethell tried to serve God's will by dispensing charity to her less fortunate neighbors. When sickness broke out, she went on a round of visits and carried the sick "something nice to eat, lightbread and rice." She loved to "visit the sick because God has commanded us to do it." But her ideas of helping the poor and needy did not always include material assistance. One day a poor woman came to Mary Jeffreys Bethell in search of "some things for her husband," who was going into the army. "I had the pleasure of giving her something for him. I sent him a Testament to read, sent him word to put his trust in God. I gave the woman advice and exorted her to seek religion." Such efforts produced the highest sense of satisfaction. "I feel cheerful and happy today, in trying to help the poor and needy I got blessed and comforted myself, my gloom and fears are all gone."[74]

Susan Davis Hutchinson was also wont to dispense religious aid. While walking one evening, she entered "a small house where poverty reigned over his votaries with indisputed sway" and "took up the Bible and read to them." The objects of her charity "were truly attentive and grateful," but just as she had finished her lecture and was about to leave, "a poor wretched woman begged me to go and see her daughter, a poor abandoned girl at the next house." This request revolted Susan Davis Hutchinson, "for it was a house of well-known infamy," but she could hardly refuse. She settled herself near the door "for somehow I had a dreadful disgust to the people and could scarcely help looking to see whether they would not attempt some violence." The poor lost girl whom she was visiting at first refused to address her, "but at last I proposed attending prayer with them, when she appeared deeply affected." The girl's mother "wrung her hands and some times appeared to be almost in despair," crying that she almost feared to go to sleep for fear of awakening in hell. "While in the detestable brothal," Susan Davis Hutchinson "felt fearful lest my conduct might be misconstrued by an unserious world."[75]

Few slaveholding women risked such misinterpretation of their conduct and, as a rule, preferred to dispense charity within their own households. When, later in life, Susan Davis Hutchinson was keeping a school, one of her acquaintances "brought a poor woman and infant both sick to stay in one of our school rooms till another place could be found." Kate Carney's mother regularly gave some money to beggar women who applied at her door. She even asked one to stay to dinner, although not to eat with the family. Meta Morris Grimball felt so bad at having had to refuse two women beggars who came to her door— she had no change and not enough extra food to give them a meal— that when subsequently she encountered one of them in the village she gave her twenty-five cents. Sarah Gayle remembered that her aunt weaned her own child to nurse a "feeble, diseased boy, a poor orphan infant," whom she restored to health and returned to his delighted and grateful father "a fat and chubby child." When necessary, some white women nursed slave infants. Eliza Clitherall frequently took in those whom she considered the deserving poor: the fatherless yeoman girl, a baby boy whose mother had run off, and a Swedish sailor who had fallen on hard times. She nursed the baby some herself during the day, had slave women nurse him at night, and mourned when, despite her best efforts, he died. Her husband settled the sailor in a vacant out-building at the top of one of their gardens with a mattress and bed clothes and under the care of a servant.[76]

At the request of friends Eliza Clitherall and her husband provided a home for "a young lady of 15 years of age—whose Father had *turn'd* her out of house & home, because she had objected to marry an *old* french man of 60 years of age—disgusting in appearance, intemperate, but rich." A few years later, Eliza Clitherall agreed to take in an eight-year-old girl who had been left with one of her acquaintances by a man who claimed that his wife had died and that he had to go on a long trip. In this instance, the child's belongings "evidenc'd she was not of vulgar Parentage." It subsequently turned out that the father was a gentleman, one I. Gibbs of Charleston, South Carolina—"(Lo, & behold a connection of our family!)"[77]

The ladies enjoyed much greater intimacy with their own slaves, especially their house servants, than with nonslaveholding white women. When they attempted to extend their charitable obligations beyond the immediate circle of their family, white and black, they preferred to do so on terms that reinforced their positions as ruling ladies. Condescension was inseparable from charity. A lady's primary obligations were to her own family and only secondarily to the occasional misery in the outside world that came to her attention. Her interest in individual cases normally depended upon the prior existence of bonds of patronage or, at best, upon the cases that fell within the purview of her church and its pastor. She assisted those whom she could in some sense assimilate into her notion of "her" people, but only on the firm understanding that her class position entitled her to their deference and protected her from their presumption. Within this context, her charitable gestures, especially those informed with a larger religious sensibility, were as important to her role as a lady as was her embodiment of fashion and the fine points of social relations.

The conventions that defined the lady included a strong emphasis on purity and chastity in the unmarried and decorum in the married. The male code of honor ascribed female sexuality to the possession and protection of the lady's male kin, but neither the convention nor the code unambiguously denied female sexuality or promoted the ideal of "passionlessness" that Nancy Cott has identified as prevalent in the Northeast. Slaveholding culture emphasized control of female sexuality; it did not deny its existence. Ladies recoiled in horror from inappropriate manifestations of sexuality and severely criticized even women of their own class who allowed their private lives to become a topic of public discussion. But within their own circles, they acknowledged the existence of passion, deploring only its ravages.[78]

Sex broke through the barriers of civility within which slaveholding conventions tried to contain it. The primary culprits were men, whose self-control was widely acknowledged to be much more fragile than that of women, but women were also acknowledged to have their share of responsibility. Walter Read recalled having been told of a cousin, Catharine, who, though "very beautiful, became a bad woman." The last he had heard from her was that she "lived with her mother Mrs. Bishop in Alexandria, & was very common." Walter Read thanked God that "she is the only one I ever did hear suspected of anything like unchaste conduct either on my father or my mother's side." Mary Austin Holley noted that, in Brazoria, Mr. Stephenson had killed Mr. Berryman in a duel (muskets at ten paces), because "Mr. Berryman was the lover of Mrs. Stephenson, now parted from her husband in consequence." On the body of the dead lover was found a lock of the lady's hair, marked "*to be placed in my coffin*," and a bundle of letters, one of which "named a place of assignation on the Mississippi, after the husband should have fallen." Meanwhile, Mrs. Stephenson had also "written back to her husband to kill berriman [*sic*] for the injury done to her name, or she would never live with him again." Mary Austin Holley marveled at what her position could now be. "Woman—when bad—how bad!!"[79]

Lucy Muse Fletcher moaned that her cousin Taliaferro Stubbins had experienced a "severe affliction" as a result of sexual impropriety. The unfortunate man had two daughters, one of whom had married a Mr. Miller, "an enterprising merchant in Charlestown," and the other a Mr. Thompson, "a young lawyer of remarkably fine personal appearance, but great vanity & strongly addicted to pleasure & self-indulgence." Rumors had long been circulating that some "improper intimacy" linked Mr. Thompson to his brother-in-law's sister, Mary Miller, who was "a very plain uninteresting girl." Then those speculations became "a matter of public notoriety." The child of the shameful affair died, and Mary Miller was sent away. But the "excitement against Mr. T was so great that he was obliged to leave the country." His father-in-law had supplied him with endless amounts of money, purportedly for business trips but really, as it turned out, for pleasure trips "to visit handsome ladies," one of whom he boasted had cost him $1,000, another of whom was a married lady in Washington. He pressed "profligacy" so far that it became "a matter of real grief & surprise" to his wife's friends when she "determined to follow him to Missouri, at his earnest solicitation." Mr. Thompson subsequently "united with the Presbyterian church" and was hoped to be a changed man. When last seen on a visit to her mother, his wife "was looking very well and happy."[80]

Taliaferro Stubbins's "affliction" affected a number of women at once. Poor Mary Miller, like others in her situation, had probably ruined her chances for a proper marriage of her own. But Mr. Thompson's wife took him back, apparently without undue bitterness, and the married woman in Washington probably continued her extramarital affairs. Washington society represented a special danger, for politicians congregated there without their wives, and among too many women of suspected morals. Julia Gilmer was distressed at "the unfortunate disgraceful 'Ickles affair,'" which involved a married woman. From what she could tell from the papers, that woman "could not have ever known what it was to be a good pure woman or she could never have so forgotten herself as to be so bold in her wickedness." Mr. Ickles's friends were making a heroic attempt to prove that he was insane when he killed Key; Julia Gilmer believed him to have been so for some time, but other purportedly sane men engaged in similar adventures.[81]

David Outlaw reported to his wife, Emily, that a man who suspected his wife of infidelity had shot her presumed lover to death on the streets of that city. He reflected: "If all men who have cause to be jealous, were to shoot a man in this city, there would be a very considerable mortality here." The capital abounded with men who had affairs with married women. It happened every session. But the wives left at home had their own reasons for suspicion. David Outlaw did his best to defend his colleague, Willie P. Mangum, against Emily's charges in the name of Mangum's wife. He insisted that Mangum's "habits, if not exemplary, have been better than heretofore." He had no wish to excuse him, since it was "unmanly for a husband to shrink from any difficulties, and have his wife to encounter them." But, at least, the causes of Mangum's delay in returning home were "much less censurable than those which have been attributed to him." Six months later, Mangum's wife had sent word that she was ill, yet her husband still had not started for home. Even David Outlaw, who tried to stress Mangum's good qualities, had to admit that his "long absence, amounting to a virtual abandonment of his family, is inexcusable." In effect, he was trying to reassure his own wife that Mangum's failings were those of cowardice in the face of financial difficulties rather than sexual philandering.[82]

Other cities, towns, and even villages had their scandals, and ladies normally cast harsh judgments on women who so defied convention as to make their behavior public. Reserving a special vitriol for men who wantonly abused women's trust, most ladies, like most gentlemen, exercised restraint in their judgment of the sexual impropriety of the men of their own class. Doubtless, they understood how completely men held the upper hand. Doubtless, they also understood how much their own social position required their being seen as proper married ladies. Perhaps, above all, they never wanted to acknowledge fully the extent of their men's sexual infidelities. Emily Outlaw trusted her husband, but many others may not have. Judge Mangum's wife, David Outlaw suggested, had more important complaints than her husband's sexual peccadilloes: He was not coming home as expected and was making a mess of the family's finances. Year after year Anna Matilda King received letters from her perennially absent husband recounting his delight in the warm reception he received from the society women of Washington and elsewhere. She did not query his accounts and inundated him with assurances of her love, asking only that he confirm his love for her.[83]

William Couper, the husband of the Kings' oldest daughter, Tootie, apparently took a few years to settle into marital respectability. Anna Matilda King wrote her son, Lord, that Tootie suddenly looked "prettier and is more happy now than since her marriage." Her husband showed every sign of devotion to her and the children and "has confessed his sins & implored her pardon for all the causes he has given her for unhappiness." Tootie was reaping her reward for "her patient forebearance—her perfect conduct—as a wife—has wrought this happy change." Mr. Couper had no idea that his mother-in-law "even had suspicions of him—but acknowledged that he thought Butler & you had." Anna Matilda, in her relief at the happy outcome, told Lord to "let bygones be bygones." Perhaps Mr. Couper had been distracting himself with one of the slave women, but, as Mary Chesnut resentfully noted, ladies who knew that such things happened in everyone else's household were loath to acknowledge them in their own. And most men, by far, did not, as James Henry Hammond did, indiscreetly reveal a slave mistress as a rival to their wives.[84]

Yet Anna Matilda King knew full well what men were capable of. Replying to her husband, who had written to her of another Washington scandal, she wondered what "must be the feelings of that *wretched woman!*" She must "have been destitute of all proper feeling to have acted as she did." Anna Matilda King reserved her greatest pity for the woman's daughter, who committed suicide, but allowed that "if the husband feels that he has never been *unfaithful* to his miserable wife," he too deserved pity. But even his infidelity *"would not make her crime the more excusable.* It is a *horrid business view it as you will."* Such crimes, she reflected, seemed to be becoming more common. And, she queried her husband, "Think you not that your sex is to blame? There are too many faithless husbands." Nonetheless, despite the husbands' behavior, "(I repeat) *that* is no *excuse for the wife*—two wrongs (as you always say) do not make a right."[85]

All slaveholding women knew that marriage could turn sour, although they were more likely to talk of their neighbors' pain than of their own. Lucilla McCorkle worried about her own proclivity to differ with her husband, in full knowledge that the assertion of her own will boded ill for domestic tranquility. In retrospect, she deplored the warmth with which she had argued the other side of a case from her husband. "There is always more or less danger when husband & wife vary on any topic." And she prayed her Holy Father to forbid "that this debateableness of the differences in our sentiments be the rock on which our domestic peace & love be wrecked." She worried about the frivolity of her own mind and her "tendency to castle building that has been allowed to a woeful extent" and against which her husband had warned her. During "one of these fits of lunacy (can I call it else?) I did nothing but pick flaws in his manner and disposition—until I had well nigh lost that respect for him which is the bond of the marriage relation." Yet she also found her husband to have a spirit which "if roused by ill health or crosses—is susceptible of becoming a thorn in his flesh & to others also." His temperament was "another trial of my meekness & patience," and it behooved her to remember that she had "a nervous husband and that all my patience will be required or our fireside will become a bedlam." But her responsibilities to obedience and deference did not lie easy upon her. She admitted that she had been "trying by argument to convince him of his errors—and that spirit of debate was itself alone a kin to the error I opposed. [Whereas] a uniform gentleness would have lulled opposition."[86]

Susan Davis Hutchinson's husband's naturally "nervous disposition" was exacerbated by financial reverses during the late 1820s, when the cotton market in Augusta collapsed. When, in October 1826, she raised the question of accepting a situation as a teacher in the Augusta

Academy, her husband withdrew into total silence, "followed by another, and more forceful exhibition of violent temper." Four days later, "tranquility seems restored." Throughout 1827 and 1828 his business difficulties persisted and his temper did not improve. In August 1829, she dreamed "it my duty to converse with Mr. H. on the sin of giving way to anger." Mr. H. "broke out into the most ungovernable rage." Reading over a parcel of his letters to his deceased first wife showed Susan Davis Hutchinson "that her trials were just as deep as my own," as were those of other women of her acquaintance. Mrs. Moderwell suffered "very deep affliction on account of her husband's having been silenced for habitual intemperance," and Mrs. Smith's husband was "almost broken hearted on account of his bankruptcy."[87]

In January 1830, Susan Davis Hutchinson suffered another "night of trial on account of Mr. H's violent temper." Yet when he began compulsively to spend the little they had on personal indulgences, she herself gave way to a "trial of temper in seeing Mr. H. with a new pair of boots." They were "destitute of even one blanket and I do believe Mr. H. has twenty pairs of boots now on hand besides shoes in profusion." A month later he "expended nearly 20 dollars for stockings." The previous month, the church session had unanimously resolved to suspend Mr. Hutchinson because "the whole community both in the church and out of it were excited against him for his conduct toward me whom all regarded as a faithful and an injured and persecuted wife."[88] Susan Davis Hutchinson and her husband eventually separated, but most abused and deceived wives did not take that extreme recourse. Probably they distinguished financial disaster and personal brutality from sexual infidelity and, in the latter case, simply endured what had to be expected from men's nature and, in the case of affairs with slave women, from the nature of their society.

Whatever slaveholding women endured, there are no grounds for believing them to have been especially prone to frigidity and want of passion. The voluminous letters between husbands and wives, as well as their diaries, display the wide variety of personalities and attitudes to be found in any society, but they provide precious little evidence of sexual morbidity. To the contrary, those letters and diaries convey an impression of frequently loving relations that hint, even by the standards of that reticent society, at physical joy in each other, and of no lack of passion. Whatever price the ladies paid for being encased in a slaveholding, male-dominated society that put them on an impossible pedestal in its rhetorical war with the North, they somehow managed to come through with a striking lack of neurotic inhibition. And if the marvelous letters of countless husbands prove anything, their men loved them for it.[89]

Southern conventions of gender defined for ladies a role narrowly circumscribed by their relations with the men of their own class and the men and women of other classes and races. Many of those ladies would have viewed those imposed limitations in the spirit of Gerard Manley Hopkins:

> . . . sheer plod makes plow down sillion
> Shine, and blue-bleak embers, ah my dear
> Fall, gall themselves, and gash gold-vermillion.[90]

Some would have agreed with Marcel Proust's defense of snobbery as the articulation of civilization.[91] And others would have felt that, all things being equal (which they were not), the game was not worth the candle. But they rarely attacked frontally the standards to which their society tried to hold them. On the contrary, many turned their own aspirations to excellence and their own sense of honor toward meeting their responsibilities as gracefully as possible, although their intentions did not preclude quiet resistance by the innumerable forms of foot-dragging at their disposal. Others openly bitched, or pushed arguments with their husbands further than prudence dictated. When Mary Jeffreys Bethell's husband was contemplating a move to Louisiana, which she strongly opposed, she prayed. And God answered her prayer. Others had extramarital love affairs of their own, and a few committed the ultimate rebellion against the dominance of white males by having sexual relations with black men.

The dominant gender conventions withstood these attacks, which slaveholding women and men did their best to bury in silence. Most ladies accommodated themselves by attributing unhappiness and restlessness to the inevitable failings of human nature, rather than to the iniquity of their society. They sought, and more often than not they found, their identity—their sense of themselves as women—in the sometimes less-than-perfect realization of their roles. The same cannot be said for slave women, who, far from being suffocated by an excess of protection, suffered in their own persons the white men's systematic violation of the very conventions they themselves imposed.

The Imaginative Worlds of Slaveholding Women

Louisa Susanna McCord and Her Countrywomen

Oh! the disadvantages we labor under, in not possessing the agreeable independence with the men; 'tis shameful that all the superiority, authority and freedom in all things should by partial Nature all be thrown in their scale; 'tis bad to be a woman in some things, but preferable in others, 'tho you may cram over me, and glory in the unlimited sphere of your actions and operations, I envy you not and would not change with you today.
—Elizabeth Ruffin

You seem to be so struck with some of my reflections you ask if they are my own. Yes husband, whatever they are, they are my own entirely.
—Mary Hamilton Campbell

For slaveholding women, whatever their personal variations, the self came wrapped in gender. To be an "I" meant to be a woman as their society defined women. Specifically, it meant to be a lady. They became themselves as daughter, wife, and mother, as the mistress of slaves, as lady, and in a personal relation to God as embodied in the religious fellowship of their community. They also became themselves through membership in a literate culture—through reading and writing. Whether through light fiction, religious literature, or the prose, fiction, and poetry of their own region and general Western culture, reading helped them to define moral, political, and personal issues. Through reading they extended the implications of their everyday lives and sought models of personal excellence, sources of personal consolation, and standards of social and political good. Their culture, including personal and social relations, taught that their identity had no meaning apart from privilege and duty. The privileges of their station set them apart from white nonslaveholding and black slave women, but those privileges imposed duties to themselves and their families, to be ignored only at the peril of their class status and immortal souls.

Slaveholding women embodied the *mentalité* of their class, notwithstanding their exhibiting all the personal virtues and failings of women everywhere. Over-whelmingly, they supported slavery and its constraints as the necessary price for their own privileged position. They emerge from their diaries and letters as remarkably attractive people who loved their children, their husbands, their families, and their friends and who tried to do their best by their slaves, but who accepted and supported the social system that endowed them with power and privilege over black women.

Ultimately, our understanding of their identities depends upon our ability to read their own representations of themselves—to evaluate, in the vocabulary of literary critics, text and context. The problems of reading and the attendant problems of sources cannot be trivialized or ignored. Despite occasional forays into statistical analysis, the history of slaveholding women remains hostage to the literary sources left by them or by the men who lived with or observed them, to the accounts of occasional travelers or journalists, and to the testimony of their slaves. Even the most devoted and learned scholars must, ultimately, fall back on subjective and impressionistic evaluations of the personal papers and published writings of contemporaries. We cannot afford to denigrate the value of those impressions, on which much of the best historical scholarship rests, but we need to justify our considered judgments by paying close attention to the meanings that slaveholding women ascribed to the words they used. Those probable meanings should be sought in their explicit ideas, which linked their private writings across decades and throughout the South, and in the dominant discourses of their society, to which they regularly, if often obliquely, referred.

Louisa Susanna McCord—daughter of Langdon Cheves of South Carolina, planter, statesman, and president of the Bank of the United States—combined the typical life of a woman of her class with an atypical career as the author of articles on political economy and social theory, including the woman question. At the relatively advanced age of thirty, she married a respected jurist, David J. McCord, with whom she had three children. She spent much of her life before the Civil War quietly in Columbia or on one of their nearby plantations. In Columbia she benefited from the lively intellectual circle that centered on South Carolina College. An outspoken and polemically effective defender of slavery and the subordination of women, she testified in her poetry and drama to a deep sensitivity to women's experience. Hardly typical, either in the range of her interests or in her manner of representing them, she nonetheless offers an essential perspective on many other women's private feelings, for she mapped, more clearly than any of her peers, the logic of women's place in slaveholding society.

Little given to personal, much less confessional, narratives, Louisa McCord wrote more of political economy than of women's condition. She left no diaries or journals and few letters. She preferred to consider women's lot from the objective perspective of society rather than from the subjective perspective of their personal experience. On the rare occasions on which she wrote of that experience, she did so obliquely. Her reflections on women's feelings rarely assumed the first person, singular or plural. She did not invite the identification of other women in some purported sisterhood. More the Roman matron than the winsome young lady, she offered a forbidding picture of women's obligations. She scoffed mercilessly at any notion of women's rights that did not insist upon their duties. Yet in her political economy and antifeminist polemics, as well as in her poetry and drama, she captured the social conditions that grounded the personal identities of the women of her class. Her intrinsic and compelling merits entitle her to more attention than she has yet received. A fiercely biting and intellectually gifted polemicist, she wrote out of the marrow of her class, her race, and her gender. Her writings differed in voice and focus from the personal reflections of less talented and less politically and theoretically sophisticated "ordinary" slaveholding women, yet they made explicit attitudes and values that other women took for granted.[1]

More traits united Louisa McCord with other slaveholding women than separated her from them. The apparent differences derived primarily from the variations in their voices, styles, and intended audiences. Most slaveholding women wrote subjectively, in a personal voice and for members of their own families. Even those who wrote for publication, notably the novelists, remained close to that personal perspective and invited their readers' identification with the stories of other women. Louisa McCord wrote primarily from an objective perspective, in an intentionally political voice, and for an enlightened audience. She wrote as a woman, but primarily in the voice of a latter-day Roman matron who measured personal feelings against their social consequences. She worked, normally with success, for an impersonal voice and an objective perspective, although even she had occasional lapses. She was wont to mobilize her considerable wit, satire, and charm in the service of her causes rather than in the service of herself—or, as she would have said, in the service of narrow personal ambition, which she deplored in all, especially politicians and belles. The case for Louisa McCord as guide to the imaginative worlds of

slaveholding women lies not in her personal voice, but in her evocation of the dynamics of the external world in which those imaginative
worlds were inscribed. Through political economy, political and social theory, drama, and poetry she articulated the worldly constraints
within which other slaveholding women sought identity.

Louisa McCord wrote for the intellectual elite of the South and,
beyond it, for the Republic of Letters of the Western world. She surely
did not intend her political economy for a primarily female audience,
for it would have taken considerable effort to find a southern woman
who could even approximate her mastery of a subject taught only in
men's schools. Even her literary work did not readily fall into a distinct
domestic or female discourse. She vigorously attacked Harriet Beecher
Stowe and Harriet Martineau as apostles of misguided, dangerous,
and muddle-headed notions, much as she attacked the men—George
Frederick Holmes and George Fitzhugh, among other worthies—with
whom she disagreed. She granted Martineau and Stowe the grudging
respect of bothering to attack them at all, although she gave them no
quarter in dismissing their ideas as muddle-headed.

Unlike Margaret Fuller, she made no apparent effort to contribute
to a fledgling female intellectual tradition, although, very much like
Fuller, she assumed that her mind was a match for the other best minds
of her time. Yet, again unlike Fuller, she frequently wrote anonymously
or signed only her initials, and she never publicly asserted her right
as a woman to claim authorship. She sought to inscribe herself in a
common culture by abstracting from rather than insisting upon her
female identity. She thus implicitly identified the status of author as an
institutional role rather than as an extension of personal identity. If
pressed, she probably would have argued that provided she, as Mrs.
David McCord, maintained appropriate reticence and decorum, which
permitted the publication of her translation of Bastiat's *Sophismes* and
her play *Caius Gracchus*, she, as L.S.M., could publish as she chose.
Obviously William Gilmore Simms and J. D. B. De Bow, among the
leading magazine editors of the South, agreed, for they actively sought
to engage her talent. Her claims to publication lay in her education,
class position, and political views, not in her private identity. She
thought of her audience as an intellectual elite to which she sought to
gain acceptance on her merits.

Most other slaveholding women never made that leap of imagination. For them, the audience that shaped their self-representations lay
in their own family circle. Their private writings, much more than
McCord's published ones, resembled the writings of the domestic sen-

timentalists who were forging their own public literary tradition in the North, although, unlike McCord and the domestic sentimentalists, they rarely published. Even in their private reflections, they did not claim the same authority for women's distinct view of the world that their northern sisters were claiming. Whatever the rhetorical similarity of southern and northern women's personal and domestic concerns, it is striking that, by the 1850s, northern women writers had forged a distinct literary culture, complete with such successful novelists as Harriet Beecher Stowe and such essayists as Catharine Beecher. Southern women had not. A Carolyn Lee Hentz or a Caroline Gilman, both transplanted northerners, might publish fiction that fell within the general confines of the domestic genre, but their works merged with the general culture and fiercely defended the proslavery premises of their adopted southern culture. Hentz's polemical novel, *The Planter's Northern Bride*, constituted a direct response to Stowe and unflinchingly defended a proslavery position, complete with harsh indictments of the purported value of "free" labor and a loving portrait of the lordly slaveholder, who earned not merely the devotion of his slaves but also the adoring love of his northern bride. The private writings of slaveholding women echoed these values, which McCord's theoretical writings explicitly articulated.[2]

Authorship could not be separated from intended audience, and hence publication could not be separated from unladylike self-display. No sooner had Sarah Gayle submitted some of her poems for publication than she sent to withdraw them. Caroline Gilman, who wrote extensively and intentionally for women and children, remembered her involuntary panic at a newspaper's printing of her verses, "Jephthah's Rash Vow," when she was sixteen. "When I learned that my verses had been surreptitiously printed . . . I wept bitterly, and was as alarmed as if I had been detected in man's apparel."[3] Mary Moragne, who before her conversion had anonymously published a serialized novella, *The British Partizan*, was thrown into "a trembling fit for an hour" by the letter from a "gentleman—an entire stranger to me—" informing her that she had won first prize for tales published in the *Augusta Mirror*. "Gracious heavens! then the 'Rubicon' is *passed*, & I am indeed an authoress! No very comfortable reflection—." But she reassured herself, for the gentleman spoke of the delight he had taken in her piece. "Is it not *something* to give pleasure to others?" Mary Moragne subsequently decided, under the promptings of her minister husband, that it was not enough. Although she continued to publish numerous poems and articles in the religious press and kept a journal, she forswore the fiction that she had loved and that might have brought her renown and money. Fannie Bumpas found justification for publication in the dictates of religion. After one struggle with doubt, she decided that "it was not only my duty to write my short experience in holiness for publication but to give my real signature."[4]

The prohibitions against women's authorship prevailed throughout the rest of the country and Europe as well. Women's tradition of public self-representation developed slowly and largely within the confines of dominant attitudes toward appropriate gender roles. Even by these standards, southern women proved reticent. When they broke the barriers, they normally represented women's identity in conformity with the southern gender conventions that linked the status and identities of ladies directly to the requisites of a God-fearing, slaveholding society.[5] McCord at least partially escaped these constraints by her unswerving rejection of explicit self-representation or even undue attention to women's special concerns. She cultivated an identification with a more public, neoclassical tradition.

Many women began keeping journals at a young age, frequently under the careful supervision of their mothers. The practice encouraged them to fashion identities in conformity with the expectations of their near kin and to learn the rudiments of graceful style. Sarah Rootes Jackson noted that one evening, while she and her sister were at their lessons, "there came a light shower of rain, such as is common at this time of the year. It soon ceased, however, and was properly an April shower." In another she noted that an uncle had brought her mother "the melancholy intelligence" of the death of a young cousin. More than likely, someone else introduced her to the formulaic phrases. As girls grew older, especially if they became deeply religious, as many did, journal keeping encouraged reflection upon their own lives—upon their meeting, or failing to meet, their responsibilities as women. Many women found a special satisfaction in keeping a journal or diary, and they were unlikely to devote themselves to it without some genuine, if not always articulated, sense of personal reward. They began and sustained their journals for deeply personal reasons, which could not entirely be separated from their sense of the journal's readers. Sarah Gayle wrote her journal at least in part to combat her loneliness during her husband's long absences. She explicitly addressed it to her daughters but showed or read it to her husband, who thought it should be bound. Many others kept a journal primarily for their children, who were enjoined to read it after their mother's death, although their husbands probably read it along the way. Susan Davis Hutchinson explicitly included advice for her children. "If my children are to be spared to peruse their mother's journal let them be admonished to govern their tempers and to live in peace with all, most especially their own households."[6]

Few surviving journals suggest that mature women wrote primarily confessional records, the contents of which were not intended for the eyes of others, although adolescent girls more readily did so. Kate Carney began her journal with the self-conscious reflection: "Today I commence a journal. It may last for years, and may continue, only, a few years, or even months, but I do it, just for my own pleasure and gratification." The surviving portions of the journal contain no secrets to be kept from others, but they do contain passages that seem to have been intended for the members of her family and perhaps others. She knew that journals were not completely private matters, for on another occasion she noted that Cousin Ell, who had been visiting, had told her several secrets. "But I will not trust them to these pages for fear some prying eyes might gather what was not intended for them." She had few secrets herself, "but still don't like to make a public matter of them." Only six weeks previously, "Brother John, read to us some his old journal tonight." Yet eventually she destroyed much of what she had written. "Have burnt the rest of my journal up, & expect some day to get courage to destroy this." At that time, in 1875, she was "married now, foolishness must be laid aside. A period has been placed at the end of my old life, & a new life has begun since."[7]

Another adolescent, Anna Maria Green, quoted Frederika Bremer, "it is a curious thing to keep a diary for one's self only," but believed that hers, if regularly kept, would give her pleasure. She could not think whom she would show it to, certainly not her father or either of her sisters, although she loved them. Yet she believed that she should thereafter, "seek better opportunities to write in my journal and render it more interesting and the style less desultory." Keeping a journal should at least afford her an opportunity for self-improvement. Elizabeth Ruffin rhetorically addressed the implied reader of her diary when she noted, ". . . completed a job commenced five years ago of which sample you may judge of my *industrious habits*." An adolescent, she cultivated an artful style and teasingly explored her own attitudes toward marriage, but she also wrote much of her intellectual pursuits and welcomed an opportunity to be "united in my *indefatigable brother's* search after knowledge." Parenthetically, she noted, "(so true is the adage 'the more we have the more earnest we will be in attaining more,' but so good a thing as intellectual improvement, who can complain of superabundance?)." She sincerely wished "they would be generous enough to bestow the unnecessary superfluity on some of the deficient ones, myself for instance." The advantage of "breathing the same atmosphere" as her brother "would be great." She nonetheless hoped that neither "he nor any one else will suppose the least compliment is intended by the expression of these observations," and thus confirmed that she thought him a possible reader, although she may also have had in mind her fiance, Henry Harrison Cocke.[8]

Gertrude Clanton began her journal when she was fourteen and on a trip. After a month, she had "been writing pretty regularly ever since. I like the plan. It is improving—." At fifteen, she spent days writing in her journal and daydreaming, and she began copying it over. She wrote her first drafts in an old copy book used for scribbling, but "wishing it all connected I copied the writing off." Three years later she noted that her friend, Leahe Goodall, was keeping a journal that she promised to will to Gertrude. At that time, Gertrude Clanton was nurturing the idea "of writing a series of tales" based upon the lives of girls she knew. Her journal figured in part as a workshop for her interest in writing, but also as a workshop for exploring her feelings. Waiting for the arrival of Jeff Thomas, whom she subsequently married, she mused on her "complicated feeling" about his coming. "What was a journal ever intended for?" She vowed, when she finished writing this book, to "get me another in which I will endeavor to unbossom myself—where I will breath every thought word and action of my mind. Where I will record *all every* feeling." And she wondered when Jeff would arrive. A month later she noted that she was "constantly deriving increased pleasure from keeping of my journal. I would find it difficult to leave off writing." But a month after that, she had never "found it so difficult to keep up a journal as this summer."[9]

The goals of self-improvement and the examined life figured prominently in journal keeping. Charlotte Beatty reflected upon the deplorable lot of "those who by their situation and engagements in the great world are deprived of the necessary & sweet enjoyment of self-acquaintance." The "corruptness of human nature" precluded women's ever perfectly knowing themselves, but "the high road of fashion and pleasure" drew them even further from the possibility. She professed herself "thankful that my journey leads thro' one of its [the world's] pleasant by paths, where shade & solitude invite to self-examination and communion with one's own heart, without which there is no true enjoyment of life." For Charlotte Beatty, communion with her own heart was communion with God and her bulwark against depression.

In the opening passages of her journal, she reminded herself that "We have only to consult our own hearts to be convinced, that religion is a part of human nature not inseparable from it." Doubt and skepticism "may weaken or cloud our hopes," but they "can never bring to the mind any certain or abiding conviction of the future." Her husband's departure for New Orleans brought on the blues. Another day at home alone, "notwithstanding my resolve yesterday," led her to suffer "considerably with low spirits, poor creatures that we are—resolving & re-resolving." Even after a day of trying, the evening's "searching into our hearts" revealed "how little progress we do make!!"[10]

Religious concerns underlay many of the journals. Mary Eliza Carmichael rebuked herself for having allowed eight months to pass without writing in her journal, "and yet my heavenly father still holds out the hand of mercy to me and mine." Four years later: "More than 1 year since I have written a line in my journal, and still my Saviour holds out the hand of mercys to my loved family." Despite her failure to write, God had blessed them with health and prosperity, "would that we had more spiritual gifts." Fannie Bumpas would not write on Sundays; instead she recorded Sunday's events on Monday. On the rare Sundays on which she did not attend church, she read, prayed, and resolved to try to live better. A Methodist minister's wife, she regarded her journal as too secular an activity for the Sabbath even if it was devoted to an account of her spiritual state. Eliza Carmichael, a Presbyterian, found that a journal helped her keep her pledge to God.[11]

Lucilla McCorkle, another minister's wife, dated all her journal entries by reference to the Sabbath and devoted long passages to exploring her spiritual state and exhorting herself to greater efforts. "Oh that I could rouse me to systematic active exertion in all the various departments of duty. 1st to God—my closest duties—the keeping of my heart—religious knowledge." She carefully rehearsed her duties to her immediate circle. "To my husband—rendering his home happy respectful—honoring him before men—as far as possible giving him quiet days of study." Her duty to her child consisted in training him "to proper tempers and habits" and attending to his diet and clothing. Those to her servants required that she treat them "as rational accountable beings," clothe and feed them, and afford them "facilities for their mental & spiritual improvement." Her duties to herself seemed endless. "Self denial—in food & clothing & keeping the *tongue*. early rising—industry—economy system—cheerfulness & sobriety—keeping down & quelling the spirit of malevolence, fault finding—covetisness or rather jealousy." She feared that she suffered from "that *disease*."

She listed her duties to the church and concluded with a prayer to God, in which she admitted that she asked "great things—but thou *canst*, Jesus Master[.] I implore thee to establish my heart in thy fear & may I walk worthy of my vocation." Three months later, she again "nettered on the duties and responsibilities of another secular week" and begged for divine assistance "in the right performance of all or any of the duties of my station and relation." And two months after that she begged Jesus to aid her "to become a 'full grown woman.'" Her journal permitted her to take stock of her failings and to struggle for the right spirit in which to live as a mature woman of her station. She did not identify her intended readers, but, like Fannie Bumpas, she probably expected them to be her husband, the minister and mediator of her spiritual life, and eventually her children.[12]

Throughout the twenty years during which Mary Jeffreys Bethell kept her journal, she recorded first and foremost "God's dealings with my soul." She regularly complained of her "great temptations and trials" but relied on Jesus to keep her safe. Her great desire was to enjoy religion, to feel God's workings in her soul, but she could go weeks at a time without that comfort. "I feel that I have not made that progress in divine life that was my privilege to do. I have been too much taken up with the things of time and sense." She reproached herself for having permitted her daughter "to attend a dancing party." She had done wrong. She again did wrong in reading a novel, which so fascinated her that she could not put it down until she had finished it. She considered both novel reading and dancing parties sinful. Novel reading wasted time and distracted attention from the Bible, nay destroyed "all desire for reading the Bible." Dancing parties consisted precisely in "the art of forgetting God, young people are so carried a way with it, they forget all their religious impressions." These temptations and others bedeviled her. "I am sorely tempted." All week "I have been severely tempted and tryed." Another week, "I have been beset with many temptations, my prayers seemed to be hindered." Mary Jeffreys Bethell rarely specified her temptations, which presumably concerned the distractions of worldliness. She turned, time and again, to prayer to set her on a right course. She may have been trying to leave an uplifting record for her daughter, but she was also writing for God.

Mary Jeffreys Bethell had much company in her dwellings on her spiritual state and her allusions to dire temptations and failings. Anne Davis's journal reveals a woman wracked by spiritual torment and a deep sense of unworthiness. Anne Davis was even less specific than

Mary Jeffreys Bethell, Lucilla McCorkle, and Fannie Bumpas, as to the precise nature of her temptations and sins. There is no evidence that she suffered from the kinds of sexual fantasies and desires to which modern women testify. More likely, she denied such impulses or projected them into the more "innocent" paths of fashion, romance, jealously, and ill-temperedness. Lucilla McCorkle wanted "to bring my body under the control of my will. Appetite." She worried that she ate and drank too much and spent "idle minutes brooding instead of catching up book & work while nursing Sallie [her new daughter]." She deplored "'answering again'" to her husband and the want of system in their domestic life. "Lastly the honor which cometh from men is a snare. I covet that honor; but it presents itself in this guise 'Be all things to all men.'" She claimed to fear that her ignorance of the "courtesies & proprieties of life" would lead her to bring "discredit to the cause of the Redeemer," but she continued to worry about the world's opinion of her. A psychoanalyst could plausibly fix upon the obsessive quality of these women's self-deprecations as evidence of displaced sexuality, but even a psychoanalyst owes some respect to the images and representations into which the deeper impulses were directed. And the women for whom we have evidence, especially the more pious, did not name those impulses even to themselves, much less to their probable readers.[13]

The women kept journals as a means of coming to terms with their female identities within a particular society. The journals testify to the variety of personalities but invariably betray a sense of self as the product of specific personal and social relations. Their language invokes religion, but also the Western secular tradition. If many function as chronicles of everyday life, most also function as chronicles of personal, intellectual, or spiritual progress. Few women, if any, kept journals primarily to comment upon the society around them. That impulse was born with the Civil War and reached full pitch in the memoirs and recollections published afterwards. For that reason, if for no other, Mary Boykin Chesnut's celebrated "diary" has little to do with its antebellum predecessors. A few women wrote "autobiographies," frequently after the deaths of their husbands, as a way of accounting for their lives as a whole. Most commonly, autobiographical writings constituted running accounts of their lives as they were unfolding.

Louisa McCord did not keep a journal, at least not one that has survived or to which she ever referred. For whatever reasons—and they probably included temperament and education—she directed her authorial ambitions toward intellectual and political debates, toward the context of women's lives more than toward personal experience. Born 3 December 1810 in Charleston, to Langdon Cheves and Mary Elizabeth Dulles, she spent the years from 1819 to 1829 in Philadelphia, where her father was serving as director of the Bank of the United States. There she received an education appropriate to a young woman of her class, and then some. With her sister, Sophia, she attended an academy and then was tutored at home in French—which she learned to read, speak, and translate fluently—and Italian as well as in history, music, astronomy, and the related cultural graces that constituted the light academic course her father considered appropriate for his daughters. She also shared in her brothers' instruction in mathematics, for which she displayed a precocious "passion." According to family legend, as a ten-year-old she was so taken with the subject that, being barred from instruction in it, she concealed herself behind the door of the room in which her brothers were being tutored. There her father found her and, being touched by her interest, permitted her to join the lessons.[14]

From her early years, exposure to her father's friends and associates gave her a formidable apprenticeship in and abiding passion for politics.[15] In 1830, after the Cheveses' return to Charleston, she inherited her own cotton plantation, Lang Syne, from an aunt and began to manage it, presumably under the direction and advice of her beloved father. During the same year, her sister Sophia married Charles T. Haskell and settled on a plantation nearby. A letter from their mother, Mary Cheves, reported that both of them adapted well to their new responsibilities, especially the making of clothes for their people. Even Louisa Cheves, who had never had much experience with sewing, cut out and made up pantaloons, "Jackson" coats, shirts, and clothes for the women and children.[16]

Little evidence remains of Louisa Cheves's life during the following decade, although it apparently left her with a jaundiced perspective on the status of belle, which so many young women of her class relished. In 1839, she reported to her brother Langdon that she and Anna, her younger sister, had finally returned home. "I have surmounted a summer at the Springs, which thank Heaven *est finie* and I am again released from playing belle, which, nolens volens, seems some how or other to be my destiny when I go into company." Never again would she "go to matronize Miss Anna in the gay world" without donning "a cap, or some such distinguishing mark of age." She would give none the excuse to think that her "venerable self stepping close on nine &

twenty had any ambition to pass as young Lady, any more." She vowed to "pin a piece of paper with '*aged twenty-nine*' on my shoulder, and if that don't scare off the young seventeen year-olders who come to flirt with me, the dear knows what will." She confessed to being "tired to death with rivalling Nan in their good graces." But she was talking "of bygone ills which really seem now like the confused bustle of a dream," for they have been going through "such very different scenes of late that the contrast seems unreal." She had been attending General Hayne's widow, who was in dreadful spirits and health. Had it not been for the sudden death of her friend and the misery of his widow, she might have judged the bustle and "fooleries" of the springs "more indulgently, tho' at best, *vraiment*, they don't suit my fancy."[17]

Apart from time she spent at Lang Syne, Louisa Cheves lived an active social life in the company of her family and friends. She made and received calls and engaged in the social rounds of her set. Continuing to see her father's political friends, she deepened her understanding of the issues of the day and strengthened her fierce loyalty to the South. Many years later, she jotted innumerable notes for a memorial that would do justice to the father she deeply revered. "I have never known or read of any man equal for completeness of character (This is the verdict I think not a natural prejudice in his favor but of my well-sifted reason)." Her father never stooped to imperfect means, however worthy the cause. He never swerved from his pursuit of truth, never changed "the right to suit circumstance," never sacrificed probity to interest or ambition. His only limit lay in his conviction that one should "never act wrongly because right is unattainable," but must "wait if the glimmer of truth may prevail, when the cloud of wrong is too heavy." He delighted "in the happiness of young people." She recalled seeing him "standing & beating time to the joyous dancing of our young friends too happy for the langour of fashion & showing how he enjoyed &c."[18] The only other hint of Louisa Cheves's feelings during her protracted spinsterhood appear in the collection of poems, *My Dreams*, which she published—or her husband had published for her—in 1848, eight years after her marriage. And even those poems testify more to the love that she had found than to the loneliness of the years before she found it.[19]

The years of spinsterhood sharply differentiated Louisa Cheves's experience from that of most young women of her class. Perhaps she was already too strong and independent during her first years in society to enjoy cultivating the charms of the belle and the favors of society. Yet the fragmentary evidence reveals a woman who felt at ease in her world, enjoying the intellectual companionship of men and the domestic companionship of women. For most young women, the prospect of marriage deeply colored their sense of entry into womanhood. Kate Carney took stock on her birthday: "Today, I am seventeen, getting quite old, and am not married, and hope I will not be soon, though older than Sister Maria was when she was married, & only lacking five months to be the same age of my mother, when she took upon herself 'to love honor & obey.'" At about the same age, Elizabeth Ruffin reported that gossip had her engaged to three different men. Everyone seemed determined to "deter me from all the anticipated horrors of *old-maidenhood*." The prospect did not unduly alarm her, for "the sweets of independence are greatly preferable to that *charming servitude* under a lord and master." She dreaded to "yield freedom, render obedience, and pay homage to any *one* or the other and only alternative, sad one indeed, bearing and groaning under the curses and stings showered on the *super-annuated sisterhood*." A better option would be to retire to the monastery in Georgetown. A few days later, an essay on old maids confirmed her sense of the attendant horrors and "almost persuaded [me] to abandon the idea of enlisting myself among the honorable sisterhood; but stay 'tis only the dark side of the picture, that is so appalling." On the positive side, she found the disadvantages attributed to spinsters by an illiberal and uncharitable world "nearly balanced by some admirable virtues" and took comfort in the "reflection that it is *chose possible* one single excellence, or good quality can be attached to *old maidism*." Disliking the tone of the author of the essay, she felt bound to defend the cause of unmarried ladies.[20]

Elizabeth Ruffin also recognized, as Louisa McCord emphasized in her writings, that women labored under serious disadvantages "in not possessing the agreeable independence with the men." She would have been happy to ride some distance to church, but disliked going alone. "'Tis shameful that all the superiority, authority and freedom in all things should by partial Nature all be thrown in their scale." That inequality made it "bad to be a woman in some things, but," she added for her reader, "preferable in others, 'tho you may cram over me, and glory in the unlimited sphere of your actions and operations, I envy you not and would not change with you today."[21]

Most of the young women who, like Elizabeth Ruffin, entertained the notion of not marrying, nonetheless married by their early twenties at the latest. Louisa McCord remained single for the critical years between sixteen and thirty, during which others were marrying, bearing children, and beginning prematurely to age. Her letter to her brother in which she railed against having to play the belle, with its wry mockery of her single condition and of the world's attitude toward it, coexisted with the sadness and poignancy of some of her poetry, which she probably drafted during these years. For despite intellectual and political ambitions that exceeded those of most of her peers, she recognized the personal loneliness and social anomaly of an old maid in a society that included fewer single women, and fewer opportunities for them, than did the societies of the Northeast or Western Europe.[22]

Louisa McCord's passing experience of spinsterhood apparently undercut any inclinations she might once have had to identify with adolescent fantasies of love, belles, and even young wives. She did not aspire to collect tokens of admiration for her person. It was as if she willed herself to become a matron even before marrying and bearing her own children. By 1851, when she published *Caius Gracchus*, she was able to portray Gracchus's young wife Lucinia with sympathy, but with scant trace of identification.[23] In "Woman and Her Needs" (1852), she scathingly castigated any trace of women's personal ambition for fame, especially that of the belle. Women, she wrote, degrade themselves when they refuse to submit themselves to "a faithful adherence to the laws of God and nature." Those women who "forget the woman's duty-fulfilling ambition to covet man's fame-grasping ambition" give way to "mistaken hungering for the forbidden fruit." This "grasping at notoriety belonging (if indeed it belongs properly to any) by nature to man, is at the root of all her debasement. Look at the ball-room belle for instance." She errs not "because there is harm in the ball-room enjoyment of youth; in the joy-waking music, or the spirit-rousing dance; but because she would be talked of, and forgets duty, conscience, and heart, in the love of notoriety."[24]

Her objections to the ambitions of the belle derived neither from the religious scruples that beset more pious women, nor from her insensitivity to the lure of intellectual accomplishment. Southern society permitted and even fostered women's religious and intellectual ambitions, provided they unfolded within circumscribed social roles. Female academies and colleges proliferated, under religious leadership or a strong church influence, throughout the South during the late antebellum period. They varied dramatically in the quality of education offered, but uniformly, as Steven Stowe has argued, they were intended to strengthen a young woman's sense of family ties, including social position and responsibility, and her sense of having special religious duties. Southern female academies and colleges could offer advanced curricula, although it remains unclear how many students took advantage of all of the offerings. Most young women only attended for a year or two, although some stayed as long as four. During their stay, in addition to receiving instruction in languages, they might attend classes in science, philosophy, English grammar and literature, mathematics, history and geography, and religion. Some schools offered instruction in the classics, including Latin and Greek, but the governing intention remained that of easing young women gracefully into the responsibilities of their station. Thus, whereas the young men had to study Greek and Latin, the women were discouraged from doing so and were steered instead toward French.[25]

Judge Herschel V. Johnson, who ranked with Howell Cobb, Alexander Stephens, and Robert Toombs among Georgia's political luminaries, praised such female accomplishments to the graduating class of the Wesleyan Female College of Macon in 1853: "Thus educated, with reference to her sphere of action and her mission—her social and domestic relations, how charming and how attractive is woman! How noble as wife and mother!" Education, he continued, "does not come from scholastic books alone. . . . It begins at the cradle, it does not end even at the grave; but being the development of the soul and its faculties, it is commensurate with immortality." There could be no doubt that education "is emphatically a matter of Religion. For religion is life; life fixes character, and character determines destiny." Female education must develop and cultivate those "physical, mental and moral powers, as will qualify Woman to perform her part, in the sphere of action, to which she has been assigned, in the order of Providential arrangement." In that scheme, man "is expected to be *learned*—woman *cultivated.*" He allowed that history offered examples of "masculine women, capable of filling the place of men," although "scarcely one has ever attained celebrity in Mathematics, Astronomy, Metaphysics, History or Medicine." Indisputably, Madame de Staël was learned, and other women from classical and biblical times to the recent past have been learned at law. But those exceptions only confirmed the soundness of the general rule.[26]

According to Johnson, women's lives include two sets of relations, the one social, the other domestic. Women set the tone for society, which can never be more refined than they, for their opinions "regulate its customs, fashions and amusements" and direct its conversation and its style. Women, accordingly, must be "educated for usefulness, in the relations of life," which meant that they must be taught the difference between pleasure and happiness. The two, he held, differed as matter and mind: "The one is external gratification, the other inward joy." Acquisition of knowledge could accompany either. "The daughter may acquire a splendid book education, and yet be utterly untaught" in her true role. Book-learned, she might yet place her own comfort above every other consideration, might feel "that in the throng of fashion and gayety, she is the central point of attraction for a thousand admiring eyes—her costume the most elegant, her motions the most graceful, and her smile the most bewitching." Yet pleasure and happiness are not altogether incompatible. Pleasure has its proper place—"always that of subordination to conscience and duty."[27]

Johnson believed religion to be perfectly compatible with distinctions of rank and the exigencies of polite society. Stressing the importance of manners, he urged young ladies to be polite and graceful. "The polite lady is always condescending and gracious to those below her." Politeness and gracefulness "invariably mark the well bred lady, and they throw a charm over every other accomplishment." Within this essential context, the other accomplishments, especially music and art, had their place, but they could not substitute for proper manners. Within it, even carefully supervised novel-reading could be tolerated. But all had to converge on training young women to fulfill their natural and divine destinies. Beyond turning out ladies, a proper female education should also shape wives and mothers. "The relation of wife and mother is the consequence of marriage, which is, at once, the foundation of the social state and the image of Heaven reflected to earth." Johnson held an exalted view of marriage, which he believed must never be reduced to a civil contract, or even a religious institution, if by that "we simply mean, that it is of Divine appointment. True marriage exists prior to and is independent of its public solemnization." For true marriage unites those distinctions of sex which do not consist only in physical differences, but which "are the results of real pre-existent distinctions of mind." Most slaveholders would not have shared his cavalier attitude toward the civil and religious solemnization of marriage, but would have warmly embraced his conviction that a woman's education should, above all, fit her to take her ordained social and familial place as lady, wife, and mother.[28]

Young ladies understood the purpose of their education, although not all resisted the temptation to seek the admiration that Johnson, like Louisa McCord, so deplored. Many also understood the importance of at least a smattering of intellectual culture to their future roles. Almost none looked to education to prepare them for an occupation. Teaching was the only profession open to women, and teacher training appeared, if barely, toward the end of the antebellum period. Women who contemplated a career normally encountered fierce parental opposition and risked community disapprobation. Although outrageous fortune, in the form of widowhood or a husband's or father's financial disaster, could force some women to seek work, such a situation normally occurred later in a woman's life. The acquisition of culture was another matter. As Johnson and many like him insisted, cultural training prepared a woman to adorn the family circle and polite society. Some young women did acquire a deep love for the intellectual life, but even they rarely valued systematic learning. The leisure afforded by the labor of slaves, combined with the retirement of rural households and villages, provided ample time for reading, and many young ladies took full advantage of the opportunity, even if most, like Sarah Gayle, had difficulty in moving beyond fiction. Frequently, they berated themselves for their failure to do so. Many women read primarily religious literature in their continuing efforts to improve themselves as Christians. Almost all read the Bible, but the more intellectual or determined also read broadly in the high culture of their day. Mary Chesnut, Louisa McCord, and Octavia LeVert were not alone in reading French as well as English.

The novels of which Herschel Johnson approved included those of Sir Walter Scott, James Fenimore Cooper, Frederika Bremer, Maria Edgeworth, and Washington Irving, all favorites among slaveholding women and considered appropriate reading for their daughters. As a young girl, Sarah Rootes Jackson was already reading Edgeworth's novels and works on education. As a mature woman and a novelist herself, Caroline Lee Hentz admiringly reread Edgeworth's works: "Almost divine enchantress; who will wear thy mantle of inspiration when thou art gone—?" In the evenings, Anna and Kitty Carmichael read to their parents from one of Scott's novels. Kate Carney read through the six volumes of Irving's *Life of Washington* in four months. But Elizabeth Ruffin had no patience for *The Last of the Mohicans*, in which she could find little to commend. She found it "of a most ferocious nature," notably in its presentation of "an exact delineation of the Indian character, mode of life, and disposition." The hero's "virtues and magnanimity would put many a civilized being to the blush," and the novel "ends horridly . . . the Indian trait of revenge is pictured and ruined to the very last."[29]

Mary Campbell, during one of her husband's protracted absences, planned to use the winter months "to read and endeavour all in my power" to store her mind with useful knowledge in order to "converse with you when you returned, on such subjects as had engaged your attention when absent and such others as would be improving to us both." She failed in the execution of her resolution. When in company, she could not read; when alone, she suffered too much from loneliness for him. She read "nothing with interest but select poems by Armstrong, Beaties, Akenside and Cowper—and our favorite Campbell's Pleasures of Hope." She had promised him that she would read history and other improving subjects but had slid back into reading books from the circulating library and the libraries of her neighbors, which "were of the light kind and most of them might be properly termed trash." She knew that novels conveyed "erroneous" views of real life yet admitted to being fond of good ones, by which she meant "such as have obtained a high reputation with the intelligent part of society and have no bad tendency." Reading the bad ones "affects one like any other stimulant, taken improperly—as soon as the stimulation passes off the mind is more prostrate than ever."[30]

Novels, including the novels that they considered escapist, influenced the imaginative worlds of slaveholding women. Fannie Page Hume reflected on her delight in the "sweet" novel, *Lady Mary, or Not of the World*. It made her feel "so dissatisfied with self—I do wish I was better, a more decided Christian." She bemoaned how little she did "to promote my Master's cause. may he lead me to higher things in the way that seemth to Him best." She also delighted in *The Curate of Linwood*, which contained "a true description of Mr. Davis's style of sermon—'Modeled upon the pattern of the free & full declaration of the Gospel of Salvation—the earnest setting forth of Christ crucified, in all the beauty of his character—& in all the suitableness of His offices to the sinner's wants.'" Eliza Clitherall took a more secular pleasure in reading William Gilmore Simms's *The Forayers*, the revolutionary narratives of which made her feel "as if the Past happy days were almost present . . . the scenes—& places, so often spoken of by my dear Mother, & some of them I have visitted." Not all novels were so uplifting. Susan Davis Hutchinson greatly regretted "having looked into an old novel—Richardson's Pamela—I am conscious that it was wrong." Elizabeth Ruffin admitted to having taken "a small peep in Tom Jones" and admonished her "delicate readers" not to be alarmed by "such an *unlady-like* and ungenteel confession."[31]

Few explained what especially attracted them in the novels they ruefully dismissed as escapist. Elizabeth Ruffin, who also read widely in more acceptable literature, noted that she had spent an entire day "lolling and reading; finished the first volume of ——— shall not say what, but leave you to guess having given you a previous hint." In this instance, she was almost certainly engulfed in *Tom Jones*, but she assimilated the particular work to

> the strange infatuation of novel-reading so popular with us *silly, weak* women whose mental capacities neither desire nor aspire to a higher grade, satisfied with momentary amusement without substantive evaluement [*sic*], and a piece of *weakness rarely indulged* (laying aside all enjoyment) by the more *noble, exalted* and *exemplary* part of society the men of course who seek alone after *fame, honor, solid benefit* and *perpetual profit*: construe the compliment as you please, exacting not from me an explanation which might be unwelcome to your superior ears.

Five days later, she had finished the novel but still would not admit its name and hoped that her reader would "pardon and pity my depraved and ungenteel taste for liking and feeling much interest in it." She was also intrigued by *Peregrine Pickle*, which she took up accidentally, "not *intentionally*, since," she mocked, "books of that *character* are ever *shunned* by the *fair sex*; more especially by such *purity of sentiment*, and *refinement of taste* as *my own uncommon degree*." To supplement her deficiencies, she then turned to the "Ladies department" of an issue of the *American Farmer* and "pored over a long letter from a father to his newly married daughter," which contained admirable advice "with the exception of the part where she is particularly cautioned against all endeavors of getting the upper-hand."[32]

Novel reading offered women a context for their private fantasies. In the midst of bustling households, they retreated to novels as a way of shutting out the world and letting their own imaginations play with the forbidden delights of romance and adventure. On their own telling, they "lost" themselves in novels. Doubtless in this losing they also found parts of themselves that their society denied or attempted to discipline. Most of the novels that they deprecated have disappeared, but there is no reason to believe that most were particularly risqué, *Tom Jones* and *Pamela* notwithstanding. More likely, they recreated—in innumerable and repetitive plots, and in acceptably chaste discourse—the dreams of women's adolescence and invited women's subjective identification. Objections to the novels, as the women were the first to admit, lay less in their specific content, however trivial, than in their capacity as drugs—their ability to free women, at least temporarily, from their responsibilities.

Novels represented a personal indulgence and a temporary release from the more demanding claims of instructive and sociable culture. In principle, women were supposed to read works that would draw them toward rather than away from their families in particular and cultivated society in general. Thus the Reverend Dr. Charles F. Deems, president of Greensboro Women's College in the early 1850s, admonished his students never to read a book if they had to do so in secret and to beware of all books that came in cheap paper covers. Women's reading was also gently guided by the common practice of having one member of the family read aloud to the others and by the readiness of husbands and fathers to recommend and buy books for the women. Mothers also read aloud to daughters, a practice that, in the case of the nine-year-old sister of the eminent divine Benjamin Morgan Palmer, appears to have been an uncommon treat: Her mother did her the great favor of reading to her from Locke's *Essay on Human Understanding*.[33]

Young Miss Palmer's travail notwithstanding, southern women in general were not required to be learned, but they were urged to be able to converse intelligently on a broad range of topics. Some novels, including some women's novels, had a place in this general culture and constituted a bridge between reading for entertainment and reading for improvement. Fannie Page Hume reread novels she both admired and enjoyed: Charlotte Brontë's *Shirley*, Augusta Evans's *Beulah*, Mrs. Humphrey Ward's *John Halifax, Gentleman*, and especially her "old friend" *Nicholas Nickleby*, which, once picked up, she found difficult to put down. She was "delighted with it—the characters so admirably sustained—don't feel as if the time had been misspent." Mahala Roach felt the same about *Dombey and Son*, which she liked as much as if she had never read it before. *John Halifax* ranked as one of Fannie Hume's favorites "because of its noble sentiments" and because it drew a "*noble picture* of what a *home may* be when husband & wife are truly one." *Shirley* held a "strange charm" for her. She also found Hawthorne's *The Marble Faun* beautifully written, but strange and "wierdlike." She did not "admire Hawthorne's style much. There is always something *terrible* & mysterious." She noted having received George Eliot's *The Mill on the Floss* from her cousin, Carter Braxton—who had also brought her the *The Marble Faun*, various periodicals, and a chess set—but not what she thought of it. She had been much moved by *Adam Bede*, "that prayer & sermon of Dinah's is so sweet—some of the descriptions are too beautiful."[34]

Like others, Fannie Page Hume interspersed novel reading with perusals of the Bible, religious tracts, prescriptive literature, magazines, history, and politics. Periodical literature linked women to each other and to the men of their class in a common cultural network. Fannie Hume read the *Southern Literary Messenger*, Littell's *Living Age*, *Harper's*, *Godey's Lady's Book*, occasionally the *Herald*, the *Home Journal*, and the *Chronicle*, and frequently the Richmond newspapers. Gertrude Clanton received *Godey's* and *Graham's Magazine*. David Outlaw sent the same periodicals to his daughters, Harriet and Betty, along with *Sartain's Magazine*. Sarah and Martha Jackson's father subscribed to the *North American Review*, the *Museum*, and the *Southern Banner*. The King family received a variety of periodicals, which Josey King referred to only as "the papers," but which contained reports on women's fiction. In Vance County, North Carolina, the postmaster regularly delivered copies of *Harper's*, *Godey's*, *Putnam's Magazine*, *Graham's*, *Blackwood's*, and the *Literary Miscellany*. Periodical literature kept women abreast of developments in the world beyond their households, including various aspects of fashion and culture.[35]

Many women's journals and letters testify to a broad, if not always deep, conversance with a range of historical, cultural, and political topics. Fannie Page Hume noted with dismay the death of Macaulay. "Another great man gone! They seem to follow in rapid succession— & who, alas! are fitted to take their places?" A few months later, she read an interesting article in the *Southern Literary Messenger* on "'Great Men,' also an able criticism on 'Macaulay,' & Irving's imaginary funeral procession." In Littell's *Living Age*, she read a lecture by Thackeray that portrayed George IV as "nothing more or less than a *dandy*— made up altogether by his tailors," as well as "a fine portraiture of Garibaldi drawn by a lady." Not surprisingly, for one concerned with the events of 1860, she remained preoccupied with the problem of leadership. She endeavored to begin 1861 in a proper frame of mind by following her morning's reading of the Bible with "'The Convention of 1776'—that famous Convention that drafted our glorious 'Declaration of Independence' composed of so many gallant spirits." She wished only "that some of their descendants could be [imbued] with similar patriotism and true worth—they are needed now." A few days later, she read some more in the convention and then "that famous speech of Vorhees delivered at the University of Va, 'The American Citizen'—it is fully worthy of its reputation—most eloquently written." A month later she "got so much interested in some extracts of speeches from American & English Statesmen (met with in 'Laggert's Standard Speeches')" that she "almost forgot sewing entirely."[36]

Eliza Clitherall read some excellent remarks in the *Albion* about

Bust of Louisa S. McCord by Hiram Powers, ca. 1850.
Courtesy of South Caroliniana Library

McCord House, Columbia, South Carolina, built ca. 1849. Home of
Louisa S. McCord and David McCord from the 1840s through the 1860s.
Courtesy of South Caroliniana Library

the "Hindoo War—The tragic cruelties, upon defenceless women &
Innocent children, surpass the most thrilling accounts, History has
presented—." She also pondered a set of resolutions which she had
found in the "Memoirs of Mrs Godolphin—Maid of Honor in the
Court of the Libertine Charles II," and which she hoped to impress
upon her own mind and conduct. She turned to history and especially
to memoirs and biographies to enlighten her on exemplary conduct
in the world. She was "partial to Biography," especially accounts of
the Friends, for her "sainted Mother was a Quakeress, and perfect
Christian—." She became deeply interested in "The Blind Girl of Wit-
tenburg & the Times of Luther"; "much engaged in Miss Sewell's
'Experience of Life'"; and she especially enjoyed "'the Memoirs of E.
Fry,'" whom she deemed "a blessing to Society, to her family & all
connected with her[,] a Blessing to the rich teaching the true enjoyment of wealth, to make others happy;—to clothe the naked, feed
the hungry[,] visit the sick[,] do good to all." Miss Sewell offered
not merely comfort, "but the way to obtain spiritual existence." Eliza

Caroline Georgia Wylly Couper, ca. 1830.
Courtesy of Georgia Department of Archives and History

Clitherall sought models for her own conduct in historical and biographical accounts.[37]

Elizabeth Ruffin and Lucilla McCorkle both read accounts of the
history of the Protestant Reformation, which was considered especially
relevant to the concerns of a deeply Protestant society. "A cursory
account of the religious reformation" impressed Elizabeth Ruffin with
"the obstacles and difficulties to be encountered and surmounted previous to its establishment." She broke off her first day's reading with
the decline that attended the succession of Mary Tudor, "whom I left
exercising her authority *unwoman-like* and the results and consequences
of whose power shall pry into at my leisure." The prying left her

Lucy Muse Walton Fletcher and the Reverend Patterson Fletcher, 1850s.
Courtesy of William R. Perkins Library, Duke University

wondering and astonished at "the almost incredible proceedings of
that 'bloody Queen' a most suitable appellation indeed." After the
"barbarity and bloodshed" had run their course, she came to the account of the martyrs, "whose burnings have shed an imperishable and
inextinguishable lustre and glory to be handed down to the latest
generation." Indeed, the ashes of their martyrdom "ought to awaken
from stupor and stimulate to effort and industry all professors of
Christianity in the present day." Lucilla McCorkle, in contrast, found
D'Aubigné's history of the Reformation difficult to read. She did "not
think it altogether the book for Sab. but I think it an excellent work &
one that should be read by every protestant and it seems that I must
read on this day or not at all." She regretted that her duties left her
little time for reading, and when she found the time, she frequently
found her progress retarded by "vain imaginations." After D'Aubigné,
she turned to Bunyan's *Holy War*, "and hope I shall be profited by it."
The young and the married lady alike viewed the history of Protestantism as of direct concern.[38]

Lucy Fletcher read even more widely in European history and literature. One winter she read Mme de Staël's *Corinne* in the original, and
Butler's *Analogy*. One summer her days were "beguiled" with Mrs.

Anderson's reading of Bancroft's *History,* "which she read entirely through to us." The following summer she reflected that she had been very much interested in Mme de Staël's *De l'Allemagne.* Despite not having read French for a long time, she found it no problem. She was especially taken with Mme de Staël's "interesting account of Schlegel who was said to be the original Prince Castel Forte in her Corrine." She recalled that Mrs. Jameson also presented an interesting sketch of Schlegel in her *Diary of an Ennuyée, "Sketches of Art, Literature &c."* The same summer Lucy Fletcher also read Prescott's *Conquest of Mexico* "with absorbing interest having previously read his Ferdinand & Isabella—both histories equal in point of interest and excitement to any romance." But Mme de Staël remained a special interest, and one night, when she could not sleep, Lucy Fletcher read a biography of her straight through, making notes of what she especially wanted to remember. Impressed with Mme de Staël's intellectual accomplishments, she was no less impressed with her personality, and carefully recorded:

> When in perfect repose her long eye lashes gave something of heaviness and languour to her countenance, but when excited, her magnificent dark eyes flashed with genius & seemed to announce her ideas before she could utter them, as lightening precedes the thunder—as she talked she always seemed to have present to her thoughts, the best actions & qualities of those whom she addressed—used to say, "politeness was only the art of choosing among our thoughts."[39]

In their different ways, Fannie Hume, Eliza Clitherall, Elizabeth Ruffin, Lucilla McCorkle, and Lucy Fletcher were, like Mary Boykin Chesnut, Louisa McCord, and others, deeply engaged in the culture of their day, which in turn shaped their sense of themselves as women. Literacy itself mattered to them as a sign of personal excellence and social station, and as the access to a network of communication with the men as well as the other women of their class. Their identifications with various forms of heroism delineate a special sense of personal honor for which men as well as women could offer models. Elizabeth Ruffin, for all her fascination with single blessedness, could castigate Queen Mary's unladylike barbarity, thereby acknowledging limits to women's independent action. And Lucy Fletcher, for all her marital stability, could delight in the flash of Mme de Staël's genius, thereby implicitly condoning her lapses from conventional domesticity. Most found ways of balancing the tensions between their society's constraints upon female ambition and independence and their own ideals of personal valor. Rather than rebel against their position, they strove as women to shine within it, but they never limited their vision exclusively to a world of female domesticity. For most, the paths of excellence remained those of duty, but duty to class and culture as well as to gender. For some, enjoyment of high culture always remained a struggle, for others it came more easily, but for most it constituted not merely an external grace but an important source of the language of identity.

The culture of less literate and wealthy white women remains elusive. Yeoman women were not much more likely than slave women to leave diaries or journals, in part because their lives did not include sufficient leisure time for keeping one. The better off among them were likely to have had some minimal education, but in the absence of a network of common schools, they probably received it from the ubiquitous Sabbath schools. Legal documents suggest that many of them could not even sign their names, and many of those who could probably could not write very well. Even among the slaveholding women grammar, punctuation, and spelling left a good deal to be desired. But, as Margaret Spufford has argued, writing—especially in the case of women—is not as good a proxy for literacy as some scholars have liked to assume. Women who cannot write may still read and be deeply engaged in a literate culture. In truth, we simply do not know much about the literate status of yeoman women, although we can be sure that for them, as for many slaveholding women, the Bible enjoyed pride of place among the books of their houses.[40]

Secular culture merged imperceptibly with sacred as a standard against which southern women measured their own progress. Above all, they turned to the Bible. Shortly after Kate Carney's seventeenth birthday, she finished the New Testament for the eighth time, and the next night she began it again. Charlotte Beatty proudly noted the occasion on which her own daughter, Sara, finished the New Testament, "having read it through. She is 5 years old next 23 February." Susan Davis Hutchinson spent one Sunday at home reading Job and Corinthians I and II, and slightly less than a year later she was finishing Job again. Lucy Fletcher noted that she was privately reading Galatians II. Sarah Adams spent Sundays after church reading the Bible. Elizabeth Ruffin spent a Sunday "reading chiefly my Bible." Despite variations in personal piety, most women viewed the Bible as the fundamental text for their religious identity, the bedrock for their hopes in this world and the next. The more pious also read extensively in religious tracts and church history. Susan Hutchinson read Gleig's history of the Bible, Romaine's life of faith, and, like others, was deeply impressed with the life of Henry Martyn. The latter work left Eliza Clitherall with the "deep conviction of my own sinful heart, contrasted with the sweet humble strains of these righteous men & I feel led to more earnest pleadings for God's blessing upon these devoted Missionaries." Sarah Adams's daughter, Emma, read to her from a history of the Christian religion and she, like Anne Davis, also read Lanvin's sermons. Fannie Hume found the work on infant baptism by Mr. Sprigg of Alexandria admirable and delighted in "Eighteen Christian Centuries." Most women read one or more of Hannah More's works. The specific readings varied, but one woman after another turned to religious literature as the ultimate guide to the good life, the ultimate standard for identity, and the ultimate source of comfort.[41]

Fannie Page Hume read extensively in religious fiction, from which she drew guides for exemplary behavior. After finishing "that sweet book, 'Edith's Ministry,'" she lamented: "Oh that I could imitate one half of her lovely Christian graces. Reading such books always depresses me, makes me feel so acutely my own unworthiness." She felt that she had made little progress in religion, that her heart was "still the seat of worldliness & pride. Oh, Father, give me strength to combat it." A month later she began "Kate Vinton or Sunshine," another "sweet book" that made her "long for greater holiness." Upon finishing it, she judged it "sweet & instructive" but "the characters are too perfect, some of them." She almost began "to doubt the existence of any true religion in my heart when I read of such, & compare my own *actions* & *motives*." Again she prayed: "Oh, Father! Help me to love Thee more, to live nearer to Thee. My temptations are so many & my resistance, at times, so weak." *Kate Vinton* continued to haunt her and she copied extracts from it, but she almost regretted having read it, for it so powerfully brought home her own lack as "a true self-sacrificing Christian—Teach me Holy Father!"[42]

Women sought in religious as in secular literature guides for correct conduct in this world and entrance into the next. They deeply regretted their difficulty in living up to the proffered standards of excellence. They nonetheless persisted, for they viewed reading as directly relevant to their lives, which—especially those of the younger women—encoded a fragile balance between the self-promotion of the belle and the self-abnegation of the Christian wife and mother. They frequently ranked works according to standards of execution and elegance, but they also ranked them according to the power of the human struggles they depicted. They measured characters for their ability to resolve human problems or to meet divine expectations. They expected their reading to illuminate and to help them live their own lives. Religious literature, although it enjoyed a special status, overlapped with secular in their minds as sources of an ideal of female honor. Both helped women to fulfill their highest potential as women.

By the time Louisa Cheves married Col. David J. McCord in 1840, she had forged a strong, independent character. Yet her fifteen years of marriage to a respected lawyer consolidated the apprenticeships of her youth and laid the foundation for the strengths she displayed during her own widowhood and the travail of the Confederacy. The testimony to her love for her husband remains strong, if indirect. Her poetry, much of which she probably wrote before meeting him, and her drama *Caius Gracchus*, which she wrote before he died, both evoke the place of love in a woman's life, but only one poem, "'Tis But Thee, Love, Only Thee," explicitly portrayed her own experience. Her marriage remained her great silence, but every word she published testified to its centrality. For Louisa McCord published only during the years of her marriage. And, according to family legend, she would never have published her most personal writing, the poems of *My Dreams*, had David McCord not sent them to a publisher without her permission.[43]

Louisa McCord's silence evokes, as poignantly as do the words of others, the importance of marriage to her and to her countrywomen. Slaveholders' marriages were as likely as the marriages of members of other classes to contain misery, infidelity, and even violence. But slaveholding women, in their own way, echoed the sentiments of the articulate freedman who harangued his brothers: "The Marriage Covenant is at the foundation of all our rights."[44] Louisa McCord believed, although she never said in so many words, that marriage constituted the bedrock of adult women's natural and, especially, their social identities. Where others sought the truth of women's experience in personal feeling, she sought it in their social roles or in the logic of nature. Her poem "Pretty Fanny" represents a young woman who challenges her "Grandame" about the desirability of marriage. The grandmother does not dispute:

> That man's a heartless, false deceiver;
> Believes from him, a maiden's ways,
> 'Tis Heaven's best mercy to deliver;
> Owns that wives have much to suffer;
> That such fate 'tis wise to dread.

And Fanny ponders,

> How that false deceiver, —man
> With his tongue could do such wonders,
> More than Grannie's wisdom can.

During Fanny's pondering, her prudence falls asleep, and "love's radiance beaming" intrudes, "Oped such worlds to her wild dreaming / That quite forgot was poor old Grannie." Fanny, like her grandmother before her, "soon was what she dreaded, / And a wedded life her lot." Only in one poem, "'Tis But Thee, Love, Only Thee," does Louisa McCord evoke love from a personal perspective. In it she wrote that, as in the glancing of sunbeams, "There my love, I think on thee," so in "fear, or dark misgiving," only one angel hovers near, "Who but thee, love? only thee!"

> Thus in hope, and thus in sorrow,
>   Fancy paints thy shadow near,
> Thou the brightener of each morrow,
>   Thou, the soother of each care.
> And the sun which gives me light,
> And the star which gilds my night,
> And the lingering hope to cheer me,
> 'Tis but thee, love! only thee![45]

Louisa McCord's sociological and precociously naturalistic perspective encoded the wisdom of those slaveholding women who bemoaned their own marriages and even those who rejected the married state, as well as the wisdom of those who delighted in their marriages. Marriage provided the standard against which they assessed their own lives. And how else could it have been among a preeminently rural social class that presided over a slave society, in which women had no viable adult alternative to marriage except widowhood? If women were fortunate, marriage anchored their personal and social lives.[46]

Sarah Gayle's deathbed testimony to her husband captured the powerful emotions with which others also invested their marriages. John Gayle reciprocated her devotion, but even women who had more reason to doubt reciprocation clung to their love for their husbands as the mooring for their personal lives. Anna Matilda Page King disagreed with her perennially absent husband that they were "too old to talk love to each other." She felt "that years have but increased my love for you" and felt "as much pleasure in writing to you now as the most love sick damsel of 17 would to her lover. More a great deal—no woman can love lover or husband more ardently than I do you." When, during 1863, pressing business detained John Grimball in Charleston, Meta noted the anniversary of her wedding, "the first time we have not passed it together."[47]

Many women had reason to know that their husbands also valued and cherished them. Mahala Roach noted of her anniversary: "I have been married *nine* years today, and I am sure that nine years of such pure, unalloyed happiness seldom falls to the lot of a mortal!" She hoped that she was sufficiently grateful for her blessings "Tho' I cannot be too grateful—with such a kind devoted husband, four good children, and good health, I have nothing to wish for." Men as well as women regarded marriage as necessary for their happiness. When nursing a sick relative kept Martha Jackson away from home, her husband, Henry, wrote mournfully to her of his loneliness and love. Everard Jackson noted in his diary after receiving a letter from Laura, his fiancée: "I am sure if a man is not happy in the selection of a consort for life he is truly of the wretched of the earth."[48]

An Episcopalian minister, the Reverend Mr. John Hamilton Cornish, captured after his wife's sudden death the essence of the role of wife as set forth in Proverbs: "Peace be with thee. Thou hast been lovely & pleasant in thy life, a faithful & loving wife—well & faithfully hast thou performed the vow as covenant between us made till death do us part. Thy children have risen up & called thee blessed. Now thou restest from thy labours with, we have good hope, the blessedness of those who sleep in the Lord. God be merciful to us who are left, especially the dear children." Women understood their married lives as the fulfillment of official roles, but the lucky ones also understood them as the realization of their personal dreams for happiness. Women made two great choices in life: a husband and a church. Most did their best to reap joy from those choices, for repudiation of them, especially the choice of husband, remained difficult and fraught with humiliation. Marriage required women to put aside the personal ambitions of the belle to seek satisfaction and reward in new "opportunities of usefulness."[49]

Louisa McCord's attack on women's quest for personal fame was derived, I suspect, from intimate personal knowledge of the temptations she deplored. She, not unlike Emily Dickinson, had wrestled with those tendencies in herself and had vanquished them young. Caroline Lee Hentz also understood those temptations and worried about them for her own daughter, sighing "to think when that innocent being, would become elated by vanity & learn to feed on the world's applause." She prayed that her daughter would be "shielded from a too ardent love of admiration—by the aegis of moral rectitude." Louisa McCord may have been troubled by her spinsterhood and the prospect of its permanence, but by the time her writings were published she had integrated her personal experience into a theoretical perspective on society and her place as a woman in it. In her view, the personal experience of women must serve the larger good of nature's purpose and society's needs. Louisa McCord may be counted among the lucky—or the deserving—in having found such deep personal satisfaction in meeting her self-defined responsibilities. During the years of her marriage she divided her time between Columbia and Lang Syne, in the management of which she continued to take an interest. She especially attended to the "comfort & well-being of a large number of slaves (to whom she was ever a kind and attentive mistress)." The demands of her life ensured that she could give only episodic attention to her own writing, although her husband encouraged her. Their identical worktables stood in different corners of the library at Lang Syne, and, according to their daughter, they delighted in the time spent there.[50]

Louisa McCord's daughter, Louisa, remembered her father as a warm man "who dearly loved a joke," told wonderful stories, and "loved to give dinner parties, not stylish dinner parties . . . , but with good cooking, good friends, and best of all, good talk." She especially remembered his "quiet, witty voice and keen bright eyes" and his close attention to his children, whom he watched with the utmost enjoyment, especially when anything in them "seemed to come up to his ideas." Louisa McCord appears to have loved those qualities in him, although she did not count on him always to attend to domestic responsibilities. He entranced the children by occasionally calling them into his room to read to them, for "the reading was sure to be something so original, so different from anything we ever heard from anybody else—so delightfully funny." But their mother read to them every day, beginning, as soon as they could understand, with Scott's novels, which continued as a standby but were gradually supplemented by "French books." She undertook much of their schooling and occasionally chafed at her husband's lack of assistance. "I school them all morning," she wrote to her cousin Mary Middleton, "& of course in the afternoon am too stupid & tired to do any thing for myself." Until another solution could be found, she remained a schoolmistress. "Mr McCord offers to read a little history & geography with them, but I do not count much upon his help. He does not like trouble much."[51]

Louisa McCord nonetheless benefited from considerable assistance in her domestic responsibilities. Her daughter fondly recalled Maum Di, who had primary charge of the McCord children. "Maum Di was our stay and comfort in trouble, our companion and sympathizer in happiness." According to family legend, on one occasion the younger Louisa ran to Maum Di with the complaint that "Mamma with her busy-body gone and slap me!" But Maum Di could also enforce standards and was known to inform the young ladies that they were nothing more than "little ha'ad head spitfires." As the children grew older and no longer needed her attention, Maum Di gradually assumed charge of the pantry, where she made the preserves and cut the sandwiches for tea. Maum Di had two sisters, both of whom also helped with the children, but Maum Rache in particular took turns with Maum Di in putting them to bed and occasionally sleeping in the nursery. Normally, one of two younger slave women, Fanny or Nora, slept there and also assisted in dressing the young ones. The slave women rivaled Louisa McCord in shaping her children's early cultural life, for their stories and music provided sources of endless bliss.[52]

The girls, as they grew older, shared with their mother a concern for clothes. Louisa McCord thanked Mary Middleton for sending a trunk of northern goodies to Columbia for all of them. For herself, she found the silk "very handsome, so much so that I will certainly have to leave home some time or other to get a chance to wear it out." The dyed one would do nicely for second best. Her daughters were as pleased with their bonnets as she was with the sleeves, "which give me a new idea & a new pattern." Except for such a lucky gift, she found that she got "sadly behind hand in my fashions & am often tempted to turn quaker—just because their fashions I believe never change." On another occasion, she sent a silk to her cousin to be dyed and allowed that she would feel quite magnificent with "two black silks, if I can ever get them made, & with 'darts' (is that the word?) in the right place." She would also welcome some trimmings, especially some "worsted braid to put round the skirt as I saw you do in Phila. I cannot get it here."[53]

Sally Baxter, who subsequently married Frank Hampton, visited the McCords at Lang Syne in 1855 and wrote a description to her father in New York. Nothing she could say could give him an idea of the beauty of the place. The plantation was "considered rather a model place even in South Carolina" where there were so many fine ones. Not very large, it included only about three thousand acres and two hundred slaves, but of the slaves only about fifteen had not been born on the place. Nobody could pity the condition of those slaves: "well tended, well cared for, they idolize their mistress, who, in her turn, devotes her whole time and energy to their improvement and comfort." Sally Baxter wished that her father could see Mrs. McCord's review of Mrs. Stowe's *Uncle Tom's Cabin*. Mrs. McCord, like the other members of the Cheves and McCord family, "is hotly engaged in the strife and almost all her feeling and intellect seem to be expended on that one topic." But above all, he should see "this kind of life on a plantation and among the slaves themselves," for it embodied "what southern life is."[54]

Louisa McCord's marriage, like her motherhood, brought her a personal fulfillment that searing personal loss could not negate. The lasting ache caused by the death of her son during the war did not cripple her efforts on behalf of other mother's sons. Unlike her friend Mary Chesnut, she was able to face the pain, suffering, and mutilation of southern soldiers. Chesnut, despite her sound allegiance to the Confederacy and her deep admiration for Louisa McCord, could not bring herself to undertake the labor of nursing or to face the anguish of the wounded. Chesnut preferred to express her devotion to the cause in the social and political circles of Richmond. Her conversational brilliance, like the biting commentary recorded in her diary, derived from her persisting identification with the belle, whereas McCord's work in the Confederate Hospital at Columbia confirmed her chosen identity as a true Cornelia.[55]

McCord never wrote directly on motherhood as woman's vocation, but she regularly evoked it. She left none of those tracts on mother's nurture which readily flowed from the pens of northern women. Nor did she leave private testimony to her feeling for her children, as did many of her southern counterparts. Her dedication of *Caius Gracchus* contains the most direct expression of her feelings as a mother: "To My Son." The moving testimony of the dedication describes the mother's heart as "that quenchless fount of love," which can never "idly rest / From the long love which ever fetters it / In bondage to her child." Reading these lines, one day, her son may catch "the shadow of my love, / Thy soul may guess its fullness." A mother's heart might throb and even break, "but never, never / Could deem her child a thing of vice or shame." Even more than this passage, her many references to women's roles as mothers provide an objective perspective on her countrywomen's subjective experience.[56]

Visiting a cousin after ten years' separation, Mahala Roach could not but contrast "my *then* self—and *my present self—then* a *young* gay girl, full of life—and *flirtations*—*now* a *happy* wife, and *Mother* of three sweet good children, a sedate *Matron* full of the pleasant cares of life." She could not "*sigh* for my happy girlhood—my womanhood *is so much happier.*" Charlotte Beatty noted her little Sara's fourth birthday with pleasure: "4 years old & she reads beautifully & is becoming very interesting. I am greatly blessed in my children." Mary Eliza Carmichael, who was devoted to her husband, nonetheless referred proudly to "my" boys and "my" girls. Eliza Clitherall, Meta Morris Grimball, and Mary Jeffreys Bethell, among many, took special pride and delight in their grown daughters. Many grown children passionately reciprocated the devotion their mothers bestowed upon them.[57]

Motherhood anchored women's personal and social identities, but it did not always come easily to them. Women knew too well the dangers that attended childbirth itself. Anne Davis awaited the birth of her first child with trepidation, knowing it to be "the most severe trial of nature." She knew "not but it is my Master's will that in giving birth to my first born he may call me home, but glory to his ever-blessed name." Fannie Bumpas frequently reflected during her confinement on "its sufferings & its dangers" and prayed to be prepared for the event, "whatever it may be. What if death should come! Am I prepared? Do not doubts arrive?" Lucilla McCorkle struggled with anguish during her confinement: "None but a *mother* can sympathize with a *mother.*" She praised the Lord that she had been safely delivered and "now my little bud of promise is repaying me amply for all the pain I suffered." As a young wife, Mary Jeffreys Bethell gave birth while her husband was away in Louisiana and worried that she might "die in my confinement and be buried before he reached home, no one but my heavenly Father knows what I suffered in my mind." Later in life, she accepted her own frequent confinements with considerable calm, but thanked God each time for her safe delivery. She worried deeply, however, about her oldest daughter's first confinement and longed to be with her. Mary Henderson dreaded the time of her confinement "beyond measure."[58]

All women knew that they risked their lives to bear children, and that the children's lives would remain at high risk for at least their first five years. The recurring dangers deeply informed their religious convictions, which functioned first to prepare them to meet unexpected as well as predictable deaths. To carry them through these ordeals, many relied not merely upon institutionalized religion, but upon their own pacts with God. Inclement weather prevented Susan Davis Hutchinson from taking her infant son, Ebeneezer, to church to be baptized.

She consoled herself that, although "I esteem it a duty to offer up our offspring," if circumstances providentially intervened "I consider it not so important as many do who have it performed even while the infant is dying." She had, she hoped, "solemnly given him to the Lord even long before his birth," and "the merciful Redeemer will I trust take him especially under his care either living or dying." Lucilla McCorkle dedicated her infant son to God "in private as well as in the face of the congregation and I now rely upon the promises—that I shall have grace to train him to become a preacher of righteousness."[59]

Responsibilities toward children, which began with the commitment of their souls to God, weighed heavily upon many mothers. Mothers had to expect to lose at least one child in infancy or early childhood, and frequently they lost two or more. Mothers and fathers felt the losses deeply and did their best to accept God's will. But mothers especially searched their consciences to discover if the death resulted from some failing of their own. Mary Jeffreys Bethell kept reminding herself that trouble worked for her spiritual good, that we are but "pilgrims, traveling to a better country, to a home in our Fathers house in heaven." Trials served to cut "the cords that bind us to earth." Yet she could hardly bear the loss of her lovely child, Phereba Hinton. Phereba followed her around, "seemed fond of me," and "would say Ma, you are sweet." Phereba's sweetness led her mother to exclaim, "we must not love her too much the Lord might take her." But at age three years and seven months, Phereba "caught fire and was burned dreadfully." She died the next day, and "is now an angel in Heaven." Yet Mary Jeffreys Bethell kept replaying the accident in her mind, asking herself what she might have done differently, and trying to bring herself to accept her loss. Mary Henderson, who bitterly regretted the two infants she had already lost, could not reconcile herself to the loss of her boy, Baldy. Every detail of his life, his last illness, and her own imagined failings pressed upon her distracted mind. Over and over she rehearsed the symptoms to which she might not have attended properly. Over and over she replayed in her mind his winning ways and trusting nature. She could not recover from the grief that "overshadows me with gloomy foreboding and shuddering dread." For eighteen months after his death, she had known nothing "but incessant mental suffering of the most intense kind, prostrating my feeble physical powers, enervating mind and body and almost overturning my reason—I do not feel rational at times, am either heartbroken or deranged." Anna Matilda King died of grief a year after the death of her adult son, Butler.[60]

Then as now, a mother's love for her children did not prevent her from finding them taxing. Most women bore a child every year or two during their adult lives. Their maternal responsibilities, which merged with those of household management, could be crushing and tried the patience of even the most loving. Mary Jeffreys Bethell always prayed for divine assistance when vexed by the demands of managing a large family of "seven children and four orphan children, I *want* to discharge my duty to *these* children, none but my *Heavenly* Father knows the sorrows and *trials* I have, but I look to God in every trial for comfort and support." Fannie Bumpas prayed: "O! for grace to enable me to govern my family aright." She had trouble managing both servant and child. From the birth of her little daughter, Eugenia, she had been concerned to manage her properly and had feared that she would fail. She was afraid that the child's fretfulness was a sign of "temper and peevishness" and was at a loss for what to do. Only God, she felt, could help her. Mahala Roach reproached herself for being "too *cross* today to live." The illness of her child's nurse had compelled her "to take entire care of the baby." The unaccustomed responsibility left her "idle, cross, and listless," unable to do anything useful but nurse the baby. Two months later she again had to nurse the baby, "and that is tiresome." Yet she, like the others, worried about doing right by the children, whom she deeply loved.[61]

Mahala Roach, like many others, did not consider nursing the baby part of her normal responsibilities as a mother. Nonetheless, southern women did not entirely escape the ideological pressure to nurse their own children. At the opening of the nineteenth century, Elizabeth Eve noted in her commonplace book: "'No mother, no child,' says the eccentric but kind hearted Rousseau." She was inclined to agree with him that it was a grievous error to leave helpless infants "to the care of sordid and mercenary hirelings—to people no way interested in their welfare: they are incapable of feeling for them that tenderness, however they may feign it, which their mothers would have felt, had they not crossed the designs of nature, and, to avoid a little trouble and confinement suffered their hearts to becoming insensible to the sweet transports of maternal love." She admitted that even mothers who fell prey to the temptations of dissipation still harbored some love for their children, for "nature is imperious." But she was certain that pursuit of the fashionable life to the neglect of sacred duties dulled maternal feeling, which would have been fully activated "if they pursued the dictates of nature and nourished their innocent infants with that food which the hand of Providence prepared for them." In her judgment, "that woman is but half a mother who does not suckle her own children."[62]

The rhetoric of maternal duty and privilege persisted throughout the antebellum period, but it was not inexorably bound to the idea of nursing mothers. Many women did nurse their own children, even until the end of their second year, but the vast majority of children were not nursed by their mothers alone. For slaveholding as for slave women, the core of maternal obligation lay in lovingly, but firmly, rearing children to assume their rightful place in society. Nursing did not constitute the primary aspect of that obligation, any more than did supervising infants and toddlers.

Doing right by one's children meant loving and disciplining them. Mahala Roach sought in vain to establish correct principles. Once, having awakened late and being cross as a consequence, she "had a serious time" with her son, Tommy. "I fear I was too hasty and severe, much good it does me to have 'Rules' or anything else." She knew that she was "too hasty at all times—and to my poor boy particularly, but he tries me too much." When her daughter, Sophy, behaved badly, she whipped her, "but hated to do it." At another time, "Sophy has been very bad today, have had to whip her *three* times, quite unusual for her, so I think she can't be well." Mahala Roach struggled continuously with her own temper. "Cross tonight! shameful too! I ought to be slap'd for it." Presumably her own mother had also used the whip to educate her daughter. Fannie Bumpas admitted to having indulged her little daughter too much, and "by trying to prevent crying have occasioned more." She recognized that she "must now learn her that our will is to be her law, for the longer I defer teaching her this lesson, the greater difficulty I may have to encounter." Yet from the start, many mothers found their daughters a source of comfort. When Fannie Bumpas's Eugenia saw her weeping, she "came to me, & kissing me put her arms around my neck, & with much concern, inquiringly said cry, cry. She is a great comfort."[63]

Motherhood brought the complexity of women's identities into focus. It confirmed a woman's place in the succession of generations, reaffirming her ties to her family of origin, especially to her mother, while it consolidated her ties to her husband. Women expressed different aspects of their identities in their special feelings for their sons and their daughters. Sons became the standard-bearers of their mothers' honor, their representatives in the world, and the objects of their intense devotion. Daughters became companions, best friends, and, in some measure, embodiments of their younger selves. It would be futile to try to ascribe greater intensity of feeling in one case or the other, although the differences in kinds were commonly sharp. A mother was, in the full sense, the mother of sons and of daughters. She was the focal point and anchor of family life, from which her own identity could not be separated. Susan Davis Hutchinson dreamed one night a dream "so singular that I thought it foreboded death, and as such an impression rested on my mind I deem it right to leave it in my journal because I cannot find it in my heart to converse with my family upon the subject." She dreamed that every member of the family was re-moved from the house and that she was left "alone to occupy one room, all the furniture was packed away except a bed." She recalled that "they put away the looking glass saying I should not want it." Yet she remembered not having "felt the slightest dread of being left only I wanted the time to come when we should meet at home again." Since that dream, she found that "when I think of death, no melancholy is attached to it." Left without her family, she needed no furniture but a bed and no glass in which to seek her own reflection. Her identity, like her reflection, depended upon her family's presence. The conviction that they should be reunited in what Sarah Gayle called the "house-hold above" triumphed over the fear of death. The melancholy of abandonment gave way to calm certainty in the recognition of her family as her self.[64]

For Louisa McCord, women's natural, personal, and social identities converged in the role of mother, which she delineated in a manner that departed significantly from the model that was being offered to white, middle-class women in the North. Nature might endow all women with an instinct for motherhood, but the realization of that instinct depended upon the broad social relations in which it was embedded as well as upon the character of the individual woman. Other women endorsed her view, in the same breath writing of their difficulties in governing their children and their servants and reminding themselves of their duties to both. Louisa McCord's doughty defense of women's true vocation as mothers rested not upon a sentimental view of wom-en's "empire" in the home, but upon a view of southern society as a slave society.[65] Her theory of gender relations proved inseparable from her theories of class and race relations. Her political economy thus furnishes the context for her discussions of women.

Louisa McCord established her intellectual reputation as a political economist, notably as the translator of and enthusiastic commentator on the work of the French political economist Frederic Bastiat. Al-though she probably read Bastiat after her formation as a woman of strong views on political and social questions, she embraced his work as the commanding formulation of her own convictions.[66] Bastiat's unmitigated defense of liberal political economy, understood primarily as free trade, derived from his understanding of the logic of French capitalist development, but it rested on a social conservatism that proved eminently adaptable to Louisa McCord's own understanding of the needs of southern slave society. She had to ignore Bastiat's resolute condemnation of slavery, but she somehow rose coolly to that task.[67]

In effect, Louisa McCord passionately espoused liberal, free-trade principles as they affected the relations between free, preferably propertied, white men in the marketplace. Free trade governed the relations among men, understood as the delegates and lords of households, but should, under no conditions, penetrate the walls of the household to influence its internal relations. This implicit notion of the household, which became explicit in the writings of her fellow proslavery theorist, Henry Hughes of Mississippi, permitted her to bind the liberal free-trade principles of bourgeois political economy to apparently contradictory particularistic and hierarchical proslavery convictions. Unfortunately—at least for her antislavery, antiracist admirers—her deep and systematic commitment to racial slavery strengthened her position and helped her to avoid the deepest contradictions that plagued the thought of her impressive predecessor, Thomas Roderick Dew.[68] Yet the central implications of her political economy for her views on "the woman question" lay in her arbitrary divorce of the principles of the market, which must govern political economy in the aggregate, from the principles of social and gender relations. She understood gender as a social question that must conform to the overriding claims of social order.

Louisa McCord never fully faced the inescapable contradiction between the market, the wondrous workings of which she so admired, and the social views that articulated her commitment to slavery as the foundation of the southern social order. She appears to have reasoned from the specific case of the needs of social order in a slave society to the general case of woman's proper identity and role, but she presented her views on women as if they reflected a general or natural law. Precocious in this respect as in others, she foreshadowed the systematic sexism of late-nineteenth-century thought even as she hearkened back to older, traditional views.[69] But she cast both tendencies in her own thought in the common language of early-nineteenth-century bourgeois culture. Her observations on women can, superficially, be read as corresponding to those of European and American bourgeois culture. To settle for that reading is to miss entirely the true referents for her words—is to misunderstand her thought and that of other women of her class.

Louisa McCord defended the innate differences between men and women as staunchly as any bourgeois sentimentalist of true womanhood. She even used the term "true woman."[70] She peppered her writings on women with evocations of motherhood, women's duty, women's charity, the unique power of women's love, and almost every imaginable prevailing piety. She forcefully insisted upon woman's special excellence and mission. But she offered a quintessentially southern interpretation of that common vocabulary. She equated gender spheres with moral and physical attributes. She had a high opinion, as well as extensive personal experience, of women's talents and capabilities, but she viewed them as confined within clearly defined channels. Above all, she dismissed with unveiled contempt the concept of systematic individualism and its permutations and corollaries, especially the concept of universal rights.

Louisa McCord, like other southerners who expressed themselves less rigorously, viewed rights as particular, not general. Rights, like the duties that must accompany them, adhere to particular functions. "It is the high duty of every reasoning mortal to aim at the perfecting of his kind by the perfecting of his individual humanity. Woman's task is, to make herself the perfected woman, not the counterfeit man." Elsewhere, she underscored the concept: "God, who has made every creature to its place, has, perhaps, not given to woman the most enviable position in his creation, but a most clearly defined position he has given her. Let her object, then, be to raise herself in that position. Out of it, there is only failure and degradation."[71]

Her view of the perfected woman owed nothing to the bourgeois ideal of female passivity. Freed from any universalist notion of woman's possible equality with man, she felt no need to protect men from women's legitimate self-assertion or strivings. She assuredly held women to possess the same intellectual capabilities as men. Conversely, she castigated any irresponsible celebration of the higher powers of intuition: "The rule of intuitions is the rule of brute force." In attacking intuition as women's distinctive mode of understanding social relations, she was attacking the women's rights advocates who advanced it as justification for their own claims. Man, too, she impatiently reminded them, has his "spontaneities and intuitions," with "the indisputable advantage of being backed by physical force, which will secure, as it always has secured, male supremacy, in case of a clash between contending spontaneities."[72]

She gave no quarter to Harriet Martineau, Fanny Wright, Elizabeth Smith, and their fellow champions of women's rights, ridiculing them mercilessly and always returning to the absurdity of their claim for universal equality. "*Fraternité* extended even to womanhood! And why not? Up for your rights, ladies! What is the worth of a civilization which condemns one half of mankind to Helot submissiveness?" Reform of this kind would destroy civilization. For reform, as she time and again insisted, betokens an entire ideology, not piecemeal tinkering with social arrangements. Touch one part of the system and you destroy the whole. She likened women's rights reformers to Sganarelle, the doctor in Molière's play *Le médecin malgré lui*, who decided that the heart lies on the righthand side of the human body. When his opinion was challenged, he replied that it used to lie on the left side, "but we have changed all that." Martineau's views, according to Louisa McCord, followed that enlightened model:

> If Miss Martineau and her sisterhood should prove powerful enough to depose *Le Bon Dieu*, and perfect their democratic system, by reducing *His* influence to a *single vote*, we do not doubt that, according to the approved majority system, it will be clearly and indisputably proved that Cuffee is Sir Isaac Newton, and Mrs. Cuffee, Napoleon Buonaparte, and Miss Martineau herself may stand for Cuffee, unless, indeed, she should prefer (as some of her recent works seem to indicate) to have it decided that she is *Le Bon Dieu* himself.[73]

She never settled for some fatuous notion that all is for the best, much less that women's lot is uniformly a happy one. "Woman's condition certainly admits of improvement, (but when have the strong forgotten to oppress the weak?)." But she saw no amelioration that could result from the projects of the prophets of women's equality. Woman does suffer from "*compression*." But so may man. "Human cravings soar high. Perhaps there is no human being, not born in a state of imbecility . . . who does not suffer, or fancy that he suffers, from compression." The solution surely did not lie in encouraging everyone to pout for the moon. Instead, it lay in striving for perfection, rather than in agitating for reform. "Here, as in all other improvements, the good must be brought about by working with, not against—by seconding, not opposing—Nature's laws." Above all, women should be mindful that, should they attain the equality they claimed to want, they would rapidly find themselves more oppressed than ever before. In sum, "are the ladies ready for a boxing match?" If so, they would be bested. For whatever men's and women's respective virtues, men would carry the day with respect to physical strength. Man, being "corporeally stronger than woman," has used his strength unjustly and has "frequently, habitually (we will allow her [Martineau] the full use of her argument,) even invariably, oppressed and misused woman." But surely the abuse is not to be corrected by

> pitting woman against man, in a direct state of antagonism, by throwing them into the arena together, stripped for the strife; by saying to the man, this woman is a man like yourself, your equal and similar, possessing all rights which you possess, and (of course she must allow) possessing none others. In such a strife, what becomes of corporeal weakness?[74]

Louisa McCord had no doubt of the outcome. The woman would lose, the world would become a "wrangling dog kennel," and life would be as nasty, brutish, and short as anything Hobbes imagined. Worse, it would become a topsy-turvy, dyspeptic nightmare—"a species of toothache, which, by some socialistic, communistic, feministic, Mormonistic, or any other such application of chloroform to the suffering patient, may be made to pass away in a sweet dream of perfection." So, with impatience, Louisa McCord dismissed all the "isms" that pretend to fell Evil, "which the poor, ignorant world has so long imagined inexplicable and incurable." So she warned against any pretense of transforming the order of God and Nature. "Wo to the world which seeks its rulers where it should but find its drudges! Wo to the drudge who would exalt himself into the ruler!" Thus her argument returns to the problem of Cuffee and of slavery as a social system. "Nature is vigilant of her laws and has no pardon for the breakers of them." The struggle for women's rights, as she saw it, challenged natural and divine intentions. Regrettably, it could only be attributed to native American genius. Happily, "our modest Southern sisters" had not succumbed to its deceptive appeal. It remained "entirely a Yankee notion."[75]

"Woman," Louisa McCord wrote, "is designed by nature, the conservative power of the world."[76] Catharine Beecher would doubtless have concurred. McCord intended a compliment to her gender, the capacities of which she, like Beecher, held in high esteem. All the more reason that she could not bear to see social disorder promulgated upon the world in the name of women's rights. The defense of women's rights constituted the cutting edge of all the baleful "isms" she deplored. Her countrywomen's accounts show that they agreed, even if few cast the question, as she did, in an objective perspective. In truth McCord, like many other slaveholding women, celebrated many of the same qualities in women as did Beecher, yet in using the same words she frequently meant different things. For Beecher represented the conservative wing of northern individualism, whereas McCord openly espoused hierarchical distinctions among human beings. Beecher, drawing the core of her identity from her New England heritage, declared war on many aspects of its Calvinist foundations, notably the institution of the church and original sin. McCord, who did not openly enter the lists of religious controversy, unmistakably drew upon the values of institutions and original sin to justify modern slavery and the subordination of women that it necessarily entailed. It gives one pause to imagine just what she would have thought of Beecher's emphasis on women's scientific management of their kitchens.[77]

The current view of Mary Chesnut and other slaveholding women as critics of slavery and "patriarchy" appears to dismiss Louisa McCord as exceptional. That view rests on a misunderstanding. Louisa McCord never denied women grounds for discontent: She opposed generalizing from individual unhappiness. Ever mindful of the prevalence of evil and of the frailty of human nature, Louisa McCord admitted that southern society left room for improvement, but she denied that the need for improvement justified "reform."

To Louisa McCord "reform," Yankee style, meant nothing less than revolution. She shrewdly linked the goals of the agitators for antislavery and women's rights to those of the French revolutionaries of 1848 and, before them, to those of the Jacobins. Behind the sanctimonious talk of individual right and universal equality, she believed, lurked the specter of landless men and women who thronged the streets, erecting barricades and toppling civilization. Louisa McCord had her private moments of despair, but she endured them as the inevitable dark side of everything she valued.

She drew her strength from the particularist, hierarchical slave society she so steadfastly defended. Elitist to her core, she anticipated all the tendencies that threatened it. At her least attractive, she embraced the pseudoscientific theory that consigned blacks to subhumanity and that her neighbor in Columbia, the Reverend Dr. James Henley Thornwell, the great Presbyterian theologian and jewel of the southern church, denounced as unscriptural and infamous. She admired modern science, bourgeois political economy, and modern culture, but she sought to bend them to the service of her class and society—to the perpetuation of a slaveholding elite within a slave society. Women's clearly defined roles as women—in a word, gender relations—constituted an integral aspect of this project. Women who challenged those prescribed roles threatened the foundations of slave society, of Christian society, of all civilized society. Women who accepted them inevitably accepted limitations. In return, they gained protection against their weakness, respect for their particular excellence, and an unchallenged status as ruling ladies.[78]

Caius Gracchus offers a marvelous panorama of Louisa McCord's view of the world and her own place in it. *Gracchus* features the widowed Cornelia; her son, Caius; her daughter-in-law, Lucinia; her infant grandson; a variety of senators and citizens; and, as a setting, Rome in turmoil. The plot carries Caius to his death at the hands of the corrupt Senatorial party and confirms the collapse of the Republic. Significantly, Caius himself bears heavy responsibility for the defeat of his cause. For, heedlessly, he has mobilized the lower ranks of the citizenry and unleashed on Rome the irresponsibility of the landless mob. The senators are a bad lot, from whom Rome deserved deliverance, but not at the price of the rabble's triumph. Although bad representatives of their kind, the senators nonetheless represent the shreds of proper order. The mob represents wanton anarchy.

Some years before the loss of her husband, and a good decade before the loss of her son, Louisa McCord depicted herself in *Caius Gracchus* as a widow who understands the implications of political choices better than the son she cherishes. She never explicitly wrote of her identification with Cornelia, although the bust of her as a Roman matron suggests that she and others took it for granted. Certainly the neoclassical overtones of republican motherhood persisted longer in southern than in northern culture. To take but one example, at the famous dinner, during the height of the Nullification controversy, at which Andrew Jackson toasted "our Federal Union—It must be preserved," the eighteenth toast was to Virginia—likened to the mother of the Gracchi. But the sensibility was general and McCord, although not usually given to displays of personal vanity, had reason to hope that she embodied it. As her tragedy ineluctably unfolds, she further depicts herself as possessed of a genuinely public vision. When Lucinia seeks to bind Caius to herself and their son, to retreat to private comforts rather than face the destiny his actions have set in motion, Cornelia gently chides her:

> Alas! I cannot in your cause, my child.
> Our life is for the world. Man doth forget
> His every highest purpose, scorning it;
> And from the level of his high intent
> Doth thus degrade himself.[79]

After Caius's departure, Cornelia experiences her own moment of crippling grief. Yet after a thoughtful pause, she reproves herself for weakness:

> My task is not yet done. Up! up! and work!
> Life yet has duties, and my comfort is
> Yet to fulfil them. Daughter! Daughter! wake!
> We must go seek our boy, who waits us still,
> To show us how his wooden horse can trot!
> Oh! what a motley is this struggling world![80]

It is tempting to leave Louisa McCord there, with her own words that testify to her double grasp of the duties that pertain to life and station and their incarnation in children's toys. Such were the boundaries and the furniture of the imaginative worlds of slaveholding women: duties to their society and their class, made manifest in daily responsibilities to succeeding generations of their families, white and black. But there is more. Although few slaveholding women matched Louisa McCord's breadth and depth of cultural literacy, many of them participated in the same discourse. Louisa McCord presented her self-portrait as Cornelia in the form of a Shakespearean tragedy. Phrases in her poetry unmistakably echo Keats. She liberally sprinkled her writings with French and Latin phrases. And, in choosing Cornelia as her model, she had to know that she was invoking the image of a woman widely celebrated among the leading men of southern politics and letters, who were well read in ancient history. To Robert Y. Hayne, Henry W. Washington, Nathaniel Beverley Tucker, and Benjamin F. Perry, among others, Cornelia, mother of the Gracchi, whose jewels were her sons, stood as a Roman beacon to the true men of the South—just as, to so many of their women, she stood as the embodiment of the virtues of republican motherhood that they aspired to emulate.[81]

Louisa McCord, and innumerable women of her class, wrote in the idiom of the canon, which they adapted to their own specific perceptions. Identifying with the canon, they accepted a discourse predominantly fashioned by men. They regularly employed the generics "he" and "man" to represent the aspirations of humanity, including their own. Writing privately, they wrote directly as women. But when they moved to inscribe their personal experience in the general culture, they accepted man as its embodiment. Their experience as women influenced their appropriations from the canon, but they never wrote as if that experience should result in a separate women's culture. In this respect, they lagged behind or ran ahead of their northern sisters. But then, they assumed culture to be more a matter of class than of gender. Even if they took second place to their men in education and intellectual ambition—and Louisa McCord did not—they viewed themselves, together with the men of their class, as heirs and custodians of a great Christian civilization.

6   *Women Who Opposed Slavery*

White notions of the appropriate relations between women and men circumscribed many aspects of black lives, but although slave women suffered the restrictions of white gender conventions, they enjoyed few of the attendant protections. Slave women did not embrace white conventions as the model of their own womanhood, but those conventions did figure among the conditions within which they shaped their own ideals. The slaves' gender conventions resulted from a combination of West African traditions, white influences, and their own experiences within the Afro-American slave community. Transplantation to the New World, however violent and disorienting, never eradicated African conventions but did divorce them from the material and institutional conditions in which they had flourished; and it exposed the slaves to the power of masters with views and attitudes different from their own.[1]

The masters' conventions, as they developed, established the dominant pattern for gender relations in the South. That dominance hardly determined the ways in which slave women viewed themselves or even the gender relations of the slave community, but it did delineate the prevailing patterns of southern society confirmed by law and religion. Dominance, however, provided no guarantee that the slaveholders would observe their own conventions in their relations with their slaves. Minimally, slaveholders viewed their slaves as women and men and even tried to promote orderly gender relations, notably marriage, among them, but they did not consider themselves bound by gender conventions in their treatment of slaves.

The slaveholders' refusal to view their slaves as ladies and gentlemen entailed more than a refusal to grant them genteel social status. It withheld minimal respect for those attributes of masculinity and femininity that the slaveholders prized most highly for themselves. The popular images of "Buck" and "Sambo" and "Jezebel" and "Mammy" captured dominant white views of gender roles among slaves and, not least, white anxieties about their relations with servants whom they had tried to deprive of autonomy in gender roles as in all else. These conventions did not reflect the slaves' views, although there is painful irony in their having sometimes represented caricatures of slave values—the strength of men and the motherhood of women.

The notion of Buck—a white gender convention—represented a caricature or reversal of the notion of cavalier. It encoded white male fears of black sexuality in particular and of virility in general. The convention of the Buck emphasized white views of the single, sexually active black male as divorced from other social roles. As a shadow image of the cavalier, it reflected whites' bad faith about the master-slave relation. Since slave law denied the legality of black marriage and ownership of property, it is hardly surprising that the white image of the black man should have divorced sexuality from reproduction and social responsibility, including the protection of women. The Buck evoked a sexually active, perpetual adolescent. Implicitly, it also evoked the threat of black sexuality to white women—a fascinating reversal since the main interracial sexual threat was that of white predators against black women. The presumed threat of black male sexuality never provoked the wild hysteria and violence in the Old South that it did in the New, but self-proclaimed slaveholding paternalists harbored their own anxieties.

The image of Sambo inverted that of Buck and embodied a reversal of white attitudes toward masculinity. For Sambo captured an image of docility in direct opposition to the white ideals of male honor. Divorced from the image of Buck, it offered an image of the black man as naturally subservient to the will of the white, as too lazy and supine to care about self-defense, much less the honorable attributes of freedom. The image reassured whites of their own ability to control their slaves—and of their safety within households in which slaves outnumbered them.

Similarly, the convention of the Mammy reflected recognizable white values. If implicitly the idea of the Mammy referred to motherhood and reproduction, it also claimed those privileges for the masters rather than for the slaves themselves. Just as Buck signaled the threat of master-slave relations, Mammy signaled the wish for organic harmony and projected a woman who suckled and reared white masters. The image displaced sexuality into nurture and transformed potential hostility into sustenance and love. It claimed for the white family the ultimate devotion of black women, who reared the children of others as if they were their own. Although the image of the Mammy echoed the importance that black slaves attached to women's roles as mothers, it derived more from the concerns of the master than from those of the slave. Presumably, it bore some relation to the masters' complex feelings about motherhood and, like the image of the Buck, testified to an abiding childishness that informed the appearance of command. Yet neither Buck nor Mammy faithfully captured the most common and direct influences of the gender conventions of the masters on the lives of the slaves.[2]

The image of Jezebel explicitly contradicted the image of Mammy and that of the lady as well, although, like that of Mammy and unlike that of the lady, it presented a woman isolated from the men of her own community. Jezebel lived free of the social constraints that surrounded the sexuality of white women. She thus legitimated the wanton behavior of white men by proclaiming black women to be lusty wenches in whom sexual impulse overwhelmed all restraint. The image eased the consciences of white men by suggesting that black women asked for the treatment they received.[3]

These four images betrayed the whites' discomfort with their own attitudes toward their slaves' relations to gender conventions. Each image represented a caricature of attributes that whites celebrated in themselves. Each emphasized physical attributes over social, as if whites had difficulty depicting their slaves in adult gender roles. In many instances, slaveholders did recognize their dependents as women and men with distinct personalities, but they had difficulty in recognizing them as social beings. This conflicted attitude on the part of the whites permeated the slaves' experience of the gender conventions by which they were constrained but by no means defined.

Sojourner Truth, in her famous speech to the women's rights advocates of the North, directly addressed the relation between the experience of slave women and the white conventions of womanhood. Those conventions, she angrily insisted, had not applied to slave women, who nonetheless remained women. White men had denied, and slave men had been unable to provide, slave women with the protection

conventionally accorded white women. Sojourner Truth was address-
ing a northern audience for whom the status of woman essentially
subsumed that of lady in an ideological commitment to equality
among women and the recognition of womanhood itself as the social
role of all women, whereas in the South, even a white woman required
the status of lady in order to enjoy the full social protection of gender
conventions. And Truth might also have pointed out that southern
slave women were doubly removed from that protection. As slaves
they had no claim to the status of lady, and as blacks they had trouble
establishing even their claim to the status of woman. Much more
readily at risk than their white sisters in the turbulent public sphere of
the antebellum South, they were at risk in the domestic sphere as well.
The conditions of slavery stripped slave women of most of the attributes of the conventional female role.[4]

For the slaveholders, gender conventions included a strong component of social stratification as well as a foundation for personal identity. For the slaves, many of whom also responded to the appeal of
social "quality," gender conventions derived their primary importance
from their role in organizing and perpetuating the slave community.
Both groups recognized the importance of gender conventions in the
life of black people, but the slaveholders saw them primarily as a means
of control, whereas the slaves saw them primarily as an anchor for
individual and collective identity. Gender conventions, as manifested
in the everyday lives of slaves, penetrated the continual struggle in
which they defended their own views as forcefully as their condition
between white household and slave community would permit.[5]

If, in assigning tasks, masters normally assigned most slaves to separate women's and men's gangs, they also assigned slave women to
work that they would not have considered appropriate for white
women. They were less likely to assign slave men to tasks that would
not have been considered appropriate for white men. Bennet Barrow
perversely confirmed a master's awareness of the importance of gender
conventions to slaves' sense of themselves, for he violated those conventions as a means of humiliation. On one occasion he set three
rugged field hands to washing clothes; on another he forced certain
"Bucks" to wear women's clothing. Lizzie Barker's mother's mistress
punished her for a theft of which she had been wrongfully accused by
making her wear trousers for a year. Once, when her mistress was
away, Victoria Adams put on a pair of pants "an scrub de floor wid
them on." Another slave reported her, and "Missums told me it was a
sin for me to put on a man's pants, and she whip me pretty bad." The

mistress claimed that the Bible said that "A man shall not put on a woman's clothes, nor a woman put on a man's clothes." Victoria Adams never saw that in the Bible, "but from then 'til now, I ain't put on no more pants." Most slaveholders probably did not indulge in malicious perversity or invoke the Bible to enforce observance of dress codes, but neither did they underestimate the importance of gender identity to their servants.[6]

For self-interested or disinterested reasons masters encouraged their slaves to observe facsimiles of white gender conventions. They encouraged "marriage" among their slaves, and motherhood even more. They valued piety among their slaves, much as among their own women—provided that it did not lead to independent thought. They provided women with skirts and men with pants. At worst, they reduced gender to mere sexuality in their relations with their slaves, ignoring the attributes of manhood and womanhood that might encourage an independent identity for individuals or for the slave community. Unable to reduce their slaves to mere chattel, they could still dominate them in innumerable ways, notably through their own sexual exploitation of slave women. Despite occasional examples of tenderness and loyalty between masters and slave concubines, the masters' unchecked power over their slave women brought into the center of the household that public violence against which white women were protected. And while it demeaned slave women, it also threatened to unman slave men. Violation of the conventions emerged as the attack of one people and one class upon another.[7]

Gender conventions never provided slave women with a seamless casing for their own identities. One facet of those identities derived from their membership in the plantation household, in which they functioned primarily as individuals in relation to the other members of "the family, white and black." Their gender carried significance for the ways in which others related to them, but little significance for their identities as members of a larger social system. Another facet of their identities derived from membership in the community of slaves, which overlapped with but also frequently transcended the plantation household, and within which gender did constitute an important form of social organization. Slave women drew from that community their most important sense of themselves as women in relation to men, children, and other women, for it provided the context for their independent lives as sisters, wives, daughters, mothers, and friends. The household nonetheless cast a long shadow over the slave community, which remained bound by the white society that encircled it and which it permeated.

In most of North American slave society, the overwhelming majority of slaves lived closer to the whites, who outnumbered them, than did slaves in the Caribbean or even in the Carolina-Georgia low-country. In 1860, 75 percent of all American slaves lived on plantations of fewer than fifty slaves, and more than half lived on farms of twenty or fewer. Yet the slave community remained rooted in the households of twenty or more slaves, which had clusters of slaves large enough to support a solid community life. From these clusters, ties among slaves extended throughout the county or district and beyond them throughout the state and region. Kinship ties established interlocking networks of slaves, as did the churches, whether established by whites or blacks. Since well over 90 percent of the slaves were illiterate, the threads that bound them together were primarily oral. Yet word-of-mouth transmissions traveled like the echoes of African drums, with successive recipients' picking up the relay and passing it on. Letters written for slaves by members of their white families helped to sustain the links, but they could not possibly reveal all the slaves were thinking. Afro-American religion and folklore testify to the slaves' determination to preserve and transform their discrete African heritage, but they were never able to do so in complete isolation from white influence.[8]

In the Caribbean—where blacks vastly outnumbered whites, slaves customarily grew their own food on individual plots, and continual importation ensured a high proportion of native Africans among the slave community—slave women enjoyed much greater opportunity to preserve or recreate African patterns intact. In North America, such opportunities were rare. The dominant white conventions did not, as many West African societies did, ascribe to women a special association with agricultural labor and marketing. Slave women's participation in the heaviest forms of agricultural labor violated white conventions and thereby emphasized the status of slave over that of woman. Many Caribbean slave women at least partially retained a positive association with agriculture and marketing, but largely because of their greater separation from white cultural influences. In the South, most slave women could not do the same. To the extent that they participated in incidental gardening and marketing, they did so to contribute an "extra" rather than basic subsistence. They clearly had a strong sense of themselves as women in relation to slave men, but if that sense owed something to their African past, it derived from remembered tradition rather than from the daily reenactment of fundamental social relations of production.[9]

During the nineteenth century, middle-class domesticity emerged as the dominant model of gender relations for American society. White southerners, especially slaveholders, embraced important features of it, even though the social relations of slavery contradicted some of its fundamental premises. Features of that model, especially the emphasis on bonds between parents and children, appealed to slaves as well as to slaveholders; yet in the case of slaves, in contrast to slaveholders, the model did not derive directly from their own traditions. The slaves came, not from European societies that had long been developing an interrelated system of ideas about conjugal relations, motherhood, and absolute property, but from African societies with very different ideas about personal and property relations.[10]

Relations of property and marriage constitute fundamental systems whereby all societies establish links between their deepest beliefs about gender relations (relations between men and women) and relations of power (who rules whom and in the name of what). Since the relations between men and women lie at the core of any viable society and individual identity, the most extreme consequence of ruthless domination may well consist in the destruction of those relations. Conversely, the successful domination of one people by another almost invariably includes concessions to those relations and attempts to bind them to the acceptance of that domination as a legitimate order. All societies attach importance to the differences between women and men and draw upon them in their elaboration of social and political institutions, but they vary widely in their interpretation of the differences.[11]

The southern model of womanhood did not protect slave women from hard physical labor or undermine their emotional self-reliance, any more than it protected them from the abuse of white—or black— men. For slave women did not institutionally suffer the domination or enjoy the protection of their own men. As husbands and fathers, slave men lacked the backing of the law. Among the slaves conjugal domesticity figured more as an act of faith, and the domination of women figured more as personal violence, than either did as established practice in the larger society. Enslavement prevented them from simply adopting white models of gender relations. Slave women and men could hardly ground their personal and community identities in "normal" middle-class models of the proper relations between women and men, for they could not establish legally binding marriages or assert legal authority over their own children.

Slaveholders, with varying degrees of enthusiasm and good faith, encouraged slaves to observe the patterns of conjugal domesticity that they valued for themselves, and the slaves, for their own reasons, frequently did. But slaveholders and slaves both knew that the forms remained fragile in the absence of solid institutional foundations. Slavery, as abolitionists were quick to point out, made a mockery of marriage and family life. Afro-American slave women transmitted their condition to their offspring even if the fathers were free. Their "marriages" to black men, slave or free, had no status at law. They could be separated from spouse or children without any recourse except personal pleas. Slave men could not protect their "wives" from the sexual assaults of white men. The slave "family" depended entirely on personal ties, which historically have required the support of legal, economic, and social sanctions. "Husbands" did not support their wives, who worked at the will of the master. They did not provide for their children or even fully determine their preparation for adult life. Under favorable conditions, a slave couple might lead a life comparable to that of rural or urban workers, but the similarities are more deceptive than instructive. The slaves' legal status weighed heavily on them. A recently emancipated slave made the point in the words with which Louisa McCord would so heartily have concurred: *"I praise God for this day!* I have long been praying for it. The Marriage Covenant is at the foundation of all our rights. In slavery we could not have *legalised* marriage: *now* we have it. Let us conduct ourselves worthy of such a blessing—and all the people will respect us—God will bless us, and we shall be established as a people."[12]

With time, Afro-American slaves absorbed a heavy dose of the larger society's attitudes. Evidence reveals that a concern for family held consuming importance for Afro-Americans both in slavery times and after emancipation. Hence, historians have stressed the semblance of conjugal domesticity that many slaves sought to sustain, and they have implicitly reasoned from it to a picture of the slave cabin as a bravely defended if precarious home. Doubtless some commitment to an idea of home did inform slaves' attitudes toward their cabins, but the slaves knew better than any that the cabin home did not benefit from any of the supports, in absolute property or even legal marriage, that buttressed its free equivalent. After slavery, Afro-American men and women struggled mightily to implement their own free homes, complete with primarily domestic wives, and they resisted to the best of their abilities the need for a married woman to work outside the home. Under slavery they did not have such opportunities to protect family life, however much they nurtured an ideal of parents and children as a primary unit. It remains difficult to determine whether they found the white version of middle-class domesticity a compelling ideal, although it is clear that antebellum free blacks, like late-nineteenth-century, middle-class blacks, valued it highly as a sign of respectability.[13]

Both in their acceptance of and resistance to white norms, the slaves established distinct limits to the power of the slaveholders, which always fell short of the total power that the latter desired. Had such limitations not applied, there would be scant justification for talking about the slaves' gender relations and roles, for total power strips away the wrappings of gender, race, and class in which the sense of self normally comes swathed. Conversely, had the slaveholders not exercised considerable power over the daily lives of their slaves, those slaves might, like many Caribbean slaves, have more readily built upon their African cultural inheritance. Behind Sojourner Truth's angry question—"and ar'n't I a woman?"—lay the implicit corollary: And whereby am I a woman? For slave women the answer lay astride the household and the slave community, astride two competing sets of gender conventions.

The lives of slave women, which unfolded between the plantation household and the slave community, constituted a compromise between an African past and a slaveholder-dominated American present, but the compromise was grounded in the slaves' own Afro-American present, which owed something to both and replicated neither. The American model of gender relations was predicated upon the ideal of the freedom of the individual man. But because, in the South, that ideal was predicated upon slavery as a social system, a fundamental contradiction informed the slaves' relation to it. However attractive, the essence of the ideal remained beyond the slaves' grasp. Yet the contradiction itself rendered the ideal compelling. African models of gender relations also remained influential, and kin networks persisted that granted, for example, special roles to the mother's brother. But in the absence of material foundations in African kin and productive relations, they could not fully ground the slaves' sense of themselves as members of the larger society.

Nor could slave women develop an "African" model of womanhood that emphasized their independence and self-reliance as women in contrast to white women's dependence on and subordination to white men. However attractive the view that they did, it does not take adequate account of slave women's relations with the men of their own community or with those of white society. The strongest case for the autonomy of slave women lies in their freedom from the domestic domination of their men—in their independent roles as working members of the household. Yet to emphasize their independence vis-à-vis slave men means to underscore their dependence upon—or subjection to—their owners. Slave women did not live free of male domination; they lived free of the legally enforceable domination of "their own" men. White slaveholding men did exercise legal power over slave women. White male heads of slaveholding households provided slave women with food, lodging, clothing, and medical care, assigned them tasks, supervised their work, disciplined them, determined the destiny of their children, and could impose nonnegotiable sexual demands. Those same white masters presumed to intervene forcefully and by legal right to "protect" black women against abusive husbands. The power of the master constituted the fundamental condition of slave women's lives, however much it was hedged in by the direct and subtle resistance of the women themselves.

Slave women, like slave men, lived in a world in which no solid or independently guaranteed institutions mediated between their basic relations of gender and the master's power. Under adverse circumstances they did their best to develop a collective sense of community legitimacy to substitute for institutions grounded in law. Their ideal lay somewhere between the whites' notions of domesticity and African notions of tribe and lineage. Both systems predicated fundamental distinctions and appropriate relations between men and women, but they organized those relations in different social forms that expressed their discrete politics and political economies. Slave women forged their own identities as women in their relations with slave men, but they did so under the political and economic domination of their masters.

In Africa, gender relations articulated and frequently constituted social relations of production as well as reproduction. The experience of slave women displayed important continuities from Africa to the New World, but the gender relations of precolonial African society derived much of their cogency from their articulation of the kinship systems that accounted for much of African social relations. Forced transplantation to the Americas disrupted those kinship relations, which Afro-American slaves could only attempt to reconstitute and adapt under the specific conditions of enslavement.[14]

In precolonial West Africa, women lived and worked primarily within households that might be, but frequently were not, composed exclusively of family members. During the seventeenth and eighteenth centuries, West Africa remained overwhelmingly but not exclusively agricultural, and the patterns of women's occupations varied from one society to another. In Bamenda (Cameroon), women played important roles in farming; in Yorubaland they were active in trading; and in all societies they engaged in occupational specializations that cut across gender lines. Throughout the precolonial period, African peoples were developing increasingly complex states based upon increasingly intricate social stratification. Conquest and interregional trade complicated and accelerated the process and brought indigenous forms of slavery and servitude. The need for labor within a growing preindustrial economy also encouraged polygyny. Throughout these manifold changes, West African women from the peasantry to the upper classes continued to enjoy traditional rights in the property of their lineage that permitted them some independence within marriage—at least among the non-Muslim peoples. Although divorce was possible upon the initiation of either party, marriage remained a fundamental institution and was not taken lightly.[15]

In many West African societies, gender persisted as a primary form of social organization that influenced the development of such political institutions as the position of Queen Mother among the Ashanti. In many others, in which family affiliation outweighed gender identification, some women continued to exercise positions of great power as the delegates of families. Even among peoples who had been influenced by Islamic ideas of domestic confinement, women frequently continued to exercise their marketing functions by substituting the family compound for the village square as the site of their activities. By the seventeenth and eighteenth centuries, West Africa, with growing cities, markets, and states, was far removed from a simple society of peasant families and lineages, although it had not embarked on capitalist development and although the peasantry continued to constitute its basic social class. If it remained a congeries of societies in which free women of different classes continued to enjoy substantial rights as members of lineages and sometimes as members of a gender, it nonetheless constituted an aggregation of hierarchical societies in which some women enjoyed substantially greater privileges than others and in which men generally held a monopoly of positions of military and political power.[16]

Our knowledge of the status of West African women during the precolonial period remains woefully inadequate, but the little we do know defies any utopian picture of women's independence and power. At best we can speculate that their position within lineages and communities permitted them considerable independence in their everyday lives and required that they contribute fully to economic production. In these ways, and possibly in others, West African society may well have encouraged women to develop a high degree of self-reliance and self-respect, especially within a defined sphere. But an African peasant society was no more likely than any other peasant society to have encouraged women to view themselves as autonomous, much less to view themselves as natural political and military leaders of men. In the long run, the coming of the Europeans strengthened the domination of African men over women and above all increased men's economic opportunities relative to those of women, but during the early colonial period some women managed to carve out powerful positions for themselves as mediators between African and European slavetraders and even by entering the trade themselves. In conformity with their personal, social, and economic opportunities, women might become slaves, slaveowners, or slavetraders.[17]

In African communities, as in other premodern societies from ancient Babylonia and Israel to early modern Italy, slavery took a variety of forms ranging from a harsh chattel slavery to a relatively mild domestic slavery that approximated indentured servitude. Enslavement for women could frequently continue their free gender roles, albeit under unfree conditions. Yet Claude Meillassoux has argued that enslavement in Africa could also strip women, as it could strip men, of all kinship ties and, in effect, subject them to a social neutrality that included depersonalization and, especially for women, desexualization. If precolonial West African societies exploited women's labor, they also endowed femininity in general and motherhood in particular with a sacred character. Slavery negated the sacredness—in effect negated womanhood as an ideological category. In the absence of an ideology of womanhood—an ideology of gender difference—female slaves lost a vital part of the basis for gender solidarity and identification.[18]

Meillassoux assumes a worst-case scenario of the effects of enslavement: a dehumanization of the slave reminiscent of Stanley Elkins's flawed view of the experience of Afro-American slaves. Whatever the African case, Afro-American slaves did build communities in enslavement, did not suffer total alienation and depersonalization, and did adapt at least some of their African traditions to new conditions. The traditions underwent drastic transformation but were not eradicated and, in interaction with the imposed gender conventions of the slaveholders, reemerged as part of Afro-American culture. Orlando Patterson's concept of slavery as "social death" illuminates the dark side of the picture. For the relations among slave women and men remained essentially personal rather than social, to the extent that they lacked institutional grounding. The reconstitution of gender relations among slaves required time. For slaves drawn from a variety of peoples and places, even if they had already been enslaved in Africa, the initial period of the middle passage and relocation in the southern colonies inescapably entailed an experience of uprootedness and personal isolation.[19]

If prior enslavement in Africa had not already uprooted women, their purchase and transportation by European slavetraders normally separated them from the men of their own kinship and probably disrupted accepted patterns of relations between men and women. Under these conditions, women experienced their own enslavement as isolated individuals.[20] Their arrival in the southern colonies during the late seventeenth and early eighteenth centuries did not introduce them to a more settled world. Many planters, with an eye to quick profits, exploited female slaves to the limits of physical endurance and sometimes beyond, with little regard to the niceties of male and female tasks. Many women initially found themselves enslaved to small households, in regions in which whites outnumbered blacks, and accordingly had no substantial slave community to turn to. Under unsettled frontier conditions, they married late and bore even fewer children than did white women in the same areas.[21]

Throughout the eighteenth century, southern slave society gradually took shape, albeit at different rates according to region, and also with considerable variation in women's experience, especially according to the size of slaveholdings and the concentration of blacks. It remains unclear how rapidly the contours of a slave community appeared, much less how gender relations among slaves and between slaves and whites developed, although some scholars believe that slave communities had begun to coalesce by the middle of the eighteenth century. Frontier conditions led whites—and not only indentured servants—to engage in sexual relations with and even to marry slave women. From the earliest period, whites displayed a strong sense of gender differences, although initially they may have had a less strong sense of class and racial differences. This social fluidity opened spaces in which slave women could establish personal relations with whites and test the limits of their enslavement, although in general their resistance helped to provoke the consolidation of white domination. Unsettled conditions also permitted slaves to withdraw completely from white society by founding maroon colonies, or to attempt to reshape it by forging class alliances with poor whites and Indians, especially on the frontier. In the face of concerted opposition from the slaveholding elite and a steady increase in the white population, those attempts ultimately failed, but slave women participated actively in all of them, including maroon colonies and outright revolts, in which they frequently figured among the leaders. Such struggles varied according to time, place, and size of plantation, but they never matched the massive rebellions or powerful maroon societies that marked other areas of the Western Hemisphere. Each successive strengthening of white authority further tied slave women's possibilities for resistance to gender lines.[22]

We do not know whether slave women played such active roles in the early slave revolts because African traditions of independence prompted their assertiveness or because the dislocation of the middle passage and unsettled conditions had cut them adrift from conventional gender expectations. We do know that white men's attitudes toward the roles of women—including slave women—reduced their ability to recognize and record women's active rebellion and reduced the punishments they allotted to those women whose rebellion they were forced to acknowledge. Following a revolt in Louisiana in the early 1770s, Mariana received one hundred lashes and lost her ears for her part—a substantially lighter punishment, notwithstanding its cruelty, than that meted out to her male coconspirators, Temba and Pedro, despite her apparent status as leader. The law did not distinguish between male and female slaves, but the determination of punishments was left to individual judges who might. Sometimes, to be sure, women were punished as severely as men for their roles in conspiracies or for suspicion of arson. Some were burned alive. Yet on balance, at least if we take the slave period as a whole, Mariana's experience was closer to the norm, and some women escaped punishment altogether.[23]

The easiest form of personal resistance to slavery was simply to run away, yet apparently by the eighteenth century in Virginia and South Carolina women were less likely than men to do so. Perhaps white preconceptions about gender hedged women in more stringently than men; perhaps as slave communities gradually developed women were more loath to leave friends and kin. Whatever the reasons, the eighteenth-century advertisements for runaways include far fewer references to women than to men: in South Carolina, about 25 percent during the middle decades of the century; in Virginia, 11 percent between 1736 and 1801; in Georgia, 13 percent during the thirteen years before the Revolution. It would be rash to conclude that women were intrinsically more docile or reconciled to slavery than men. They may have had more trouble in passing unobserved outside the plantation, and they clearly felt a more direct responsibility for their children than their men did.[24]

Some slaveholders simply assumed that a missing woman had only gone to visit kin in the neighborhood. In 1818, an advertisement from the *Carolina Centinel* of New Bern, North Carolina, requested help in securing the return of a female runaway who had already been known to be absent for a considerable period of time, during which she had been "harboured" by slaves on various plantations in the neighborhood. Another advertisement from the *Virginia Gazette* of Williamsburg, in 1767, sought assistance in recovering a female slave who clearly had been anything but docile: "Hannah, about 35 years of age, had on when she went away a green plains petticoat, and sundry other clothes, but what sort I do not know, as she stole many from the other Negroes." Hannah was described as having remarkable "long hair, or wool," as being "much scarified under the throat from one ear to the other," and as having "many scars on her back, occasioned by whipping." The master clearly regarded Hannah as a serious runaway. "She pretends much to the religion the Negroes of late have practised, and may probably endeavour to pass for a free woman, as I understand she intended when she went away, by the Negroes in the neighbourhood." He believed that, under the pretense of being a "free woman," she was heading for Carolina. The two advertisements reflected the combination of actual conditions and masters' perceptions: A slave woman might "visit" on neighboring plantations on which she would disappear among the other slaves without causing comment or provoking a search—at least initially. If she undertook serious flight, she would probably have to attempt to pass for a free woman in order to have a plausible reason to be abroad. Some women ran away to join groups of maroons, but apparently in much fewer numbers than men and with diminishing frequency as the possibilities for establishing maroon societies were eroded. During the Revolution women, like men, ran away to the British and, at least in Georgia, constituted the larger proportion of all runaways.[25]

Unsettled conditions had permitted slaves to seize a variety of personal opportunities to which they had no official right, but one colony after another gradually implemented laws that defined and circumscribed the condition of the slave. In South Carolina, the comprehensive Negro Act of 1740, which followed in the wake of the Stono Rebellion, explicitly proscribed slaves from "freedom of movement, freedom of assembly, freedom to raise food, to earn money, to learn to read English." This legislation and the determination it represented established the ownership and discipline of slaves as a matter of class, not merely individual, responsibility. It may also have sharpened the distinction between male and female forms of resistance and revolt, if only by systematizing the constraints of enslavement and thus making some forms of women's activity more visible. To put it differently, the law may have begun to subject female slaves to the same structural constraints that relegated white women to households and male supervision.[26]

By the time of Stono, slave revolts had become primarily male affairs. At least, no women are known to have participated as leaders. During the eighteenth century some revolts had begun to assume a distinct military—and masculine—cast, which distinguished them from the ubiquitous, informal peasant and servile rebellions known throughout the world. Stono started with twenty black men, who marched southwest toward St. Augustine with "colors flying and two drums beating." Vincent Harding emphasizes the importance that those rebellious slave men attached to their having become soldiers: "Sounding the forbidden drums, they were warriors again." In Africa, women did occasionally fight as soldiers, but Africans, like Europeans, normally viewed organized warfare as primarily a male affair. In this matter, as in many others, the models promoted by white society may well have corresponded to the Africans' own traditions.[27]

Although the eighteenth century witnessed a growing tendency for men to specialize in military revolt, they continued to conspire with women to kill overseers and slaveholders. In December 1774, the *Georgia Gazette* of Savannah reported the "following melancholy account, viz.":

That on Tuesday morning the 29th ult. six new Negro fellows and four wenches, belonging to Capt. Morris, killed the Overseer in the field, after which they went to the house, murdered his wife, and dangerously wounded a carpenter named Wright, also a boy who died the next day; they then proceeded to the house of Angus McIntosh, whom they likewise dangerously wounded; and being there joined by a sensible fellow, the property of said Mc-Intosh, they went to the house of Roderick M'Leod, wounded him very much, and killed his son, who had fired upon them on their coming up and broke the arm of the fellow who had joined them. Their leader and McIntosh's negro have been taken and burnt, and two of the wenches have returned to the plantation.

Again, for reasons best known to themselves, the white authorities did not see fit to punish the "wenches" as severely as the men. Perhaps such concerted actions, which often began in the fields, declined during the nineteenth century because women were increasingly separated from men in the fields.[28]

During the eighteenth century, at least in such settled regions as the Virginia tidewater and the South Carolina lowcountry, specialization of skills according to gender offered female slaves other opportunities for resistance. As cooks and house servants, they were in a privileged position for poisoning, the ubiquitous fear of which did much to exacerbate the disquiet of the slaveholding class. The South Carolinians, especially concerned to control their large slave and free black population, did their best to anticipate danger through legislation. In 1751, they passed an addition to the Negro Act of 1740 that prescribed punishment for any black who should instruct another "in the knowledge of any poisonous root, plant, herb, or other poison whatever, he or she, so offending shall upon conviction thereof suffer death as a felon." The law also prohibited physicians, apothecaries, or druggists from admitting slaves to places in which drugs were kept or allowing them to administer drugs to other slaves. This kind of legislation and the cautious spirit it reflected may have decreased slaves' access to drugs but could not abolish it entirely. It was completely ineffective in controlling black women's knowledge of and access to poisonous herbs, gleaned from African as well as Indian and other American lore, which they transmitted down through the generations.[29]

Even when poison could not be detected as the cause of death, it was frequently suspected. In Georgia, "an old sullen house negress" complained to a fellow slave, who reported her, of having misjudged the necessary amount of arsenic: "I thought my master and mistress would get enough, but it was not sufficient." Another slave woman profited from her position as a nurse to poison an infant and to attempt to do the same to her master. She was burned alive in Charleston, together with the slave man who had supplied the poison.[30]

Charlestonians, who lived in the midst of an expanding slave and free black population that could never fully be contained within slaveholding households, were especially vigilant about any sign of disrespect for the conventions of hierarchy. In 1808 a group of them requested that the legislature consider slave apparel with the gravity it deserved. The dress of persons of color had become so expensive "as to tempt the slaves to dishonesty; to give them ideas not consistent with their conditions; to render them insolent to the whites, and so fond of parade and show as to cause it extremely difficult to keep them at home." They should only be allowed to wear coarse materials. Liveries were another matter, for they, no matter how elaborate, constituted a badge of servitude. But it was necessary "to prevent the slaves from wearing silks, satins, crapes, lace muslins, and such costly stuffs, as are looked upon and considered the luxury of dress." An orderly slave society required that "every distinction should be created between the whites and the negroes, calculated to make the latter feel the superiority of the former."[31]

By the 1820s, southern society had drawn tight lines around the condition of slaves and, in the interest of securing control of its troublesome property, increasingly curtailed the freedoms of free blacks. The Gabriel Prosser (1800) and Denmark Vesey (1822) revolts had starkly revealed the dreaded possibilities, which were terrifyingly confirmed by the Nat Turner revolt in 1831. In the absence of legally binding slave marriage, and because slaves's access to property was negligible and therefore devoid of political significance, the law of slavery had no cause to differentiate between women and men. Its gender blindness, which acknowledged women only as the transmitters of the condition of slavery—and which did not recognize the rape of slave women as a crime—stolidly proclaimed that, in all formal respects, a slave was a slave was a slave. Yet as southern society coalesced, slaveholders and slaves alike showed a growing propensity to differentiate slave women from their men. This tendency reflected the growing cohesion of both white southern society and the slave community, as well as a growing recognition of the class divisions and antagonisms that separated slaveholders from slaves, notwithstanding the persistence of a paternalistic ethos.[32]

Within the slave community, these tendencies resulted in a view of violent, organized revolt as a specialized political and insurrectionary male responsibility. None of the most visible revolts took a woman's name; none of them were attributed to a woman's leadership. Nor did slave women organize any of those "women's" revolts which were common in Europe and Africa. No major rebellion was composed entirely, or even primarily, of women and ascribed to the defense of woman's sphere. North American slave society generated no "Nanny," no Igbo "Women's Riot," no protest that can be compared to women's subsistence protests in early modern Europe.[33]

During the antebellum period, slave women's resistance was likely to be individual rather than collective. Even their forms of individual resistance differed somewhat from those of men, in part because of their reproductive capacities, in part because of Afro-American attitudes toward womanhood, and in part because of the various opportunities offered and denied by white gender conventions.[34] In innumerable ways, from biology to interlocking social relations with slaveholders and with other slaves, women's everyday lives were organized by gender. Both slaves and slaveholders had strong, if different, reasons to view their lives as in some sense organically linked and as bound by mutual obligations and responsibilities. This view, which always consisted of both substance and froth, depended heavily on the recognition of gender relations as the anchor for individual identity. Yet the relations of slavery in the abstract, notably the law of slavery, barely recognized slave women as women, and testy masters and mistresses frequently failed to do so in daily practice. Slaveholders always wrestled with the temptation—to which they frequently succumbed— to view slaves above all as the extensions of their own wills, the instruments of their own responsibilities. When provoked, slave women, who were never deceived on the matter, responded in kind.

Mistresses and slaves lived in tense bonds of conflict-ridden intimacy that frequently exploded into violence on one side or the other. Everyday proximity to mistresses permitted slave women special kinds of psychological resistance, the consequences of which are almost impossible to assess. Impudence and "uppityness," which derived from intimate knowledge of a mistress's weak points, demonstrated a kind of resistance and frequently provoked retaliation out of all proportion to the acts, if not the spirit. Because the mistress lacked the full authority of the master, her relations with her servants could easily lapse into a personal struggle. When servants compounded sauciness and subtle disrespect with a studied cheerful resistance to accomplishing the task at hand, the mistress could rapidly find herself losing control—of herself as well as her servant. "Puttin' on ole massa" must have been, if anything, more trying when practiced by slave women against the mistress. But slave women who worked in the big house were uniquely positioned to resist the message of deference, to undermine the distinctions, and to make the lives of privileged mistresses an unending war of nerves. Withal, it was the mistress, not the servant, who held the whip and who, much more often than not, initiated the violence.

Ida Henry's unpredictable mistress could be either tolerant or mean. One day the cook was passing potatoes at table and "old Mistress felt of one and as hit wasn't soft done, she exclaimed to de cook, 'What you bring these raw potatoes out here for?' and grab a fork and stuck hit in her eye and put hit out." Once Anna Dorsey, failing to hear her mistress call her, continued with her work until the mistress "burst out in a frenzy of anger over the woman not answering." Despite Anna Dorsey's protestations, her mistress "seized a large butcher knife and struck at Anna," who, "attempting to ward off the blow, . . . received a long gash on the arm that laid her out for some time." Hannah Plummer's mother's mistress "whipped her most every day, and about anything. Mother said she could not please her in anything, no matter what she done or how hard she tried." Once, the mistress returned from town especially angry and "made mother strip down to her waist, and then took a carriage whip an' beat her until the blood was runnin' down her back." Hannah Plummer's mother took to the woods, vowing never to come back.[35]

Mistresses and servants did not readily agree about the appropriate standards for work, and resentful slave women frequently shirked to make their point. Years after the event, Tempe Pitts claimed to have deserved a whipping her mistress administered. She had been sent "out in de yar ter scrub de silverware wid some san'." She knew that she was supposed to give it a good scrubbing and wash it off, "but 'sted of dat I leaves hit layin' der in de yard wid de dirt on it." Another woman, who was charged with fanning her sick mistress to keep off the flies, "would hit her all in the face; sometimes I would make out I was sleep and beat her in the face." The mistress, who was so ill that she could not talk, tried to make her husband understand what was going on, but he only understood that the slave woman had fallen asleep and would only send her out to the yard to wake up. This slave was reaping her revenge for years of mean treatment. In innumerable other instances, house maids dusted inattentively, young nurses pulled children's hair, and everyone pretended not to hear or understand instructions. After the war, Frances Butler Leigh noted with exaspera-

Women pounding rice, Sapelo Island, Georgia, late nineteenth century.
Courtesy of Georgia Department of Archives and History

"Old Sarah," ca. 1840. Sarah belonged to five generations and nursed three generations of the Sutton family of Dougherty County, Georgia.
Courtesy of Georgia Department of Archives and History

"Old Sibby," a midwife in Petersville Community, Glynn County, Georgia, ca. 1930.

Courtesy of Georgia Department of Archives and History

tion that, to get blacks to do anything, she had to tell them to do it, show them how to do it, and then do it herself.[36]

In theory slave women had to take the whippings, although they normally viewed them less as a merited punishment than as the price for asserting their own wills in a continuing struggle. As many slave women knew, mistresses' whippings did not represent the ultimate authority. Lou Smith's mistress always played the devil when the master was away. When the master was there, "He made her treat us good but when he was gone she made our lives a misery to us." In other instances, the master's discipline proved more exacting. Easter Wells's mother, a cook, had a master with "some purty strict rules and one of 'em was iffen you burnt de bread you had to eat it." On an especially busy day, her mother burned the bread and, knowing what was coming, took off to the woods for two weeks. Upon her return her master whipped her, but not seriously. "He was glad to get her back."[37]

Sometimes the master's severity threw slave woman and mistress into each other's arms. When Luzanne Kaze burned the biscuits, her master, Marse Drew, whipped her, but her mistress, Miss Cary, gave her salve to rub on her wounds. When Marse Drew found out about Miss Cary's kindness, he told her "dat he gwine touch her up wid his whip . . . dat when he wants his niggers doctored he gwine doctor dem heself." And he "got to use his lash a little bit to make her remember." Fanny Cannady's mistress, Miss Sally, was all sweetness when her husband, Jordan, was away, but when he was there she did anything he told her to do. Fanny's mother spilled some coffee that she was serving him, and he ordered Miss Sally to slap her. Miss Sally's first gentle slap did not satisfy his anger and he ordered, "'Hit her, Sally, hit de black bitch like she 'zerve to be hit.'" After administering the blow, Miss Sally returned to her place at the table and pretended to eat, but as soon as her husband left "she come in de kitchen an' put her arms 'roun' Mammy an' cry, an' Mammy pat her on de back an' she cry too. I loved Miss Sally when Marse Jordan wuzun' 'roun'."[38]

Slave women had their own ideas about the limits of whipping. Some rare women, like Susan Shaw's "mean" African mother, defied all whippings by man or woman, black or white. Lila Nichols knew a woman who once said to her mistress, who had decided to whip her for some offense, "'No Sir, Missus, 'ain't 'lowin' nobody what wa'r de same kind of shirt I does ter whip me.'" Presumably, she would not tolerate being whipped by another woman. Eliza Washington's mother, at about the age of sixteen, got into a fight with her master's son, who was roughly the same age. She was in the kitchen, and he came in with some other white boys to put on dog. He kept threatening her with what he would do if she "didn't hush her mouth." She told him "to just try 'hit, and the fight was on." At the end of an hour's fighting, with the other boys egging them on, she told him "that her old master never did whip her, and she sure wasn't going to let the young one do it." Eliza Washington never heard "that they punished her for whipping her young master."[39]

Young masters could be a problem, especially when they were beginning to taste their power without yet acknowledging its responsibilities. Phoebe Henderson's young master, with no apparent provocation, kicked "my aunt, an old woman who had raised and nursed him." Ellen Cragin's mother had her own reasons for refusing to be whipped by a young master. Once she fell asleep over her loom and the master's boy reported her to his mother, who told him to wake her up with a whip. He grabbed a stick and beat her awake, whereupon "she took a pole out of the loom and beat him nearly to death with it." He backed off begging her to stop. She replied "'I'm goin' to kill you. These black titties suckled you, and then you come out here to beat me.' And when she left him, he wasn't able to walk."[40]

Mary Armstrong never forgave her mistress, Polly, for beating her sister to death and eventually "got some even." One day when Polly tried to give her "a lick out in the yard," she picked "up a rock 'bout as big as half your fist and hits her right in the eye and busted the eyeball, and tells her that's for whippin' my baby sister to death. You could hear her holler for five miles." Polly, to whom Mary Armstrong denied the title "Miss," must have been an unusually unpleasant woman, for her daughter, Miss Olivia, responded to the incident by saying, "'Well I guess Mama has larnt her lesson at last.'" Other mistresses did not get off so lightly. Mrs. Bowman, finding fault with one of her female servants, undertook to punish her herself, "but the girl returned the blow and proved too strong for her mistress—threw her down and beat her unmercifully on the head and face." Rachel O'Connor, who recounted the incident, concluded: "The girl is confined and I expect will be hung. She is an uncommonly smart yellow woman & a first rate house servant." Frederick Law Olmsted noted the case of the beautiful young Virginia Frost, who reproved her servant for insolent language. The servant shot her dead. Another slave woman of whom he heard responded to an admonition from her mistress: "'You can't make me do it, and I won't do it: I ain't afeard of you whipping me.'" He also noted that ladies who did not wish to take on their servants themselves commonly sent them to the public guard house for whipping, but he did not speculate about what the mistresses might expect upon the servants' return.[41]

The personal relations between house slaves and the white family could range from love to hatred, but whatever their emotional quality, they were more likely than not to include a high level of intimacy. Mistresses whipped slave women with whom they might have shared beds, whose children they might have delivered or who might have delivered theirs, whose children they might have suckled and who frequently had suckled theirs. Young masters fought with young slave women with whom they had played as children and whom they might already be attempting to seduce. And masters, who embodied the ultimate authority, might have sexual relations with the women they disciplined and who indeed might be their daughters. Not surprisingly, house slaves felt that they had grounds to resist abuses of authority and even to claim a role in determining its legitimate bounds. Whether the tensions were openly acknowledged or not, slave women's lives in the big house constituted a dense pattern of day-to-day resistance that could at any moment explode into violence.[42]

House slaves believed they had a right to a just share of the goods of the household, to which they enjoyed easier access than other members of the slave community. Cooks and others benefited from their positions to supplement their diets and those of families and friends. House servants were also likely to know who was pilfering what around the place. Fannie Dorum bargained with her master that, if he would not hit her anymore, she would tell him who had been stealing all his eggs. No naïf, he queried, "'Will you tell me, sure 'nough?'" She said she would. "But I never done it." As a rule, house slaves did not look on the lifting of an odd biscuit or cookie or even a helping of meat as a theft, but rather as a perquisite. Slaveholders were much more likely to label small disappearances as thefts, although they were not likely to recognize them as acts of defiance.[43]

Life in the big house also opened opportunities for resistance that could less easily be mistaken. Clara used her position in the big house to search for bullets for her son, who intended to murder his master. He succeeded, and she was convicted with him. Poison was a much more common weapon than bullets, and much more peculiarly women's own. Slaveholders were especially conscious of the threat of poison, although they rarely acknowledged it as a regular feature of their everyday lives. Eliza Magruder noted that a female slave in a neighboring household had tried to poison her mistress and was expected to hang. Betsey, a servant in the Manigault household and "a very wicked woman," was said to have poisoned several children. Mary Chesnut reported the tale of a nurse who killed a child she was nursing. The fears that such tales provoked could lead mistresses into violence against suspected offenders. A slave named Alice brought her sick mistress some water and food, and the mistress got sick to her stomach. "She sez dat Alice done try ter pizen her. Ter sho yo' how sick she wuz, she gits out of de bed, strips dat gal ter de waist an' whips her wid a cowhide till de blood runs down her back. Dat gal's back wuz cut in gashes an' de blood run down ter 'er heels." Thereafter she was chained down until she recovered from her wounds and then "carried off ter Richmond in chains an' sold."[44]

The resistance of house slaves combined features of their identity as women with features of the white gender conventions that assigned them to women's work. Like the resistance of other women, it also embodied a determination to lighten work loads and to reject the worst consequences of enslavement, with no special relation to gender. The resistance of house slaves was, nonetheless, complicated by their personal relations with their mistresses, their masters, and other members of the white family. The resistance of field slaves manifested few of these complications. Like house slaves, field slaves ultimately resisted the master, but in their case his delegate was not the mistress, but an overseer or driver. The overseer, who belonged neither to the white family nor the slave community, was frequently perceived as lacking all claim to legitimate authority. Field women did more than their share to unsettle the overseer's position and to ensure that, on the average, he held his job for no more than three years.[45]

As field workers, women resisted in the same ways as men. Male slaves held no monopoly on the breaking of tools and the challenging and even the murdering of overseers. Even when female slaves worked in the field with other women, they did not work at specifically women's tasks or normally work under the supervision of a woman. Frequently, especially on large plantations, they worked under the supervision of an overseer or a black driver, whom they regarded more as a taskmaster than as a person. Field women fiercely defended their sense of acceptable work loads and violently resisted abuses of power, which for some meant any discipline at all. When anyone started to whip Lily Perry, "I'd bite lak a [rum?] mad dog so dey'd chain my han's." The chains left permanent scars, but the pain did not induce her compliance. "Dey'd also pick me up by de years an' fling me." Once Lily Perry was working around the yard, carrying slops, and, not feeling well, she poured some of the slops out on the ground. The overseer, who observed her, grabbed her up to whip her. "De minute he grabs me I seize on ter his thumb an' I bites hit ter de bone, den he gits mad an' he picks me up an' lifts me higher dan my haid an' flings me down on de steel mat dere in front of de do." She had to be revived with cold water and was sick for a week. Once when Martha Bradley was working in the fields, the overseer "come 'roun and say sumpin' to me he had no bizness say." She took her hoe and "knocked him plum down." Nancy Ward fought with her overseer "for a whole day and stripped him naked as the day he was born."[46]

Some overseers rashly sought confrontations. Irene Coates remembered that one day when a group of women were hoeing, the overseer rode by and struck one of them across the back with a whip. A woman nearby said "that if he ever struck her like that, it would be the day he or she would die." The overseer overheard her and took the first opportunity to strike her with his whip. As he started to ride off, the woman whirled around, struck him on the head with her hoe, knocking him from his horse, and then "pounced upon him and chopped his head off." Then, going temporarily mad, she "proceeded to chop and mutilate his body; that done to her satisfaction, she then killed his horse." Her work completed, she "calmly went to tell the master of the murder." The master asked if she really meant to say that she had killed the overseer and she said yes, and his horse as well. Without hesitation, the master pointed to a small cabin and told her to collect her belongings and move into it. "You are free from this day and if the mistress wants you to do anything for her, do it if you want to." Irene warmly recalled the effect of the incident on subsequent overseers' treatment of the slaves.[47] Irene's story bears all the earmarks of a folktale that was embroidered in transmission, but, whatever its value as fact, it betrays the confidence that slave women could defend themselves and the hope that the master could—at least on occasion—exercise his power on behalf of justice.

Masters were more likely than overseers to take a long-term view of their relations with slave women, and were known to dispatch overseers who could not handle them. Ruben Laird recalled an overseer who started to whip a young field woman for not doing her share of the work. She turned on him "and chased him out of the field with her hoe, whereupon the overseer resigned, stating that Dr. Laird's slaves were too 'ambitious' for him to manage." But masters had to reach their own accommodations with slaves or else sell them. Selina Jordan, who had a merited reputation as a fighter, could not stand life with her master, who "was always whipping and beating his slaves." She figured that she "would be better off dead and out of her misery," so one day when the master claimed to find fault with her work and started to raise his whip, "she fought back." When "the ruckus was over the master was laying still on the ground," as if dead from the whipping. He was not, but she was sold to a new master. On her second day at the plantation, the new master "acted like he was going to whip her for something she'd done or hadn't, but mammy knocked him plumb through the open cellar door." Presumably he had only been testing her, for he climbed out unhurt and laughing, saying "he was only fooling to see if she would fight." Although masters could turn to the law and the public authorities for assistance in controlling their slave women, they—like those women—knew better than any that, to the fullest extent possible, day-to-day resistance had to be dealt with within the household.[48]

Although slave women frequently viewed their confrontations with overseers and masters as personal business, on occasion they banded together. Working so much together, they shared much of their everyday experience, including a distinct women's culture, the standards of which they enforced through their network of gossip. Gossip constituted a primary form of socialization and censorship for the slave community, but it especially monitored the behavior of women and disseminated knowledge of current household goings-on as well as a large body of folklore. Whether in field gangs or the trash gang around the yard, they worked with younger and older women and helped to integrate diffuse social bonds into a daily routine. These work groups, supplemented by religious gatherings or other possible informal women's associations, permitted women to share a body of knowledge about medicine, herbs, and childbirth and a larger system of beliefs about womanhood. They also occasionally provided the core of a concerted women's resistance. Sometimes that collective resistance began as nothing more than a desire for a little free time. Clara Littlejohn remembered that the women sometimes "played off sick an' went home an' washed an' ironed an' got by wid it." When an overseer once tried to make two of them return to work, "dey flew at him an' whipped him." Upon being told of the incident, the master incredulously asked the overseer if he had allowed the women to whip him. The overseer owned that he had, and the "marster tole him if women could whip him he didn't want him," although in the end he allowed the overseer to stay. Women also combined forces with men to put an unacceptable overseer in his place. In 1857 a slave, David, appealed his conviction for the murder of the overseer, whom he had assisted another slave, Fanny, in killing. Prior to the act, Fanny had been heard to say that she was not about to allow that overseer to mess in her affairs—and the affairs in question had nothing to do with sexual exploitation.[49]

Sometimes women also responded collectively to the abusive whipping of one of their number. Fannie Alexander heard from her mother-in-law, who had been a field hand on a plantation where "the women worked together and the men worked together in different fields," that when one overseer tried to whip a woman "'bout sumpin' or other" all of the women turned on him with their hoes and "run him clear out of the field." They "would have killed him if he hadn't got out of de way." For a while after the incident, the master left the women to work without supervision, but finding that "some of 'em wouldn't do their part," he assigned them a "colored foreman." Annie Coley's master had a mean overseer "who 'tuk 'vantage of the womens in the fiel's." Once he knocked down a woman who "was heavy, en cause her to hev her baby—dead." Retribution came swiftly. "The niggah womens in the quarters jumped on 'im and say they gwine take him to a brushpile and burn him up. But their mens hollered for 'em to turn him loose." The master made the women return to the quarters and said "'I ain' whipped these wretches fer a long time, en I low to whip em dis evenin!'" The women spent the evening hiding in the woods, and the master let the matter drop. He dismissed the overseer.[50]

Running away provided an important safety valve for slave women's frustrations with the demands on their lives. Since women did not figure prominently among the visible fugitives who escaped to the North and wrote of their experiences, it is easy to assume that they were not among the more frequent runaways, but for reasons that had less to do with resolve than with opportunity. Whether as a result of white or black male bias—or more likely a combination of the two—female slaves were unlikely to be trained in carpentry, blacksmithing, masonry, coopering, or other specialized crafts that would lead them to be hired out. Accordingly, they were less likely than men to have an excuse to be abroad alone. The pool of skilled craftsmen, who could not only move about with less attention but who also stood a much better chance of being literate, provided the leadership for the most important slave revolts and also the largest number of fugitives. When Ellen Craft fled to the North with her husband, she dressed as a man. Furthermore, because, under the laws of slavery, children stayed with their mothers (at least until they were sold away from all kin), fathers more often than mothers were forced to run away in order to visit the rest of the family. Women, too, sometimes ran away to visit kin in other households, but slaveholders, for reasons best known to themselves, were much less likely to advertise for them than for men. The advertisements for runaways misrepresent—perhaps to a great degree—the proportion of women to men. We know that innumerable women, who lacked men's opportunities for mobility and who never ran to freedom, regularly ran away to avoid work, to avoid punishment, or simply to have some time to themselves.[51]

Ordinarily, slave women did not run far. They visited in neighboring households or took to the woods, and up to a point at least some masters tolerated their absences, although the woman could count on some form of punishment upon her return. Joe Rollins was born in the woods, where his mother had hidden from her master. Her mistress came out to see her and took the newborn back to the household. Some slaves went visiting kin or friends in neighboring households or dallied when sent on errands. The slaves of Celestia Avery's household in Troup County, Georgia, would steal off at night to go to La Grange to sell chickens. Some slaves ran off after particularly brutal or undeserved whippings. Mattie Farmer's mother and some other women were tied to trees and "just whooped across their backs . . . 'cordin' to what they had done." Some then ran off "to the woods and stay a week or a month. The other niggers would feed them at night to keep them from starving." Julia Green's mother ran away after her master broke his leg because "the rest was so mean to her." After the master's death, her mistress got so mean that the slave repeatedly ran away "till her ole missis sold her." Sarah Wells's mother would run off to the woods for two to three months at a time, but "she never took me with her when she ran away." Martha Jackson remembered a house servant named Tishie who took off one day "case dey so mean to her, I reckon." The other slaves hid Tishie in the grain house "wid de peas and sech lac' stedder down in de corn crib." Martha Jackson still was not saying "who 'twuz 'trayed her . . . but a crowd uv der Patterrollers come and got 'er one night, and tuck her away, and I ain't nebber seed Tishie no mo'."[52]

The patrols, which so many former slaves remembered with terror, played an important part in keeping unattended slaves off the roads and helping masters to find them in the woods. Evie Harris's mother was a smart and accomplished housemaid, who one day "got mad about something what happened at the big house." She ran away and when she could not be found, "they hunted her with dogs. Them dogs went right straight to the ditch where my mother was hid, and before the men could get to them, they had torn her clothes off her and had bitten her all over." When she was brought back, covered with blood and dirt, her mistress "flew into a rage, and she told those men to never again hunt nobody on her place with dogs." The slaves took their own measures to forestall the fearful dogs. They would carry "plenty pepper with them to rub on the bottom of their feet at nights when they slipped off so that the dogs couldn't scent them." Other masters tried to prevent slave women from running away to avoid work by chaining them around the neck. "The chain would hang down the back and be fastened on to another 'round the waist and another 'round the feet so they could not run." For three or four months they would have to work and sleep in the chains.[53]

Personal ties kept many slave women from running too far or for too long, although many, however much they may have loved their men or their children, did not feel bound by conventional notions of domesticity and motherhood. Those who escaped alone, in contrast to those like Ellen Craft, who ran with her husband, felt themselves isolated individuals. Sarah Wells's mother left her behind when she took to the woods. Hamp Kennedy remembered a woman, Nancy, "who stayed in the woods three years," although he did not mention whom, if anyone, she left behind. Rulen Fox's mother was "the only person that ever ran off." She was determined to try to make it to "the free country. She didn't have no cause for leaving, sept she wanted to be free." But she did not get very far "before them patrollers catched her and brought her back." When John Elliott's mother was about thirteen, she ran away from Virginia with "a pretty good flock of them." Wherever they had intended to go, they ended up in Wayne County, North Carolina, where a white man named John Elliott found them. "They was in a pretty bad way. They didn't have no place to go and they didn't have nothing to eat. They didn't have nobody to own 'em. They didn't know what to do." The white John Elliott offered himself as their new owner and presumably the black John Elliott's mother registered her gratitude by giving her son his name. The problem of where to go and what to eat was not a trivial one for runaways. Nancy Thomas remembered that slaves from adjacent households in Texas would get passes, go to the Colorado River, and start swimming across it. "Nobody would hear f'om 'em agin. Alot of 'em would hide out in de woods and bottom lands fo' awhile, and den go back to dere mawsters. If dey runaway f'om dere mawsters, dey didn't have noplace to go."[54]

At first glance, it is tempting to argue that if, in the case of runaways, southern gender conventions favored slave men over women, they compensated by affording slave women some protection as women, especially as mothers. Slaveholders did permit women greater latitude than men in feigning illness, especially if they claimed to be pregnant, but not necessarily out of solicitude for female delicacy or maternal feeling. Because the condition of slavery was passed on through the mother, all children born to slave women were slaves, no matter what their father's status. No slaveholder could lightly dismiss potential increases to his human property, and most felt themselves obliged to give women who claimed illness related to pregnancy the benefit of the doubt. Slave women perfectly understood their masters' motives and were quick to use the excuse even when they were not pregnant, or to claim unusual discomfort or weakness when they were. The tactic, which did not always work, embodied a marvelous challenge to the master: You want me to reproduce as a woman, treat me as a woman. Most masters did not view their slaves' maternity the way they viewed that of their wives and daughters, but self-interest led many, like George J. Kollock, to go easy on pregnant slave women, especially in their third trimester. This attitude, whatever prompted it, unquestionably contributed to Afro-American slave women's success in bearing enough children to make their people the only self-reproducing slave population in the Western Hemisphere. If a slave woman's resistance in this matter lightened her work, it also contributed to strengthening her people.[55]

Many slave women took pride and joy in motherhood. Deborah White has convincingly argued that for Afro-American women, as for their African foremothers, motherhood was of much greater significance than marriage in a young woman's coming of age and identity. Slaveholders and slaves both acknowledged the special pain of separating mothers and children by sale. Slave children frequently took great pride in their mothers, whom they deeply loved. They also frequently displayed a healthy respect—sometimes fear—for the sharpness of their mothers' tongues and the power of their blows. Slave women inescapably bore children into slavery and had every reason to try to prepare them to survive in the dangerous world that awaited them. They also bore them into a slave community that nurtured its own ideals of relations among human beings. It is next to impossible, and probably presumptuous, to attempt to understand fully how slave women felt about their identities as mothers, but it is safe to assume that those feelings did not necessarily correspond to white models.

Mothers throughout the world have loved children without subscribing to a modern Western ideal of motherhood, and loving mothers have defined themselves by more than their identities as mothers.

Anna Baker remembered that, "when I was too little to know anything 'bout it," her mother "run off an lef' us." She did not remember much about her mother from that time, but after the war her mother returned to get them and explained why she had had to go. "It was 'count o' de Nigger overseers. . . . Dey kep' a-tryin' to mess 'roun' wid her an' she wouldn' have nothin' to do wid 'em." Once, when one of the overseers asked her to go to the woods with him, she said she would go ahead to find a nice place, and she "jus kep' a'goin. She swum de river an' run away." She hired herself out to some "folks dat wasnt rich 'nough to have no slaves o' dey own" and who were good to her, and once or twice she slipped back at night to see her children. Her resistance to the sexual abuse she could not safely refuse forced her to desert her children, although she could count on their being fed by the master and reared by the other women of the slave community.[56]

Anna Baker's mother could rely upon the cohesiveness of the slave community to provide a stable world for her children, but she could not tolerate the sexual abuses to herself. Other women, who could live with their own situation but who could not accept what was done to their children, took more drastic measures. Lou Smith's mother told her of a woman who had borne several children, only to see her master sell them when they were one or two years old. "It would break her heart. She never got to keep them." After the birth of her fourth baby, "she just studied all the time about how she would have to give it up," and one day she decided that she just was not going to let her master sell that baby. "She got up and give it something out of a bottle and purty soon it was dead. 'Course didn't nobody tell on her or he'd of beat her nearly to death." Enough slave babies died from a variety of causes that a master would not necessarily recognize infanticide when it occurred. Slave women who slept with their children could unintentionally roll over on them and smother them during the night, and some slaveholders expressed compassion for their loss. Many infants died from natural causes, ranging from what is now called sudden infant death syndrome (SIDS) to the ubiquitous diseases that carried off white children as well. Many others may have died because their mothers were not allowed to nurse them for longer than a year, and they lacked adequate nutrition. Even mothers who were still nursing but who had been returned to their labor in the fields could not always feed their infants enough. When Celia Robinson's mother had a young child, the overseer would tell her it was time to go home to suckle it and she had better be back at her work in fifteen minutes. "Mother said she knowed she could not go home and suckle dat child and git back in 15 minutes so she would go somewhere an' sit down an' pray de child would die."[57]

For women who loved their children, infanticide and even abortion constituted costly forms of resistance. Whether women turned to such desperate measures depended upon a variety of factors that defy generalization, but those who did were, at whatever pain to themselves, resisting from the center of their experience as women. More, they were implicitly calling to account the slaveholders, who protected the sexuality and revered the motherhood of white ladies while denying black women both. From slave women's perspective, the slaveholders' behavior arrogantly assimilated the essence of womanhood to the prerogatives of class and racial status. Slave mothers knew that if their infanticide were discovered, it would be recognized as a crime against their master's property. Perhaps that knowledge led some of the more desperate to feel that, by killing an infant they loved, they would be in some way reclaiming it as their own. Jane, "a mulatto woman, slave," who was indicted for the murder of her infant child, had resisted, at however high a cost to herself. But she had also implicitly acknowledged that the oppression of slavery had, at least in her case, won out over the vigor and vitality of the slave community—and even more, over the slaveholders' cherished paternalistic ideal of the family, white and black.[58]

When slaveholders lived up to their side of the paternalistic compromise, they undercut some aspects of slave women's active resistance. Sarah Wilson had been called Annie until she was eight years old. "My old Mistress' name was Annie and she name me that, and Mammy was afraid to change it until old Mistress died, then she change it." Sarah's mother hated her mistress, but the mistress, perhaps impervious to the woman's feelings, symbolically claimed the woman's child as her own. She also claimed Sarah's half-sister, Lottie, whom she insisted also be called Annie. Sarah's and Lottie's mother changed Lottie's name "in her own mind but she was afraid to say it out loud, a-feared she would get a whipping." When Lottie was sold, her mother told her "to call herself Annie when she was leaving but call herself Lottie when she git over to the Starrs. And she done it too. I seen her after that and she was called Lottie all right." Martha Jackson gave one of her favorite servants a fancy wedding and expected her to name her first daughter

Patsy. There was no evidence of special friction between mistress and servant, but we may doubt that Patsy would have been the servant's own first choice. Names held great symbolic significance for slaves, as for slaveholders. Especially under conditions in which families could all too easily be fractured by sales, the choice of a name could provide an important link in the delineation of kin and a statement of an independent identity. To this day, Afro-American women in the deep South make up names for their children that symbolically confirm the bearer's unique identity. Slaveholders considered it a sign of condescension and interdependence to bestow their own names on their slaves' children, but many slaves saw that benevolence as an act of usurpation.[59]

Slaveholders' sexual exploitation of slave women further shredded the illusions of a harmonious white and black family but did not easily permit resistance, especially if the master was the perpetrator. "Plenty of the colored women have children by the white man. She know better than to not do what he say." Young masters presented a more complicated problem. Whites knew as well as blacks that the young men were likely to claim sexual prerogatives with the slave women and frequently sought to remove them from temptation by sending them away to school. When Eliza Washington's mother fought with her young master, she may well have been fending off his sexual advances, which she may have found all the more distasteful for being initiated before an audience of his peers. Overseers and black drivers caused even worse problems by assuming that their positions as delegates of the masters' authority implicitly carried sexual prerogatives. Slave women did not agree with their interpretation and were wont violently to resist advances that they might have been forced to endure from the master himself. Masters, who normally did not encourage the sexual license of others, often proved sympathetic to their outrage and dispatched the presumptuous delegate.[60]

Many southerners privately concurred with the harshest northern critics of slavery that the system suffered from sexual disarray. Slaveholding women in particular found their men's relations with slave women almost impossible to bear. One white lady "slipped in a colored gal's room and cut her baby's head clean off 'cause it belonged to her husband." The husband beat her for her act "and started to kill her, but she begged so I reckon he got to feelin' sorry for her." Most ladies did not resort to such drastic measures, and many husbands never repented of their ways. Annie Young's master was determined to have her aunt. Her aunt ran into the woods, but the master set the bloodhounds on her. When he caught her "he knocked a hole in her head and she bleed like a hog, and he made her have him." She told her mistress, who told her that she might as well be with him "'cause he's gonna kill you."[61]

The power of the master constituted the lynch pin of slavery as a social system, and no one ever satisfactorily defined its limits. If, as many jurists, echoing Thomas Ruffin, insisted, the power of the master must be absolute, how could it be curtailed in domestic affairs, especially when its victims had no identity as women at law? The supreme court of Alabama conceded the difficulty with respect to punishment: "Absolute obedience, and subordination to the lawful authority of the master, are the duty of the slave. . . . The law cannot enter into strict scrutiny of the precise force employed [by the master], with the view of ascertaining that the chastisement had or had not been reasonable." The law did hold masters accountable for what it defined as wanton murder, but not for accidental deaths and assuredly not for sexual assault. By the late 1850s, some jurists, theologians, and uncommonly conscientious masters were beginning to worry about the total lack of legal protection for slave women as women and were beginning to argue that the rape of slave women should be regarded as a crime. But convention and attitude alike militated against a serious hearing for their views. White male sexual power followed naturally upon white male social power, oppressing both white ladies and black slaves, however unequally, but white ladies often displaced their anger at the husbands who "protected" them onto the slave women whom their husbands' power entitled them to bully.[62]

Slave women's husbands, legally not husbands at all, lacked any power to defend their wives, short of placing their own lives at high risk. Slave women's freedom from the legal domination of their own men ensured that in most instances they would confront the power of their masters alone. The lack of legal guarantees, however, did not preclude slaves from developing intense loyalty to their mates and even a deep commitment to the substance of marriage in the absence of its forms. Annie Tate's grandmother drowned herself "'cause dey sold her husban'." Lily Perry grew up with her husband, Robert, who always tried to defend her. Robert hated to see her beaten and would beg her "not ter let my mouth be so sassy, but I can't help hit." Any number of times he sneaked out to the fields in the evening to carry the slops to the pigs for her, and whenever he could he tried to take her beatings. Once, when the master was beating her, Robert ran up and begged him to "put de whuppin on him 'stead of me. De result was marse whupped us both an' we 'cided ter run away." They did run away, but the master brought them back to yet another whipping and they never tried to run away again. Sallie Carder's father tried to protect his wife from a whipping. The overseer had tied her up and her husband untied her. "De overseer shot and killed him." When Harrod C. Anderson sold the husband of one of his women, she put ground glass in his milk. He found her out in time and made her drink the milk herself, and then gave her an emetic. But he subsequently sold her out of fear that the next time she would succeed.[63]

Slave husbands and wives could vary in their mutual loyalty and devotion, like husbands and wives throughout the world and throughout history, but the absence of legal standing for their marriages confronted them with especially difficult conditions. Men who lacked all external supports for their domination of their women frequently lost them to other men or were faced with the women's more or less open infidelity. Sexual fidelity is not exclusively a modern Western virtue: Many African societies, like medieval Christian and Islamic societies, prized it highly. Slave men fought and even killed other men who had sexual relations with their women. Women also fought and sometimes killed each other over men. The complexities of modern attitudes toward sexuality and the sexual values of other peoples should not prevent us from recognizing that a high level of violence resulted from slave men's inability to exercise the domination over women that most societies have awarded to men.[64]

If struggles among slave women and slave men testified to the oppressive power of masters, they hardly constituted effective resistance to it. The lack of sanction for slave marriages placed an almost unbearable burden on individuals who were forced to defend their personal commitments without the assistance of enforceable conventions. The slave community developed its own conventions, but even those informal collective sanctions were vulnerable to wanton intervention on the part of whites who, whatever their commitment to the decorous behavior and orderly conduct of their people, had little personal stake in their slaves' independent community life. Slaveholders who were committed Christians had strong reasons of conscience as well as of social stability for encouraging monogamy and family life among their slaves, but even they remained torn between their ideals and the economic exigencies that could lead them at any time to break up marriages and families through sale. And even Christian masters dealt with slave women primarily as individuals rather than as socially defined wives, daughters, and mothers.[65]

The churches did better than the masters in supporting slave marriage, but even they remained essentially powerless. By the 1830s they had irrevocably committed themselves to the defense of slavery and could at best deal with individual cases on their own merits, without considering the context from which they derived. Thus a church could censure or expel a slave "husband" who beat his wife, just as it could a white husband, but such discipline remained more symbolic than real. Many slaveholders were committed to converting their slaves to Christianity, both to prove to themselves that they were indeed good Christian masters and mistresses and to encourage their slaves to observe their standards of personal probity. Christian slaves drew upon their own faith to reject the messages of docility and blind obedience and to project a future world in which the last would indeed be first. Their Afro-American Christianity contained the seeds of resistance and in many instances probably helped to spark outright rebellion, but in everyday life it did not offer an unambiguous model of resistance.[66]

Fannie Moore's mother "was trouble in her heart bout de way they treated. Ever night she pray for de Lawd to git her an' her chillun out ob de place." One day in the fields the light descended and she let out a big yell. "Den she sta't singin' an' a shoutin', and' a whoopin' an' a hollowin'." She seemed to plow all the harder. Upon her return, the master's mother asked her what had been going on and reminded her that she was out there to work and if she did not they would have the overseer whip her. "My mammy jes grin all over her black wrinkled face and say: 'I's saved. De Lawd done tell me I's saved. Now I know de Lord will show me de way. I ain't gwine a grieve no more. No matter how much yo' all done beat me an' my chillun de Lawd will show me de way. An' some day we nevah be slaves.'" The mistress got out her cowhide and set to work, but Fannie Moore's mother did not let out a peep and returned to the fields singing. Faith permitted Fannie Moore's mother to endure with equanimity and inner certainty and could, accordingly, be viewed as a source of resistance. But, like Celia Robinson's mother, who prayed for her infant to die, she did not resist in a way that threatened the everyday operation of the system.[67]

Slave women resisted within the system by setting limits to the work they considered tolerable and the punishments they could endure. Afro-American Christianity and the fellowship of the slave community strengthened their internal resistance to slavery by strengthening their sense of identification with their own society and beliefs, by offering them a place in the world and an identity as members of a gender. The sources of their internal resistance helped to undercut the logic of slavery that reduced them to isolated individuals, but it also tended to undercut the more extreme forms of resistance by binding them to a viable community in this world and to the hope of salvation in the next. If the community or the faith failed them, or if the master decisively exceeded the limits of an authority that could begrudgingly be accepted as legitimate, they found themselves once again confronting the master in social and psychological isolation. Women in that situation frequently turned to a violent and contemptuous resistance for which they might pay with their own lives. One of Nancy Bean's aunts "was a mean, fighting woman." Her master, presumably because he could not master her, determined to sell her. "When the bidding started she grabbed a hatchet, laid her hand on a log and chopped it off. Then she throwed the bleeding hand right in her master's face." T. W. Cotton's aunt, Adeline, was another woman who refused to be whipped. One day when she thought that she would be, "she took a rope and tied it to a limb and to her neck and then jumped. Her toes barely touched the ground." Charlotte Foster knew a young girl of about sixteen who said "she'd as leave be dead as to take the beatings her master gave her." One day she simply went "into the woods and eat some poison oak. She died, too."[68]

Resistance was woven into the fabric of slave women's lives and identities. If they defined themselves as wives, mothers, daughters, and sisters within the slave community that offered them positive images of themselves as women, they were also likely to define themselves in opposition to the images of the slaveholders for whom their status as slave ultimately outweighed their identity as woman. The ubiquity of their resistance ensured that its most common forms would be those that followed the patterns of everyday life: shirking, running off, "taking," sassing, defying. The extreme forms of resistance—murder, self-mutilation, infanticide, suicide—were rare. But no understanding of slave women's identities can afford to ignore them, for, if they were abnormal in their occurrence, they nonetheless embodied the core psychological dynamic of all resistance. The extreme forms captured the essence of self-definition: You cannot do that to me, whatever the price I must pay to prevent you.

Slave women normally resisted in forms determined within the household and in direct confrontation with masters, mistresses, and especially overseers. In most cases, they were punished within the same context, as befitted what was most comfortably viewed as a private matter. Murders, poisonings, infanticide, and arson could bring them to the courts, which recognized such acts as attacks against the system and accordingly recognized the slave woman's legal standing as a criminal. Richard Mocks remembered a mulatto girl "of fine stature and good looks," who was put on sale. "Of high spirits and determined disposition," she refused to be coerced or forced. While she was awaiting sale, one of the traders took her to his room "to satisfy his bestial nature." During the ensuing struggle, she "grabbed a knife and with it, she sterilized him and from the result of injury he died the next day." She was tried for murder, but with the advent of the war she was taken to Washington and freed.[69]

Arson, another favored form of violent resistance, was guaranteed to provoke the wrath of the law, for arson, even when directed at an individual master, constituted a danger to the whole area. Lee Guidon knew an old woman who set "Stingy Tom's" barn on fire "and burned thirteen head of horses and mules together." Stingy Tom called the sheriff to try to get her to tell "what white folks put her up to do it. He knowed they all hated him cause he jes' so mean." The woman "never did tell but they hung her anyhow. There was a big crowd to see it." The courts did not view women accused of arson as mere extensions of their masters' wills: "The Rolling-house was maliciously burnt by a Negro woman of the Defts. [defendant] whereof she was Convicted . . . and Executed for it." The court, which was unwilling to convict the woman's master for the crime, held that he "is not Chargeable for the wilful wrong of his servant."[70]

Slave women resisted their enslavement, as women and as individuals, in all the ways available to them, according to their particular situations and their particular temperaments. Like other women of oppressed groups everywhere, they participated in their people's struggle for national liberation and self-determination. Like other women in comparable struggles, depending upon specific conditions, they were found in almost any role from leadership to armed combat to spying to a variety of less dramatic ones. As in other struggles for national or class liberation, at least some women resisted with no regard for their ascribed gender roles. There was no form of insurrectionary struggle in which some women did not, at some time, engage. Nonetheless, with the consolidation of white slaveholding society and the slave community, slave women effectively disappeared from the leadership of formal revolts. That disappearance had nothing to do with the ferocity of their personal opposition to slavery, but it probably had much to do with the emergence of a slave community that naturally viewed the reestablishment of gender relations as the necessary foundation for long-term collective resistance.[71]

The disappearance of women from visible roles in formal revolt does not mean that they did not continue to support those efforts in decisive ways. Enslaved and oppressed peoples, as Frantz Fanon movingly demonstrates in "Algeria Unveiled," have readily taken advantage of the "invisibility" of their women in the interests of a victorious struggle. For the black men who left firsthand accounts of their struggle against slavery, the invisibility of women was essential, because in struggling against oppression they regarded the affirmation of their own independent manhood as central to the argument that they and their people deserved freedom. The records that they constructed constituted an integral part of the struggle itself.[72]

Yet, as Vincent Harding has particularly insisted, the various records of revolts invariably make some mention of churches or funerals or religious gatherings as a backdrop for rebellion. Afro-American religion, including secret black churches and religious meetings and networks, provided a focal point for slave organizations. Those churches and secret religious networks undoubtedly provided the institutional links between acts of individual resistance and collective revolts. Women were not much more prominent as religious than as military leaders, although they occasionally held high positions in the churches, especially in New Orleans and in conjunction with the persistence of voodoo. It is nonetheless difficult to believe that informal—and perhaps formal—associations of women, or sisterhoods, did not extend women's networks into slave religious communities. Especially after the prohibition of separate black churches, such associations would likely have been as secret as the congregations to which they were linked.[73]

Like black men, whose associations took shape so rapidly during Reconstruction, black women probably developed associations under slavery that were rooted in African culture. Such gender groupings are reasonably common in societies in which gender constitutes one of the principal forms of social organization, as it did among many West African peoples, and the same spirit doubtless informed the female community of slaves. It is plausible to assume that the community of female slaves generated some kind of religious sisterhood, however fragile and informal. At the least, slave women indisputably saw themselves as sisters in religion, as essential members of the religious community of slaves. To the extent that the religious community provided the context or underpinnings for slave revolts, the women of that community constituted its backbone—not least because, not being active members of the revolt, they did not risk being cut down with their brothers. They would live to keep the tradition alive.[74]

Slave women participated in discussions of revolts and in shaping the emerging political goals of their people. Daniel Goddard's parents and their friends frequently discussed political matters in his presence. They spoke of the Nat Turner insurrection in Virginia and the Vesey plot in Charleston. "I learned that revolts of slaves in Martinique, Antigua, Santiago, Caracas and Tortigua was known all over the South. Slaves were about as well aware of what was going on, as their masters were," although the masters tried not to share such information with them. The masters had reason to be cautious. Maria Thompson was present at many discussions in which "de scared slaves would git together and talk about dere freedom. Dey would git together, polish up dere huntin' guns and be ready to start somethin'." The slaves had one main ambition: "to git dere freedom, but de mawsters had better not hear about it." Slave women, nonetheless, did their best to make sure that the slaves learned of the masters' discussions. During the war, Elizabeth Russell was still small, "yet I served my people as a secret service agent." She spent her days in the big house to "attend the babies" and "would often pretend to be asleep" in order to overhear "the folk at the big house" talk about the battles "and which side was winning or losing and when the word came that the north had won and the slaves were free, it was I who carried the word to the hundreds of slaves in our section." Though she was only a little child, "God used me as a bearer of good news to my people."[75]

Withal, the common denominator of the innumerable ways in which slave women opposed their own enslavement lay in the individual will. Normally, that will does not appear naked, but comes wrapped in gender, in race, in class—in the complex of relations that composes any social system. Absolute rejection of slavery results in the stripping away of those wraps, of those components of self as a social being. Slave women's absolute rejection of their own enslavement has, at the extreme limit, no history and is not gender specific. The recognizable patterns of slave women's resistance to and of their participation in revolts against slavery as a social system has a history and is gender specific. These patterns of resistance and revolt derive from the interaction of slaves with other slaves, with slaveholders, with non-slaveholding whites, and with free blacks in specific societies.[76]

There is a danger in insisting upon the specific experience of women as women: We can miss the determined struggle of the individual soul and consciousness against reduction to the status of thing. However deeply slave women themselves felt their exploitation and vulnerability as women, they also seem to have insisted, in the end, on their oppression as slaves. Despite the extensive commentary that has arisen from Judge Thomas Ruffin's celebrated decision in *State* v. *Mann* (1824), there has been almost no comment on the sex of the slave who provoked the action that led to the case. Lydia "had committed some small offence, for which the Defendant undertook to chastise her—that while in the act of so doing, the slave ran off, whereupon the Defendant called upon her to stop, which being refused, he shot at and wounded her." The supreme court of North Carolina reversed the conviction of the white man. In Ruffin's words: "The Power of the master must be absolute to render the submission of the slave perfect."[77] Power and submission: The conflict pitted one will against another. Time and again, slave women in their resistance confirmed that they, too, saw the conflict as one between the master's will and their own.

The ultimate resistance lay in the ultimate loneliness—the absolute opposition of power and submission, of one will to another. In that extreme case, gender counted for little. Gender counted increasingly as the vitality and vigor of the slave community and slave culture anchored individuals into a viable world—anchored them as women and as men in relation to other women and other men. The political division of labor by gender that came to characterize Afro-American slaves' resistance to slavery testifies to a growing commitment not merely to escaping from or defying their enslavement as individuals, but to replacing the prevailing social system with a more just one.

7   *And Women Who Did Not*

Slaveholding women did not share their slaves'
opposition to slavery. Nor did slaveholding
women embrace the fledgling cause of women's
rights, which was gaining ground among northerners and which they, like others, viewed as intimately linked to abolitionism. They were known
to grumble in private about certain aspects of
their lives and even, on occasion, to blame slavery for the most disagreeable ones. Women, like
men—black and white, northern and southern—
will sometimes grumble. But the complaints of
slaveholding women never amounted to a concerted attack on the system, the various parts
of which, as they knew, stood or fell together.
Slavery, with all its abuses, constituted the fabric of their beloved country—the warp and woof
of their social position, their personal relations,
their very identities.

The antislavery and women's rights movements derived their initial impulse from a determination to apply the logic of bourgeois individualism to those excluded from its benefits.
The language of bourgeois individualism, which
had been formulated by men to establish their
claims to individual right, embodied universal
claims that served their progenitors well, even
when they were not applied to all members of
society equally. By defining individual right as an
absolute, bourgeois individualism defined slavery, which had long been viewed as one form of
unfree labor among many, as the antithesis of
individual freedom. This definition made possible the corollary view that the subordination of

women, heretofore accepted as a simple manifestation of natural differences, contradicted the fundamental principle of individual right. It did not take some women long to see the contradiction as it applied to their own condition. Indeed, astute male political theorists like Thomas Hobbes had been bothered by the obvious contradiction posed by the relation of women to society and the polity. Women of the Revolutionary generation, like Abigail Adams and Judith Sargent Murray, insisted only that men refrain from tyranny at home and that women receive an education appropriate to their station, but their identification with what Linda Kerber has called "republican motherhood" paved the way for their daughters' escalating claims on behalf of their gender. Logically, the language of bourgeois individualism that informed the Revolutionary legacy applied equally to all members of society. The obstacles to such radical application of the doctrine derived not from its internal logic, but from—as Locke had so presciently written—the "laws and customs of the country."[1] Those laws and customs had prescribed the subordination of women to men as the necessary foundation of social order.

The eighteenth-century revolutions, including the Enlightenment, had fundamentally challenged received laws and customs and opened innumerable possibilities. The men who steered the revolutions to their successful landing at the docks of bourgeois freedom rapidly lost patience with the various left flanks that had helped to guarantee their triumph, including those that championed women's individualism. In the event, "the woman question" caused them little trouble. Most middle-class women proved ready to accept the new view of themselves as republican mothers and, shortly thereafter, as true women. In the transaction, women forswore their pretensions to individualism in return for a newly favorable image of themselves as women. In the capitalist and rapidly industrializing northern states, this image emerged naturally, if not smoothly, from the new social conditions that featured the separation of home and work and their respective ascriptions to female and male spheres.

From the opening decades of the nineteenth century, northern women drew upon the model of gender relations embodied in the doctrine of separate spheres to justify their own collective efforts as women. Thus, well before women began to organize on behalf of women's rights, they had been organizing on behalf of women's special concerns, notably the plight of less fortunate women and women's roles as mothers. Their organizations drew upon the idea of women's special mission to justify action outside the home. The mid-nineteenth-century flurry of the women's rights and antislavery movements brought together the two tendencies of women's rights as individuals and women's rights as women. Only after the Civil War would the fissure between the two ideals widen. At midcentury they coexisted the more easily since they originated in the same social and ideological revolution. For whether northern women favored women's rights as individuals or women's rights as women, they accepted the basic premises of their capitalist society and bourgeois culture. Their "feminism" borrowed its logic and its claims from the dominant culture of their region.[2]

The logic of women's rights as individuals derived from bourgeois individualism in its implicit insistence that physical attributes did not constitute an adequate basis for distinguishing between any group of individuals and any other—or better, did not constitute an adequate basis for excluding any group of individuals from the rights that in principle adhered to all individuals. It also embodied the universalist assumption that women, like men, should be viewed as equals across class lines. In the minds of the early proponents of women's rights, the struggle entailed practical considerations as well as principles. In particular, they believed that women should remain adult individuals after marriage and should therefore be able to hold property in their own names. Some northern jurists agreed, but less out of a commitment to women's rights than out of a commitment to the freedom of property from all particularistic encumbrances. In this climate a growing circle of northeastern and midwestern as well as some mid-Atlantic women formed organizations to promote the improvement of women's position in society. These women—among whom Elizabeth Cady Stanton, Susan B. Anthony, Lydia Maria Child, Lucy Stone, and the southern émigrés, Sarah and Angelina Grimké, remain the best known—espoused a variety of related causes, notably woman suffrage. All the leaders and many of their followers identified with the antislavery movement, the rhetoric of which they frequently adapted to their struggles on behalf of women. In so doing, they borrowed from the dominant bourgeois discourse of individual right.[3]

The nascent "feminism" of those women, whatever its shortfalls, belonged to the mainstream of modern feminism that runs from Mary Wollstonecraft to the contemporary women's movement. It rested squarely on the principle of universalism: All individuals should enjoy equal rights by virtue of their status as individuals and independent of their other innate attributes. This feminism specifically expressed the aspirations of women as members of a capitalist society and democratic polity. In this respect, it portrayed all women as bound by gender rather than divided by class and race. Gender figured as a universal classification that transcended other possible forms of social classification. In this respect also, feminism did have a natural relation to antislavery, if not necessarily to abolitionism in the strict sense. For both feminism and antislavery insisted that the bondage of any individual to any other mocked the fundamental principles of bourgeois individualism. This attribute of universalism distinguishes modern feminism from previous defenses of women's rights or excellence as women and identifies systematic feminism as the defense of women's rights within the context of bourgeois individualism.[4]

Yet the defense of women's rights as individuals gained ground in conjunction with a new discourse of women's rights as women. Especially in those northeastern regions in which industrial capitalism was proceeding apace, women drew upon the logic of separate spheres to declare themselves the natural custodians of a different and higher morality than men. Their concerns, which centered on religion, the preservation of the home, the care of children, and the protection of female virtue, provided the most telling critique of the excesses of individualism, which, especially in its unbridled pursuit of profit, promised to lead the world ever deeper into sin, corruption, and greed. Many women who espoused this view did not see that it contradicted the quest for women's rights, which they saw as the necessary means for implementing their higher goals. From their belief in a separate and better female nature, they concluded that women would have to enter the world in order to redeem it. Other women, who shared the assumption of women's special nature, recoiled at the prospect of women's meddling in politics and even doubted the wisdom of an all-out war on slavery.

The relation between domesticity and the defense of women's rights complicates the attempt to evaluate the "feminism" of northern women, but both strands bear the mark of a distinctly bourgeois society. Women, like men, were split in their progressive and conservative responses to the problems engendered by emerging industrial capitalism, for both women and men belonged to a society that was repudiating the principle of particularistic and hierarchical social relations. Practice lagged well behind principle, but the diversity of practices did not coalesce in an alternate ideology. The arguments for class distinctions increasingly became matters of policy rather than matters of principle. The arguments for gender and racial distinctions persisted more flagrantly and moved toward the new ground of scientific racism and sexism. The women who opposed discrimination against themselves, like those who opposed slavery, forged their goals from the practices and discourses of their society, which they primarily reproached for failing to live up to its own highest ideals.

Southern women also fashioned aspirations for themselves in conformity with the dominant culture and social relations of their society, which differed in essential respects from northern society. The principles upon which northern feminism rested constituted—indeed were formulated as—a direct challenge to the principles of southern slave society. Southern women who might have participated in these discussions, notably articulate slaveholding women, were known to rail against the injustices that women endured at the hands of men. But their discontents hinted at feminism only in rare and scattered cases. Overwhelmingly they had another meaning, which rested on the conviction that the system of southern civilization "obeys and displays the great law of nature—series, gradation, order."[5]

To view slaveholding women as the opponents of southern social relations is to extrapolate from their depictions of slavery as a personal burden to an assumed opposition to the social system as such. That southern women complained about slavery and sometimes about men does not mean that they opposed slavery as a social system or even the prerogatives with which its class and race relations endowed men. Slaveholding women did not accept bourgeois feminism's claims to universality, did not accept its claims to be an accurate statement about the relations between women and men in all times and places. Nor did they agree that northern women's rights advocates primarily proposed a radical critique of their own bourgeois society. In fact, they assumed that those advocates were advancing a radical critique of someone else's society—namely southern society. Literate southern women responded to this perceived attack in kind, repeatedly denouncing the evils and immorality of free society and comparing it unfavorably to the slave society they overwhelmingly favored, despite its acknowledged failings.[6]

Bourgeois feminism followed bourgeois individualism in enunciating its claims as universal truths. Therein lay its great strength and its capacity to denounce slavery as an absolute evil, but its claims to universality only partially succeeded in obscuring its ties to a specific historical period and a specific class. Even within the context of bourgeois society, the struggle for women's rights as women, however critical of men's mismanagement of the world, did not constitute a frontal attack on society; it called for a broad reformation. From the southern perspective, as Louisa McCord scathingly noted, that modest call for reform looked a great deal like revolution. But even McCord pulled her punches. In truth, the struggle exposed the extent to which northern society embodied the principles of revolution—as George Fitzhugh, an eminently logical reactionary, understood perfectly. Northern bourgeois women who sought to improve their own position were engaging in a form of sibling rivalry: They sought to claim for themselves the prerogatives that their brothers enjoyed.[7]

In truth, southern women shared many values with northern women and fashioned their identities in reference to many of the same discourses. But as Frederick Porcher insisted, that conventional language was "drawn from scenes totally at variance with those which lie about us." Slaveholding women's commitments to their own versions of evangelicalism, motherhood, and companionate marriage do not constitute proof that they shared some northern women's commitments to feminism and abolitionism, nor do their complaints about the flaws of the society to which they belonged. Those complaints must be understood within the context that gave them utterance. How, for example, do Mary Boykin Chesnut's pithy and scathing broadsides on slavery and the men who presided over it—"Poor women, poor slaves!"—relate to the beliefs and feelings of other slaveholding women? Mary Chesnut as "feminist-abolitionist" cannot pass muster as a typical slaveholding woman. She cannot even pass muster as representative of a significant minority of southern women, for although quasi abolitionists and quasi feminists existed, they were few and far between. Perhaps she should simply be understood as an anomaly— charming and talented, but no less an anomaly. Or perhaps she did not intend her scathing words in an abolitionist or feminist spirit at all.[8]

Mary Chesnut was, in fact, typical of the women of her class in some respects. At the least, her class attitudes—not to mention her conscious and abiding loyalty to her fellow slaveholders and to the Confederate cause—should occasion, as Drew Faust has argued, some second thoughts about her allegedly advanced social views. For Mary Chesnut participated in the same social and imaginative worlds as her dear friend, the more forthrightly polemical Louisa McCord.[9]

Born in Statesburg, South Carolina, in 1823, Mary Boykin Chesnut, like Louisa McCord, grew up among the slaveholding elite. Her father, Stephen Decatur Miller, whom she adored, had married Mary Boykin, daughter of a distinguished South Carolina family, which accepted him as one of their own. Mary Miller grew up on the plantation that her father purchased adjacent to the plantation of his wife's father.

Her early memories abounded with pictures of life in the company of her maternal grandmother, whom she accompanied in her daily round of responsibilities. She remembered Mary Whitaker Boykin as a woman who did her best to meet her responsibilities as a Christian mistress. Mary Whitaker Boykin oversaw the making of cakes and pastries, visited the weaving room, dispensed medicine to the slaves, and cut "negro clothes." After the clothes had been cut, young Mary settled herself in the seamstress's room, alternately listening to the slaves' singing and reading to them from her favorite books. In 1828, when she was five, her father was elected governor of South Carolina.[10]

During the years of her father's governorship, Mary Miller developed her own lifelong passion for politics. Although she episodically attended two schools in Columbia, her mother took primary responsibility for her education. The Miller house bustled with the comings and goings of political visitors, to whose conversations she listened whenever she could. Politics, according to her biographer, Elisabeth Muhlenfeld, "was in the air she breathed." She inhaled it with a relish attuned both to the play of opinion and to her mother's role as hostess, which she hoped to fill one day. The politics she absorbed in her girlhood was that of nullification, which her father strongly supported. During the early 1830s, when her father's election to the U.S. Senate took him to Washington, she began to attend Miss Stella's school in Camden. In 1833, her father resigned his seat. In 1835 he sold the plantation and determined to move to Mississippi, but before the move he settled Mary with the Roman Catholic Mme Talvande in her celebrated French School for Young Ladies in Charleston.[11]

Mme Talvande's school catered to elite young women of the lowcountry, among whom Mary Miller stood out as a charming and witty conversationalist. At Mme Talvande's she studied literature, music, history, rhetoric, and natural science, in addition to singing and dancing. She apparently excelled at languages, for she not only learned French, which in later years she spoke and read like a native, but also German, which she read well and wrote in an elegant script. Although only fourteen by the end of her second year at the school, she must have begun to develop into an engaging belle, for she attracted the serious attention of a twenty-three-year-old lawyer, James Chesnut, the brother of her dear friend, Mary Chesnut. Her parents opposed so early an attachment, especially since they thought that their daughter reacted more with excitement than love. They withdrew her from school to join them in Mississippi. After six months of "frontier" life, for which young Mary had no more taste than Julianna Conner, the family moved to Charleston and once again enrolled her in Mme Tal-vande's. Her father's unexpected death in 1838 caused her to be with-drawn again to accompany her mother and sister to Mississippi. By this time James Chesnut had declared his intentions and, despite her family's opposition to a premature marriage, she was beginning to attend to them. In April 1840 they were quietly married at the old Boykin plantation, in the company of a mere fifty guests. Mary and James Chesnut took up residence at Mulberry, his parents' plantation three miles south of Camden, South Carolina.[12]

The thirteenth and youngest surviving child of James Chesnut, Sr., and Mary Cox Chesnut, James Chesnut had attended Princeton and thereafter read law in the office of James Petigru, the Charleston Unionist. By the time he married Mary he was embarked on a promis-ing career solidly grounded in his own talent and in his family's social connections and great wealth. The unexpected death in 1839 of his favored older brother, John, from complications following measles had promoted him to the position of heir apparent. The household into which he brought his young bride embodied the wealth and social position of his parents, who continued to dominate it. Mary Chesnut felt like something of a permanent guest. With servants to attend to her every need and with her mother-in-law firmly in charge of the household, she spent the early years of her marriage rather aimlessly, reading and visiting. In return for her sacrifice of the excitement of being a belle, she gained none of the independence that would have resulted from control of her own household.[13]

By 1846, after spending the first five years of her marriage in appar-ent quiet at Mulberry, she was seeking as many excuses as possible, notably her own purportedly poor health, to accompany her husband on trips to northern cities and spas and to Europe. During these years, James Chesnut embarked on a political career in earnest. In 1840 he had been elected to the South Carolina state legislature, and by 1850 his growing political stature had resulted in his being sent as one of the delegates to the Nashville Convention. In Mary's accurate reading, James stood for "the conservative and moderate wing of the southern rights party." In 1848, upon their return from a trip to the North, the Chesnuts finally moved into their own house, Frogvale, in Camden. There, Mary Chesnut assumed control of her own household, however modest in comparison with that of Mulberry. By then, also, it was clear that they would have no children. During the years at Mulberry, Mary Chesnut avidly pursued her reading; cultivated her deep, if very pri-vate, religious sensibility; developed warm, if complicated, relations with her in-laws, especially James Chesnut, Sr.; and began writing bits and pieces of journals and memoirs.[14]

The Mary Chesnut who, in 1861, began the journal that, after rewriting and revision, later launched her into a long posthumous career, was a vivacious, complicated, and dissatisfied woman. Throughout the 1850s, with her husband's growing political success, she plunged with ever-greater verve into her career as a hostess. In 1856, the Chesnuts moved from Frogvale to a more fashionable house in Camden, Kirkwood. James Chesnut had been elected to the state senate in 1852 and from 1856 to 1857 served as its president; in 1858 he won unanimous election to the U.S. Senate, from which he resigned when South Carolina seceded. Mary Chesnut accompanied him to Washington, where she relished the unending social and political whirl. Her husband, whom she viewed as cold and conservative in temperament as well as politics, left his social schedule to her. Unlike many Washington wives, she had no call to doubt his fidelity, but she frequently chafed at his want of enthusiasm for the society she adored. She especially delighted in her lifelong ability to attract the attention and admiration of men of all ages, who, even as she reached middle age, continued to flock around her.[15]

And she loved the politics and the endless and animated discussions in which she regularly participated. Politics, which she indirectly entered by appropriating her husband's career to herself, provided an outlet for her gnawing ambition. During the first year of the war, from August to December 1861, her journal contained a running commentary on her feelings. Should James Chesnut not be reelected to the Senate, she would be looking the "*defeat* of my personal ambition in the face." She tried to stifle her urge to have him pursue military fame, for if anything should happen to him, how could she live with herself: "Why was I born so frightfully ambitious." Mr. Slidell was appointed minister to France instead of Mr. Chesnut: "So 'all my pretty chickens at one fell swoop.'" What if the worst should befall? "Now if we are not reelected to the Senate! . . . pride must have a fall—perhaps I have not borne my honours meekly." Throughout the war, her ambition steadily grew, always merging with her ambitions as a belle but increasingly leading her to fret that she was not in a position to execute well the political and military tasks that the men about her were executing badly.[16]

By the time Mary Chesnut began to keep the first version of her journal, she was close to forty, married, and childless. Her birth, her marriage, and her social and political position rooted her in the center of the South Carolina slaveholding elite, as embodied in the gentle-men and ladies of her family and her circle. Her identification with this intransigently proslavery elite was never simple, especially since she remained torn about her personal identification and relations with both women and men in her circle. Following the death of her father, she, who had no brothers, remained especially conflicted about her relations with her closest male kin, her husband and his father. Despite her deep love for her mother and her sister, Kitty, and her attachment to her mother-in-law and her women friends, her feelings about the sisterhood of women remained no less complicated. In the apt words of Elisabeth Muhlenfeld, she regarded herself "as superior to most people she knew—male or female." She nonetheless enjoyed and ex-ploited the power of her femininity even as she coveted the powers of men from which it excluded her. Although her writings never focused directly on those relations and feelings, evidence of them abounds.[17]

Mary Chesnut took the world—at least her own country and its history—as her subject and continually struggled to subordinate the subjective perspective to an objective account of events. Less than a month after she began her Civil War diary, she started to reflect upon her husband's character and upon the reticence that led her to doubt whether she knew him any better after twenty years of marriage than she had when they first met. Abruptly, she caught herself. "What non-sense I write here. However this journal is intended to be entirely *objective*. My subjective days are over. No more *silent* eating into my own heart, making my own misery, when without these morbid fanta-sies I could be so happy." Yet her journal relentlessly beckoned her to an introspection she feared would be disadvantageous, "for I spend the time now, like a spider, spinning my own entrails instead of reading, as my habit was at all spare moments."[18]

Mary Chesnut never fully disentangled her personal feelings from her politics. If personal loyalties and sectional identification bound her unswervingly to the fate of the Confederacy, personal resentments led her to challenge those about her. In 1850 she had written to her hus-band that she was considering transferring her allegiance from John C. Calhoun to Henry Clay, "particularly as I am not the *hearty* lover of slavery this latitude requires." She confessed herself to be not as "*sound* on certain important *topics* now so constantly discussed—indeed so very heterodox am I—that I principally *hate* the abolitionist [*sic*] for their *cant* & abuse of us—& worse than all their using this vexed question as a political engine & so retarding beyond all doubt the gradual freeing of our states which seemed to be working its way down in Maryland & Virginia."[19] She did not, in this letter, elaborate her reasons for disliking slavery, but they would surface in her diary. Her references to Clay and Calhoun confirmed her interest in politics and even suggested that she might have had more interest than she elsewhere revealed in political economy. Her other letters and diary offer no answers.

In 1848, eight years after Mary Chesnut's marriage, she plunged into a deep depression. Her beloved sister Kitty had given birth to her first child, and she herself may have had a miscarriage in 1846. In any case, by 1848 the odds were lengthening that she would remain childless in a society that grounded a mature woman's identity in motherhood. Southern delicacy drew an impenetrable veil over the reasons for the Chesnuts' failure to have children, but at moments Mary seems to have blamed James or, blaming herself, to have projected her anger and frustration onto him. Irresponsible speculation will not do, and the sources discourage responsible speculation. Yet statistics do not suffice to explain individual cases, and the historians who implicitly attribute the Chesnuts' childlessness to her incapacity rather than his have yet to offer more than an assumption based upon statistical probability. The acerbic tone of her writing should caution that in this matter, as in others, she might have resented such prevailing assumptions as the inference that a woman's barrenness accounted for a couple's child-lessness. If she did not, her veiled hints that her husband was lacking in manly vigor amounted to perverse liberties with a style she was worldly enough to know could arouse suspicions.

Some things are clear. Mary Chesnut, who married young and spent the early years of her marriage in the household of her husband's parents, was never able to ground her marriage in the pleasures of and obligations to children that fulfilled the lives of her peers. Her feelings for James Chesnut were, at their warmest, marked by affection and companionship but not by passion or even deep devotion. At their coldest, they were marked by competition and impatience. During the late 1840s and the 1850s she was reaching, more or less gracefully, a truce with her destiny. As she did so, she moved steadily toward the center of her husband's political world, which, after all, recalled that of her father. Never able to rival her husband in the corridors of power, she could not resist challenging his judgment while she worried about his want of ambition. The letter that announced her secret doubts about slavery no doubt had several meanings, but one of them repre-sented a taunt and a challenge to his political opinions and loyalties. The choice of Clay over Calhoun had to appear preposterous from the daughter of the nullifying Governor Miller. She later remarked in the opening passage of her diary: "My father was a South Carolina Nullifier—Governor of the state at the time of the *N* row & then U.S. Senator. So I was of necessity a rebel born." And she allowed that, in the early days of her marriage, the Unionism of her husband's family "rather exasperated my zeal." Rebel that she was, she was known to defend a variety of opinions out of a spirit of contradiction.[20]

The letter may well have cloaked even deeper bitterness and represented a challenge to the society that denied her a satisfactory identity. Significantly, she wrote that she might not love slavery as much as "this latitude" required. "Latitude" explicitly transformed her country and her people into a site. Yet the geographic attribute could not encompass her feelings, loving or resentful, about the society with which she identified. Even as she taunted her husband about shifting her allegiance to Clay, she admitted that Daniel Webster, notwithstanding the "Seventh of March," lay beyond the pale.[21] We would gain nothing by trying to ignore this open expression of her doubts about slavery, but neither can we gain anything by divorcing the sentiment from her personal relations. However deep her doubts ran, they remained internal to her world; they were not the harbinger of an alternative to it. That Mary Chesnut had moments of doubt about slavery we may be sure, but then so did many proslavery men, even among the fire-caters. Sensitive, intelligent southerners, like other people, normally did have doubts about many things—even about God, as James Henley Thornwell, her father's cousin and South Carolina's great theologian, reminded his parishioners. The struggle against doubt, he added, guarantees the depth of the certainty. And, despite all attempts to interpret Mary Chesnut's occasional outbursts out of context, her life demonstrated nothing so much as certainty that her world, however flawed, was on balance the best available.

The letter to her husband remains an isolated example of her possible feelings before the war. The main case for her opposition to slavery and to women's position within a slave society must be made on the basis of her diary. But the diary poses formidable problems, most important of which is that Mary Chesnut crafted and recrafted her purportedly spontaneous response to the unfolding of events as she set her sights upon eventual publication. The implications of the revisions, in particular those which concerned her intended audience, raise questions about the views she claimed to hold.[22]

Other slaveholding women took up diaries at the outbreak of secession, and even more did so as the war unfolded. Their diaries betray a marked shift in tone from those written before the war. One after another, they responded to the crisis as to a rendezvous with destiny, for almost overnight they knew their private lives to have become witnesses to a great historical confrontation. One after another, they began implicitly to write for posterity—to write in support of their cause and to justify their ways to God, to each other, to their enemies, to the world. One "Virginia Girl" began her diary with the recollection of a prominent Baltimore lawyer's comment that the Charlestonians had a habit of dating everything from before the war, reporting that one citizen had even said of the moonlight on the Battery, "'You should have seen it before the war.'" Having begun by laughing, she later became reflective and even caught herself "echoing the sentiment of that Charleston citizen to visitors who exclaimed over the social delights of Norfolk. For really they know nothing about it—that is about the real Norfolk." From the time the first shots were fired on Fort Sumter—or perhaps even from Lincoln's election and the events that led up to it—slaveholding women assumed a heightened self-consciousness, usually to defend slavery and the way of life it engendered, but sometimes to establish themselves as independent minds that would not shrink from criticism. The tone of the diaries shifted again in the autobiographies and reminiscences of life under the old regime that were written after Reconstruction. The destruction of the writers' society accounted for part of the difference, their expectations of their prospective readers for another part. By the end of the century, those who wrote of their lives before the war—loyal though they might be to their people and their region—were likely to present themselves as having always opposed slavery or supported a better position for women, or both.[23]

The drafting and revising of Mary Chesnut's diary cut across the period of Civil War and Reconstruction; she began the original in 1861 and revised most heavily during the 1880s. In between she tried her hand at writing novels, which she never published. Her attempt to find her voice as an author before she returned to the extraordinary diary that has earned her the fame she always coveted constitutes part of the history of the diary's final form—and part of the history of its original draft. Success eluded her attempts at social portraiture in the manner of Thackeray and autobiographical fiction, yet her chosen themes remained the great canvas of history and herself. The diary, better than any other genre, permitted her to join those themes in a manner that remains, even among the ranks of accomplished diarists, very much her own. But the ambition for authorship was there from the start. However much she attempted to discipline her own subjective melancholy, it, like her charming exhibitionism, lay at the core of her "objective" account of persons and events.

Anger, bitterness, and disappointment surely account for Mary Chesnut's inability to write the story of her life to her own satisfaction. There were always things with which she did not trust herself or her readers, always things that could not, for whatever reason, be written. From the start, she kept her diary under lock and key. Hers was not an account for children, for husband, for the private edification of the family circle. But the diary did not and could not have contained the secrets she dared not reveal. She kept it under lock and key, but not because she did not wish James Chesnut or her beloved nephew Johnny or her devoted friends to read "poor women, poor slaves" or to read that she thought slavery a "monstrous system." And James Chesnut, and presumably others of her circle, knew that she took opium but tried to curb the habit. He and her women friends had had their taste of her sharp tongue and craving for gossip, even about the philandering of respected citizens like her father-in-law. Mary Chesnut revealed little more than most slaveholding women, although she frequently expressed herself more pithily. Why, then, the secrecy?

Mary Chesnut kept her diary to herself because she aspired one day to share it with the world. She hid it not because of its contents, but because of the unladylike spirit that informed its writing. The diary testifies above all to her ambition to authorship, and not the authorship—already dangerous enough—of the occasional verse or fiction or religious views that were, at the margin, considered appropriate to her gender. She had her sights set on authorship in the grand manner. Her diary would permit her to marry the charms and ambitions of the belle to the command and ambitions of the military officer or statesman. In her pages, she could command armies and determine events. Her criticisms of her society, especially of its men, constituted her revenge for the miseries she had suffered. Had the war not come, she might never have found a public voice. As she noted, bemoaning her confinement at home while the battle raged elsewhere, one day was so like another that she forgot she had a journal. But as the southern divines increasingly insisted, the war represented God's testing of and judgment upon his chosen people. She, like the God evoked by the divines, proposed not to abandon that people but to call it to account. To be sure, the subjective perspective that she could never shake gave a personal edge to her judgments and robbed her of the social perspective that informs grand visions. The aspiration to emulate Thackeray haunted her work, always returning her from the destiny of nations to the comedy of manners. But her attempt to catch, however personally, the "scheme of things entire" heavily influenced the way in which she represented her world, just as her personal ambition to represent herself as *of*, but never determined *by*, her country led her to attempt to present personal complaints as social judgments.

She succeeded well beyond anything she might have expected. Her fellow southerners would not likely have taken her criticisms of their world as evidence of the feminism and abolitionism against which she and they were fighting. They had heard such criticism many times, especially from their respected ministers, and they had long trained themselves not to confuse criticism of abuses with criticism of their basic values and social relations. They would probably have recognized her passion for display and her habitual grumbling and would have taken both as facets of the woman they knew and valued. But her subsequent readers, not rooted in her antebellum southern world, have read her through different eyes. Mary Chesnut's complaints about slavery and slaveholding men were part of a presentation of herself and were always intended for the widest possible audience. The question, therefore, must be: What secrets lie behind that public garb?

Those who wish to see Mary Chesnut as a feminist and abolitionist refer to the celebrated passages in her diary in which she bemoaned the related fates of women and slaves in southern society. For the date of 4 March 1861 she offered, in the published version:

> So I have seen a negro woman sold—up on the block—at auction. I was walking. The woman on the block overtopped the crowd. I felt faint—seasick. The creature looked so like my good little Nancy. She was a bright mulatto with a pleasant face. She was magnificently gotten up in silks and satins. She seemed delighted with it all—sometimes ogling the bidders, sometimes looking quite coy and modest, but her mouth never relaxed from its expanded grin of excitement. I daresay the poor thing knew who would buy her.
>
> I sat down on a stool in a shop. I disciplined my wild thoughts. . . .
>
> You know how women sell themselves and are sold in marriage, from queens downward, eh?
>
> You know what the Bible says about slavery—and marriage. Poor women. Poor slaves.[24]

This passage bears comparison with the version that Chesnut drafted in her original diary:

> I saw to day a sale of Negroes—Mulatto women in *silk dresses*—one girl was on the stand. Nice looking—like my Nancy—she looked as coy and pleased at [as?] the bidder. South Carolina slaveholder as I am my very soul sickened—it is too dreadful. I tried to reason—this is not worse than the willing sale most women make of themselves in marriage—nor can the consequences be worse. The Bible authorizes marriage & slavery—poor women! poor slaves![25]

Consider the differences between the original and the published versions. In the original, Chesnut began her entry by noting, "I saw something to day which has quite unsettled me. I was so miserable [several illegible words] that one character in the world is lost—it knocks away the very ground I stand on—but away night mare." Although it might be tempting to identify the unsettling sight with the slave auction, the text discourages that interpretation. Rather, it appears that, as with other southern women, Chesnut's unhappiness about other matters brought slavery to mind as a target for the displacement of other grief. Before she even saw the slave auction, she had "sat at home this morning eating my own heart—but knew that it would never do." So out she rushed to distract herself with shopping and calls.[26]

In the published version, all references to her personal misery have disappeared. In addition to the changes in context, the original and published versions reveal significant differences in the description of the slave auction itself. The published version records the magnificence of the mulatto woman's attire; the original version all but sneers at the generic inappropriateness of mulatto women in *silk dresses* (her italics). South Carolina slaveholder that she was, she might sicken at direct confrontation with slave auctions, but she also scorned a slave woman's espousal of upper-class garb and ladylike wiles. From my reading of the diaries and private papers of the slaveholders, I have sadly concluded that the racism of the women was generally uglier and more meanly expressed than that of the men. The published version of Chesnut's diary reveals a hardening of her own always deep racism: witness her description of the slave woman "ogling the bidders" and her "expanded grin of excitement."[27]

Mary Chesnut's class and racial attitudes recur with a vengeance in

Mary Boykin Chesnut, ca. 1840.
Courtesy of South Caroliniana Library

Lucy Muse Walton Fletcher, ca. 1870.
Courtesy of William R. Perkins Library, Duke University

Mulberry Plantation, near Camden, South Carolina, built ca. 1820. Home of
Mary Cox Chesnut and Colonel James Chesnut.
Courtesy of South Caroliniana Library

her other frequently cited outcry against the oppression of women and
slaves. "I wonder," she mused in the entry for 18 March 1861, "if it be a
sin to think slavery a curse to any land." Northern opponents of slavery
speak true: "Men and women are punished when their masters &
mistresses are brutes & not when they do wrong—& then we live
surrounded by prostitutes. An abandoned woman is sent out of any
decent house elsewhere. Who thinks any worse of a Negro or Mulatto
woman for being a thing we can't name. God forgive *us*, but ours is
a *monstrous* system & wrong & iniquity." She continued with scathing remarks about every family's mulatto children who resembled the
white children and about women's unwillingness to recognize their
husbands' responsibility for the children's conception. Yet she concluded by defending the women of her class and region, who were, she
believed, "in conduct the purest women God ever made." The men
were another matter: "No worse than men every where, but the lower
their mistresses, the more degraded they must be."[28]

In both versions of the diary, this passage falls between reflections
on her husband and father-in-law. The paragraph that precedes it
records her distress at her husband's wishing aloud, while they were
on a trip, that they "had separate coaches. . . . That we could get away

Virginia Tunstall Clay-Clopton, 1860s.
Courtesy of William R. Perkins Library, Duke University

from these whiskey-drinking, tobacco-chewing rascals and rabble."
The rabble, she pointed out, was armed. Following her musing on
their "monstrous" system, she pursued a train of thought that led from
the behavior of "patriarchs," who insisted on adding "wives" to their
households, to the ungenerous way in which her wealthy father-in-law
had treated her husband—leaving him to live from his earnings as a
lawyer—although her husband did not see it. She concluded with
slightly different wording from the unpublished version, "And again I
say, my countrywomen are as pure as angels, tho' surrounded by another race who are the social evil!"[29]

Chesnut associated her attack on the monstrous system with the
misery suffered by childless women. She reported that she did a kindness to Mrs. Browne by informing other women that, although childless now, Mrs. Browne had once had three children. The lie, she knew,
would "be of service to her. Every body (women I mean) despise a
childless old woman." And she added, doubtless referring to the childlessness that haunted her: "In the gall of bitterness once more. The
Trail of the Serpent is over it all." One entry later, she made the point
in a yet more personal way. She reported that her father-in-law had
told his wife that she could not feel she had been useless since she had
twenty-seven grandchildren. Bitterly, Mary Chesnut reflected, "Me a
childless wretch. . . . And what of me! God help me—no good have I

done myself or anyone else, with this I boast so of, the power to make myself loved." And in a yet more bitter parenthetical aside: "(*He did not count his own children!!*)."[30]

Mary Chesnut associated the evils of slavery and the subordination of women with her own resentments, specific and general, against the men of her own class, with whom she nonetheless identified. Her style permits no neat analysis, but she made clear enough that powerful men—"patriarchs" like her father-in-law—enjoyed the power to deceive and humiliate their wives, who were forced to suffer men's indulgence in prostitution within their own homes, and to deprive their sons of the full powers of manhood. By this logic, James Chesnut, Sr., became responsible for Mary Chesnut's childlessness, which deprived her even of the respect and kindness of her pure and normally considerate countrywomen.

In a biting and brilliant passage drafted well after the event, she insisted that war brought the differences between men and women to the fore. In a sarcastic reference to antebellum gender conventions, she noted that women "who come before the public are in a bad box now." Should they appear alone on the thoroughfares, they risk having their false hair searched for papers, their "cotillions renversés" searched for pistols. "Bustles are 'suspect.'" And, it was said, all manner of things crossed the border under the huge fashionable hoops. "So they are ruthlessly torn off. Not legs but arms are looked for under hoops. And sad to say, found." The war had made mockery of the gender conventions that protected ladies, had stripped the illusion of fashion from the decay of flesh. How could such experiences not have humiliated women? Their modesty was exposed—and even more, their artificial efforts at self-presentation. War denuded the lady of her pretenses and protections and reduced her to a mere woman.[31] In the original version of this passage she had written, in the same spirit but with revealing differences:

> Our women are now in a nice condition—traveling, your false hair is developed & taken off to see if papers are rolled in it—& you are turned up instantly to see if you have pistols concealed—not to speak of their having women to examine if you are a *man*—in disguise. I think *these* times make all women feel their humiliation in the affairs of the world. With *men* it is on to the field—'glory, honour, praise, & power.' Women can only stay at home—& every paper reminds us that women are to be *violated*—ravished

& all manner of humiliation. How are the daughters of Eve punished.[32]

In both versions the passage follows a discussion of a letter by William H. Russell in the *London Times* about the battle of Manassas. In the later version, Mary Chesnut adopted a balanced and witty tone and credited the author with understanding the flaws of the Yankees as well as those of the Confederates. In the original, she admitted to being enraged even if the author did, in spite of himself, show gleams of truth. "We are Americans as well as the Yankees—& Russell cannot do us justice," especially since he repeated hideous falsehoods. From that sentiment she moved directly into a discussion of the condition of women in such times. The Yankees, her logic ran, were depriving her countrywomen of the status of ladies. No wonder they felt humiliated. But that was not the whole story. In both versions, her complaint about women's being ravished and violated came between her complaints that women were kept at home and that to men accrued the glory and the power. She was not arguing for women's rights but for the exceptional woman's opportunity to display excellence. She used women's humiliation as a code to cloak her own frustration at being left to twiddle her thumbs at home when she might have been directing the battle and receiving the applause. Her diary was her response, the repository of her fantasies of glory and power.[33]

Mary Chesnut's complex and conflicted attitudes toward James Chesnut, Sr., lie at the heart of the matter. She regularly invoked him, directly or indirectly, as the prototype of the male behavior and prerogative she resented. Yet she not only respected but liked him, and she took pleasure and pride in his fondness for her. In the same passage in which she bristled at his implicit insensitivity to her own childlessness, she added, plaintively, "Colonel Chesnut, a man who rarely wounds me."[34] At the risk of simplification, I would suggest that she saw her father-in-law as the embodiment of that southern "patriarchy" with which she flirted and which she tried to charm, but which she nonetheless resented. Men like Colonel Chesnut guaranteed the status of lady in which she delighted. Yet, in her subtle psychological speculations, she seems to have believed that Colonel Chesnut cast a shadow over his son that denied her the children she needed for full status and comfort.

Never fully accepting an identity as matron, Mary Chesnut remained very much the belle. She never directly took up the challenge of Louisa

McCord's taunt that if the ladies wanted a boxing match they would be bested, but she displayed a sizable dose of the ambition that McCord so deplored in politicians and belles. No reader of Chesnut's diary could miss her concern with pleasing, charming, being at the center of attention. These preoccupations amount to a special form of female ambition. She sought to excel as a woman in the eyes of men. Her uneasy identification with the other women of her class informed both her bitter critiques of their lack of charity to childless women and her formulaic praise of their excellence. She remained, in some ways, their observer rather than their sister—remained a shade apart from the company of women. She harbored mixed feelings toward powerful men, as represented by James Chesnut, Sr. Some deeply buried part of her surely aspired to equal them. She did not refrain from criticizing generals and politicians as if she could have met their responsibilities better than they. Yet she wrote her husband asking to be instructed in political matters, as if such things exceeded the comprehension of a mere woman. It is easy to imagine her bringing that coy deference to her relations with Jefferson Davis, Louis Wigfall, Francis Pickens, and other powerful men of her acquaintance, even as some part of her continued to covet their glory and power for herself. "If I was a *man* I would not doze & drink & drivel here until the fight is over in Virginia," she noted in the original diary. Later she changed the sentence to read that Johnny "reproved" her for saying that were she a man she would join the fight, saying that it was not her duty to talk so rashly. In short, having been blocked from the full identification with the maternal role that her society preferred for mature women, she was torn between her ambitions as a belle and her more repressed ambitions to equal men.[35]

This personal history imperceptibly merged, as do all personal histories, with her social attitudes, deftly captured in her passing reference to nonslaveholding whites as an armed rabble, and subtly evoked in the manifest racism of her comments on black and mulatto women. In the end, the presumed lasciviousness of slave women merged with the domination of slaveholding men and the blindness and cruelty of slaveholding women in a seamless social web. Under the combined influences of personal misery and the opium she took to alleviate it, Mary Chesnut could momentarily condemn the system as monstrous.[36] But she never mounted a critique of her society's fundamental social relations, which her own social and racial attitudes clearly supported. She offered no hint that she favored equality among individuals. She compared the woman on the auction block with "my

Nancy," never suggesting that Nancy should be anything other than her personal possession. She deplored the sight of slave women's sporting the finery of their betters. She worried about her husband's reference to other white men as rabble only because they, being armed, might react violently. "Poor women! Poor slaves!" constituted, not a call for emancipation and equality, but a lament for the human condition.

Mary Chesnut was well schooled in the opinions of abolitionists, notably those of Harriet Beecher Stowe, whom she mentioned with the same contempt expressed in print by Louisa McCord. Like many other southern women, she bristled at the presumption of northerners in judging southern social relations and regularly insisted that they had no idea what they were talking about. Reading Charles Kingsley's *Two Years Ago*, she admitted to finding the main character, Tom Thurnall, deeply stirring. But Kingsley knew nothing about negroes. "These beastly negroes—if Kingsley had ever lived among them! How different is the truth." She knew a wretched mulatto slave woman "who is kept a mistress—& her son a negro boy—with a black father—beats her white lover for giving her brandy to drink—& white people say well done! to the boy!" And she wondered if there were more impure women, "Negroes & all, North or South." In her revisions, she directly confronted the question of northern attitudes. Northerners' antislavery amounted to little more than the most lucrative hobbyhorse for New Englanders, snug and smug in their "clean, clear, sweet-smelling" homes or shut up in their libraries, "writing books which ease their hearts of their bitterness to us, or editing newspapers—all [of] which pays better than anything else in the world." She condemned them all: Stowe, Greeley, Thoreau, Emerson, Sumner. Even among the politicians, "antislavery is the beast to carry him highest." Did they practice self denial? No, theirs was "the cheapest philanthropy trade in the world—easy. Easy as setting John Brown to come down here and cut our throats in Christ's name. These people's obsession with other decent people's customs reduced to self-serving and sanctimonious nonsense."[37]

Against them she arrayed her mother, her grandmother, and her mother-in-law. Who were these Yankees, she asked, to lecture pure southern women, many of whom were educated in northern schools and who read "the same books as their Northern contemners, the same daily newspapers, the same Bible—have the same ideas of right and wrong—are highbred, lovely, good, pious, doing their duty as they conceive it." Southern women faced a reality that their northern sisters could not begin to understand. Southern women lived in "negro villages"; rather than preaching insurrection, they attempted to ameliorate the lives of those in their charge. "They set them the example of a perfect life—life of utter self-abnegation." How would these "holy New England women" feel if they were "forced to have a negro village walk through their houses whenever they saw fit—dirty, slatternly, idle, ill-smelling by nature (when otherwise it is the exception)." Southern women could not have done more for negroes if they had been African missionaries. "They have a swarm of blacks about them as children under their care—not as Mrs. Stowe's fancy paints them, but the hard, unpleasant, unromantic, underdeveloped savage Africans."[38]

Slaveholders, Chesnut insisted, were doing their duty as well as possible, and it had crippled them with debt. In the end, only northerners and negroes profited. Her father-in-law's money went to support "a horde of idle dirty Africans—while he is abused and vilified as a cruel slave-owner." Everything he made went back to his laborers, "those here called slaves and elsewhere called operative, tenants &c . . . peasantry &c." The slaveholders, who were "good men and women, are the martyrs." They were "human beings of the nineteenth century—and slavery has to go, of course." Mary Chesnut believed, as did southern intellectuals like Thomas Roderick Dew and George Tucker, that history would sooner or later outrun the kind of slavery that existed in the South. But she insisted that northern and European bourgeois, with their sanctimonious platitudes and callous disregard of the laboring classes, had nothing better to put in its place. "I hate slavery," Mary Chesnut wrote. But she immediately added, in a manner designed to draw the teeth of any charge of abolitionism: "I even hate the harsh authority I see parents think it their duty to exercise *toward their children.*" Harriet Beecher Stowe could make one feel "utterly confounded at the atrocity of African slavery." Yet, "at home we see them, the idlest, laziest, fattest, most comfortably contented peasantry that ever cumbered the earth—and we forget there is any wrong in slavery at all." In expressing these sentiments, she did not veer from the view, loudly trumpeted by southern divines as well as by other social theorists during the 1850s, that a more humane slavery or personal servitude would characterize the society of the future. Nor did Mary Chesnut substantively depart from Caroline Lee Hentz's avowed apology for slavery, *The Planter's Northern Bride*, which depicted the frail female worker, dismissed from her job because she was dying of tuberculosis, and thrown back to starve in the arms of the widowed mother she had been supporting; the arrogant and ignorant abolitionist, who was robbed by the fugitive slave whom he had taken into the sanctity of his domestic circle as a matter of principle; the lordly, beneficent slaveholder who brought happiness to his bride, the abolitionist's daughter.[39]

Was slavery wrong in the abstract, as the abolitionists argued and the proslavery theorists denied, or was it wrong only in its abuses? Mary Chesnut did not devote much attention to slavery as a social system. She did insistently call attention to the pain—the martyrdom—it imposed on women. But her pervasive racism suggests that she believed that blacks had to be enslaved. She betrayed scant concern for their rights. "Topsys," she averred, "I have known—but none that were beauties—or ill used. Evas are mostly in the heaven of Mrs. Stowe's imagination. People can't love things dirty, ugly, repulsive, simply because they ought, but they can be good to them—at a distance." And, confirming the personal nature of her own response, she admitted, "You see, I cannot rise very high. I can only judge by what I see."[40]

Mary Chesnut took slavery for granted as the foundation of her world. Time and again she referred to slaves who did one thing or another for her. After emancipation she expected them to stand by her. With dismay she noted that when, in February 1865, the Martins left Columbia, "their mammy, the negro woman who had nursed them, refused to go with them. That daunted me." She might have been borrowing from Caroline Lee Hentz when she noted the death of Burwell Boykin (the son of her uncle), whom her sister called "the very best man I ever knew, the kindest," from the typhoid he contracted by attending to his sick slaves. By limiting her expressed hatred of slavery to stylized, polemical passages, and by linking it to her hatred for the abuse of parental authority, she rhetorically equated slavery with men's domestic power and public advantage. Her heated assertion, "There is no slave, after all, like a wife," said just that. But nowhere did she challenge Louisa McCord's theoretical defense of the legitimacy of men's authority over women and slaves. Rather, like McCord, she cried out against abuses of that authority.[41]

Mary Chesnut read *Uncle Tom's Cabin* more than once, as if she were engaged in a private debate with the author. In March 1862, she "read *Uncle Tom's Cabin* again," and again in June, "tried to read *Uncle Tom*. Could not. Too sickening. It is bad as Squeers beating Smike in the hack. Flesh and blood revolts." In May 1864, she met a lovely relative, "the woman who might have sat for Eva's mother in *Uncle*

Tom's Cabin." The beautifully dressed, graceful, languid woman made eyes at all comers and "softly and in dulcet accents" regretted the necessity under which she labored, "to send out a sable Topsy who looked shining and happy—quand même—to her sabler parent, to be switched for some misdemeanor—which I declined to hear as I fled in my haste." She wrestled with Stowe's views, and probably with her success as an author as well. She did not embrace Stowe as an authority on the woes of southern women, black or white. Negro women in the South "have a chance here women have nowhere else. They can redeem themselves. The 'impropers.'" In the South, they "can marry decently—and nothing is remembered against them, these colored ladies." The topic was not nice, yet she felt that Stowe reveled in it. "How delightfully pharisaic a feeling it must be, to rise superior and fancy we are so degraded as to defend and like to live with such degraded creatures around us."[42]

However indirectly expressed, Chesnut's resentment of Stowe, like her reservations about Stowe's picture of southern social relations, had much in common with Louisa McCord's frontal attack. She could only have concurred with Louisa McCord's sneering association of *Uncle Tom* with the sensationalist fiction of their day. Nor would she have differed with Louisa McCord's judgment that the "public feeling with us is, we believe, as delicate and as much on the alert upon such points, as in any part of the world." The transgressions and wanton violence that Stowe depicted were not sanctioned by southern laws, which held masters to account in their treatment of their people. Louisa McCord asserted that "the existence of a system of slavery rather tends to increase than diminish this feeling, as, leaving a larger portion of society in a state of tutelage, naturally and necessarily greater attention is turned to the subject." What must Mrs. Stowe's social background be, for her to assume that slaveholders admitted slave traders into their houses? "We have lived at the South, in the very heart of a slave country, for thirty years out of forty of our lives, and have never seen a slave-trader set foot in a gentleman's house." Here, Louisa McCord pressed her polemic beyond reasonable limits. No doubt, she did not admit slave traders into her house, but others did, although they distinguished between the "gentlemen slave traders," who owned plantations and married into the high planter class, and the rest. Louisa McCord exaggerated in order to label Harriet Beecher Stowe as hopelessly middle class—lower middle class at that. To Louisa McCord, Stowe's assertions offered a dubious impression of the society "with which madame and her clerk-brother have associated, and prepares us for some singular scenes in the elegant circles to which she introduces us." Stowe, in McCord's belief, did not know what she was talking about. Worse, she lacked the social standing to write authoritatively of gentle folks.[43]

Mrs. Stowe, Louisa McCord continued, knew no more of morals than she knew of manners. How could she believe that slaveholding men and women labored under a cloud of guilt? How could she believe that slaveholders were good to their slaves only to repay them in part for the fraud of owning them at all? "To rob a man and pay him back a moderate per-centage on the spoils of his own pocket, is not Southern honour." Neither slaveholders nor other honest people degraded their laborers. Louisa McCord, who was exceptionally well read in the political economy of her day, insisted that only economic illiterates could think that any laborers, slave or free, earned more than the subsistence they in fact got. Southern men and women, "who do what they think right," did not live "with a constant lie on their lips and in their hearts." They owned slaves because "they believe 'the system' to be the best possible for black and white, for slave and master." They could, on their knees, "gratefully worship the all-gracious providence of an Almighty God, who has seen fit, so beautifully, to suit every being to the place which its nature calls it." There were, McCord asserted,

> pious slaveholders; there are christian slaveholders; there are gentlemanly slaveholders; there are slaveholders whose philosophic research has looked into nature and read God in his works, as well as in his Bible, and who own slaves because they think it, not expedient only, but right, holy and just so to do, for the good of the slave—for the good of the master—for the good of the world. . . . There are men, and women too, slaveowners and slaveholders, who need no teachings to act as closely as human weakness can, to such a rule.

With the arrogance of those who claim a monopoly on absolute truth and who have no sense of human nature, Harriet Beecher Stowe had, McCord felt, dismissed an entire people. "If we answer that there is no more moral population in the world than that of our Slave States (few, indeed, equally so) we are answered with a sneer of derision."[44]

Above all, Louisa McCord contemptuously inquired, what did Mrs. Stowe know of southern ladies? They included their share of those who had been spoiled and indulged from birth—women who might neglect a child, snub a husband, or be "peevish and exacting" with their servants. But a southern lady "could not be the vulgar virago." Southern character "has its faults—faults, too, which take their stamp, in part, from our institutions and our climate, as do those of our Northern neighbors from theirs." But no southern woman, "educated as a lady," could have provided the model for Mrs. Stowe's portrait of Mrs. St. Clare. Louisa McCord drew the link between Stowe's outrageous views and the women's rights theory "that is putting ladies in their husbands' pantaloons." Where such views might lead, God alone could tell. With this argument Mary Chesnut, complaints notwithstanding, concurred: Harriet Beecher Stowe knew nothing about human nature—and less about southern ladies.[45]

Mary Chesnut's insistence on the enslavement of wives would have found ready acceptance among northeastern feminists, who were quick to use the rhetoric of antislavery in the service of their own cause. An immensely talented and well-read woman, Chesnut was familiar with the issues in the debate over slavery and with the uses to which supporters of women's rights put those issues. Yet she barely touched upon them in her own writing. She regularly linked her private debate with Harriet Beecher Stowe and other abolitionists to what she deemed the incontrovertible evidence of racial inequality and to the realities of daily life among Africans. She did not usually follow Caroline Lee Hentz, among many others, in explicitly juxtaposing the harmony of slave society with the chaos and cruelty of a society based on wage labor. Indeed, even Louisa McCord waffled on that question, for, as a devoted exponent of both classical political economy and the proslavery argument, she remained deeply conflicted about the proper status of white labor. Mary Chesnut never joined the debate with such feminists as Harriet Martineau or Frances Kemble, of whom she knew but whom she did not mention. She tried to read Margaret Fuller Ossoli, "but could not." Her repeated linking of the abuses of slave society and the unhappiness of women implied no sympathy for emerging feminist-abolitionist opposition to restrictions on the rights of any individual. Her complaints lacked all reference to a concept of individual rights.[46]

In the revised version of her diary, Chesnut constantly strove for literary effect. She never achieved the unity and control of a novel, although she frequently sought to capture the wise and impersonal voice of the great depicters of human nature in all its variety. Reaching to find her own voice, she subtly varied the presentation of her views in different entries. In August 1861, William H. Russell again provoked her wrath, this time for expressing "indignation because there are women on negro plantations who were not vestal virgins!" His attack prompted an unambiguous response: "Negro women are married and after marriage behave as well as other people. Marrying is the amusement of their life. They take life easily. So do their class everywhere. Bad men are hated here as elsewhere." She followed that unqualified statement with the account of a long conversation among her women friends, in which she did not identify who was saying what. She simply presented a succession of interlocking opinions as if they represented the full range of views. The conversation began with an unidentified speaker who announced: "I hate slavery. I hate a man who ———." What, the speaker inquired, could be said of a "magnate who runs a hideous black harem and its consequences under the same roof with his lovely white wife and his beautiful and accomplished daughters?" That man demanded purity from his women, as if he himself had never done wrong in his life. And probably, another speaker added, he forbade his daughters to read *Don Juan*.[47]

The conversation progressed to Stowe, to her mistake in making Legree a bachelor—and was it an accident that her villain was named Legree and thereby identified with a prominent South Carolina family, the Legarés, that in fact pronounced its name "Legree?"—and on to the purity of the wife and daughters he might have had and to the abuse they would have suffered at his hands. "*Now*," another voice interjected, "now, do you know any woman of this generation who would stand for that sort of thing?" Another responded, "No, never— not for one moment." The condition of women was said to be improving. But what of southern men? Were "they worse because of the slave system and the—facile black woman?" No, they were not, for they saw too much of the black women to be tempted. And then, some men were drunkards. Not that women could not be, "well, the very devil and all his imps." But did not girls cower before a fierce brute of a father? "Men are dreadful animals." Yet, as one of the group reminded the others, "those of you who are hardest on men here are soft enough with them when they are present. Now, everybody knows I am 'the friend of man,' and I defend them behind their backs, as I take pleasure in their society."[48]

Without resolution, the conversation moved off along the trail of Mirabeau, author of *The Friend of Man*, and on to the women's husbands' present and future political and military assignments. Had anyone seen any of the Yankee letters from Manassas? "The spelling is often atrocious. And we thought they had all gone through a course of blue-covered Noah Webster spelling books." In contrast, "our soldiers do spell astonishingly." (In truth, as every historian of the South knows, the spelling even of elite southerners ranged from poor to atrocious.) And what about Horace Greeley? It was said that he could not even read his own handwriting. At least, though, he was man enough to say "that in our army *they* have a hard nut to crack." Another of the women interjected, "Bully for our boys!" Greeley even said that "the rank and file of our army is superior in education and general intelligence to theirs." The difference was that southern gentlemen themselves served in the army, whereas the Yankees got an Irishman or a German to take their place.[49]

This passage, like the one that follows it about women's vulnerability in public during the war, represents Mary Chesnut at her most skillful, urbane, and sophisticated. She did not trivialize women's complaints against the men their society bred, nor did she raise them to a theoretical rule. Conditions and personalities varied. Human nature remained problematic. Her perspective inspired her with no patience with the pieties of northern women's domestic fiction. In May 1861, she read Anna and Susan Warner's novel, *Say and Seal*. "New England *piety* & love making—*pie* making. Such baking & brewing—house maid's duties elevated to the highest scale of human refinement." The hero fared no better in her estimation than the housemaid heroine: "Quoting scripture & making love with equal *unction*. Never takes a kiss without a text to back him—& every *embrace* & every kiss is duly chronicled, *several* a page—& not one *breakfast*, dinner or *tea* spared the reader." This hero, who "manfully admires the heroine through her butter making, pie making, cooking & bed making, scrubbing, &c, is finally dreadfully shocked to find she clandestinely makes dresses." For the revised version of her diary, Mary Chesnut honed and polished this passage, but dropped none of the essentials. The novel presented "housemaid's duties made divine." But why should the hero, who admired his beloved's "butter-making, scrubbing, making up beds, and all the honest work she glories in," draw the line at dressmaking? "One must draw the line somewhere." She herself would have drawn it sooner. Domestic fiction did not inspire her to reflect upon the sisterhood of women.[50]

Mary Chesnut could envision no alternative to the system she could momentarily describe as monstrous. Piety and piemaking, not to mention scrubbing and bedmaking, did not interest her. She may have deplored the ways in which slaveholding men abused their prerogatives, but she did not propose stripping them, much less their women, of their privileged social positions. Mary Chesnut criticized her society, in precisely the way the militantly proslavery divines—for example, the Reverend Dr. James Henley Thornwell, whom she much admired—did. She criticized its imperfections and abuses, but not, despite an occasional rhetorical flourish, its social relations. She may have wanted to reform the men of her class, or even to punish them for certain transgressions, but she did not want to dissolve that class into some great mass of human equality.[51]

Other slaveholding women occasionally voiced similar complaints about the baleful effects of slave society on their lives. Anna Matilda Page King, who, like Mary Chesnut, wrote from the marrow of the slaveholding elite, once wrote plaintively to her husband of how bad slavery was for boys—and girls. She wished they could sell their slaves, "get rid of *all* at *their value* and leave this wretched country." The slave South was no place to rear children. "To bring up boys on a plantation makes them tyrannical as well as lazy, and girls too." On the day this letter was written, it had been raining, seemingly forever, on St. Simon's Island. The walls of the house were leaking. Servants and children were sick. Unexpected guests had descended. The mountain of debts was staggering. Poor Anna had been forced to retreat to a closet to nurse her headache and write to her absent husband. How was a woman to preside over a plantation and to rear children without her husband? Small wonder that she found the burdens of life too much to bear. But her heartfelt complaints, rather than developing into a critique of her society, later disappeared from her correspondence. The mood passed, and with it her criticism of the society that gave her an identity. Her protests at her husband's absence recurred but focused on other objects. And in 1861 her devoted daughter, Georgia, attending Georgia's secession convention with her father, wrote home to her brother, Fuddy: "All the women here are 'right' but it is strange to say, there are *many men*, quite willing to be ruled by the Yankee and the nigger." In horror, she added that she supposed he knew "that New York has passed the law for *universal suffrage—all* the niggers!"[52]

Keziah Brevard, who had never married and who managed her own affairs without suffering the immediate burdens of male domination, railed against life among slaves without mentioning women's condition. Brevard bitterly resented her slaves for the troubles they imposed upon her: theft, disrespect, laziness. Her complaints might even be read as an indictment of slavery's subjugation of slaveholding women, but only with the understanding that she feared and mistrusted the slaves much more than she disliked slavery. Her dislike of slavery, like that of other women of her class, could be traced to extreme racism:

How was it possible for a decent woman to live among such people? She would solve the social problem by shipping them all back to Africa as soon as possible. Should that prove impossible, then obviously they must remain slaves, whatever the burdens on long-suffering women. Some semblance of social order had to be preserved.[53]

Many slaveholding women may have secretly felt that in everyday life slavery contributed as much to disarray as to order. Some expressed doubts in their diaries and letters, but, like the southern clergy to whom they readily turned for guidance, they were more likely to stress the need for reform of the system than its abolition. Most of their doubts concerned the effects of slavery on the character and behavior of slaveholders, notably boys and men. Although they might blame slavery for aspects of their lives that they found painful and occasionally intolerable, they rarely opposed it on principle or in the abstract. Writing long after the war, Elizabeth Meriwether claimed to have opposed slavery on principle, but her principles did not prevent her from accepting a slave to relieve her of the unacceptable responsibility for her own housework. Even Mary Minor Blackford, who did oppose slavery on principle, hired a slave nurse for her children and lived to see both of her sons fight for the Confederacy. Many slaveholding women understood that abuses of sexuality and power could be directly linked to slavery but had difficulty understanding that the main victims were the slaves. They were not much concerned with justice to the slaves and not at all concerned with individual freedom and with justice in the abstract.[54]

Before the war Gertrude Thomas, who has been advanced as an example of slaveholding women's "feminism," did not protest slavery, but she did express reservations about prevailing attitudes toward women. After the war she actively supported women's rights; before the war, if we are to credit her journal, she did not. During the 1850s she wrote primarily of her daily activities, her extensive reading, her religious feelings, and her family relations. Her husband, who would subsequently disappoint her, at that time constituted the source of all her stability and happiness, and she thanked God for her good fortune. In her view, Jeff Thomas combined "such moral qualitys, such an affectionate heart, with just such a master will as suits my womans nature, for true to my sex, I delight *in looking up*, and love to feel my womans weakness protected by man's superior strength."[55]

She noted that women did not always remain true to their nature. At a prayer meeting during which the minister invited all to speak their minds, "one lady addressed us with a few words." Presumably, she had been prompted to her boldness by the minister's text on the previous night: "Quench not the spirit." Gertrude Thomas had no doubt that "many felt it their duty to speak but quenched the spirit." Had not Paul said, "'Let not your women speak in public'"? This admonition, "aside from their natural diffidence would cause a female to remain silent upon such an occasion." She nonetheless thought that there was a case for treating women more equally with men. "*Christine or Womans Trials and Womans Triumphs*" differed dramatically from her normal reading, "being very decided womans rights book advocating women—Their perfect equality with the other sex." Thomas admitted that the author made some very good arguments, although the denouement of the plot disappointed her, because the Christian heroine "*marries* and then confesses that she is glad that the tie of marriage is so strong that it cannot be broken, this too after she has been advocating to the contrary." Gertrude Thomas believed strongly in the indissolubility of marriage but reproached this author for a muddled argument. At the same time, she had been reading a book, *Caste*, by "a decided Abolitionist." In this work, the orphan heroine's proposed marriage to the son of the household to which she had gone as governess was called off when she was discovered to be the child of a mulatto slave and a neighboring planter. Gertrude Thomas had to "confess I was sufficiently *Southern* to think him justifiable in breaking off the engagement."[56]

White women's trials remained closer to Gertrude Thomas's heart than those of slaves. She referred regularly to her own slaves, noting the tasks they accomplished or failed to accomplish, her dependence on them for the care of her children, their nursing of her children, and their thefts. Tamah was caught red-handed. Isabella was incorrigible. A slave preacher won her admiration for his moving rhetoric. But we catch here not a breath of their deserving freedom, not a breath that they complicated the lives of white women beyond taxing their powers of discipline. Thomas admitted that some women suffered from the "general depravity" of men, but she was not among their number. Men were mostly bad, but there "were some *noble exceptions*," among whom she classed her husband. She had staked her "reputation upon his" and, perhaps, had "acted rashly," but did not think so. Were her faith "dissipated by *actual experience* then would be dissolved a dream in which is constituted my hope of happiness upon earth." After three years and six months of marriage, she allowed that there had been the normal little trials of which the human lot was composed, but still had "unbounded love and confidence in my husband." She frequently wondered "what the feelings of a woman must be when she finds she has been trifled with and her affections slighted. I can imagine the wild . . . contending feelings. The indignation, insulted pride and &c." She had read of such things.[57]

Thomas doubted the justice of a double moral standard. After reading *Ruth*, a beautiful novel about a fallen woman, she deplored the hard spirit displayed toward such unfortunates "*by our own sex*. Oh how many of these women are more sinned against than sinning." She did not condone the sin and counted herself "as strong an advocate for purity, perfect purity in women as any one can be." Yet she thought it time to "change some of our ways of thinking and acting." What a shame it was that "what is considered a venial thing in man should in a worldly point of view *damn* a woman and shut her out from every form of employment." She never intended, however, to make women less moral and inveighed strenuously against another novel, *Light and Darkness*, finding it objectionable "that any *unmarried* woman should write so freely and express herself, on *certain* subjects so independent." George Sand she charged with disseminating "licentious literature" and "intellectual poison." "What a libel upon womanhood is this George Sands, Madame." The only thing to be said in Sand's defense was that she refused "to sign the name given her by *her mother* to her infamous productions."[58]

Gertrude Thomas knew that serious trials abounded in her own world as well as in fiction. She bemoaned the fate of an unfortunate wife whose husband was living with another white woman and her children and supporting them all off the resources that his wife's labor provided him. But women, too, could turn bad. A Mrs. McDonald left her husband and children to run off with a gambler. Yet why, Thomas pondered, would it be considered perfectly correct for Dr. McDonald to refuse to take his wife back, whereas she, in a similar position, would be expected to forget and forgive? Social ethics admitted of great improvement. "But I mount my hobby when I commence on the subject of woman and her wrongs." Her concern for women's wrongs should not be misinterpreted. "I am no 'Womans Rights Woman' in the northern sense of the term." She only warred against the injustice of "womans being forever 'Anathema Masanatha' in society for the *same offence* which in a man, *very* slightly lowers, and in the estimation of some of his *own sex* rather elevates him." This distinction she found "to be a *very very* great injustice." She remained "the greatest possible advocate for womans purity, in word, thought, or deed," yet thought that "if a few of the harrangues directed to *women* were directed in a point where it is needed more, the standard of morality might be elevated."[59]

It should surprise no one that examples of this kind could be multiplied. Women, like men, rail against the unpleasant aspects of their lives. But their railing should not ipso facto be taken as a rejection of their society or its reigning worldview. Southern society extracted its price from slaveholding women, but it also offered compensations. In 1862, Susan Becton, a North Carolinian who had been educated in New Jersey and was trapped in the North by the outbreak of hostilities, wrote to a friend at home that she had recently embarked on a new phase of life: "And true, democratic life it is; one in which every body labours; the men earning their bread by hard toil, and their wives, alternately mistress & maid, performing with their own hands, the drudgery, which, with us, devolves upon slaves." At first, the novelty rather pleased her. She met men who "had worked all day in the field," yet in the evening "appeared intelligent, educated gentlemen." She saw a lady move from parlor to kitchen "and perform her duties with equal ease and facility in each." Within six months, however, she had been disillusioned: "The nobility and elevating influences of labour are lost in the daily, hourly strife with petty cares and means; men become narrow-minded and pernicious; women sink beneath the double burden of natural and assumed duties—Care for the body usurps care for the mind and the tone of society is inevitably lowered."[60]

The Anna Kings and Keziah Brevards did not even mention such matters, but had they been forced to, they, like Mary Chesnut, probably would have concurred wholeheartedly with Susan Becton's opinion—as did Thomas Roderick Dew, who fully understood that slavery permitted the freedom from labor that made possible a civilization worthy of the name. Normally, southern women did not write in an abstract or sociological mode. They wrote primarily from a subjective perspective and envisioned women as members of a sex—a biological category. Louisa McCord, in contrast, wrote primarily from an objective perspective and envisioned women as members of a gender—a social category. If Mary Chesnut wrote as a perennial belle, bedeviled by personal ambition, Louisa McCord wrote as a matron who measured personal feelings against their social consequences. McCord, in contrast to Chesnut and many other slaveholding women, addressed the debate about feminism directly. She made explicit what others took for granted: the necessary link between women's position and the social relations of the society to which they belonged.

To view Mary Chesnut and other slaveholding women as critics of slavery and "patriarchy" is implicitly to challenge McCord's wisdom on the "woman question," and to cast McCord herself as exceptional. In reality, McCord knew as well as any that women had grounds for discontent, just as she knew that Mary Chesnut was not alone in railing against the monstrous system that hedged slaveholding women in. She merely opposed generalizing from individual unhappiness, and she understood that few slaveholding women, least of all Mary Chesnut, would have chosen to mingle in equality with the white—much less with the black—masses. Mary Chesnut's bitterness at the self-indulgence and arrogance of her father-in-law and his kind did not justify a broadside attack on the system simply because it left room for abuse. For that system provided privileges and amenities for its women that they had no intention of surrendering.

Gertrude Thomas resumed her journal, after a brief lapse, on 15 July 1861. "Events transcending in importance any thing that has ever happened within the recollection of any living person in *our* country, have occurred since I have last written in my journal." Since then war had come. Thomas noted that the southern ministers sent north to negotiate terms of peace were treated with "cool indifference," but that southern forts, with the exception of Sumter, were in southern hands. "*There* the ever memorable victory was achevied which added fresh laurels to the glory of the gallant little state of South Carolina." Georgia had responded well. "I have always been proud of my native state but never more so than now." Duty and honor had called her husband to battle. "Our country is invaded—our homes are in danger—We are deprived or they are attempting to deprive us of that glorious liberty for which our Fathers fought and bled and shall we tamely submit to this?"[61]

In 1860 the spurs of history had turned Catherine Edmonston to her journal. "I have," she began, "many times in my life commenced a journal, faithfully kept it for a few months and then gradually left it off, perhaps from weariness, perhaps from an absolute dearth of events." How could a woman's daily round hold the attention of writer or reader? To be readable, a journal must have "plenty of Plums in it! None of your Milestone puddings but a real Christmas Pie, wherein no 'Jack Horner' can 'put in his thumb' without 'pulling out' a juicy sugar of 'plum'!" The time for her own journal had come, for "in these troublesome times a lack of incident can be no excuse for dullness." Throughout the South, many women responded in kind, adding only that the danger of their country left no excuse for doubts about the justice of the cause.[62]

Mary Chesnut was among their number. Yankee aggression reinforced her identification with the society of which she was so deeply a part. The subjective drowned in the flow of objective events, or at least henceforth was kept under control. Although she never succeeded in banishing the subjective entirely, she unambiguously opened her diary under the aegis of history: "Conecuh. Ems. I do not allow myself vain regrets or sad foreboding. This Southern Confederacy must be supported now by calm determination and cool brains. We have risked all, and we must play our best, for the stake is life or death."[63]

By opening her diary with that pronouncement, portrayed as a private moment of truth, Mary Chesnut assumed the prerogatives of craft to distinguish between historical contingency and personal conviction. History had forced her to choose. Nonetheless, within historical exigency her true self persisted. The tension between her historical and private selves accounts for much of the richness and fascination of her diary. Yet ultimately she lacked sufficient control of her material to forge it into a coherent story. Apparently unable or unwilling to decide between the historical and the personal, she let them coexist and thus provoked understandable confusion about her true views.

Louisa McCord unflinchingly accepted the priority of historical over personal claims. This acceptance permitted her also to accept the logical relation between social and gender relations. Loyalty to southern society led inescapably to the defense of slavery, which led inescapably to the subordination of women to men. Social order stood or fell as a whole. Mary Chesnut would have preferred to have had it both ways—to have had the delights of southern civilization without the inconveniences of slavery; to have retained her privileges without suffering the abuse of men. Her deepest secrets, which remain buried beneath the breathless flow of those thoughts and events that she was willing to expose to the world, probably concerned her angers and her ambitions: anger at the men who caused her childlessness, ambition to excel on the great stage of the world. To confuse that consuming ambition with a desire to share equally with men and other women in pie(ty)-making, or with a commitment to equal rights for all women, is to mistake her. Had she been able to choose, she would—I suggest—have chosen to follow that quintessential hero and belle, Elizabeth I, in her announced role of Prince.

Epilogue

For a slaveholding woman, the self came wrapped in gender, and gender wrapped in class and race. From her earliest consciousness, when a slaveholding girl thought of herself as "I," she thought of herself as a female. As her earliest consciousness grew into a personal identity, she naturally thought of herself as a privileged white woman—a lady. Everything in her society conspired to reinforce her identity as a woman. Everything discouraged her from thinking of herself as an individual in the abstract.

For most antebellum white women, northern as well as southern, gender constituted the invisible, seamless wrapping of the self. Even the northeastern women who were beginning to challenge the restrictions on women in the name of individual rights were not radically questioning their own identifications as women. White women's identities as women emerged directly from the gender relations of their society. To be an "I" at all meant to be a female self, to be a member of a gender. Gender relations thus linked the individual woman to the larger world. The gender roles through which she was encouraged to realize her identity defined the place of her self in that world. However limiting slaveholding women might find their gender roles as ladies, they overwhelmingly accepted them as the proper articulation of their selves in the world. Gender conventions might limit their possibilities, but they delineated an order that confirmed the women's deepest sense of who they were.

A slave woman, in contrast, remained caught

between the gender conventions of southern society and the gender relations of the slave community. She never enjoyed—or was never entirely imprisoned by—a definition of womanhood so all-pervasive that it constituted the core of her identity. Her relations with members of the slave community and, in lesser measure, with whites offered her interlocking networks of gender relations and gender roles, but both networks were subject to constant violation. Slave women and men developed their own model of gender relations, but never in isolation from the conditions of their enslavement. And they lacked the power to develop gender roles that derived from their gender relations. We may never be able to evaluate precisely the African contribution to an evolving Afro-American culture, but we can be sure that the African and the American intermingled under conditions in which African traditions were uprooted from African society and in which American models were not grounded in those institutions—marriage, property relations—on which white Americans relied. Afro-American slaves forcefully resisted the extreme dehumanization and desexualization of enslavement, but they were not free to ground their particular vision of the proper relations between women and men in their own institutions.

Slave women could not experience gender as a seamless wrapping of their selves. Slavery forced upon them a double view of gender relations that exposed the artificial or problematic aspects of gender identification, for by stripping slave men of the social attributes of manhood in general and fatherhood in particular, it afforded women no satisfactory social definition of themselves as women. This social "unmanning" of slave men, whatever its negative consequences for women, had nothing to do with some purported personal emasculation of the men, but it had everything to do with slaves' ability to create a community in which they could protect the gender identities and roles of their people. When a slaveholding woman lost a child, she had to do her best to reconcile herself to the will of God, who had seen fit to take the child from her. The loss did not threaten her role or her identity as a mother. A slave woman had more than one way to lose her child. If the child died, she could hope that the death was sanctified by God, but if the child lived and was sold, she had to reconcile herself to the power of a master who could wantonly make a mockery of her motherhood. Alternatively, she had to find a way to reject the legitimacy of the master's action and a way of opposing her will to his beyond the bounds of gender. No black man, however loving—even if he were her child's father—could readily help her. He could try. He could sacrifice himself to prevent or avenge an assault on her. But he could not defend his wife and child without subjecting himself to a risk that she herself would regard as unacceptable and would try to keep him from assuming. His claim to the status of father had no basis in law, no confirmation from the society in which he lived.

Many slaveholders did their best to soften these harsh realities. Some encouraged "marriage" and tried to avoid separating slave "families," especially mothers and young children. But few considered a slave woman's sexuality as being under the protection of a particular man. Those whose personal morality did not restrain them believed that they had a right to enjoy that sexuality without anyone's by-your-leave. To argue that their very sexual advances implicitly recognized slave women's womanhood misses the point. Their advances above all reflected their appreciation of a sexuality freed from the constraints of social and gender conventions, freed from the bonds in which sexuality is normally embedded and through which it is normally experienced. Sexual advances by slaveholders did not differ significantly, in their underlying rationale, from the separation of mothers and children, the assigning of women to "men's" work, or physical brutality. All subjected slave women to a sense of atomization. As a slave woman and her master confronted each other, the trappings of gender slipped away. The woman faced him alone. She looked on naked power.

Since almost no slave women left direct testimonies of their experience, it remains difficult, if not presumptuous, to try to reconstruct their lives. But Harriet Jacobs, a remarkable slave who fled to the North, did write *Incidents in the Life of a Slave Girl*, a powerful account of her enslavement, her escape, and her freedom. To protect her relatives and those who had assisted in her escape, Harriet Jacobs wrote under the name Linda Brent, but she insisted on her own (disguised) authorship by her subtitle, *Written by Herself*. For decades, while her identity remained largely unknown, the authenticity of her account was doubted. Critics assumed that Lydia Maria Child, Jacobs's editor, had written *Incidents*, for how could a slave woman have written in the flowery style of middle-class domestic fiction? Jacobs's surviving correspondence proves them wrong, and, thanks to the meticulous research of Jean Fagan Yellin, her authorship can no longer be doubted. But the problem of her idiom persists, for she did write in the discourse of domestic fiction and did cast her travail in the rhetoric of true womanhood. Her account thus poignantly reveals the ways in which she and other black women, slave and free, were simultaneously alienated from and bound to the dominant white models of womanhood and the discourses through which those models were developed.[1]

In self-consciously writing for a white, northern, middle-class audience, Jacobs did not differentiate herself from the most celebrated male authors of slave narratives. Frederick Douglass, for example, firmly identified himself with the triumph of manliness and individualism that slavery suppressed. In so doing, he explicitly called upon his northern readers to recognize that the sufferings and inequities to which he had been subjected by the very condition of enslavement directly contravened their deepest principles of individualism. He assumed that the most effective way to reach his readers was to remind them that he was a man like themselves. Slavery, he argued, using his own case as the prime example, mocked the laws of God and man by unjustly subjecting one man to the will of another. Slavery defied the principle of individualism itself. An insult to his manhood was an insult to theirs; a violation of his innate rights was a potential violation of theirs. Thus did Douglass locate himself squarely in the mainstream of universalist and individualist thought and repudiate southern particularism and hierarchy. Slavery was not a particular case of various gradations of dependency and unfreedom; it was the absolute contradiction of freedom itself. So long as it was allowed to persist, no man's freedom would be secure.[2]

Harriet Jacobs faced a more difficult task. For her, a woman, to claim that her enslavement violated the principles of individualism would be to risk having her story dismissed. A few northern white women were beginning to work out the analogy between slavery and the oppression of women, but their view had not won general sympathy. Inequalities between women and men still appeared to many northerners, even those who opposed slavery, as manifestations of natural differences. Northern women who sought improvement in their own condition clung to the discourses of true womanhood and domesticity to help to make their case. Northern gender conventions differed from southern ones, but they, too, dictated that a woman address the public modestly and deferentially, if at all. A poignant account of the violation of a woman's virtue stood a much better chance of appealing to northern sensibilities than a pronunciamento for woman's individual rights, if only because it reaffirmed woman's essentially domestic nature. Perhaps Jacobs would have written differently had she been able to write for an audience of slave women, but few slave women could read, and she could not, in any case, have reached them. Her only hope for a hearing lay in reaching the same people who avidly read Harriet Beecher Stowe. Jacobs left no doubt about her intended readers: "O, you happy free women, contrast *your* New Year's day with that of the poor bondwoman!"[3]

Jacobs, like slaveholding women who kept diaries or journals, shaped her presentation of herself to conform, at least in part, to the expectations of her intended readers. Like Douglass, who invoked the rhetoric of male individualism to encourage identification with his narrative, she had to try to make her readers take the oppression of slave women personally, to see it as a threat to their own sense of themselves as women. To touch their hearts, she had to address them in their own idiom, tell her story in a way with which they could identify. For her readers to accept her as a woman, she had to present herself as a woman like them. Understanding that their ideas of womanhood were intimately linked to the specific gender relations and conventions of their society, she represented her own travail as an assault on true womanhood and the triumph of virtue. She exposed slavery as a violation of the norms of womanhood and portrayed slave women as essentially like their northern white sisters in their goals and sensibilities. Slavery, in this portrayal, constituted a crime against woman's essential nature—her natural yearning for virtue, domesticity, and motherhood. Jacobs followed Douglass in accepting the norms of northern society as absolutes—the articulations of innate human nature—which were directly contradicted by slavery.[4]

In her preface, Jacobs assured her readers that her narrative "is no fiction," however incredible some of the adventures might seem, and that she was not writing to call attention to herself, nor to "excite sympathy for my own sufferings." Rather, she sought "to arouse the women of the North to a realizing sense of the condition of two millions of women at the South, still in bondage, suffering what I suffered, and most of them far worse." She only wished that she were more competent to perform the task, but, having been born and reared in slavery, having lived in slavery for twenty-seven years, and having, since her arrival in the North, been obliged to work for her living, she had not had much leisure "to make up for the loss of early opportunities to improve myself." She presumed to write only out of the conviction that experience alone could reveal "how deep, and dark, and foul is that pit of abominations." So she dared to offer "this imperfect effort on behalf of my persecuted people."[5]

Intending her narrative as an exposé of slavery as the violation of woman's nature, Harriet Jacobs began by distancing the self—her fictional self, Linda Brent—from the condition. "I was born a slave; but I never knew it till six years of happy childhood had passed away." Yet the possible effects of the condition haunted her. Her father, she insisted, "had more of the feelings of a freeman than is common among slaves," and thereby she implicitly acknowledged the difference between slavery and freedom in the development of an independent self. Not all slaves naturally developed the innate appreciation of individualism and freedom. By representing her legacy of upstanding individualism as having come from her father, Jacobs attempted to provide a social fatherhood that slavery denied. Yet she quickly revealed its limitations. On one occasion, her father and mistress called her brother at the same instant. After a moment's hesitation, the boy went to the mistress. The father sharply reproved him: "You are *my* child . . . and when I call you, you should come immediately, if you have to pass through fire and water." But no law backed the father's claim. His desire to command the primary obedience of his child flowed from instinctive feelings of freedom, the social legitimacy of which his condition denied. By the law of slavery, his son was not his child at all: He was the child of his slave mother. Even a free father could not call "his" child by a slave wife his own. Yet Jacobs had reason to introduce her own story of resistance with the representation of Linda Brent's father's spirit of manliness and instinctive grasp of the virtues of freedom.[6]

Linda Brent's early years had been sheltered. Her parents, who were both "a light shade of brownish yellow, and were termed mulattoes," lived together in a comfortable home. Her father hired himself out as a carpenter and, on condition of paying his mistress two hundred dollars a year, managed his own affairs. Her mother was "a slave merely in name, but in nature was noble and womanly." Her grandmother lived nearby in the household of the mistress, where she had become indispensable "in all capacities, from cook and wetnurse to seamstress." This sheltered universe collapsed when Linda Brent's mother died, and then, when she was six, "for the first time, I learned, by the talk around me, that I was a slave." Between the ages of six and twelve, Linda Brent experienced the gentle face of slavery. Her kind mistress imposed no harsh duties upon her and "was so kind to me that I was always glad to do her bidding, and proud to labor for her as much as my young years would permit." At her mistress's side, Linda Brent sat for hours, "sewing diligently, with a heart as free from care as that of any free-born white child" (pp. 5–7).

When Linda Brent was nearly twelve, her mistress sickened and died. Watching the cheek grow paler, the eye more glassy, "how earnestly I prayed in my heart that she might live! I loved her; for she had been almost like a mother to me." She had taught "me to read and spell; and for this privilege, which so rarely falls to the lot of a slave, I bless her memory." But the reading of the will did not bring Linda Brent the freedom that her mistress's attachment seemed to promise. The will bequeathed Linda Brent to the five-year-old daughter of her mistress's sister. Thus even the most beneficent mistress followed the dictates of slavery, and by means of this female succession from a motherly mistress to a five-year-old child, Linda Brent, poised on the threshold between childhood and womanhood, first came under the control of a master (pp. 7–8).

That master was the father of her new mistress, a Dr. Flint, "a physician in the neighborhood." Harriet Jacobs opened the chapter that introduced Dr. Flint with the passage on her own father's manliness. Presumably, she sought, however mutedly, to underscore the contrast between the slave man who was a true father and the slaveholder who was none at all, sought to expose the bankruptcy of the metaphor of family that cast the slaveholder as the father of his dependents. But by juxtaposing her father and his instinctive feelings of freedom with her introduction of the master, with whom she would engage in deadly combat, she also underscored the limitations of feelings of fatherhood relative to the powers of "fatherhood." And in moving from her father to her master, she brought her reader from the gentle world of her parents' domesticity and her first mistress's motherliness into the harsh reality of slavery. Linda Brent's entry into slavery also coincided with her entry into womanhood, which, as her subsequent trials revealed, offered slave women no protection at all.

Dr. Flint's wife offered no antidote to his cruelty. "She was totally deficient in energy." Lacking the strength to superintend the affairs of her household, she nonetheless had nerves so strong "that she could sit in her easy chair and see a woman whipped, till the blood trickled from every stroke of the lash." A member of a church, she drew no spirit of charity from the services. Niggardly with her slaves, she would spit into pots after the white family had been served to prevent the cook and her children from enjoying the scraps, and she permitted them nothing to eat but what she herself gave them. "Provisions were weighed out by the pound and ounce." No slave dared eat from her flour barrel. "She knew how many biscuits a quart of flour would make, and exactly what size they ought to be" (p. 12).

Dr. Flint owned a fine house in town and several farms; he also owned about fifty slaves, in addition to those whom he hired. He embodied all the pretensions to civility that supposedly characterized men of his class, but his refined tastes formed only a thin veneer for his boundless sadism. He terrorized the cook and brutally whipped any servant who displeased him. During Linda Brent's first weeks in his house she heard, for the first time, "hundreds of blows fall, in succession, on a human being." The victim of the terrible punishment was a man from one of the plantations. Opinions varied about the cause, but one story held that the slave had quarreled with his wife in the presence of the overseer and "had accused his master of being the father of her child. They were both black, and the child was very fair." A few months later Dr. Flint sold both man and wife, telling her, when she protested, that she had let her tongue go too far. "She had forgotten that it was a crime for a slave to tell who was the father of her child" (pp. 15, 12–13).

Linda Brent's first few years in Dr. Flint's house introduced her to petty cruelties she had not previously known, but her lingering childhood protected her from the worst. Then she "entered on my fifteenth year—a sad epoch in the life of a slave girl." Her master began "to whisper foul words in my ear," and, young as she was, she grasped their meaning. When she tried to avoid and resist him, he told "me I was his property; that I must be subject to his will in all things." Her soul revolted, but where "could I turn for protection?" Be the slave girl as black as ebony or as fair as her mistress, "there is no shadow of law to protect her from insult, from violence, or even from death; all these are inflicted by fiends who bear the shape of men." And the mistress who ought to protect her feels only jealousy and rage. The slave girl thus becomes "prematurely knowing in evil things. Soon she will learn to tremble when she hears her master's footfall. She will be compelled to realize that she is no longer a child. If God has bestowed beauty upon her, it will prove her greatest curse. That which commands admiration in the white woman only hastens the degradation of the female slave." Some may be too brutalized by slavery to feel the horror of their position, but others feel it acutely (pp. 27–28).

Linda Brent was among those who felt it. Jacobs depicts her position by contrasting two beautiful children, one white, one black. Whereas the fair child had in front of her a pathway of flowers, her slave sister, who was also beautiful, had a road of misery. "She drank from the cup of sin, and shame, and misery, whereof her persecuted race are compelled to drink." In the previous chapter, in which she wrote of Linda Brent's first few years in Dr. Flint's house, Jacobs had included a narrative of her Uncle Benjamin's successful flight to the North. When word finally arrived that he was safe, her family proudly concluded: "'He that is *willing* to be a slave, let him be a slave.'" The relation between the slave girl's being compelled to drink the bitter cup of sin and the triumph of Uncle Benjamin's will to freedom invite reflection. They frame Linda Brent's dawning awareness of her master's intentions: "My master met me at every turn, reminding me that I belonged to him, and swearing by heaven and earth that he would compel me to submit to him" (pp. 26–28).

Through the narrative of Linda Brent's unfolding struggle with her master, Jacobs underscored that the unfortunate slave girl had no one to turn to, especially not white slaveholding women. Some mistresses, like Dr. Flint's wife, were jealous of the slave women their husbands pursued; some, who married knowing that their husband was the father of slave children, "do not trouble themselves about it"; some, who had true moral sensibilities, prevailed upon their husbands to free the slaves toward "whom they stood in a parental relation." Jacobs admitted that although slavery as a "bad institution deadens the moral sense, even in white women, to a fearful extent," it did not entirely extinguish it. Some women were known to say of men's behavior: "'I declare, such things ought not to be tolerated in any decent society.'" But even they could offer unfortunate slave women scant protection (p. 36).

Why, Jacobs had Linda Brent wonder, would a slave, constantly exposed to the tyrannical will of the master, ever love? Separations caused by death might invite the pious to resign themselves to God's will. "But when the ruthless hand of man strikes the blow, regardless of the misery he causes, it is hard to be submissive." Yet youth will be served, and Linda Brent fell in love with a "young colored carpenter; a free born man," who loved her and wanted to marry her. Never! thundered her master. During the confrontation in which he told her he would not tolerate her marrying "a free nigger"—a man who might think he could protect her—she enraged him by openly stating that she loved her free black "lover." How dared she tell him such a thing? And he struck her. She responded: "'You have struck me for answering you honestly, How I despise you!'" Momentarily confounded, he asked her if she knew what she had said. She replied that she did, "but your treatment drove me to it." And he asked her if she knew that "'I have a right to do as I like with you,—that I can kill you, if I please?'"

(Legally, he had no such right, but he did have the power, as she doubtless knew.) She did know. He had already tried to kill her, and she wished he had succeeded, " 'but you have no right to do as you like with me.' " Enraged, he insisted that she forgot herself and asked her if she were mad. Most masters in his position would already have killed her. She admitted to having been disrespectful, " 'but you drove me to it; I couldn't help it.' " She would prefer jail to her current situation. For a fortnight after the interview, Linda Brent heard nothing more from her master, and then he sent her a letter to inform her that he was thinking of moving to Louisiana and would take a few slaves with him. He proposed that she come with him and promised that his wife would stay behind. "He begged me to think over the matter, and answer the following day" (pp. 37–41).

In this passage, Jacobs depicts Linda Brent as if she were, in essential respects, her master's social and racial equal. Twice Linda Brent tells him that he drove her to her rebellious actions, that she could not help herself—presumably because her feelings of decency and self-respect had been abused. The interchange between master and slave strains credulity. The sending of a letter certainly had more to do with the conventions of domestic fiction than with actual relations between masters and slaves. But the familiar picture of female virtue had another side, for Linda Brent felt more than the outrage of offended virtue. "Reader, did you ever hate? I hope not. I never did but once; and I trust I never shall again." Knowing that she would never be allowed to marry the man she loved, knowing that the path to respectability was barred forever by her master's power, she resolved to tell her lover to forget her and to continue the struggle alone. She knew her master would never consent to sell her, especially not to a man who would marry and protect her. "He had an iron will, and was determined to keep me, and to conquer me." Coolly acknowledging the end of her dream, she prepared for the next round of struggle (pp. 40, 42).

Gradually her potential allies and supporters were being stripped away. Nothing could be hoped from her jealous mistress. Nothing could be hoped from her devoted lover. Little could be hoped from the other slaves, especially the men, whom she perceived as living in a state of ignorance and degradation. Some had been so "brutalized by the lash" that they would sneak away to leave their masters "free access to their wives and daughters." She did not mean that such behavior proved "the black man to belong to an inferior order of beings." What could be expected of one who had been reared a slave, "with generations of slaves for ancestors"? She admitted that "the black man *is* inferior." But she argued that his inferiority resulted from "the ignorance in which white men compel him to live," the "torturing whip that lashes manhood out of him," and the "fierce bloodhounds of the South, and the scarcely less cruel human bloodhounds of the north, who enforce the Fugitive Slave Law. *They* do the work" (p. 44).

Increasingly isolated in her struggle with her master, Linda Brent toughened her resolve. She was determined "that the master, whom I so hated and loathed, who had blighted the prospects of my youth, and made my life a desert, should not, after my long struggle with him, succeed at last in trampling his victim under his feet." She vowed to "do any thing, every thing, for the sake of defeating him. What *could* I do?" She begged her readers—"ye happy women, whose purity has been sheltered from childhood, who have been free to choose the objects of your affection, whose homes are protected by law"—not to judge "the poor desolate slave girl" too severely. She was "struggling alone in the powerful grasp of the demon Slavery; and the monster proved too strong for me." She felt as if she had been "forsaken by God and man; as if all my efforts must be frustrated; and I became reckless in my despair." Yet she refused to hide behind the "plea of compulsion from a master; for it was not so." She could not plead "ignorance or thoughtlessness." The influences of slavery had taken their toll on her as on others, "had made me prematurely knowing, concerning the evil ways of the world. I knew what I did, and I did it with deliberate calculation" (pp. 53–54).

She took a white lover, "a white unmarried gentleman," Mr. Sands, who had learned the particulars of her condition, expressed sympathy for her, "and wrote to me frequently. I was a poor slave girl, only fifteen years old." Naturally, she found the attentions of such a "superior person," of "an educated and eloquent gentleman," flattering. To be an object of interest "to a man who is not married, and who is not her master, is agreeable to the pride and feelings of a slave, if her miserable situation has left her any pride of sentiment." Above all, it seemed "less degrading to give one's self, than to submit to compulsion. There is something akin to freedom in having a lover who has no control over you, except what he gains by kindness and attachment." She also hoped that her master might sell her to Mr. Sands, who then might free her. Reflecting upon these and other considerations, "and seeing no other way of escaping the doom I so much dreaded, I made a headlong plunge." She could only beg her virtuous reader to pity her. For the virtuous reader had never known "what it is to be a slave; to be entirely unprotected by law or custom; to have the laws reduce you to the condition of a chattel, entirely subject to the will of another" (pp. 55–56).

A struggle of wills lay at the core of this incident, although Jacobs tried to disguise it by having Linda Brent express lifelong regret for her fall from virtue. But, she added, "the slave woman ought not to be judged by the same standard as others." At the time, only Linda Brent's beloved grandmother judged her harshly: "'O Linda! has it come to this? I had rather see you dead than to see you as you now are. You are a disgrace to your dead mother.'" The grandmother eventually relented, but even when she expressed pity, she did not say that she forgave Linda. During the next few years, Linda Brent bore Mr. Sands two children. Both pregnancies enraged Dr. Flint, who had not abandoned his pursuit of Linda. Once, in a fury, he pitched her down a flight of stairs. Another time, he cut off the hair she was so proud of and, when she replied to his abuse, struck her. Throughout, he heaped upon her insults she could not repeat. The birth of her second child, a girl, brought her miseries home with full force. "Slavery is terrible for men; but it is far more terrible for women. Superadded to the burden common to all, *they* have wrongs, and sufferings, and mortifications peculiarly their own" (pp. 56–57, 77).

The baptism of her children exposed the isolation of their, and her own, situations. She always regretted that they had "no lawful claim to a name." Mr. Sands offered his, but she dared not accept while her master lived. And she knew that "it would not be accepted at their baptism," for Dr. Flint would have forbidden any baptism at all. But one Sunday when he was called from town, Linda Brent's grandmother arranged it. As Linda Brent entered the church, she was suffused with memories of her mother, who had presented her for baptism with no cause for shame. "She had been married, and had such legal rights as slavery allows to a slave." Her vows had been sacred to her, and she had never violated them. Why should Linda Brent's situation be so different? "*Her* [mother's] master had died when she was a child; and she remained with her mistress till she married. She was never in the power of any master" (pp. 76–79).

Motherhood, far from releasing Linda Brent from Dr. Flint's persecutions, intensified them. Mr. Sands tried to buy her and the children, but to no avail. "Dr. Flint loved money, but he loved power more." Not content with tormenting her, he abused her children. After months of abuse, followed by months of quiet, he suddenly changed tactics. Still determined to have his way with her, he offered freedom for her and her children if she would agree to live in one of his small cottages and have no further communication with the children's father. She refused. Curbing his anger, he told her that she had answered too fast. Should she persist in rejecting the offer, he would send her children to one of the plantations, where they would "fare like the rest of the negro children." The threat shook Linda, who viewed the plantation as the embodiment of slavery. At the end of the week, she told him that she was ready to go to the plantation, thus sacrificing the mobility and status of life in town in order to thwart her master's will. He retorted that she could go with his curse and that her boy would be put to work in preparation for being sold; her daughter would be raised "for the purpose of selling well." Linda Brent's grandmother despaired. Linda herself, however, claimed: "I had my secret hopes; but I must fight my battle alone. I had a woman's pride, and a mother's love for my children; and I resolved that out of the darkness of this hour a brighter dawn should rise for them. My master had power and law on his side; I had a determined will. There is might in each" (pp. 80–85).

Life at the plantation proved less degrading than Linda Brent had feared, although it constituted a further step away from the family and privileged status that had grounded her life. Dr. Flint, hard pressed for competent house servants, entrusted the entire management of the house to her, and she did her work "faithfully, though not, of course, with a willing mind." But the descending spiral was accelerating. Not long after her arrival, she learned that Dr. Flint intended to send her children to join her on the plantation to be "broke in." That knowledge determined her to set in motion the plan she had been contemplating. She would flee, assuming that, once she was gone, Dr. Flint would put the children up for sale and Mr. Sands would buy them. Her grandmother questioned the wisdom of the plan and advised her not to trust to Mr. Sands's promises: "Stand by your own children, and suffer with them till death. Nobody respects a mother who forsakes her children; and if you leave them, you will never have a happy moment" (pp. 86–95).

In Harriet Jacobs's representation, Linda Brent left her children in order to protect them from the brutalization of plantation life and to improve their situation. Her resistance to Dr. Flint's will had jeopardized their well-being. Rather than submit, she raised the level of her resistance and entrusted her children to the good intentions of others. The rhetoric of motherhood constitutes an important strand in *Incidents*, but it remains difficult to determine how faithfully it reflected

Harriet Jacobs late in her life, ca. 1890.
Courtesy of anonymous donor

Letter from Harriet Jacobs to Amy Post, 23 May [n.d.].
Courtesy of Department of Rare Books and Special Collections, University of Rochester Library

Jacobs's own feelings, as depicted through Linda Brent. Motherhood, like love and marriage, frequently evokes an ideal rather than a reality. At issue is not Linda Brent's love for her children, but her sense of the relation between that love and the role of mother and the relation between that love and her own identity. The lack of a husband left her and her children without a man to protect them and left the children without a name and a legal identity. Slavery made it impossible for her to fulfill the role of mother, and increasingly her love for her children became divorced from any attempt to do so. Unable to act as their mother, she could offer them nothing but love. She had no power to shape their lives and, accordingly, did not feel bound to remain with them at any cost. If the cost were her own integrity—her own will— what kind of mother could she be? Jacobs did not spell out the logic of her narrative, but the succession of events leaves little doubt of her intent. Like other slave women who ran away, leaving their children behind, Linda Brent also ran away, trusting her grandmother and the other members of the slave community to take care of little Benjamin and Ellen and hoping that she could trust their father to buy them.

Linda Brent's protracted flight from her master began with her flight from the plantation and depended, for its initial success, not upon the assistance of her grandmother—who would, she knew, say "'Linda, you are killing me'"—but upon that of another slave woman, Sally. Unlike the members of Linda Brent's family, whom Jacobs portrayed as speaking the purest English, Sally was portrayed as speaking dialect. But Sally, unlike Linda Brent's grandmother, could understand and approve the reasons for Linda's flight. At first, Sally advised her not to flee because of the pain she would cause her grandmother. But Linda replied that Dr. Flint was going to move her children to the plantation and would never sell them to anyone else so long as she remained in his power. Under such conditions, would not Sally advise her to flee? She would: "'When dey finds you is gone, dey won't want de plague ob de chillern; but where is you going to hide?'" Sally's last reservation concerned the danger to Linda Brent of running alone: "Let me call you uncle." Linda Brent thanked her but said no. "'I want no one to be brought into trouble on my account.'" She was reaching that core of isolation in which no one could share her rage or determination (pp. 95–96).

Linda Brent's flight lasted a proverbial seven years, which she spent in the South, in the very neighborhood in which she had lived, and practically under her master's crazed and jealous eye. The initial stages of her flight took her to the house of a trustworthy friend, from whence fear of searchers drove her outside to hide in a thicket. While in hiding, she was bitten in the dark by an unidentified reptile. Her friend prepared a "poultice of warm ashes and vinegar," which gave some relief but did not reduce the swelling. The friend then asked "an old woman, who doctored among the slaves," what to do for such a bite. The woman advised her "to steep a dozen coppers in vinegar, over night, and apply the cankered vinegar to the inflamed part." Again, the women of the slave community devoted their resources and skills to assisting one of their own. Linda Brent's relatives were, initially, less stalwart. Being threatened on account of her absence, and despairing of her ability to escape for good, "they advised me to return to my master, ask his forgiveness, and let him make an example of me." Their counsel left her unmoved. When she had started upon her undertaking, she "had resolved that, come what would, there should be no turning back. 'Give me liberty, or give me death,' was my motto." And once her friend had told her relatives of her dangerous and painful situation, "they said no more about my going back to my master." But something had to be done (pp. 98–99).

Help came from the unexpected quarter of a beneficent slaveholding woman who had long taken a friendly interest in Linda Brent's grandmother and her family. Moved by Linda's story, she offered a hiding place in her own house—a small storage room over her sleeping apartment. No one would presume to look in that respectable slaveholding household for a fugitive slave. In her hideaway, Linda Brent could lie "perfectly concealed, and command a view of the street through which Dr. Flint passed to his office." Anxiety notwithstanding, she could not but feel "a gleam of satisfaction" in observing him. "Thus far I had outwitted him, and I triumphed over it." What reader would presume to blame slaves for their cunning? "They are constantly compelled to resort to it. It is the only weapon of the weak and oppressed against the strength of their tyrants." Linda Brent's cunning was not unique, nor could it alone have assured her of victory. One night it appeared that Dr. Flint had learned of her whereabouts. Her friend, Betty, a slave of the woman who was hiding her, came to her, told her to rise and dress, and moved her to a crawl space beneath the kitchen floor. Betty instructed Linda to remain concealed until she could determine what was known. "'If dey *did* know whar you are, dey won't know *now*. Dey'll be disapinted dis time. Dat's all I got to say. If dey comes rummagin 'mong *my* tings, dey'll get one bressed sarssin from dis 'ere nigger.'" Throughout the day, Betty walked back and forth above Linda's hiding place, chuckling to herself. "'Dis nigger's too cute [acute] for 'em dis time." And at night, when the household was asleep, she returned to let Linda out. "'Come out, chile; come out. Dey don't know notin 'bout you. 'Twas only white folks' lies, to skeer de niggers'" (pp. 100–103).

Betty enfolded Linda Brent in the sisterhood of slave women and, in her generous care, identified her as one of "de niggers." For Linda Brent, whose father had the feelings of a free man, that identification came when she was approaching the nadir of her ordeal. In fleeing, she abandoned the attributes of breeding, color, and situation that distinguished her from the normal run of slaves. In fleeing, she cast herself not only as the unconditional opponent of her master, but also as the unconditional opponent of the system, and thereby identified herself as just another fugitive slave. She retained the will that preferred death to liberty, that would not let her submit, but her ability to execute that will depended heavily on the assistance of others. As she plunged toward her ultimate isolation, she became, more than ever before in her life, a slave woman among slave women. Betty's dialect signaled the true community with which Linda Brent was identified, and Betty's own acuteness identified Linda Brent's cunning as an attribute she shared with the other women of her race and class.

Finally Dr. Flint, despairing of recapturing his prey, was tricked into selling her children to their father. Betty brought her the news, and tried to quiet her hysterical weeping. "'Lor, chile,' she said, putting her arms round me, 'you's got de highsterics. I'll sleep wid you to-night, 'cause you'll make a noise, and ruin missis.'" Betty had seen the children, who were "'well, and mighty happy. I seed 'em myself. Does dat satisfy you?'" The next day Betty reported more fully. "'Brudder, chillern, all is bought by de daddy. I'se laugh more dan nuff, tinking 'bout ole mass Flint. . . . He's got ketched dis time, any how.'" When Betty went back to her kitchen, Linda Brent said to herself: "'Can it be true that my children are free? I have not suffered in vain. Thank God!'" Knowing that, whatever slavery might now do to her, "it could not shackle my children," she enjoyed her season of thanksgiving. "If I fell a sacrifice, my little ones were saved." They were saved from Dr. Flint, yes, but only precariously from slavery, for Mr. Sands, who had promised to free them, dared not free them in the South. Dr. Flint still claimed that because the children belonged to his daughter, who was not of age at the time of their sale, the contract was not binding. Mr. Sands arranged to have Ellen, Linda Brent's daughter, sent North, but only years later would Linda Brent finally succeed in buying her children's freedom. Nonetheless, their purchase by Mr. Sands and their return to her grandmother's house severed the most powerful fetter on Linda Brent's actions and set the scene for the final stages of her flight (pp. 105–7).

Dr. Flint, incensed by the outcome of the sale of Linda Brent's children, renewed his attack by trying to take revenge on her relatives. He had her uncle Phillip jailed on the charge of having aided her flight. Although Phillip was eventually released, "the movements of all my relatives, and of all our friends, were very closely watched." It was clear that Linda Brent could not remain much longer in her place of concealment. Once someone scared her by trying to get into the room. She reported the incident to Betty, who knew exactly who it must have been. "'Pend upon it, 'twas dat Jenny. Dat nigger allers got de debble in her.'" Linda Brent worried that Jenny might have heard something that aroused her suspicions. Betty dismissed the fear. Jenny "'ain't seen notin', nor hearn notin'. She only 'spects something. Dat's all. She wants to fine out who hab cut and make my gownd. But she won't nebber know. Dat's sartin. I'll git missis to fix her.'" But Linda Brent felt she could not count on the power of a mistress, however good, to quell jealousies among house servants over finery. After a moment's reflection, she told Betty that she would have to leave that night. Betty's mistress intervened to keep Jenny busy in the kitchen and sent word to Linda Brent's uncle Phillip. That night, Betty brought her "a suit of sailor's clothes,—jacket, trowsers, and tarpaulin hat." Wishing her Godspeed, she burst out: "'I'se *so* glad you is gwine to free parts! Don't forget ole Betty. P'raps I'll come 'long by and by'" (pp. 110–11).

Dressed as a man, Linda Brent bade farewell to the slave sister who had befriended her and prepared for what she expected to be the final dangerous lap of her journey. Betty would accept no thanks and was only glad to have helped. Her parting words were, "'Put your hands in your pockets, and walk ricketty, like de sailors.'" At the gate Linda Brent found a young man, Peter, who had been apprenticed to her father. She did not fear to trust him, and he enjoined her to take courage. "'I've got a dagger, and no man shall take you from me, unless he passes over my dead body.'" On Jacobs's evidence, hideaways within the confines of the household depended upon the protection of women, whereas progress on the thoroughfares beyond depended upon the weapons of men (p. 112).

Under the protection of Peter and her disguise, she walked safely to the wharf, where her aunt Nancy's husband, a seafaring man, rowed her out to a nearby vessel. They then told her that the plan was for her to remain on board until dawn, when they would hide her in Snaky

Swamp until her uncle Phillip had prepared her hiding place. Even had the vessel been bound for the North, it would have done her no good, for the ship would have been searched. The swamp represented the very pit of hell, but submission to her master would be worse, so she steeled herself to face the dreaded ordeal. Peter cut a way for her through the bamboos and briars and then returned to carry her to a seat he had made for her among the bamboos. Even before they reached it, her skin was poisoned by the hundreds of mosquitoes. As the day rose, she looked out on a sea of snakes, larger than any she had ever seen. With the approach of evening, their numbers increased so much that she and Peter had to beat them off with sticks. The high, thick bamboos made it impossible to see for any distance. As darkness began to fall, they moved closer to the entrance of the swamp in order to be sure of finding their way back (pp. 112–13).

Nightfall permitted them to return to the vessel, where she passed a fitful, terror-ridden night. The following day she could barely summon the courage to rise and return to the infested hiding place. "But even those large, venomous snakes were less dreadful to my imagination than the white men in that community called civilized." Finally, the following evening, when Peter decided that she could endure no more, "they told me that a place of concealment had been provided for me at my grandmother's. I could not imagine how it was possible to hide me in her house, every nook and corner of which was known to the Flint family." She was told to wait and see. Having been rowed ashore, she and Peter walked boldly through the streets to the house. Wearing her sailor's clothes, and having blackened her face, she passed many whom she knew without being recognized. Peter advised her to make the most of her walk, for she was unlikely soon to have another. "I thought his voice sounded sad. It was kind of him to conceal from me what a dismal hole was to be my home for a long, long time" (p. 113).

What Harriet Jacobs called Linda Brent's "loophole of retreat" consisted in a minute garret, which was squeezed between the ceiling and the roof of a small shed attached to her grandmother's house. "The air was stifling; the darkness total." Rats and mice ran over the bed on the floor. The garret was but nine feet long, seven feet wide, and, at the highest point, three feet high. She could not stand, and the darkness was oppressive. No hole or crack permitted her to peek at her children, whom she heard chattering below. "It seemed horrible to sit or lie in a cramped position day after day, without one gleam of light. Yet I would have chosen this, rather than my lot as a slave, though white people considered it an easy one; and it was so compared with the fate of others." Harriet Jacobs thought her readers would not believe that Linda Brent "lived in that dismal hole, almost deprived of light and air, and with no space to move my limbs, for nearly seven years. But it is a fact. . . . Members of my family, now living in New York and Boston, can testify to the truth of what I say" (pp. 114, 148).

According to Harriet Jacobs, for six years and eleven months Linda Brent lay concealed in a garret in her grandmother's house in Edenton, North Carolina. From that confinement, she arranged to have her daughter, Ellen, sent North by her father, and from it she herself finally made good her escape. But in the narrative, the period of hiding, at the center of her circle of family and friends, represented more than a factual account. It also represented the depth of the social isolation to which total resistance consigned a slave woman—represented the sign of her single will, cut off from all normal ties of family and friendship. For Linda Brent, the loophole of retreat betokened a rebirth into freedom before the event. In accepting that confinement, she lived out her determination to settle only for liberty or death. She manifested her deepest purpose of setting her will against that of her master.

Testimony does exist to corroborate Harriet Jacobs's account of a biblical seven-year travail, but our skepticism is permissible. Probably she and her witnesses, in accordance with the literary conventions of the day, embellished an account that was true in its essentials. No matter. If specific details such as the duration of her hiding, the size of her hiding space, and the letters from her master are altogether improbable, their very improbability serve as reminders that Jacobs's book should be read as a crafted representation—as a fiction or as a cautionary tale—not as a factual account. Its purpose, after all, was to authenticate her self, not this or that detail. And even that pivotal authentication of self probably rested upon a great factual lie, for it stretches the limits of all credulity that Linda Brent actually eluded her master's sexual advances. The point of the narrative lies not in her "virtue," which was fabricated for the benefit of her northern readers, but in her resistance of domination, which the preservation of virtue imperfectly captures.[7]

Harriet Jacobs was a politically and intellectually serious woman as well as an aspiring writer, and we would do well to take seriously the message she was determined to transmit. Her narrative of a successful flight from slavery can be read as a progress from her initial state of innocence through the mires of a struggle against her social condition, to a prolonged period of ritual, or mythic, concealment, to the flight itself, and finally to the state of knowledge that accompanied her ultimate acquisition of freedom. The pivot of the narrative lies in the account of the years of confinement, which also effectively constitutes the tale's climax. The sections that follow it lack the drama and tension of those that precede it. As the ship on which Linda Brent and her friend, Fanny, finally escaped sailed north, it passed the Snaky Swamp, in which Linda had briefly been concealed, then came into Chesapeake Bay. "O, the beautiful sunshine! the exhilarating breeze! and I could enjoy them without fear or restraint." Then they arrived in Philadelphia. On the morning they were to disembark, she and Fanny stood on the deck to watch the sun rise, "for the first time in our lives, on free soil; for such I *then* believed it to be." As the sky reddened, the sun rose slowly from the water, "the waves began to sparkle, and every thing caught the beautiful glow. Before us lay the city of strangers." Both women's eyes filled with tears: "We had escaped from slavery, and we supposed ourselves to be safe from the hunters. But we were alone in the world and we had left dear ties behind us; ties cruelly sundered by the demon Slavery" (p. 158).

In the end, Linda Brent's freedom resulted not from her heroic escape, but from an economic transaction. Some years after her escape, when she had bought—so she believed—her children's freedom and was settled in secure employment with a Mrs. Bruce, a Mr. Dodge, who had married Dr. Flint's daughter, Emily, claimed her as his property. For all those years, he claimed, she had belonged to the young woman who, as a five-year-old girl, had inherited her. When, years later, Mr. Dodge arrived in New York, a friend of Linda Brent went to see him. Mr. Dodge offered to let her buy her freedom from him. The friend replied that he had heard her say that "she would go to the ends of the earth, rather than pay any man or woman for her freedom, because she thinks she has a right to it." Mr. Dodge was enraged and initiated proceedings to claim her or her children, to whom, he insisted, his wife had never signed away her right. Linda Brent's employer, Mrs. Bruce, finally prevailed upon her to flee to New England and then arranged to buy out Mr. Dodge's final claims to her and the children. When Linda Brent received the news from her benefactress, the words "bill of sale" struck her like a blow. "So I was *sold* at last! A human being *sold* in the free city of New York. The bill of sale is on record and future generations will learn from it that women were articles of traffic in New York, late in the nineteenth century of the Christian religion." Yet for all her objections to the transaction, "I felt as if a heavy load had been lifted from my weary shoulders" (pp. 195–200).

Linda Brent advised her readers that her story "ends with freedom; not in the usual way, with marriage." She also admitted that her dreams were not yet complete, for "I do not sit with my children in a home of my own. I still long for a hearthstone of my own, however humble . . . for my children's sake far more than for my own." But God so ordered the world as to keep her in the service of her friend, Mrs. Bruce. "It is a privilege to serve her who pities my oppressed people, and who has bestowed the inestimable boon of freedom on me and my children." In the end, it was painful for her to recall her dreary years of bondage, which she would gladly have forgotten if she could. "Yet the retrospection is not altogether without solace; for with those gloomy recollections come tender memories of my good old grandmother, like light, fleecy clouds floating over a dark and troubled sea" (p. 201).

Harriet Jacobs was as exceptional in the fact of her flight as in her account of it. Yet many of her responses must have been shared by the innumerable other slave women who fiercely resisted enslavement, even though Jacobs herself emphasizes the exceptional over the typical in her self-representation. She endows herself with a special pedigree of physical, mental, and moral comeliness. She distinguishes herself from the other slaves among whom she lived, especially in her capacity to rise above her condition. She offers something less than a coherent picture of the relation between the identity and behavior of Afro-American slaves, including herself, and the effects of slavery. If slavery were as evil as she claimed—and it was—then it had to have had consequences. If the consequences included, as she claimed, a breaking of the spirit of the enslaved, how could slaves be credited with character and will?

The questions may not so much have clouded Harriet Jacobs's sense of her self as they clouded her sense of how best to present that self to others. At issue were the relations between her self and her gender, between her self and her social condition. Writing her narrative for white readers, Jacobs wrote from behind a mask. She struggled to create, in Linda Brent, a persona her readers could recognize and for whom they could feel pity. But woven through that discourse for others, Jacobs also constructed a discourse for herself. The woman who defied Dr. Flint did not seek pity and condescension. She sought recognition of her independent spirit. The issues between Linda Brent and her master did not primarily concern virtue, chastity, sexuality, or any of the rest. They concerned, as she said almost parenthetically, the conflict of two wills. The scene in which Linda Brent, after much anxious delay, confesses her past to her daughter drives the point home. When she began to tell "how slavery had driven me into a great sin," Ellen cut her off. "O, don't mother! Please don't tell me any more." Linda Brent persisted. She wanted Ellen to know something of her father. Ellen knew all about it. "I am nothing to my father, and he is nothing to me. All my love is for you." Far from confirming the "sinfulness" of Linda Brent's actions, Jacobs rewards them with the status of motherhood and fatherhood in one (pp. 188–89).

Jacobs worked with a metaphor of the journey to selfhood that carried a special resonance for the Protestant culture of her day, but she did not conceive of the journey as one from sin to salvation. For if slave society embodied sins against humanity, free society, too, left much to be desired. The values of free society labeled her actions sinful and pushed her to defend her fall from virtue. Jacobs borrowed from the discourse of free society's convention of womanhood in order to gain a hearing for her tale, but that convention did not penetrate beneath the surface—did not shape her deeper sense of her self. The end of the journey, for all her rhetoric of gratitude, figured as a rather bleak dawn on a troubled landscape. It offered no pot of gold at the end of the rainbow; instead, it offered new confrontations with racism and injustice, new challenges for the isolated self. The self-knowledge that accrued from the struggle consisted above all in the recognition that there was no resting place for the fugitive. The struggle for the dignity of the self persisted. That struggle required that Jacobs represent herself to her readers as a woman like themselves, even as she underscored the abominations of slave society that justified her "un-womanly" behavior.

Harriet Jacobs told a story—sometimes lurid—of extraordinary cruelty but also of courage and nobility. She described some men without social power who retained instinctive feelings for freedom, and some women who, through terrible suffering, retained instinctive feelings of decency. Even the dehumanizing system of slavery could not crush out all humanity. Here and there a slaveholder showed compassion for a slave; here and there slaves created a rich and mutually loyal community life. But in both instances, the law—the very register of society—conspired against their efforts, which, even at their most moving, remained personal gestures and acts of faith. The system endowed masters with a power that few could defy and that the law could barely check. A slave woman, in resisting her condition, risked assaults on her person, the gradual erosion of ties to her community, and, ultimately, isolation or death. Neither well-intentioned slaveholding women nor determined slave men could withstand the power of the master. Neither had any legal right to take the slave woman's struggle upon themselves. Slave sisters and kin could and did help, and without them nothing would have been possible. But in the end it was will against will, and the struggling slave woman sought, not virtue, but triumph.

Virtue would have to come later, when the Afro-American people, as a people, had won their struggle for freedom. Only then could they ground the relations between women and men in institutions, without which no people could hope to determine its destiny, shape its young, and define its own virtues. Freedom alone did not guarantee success, although it permitted renewal of the struggle on new and more solid foundations. Race and class continued to expose Afro-American women to indignities against which their men could not always protect them and from which their white "sisters" continued to benefit. But freedom, in destroying the master, laid the foundation for future victories. So long as his power persisted, the slave woman lived always on the edge of an abyss, always confronted a dangerous world in which her naked identity would challenge his in solitary combat.

Notes

Abbreviations

ADAH   Alabama Department of Archives and History, Montgomery,
       Alabama
AHS   Atlanta Historical Society, Atlanta, Georgia
AUA   Auburn University Archives, Auburn, Alabama
DU   Duke University, Durham, North Carolina
EU   Emory University, Atlanta, Georgia
GDAH   Georgia Department of Archives and History, Atlanta, Georgia
HSC   Hoole Special Collections, University of Alabama, University,
       Alabama
ILSG   Harriet Jacobs, *Incidents in the Life of a Slave Girl*
LC   Library of Congress, Washington, D.C.
LSU   Louisiana State University, Baton Rouge, Louisiana
MBC   Elisabeth Muhlenfeld, *Mary Boykin Chesnut: A Biography*
MCCW   C. Vann Woodward, ed., *Mary Chesnut's Civil War*
MDAH   Mississippi Department of Archives and History, Jackson,
       Mississippi
PMC   C. Vann Woodward and Elisabeth Muhlenfeld, eds., *The Private
       Mary Chesnut*
SCHS   South Carolina Historical Society, Charleston, South Carolina
SCL   South Caroliniana Library, University of South Carolina,
       Columbia, South Carolina
SHC   Southern Historical Collection, University of North Carolina
       Library, Chapel Hill, North Carolina
TSLA   Tennessee State Library and Archives, Nashville, Tennessee
TU   Tulane University, New Orleans, Louisiana
UTLA   University of Texas Libraries, Austin, Texas
VHS   Virginia Historical Society, Richmond, Virginia

Listings of state *Narratives* refer to volumes in Rawick, *The American Slave*.

Prologue

1. See Bayne and Gayle Family Papers, esp. the journal (1829–35) and correspondence (1820–35) of Sarah A. (Haynsworth) Gayle, SHC. See also Gayle and   *397*

Crawford Family Papers, SHC; Sarah Haynsworth Gayle Diary (1827–31), 10 Apr. 1828, HSC; and Johnston with Lipscomb, *Amelia Gayle Gorgas*.

2. Sarah Haynsworth Gayle Diary, Tuesday [n.d.] 1827, HSC. Ella Gertrude Clanton Thomas used the same metaphor in reflecting on her own experience as a girl-become-young-mother: "My bark has glided calmly and *swiftly* oer the sea of life" (Diary, 11 Apr. 1855, DU).

3. Sarah Haynsworth Gayle Diary, Tuesday [n.d.] 1827, 14 July 1828, HSC.

4. Ibid.

5. Sarah A. Gayle to John Gayle, 14 July 1832, Bayne and Gayle Family Papers, SHC.

6. Sarah A. (Haynsworth) Gayle Journal, Friday [n.d.] June, 1833, SHC; Sarah Haynsworth Gayle Diary, Thursday [20 Nov.] 1828, HSC.

7. Sarah Haynsworth Gayle Diary, 10 Sept. 1828, HSC; Sarah A. Gayle to John Gayle, 21 Sept. 1827, Bayne and Gayle Family Papers, SHC.

8. Sarah Haynsworth Gayle Diary (1827–31), HSC; Sarah A. (Haynsworth) Gayle Journal (1829–35), SHC. Also, in addition to the family papers, see Johnston with Lipscomb, *Amelia Gayle Gorgas*; for glimpses of Gayle's role in Alabama politics, see Thornton, *Politics and Power*. John Gayle, son of Matthew and Mary (Reese) Gayle, was born in the Sumter District of South Carolina. In 1815 he graduated from South Carolina College and became a resident of Alabama, where his parents had moved a few years earlier. See *Dictionary of American Biography*, s.v. "Gayle, John."

9. Sarah Haynsworth Gayle Diary, 14 July 1828, HSC. Indeed, later in life she retained an almost romantic interest in Indians and deplored their mistreatment by whites. Juliana Margaret Conner Diary, June–Oct. 1827, SHC.

10. See "Sarah Haynsworth Gayle and Her Journal" (ADAH), an account that clearly was written for the family by one of her descendants (she is identified as "Hugh's great-grandmother") and that identifies her parents as Richard Haynsworth (1785–1830) and Sarah Ann Pringle. Her grandmother, Sarah Furman Haynsworth, was the sister of the Baptist minister, Richard Furman, after whom Furman University was named. Her father's father and all of her maternal grandmother's brothers fought in the American Revolution. Her maternal grandmother's father, Judge Wood Furman, was a signer of the South Carolina "Declaration of Rights." On other migrants to Alabama, see Jordan, *Hugh Davis*; Mathis, *John Horry Dent*; Thornton, *Politics and Power*. Minnie Boyd (*Alabama in the Fifties*) presents an illuminating general picture of life in Alabama in the high antebellum era. On the Gayles' slaves, see Sarah Haynsworth Gayle Diary, HSC. Sarah Gayle never provided a hard-and-fast number, but she periodically listed the names of slaves and referred to their children.

11. See Yerby and Lawson, *History of Greensboro*, pp. 5–9. The settlement that would become Greensboro was initially named Troy. In 1819 the inhabitants of Troy moved to the present site of Greensboro but retained the name of Troy until 1823, when Greensboro was incorporated. Mail service actually began before Greensboro's incorporation. The first postmaster was Frederick Peck, who also sold groceries and dry goods; Sarah Gayle knew him, and his name still appears in the address of a letter she wrote to Miss Amanda Hobson from Tuscaloosa in May 1835 (Gayle Family Papers, ADAH). The stores in the early town included a barroom, a saloon, two general stores, and a hotel. On the churches, see Yerby and

Lawson, *History of Greensboro*, pp. 3–4: The Methodists began preaching in Troy in 1818, and the Baptists arrived the following year. The area's first Presbyterian minister, Mr. Hunter, preached in Greensboro in 1822. In the same year, Rev. James Hillhouse of South Carolina began preaching and established a Presbyterian church; Sarah Gayle refers frequently to the Reverend Mr. Hillhouse. Episcopalians entered the region in 1834 but did not incorporate their parish, St. Paul's, until 1840.

12. Sarah Haynsworth Gayle Diary, 16 June 1831, 13 July 1830, HSC.

13. Ibid., Monday [25 Aug.] 1831, 30 Aug. 1831.

14. Ibid., Sunday [first half of the year] 1828; Sarah Gayle to Miss Amanda Hobson, 3 Mar. 1833, Gayle Family Papers, ADAH.

15. Sarah Gayle to Miss Amanda Hobson, 3 Mar. 1833, 23 Mar. 1833, May 1833, Gayle Family Papers, ADAH.

16. Sarah A. (Haynsworth) Gayle Journal, Mar.–June 1833, SHC. Sarah Haynsworth Gayle Diary, 7 Dec. 1829, HSC.

17. Sarah Haynsworth Gayle Diary, 5 July 1828, HSC.

18. Sarah Gayle to John Gayle, Dec. [before the 12th] 1827, Bayne and Gayle Family Papers, SHC.

19. Sarah Haynsworth Gayle Diary, 29 Nov. 1827, 1 Sept. 1827, 23 Jan. 1828, 7 [Feb.] 1828, HSC.

20. Ibid., Saturday [probably early Dec.] 1827.

21. Ibid., 21 Apr. 1828, 3 May 1829; Sarah Gayle to Miss Amanda Hobson, 3 Mar. 1833, Gayle Family Papers, ADAH.

22. Sarah A. (Haynsworth) Gayle Journal, Thursday [presumably Dec.] 1829, 8 Apr. 1832, 29 June 1832, SHC.

23. Ibid., 13 Jan. 1833, 16 May 1832.

24. Sarah Haynsworth Gayle Diary, 5 May 1829, HSC.

25. Ibid., 5 Sept. 1829.

26. Ibid., 19 Feb. 1828, 15 Sept. 1828; Sarah A. (Haynsworth) Gayle Journal, 13 Jan. 1833, SHC.

27. Sarah A. (Haynsworth) Gayle Journal, 1827 and throughout, SHC. Gayle's journal periodically refers to her friend Amelia Ross, with whom she corresponded. Maria was a member of her youthful circle of the Haynsworth and Gayle families, and Sarah Gayle loved her "as my play fellow and only friend." Maria's identity is not clear. See Sarah Haynsworth Gayle Diary, 14 July 1828, HSC. Sarah Gayle named her male children for kin but, after naming her oldest daughter for her mother (and herself), she named her other daughters for friends. Her son Matt was named for John Gayle's father.

28. Sarah Haynsworth Gayle Diary, 15 Sept. 1829, HSC. For references to her reading, see the Sarah Haynsworth Gayle Diary and Sarah A. (Haynsworth) Gayle Journal generally.

29. Sarah Haynsworth Gayle Diary, 12 Dec. 1829, HSC.

30. Sarah A. (Haynsworth) Gayle Journal, 16 May 1832, SHC.

31. Ibid., 10 Mar. 1834.

32. Sarah Haynsworth Gayle Diary, 13 Apr. 1828, 30 Dec. 1830, HSC.

33. Ibid., 20 Mar. 1830.

34. Ibid., 14 Sept. 1832, 3 Jan. 1829, 4 Sept. 1829.

35. Sarah A. (Haynsworth) Gayle Journal, 19 July 1835, 28 Oct. 1832, SHC.

36. Ibid., 2 July 1832, 31 June 1832.
37. Sarah Haynsworth Gayle Diary, Sunday [25 July] 1831, 1 Feb. 1830, HSC.
38. Ibid., 16 May 1832.
39. Sarah Gayle to John Gayle, 10 Jan. 1832, Bayne and Gayle Family Papers, SHC; Sarah A. (Haynsworth) Gayle Journal, Thursday [presumably Dec.] 1829, 16 Nov. 1832, SHC.
40. Sarah Haynsworth Gayle Diary, Wednesday [no date] 1827, HSC; Sarah A. (Haynsworth) Gayle Journal, 6 July 1835, SHC.
41. Sarah Haynsworth Gayle Diary, 21 July 1828, HSC.
42. Ibid., Thursday [presumably Dec.] 1829.
43. Ibid., 15 Sept. 1833; Johnston with Lipscomb, *Amelia Gayle Gorgas*, p. 2.
44. There is considerable, if scattered, evidence that male and female slaves found it difficult to take seriously young mistresses whose parents had owned them and whom they had known as girls. See chaps. 3 and 6.
45. Brown, *Planter*, p. 118; Sarah Gayle to John Gayle, 17 Dec. 1831, Bayne and Gayle Family Papers, SHC; Sarah A. (Haynsworth) Gayle Journal, 30 July 1833, 15 Dec. 1833, SHC.
46. Sarah Gayle to John Gayle, 17 Dec. 1831, Bayne and Gayle Family Papers, SHC; Sarah A. (Haynsworth) Gayle Journal, 17 Feb. 1835, SHC.
47. Sarah A. (Haynsworth) Gayle Journal, 4 May 1834, SHC.
48. John Gayle to Sarah Gayle, undated [ca. 5–12 Apr. 1833], Bayne and Gayle Family Papers, SHC.
49. Sarah Gayle to John Gayle, 19 May 1831, ibid.
50. Gorgas, *Extracts from the Journal of Sarah Haynsworth Gayle*, p. 7.

Chapter 1

1. See the bibliography and the notes throughout for references to slaveholding women's journals, diaries, and letters. Other literary sources—notably the accounts of literate men, who outnumbered literate women in every class and race, and of visitors and travelers—provide invaluable supplements, as do legal records and other public sources. For examples of accounts of southern men, see Rosengarten, *Tombee*; Faust, *James Henry Hammond*; May, *John A. Quitman*. Suzanne Lebsock, in *Free Women of Petersburg*, has demonstrated how much information about women can be gleaned from court records. See also Salmon, *Women and the Law of Property*.

2. See Fox-Genovese, "Antebellum Southern Households," and, for additional references, the remainder of this chapter. In addition, among many works on the economic transformation of northern households, see Clark, "Household Economy" and esp. "Household, Market and Capital"; Merrill, "Cash Is Good to Eat"; Tryon, *Household Manufactures*, pp. 164–87, 242–376; North, *Economic Growth*; Bidwell, "Agricultural Revolution in New England"; Taylor, *Transportation Revolution*; Johnson, *Shopkeeper's Millennium*; Wallace, *Rockdale*; Prude, *Coming of Industrial Order*. For a helpful overview, see Hahn and Prude, *Countryside in the Age of Capitalist Transformation*. For an examination of the impact that the separation of home and work had on northern women, see esp. Cott, *Bonds of Womanhood*; Kerber, *Women of the Republic*; Douglas, *Feminization of American*

Culture; Smith-Rosenberg, *Disorderly Conduct*; Jensen, *Loosening the Bonds*; Bloch, "American Feminine Ideals in Transition"; Ryan, *Cradle of the Middle Class*; Hewitt, *Women's Activism and Social Change*; Sklar, *Catharine Beecher*; Beecher, *Treatise on Domestic Economy*.

3. Mary Kendall to "Sister Lydia," 20 June 1853, Hamilton-Kendall Family Papers, GDAH.

4. Fox-Genovese, "Placing Women's History in History." For recent work that takes seriously the distinctive cast of southern women's experience, see Friedman, *Enclosed Garden*, and Janiewski, *Sisterhood Denied*. Suzanne Lebsock, who is one of the few authors to consider black and white women in the same book, does not emphasize the centrality of slavery in southern society (see *Free Women of Petersburg*). Catherine Clinton, in *Plantation Mistress*, explicitly attacks the "New Englandization" of American women's history, but she also advances the unsupportable theory that slaveholding women were oppressed in a manner that made them the "slave of slaves." In "Caught in the Web," Clinton allows that color and class gave slaveholding women some advantage over their black female slaves but nonetheless maintains her basic interpretation. See also Hawks and Skemp, *Sex, Race, and the Role of Women*; Gwin, *Black and White Women*.

5. See esp. Bordin, *Women and Temperance*; Schlesinger, "The Role of Women in American History"; Degler, *At Odds*; Melder, *Beginnings of Sisterhood* and "Ladies Bountiful," pp. 101–24; Freedman, *Their Sisters' Keepers*; McCarthy, *Noblesse Oblige*; Flexner, *Century of Struggle*; Blair, *Clubwoman as Feminist*; Sklar, "Hull House in the 1890s"; Lemons, *Woman Citizen*; Chafe, *American Woman*; Brown, *Setting a Course*; Ware, *Beyond Suffrage*; Hartman, *Home Front and Beyond*; and Klein, *Gender Politics*. For the dynamics of race and class within mainstream women's history, see Stansell, *City of Women*; Dublin, *Women at Work*; Smith-Rosenberg, *Disorderly Conduct*; Epstein, *Politics of Domesticity*; Blackwelder, *Women of the Depression*; Wandersee, *Women's Work and Family Values*; Hall, *Revolt against Chivalry*; Janiewski, *Sisterhood Denied*.

6. Stansell, *City of Women*; Smith-Rosenberg, *Disorderly Conduct*. See also DuBois, "Working Women, Class Relations, and Suffrage Militance."

7. On the expansion of New England nativism and the rise of antislavery republicanism, see Turner, *United States, 1830–1850*, and Foner, *Free Soil, Free Labor, Free Men*. For the values of the women of New England and their dissemination, see Cott, *Bonds of Womanhood*; Sklar, *Catharine Beecher*; Welter, *Dimity Convictions*; Ryan, *Cradle of the Middle Class*; Smith-Rosenberg, "Beauty, the Beast and the Militant Woman"; Lerner, "Lady and the Mill Girl."

8. Jensen, *Loosening the Bonds*.

9. See Fox-Genovese, "Culture and Consciousness." For other recent discussions of the issues, see DuBois et al., "Politics and Culture in Women's History"; Kaplan, "Female Consciousness"; Fox-Genovese, "The Personal Is Not Political Enough." On working-class women, see, among many, Cantor and Laurie, *Class, Sex, and the Woman Worker*; Kessler-Harris, *Out to Work* and *Women Have Always Worked*; Kennedy, *If All We Did Was to Weep at Home*; Wertheimer, *We Were There*; Tentler, *Wage-Earning Women*; Davies, *Woman's Place Is at the Typewriter*; Dye, *As Equals and as Sisters*. For works that address the experience of working-class ethnic women, see Yans-McLaughlin, *Family and Community*, and Diner, *Erin's Daughters in America*. Among works that take into account the centrality of

class relations to working women's experience, see Stansell, *City of Women*; Dublin, *Women at Work*; Katzman, *Seven Days a Week*; Tax, *Rising of the Women*; Eisenstein, *Give Us Bread but Give Us Roses*. For recent works on black women's history, see Harley and Terborg-Penn, *Afro-American Woman*; Sterling, *We Are Your Sisters*; Giddings, *When and Where I Enter*; Jones, *Labor of Love, Labor of Sorrow*; Noble, *Beautiful, Also, Are the Souls of My Black Sisters*; Davis, *Women, Race, and Class*; Loewenberg and Bogin, *Black Women in Nineteenth-Century American Life*; and Lerner, *Black Women in White America*.

10. For a fuller development of these arguments, see Fox-Genovese, "Placing Women's History in History" and "Gender, Class, and Power."

11. For yeoman women, see Bryant, "Role and Status of the Female Yeomanry"; McCurry, "'Their Ways Are Not Our Ways'"; Wyatt-Brown, *Southern Honor*; Nesbitt, "To Fairfield with Love." For relations between slaveholding women and slave women, see Clinton, *Plantation Mistress*; Friedman, *Enclosed Garden*, pp. 87–91; Scott, *Southern Lady*, pp. 46–48; Genovese, *Roll, Jordan, Roll* and *In Red and Black*; Bartlett and Cambor, "History and Psychodynamics"; Sides, "Women and Slaves"; Parkhurst, "Role of the Black Mammy"; Pugh, "Women and Slavery."

12. See, e.g., Boatwright, "Political and Civil Status"; Gundersen and Gampel, "Married Women's Legal Status"; Basch, *In the Eyes of the Law*; Rabkin, *Fathers to Daughters*; Jenson, "Equity Jurisdiction"; Lebsock, "Radical Reconstruction"; Salmon, *Women and the Law of Property*, "The Debtor's Wife," and "Women and Property in South Carolina." On divorce, see Censer, "'Smiling through Her Tears'"; McDonnell, "Desertion, Divorce, and Class Struggle." On the effect of the rural character of southern society, see Kolchin, "Reevaluating the Antebellum Slave Community"; Clinton, *Plantation Mistress*, pp. 34–58, 164–80; Friedman, *Enclosed Garden*, pp. 3–38; White, *Ar'n't I a Woman?*, pp. 142–60.

13. Jean Friedman (*Enclosed Garden*) offers the best recent discussion of southern women and religion, but see also Mathews, *Religion in the Old South*; Scott, *Making the Invisible Woman Visible*, pp. 190–211; Van Zandt, "The Elect Lady"; McBeth, "Role of Women in Southern Baptist History"; Lumpkin, "Role of Women in Eighteenth-Century Virginia Baptist Life"; Gundersen, "Non-Institutional Church"; Sweet, *Minister's Wife*, pp. 44–56; Leloudis, "Subversion of the Feminine Ideal"; Kincheloe, "Transcending Role Restrictions"; Lewis, *Pursuit of Happiness*; Jordan with Manning, *Women of Guilford County*, pp. 34–39. For general studies, see Bruce, *And They All Sang Hallelujah*; Smith, *Revivalism and Social Reform*; Boles, *Religion in Antebellum Kentucky* and *Great Revival*. The modern work on southern women and religion remains sparse, yet I have not read a single journal or diary by an antebellum slaveholding woman that makes no mention of church, and few that do not comment on the texts of sermons, the quality of preaching, or even points of theology. Not surprisingly, ministers' wives are especially concerned with such questions and especially informative on women's religious attitudes. See, e.g., Moragne, *Neglected Thread*; Anne Turberville (Beale) Davis Journal, SHC; Lucilla Agnes (Gamble) McCorkle Diary, SHC; Frances Moore (Webb) Bumpas Diary, SHC; Butler, *Frances Webb Bumpas*; Lucy Walton Muse Fletcher Journal, DU; Dow, *Vicissitudes*. On American women and religion in general before the Civil War, see James, *Women in American Religion*; Ruether and Keller, *Women and Religion in America*, vols. 1 and 2; Keller et al., *Women in New Worlds*, vols. 1 and 2; McDannell, *Christian Home*; Sizer, *Gospel Hymns and*

Social Religion; Porterfield, *Feminine Spirituality*; Cross, *Burned-Over District*; Cowing, "Sex and Preaching"; Shiels, "Feminization of American Congregationalism"; Sweet, *Minister's Wife*; Deweese, "Deaconesses in Baptist History"; Hays, *Daughters of Dorcas*; Boylan, "Evangelical Womanhood"; Gillespie, "Modesty Canonized"; Ryan, "Women's Awakening"; Douglas, *Feminization of American Culture*.

14. In a separate project, Eugene D. Genovese and I are looking at these problems from the perspective of the entire slaveholding class. We are considering the high culture of the antebellum South as encoded in printed texts and the private papers of slaveholding men and women. We are trying to identify the links that bound the two and also the links between texts on various subjects—e.g., literature, theology, political economy, political theory, sociology, history. In both cases we have found extraordinary continuities, both between the texts and the lives of the people that produced them and among the different kinds of texts themselves. For some preliminary statements, see Genovese and Fox-Genovese, "Slavery, Economic Development, and the Law" and "Religious Ideals of Southern Slave Society"; Fox-Genovese and Genovese, "The Divine Sanction of Social Order."

On Louisa S. McCord, see chap. 5; Lounsbury, *"Ludibria Rerum Mortalium"*; and see O'Brien and Moltke-Hansen, *Intellectual Life*, on the intellectual life of Charleston in general. For running references to theology, literature, or history, see, among many, Quitman Family Papers, SHC; Fannie Page Hume Diary, SHC; Ella Gertrude Clanton Thomas Diary, DU; Martha Foster Crawford Diary, DU; Jackson and Prince Family Papers, SHC; Eliza Carolina (Burgwin) Clitherall Books, SHC; Elizabeth Ruffin Diary, SHC; Thomas Butler King Papers, SHC; Mary Eliza (Eve) Carmichael Diary, SHC; Sarah Eve Adams Diary, DU; Susan Davis (Nye) Hutchinson Diary, SHC; Charlotte Beatty Diary, SHC; Sarah A. (Haynsworth) Gayle Journal, SHC; Octavia LeVert Journal, ADAH; Campbell Family Papers, DU; King, *Ebb Tide*; Moragne, *Neglected Thread*. William W. Reavis ("Accounts," DU) offers a fascinating picture of the newspapers, magazines, and periodicals being delivered in the county.

We do not have even a preliminary intellectual history of southern women to put beside Susan Conrad's *Perish the Thought*; but see Forrest, *Women of the South*, and Hart, *Female Prose Writers*. Southern women novelists often betray intellectual concerns. See, e.g., Stowe, "City, Country, and the Feminine Voice"; Fidler, *Augusta Evans Wilson*; Meriwether, *South Carolina Women Writers*; Murchie, "'Copperhead? I Thank You for It!'" Anne Goodwyn Jones (*Tomorrow Is Another Day*, pp. 3–50) is interested in southern women's writing as evidence more of their struggles with society than as their acceptance of it, but she does also recognize the tension between self-assertion and conformity in Augusta Evans Wilson (pp. 51–91). Among the many novels by southern women, see, in particular, Gilman, *Recollections of a Southern Matron*; Hentz, *Planter's Northern Bride*; and Evans, *Beulah*.

15. The fine work on slave religion does not, on the whole, directly address slave women's experience, but see Harding, *There Is a River*; Raboteau, *Slave Religion*; Sobel, *Trabelin' On*; Genovese, *Roll, Jordan, Roll*; Joyner, *Down by the Riverside*, esp. pp. 141–74; Bruce, "Religion, Society, and Culture in the Old South"; Daniel, "Virginia Baptists and the Negro"; Franklin, "Negro Episcopalians." Eugene D. Genovese and I plan to address men's and women's attitudes toward religion in

our study of the slaveholders. Provisionally, it is noteworthy that innumerable adult slaveholding women wrote of staying home from church while their men attended, and that young women wrote of being escorted to church by men or of hoping to meet some man there. See, e.g., Charlotte Beatty Diary, SHC; Kate S. Carney Diary, SHC; Mary Eliza (Eve) Carmichael Diary, SHC; Thomas Butler King Papers, SHC; Sarah Gayle Journal, SHC. For a northern woman's description of the social aspects of a country congregation, see Eleanor Jackson Diary, 25 Feb. 1848, ADAH. It is also true that yeoman and town women may have outnumbered their men in church membership, but we still lack a systematic study of the figures. See Friedman, *Enclosed Garden*; Burton, *In My Father's House*, pp. 21–28.

16. Meta (Morris) Grimball Journal, 10 Jan. 1866, SHC. There is no systematic study of women's education during the antebellum period, but see, e.g., Scott, *Southern Lady*, pp. 61–79; Clinton, "Equally Their Due"; Stowe, "Not-So-Cloistered Academy"; Blandin, *History of Higher Education*; Woody, *History of Women's Education*, 1:238–300, 363–96; Griffin, *Less Time for Meddling*; Allen, "Historical Study of Moravian Education"; Bowie, "Madame Greland's French School"; Green, "Higher Education of Women in the South"; Coulter, "Ante-Bellum Academy Movement in Georgia"; Pierce, "Georgia Female College"; Farnham-Pope, "Preparation for Pedestals"; Barbour, "College Education for Women in Georgia"; "Catalogues," EU. The archives of Salem College in Winston-Salem, North Carolina, contain a variety of papers pertaining to young women's education, including curricula, class lists, and correspondence with parents. For the experience of a single teacher, see Lines, *To Raise Myself a Little*. For the experience of widows or married women, see Eliza Carolina (Burgwin) Clitherall Books, SHC; Caroline Lee (Whiting) Hentz Diary, SHC; Susan Davis (Nye) Hutchinson Diary, SHC. For an account of a slaveholding woman's opposition to her daughter's teaching, see Meta (Morris) Grimball Diary, SHC. On the difficulty of finding teachers and the tendency to seek them from the North or Europe, see Kate S. Carney Diary, SHC; Campbell Family Papers, DU. On northern women's espousal of teaching, see Sklar, *Catharine Beecher*; Chambers-Schiller, *Liberty a Better Husband*; Kaufman, *Women Teachers*; Filler, *An Ohio Schoolmistress*; Green, *Mary Lyon and Mount Holyoke*.

17. On the eighteenth-century commitment to gentlewomen's education, see esp. Kerber, "Daughters of Columbia" and *Women of the Republic*. See also Gordon, "Young Ladies Academy"; Norton, *Liberty's Daughters*; Cott, *Bonds of Womanhood*. On women teachers in the nineteenth century, see Bernard and Vinovskis, "Female School Teacher"; Kaestle and Vinovskis, *Education and Social Change*; Vinovskis, *Origins of Public High Schools*; Nelson, "Vermont Female School Teachers"; Scott, *Making the Invisible Woman Visible*, pp. 64–88; Chambers-Schiller, *Liberty a Better Husband*; Kaufman, *Women Teachers on the Frontier*; Rosenbloom, "Cincinnati's Common Schools." David Allmendinger ("Mount Holyoke Students") shows that 53 percent of Mt. Holyoke graduates during the antebellum period were farmers' daughters.

18. See *PMC*; *MCCW*, pp. xv–liii; Scott, *Southern Lady* and "Women's Perspective on the Patriarchy"; Clinton, *Plantation Mistress*; Atkinson and Boles, "The Shaky Pedestal"; Seidel, "Southern Belle"; Wolfe, "Southern Lady"; Bartlett and Cambor, "History and Psychodynamics"; Grantham, "History, Mythology, and the Southern Lady"; Leslie, "Myth of the Southern Lady."

19. C. Vann Woodward (*MCCW*, pp. xlvii–liii) and Catherine Clinton (*Plantation Mistress*, pp. 16–35) formulate the two positions. Anne Firor Scott (*Southern Lady*, esp. pp. 46–63) claims that resentment of slavery and comparison of the condition of women and slaves was widespread, but that Sarah Grimké was virtually unique in her critique of the relations between men and women. Scott is less willing to acknowledge that even women's most bitter resentment of slavery rarely resembled the Grimké sisters' opposition to the institution as a social system. On these questions, see chapter 7 below. On women's relation to abolitionism, see Grimké, *An Appeal*; DuBois, *Elizabeth Cady Stanton, Susan B. Anthony*, pp. 72–74, 79–85; Stowe, *Uncle Tom's Cabin*, chap. 16, pp. 260–83; Hersh, *Slavery of Sex*.

20. The large amount of work on Afro-American slave life and culture produced in the 1960s and 1970s did not directly address women's history, even though many of the historians were sensitive to women's experience. Most of the male authors had done a large part of their work before the development of women's history as a discipline, and even the most sensitive were hampered by a paucity of sources and by unfamiliarity with the questions feminists would soon raise. See esp. Blassingame, *Slave Community*; Rawick, *From Sundown to Sunup*; Fogel and Engerman, *Time on the Cross*; Genovese, *Roll, Jordan, Roll*; Gutman, *Black Family*; Owens, *This Species of Property*; Levine, *Black Culture*. For a recent critique of the literature on the slave community, see Kolchin, "Reevaluating the Antebellum Slave Community."

21. The best recent treatment of slave women's work can be found in White, *Ar'n't I a Woman?*. See also idem, "Female Slaves"; Davis, "Reflections on the Black Woman's Role"; Jones, *Labor of Love*, pp. 13–29. For recent developments in Afro-American and Pan-African feminism that underlie the new interpretation of slave women, see Hooks, *Ain't I a Woman?*; Dill, "Dialectics of Black Womanhood"; Steady, "Black Woman Cross-Culturally."

22. Recently, historians of black women have been challenging their work for failing to pay adequate respect to slave women's independence, strength, and self-assertion (see, e.g., White, *Ar'n't I a Woman?*). Despite my differences with Deborah White on this matter, she offers the best introduction to the theoretical problem. See also chap. 6 below.

23. Joan Scott ("Gender: A Useful Category," p. 1067) proposes that we consider gender as "a constitutive element of social relationships based on perceived differences between the sexes" and as "a primary way of signifying relationships of power," but she does not address relations of class and race. Bertram Wyatt-Brown, in his valuable book *Southern Honor*, does not address the specific class component of slaveholding southerners' idea of honor—and does not discuss slaveholding women's special sense of honor at all.

24. Du Bois, *Darkwater*, p. 172; Sojourner Truth's words are reprinted in Loewenberg and Bogin, *Black Women in Nineteenth-Century American Life*, pp. 235–36. The original was privately printed in Boston in 1854. See also Gilbert, *Sojourner Truth's Narrative*.

25. See Genovese, *Roll, Jordan, Roll*, for discussions of hegemony and paternalism. See also Aptheker, *American Negro Slave Revolts* and *Essays in the History of the American Negro*; Genovese, *From Rebellion to Revolution*; Harding, *There Is a River*; Okihiro, *In Resistance*. For discussions of the balance between African origins and white influences, see Sobel, *World They Made Together*; Littlefield, *Rice and Slaves*;

Wood, *Black Majority*; Morgan, "Black Life in Eighteenth-Century Charleston" and "Black Society in the Lowcountry"; Berlin, "Time, Space, and the Evolution of Afro-American Society"; Kulikoff, "Origins of Afro-American Society"; Rodney, "Upper Guinea and the Significance of the Origins of Africans"; Joyner, *Down by the Riverside*; Levine, *Black Culture*. For a more extended discussion of slave women and resistance, see chap. 6 below.

26. Horton, "Freedom's Yoke." See also Horton and Horton, *Black Bostonians*; Jones, *Labor of Love*, pp. 58–68, 99–100; Berkeley, "'Colored Ladies Also Contributed'"; Frazier, *Negro Family*; Brooks, "Women's Movement in the Black Church." See also Drago, "Militancy and Black Women."

27. Lebsock, "Free Black Women"; De Bow, *Statistical View*. Michael Johnson and James Roark (*Black Masters*, pp. 209–10) offer an excellent discussion of the marriage practices of free black women. I am grateful to Virginia Gould for sharing her work-in-progress on the free black women of Mobile and New Orleans. On female heads of households, see Kuznesof, "Household Composition." On the commitment of former slaves to marriage, see, among many, Gutman, *Black Family*; Litwack, *Been in the Storm So Long*, esp. pp. 229–47, 417–48; Berlin et al., *Freedom*, vol. 1.

28. See chap. 6 below. See also Mintz and Price, *Anthropological Approach*; Krige, "Woman-Marriage"; Netting, "Marital Relations"; Mullin, "Jamaican Maroon Women" and "Women, and the Comparative Study of American Negro Slavery." See also Aptheker, *American Negro Slave Revolts*; Bush, "'The Family Tree Is Not Cut'" and "Defiance or Submission?"; Gaspar, "Slave Women and Resistance in the Caribbean"; Patterson, "Slavery and Slave Revolts"; Kilson, "Towards Freedom"; Obitko, "'Custodians of a House of Resistance'"; Wood, "Some Aspects of Female Slave Resistance."

29. Fox-Genovese, "Placing Women's History in History" and "Gender, Class, and Power." Those who use capitalism in a heuristic fashion include scholars as diverse as Fernand Braudel, Paul Sweezy, and Immanuel Wallerstein. See Braudel, *Capitalism and Material Life* and *Afterthoughts*; Sweezy, contributions to Hilton, *Transition from Feudalism to Capitalism*; Wallerstein, *Modern World-System*. For critiques, see George, "Origins of Capitalism"; Brenner, "Agrarian Class Structure" and "Origins of Capitalist Development." For a more extended development of my own view, see Fox-Genovese and Genovese, *Fruits of Merchant Capital*, esp. pp. 3–25. These debates have not addressed gender relations in general or the role of women in particular.

30. The practice was more complex than the principle, even though the secular tendency toward absolute property was clear. Conflicts over absolute property in land persisted in England, and even in New England colonists could not buy unallocated land, which remained communal. See Fox-Genovese, "Many Faces of Moral Economy"; Fox-Genovese and Genovese, *Fruits of Merchant Capital*, esp. pp. 61–75; Dobb, *Studies*; Hilton, *Transition from Feudalism to Capitalism*.

31. See, e.g., Horowitz, *Transformation of American Law*; Foner, *Tom Paine*; Nash, *Urban Crucible*; Prude, *Coming of Industrial Order*; Wilentz, *Chants Democratic*; Stansell, *City of Women*; Cott, *Bonds of Womanhood*; Mutch, "Yeoman and Merchant"; Merrill, "Cash Is Good to Eat"; Simler, "Tenancy"; Rothenberg, "Market and Massachusetts Farmers" and "Emergence of a Capital Market";

Henretta, "Families and Farms"; Clark, "Household Economy"; Morgan, *American Slavery, American Freedom*; Kulikoff, *Tobacco and Slaves*.

32. Simpson, *Dispossessed Garden*, pp. 1–33; Morgan, *American Slavery, American Freedom*; Fox-Genovese and Genovese, *Fruits of Merchant Capital*, esp. pp. 34–60, 90–135; Kulikoff, *Tobacco and Slaves*, epilogue. For the debates over slave and plantation modes of production, see, e.g., Mandle, *Roots of Black Poverty*; Hindess and Hirst, *Precapitalist Modes of Production*.

33. Simpson, *Brazen Face*, pp. 3–22. Lewis Simpson, here and elsewhere, refers to the republic of letters as the "Third Realm," which arose "as a result of the differentiation of a power struggle between Church and State—a struggle, not previously known in history, between a transcendent order of Being and the temporal order of existence—a Republic of Letters emerged from the Republic of Christ" (p. 5). See also Price, *France and the Chesapeake*; Woodman, *King Cotton*; Morgan, *American Slavery, American Freedom*; Clemens, *Atlantic Economy*; Wright, *Political Economy of the Cotton South*, pp. 90–97; Main, *Tobacco Colony*; McCusker and Menard, *Economy of British America*; Dunn, *Sugar and Slaves*; Tate and Ammerman, *Chesapeake in the Seventeenth Century*; Land et al., *Law, Society, and Politics*.

34. Genovese, *Political Economy of Slavery*; Bateman and Weiss, *Deplorable Scarcity*; Fox-Genovese and Genovese, *Fruits of Merchant Capital*, pp. 90–171; Woodman, *King Cotton*; Fox-Genovese, "Antebellum Southern Households."

35. Finley, *Ancient Slavery*. For two other recent overviews of slavery, see Davis, *Slavery and Human Progress*; Patterson, *Slavery and Social Death*.

36. The concept of a slave mode of production unnecessarily complicates our understanding of the place of slavery in the development of North American society and has not proven useful for the solution of important historical questions. It remains an abstraction and a distraction that has yet to help solve any important problem in antebellum southern history. For a related discussion of these problems in North American society in general, see Palmer, "Social Formation and Class Formation." See also Starobin, *Industrial Slavery*; Shryock, "Early Industrial Revolution"; Stavinsky, "Industrialism in Ante Bellum Charleston"; Lewis, *Coal, Iron, and Slaves*; Bateman and Weiss, "Manufacturing in the Antebellum South"; Wade, *Slavery in the Cities*. Michelle Gillespie's dissertation-in-progress at Princeton on the workers and artisans of antebellum Georgia reveals a sharp difference in experience, organization, and values between southern and northern workers. See, e.g., Wilentz, *Chants Democratic*.

37. Thus, even after the war, southern farmers proved reluctant to adopt new forms of technology. See Ferleger, *Tools and Time*. On the general problem of social relations and economic development, see Confino, *Systèmes agraires*.

38. In fact the literature normally refers less to capitalism than to the American Revolution or industrialization or modernization. Linda Kerber, in *Women of the Republic*, offers the most balanced and intellectually sophisticated view. The case for a decline in women's status has been made most cogently by Wilson, "Illusion of Change." The various modern arguments for the decline in women's position with the rise of capitalism originate with Clark, *Working Life of Women*. The strongest proponent of improvement has been Mary Beth Norton (*Liberty's Daughters* and "Evolution of White Women's Experience"). See also Fox-Geno-

vese and Genovese, *Fruits of Merchant Capital*, pp. 299–336; Maclean, *Renaissance Notion of Women*; Fox-Genovese, introduction to *French Women and the Age of Enlightenment*, "Women and Work," and "Women and the Enlightenment"; Davidoff and Hall, *Family Fortunes*; Davidoff, *Best Circles*.

39. See MacPherson, *Political Theory of Possessive Individualism*; Fox-Genovese, *Autobiography of Du Pont de Nemours*, pp. 1–74; Heller et al., *Reconstructing Individualism*.

40. See Fox-Genovese, "Women, Affirmative Action, and the Myth of Individualism." For a comparable argument about particularism and universalism, albeit developed for the case of early modern French Protestantism and Catholicism, see Davis, *Society and Culture*, pp. 65–95.

41. This problem is fundamental to comparative women's history. See esp. Rosaldo, "Use and Abuse of Anthropology"; Harris, "Households and Their Boundaries"; George, "From 'Goodwife' to 'Mistress'"; Friedl, "Position of Women"; Rogers, "Woman's Place"; Fox-Genovese, "Women and Work"; Brown, "Anthropological Perspective."

42. Fox-Genovese and Genovese, *Fruits of Merchant Capital*, pp. 299–336; Fox-Genovese, "Gender, Class, and Power," "Culture and Consciousness," and introduction to *French Women and the Age of Enlightenment*. See also Davidoff, *Best Circles*; Hall, "Early Formation of Victorian Domestic Ideology"; Burstyn, *Victorian Education*.

43. Kerber, *Women of the Republic*; Cott, *Bonds of Womanhood*; Basch, "Invisible Women" and "Equity vs. Equality"; Rabkin, *Fathers to Daughters*; Salmon, "Life, Liberty, and Dower"; De Pauw, "Women and the Law"; Gundersen, "Independence, Citizenship, and the American Revolution"; Kenny, *History of the Law of England*; Ostrogorski, *Rights of Women*.

44. Faragher, *Women and Men*, "History from the Inside Out," and *Sugar Creek*; Jeffrey, *Frontier Women*; Stratton, *Pioneer Women*; Schlissel, *Women's Diaries*; Myres, *Westering Women*; Riley, *Frontierswomen*; Kolodny, *Land Before Her*.

45. Du Bois, *Feminism and Suffrage*; Griffith, *In Her Own Right*; Rabkin, "Origins of Law Reform"; Basch, "Invisible Women"; Fox-Genovese, "Women, Affirmative Action, and the Myth of Individualism"; Alcott, *Work*.

46. Wyatt-Brown, *Southern Honor*.

47. See, among many, Stone, *Family, Sex, and Marriage*; Trumbach, *Rise of the Egalitarian Family*; Smith, *Inside the Great House*; Lewis, *Pursuit of Happiness*; Greven, *Protestant Temperament*; Kuhn, *Mother's Role in Childhood Education*; Fox-Genovese and Genovese, *Fruits of Merchant Capital*, pp. 299–336.

48. Both Eugene Genovese (*Roll, Jordan, Roll*) and Rhys Isaac (*Transformation of Virginia*) use the term, albeit somewhat differently, to characterize southern relations of dependence and inequality after the demise of a genuine patriarchy. See also Treckel, "English Women" and "Women in Early Virginia." For different formulations, see Kulikoff, *Tobacco and Slaves*, pp. 165–204; Clinton, *Plantation Mistress*; Johnson, "Planters and Patriarchy."

49. White, *Ar'n't I a Woman?* and "Female Slaves"; Davis, "Reflections on the Black Woman's Role."

50. Kulikoff, *Tobacco and Slaves* and "Colonial Chesapeake"; McCusker and Menard, *Economy of British America*; Greene and Pole, *Colonial British America*. In addition, see Isaac, *Transformation of Virginia*; Beeman and Isaac, "Cultural Con-

flict and Social Change"; Beeman, *Evolution of the Southern Backcountry*; Lewis, *Pursuit of Happiness*; Smith, *Inside the Great House*. For the impact of the American Revolution on Afro-American thought, see Genovese, *From Rebellion to Revolution*; Fox-Genovese, "Strategies and Forms of Resistance" and chap. 6 below. Unfortunately, Mechal Sobel's important new book, *The World They Made Together: Black and White Values in Eighteenth-Century Virginia*, appeared too late to be discussed at length here. However, her interpretation is essentially compatible with my own. On the effect of the Revolution on slaves and slaveowners, see Quarles, *Negro in the American Revolution*; MacLeod, *Slavery, Race, and the American Revolution*; Mullin, *Flight and Rebellion*; Crow and Tise, *Southern Experience in the American Revolution* (esp. Mullin, "British Caribbean and North American Slaves," and Wood, "'Taking Care of Business'"); Quarles, "Revolutionary War"; Klein, "Frontier Planters and the American Revolution"; Sheridan, "Jamaican Slave Insurrection Scare"; Frey, "'Bitter Fruit'"; Newman, "Black Women in the Era of the American Revolution."

51. Morgan, *American Slavery, American Freedom*; Miller, *Wolf by the Ears*; Albert, "Protean Institution"; Shaffer, "Between Two Worlds"; Sokoloff, "Industrialization and the Growth of the Manufacturing Sector"; Goldin and Sokoloff, "Women, Children, and Industrialization"; Goldin, "Economic Status of Women"; Bateman and Weiss, "Comparative Regional Development"; Williamson, "Urbanization in the American Northeast."

52. For an introduction to the many variations among Euro-American households that takes a theoretical perspective very different from my own, see Laslett, *Household and Family*. See also Mendras, *Sociétés paysannes*, esp. pp. 57–72, on the complexities of what he calls "domestic groups"; Shanin, "Nature and Logic"; Medick, "Proto-Industrial Family Economy"; Klapisch-Zuber, *Women, Family, and Ritual*, esp. pp. 23–35, 36–67. Despite growing recognition of the household as a distinct grouping, many studies tend to collapse into discussions of the "family." For a critique, see Mitterauer and Sieder, *European Family*, pp. 1–23. On gender relations within peasant households, see also Segalen, *Mari et femme*, which, despite some problems, provides a useful introduction; and Fox-Genovese, "Women and Work." The literature on the family also contains instructive information on the variety of households in relation to different socioeconomic tendencies. See, e.g., Berkner, "Use and Misuse"; Planck, *Der bäuerliche Familienbetrieb*; Levine, *Family Formation*, and his essay in Levine, *Proletarianization*. On merchant capital and southern development, see Fox-Genovese and Genovese, *Fruits of Merchant Capital*. For recent interpretations of the development of southern society, see Isaac, *Transformation of Virginia*; Rutman and Rutman, *Place in Time*; Beeman, *Evolution of the Southern Backcountry*; Kulikoff, *Tobacco and Slaves*; and Sobel, *World They Made Together*.

53. See, most recently, Shore, *Southern Capitalists*. For an introduction to "yeoman" households in the North, see Hahn and Prude, *Countryside in the Age of Capitalist Transformation*; Prude, *Coming of Industrial Order*; Barron, *Those Who Stayed Behind*; Kulikoff, "Rise and Destruction." On women's wage labor and households, see Dublin, *Women at Work*. For French equivalents, see Lehning, *Peasants of Marhles*; Gullickson, *Spinners and Weavers of Auffay*.

54. On yeoman women's textile production, see McCurry, "In Defense of Their World." On yeoman households and labor, see Hahn, *Roots of Southern Populism*.

55. Tönnies, *Gemeinschaft und Gesellschaft*. For an impressionistic use of the concept, see Blassingame, *Slave Community*. See also Gilmore, *Revisiting Blassingame's "The Slave Community."* Blassingame, in his response (pp. 135–68), does not offer a definition.

56. Lebsock, *Free Women of Petersburg*. For the size of cities, see U.S. Bureau of the Census, *Historical Statistics*, pt. 1, ser. A, tables 125–29, pp. 195–209.

57. James E. Davis finds that northern and southern frontier households differed slightly in demographic composition but closely resembled the households of their respective settled regions of origin: "Of equal importance, but perhaps far less conspicuous . . . the *household* . . . formed the basic economic and social unit in the wilderness" (*Frontier America*, p. 99).

58. These figures and those that follow, unless differently acknowledged, are derived from the U.S. Bureau of the Census, *Historical Statistics*. Delaware followed a distinctly northeastern pattern of urban development, increasing from 0 (by census definition) to 10 percent urban population between 1830 and 1840 and rising to 19 percent in 1860. Maryland, because of Baltimore, had 4 percent urban population in 1790, a total that increased steadily to 34 percent in 1860. On the complexities of Maryland as a slave state, see Fields, *Slavery and Freedom*; on Baltimore in particular, see Browne, *Baltimore in the Nation*.

59. Mumford, *City in History*; Dickinson, *West European City*; Kennedy, "From *Polis* to *Madina*." For a discussion of the relation between capitalism and urbanization, see Harvey, *Urbanization of Capital* and *Consciousness and the Urban Experience*.

60. Fox, *History in Geographic Perspective*; Pirenne, *Medieval Cities*; Clark, *Early Modern Town*; Clark and Slack, *English Towns*; DeVries, *European Urbanization*; Hohenberg and Lees, *Making of Urban Europe*, pp. 74–171; Willan, *Elizabethan Manchester*; DuPlessis and Howell, "Reconsidering the Early Modern Urban Economy"; Everitt, "Marketing of Agricultural Produce"; Chartres, "Marketing of Agricultural Produce"; John, "Aspects of English Economic Growth"; Price, "Rise of Glasgow"; Clemens, "Rise of Liverpool"; Price and Clemens, "Revolution of Scale in Overseas Trade"; Merrington, "Town and Country"; Harris, *Liverpool and Merseyside*; Pariset, *Bordeaux au XVIIIe siècle*; Huetz de Lemps, *Géographie du commerce de Bordeaux*; Shepherd and Walton, *Shipping, Maritime Trade*; Roupnel, *La ville et la campagne*; Ford, *Strasbourg in Transition*.

61. See esp. Briggs, *Making of Modern England* and *Victorian Cities*; Lees and Lees, *Urbanization of European Society*; Hohenberg and Lees, *Making of Urban Europe*, pp. 179–247; Wirth and Jones, *Manchester and Sao Paulo*; Vigier, *Change and Apathy*; Anderson, *Family Structure*; Ashworth, *Genesis of Modern British Town Planning*; Hartwell, *Industrial Revolution*; Smelser, *Social Change in the Industrial Revolution*; Bairoch, *Révolution industrielle et sous-développement*; Landes, *Unbound Prometheus*.

62. Wrigley, "Simple Model"; Sheppard, *London, 1808–1870*; Fox-Genovese and Genovese, *Fruits of Merchant Capital*, pp. 3–89 (esp. pp. 76–89).

63. Tucker, *Progress of the United States*, pp. 127–32 (citation from p. 127).

64. Ibid., p. 132. Eugene Genovese and I will expand this discussion of the role of the towns in our forthcoming book, *The Mind of the Master Class* (tentative title). On Tucker as a political economist, see Genovese and Fox-Genovese, "Slavery, Economic Development, and the Law." For descriptions of southern towns,

see also Olmsted, *Journey in the Back Country*, pp. 420–21; Ingraham, *South-West*, 2:82, 205–7; Featherstonhaugh, *Excursion*, pp. 17–18; Groene, *Ante-Bellum Tallahassee*; Bonner, *Milledgeville*.

65. For a general bibliography, see Berry and Pred, *Central Place Studies*. See also Christaller, *Central Places*; Smolensky and Ratajczak, "Conception of Cities"; Stigler, "Division of Labor Is Limited." Although I draw heavily upon the insights of scholars from the central-place school, I do not fully accept the theoretical implications that they attribute to their work. The sophisticated analysis of Allan Pred (*Urban Growth*) includes a systematic critique of the ways in which urban growth has been treated on the basis of census data as well as an excellent discussion of the comparative density of transportation and communication networks North and South. See also Lindstrom, *Economic Development*; Weber, *Growth of Cities*. For a different reading of the larger implications, see Harvey, *Consciousness and the Urban Experience*. Douglass North has made the case for the South's integration in the national market in *Economic Growth of the United States*. Although North does view southern economic development as qualitatively different from that of the Northeast, he does not make much allowance for the significance of its political and social differences and views the Civil War as a blunder. Among the exponents of the contrary view, see Fishlow, *American Railroads* and "Antebellum Interregional Trade Reconsidered." See also Genovese, *Political Economy of Slavery*; Bateman and Weiss, *Deplorable Scarcity*; Woodman, *King Cotton* and "Economic History and Economic Theory"; Phillips, *History of Transportation*.

66. Williamson, "Urbanization in the American Northeast." On the towns and cities of western New York, see, e.g., McKelvey's volumes on Rochester, *Water-Power City* and *Flower City*; Johnson, *Shopkeeper's Millennium*. Mary P. Ryan, in *Cradle of the Middle Class*, deals more with urban middle-class culture than with urban development per se.

67. The transformation of northern cities has been most carefully explored for one particular city by Diane Lindstrom (*Economic Development*) and as a general process by Allan Pred (*Urban Growth and the Circulation of Information* and *Urban Growth and City-Systems*). See also Albion, *Rise of the Port of New York*; Williamson and Swanson, "Growth of Cities"; Crowther, "Urban Growth in the Mid-Atlantic States"; Lampard, "Evolving System of Cities"; Bateman and Weiss, "Comparative Regional Development"; Cochran, "Business Revolution"; Goheen, "Industrialization and the Growth of Cities"; Ward, "New Look"; Earle and Hoffman, "Foundations of the Modern Economy." For eighteenth-century developments, see Gilchrist, *Growth of Seaport Cities*; Nash, *Urban Crucible*; Price, "Economic Function"; Ernst and Merrens, "'Camden's Turrets Pierce the Skies!'"; Clark, *New Orleans*; Earle and Hoffman, "Staple Crops and Urban Development." On patterns of confinement, see Rothman, *Discovery of the Asylum*.

68. On Virginia, see Goldfield, *Urban Growth*. Goldfield generalizes rashly from the Virginia experience in "Pursuing the American Urban Dream." See also Wertenbaker, *Norfolk*; Dabney, *Richmond*; Stewart, "Railroads and Urban Rivalries." On slaves and free blacks in southern cities, see esp. Goldin, *Urban Slavery* and "Model to Explain the Relative Decline of Slavery"; Fields, *Slavery and Freedom*, pp. 40–62; Wade, *Slavery in the Cities*; Starobin, *Industrial Slavery*; Curry, *Free Black*; Berlin, *Slaves without Masters*; Fitzgerald, *Different Story*. The debates over the relations among slavery, industrialization, and urban development remain

largely inconclusive, not least due to the lack of clarity about the relations between urban development and industrialization. Any consideration of slavery clearly reveals the ways in which the two should not be confused: A rural manufacture, even one that employed large numbers of slaves, posed different problems of social control than did a large slave population within a city. Furthermore, the urban slave population easily may have specialized in crafts and services that served and even helped increase a large urban population without transforming the fundamental nature of its economy. These considerations obtain in some measure independent of the related questions of whether slave labor drove out free, and whether slave ownership discouraged capital accumulation and investment in manufacturing. For a recent attempt to argue for the growth of a free, white laboring population, see Berlin and Gutman, "Natives and Immigrants"; however, Michelle Gillespie's work-in-progress shows that southern white laborers did not constitute a working class in the northern sense (Ph.D. diss., Princeton University). On the old Northwest, see Wade, *Urban Frontier*; Schnell and McLear, "Why the Cities Grew"; Easterlin, "Farm Production and Income"; Davis, Easterlin, Parker, et al., *American Economic Growth*, pp. 61–89.

69. For the percentage of the southern urban population that lived in one of nine cities, see Goldin, *Urban Slavery*, p. 12, table 1. The nine cities she uses are Baltimore, Charleston, Louisville, Mobile, New Orleans, Norfolk, Richmond, Savannah, and Washington. For other views on southern urbanization, see Brownell, "Urbanization in the South"; Dorsett and Shaffer, "Was the Antebellum South Antiurban?"; Curry, "Urbanization and Urbanism"; Goldfield, "Pursuing the American Urban Dream."

70. For purposes of comparison, Boston's share of Massachusetts's urban population declined steadily from 36 percent in 1820 to 33 percent in 1840 and 24 percent in 1860; New York City's share of New York's urban population declined from 76 percent in 1820 to 66 percent in 1840 and to 53 percent in 1860. See Andriot, *Population Abstracts*, vol. 1. See also Sharpless, "Economic Structure of Port Cities."

71. Coclanis, "Economy and Society"; Clowse, *Economic Beginnings*; Ver Steeg, *Origins of a Southern Mosaic*; Sirmans, *Colonial South Carolina*; Weir, *Colonial South Carolina*; Ward, "Early Victorian City," esp. p. 180; Rogers, *Evolution of a Federalist*, pp. 342–400; Smith, *Economic Readjustment of an Old Cotton State*.

72. See, e.g., Coulter, *Old Petersburg*; James, *Antebellum Natchez*; Meyers, *History of Baton Rouge*; Capers, *Biography of a River Town*; Jordan, *Antebellum Alabama*; Harris, *Plain Folk and Gentry*.

73. Carroll Smith-Rosenberg develops a similar position, albeit in very different terms, in *Disorderly Conduct*, esp. pp. 79–89, 109–28. Christine Stansell (*City of Women*) delineates the experience and responses of working-class women and Joan Jensen (*Loosening the Bonds*) that of mid-Atlantic farm women. On women's domestic fiction, see, e.g., Baym, *Woman's Fiction*; Papashvily, *All the Happy Endings*; Kelley, *Private Woman, Public Stage*. These three works, although they do not discuss the issue in these terms, do show the quest for rural harmony in much women's fiction. See also Smith-Rosenberg, "Sex as Symbol"; Watts, "Masks, Morals, and the Market"; Fox-Genovese and Genovese, *Fruits of Merchant Capital*, pp. 299–36. For a discussion of rural nostalgia during the expansion of capitalism, see Williams, *Country and the City*. On the idea of community, see Nisbet, *Socio-*

logical Tradition, and Plant, *Community and Ideology*. For overviews of the new community studies, see Russo, *Families and Communities*, and Bender, *Community and Social Change*. Most of those who have written on the emergence of the doctrine of separate spheres have not emphasized its base in a capitalist city-system, although most emphasize its relation to the beginnings of industrialization. See, e.g., Cott, *Bonds of Womanhood*; Welter, "Cult of True Womanhood"; Sklar, *Catharine Beecher*; Douglas, *Feminization of American Culture*; Lerner, *Majority Finds Its Past*, pp. 15–30; Smith-Rosenberg, *Disorderly Conduct*, pp. 53–76; Melder, *Beginnings of Sisterhood*. Joan Jensen (*Loosening the Bonds*, pp. 205–7) argues that the lack of an urban culture influenced the experiences, perceptions, and actions of the farm women she studied, although she considers ethnic factors even more important. Barbara Berg (*Remembered Gate*) and Carroll Smith-Rosenberg (*Religion and the Rise of the American City*) both show a close relation between women's concerns and voluntary associations and the challenge of the city. Nancy Hewitt (*Women's Activism* and "Feminist Friends") closely links women's reform activities to their experience of urban life. Barbara Epstein (*Politics of Domesticity*) provides a sophisticated critique of the class base of the ideology of domesticity but does not explore its urban dimension. Most discussions of the change in northeastern women's experience during the late eighteenth and early nineteenth centuries do not directly address the combined impact of political revolution and capitalism. Linda Kerber (*Women of the Republic*) offers the best discussion of the issues, although she does not focus on the emergence of the ideology of separate spheres.

74. For examples, see Hewitt, *Women's Activism*; Smith-Rosenberg, *Religion and the Rise of the American City* and *Disorderly Conduct*; Berg, *Remembered Gate*; Ryan, "Power of Women's Networks" and *Cradle of the Middle Class*; Flexner, *Century of Struggle*; Dannenbaum, "Origins of Temperance Activism"; Freedman, *Their Sisters' Keepers*; Wellman, "Women and Radical Reform"; Lerner, *Majority Finds Its Past*, pp. 112–28; Melder, "Ladies Bountiful"; Smith, "Family Limitation"; Tyrrell, "Women and Temperance"; Basch, "Equity vs. Equality"; Matthews, "Race, Sex, and the Dimensions of Liberty"; Baker, *Affairs of Party*; Norton, *Alternative Americas*, pp. 64–96; Walters, *American Reformers*.

75. For a preliminary elaboration, see Genovese and Fox-Genovese, "Religious Ideals." The single best discussion of southern urban culture in general can be found in Holifield, *Gentlemen Theologians*, esp. pp. 5–23; for a focus on a particular city, see O'Brien and Moltke-Hansen, *Intellectual Life*. See also Bonner, *Milledgeville*; Johnson, *Ante-Bellum North Carolina*, pp. 114–90; Rogers, *Charleston in the Age of the Pinckneys*; Murray, *Wake: Capital County*, vol. 1, esp. pp. 168–220, 300–377; and Boyd, *Alabama in the Fifties*.

76. The literature on charitable activities and associations during the antebellum period remains misleading in its failure to give much precise information on the nature of groups, the size of their memberships, the frequency of their meetings, and more. The older literature largely derived from a celebratory impulse that sought to demonstrate southern women's sense of social morality and responsibility; the more recent literature fastens on random examples in order to prove the existence of "women's networks." We sorely lack a systematic study of the subject. Until such a study is completed, see Heck, *In Royal Service*; Gray, "Activities of Southern Women"; Truedly, "The 'Benevolent Fair'"; Johnson, *Ante-Bellum North*

Carolina, esp. pp. 155–56, 162–64, 418, 423–26; Van Zandt, *"Elect Lady"*; Lebsock, *Free Women of Petersburg*, pp. 195–236. For the view that southern women organized few charitable associations, see Sterkx, *Partners in Rebellion*. Fannie Heck's papers are in the archives at Wake Forest University. See also the papers of the Charleston Ladies Benevolent Society, SCHS. For samples of travelers' reports, see Bremer, *Homes of the New World*, 2:537 (on Richmond); Buckingham, *Slave States*, 1:125–26 (on Savannah). For suggestive accounts of the character and limitations of southern women's groups, see Thompson, *Presbyterians*, 1:287–89, 292; Dale, *Sketch of St. James Parish*, pp. 44, 54; Riley, *History of the Baptists*, pp. 299–301; Jones and Mills, *History of the Presbyterian Church*, pp. 435–39. The reports and reactions of male slaveholders, including ministers, also cast doubt on the extent to which the southern women's groups corresponded to the northern. See, e.g., John Houston Bills Diary, 11 May 1854, 25 May 1866, John Houston Bills Papers, SHC; Samuel Andrew Agnew Diary, 4 May 1854, SHC; John Hamilton Cornish Diary, 30 May 1840, 16, 23 July 1842, 14 June 1853, SHC; James W. Albright Diary, 16 Dec. 1864, James W. Albright Books, SHC; R. R. Barrow to Dear Ladys, Sept. 1845, R. R. Barrow Family Papers, TU. Among the private accounts of women, which hardly substantiate claims of organized efforts on the northern model, see Mildred T. Taylor to Mrs. Gustavus A. Henry, 14 May 1847, and Marion Henry to Gustavus A. Henry, 4 Dec. 1858, Gustavus Adolphus Henry Papers, SHC. See also scattered references in sources cited elsewhere in this book, among them: Martha R. Jackson Diary, SHC; Lucilla Agnes (Gamble) McCorkle Diary, SHC; Sarah Eve Adams Diary, DU; Fannie Page Hume Diary, SHC; Lucy Muse (Walton) Fletcher Journal, DU; Susan Davis (Nye) Hutchinson Diary, SHC; Eliza Carolina (Burgwin) Clitherall Books, SHC; Mary Eliza (Eve) Carmichael Diary, SHC.

77. For women's networks and bonds among women, see Ryan, "Power of Women's Networks"; Smith-Rosenberg, *Disorderly Conduct*, pp. 53–76, and *Religion and the Rise of the American City*; Welter, *Dimity Convictions*; Melder, "Ladies Bountiful"; Berg, *Remembered Gate*. For attention to networks and spheres among southern women, see Scott, *Southern Lady*; Massey, *Bonnet Brigades*; McMillen, "Mothers' Sacred Duty"; Censer, *North Carolina Planters*; and works cited in the previous note.

78. Clark, "Household Economy" and esp. "Households, Market, and Capital"; Henretta, "Families and Farms"; Waters, "Traditional World of the New England Peasants"; Mutch, "Yeoman and Merchant." For contrasting views, see Rothenberg, "Market and Massachusetts Farmers" and "Emergence of a Capital Market." For the persisting importance of the household in rural nineteenth-century America, see Hahn, "'Unmaking' of the Southern Yeomanry"; Faragher, "Open-Country Community." And for persisting production within some northern households, see Nobles, "Commerce and Community." On the household mode of production, see Merrill, "Cash Is Good to Eat." For thoughtful preliminary attempts to link household relations to changing historical conditions, see Howell, *Women, Production, and Patriarchy*, pp. 30–43; Medick, "Proto-Industrial Family Economy." Households are ubiquitous features in historical development, and the decisive questions depend not on identifying their presence but on exploring their internal dynamics and specific relations to modes of production. The pitfalls of the "household mode of production" emerge clearly from the controversy surrounding the work of A. V. Chayanov (*Theory of the Peasant Economy*).

79. I am indebted, here and elsewhere, to personal correspondence with Sidney Mintz concerning the anthropological view of the household. See also Gonzalez, *Black Carib Household*.

80. Allan Kulikoff faithfully summarized recent work in seventeenth-, eighteenth-, and early nineteenth-century social history and developed this argument in his paper, "American Yeoman Classes." In revising and expanding the original paper for his forthcoming book, he is developing an argument that is closer to my own. This picture of colonial households took shape from many of the pathbreaking local studies of the colonial period, especially New England. Bernard Bailyn set the tone with his *New England Merchants*, in which he argued that the merchants of New England retained an essentially medieval distaste for aggressive capital accumulation and even undue profit seeking. Bailyn's successors addressed the experience of rural and small-town inhabitants whom they similarly found to be something less than modern in their behavior and attitudes. See, e.g., Demos, *Little Commonwealth*; Lockridge, *New England Town*; Greven, *Four Generations*; Zuckerman, *Peaceable Kingdoms*; Waters, "Patrimony, Succession, and Social Stability." Cf. Levy, "'Tender Plants,'" which uses an argument closer to mine.

81. Most such studies, some of which are cited below, focus on such questions as the developmental possibilities of the slave economy, the profitability of slavery, the strength of the black family, the role of scientific methods in agriculture, and the self-sufficiency or staple-dependency of southern farms. These studies draw upon specific sets of plantation records to document in detail theses that have accompanied the general questions over the nature of antebellum southern society, and they provide invaluable insights into and specific illustrations of the questions to which they respond.

82. Gray, *History of Agriculture*; Stampp, *Peculiar Institution*; Fogel and Engerman, *Time on the Cross*. James Oakes's impressionistic account in *Ruling Race* offers little to advance an understanding of southern households, which he does not mention. Robert Fogel pays more attention to gender in *Without Consent*.

83. Genovese, *Political Economy of Slavery*, *World the Slaveholders Made*, and *Roll, Jordan, Roll*; Genovese and Fox-Genovese, "Slavery, Economic Development, and the Law"; Tushnet, *American Law of Slavery*; Fields, *Slavery and Freedom*; Woodman, *King Cotton*; Hahn, *Roots of Southern Populism*. For compatible interpretations, see Kolchin, "Reevaluating the Antebellum Slave Community" and *Unfree Labor*; Faust, "Culture, Conflict, and Community" and *James Henry Hammond*; Klein, *Unification of a Slave State*; Kulikoff, *Tobacco and Slaves*; Simpson, *Dispossessed Garden*; Bradford, *Better Guide Than Reason* and *Worthy Company*; Phillips, *Life and Labor* and *Slave Economy*; Wright, *Political Economy of the Cotton South*. Gavin Wright has modified his position somewhat in *Old South, New South*. For the classic formulation of the conservative interpretation, see Twelve Southerners, *I'll Take My Stand*; Weaver, *Southern Tradition at Bay*.

84. Owsley, *Plain Folk*; Clark, *Tennessee Yeomen*; Weaver, *Mississippi Farmers*. Recently, there has been a renewed interest in the yeomanry, notably due to the influence of Steven Hahn (*Roots of Southern Populism*). See also Foust, *Yeoman Farmer*; Oakes, *Ruling Race*; Burton and McMath, *Class, Conflict, and Consensus*; Magdol and Wakelyn, *Southern Common People*. For a related interpretation of southern politics, see Thornton, *Politics and Power*; Shore, *Southern Capitalists*. See also Fox-Genovese and Genovese, *Fruits of Merchant Capital*, pp. 249–71; Hahn,

" 'Unmaking' of the Southern Yeomanry."

85. See Oakes, "Politics of Economic Development." Cf. Kolchin, *Unfree Labor*, esp. p. 360, where the author summarizes his argument that the mode of production was more significant than the mode of exchange in determining the character of southern slave society.

86. Bender, "Refinement of the Concept of Household."

87. Friedmann, "Household Production and the National Economy."

88. Fox-Genovese and Genovese, *Fruits of Merchant Capital*, pp. 90–135.

89. Gavin Wright (*Political Economy of the Cotton South*) and Eugene Genovese (*Political Economy of Slavery*) concur on the general picture, especially the dependence on the world market, despite their persisting disagreements about the fundamental dynamics of the system. Even Robert Fogel and Stanley Engerman (*Time on the Cross*) agree on many of the general features, although their interpretation of the dynamics, especially the internal dynamics of the system, diverges sharply from that of others. Fred Bateman and Thomas Weiss (*Deplorable Scarcity*) argue that slaveholders chose not to invest in industry even though the returns would have been higher than the returns from farming. See also Fox-Genovese and Genovese, *Fruits of Merchant Capital*, pp. 90–171. Some of the most fruitful new work on southern political economy is emerging from new studies of the yeomanry, e.g., Allman, "Yeoman Regions"; Ford, "Social Origins of a New South Carolina"; Klein, *Unification of a Slave State*; Weiman, "Petty Commodity Production." See also Jordan, "Imprint of the Upper and Lower South"; Weiman, "Farmers and the Market" and "Slavery, Plantation Settlement, and Regional Development." On the cultural aspect, see, e.g., Eaton, *Freedom-of-Thought Struggle* and *Growth of Southern Civilization*; Faust, *Ideology of Slavery*; Kaufman, *Capitalism, Slavery, and Republican Values*; Loveland, *Southern Evangelicals*; Mathews, *Religion in the Old South* and *Slavery and Methodism*; Bailey, *Shadow on the Church*; Freehling, *Prelude to Civil War*; Genovese and Fox-Genovese, "Slavery, Economic Development, and the Law."

90. Menard, "Why African Slavery?," "Immigrants and Their Increase," "Population, Economy, and Society," "From Servants to Slaves," and "Economy and Society"; Carr and Menard, "Immigration and Opportunity"; Shammas, "World Women Knew"; Clemens, *Atlantic Economy*; Main, *Tobacco Colony*; Rutman and Rutman, *Place in Time*; Kulikoff, *Tobacco and Slaves*, esp. pp. 3–27; Bridenbaugh, *Vexed and Troubled Englishmen*; Everitt, "Farm Laborers"; Bowen, "Agricultural Prices, Farm Profits, and Rents"; and Kerridge, *Agricultural Revolution*.

91. The relations between indentured servants and their masters may plausibly be interpreted—as some have done for the Chesapeake region—as a special and qualified hybrid of the wage relation and unfree labor. These conclusions are based on the work of the splendid group of historians studying the Chesapeake of the seventeenth and early eighteenth centuries. In addition to the works cited in the preceding note, see Shammas, "Black Women's Work"; Tate and Ammerman, *Chesapeake in the Seventeenth Century*; Land et al., *Law, Society, and Politics*. See also Greene and Pole, *Colonial British America*; Smith, *Seventeenth-Century America*; Craven, *White, Red, and Black*; Menard, "Tobacco Industry"; Galenson and Menard, "Approaches to the Analysis of Economic Growth"; Land, "Economic Base and Social Structure," "Economic Behavior in a Planting Society," and "To-

bacco Staple"; Earle, *Evolution of a Tidewater Settlement System*; Breen and Innes, *"Myne Owne Ground"*; Morgan, *American Slavery, American Freedom*; Wood, *Black Majority*; Mullin, *Flight and Rebellion*; Littlefield, *Rice and Slaves*. The decisive work on the development of the tobacco trade in the context of the Atlantic economy remains that of Jacob M. Price (*France and the Chesapeake*).

92. Shammas, "How Self-Sufficient?"; Rothenberg, "Market and Massachusetts Farmers" and "Emergence of a Capital Market." Laurel Thatcher Ulrich (*Good Wives*, pp. 15–17) charts the increase and decrease in household ownership of the tools of household production in Essex and York counties during the eighteenth century. Joan Jensen (*Loosening the Bonds*) discusses the commercialization of women's traditional labor in the farm household. On midwestern farm households, see Faragher, *Women and Men* and *Sugar Creek*. See also Davis, *Frontier America*. Allan Kulikoff (*Tobacco and Slaves*, pp. 102–4) argues that, during the late seventeenth and early eighteenth centuries, heavy investment of labor in tobacco cultivation may also have discouraged more prosperous households from such manufacture. See Edward Carrington to Alexander Hamilton, 4, 8 Oct. 1791, in Syrett, *Papers of Alexander Hamilton*, 9:275–82, 299–304. The question requires further study. For the postbellum period, see Ferleger, "Self-Sufficiency."

93. There is, in fact, no necessary relation between a particular scholar's position on the capitalist or precapitalist nature of North American slave society and his or her position on the self-sufficient or food-importing status of plantations. Both self-sufficiency and food importation would be compatible with the high level of southern profits or the underdevelopment of internal southern markets. But scholars on both sides of the debate have paid insufficient attention to the centralization of aggregate demand in the hands of a few.

94. Hilliard, *Hog Meat and Hoe Cake*. See also Woodman, *King Cotton*.

95. Rothstein, "Antebellum South as a Dual Economy."

96. See, e.g., the mounting debts of the Thomas Butler King family of St. Simon's Island, Georgia, in the 1840s, as revealed by the Thomas Butler King Papers, SHC.

97. See, e.g., House, *Planter Management*; Rosengarten, *Tombee*, pp. 83–84; and, for the best treatment of the general problem, Woodman, *King Cotton*. On relations between the smaller households and the structure of the economy, see Genovese, *Political Economy of Slavery*; Gray, *History of Agriculture*; Hahn, *Roots of Southern Populism* and "'Unmaking' of the Southern Yeomanry." On aggregate figures for comparative household manufacture, see Tryon, *Household Manufactures*. For evidence of household textile production, see chap. 3 below and, for one particularly valuable source, Wilson, *Plantation Life*. On early plantation economies, see Verlinden, *Beginnings of Modern Colonization*.

98. Gray, *History of Agriculture*, pp. 488–92, esp. p. 488; Isaac, *Transformation of Virginia*; Beeman, *Evolution of the Southern Backcountry*; Parker, "Slave Plantation in American Agriculture" and "Slavery and Southern Economic Development"; Anderson and Gallman, "Slaves as Fixed Capital"; Gallman, "Slavery and Southern Economic Growth"; North, *Economic Growth*; Genovese, "Significance of the Slave Plantation"; Fleisig, "Slavery, the Supply of Agricultural Labor"; Wright, *Political Economy of the Cotton South*; Oakes, *Ruling Race*.

99. See, e.g., Dunn, "Tale of Two Plantations"; Elkins, *Slavery*.

100. Fogel and Engerman, *Time on the Cross*. On South Carolina, see Littlefield, *Rice and Slaves*. For a fine overview, see Morgan, "Development of Slave Culture."

101. Gutman, *Black Family*.

102. See, e.g., Aptheker, *American Negro Slave Revolts*; Genovese, *Roll, Jordan, Roll*; Harding, *There Is a River*; Levine, *Black Culture*.

103. The work on yeoman women remains minimal, but see Friedman, *Enclosed Garden*; Drake, *Pioneer Life*; Buck, "Poor Whites"; Clark, *Tennessee Yeomen*; Owsley, *Plain Folks*; Thornton, *Politics and Power*; Hahn, *Roots of Southern Populism*; Harris, *Plain Folk and Gentry*; Fox-Genovese and Genovese, *Fruits of Merchant Capital*, pp. 249–64; McCurry, "In Defense of Their World."

104. For an astute discussion of the issues, see Brown, "Getting in the Kitchen with Dinah." Also see Beecher, *Treatise on Domestic Economy*; Beecher and Stowe, *American Woman's Home*; Kelley, *Private Woman, Public Stage*; Bloch, "American Feminine Ideals"; Martineau, *Views of Slavery and Emancipation*.

105. Hubka, *Big House, Little House*.

Chapter 2

1. Charles Colcock Jones, Jr., to Rev. and Mrs. Charles Colcock Jones, 24 Aug. 1854, in Myers, *Children of Pride*, p. 78.

2. See, e.g., the strong statement in Dabney, *Defence of Virginia*, p. 229.

3. Emmaline Eve's account of the Eve family, Carmichael Family Books, SHC.

4. Burke, *Reminiscences of Georgia*, pp. 111–12. On houses, see Hubka, *Big House, Little House*. Mrs. John W. Wade reported, for example, that on her grandfather's plantation in East Texas there was "a flouring mill, a grain thresher and a cotton gin, in addition to the kitchen, the smokehouse, a potato house, an apple house, and, of course, the slaves' cabins" ("Recollections," UTLA).

5. Lumpkin, *Making of a Southerner*, pp. 26, 44. Anna Matilda Page King's plantation, Retreat, had an infirmary. On nurseries, see Burke, *Reminiscences of Georgia*, pp. 233–34. On outbuildings, see Felton, *Country Life*, pp. 29, 39; Wade, "Recollections," UTLA.

6. Lumpkin, *Making of a Southerner*, p. 22.

7. Burke, *Reminiscences of Georgia*, pp. 224–25.

8. Eliza Carolina (Burgwin) Clitherall Books, Book 5, SHC; Juliana Margaret Conner Diary, 21 June 1827, SHC; Meriwether, *Recollections*, p. 5. See also Flanders, "Two Plantations," p. 8.

9. Meriwether, *Recollections*, p. 52.

10. Burke, *Reminiscences of Georgia*, pp. 104, 109–11.

11. Eliza Carolina (Burgwin) Clitherall Books, Book 5, SHC; Anna Matilda King to Thomas Butler King, 27 Dec. 1844, Thomas Butler King Papers, SHC; deButts, *Growing Up in the 1850s*, p. 71; Burke, *Reminiscences of Georgia*, p. 118. On the small size or unimpressive condition of many plantation houses, see, among others, McReynolds, "Family Life in a Borderland Community," p. 154. See also Wade, "Recollections," pp. 7–8, UTLA; Terhune, *Marion Harland's Autobiography*, pp. 7, 335; Felton, *Country Life*, pp. 29, 34; Burton, *In My Father's House*, esp. pp. 38–39; Cheatham, "Washington County, Mississippi," pp. 53–58; Anthony, "Big House and the Slave Quarters," pt. 1; Roos, *Travels in America*, p. 87; Spruill,

Women's Life and Work, pp. 20–42; Johnson, *Ante-Bellum North Carolina*, pp. 226–27.

12. See, e.g., Sarah Gayle to John Gayle, 9 Jan. 1827, Bayne and Gayle Family Papers, SHC; Sarah Cobb to Martha Jackson, 6 Mar. 1823, Jackson and Prince Family Papers, SHC (reporting on Mr. Cobb's attempt to purchase a carpet); Wilson, *Plantation Life*, p. 235 (28 May 1827).

13. The same held true for John Gayle, a lawyer and politician, and Sydney Bumpas, a Methodist minister, among many. See, e.g., Bleser, *Hammonds of Red-cliffe*; Faust, *James Henry Hammond*; Jordan, *Hugh Davis*; Mathis, *John Horry Dent*.

14. On the self-sufficiency of southern households see, among many, Coulter, *Old Petersburg*, pp. 136–37; Klein, *Unification of a Slave State*, chap. 1; Lovell, *Golden Isles of Georgia*, p. 80; Cheatham, "Washington County, Mississippi," p. 61.

15. See, e.g., Mary Bateman Diary, 29 Feb., 30 Mar., 9 May, 5, 12, 13 June 1856, SHC; Meta (Morris) Grimball Journal, 16 May 1864, SHC; Frederick Fraser to Mary Fraser, 3 Mar. 1821, Mary DeSaussure Fraser Papers, DU; Mrs. (Eleanor) Jefferson Franklin Jackson Diary, 28 July 1849, ADAH.

16. For a fuller discussion of prevailing gender conventions and their place in southern society, see chap. 4 below.

17. Crabtree and Patton, *Journal of a Secesh Lady*, p. 240 (21 Aug. 1862). On keys, see Ella Gertrude Clanton Thomas Diary, 19 Aug. 1855, DU; Mary E. Robarts to Rev. Charles Colcock Jones, 26 Apr. 1858, in Myers, *Children of Pride*, p. 411; Terhune, *Marion Harland's Autobiography*, p. 7; Martineau, *Society in America*, 1:219–28.

18. Clinton, *Plantation Mistress*, chap. 2; Ella Gertrude Clanton Thomas Diary, 24 Sept. 1848, DU; Lucilla Agnes (Gamble) McCorkle Diary, 14 Apr. 1850, SHC. See also Robertson, *Lucy Breckinridge*, pp. 52 (29 Sept. 1862), 88 (29 Dec. 1861); Kate S. Carney Diary, SHC; Anna Matilda Page's correspondence with her father before her marriage, Thomas Butler King Papers, SHC; Schoolcraft, *Plantation Life*, p. 115.

19. Jackson and Prince Family Papers, SHC; Henry Watson to Miss Amelia Dresser, 12 Sept. 1858, Henry Watson Family Papers, DU; Jessie Webb to James Webb, 8 July, 14 Nov. 1861, Walton Family Papers, SHC. See also Eliza Carolina (Burgwin) Clitherall Books, Book 5; Boucher, "Wealthy Planter Families," pp. 150–51. Charles Colcock Jones, Jr., while away at Princeton, still sent his mother a draft of an address he was to give and winced at her trenchant criticism (Myers, *Georgian at Princeton*, pp. 121–23). On fathers' roles in their daughters' formal education, see Kate S. Carney Diary, Sept. 1859, SHC. The journal of Martha R. Jackson (Aug. 1833–July 1834, Jackson and Prince Family Papers, SHC) provides a running account of her daily training and that of her sister, Sarah Rootes Jackson, by their mother and father. Their mother supervised all aspects of their lives, but their father actively participated in their school lessons. See also David Campbell to Virginia Tabitha Lavinia Campbell, 24 July 1833, in which he instructs her on continuing to improve her writing; and Lavinia (Campbell) Kelley to Margaret H. Campbell, 14 Feb. 1833, saying that now that she is married, she will no longer have time to copy over her letters (Campbell Family Papers, DU). Lizzie Ozburn, writing to her father, notes that her mother has always had twice the influence over them that he has (11 Sept. 1860, Mary Elizabeth [Lizzie] Osborn Family

Papers, GDAH). See also Terhune, *Marion Harland's Autobiography*; Clay-Clopton, *Belle of the Fifties*, p. 15; Pringle, *Chronicles of Chicora Wood*, pp. 123–29; King,
Ebb Tide, pp. 47, 49, 51, 60–62, 80, 84.

20. Meriwether, *Recollections*, p. 31.

21. On the Browns, see Bonner, *Milledgeville*, p. 151. On black cultural influence
on white girls, see Lovell, *Golden Isles of Georgia*, p. 187; Fishburne, *Belvidere*, p. 25;
Clay-Clopton, *Belle of the Fifties*, p. 4; Eliza L. Magruder Diary, 3 Jan. 1854, LSU;
Middleton, *Life in Carolina and New England*, p. 100; Watts, "Summer on a
Louisiana Cotton Plantation," pp. 105–6, Louise Taylor Pharr Manuscripts, LSU;
Pringle, *Chronicles of Chicora Wood*, p. 54; [Walton], "Autobiography of E.D.W.,"
p. 10, Lawrence Family Papers, TSLA.

22. Julia Howe to Louisa Lenoir, 31 May 1837, Lenoir Family Letters, SHC;
Sarah Haynsworth Gayle Diary, HSC; Mary Steele Ferrand Henderson Journal,
SHC; Ella Gertrude Clanton Thomas Diary, 1855, DU; Crabtree and Patton, *Journal of a Secesh Lady*, pp. 21–23 (12 Dec. 1860), 418–19 (27 June 1863). See also
McMillen, "Women's Sacred Occupation." Sally McMillen draws heavily on medical evidence and ideological prescription and does not pay much attention to the
ubiquitous presence of servants; hence she does not underscore the relation of the
ideal of motherhood to the reality.

23. Ella Gertrude Clanton Thomas Diary, 1848–52 passim (e.g., 28, 29 Sept., 3, 5,
9 Oct. 1848, 6 Jan. 1849, 2 Feb., 5 Mar. 1852), DU; Moragne, *Neglected Thread*, p. 7;
Robertson, *Lucy Breckinridge*, pp. 97–98 (18 Jan. 1863). On the lives and training of
young women, see also Kate S. Carney Diary, SHC; John Hamilton Cornish
Diary, 16 July 1849, SHC; Martha R. Jackson Diary, 1833–34 passim, SHC; Sarah
Rootes Jackson Diary, 1834–35 passim, SHC; Terhune, *Marion Harland's Auto-
biography*, pp. 111, 113, 334; David Campbell to David Campbell [dear friend], 3
Dec. 1832, Campbell Family Papers, DU (noting that since the end of school
Virginia has been employed primarily "in domestic matters").

24. Ella Gertrude Clanton Thomas Diary, 12 June 1852, DU.

25. For the experience of a circuit-riding minister's wife, who started married life
as a boarder, see Frances Moore (Webb) Bumpas Diary, SHC; for that of a young
woman who would have preferred to board rather than have to cope with difficult
servants, see Lines, *To Raise Myself*, pp. 190, 192, 197–98, 204, 211.

26. Mary Steele Ferrand Henderson Journal, 9 July 1855, SHC; Mary Hamilton
Campbell to David Campbell, 23 Dec. 1821, Mary Hamilton Campbell Letterbook,
Campbell Family Papers, DU. See also Susanna C. Clay to Clement Claiborne
Clay, 24 Jan. 1833, Clement Claiborne Clay Family Papers, DU (on her surprise at
the successful performance of a young bride); Frances Moore (Webb) Bumpas
Diary, 13, 20 Apr. 1842, SHC (on her initial uncertainty and growing confidence);
Smedes, *Southern Planter*, p. 11 (on a young woman's struggle to take control of
the servants after her mother's death). See also Pringle, *Chronicles of Chicora Wood*,
pp. 61–62; Mrs. Mary Jones to Mary Sharpe Jones, 22 Dec. 1856, and Mrs. Mary
Jones to Mrs. Mary Sharpe [Jones] Mallard, 22 May 1857, in Myers, *Children of
Pride*, pp. 278, 318–19; Terhune, *Marion Harland's Autobiography*, pp. 333–45. On
women's work in more modest households, see Lines, *To Raise Myself*, pp. 90, 187–
211 passim. In Webb, *Mistress of Evergreen*, Rachel O'Connor describes the prospective bride of a neighbor: "Miss Terry will make an excellent poor man's wife—she

can milk and wash and do anything" (Rachel O'Connor to David Weeks, 8 July 1832, p. 72).

27. *MBC*, p. 46. On Floride Calhoun, see Wiltse, *John C. Calhoun: Nationalist*, p. 343; Wiltse, *John C. Calhoun: Nullifier*, p. 116; Holmes and Sherrill, *Thomas Green Clemson*, p. 16. See also Sally Baxter to George Baxter, 15 Apr. 1855, and Sally Baxter Hampton to George Baxter, 22 Dec. 1860, in Hampton, *Divided Heart*, pp. 21–23, 80; Crabtree and Patton, *Journal of a Secesh Lady*, pp. 37 (16 Feb. 1861), 142 (13 Mar. 1862); Meta (Morris) Grimball Journal, 29 Dec. 1860, SHC; Wilson, *Plantation Life*, p. 202 (23 June 1824); Terhune, *Marion Harland's Autobiography*, p. 337 (on her mother, who was a good housekeeper, "and the wheels of her machine ran in smooth ruts"); Eliza Lucas Pinckney to Miss Bartlett, undated, in Pinckney, *Letterbook*, p. 34.

28. Rev. C. C. Jones to Mr. Charles Colcock Jones, 22 May 1854, and Miss Mary E. Robarts to Rev. C. C. Jones, 18 Mar. 1856, in Myers, *Children of Pride*, pp. 35, 197–98. Augustus Longstreet Hull painted a similar picture of his mother's responsibilities, concluding that she, like other housewives, "was the dispenser of food, clothing, and medicine for a large family of dependents whose claims and duties absorbed her waking hours" (Hull, *Annals of Athens, Georgia*, p. 284).

29. On masters' distribution of rations, see Faust, *James Henry Hammond* and "Culture, Conflict, and Community," pp. 83–98. But at Martha Campbell's Argyle Plantation, there was no resident man, so the rations were distributed by one of the senior women (Mary E. Bateman Diary, 24 Aug., 7 Sept. 1856, SHC). On the responsibilities of the mistress, see Rev. Charles Colcock Jones to Charles Colcock Jones, Jr., 22 May 1854, in Myers, *Children of Pride*, pp. 35–36; Smedes, *Southern Planter*, pp. 4–7; Emily Caroline Douglas Autobiography, pp. 109–10, Emily Caroline Douglas Papers, LSU.

30. Iraminta Antoinette Alexander to Dear Aunt, 5 Oct. 1859, Iraminta Antoinette Alexander Papers, GDAH. See also Mary E. Bateman Diary (e.g., 7 Aug. 1856), SHC; Sarah Eve Adams Diary, 11 Dec. 1813, DU. The Jackson plantation was in Georgia, near Augusta, and had more than fifty slaves (Martha Jackson to Henry Jackson, 15 June 1828, and Martha R. Jackson to Henry Jackson [brother], 22 July 1835, Jackson and Prince Family Papers, SHC). On women and poultry, see also deButts, *Growing Up in the 1850s*, p. 62. On mistresses' provision of delicacies to their servants, see Fannie Page Hume Diary, 31 Dec. 1859, 4 Nov. 1861, SHC; Martha R. Jackson Diary, 14 June 1833, SHC.

31. Anna Matilda Page King to Thomas Butler King, 5, 9 Aug. 1842, Thomas Butler King Papers, SHC; Mary Steele Ferrand Henderson Journal, 15 July 1855, SHC; Mary Hamilton Campbell to David Campbell, 19 Mar. 1813, Campbell Family Papers, DU. On women and gardens, see also deButts, *Growing Up in the 1850s*, p. 62; Charlotte Beatty Diary, 6, 28 Feb. 1843, SHC; Rachel O'Connor to Mary Weeks, 15 June 1824, Rachel O'Connor to Mary Weeks, 15 Sept. 1833, and Rachel O'Connor to Frances Weeks, 17 Apr. 1835, in Webb, *Mistress of Evergreen*, pp. 5, 116, 167; Moragne, *Neglected Thread*, pp. 234–35 (7 Mar. 1842); Robertson, "Diary of Dolly Lunt Burge," 44:453 (22 Mar. 1852), 45:57 (31 Jan., 7 Feb. 1853); Anderson, *Brokenburn*, p. 10; Virginia Tabitha Jane Campbell to David Campbell, 5 Apr. 1837, Campbell Family Papers, DU; Terhune, *Marion Harland's Autobiography*, p. 7; Wilson, *Plantation Life*, pp. 5 (21 Nov. 1814), 123 (14 Apr. 1821), 409 (17

Apr. 1839); Margaret Johnson Erwin to Eleanor Ewing Sherman, 8 June 1859, in Erwin, *Like Some Green Laurel*, p. 47; Mary E. Bateman Diary, 12 Feb. 1856, SHC (on a slave's starting to plant the garden).

32. Rev. Charles Colcock Jones to Charles Colcock Jones, Jr., 22 May 1854, in Myers, *Children of Pride*, p. 35.

33. Anna Matilda Page King to Thomas Butler King, 14 June 1849, Thomas Butler King Papers, SHC; Mary E. Bateman Diary, 2, 3, 21, 22, 23 July, 7 Aug. 1856, SHC; Martha R. Jackson Diary, 25 July, 23 Aug. 1833, SHC; Sarah Rootes Jackson Diary, 28, 29 July, 1, 9, 15, 16, 17 Sept. 1835, SHC; Kate S. Carney Diary, 12 Jan. 1859, SHC; Mary Steele Ferrand Henderson Journal, 9 July 1855, SHC. On preserves, see also Crabtree and Patton, *Journal of a Secesh Lady*, 25, 28 Aug. 1860; Robertson, "Diary of Dolly Lunt Burge," 45:57 (17 Jan. 1853); Wilson, *Plantation Life*, e.g., pp. 4 (9 Sept. 1814), 30 (18 Sept. 1816), 50 (22 Sept. 1817), 130 (21 Sept. 1821); Mrs. Mary Jones to Mr. Charles Colcock Jones, Jr., 7 Dec. 1854 and 18 Dec. 1855, in Myers, *Children of Pride*, pp. 112, 177–78. On domestic affairs, see also Susanna C. Clay to Clement Claiborne Clay, 11 June 1821, Clement Claiborne Clay Family Papers, DU; Eliza Ann Marsh Diary, 9 Jan. 1850, LSU; "Autobiography," Lucy Muse (Walton) Fletcher Journal, late 1848–early 1849, Jan. 1851, DU; Virginia Tabitha Jane Campbell to David Campbell, 5 Apr. 1837, Campbell Family Papers, DU; Sally Holmes to Elizabeth Blanks, 17 Sept. 1833, Elizabeth Blanks Papers, DU; Mary Telfair to Mary Few, 4 Aug. [1812?], William Few Collection, GDAH.

34. Sarah Eve Adams Diary, 22 Dec. 1813, 10 Feb. 1814, DU; Mary Hamilton Campbell to David Campbell, 8 Jan. 1822, Campbell Family Papers, DU; Wilson, *Plantation Life*, e.g., pp. 6 (5, 15, 19 Dec. 1814), 9 (3 Feb. 1815), 30 (7 Oct. 1816), 135 (12 Dec. 1821), 321 (13 Dec. 1832).

35. Kate S. Carney Diary, 15 Mar. 1859, SHC; Anna Matilda Page King to Thomas Butler King, 9 June 1842, Thomas Butler King Papers, SHC; Moragne, *Neglected Thread*, p. 104; Terhune, *Marion Harland's Autobiography*, p. 169; Mrs. Mary Sharpe (Jones) Mallard to Miss Mary Jones Taylor, 12 Aug. 1857, in Myers, *Children of Pride*, p. 364. On flour, see also Mary E. Bateman Diary, 29 Feb., 22 Aug. 1856, SHC. On whiskey, Mary E. Bateman Diary, 23 Apr. 1856, SHC. On sugar, Martha Jackson to Henry Jackson, [n.d.] Aug. 1831, Jackson and Prince Family Papers, SHC; Fannie Page Hume Diary, 4 Nov. 1861, SHC. On coffee, Mary Steele Ferrand Henderson Journal, 16 Aug. 1855, SHC; Mary E. Bateman Diary, 7 Mar. 1856, SHC. On poultry, Ann Matilda Page King Plantation Record Book, GDAH; Wilson, *Plantation Life*, pp. 217 (5 May 1826), 258 (26 Feb. 1828), 318 (19 Sept. 1831). On bacon, Iverson Brookes to Cornelia Brookes, 30 Apr. 1860, Iverson Brookes Family Papers, DU; On pork, Susanna C. Clay to Clement Claiborne Clay, 24 Jan. 1833, Clement Claiborne Clay Family Papers, DU; Martha R. Jackson Diary, 16 Oct. 1833, SHC.

36. Anna Matilda Page King to Thomas Butler King, 6 July 1854, Thomas Butler King Papers, SHC. On the washing of glassware, see Wilson, *Plantation Life*, p. 193; Morrill, *My Confederate Girlhood*, pp. 14–15. On fixing parlor ornaments while a servant cleaned, see Fannie Page Hume Diary, 6 Mar. 1861, SHC. On slaves' labor in cleaning, see also Mary Eliza (Eve) Carmichael Diary, 23 Apr. 1834, 4, 20 Oct. 1837, SHC; Frances Moore (Webb) Bumpas Diary, SHC; Lucy Walton Muse Fletcher Journal, DU; Julia E. Hunter to Eliza Ogletree, [n.d.] Mar. 1856, Ogletree Family Papers, GDAH; Anne Winship Copybook, 6 Feb. [1853], Winship-

Flournoy Family Papers, AHS; Wilson, *Plantation Life*, pp. 218 (22 May 1826), 224 (27 Sept. 1826), 241 (27 Sept., 1 Oct. 1827), 278 (4 Dec. 1829); Crabtree and Patton, *Journal of a Secesh Lady*, p. 398 (31 May 1863). For a well-to-do slaveholding woman who lived in Natchez and claimed to do some of her own housekeeping, see Mahala (Eggleston) Roach Diary, 19 Mar. 1853, SHC. On washing, see Mary Steele Ferrand Henderson Journal, 12 Aug. 1855, SHC; Lines, *To Raise Myself*, p. 190; Mary Jones to Mary Sharpe Jones, 22 Dec. 1856, in Myers, *Children of Pride*, p. 278. On candles, see Sarah Eve Adams Diary, 4, 21 Apr. 1814, DU; Wilson, *Plantation Life*, pp. 5 (30 Nov. 1814), 60 (24 Apr. 1818). And, on the return to candlemaking during the Civil War, Mary Sharpe (Jones) Mallard to Mary Jones, 14 Dec. 1861, in Myers, *Children of Pride*, p. 818; Crabtree and Patton, *Journal of a Secesh Lady*, p. 186 (1 June 1861); John Walker Diary, e.g., 1 May 1834 and 14 Mar. 1835 (for soap), SHC. On carrying water, see Susan Davis (Nye) Hutchinson Diary, 26 June 1833, SHC.

37. See Mary Steele Ferrand Henderson Journal, 20 Aug. 1855, SHC (on a slave's quilting for her); Catherine Carson to W. S. Walker, 26 Jan. 1836, Carson Family Papers, TSLA (on her servant's uselessness at tatting and being sent to sew for the outhands). On quilting, see also Felton, *Country Life*, pp. 29, 53. Dolly Lunt Burge noted that "only poor white folks made bed quilts" (Robertson, "Diary of Dolly Lunt Burge," 45:166 [14 Feb. 1862]).

38. On a slave's making pillow cases, see Mary E. Bateman Diary, 16 Feb. 1856, SHC. On making carpets, Wilson, *Plantation Life*, p. 34 (6 Jan. 1817). On knitting, Fannie Page Hume Diary, 31 Dec. 1859, SHC; Moragne, *Neglected Thread*, p. 159; Wilson, *Plantation Life*, p. 6 (4 Dec. 1814); Robertson, "Diary of Dolly Lunt Burge," 45:58 (29 Sept. 1853); Crabtree and Patton, *Journal of a Secesh Lady*, p. 57 (26 Apr. 1861). On tatting, Fannie Page Hume Diary, 5 Apr. 1861, SHC. On making negro clothes with slave women, Joel B. Fort Diary, 1822, TSLA. All but Sunday clothes, for white and black, were made on the plantation. On negro clothes, see also Sarah Eve Adams Diary, 6, 14 Dec. 1813, DU; Wilson, *Plantation Life*, e.g., pp. 8 (20 Jan. 1815), 144 (25 June 1822), 236 (22 June 1827), 282 (18, 20 Feb. 1830); Robertson, "Diary of Dolly Lunt Burge," 45:63 (24 Nov. 1854).

39. Olmsted, *Journey in the Back Country*, p. 352. On flax, see Wilson, *Plantation Life*, pp. 6 (10 Dec. 1814), 9 (4 Feb. 1815), 295 (13 Jan. 1831), 359 (12 Feb. 1836). Martha Ogle Forman also kept silkworms; see, e.g., Wilson, *Plantation Life*, p. 271 (11, 14 July 1829). See also Leigh, "Report." For the reassignment of field women on rainy days, see Davis, *Cotton Kingdom*, pp. 67–68; Nicholas Bryor Massenburg Books, Oct. 1836, SHC; John Durant Ashmore Book, Jan. 1856, SHC; James Monette Day Book and Diary, LSU; Sydnor, *Slavery in Mississippi*, p. 11.

40. On wool, see Mary Steele Ferrand Henderson Journal, 18 July 1855, SHC; Sarah Cobb to Martha Jackson, 21 Nov. 1822, Jackson and Prince Family Papers, SHC; Wilson, *Plantation Life*, e.g., pp. 2 (1 Aug. 1814), 30 (25 Sept. 1816), 33 (25 Nov. 1816). Charles Joyner claims that most of the planters of All Saints Parish in Georgetown District, S.C., ordered woolen cloth from England and had it made up on the plantation (*Down by the Riverside*, pp. 108–9). On spinning and weaving, see chap. 3 below; Felton, *Country Life*, pp. 29–32.

41. On the purchase of a sewing machine, see Mary E. Bateman Diary, 13 June 1856, SHC; John Hamilton Cornish Diary, 21, 27 May 1858, SHC; Virginia Ayer to her "Beloved Sister," [n.d.] Mar. 1858, Iverson Brookes Family Papers, DU; Mary

Sharpe Jones discusses relatives and acquaintances who have purchased sewing machines (Mary Sharpe Jones to Mary Jones, 27 Dec. 1856, in Myers, *Children of Pride*, p. 282).

42. Mary Steele Ferrand Henderson Journal, 12 July 1855, SHC. Three days later, although feverish and suffering, she finished "ruffling the little dimity skirt" and looked ahead to the "two pairs of linen pillowcases to ruffle—the little Salmon merino dress skirt to embroider with white floss silk and a white dress to needle work" (15 July 1855). Fannie Page Hume Diary, 2, 5, 23, 24 Apr., 20 Oct., 1860, 22 June 1861, SHC; Frances Moore (Webb) Bumpas Diary, 20 May 1842, 15 Oct. 1843, SHC. See also Mahala (Eggleston) Roach Diary, 15, 28 July, 23 Sept. 1853, SHC; Charlotte Beatty Diary, 29 May 1843, SHC; Moragne, *Neglected Thread*, pp. 114, 135, 160; Mary Telfair to Mary Few, 25 Jan. 1828, William Few Collection, GDAH; Virginia Tabitha Lavinia Campbell to Lavinia Campbell, [Sunday afternoon] Nov. 1832, and Margaret Campbell to Mary H. Campbell [draft], 9 Feb. 1833, Campbell Family Papers, DU; Meta (Morris) Grimball Journal, 15 Dec. 1860, SHC; Terhune, *Marion Harland's Autobiography*, pp. 7, 111, 113; Pinckney, *Letterbook*, p. 34; King, *Victorian Lady*, p. 66.

43. Sarah Rootes Jackson Diary, 14 Jan. 1835, Jackson and Prince Family Papers, SHC; Ella Gertrude Clanton Thomas Diary, DU.

44. Kate S. Carney Diary, 16–23, 24, 25 Feb., 22 Apr. 1859, SHC.

45. Ibid., 23 Apr. 1859.

46. Ibid., 4 Feb., 7 May 1861. Anna King reported that she, a daughter, and a cousin went up to her oldest daughter's plantation for the day to help her sew, and they planned to keep up the practice until all the sewing was done (Anna Matilda Page King to Lord King, 4 July 1853, Thomas Butler King Papers, SHC). See also Mahala (Eggleston) Roach Diary, 28 Jan. 1853, SHC; Charlotte Beatty Diary, 1 June 1843, SHC. On cutting and sewing negro clothes, see Margaret H. Campbell to Mary H. Campbell, 3 Apr. 1831, Campbell Family Papers, DU; Sarah Eve Adams Diary, 3, 6, 11, 14 Dec. 1813, DU; Pringle, *Chronicles of Chicora Wood*, pp. 153–56; Rev. Charles Colcock Jones to Charles Colcock Jones, Jr., 22 May 1854, in Myers, *Children of Pride*, p. 35. Rachel O'Connor to Alfred Conrad, 12 Apr. 1835, in Webb, *Mistress of Evergreen*, p. 167. On the master's dispensing the clothes, see J. B. Grimball Diary, 20 Nov. 1844, Grimball Family Papers, SHC. On mistresses' dispensing clothes, see Myers, *Children of Pride*, p. 265.

47. Anna Matilda Page King to Thomas Butler King, 2 June 1842, 2 Aug., 12 Oct. 1858, Thomas Butler King Papers, SHC; Thomas Butler King to Anna Matilda Page King, 7 June 1852, ibid.; Mahala (Eggleston) Roach Diary, 8 Mar., 1 Nov. 1853, SHC; Mary Eliza (Eve) Carmichael Diary, 14 Oct. 1837, 27 July 1845, SHC; Turner, *Old Field School Teacher's Diary*, p. 39. See also Mary Steele Ferrand Henderson Journal, 18, 20 Aug. 1855, SHC; Mary (Jeffreys) Bethell Diary, 12 Dec. 1853, 1 Jan., 17 Apr. 1862, SHC; Susan Davis (Nye) Hutchinson Diary, 27 Sept. 1840, SHC; Henry Craft Diary, 17 July 1863, SHC; Anna Matilda Page King to Lord King, 28 Sept. 1848, Thomas Butler King Papers, SHC; Henry Jackson to Martha Jackson, 25 July 1829, Jackson and Prince Family Papers, SHC; Rachel Weeks O'Connor to David Weeks, 14 Oct. 1824, Weeks Papers, LSU; Eliza L. Magruder Diary, 21 May 1846, LSU; Mary Telfair to Mary Few, 1 June 1837, William Few Collection, GDAH; C. C. Howard to Eliza Ogletree, [n.d.] Mar. 1846,

Ogletree Family Papers, GDAH; David Campbell to William B. Campbell, 19 Feb. 1833, Campbell Family Papers, DU; Sally Baxter Hampton to Anna Baxter, [n.d.] Apr. 1859, in Hampton, *Divided Heart*, p. 54; Schoolcraft, *Plantation Life*, pp. 113–14; Pringle, *Chronicles of Chicora Wood*, pp. 63–65; Charles Colcock Jones, Jr., to Mrs. Mary Jones, 25 May 1859, and Mrs. Mary Jones to Mrs. Mary Sharpe (Jones) Mallard, 21 Oct. 1858, in Myers, *Children of Pride*, pp. 486, 454; Rachel O'Connor to Mary Weeks, 1 Sept. 1833, in Webb, *Mistress of Evergreen*, p. 114; King, *Victorian Lady*, p. 30 (29 June 1863); Catherine Edmonston notes that all of the slave children were receiving vaccinations as preventive care (Crabtree and Patton, *Journal of a Secesh Lady*, p. 153 [13 Apr. 1862]).

48. Susan Davis (Nye) Hutchinson Diary, 25 Nov. 1826, 27 Apr. 1838, 27 Sept. 1840, SHC; Mary (Jeffreys) Bethell Diary, 12 Dec. 1853, 26 Jan. 1857, 1 Jan. 1860, 3 May 1863, SHC.

49. Eliza Carolina (Burgwin) Clitherall Books, 1 Feb., 19 Dec. 1852, 23, 24 Jan. 1853, 20 Aug., 6 Sept. 1856, SHC; Anna Matilda Page King to Thomas Butler King, 6, 17 Oct. 1858, and Anna Matilda Page King to Floyd King, 6, 12 Oct. 1858, Thomas Butler King Papers, SHC. See also Mary Steele Ferrand Henderson Journal, 19 Aug. 1855, SHC; Fannie Page Hume Diary, 22, 24 May 1860, SHC; Sarah G. Howard to Eliza Ogletree, 30 Aug. 1856, Ogletree Family Papers, GDAH; Wilson, *Plantation Life*, e.g., pp. 97 (16 Feb. 1820), 421–22 (12 May 1841); Margaret Johnson Erwin to Carrie, 5, 16 June 1859, in Erwin, *Like Some Green Laurel*, pp. 97, 99; Rachel O'Connor to Mary Weeks, 1 Sept. 1833, Rachel O'Connor to David Weeks, 22 Dec. 1833, and Rachel O'Connor to Mary Weeks, 10 Oct. 1840, in Webb, *Mistress of Evergreen*, pp. 113–14, 130, 227; Mahala (Eggleston) Roach Diary, 17, 19 May 1853, SHC. For representative expressions of grief by white women at the death of male slaves, see Antonia Quitman to John A. Quitman, 14 Sept. 1855, Quitman Family Papers, SHC; Nueremberger, *Clays of Alabama*, p. 15; Keating, *Washington County, Mississippi*.

50. Fisk University, *Unwritten History of Slavery*, p. 3. For mistresses who perceived their slaves as devoted to them, see, e.g., Eliza Carolina (Burgwin) Clitherall Books, 2 Feb. 1860, SHC; Sarah Rootes Jackson Diary, 21 May 1834, SHC.

51. Kemble, *Journal of a Residence*, pp. 206, 208, 210, 223. See also Samuel Hairston Diary, 31 Dec. 1845, MDAH. For evidence that former slaves remembered their mistresses as having made life easier, see Yetman, *Life under the "Peculiar Institution,"* p. 218; George Teamoh Journal, pts. 1–2, p. 32, Carter G. Woodson Papers, LC; Willie Lee Rose, *Rehearsal for Reconstruction*, p. 85. See also Samuel Boulware, *South Carolina Narratives*, vol. 2, pt. 1, p. 66; Andy Brice, ibid., p. 76; Philip Rice, ibid., vol. 3, pt. 2, p. 17.

52. On the dynamics of paternalism, see Genovese, *Roll, Jordan, Roll*.

53. For examples of mistresses' brutality, see chaps. 3 and 6 below. See also *MCCW*, pp. 646–47 (26 Sept. 1864).

54. Josey King to Fuddy King, 6 Oct. 1858, Thomas Butler King Papers, SHC; Mrs. Eleanor J. W. Baker Journal, 1848, p. 16, DU. See also Bonner, "Plantation Experiences of a New York Woman," p. 389.

55. Juliana Margaret Conner Diary, 22 June, 13 Aug. 1827, SHC; Mary Hamilton Campbell to David Campbell, 20 Jan. 1822, Campbell Family Papers, DU; Kemble, *Journal of a Residence*; Hentz, *Planter's Northern Bride*. See also Wilson, *Plan-*

tation Life, pp. 6 (4 Dec. 1814), 76 (18 Feb. 1819); King, *Victorian Lady*, p. 60; Rachel O'Connor to Mary Weeks, 15 Mar. 1844, in Webb, *Mistress of Evergreen*, p. 250.

56. Eliza Quitman to John A. Quitman, 20 Jan. 1836, Quitman Family Papers, SHC; Anna Matilda Page King to Lord King, 28 Sept. 1848, and Anna Matilda Page King to Thomas Butler King, e.g., 14, 20 June 1849, Thomas Butler King Papers, SHC; Kate S. Carney Diary 16, 17 June 1859, SHC; Fannie Page Hume Diary, 28 Jan., 25 Nov., 2 Dec. 1860, SHC; Eliza Carolina (Burgwin) Clitherall Books, 25 June, 18 July, 1, 15 Aug. 1852, 2 Feb. 1860, SHC. See also Robert F. W. Allston to Adele Petigru Allston, [n.d.] Mar. 1859, Allston Family Papers, SCL; Mary Hamilton Campbell to David Campbell, 8 Jan. 1822, Campbell Family Papers, DU; Eliza Ann Marsh Diary, 9 Jan. 1850, LSU; Catherine Carson to W. S. Walker, 26 Jan. 1836, Carson Family Papers, TSLA; Mary (Jeffreys) Bethell Diary, 21 Oct. 1862, SHC; Mary Telfair to Mary Few, Dec. [1832?], William Few Collection, GDAH; David Campbell to Virginia Tabitha Lavinia Campbell, 24 July 1833, Campbell Family Papers, DU (with detailed news of the servants who ask for her).

57. Emmaline Eve's account of her family, Carmichael Family Books, SHC.

58. Mrs. Isaac Hilliard Diary, 19 June 1850, LSU. See also John Osgood (*A Letter of Prudent Advice*) for advice to his son and daughter [in-law?] on the management of slaves, among other things.

59. *MBC*, pp. 45–46; Meta (Morris) Grimball Journal, 29 Dec. 1860 and throughout, SHC; Lucilla Agnes (Gamble) McCorkle Diary, 2 June, 6 July 1846, SHC.

60. Mary Steele Ferrand Henderson Journal, 8 July 1855, SHC. See Elizabeth Avery Meriwether's account of her old black mammy's cleaning her up after an accident (*Recollections*, p. 31). See also Fishburne, *Belvidere*, p. 25; *MBC*, p. 46; Smythe, "Recollections," SCHS. On regular nurses, see Mary (Jeffreys) Bethell Diary, 3 Dec. 1856, SHC; Mary Steele Ferrand Henderson Journal, 8 July 1855, SHC; Wade, *Augustus Baldwin Longstreet*, pp. 242–43; chap. 3 below.

61. Mary E. Bateman Diary, 5 Aug. 1856, SHC; Broidrick, "Recollection of Thirty Years Ago," p. 5, LSU; Meta (Morris) Grimball Journal, 30 Dec. 1863, SHC. See also, e.g., Henry Turner to John A. Quitman, 2 May 1845, Quitman Family Papers, SHC; Wade, "Recollections," p. 5, UTLA; Pringle, *Chronicles of Chicora Wood*, p. 251. On cooks, see Smedes, *Southern Planter*, p. 41; Powdermaker, *After Freedom*, p. 119; Jordan, *Hugh Davis*, p. 77; Virginia Ayer to her "Beloved Sister," Mar. 1858, Iverson Brookes Family Papers, DU; Wilson, *Plantation Life*, p. 391 (29 Dec. 1837); chap. 3 below.

62. Anna Matilda Page King to Thomas Butler King, 11, 12 Aug. 1842, Thomas Butler King Papers, SHC.

63. Meriwether, *Recollections*, p. 31. See also Wade, "Recollections," pp. 9–10, UTLA. The examples of Meriwether and Wade suggest that slaveholding girls did go into the kitchen, probably when they were in the charge of slave women.

64. Mary Steele Ferrand Henderson Journal, 1, 2, 12 Jan. 1858, 9 June 1855, SHC.

65. Mary Steele Ferrand Henderson Journal, 13, 20 July 1855, SHC. Mrs. McCollam's manuscript diary is quoted in Sitterson, "The McCollams," pp. 349–50.

66. Eliza L. Magruder Diary, 17 Apr., 11 Sept. 1846, 26 Oct. 1854, 1 July 1855, LSU. See also Genovese, *In Red and Black*, pp. 119–20. For examples of affection among mistresses and slaves and gifts from mistresses to slaves, see Sarah Rootes

Jackson Diary, 21 May 1834, SHC; Meta (Morris) Grimball Journal, 15 May 1864, SHC; Mrs. Isaac Hilliard Diary, 15 May 1850, LSU; Mary Telfair to Mary Few, 15 Jan. [?], William Few Collection, GDAH; Terhune, *Marion Harland's Autobiography*, pp. 166–67. But, for former slaves' recollections of the viciousness of mistresses, see Mary Armstrong, *Texas Narratives*, vol. 4, pt. 1, pp. 25–26; Yetman, *Life under the "Peculiar Institution,"* pp. 13, 45, 225, 226. And for contemporaneous antislavery accounts, see Weld, *American Slavery as It Is*, p. 25; Drew, *Refugee*, pp. 24, 259.

67. Fannie Page Hume Diary, 9 Jan. 1861, SHC.

68. Withers Clay to Clement Claiborne Clay, 24 Dec. 1833, Clement Claiborne Clay Family Papers, DU.

69. David Campbell's Private Journal, 7 July 1843, Campbell Family Papers, DU; Foby, "Management of Servants," p. 227. On mistresses' concerns for their servants' souls, see Lucilla Agnes (Gamble) McCorkle Diary, 24 Jan. 1847, SHC; Eliza Carolina (Burgwin) Clitherall Books, 23 Jan., 2 Apr., 3 July 1853, SHC; Mary (Jeffreys) Bethell Diary, SHC; Crabtree and Patton, *Journal of a Secesh Lady*, pp. 21–22 (12 Dec. 1860).

70. Merrick, *Old Times in Dixie Land*, p. 17.

71. Meriwether, *Recollections*, pp. 49–50, 55–56.

72. Ibid., p. 55.

73. Northup, *Twelve Years a Slave*, pp. 62–63.

74. See, Smedes, *Southern Planter*, on a very accomplished cook who, after her mistress's death, systematically disobeyed orders until she got herself sent back to the fields.

75. Merrick, *Old Times in Dixie Land*, pp. 17–18.

Chapter 3

1. For a discussion of African traditions, see chap. 6 below. For discussions of Afro-American culture, see esp. Levine, *Black Culture*; Genovese, *Roll, Jordan, Roll*; Sobel, *Trabelin' On*. Information on West African women in the seventeenth and eighteenth centuries is virtually nonexistent, primarily because West African societies did not have written records. Seventeenth- and eighteenth-century histories provide some information on gender relations at the level of politics and warfare, but next to nothing at the level of everyday life. It is possible to speculate about the lives of early-modern West African women on the basis of evidence from the late-nineteenth and the twentieth centuries, but to place too much weight on that evidence is implicitly to assume that West African societies had no history. I have preferred not to do so.

2. The best discussion of slave women's work is found in White, *Ar'n't I a Woman?* and "Female Slaves." See also Jones, *Labor of Love*, pp. 11–43; and, on South Carolina, Weiner, "Plantation Mistress/Female Slave." Adam Singleton, *Mississippi Narratives*, supp. ser. 1, vol. 10, pt. 5, p. 1949; Barney Alford, *Mississippi Narratives*, supp. ser. 1, vol. 6, pt. 1, p. 23; Gus Feaster, *South Carolina Narratives*, vol. 2, pt. 2, p. 51. On the usefulness of the slave narratives for the reconstruction of Afro-American women's history, see Goodson, "Slave Narrative Collection." On the narratives in general, see Escott, *Slavery Remembered*; Woodward, "History

from Slave Sources"; Bailey, "Divided Prism"; Sekora and Turner, *Art of Slave Narrative*. See also Fisk University, *Unwritten History of Slavery*.

3. Mary Jane Simmons, *Georgia Narratives*, supp. ser. 1, vol. 4, pt. 2, p. 562; Molly Ammonds, *Alabama Narratives*, vol. 6, pt. 1, p. 10; Mattie Fannen, *Arkansas Narratives*, vol. 8, pt. 2, p. 265.

4. "Marengo Planter." See also Julia Bunch, *Georgia Narratives*, vol. 12, pt. 1, pp. 156–57; Mom Jessia Sparrow, *South Carolina Narratives*, vol. 3, pt. 4, p. 123; Fanny Smith Hodges, *Mississippi Narratives*, vol. 7, pt. 2, p. 68; Mattie Fannen, *Arkansas Narratives*, vol. 8, pt. 2, p. 265; Candis Goodwin, *Virginia Narratives*, vol. 16, pt. 5, p. 17; Caroline Holland, *Alabama Narratives*, vol. 6, pt. 1, p. 185; Mom Genia Woodberry, *South Carolina Narratives*, vol. 3, pt. 4, p. 220.

5. Keckley, *Behind the Scenes*, p. 19.

6. Ingraham, *The South-West*, 2:125; Lyell, *Second Visit*, 1:264; Ank Bishop, *Alabama Narratives*, vol. 6, pt. 1, p. 36; James A. Tait Memorandum Book, 1850, Tait Collection, AUA; Martha Allen, *North Carolina Narratives*, vol. 14, pt. 1, pp. 14–15; Bremer, *Homes of the New World*, 2:449; Campbell, "Work, Pregnancy, and Infant Mortality"; Klein and Engerman, "Fertility Differentials." See also Matilda McKinney, *Georgia Narratives*, vol. 13, pt. 3, p. 88; Millie Barber, *South Carolina Narratives*, vol. 2, pt. 1, p. 39; Lila Nichols, *North Carolina Narratives*, vol. 15, pt. 2, p. 149; Mom Ryer Emmanuel, *South Carolina Narratives*, vol. 2, pt. 2, p. 12; Sam Polite, *South Carolina Narratives*, vol. 3, pt. 3, p. 273; Henry Brown, *South Carolina Narratives*, vol. 2, pt. 1, p. 119; Rosina Hoard, *Texas Narratives*, vol. 4, pt. 2, p. 142.

7. Susan McIntosh, *Georgia Narratives*, vol. 13, pt. 3, p. 80; Eliza Holman, *Texas Narratives*, vol. 4, pt. 2, p. 148; Maggie Black, *South Carolina Narratives*, vol. 2, pt. 1, p. 58; Ida Adkins, *North Carolina Narratives*, vol. 14, pt. 1, p. 9; Cicely Cawthon, *Georgia Narratives*, supp. ser. 1, vol. 3, pt. 1, p. 185; Betty Brown, *Arkansas Narratives*, vol. 11, pt. 8, p. 52.

8. Joyner, *Down by the Riverside*, pp. 117–19; *De Bow's Review* 10:623, quoted in Sydnor, *Slavery in Mississippi*, p. 39.

9. Kolchin, *Unfree Labor*, pp. 134–35; Kemble, *Journal of a Residence*, p. 68; Genovese, *Roll, Jordan, Roll*, pp. 524–26; Fogel and Engerman, *Time on the Cross*, 1:115–16.

10. Jordan, *Hugh Davis*, pp. 81–83; Smith, *Slavery and Rice Culture*, pp. 119–30; Sellers, *Slavery in Alabama*, pp. 81–83; Blassingame, *Slave Community*, pp. 254–55; Joyner, *Down by the Riverside*, pp. 119–20; Davis, *Cotton Kingdom*, pp. 80–81; Killion and Waller, *Slavery Time*, pp. 125–26; Singleton, "Archaeology of Afro-American Slavery," pp. 109–39. On the problem of disease, see esp. Savitt, *Medicine and Slavery*, pp. 49–80.

11. For a detailed discussion of slave housing in Maryland, see McDaniel, *Hearth and Home*, pp. 45–102 (p. 56 for African room dimensions). See also Anthony, "Big House and the Slave Quarters," pt. 2, pp. 9–15; Otto, "New Look at Slave Life," pp. 8, 16–30; Peniston, "Slave Builder-Artisan"; Julia Larken, *Georgia Narratives*, vol. 13, pt. 3, p. 37. On cabins, see also Genovese, *Roll, Jordan, Roll*, pp. 528–30; Blassingame, *Slave Community*, pp. 254–55; Finch, *Englishwoman's Experience*, pp. 294–95; Fred Dibble, *Texas Narratives*, vol. 4, pt. 2, p. 119.

12. Harrison Beckett, *Texas Narratives*, vol. 4, pt. 1, p. 54.

13. Genovese, *Roll, Jordan, Roll*, pp. 527–28; Wilson, *Plantation Life*, p. 124.

14. Mattie Logan, *Oklahoma Narratives*, vol. 7, pt. 1, p. 187; Phyllis Petite, *Okla-*

homa Narratives, vol. 7, pt. 1, p. 237; Eliza Holman, *Texas Narratives*, vol. 4, pt. 2, p. 148; Cicely Cawthon, *Georgia Narratives*, supp. ser. 1, vol. 3, pt. 1, p. 185; Jane Wilson, *South Carolina Narratives*, vol. 3, pt. 4, p. 216; Molly Harrell, *Texas Narratives*, vol. 4, pt. 2, p. 116.

15. Ellen Resnick, *South Carolina Narratives*, vol. 3, pt. 4, p. 9; Heyward, *Seed from Madagascar*, p. 71; Yetman, *Life under the "Peculiar Institution,"* pp. 69 (Katie Darling), 298 (Elizabeth Sparks); Fisk University, *God Struck Me Dead*, pp. 93, 101, 185; Botkin, *Lay My Burden Down*, pp. 140, 152; Yetman, *Life under the "Peculiar Institution,"* p. 98 (Sarah Debro). See also Lucretia Heyward, *South Carolina Narratives*, vol. 2, pt. 2, p. 279; Betty Farrow, *Texas Narratives*, vol. 4, pt. 2, p. 10; Pauline Johnson, *Texas Narratives*, vol. 4, pt. 2, p. 224; Adeline Johnson, *South Carolina Narratives*, vol. 3, pt. 3, pp. 36–37; Aunt Easter Brown, *Georgia Narratives*, vol. 12, pt. 1, pp. 138–39.

16. Alice Shaw, *Mississippi Narratives*, supp. ser. 1, vol. 10, pt. 5, pp. 1920–22; Harriet Benton, *Georgia Narratives*, supp. ser. 1, vol. 3, pt. 1, p. 51; Joanne Draper, *Oklahoma Narratives*, vol. 7, pt. 1, p. 82; Charity Anderson, *Alabama Narratives*, vol. 6, pt. 1, p. 12; Ida Adkins, *North Carolina Narratives*, vol. 14, pt. 1, pp. 9–12; Mary Island, *Arkansas Narratives*, vol. 9, pt. 3, p. 389; Aunt Ellen Thomas, *Alabama Narratives*, vol. 6, pt. 1, pp. 376–77; Mattie Gilmore, *Texas Narratives*, vol. 4, pt. 2, p. 71; Julia E. Haney, *Arkansas Narratives*, vol. 9, pt. 3, p. 151. See also Wade, "Recollections," p. 9, UTLA.

17. Taylor, *Negro Slavery in Louisiana*, p. 85; Anderson, *Brokenburn*, p. 33; Joanna Draper, *Oklahoma Narratives*, vol. 7, pt. 1, p. 82.

18. Sally Brown, *Georgia Narratives*, supp. ser. 1, vol. 3, pt. 1, p. 101; Anne Bell, *South Carolina Narratives*, vol. 2, pt. 1, p. 53; Lucretia Heyward, *South Carolina Narratives*, vol. 2, pt. 2, p. 279; Adeline Johnson, *South Carolina Narratives*, vol. 3, pt. 3, p. 36.

19. Cicely Cawthon, *Georgia Narratives*, supp. ser. 1, vol. 3, pt. 1, p. 185; Fanny Smith Hodges, *Mississippi Narratives*, vol. 7, pt. 2, p. 68; Melinda Mitchell, *Georgia Narratives*, vol. 13, pt. 4, pp. 314–15; Margaret Hughes, *South Carolina Narratives*, vol. 2, pt. 2, pp. 327–28; Adeline Johnson, *South Carolina Narratives*, vol. 3, pt. 3, pp. 36–37. Mrs. John Wade recalled that, as children, she and her sisters had a waiting maid, Rose, who "slept in our room, looked after our clothes, made beds, swept and dusted and kept our room tidy, brought up and carried down bath water." Sometimes, in what Mrs. Wade preferred to view as a "practical joke," Rose brought scalding water, and "all unaware," the young mistresses, "would thrust our feet in the basin and withdraw them with a shriek" ("Recollections," p. 26).

20. Yetman, *Life under the "Peculiar Institution,"* pp. 16–17 (Mary Anderson); Thomas Bayne, "An Autobiographical Sketch," Bayne and Gayle Family Papers, SHC; Harriet Benton, *Georgia Narratives*, supp. ser. 1, vol. 3, pt. 1, p. 46; Queen Elizabeth Bunts, *Georgia Narratives*, supp. ser. 1, vol. 3, pt. 1, p. 127; Bruce, *New Man*, p. 24; Clay-Clopton, *Belle of the Fifties*, p. 4. Mrs. John Wade retained a very one-sided, yet revealing, picture of the play of slave and slaveholding children. "There were no social restrictions than [*sic*] as now, there was no need, a good feeling of comradeship, almost of kinship existed, the negro children recognizing without envy or ill will, the relations existing between owner and slave and were yielding and obedient to the will and dictates of their white play-mates, who felt the responsibility of a superior position and pride of ownership, and they had also

deeply instilled in them, the full significance of that fine old maxim, 'Noble'sse oblige'" ("Recollections," p. 17, UTLA). We are entitled to be skeptical about the attitudes she presumed.

21. Queen Elizabeth Bunts, *Georgia Narratives*, supp. ser. 1, vol. 3, pt. 1, pp. 126–27; Harriet Benton, *Georgia Narratives*, supp. ser. 1, vol. 3, pt. 1, p. 46; Tempie Cummins, *Texas Narratives*, vol. 4, pt. 1, p. 264. On boys' hunting, see also Bruce, *New Man*. On black and white children in the big house, see also Broidrick, "Recollection of Thirty Years Ago," p. 7, LSU.

22. Betty Bormer, *Texas Narratives*, vol. 4, pt. 1, p. 110; Tempie Cummins, *Texas Narratives*, vol. 4, pt. 1, p. 264; "Autobiography," Eliza Carolina (Burgwin) Clitherall Books, 12 May 1860, SHC; Elizabeth Collier Diary, 6 Mar. 1865, SHC; Olmsted, *Journey in the Back Country*, pp. 182–83; Eliza L. Magruder Diary, 19 Nov. 1854, LSU.

23. Elsie Moreland, *Georgia Narratives*, supp. ser. 1, vol. 4, pt. 2, p. 454; Mary Kendall to Lydia Hamilton, 13 Apr. 1853, Hamilton/Kendall Family Letters, GDAH; Samuel Boulware, *South Carolina Narratives*, vol. 2, pt. 1, p. 66; Lily Perry, *North Carolina Narratives*, vol. 15, pt. 2, p. 163; Marie Smith and Grammaw, *Georgia Narratives*, supp. ser. 1, vol. 4, pt. 2, p. 572. See also Sallie Paul, *South Carolina Narratives*, vol. 3, pt. 3, p. 235; Susan Merritt, *Texas Narratives*, vol. 5, pt. 3, p. 4; Mary Overton, *Texas Narratives*, vol. 5, pt. 3, p. 163; Caroline Farrow, *South Carolina Narratives*, vol. 2, pt. 2, pp. 39–40; Jennie Brown, *Alabama Narratives*, vol. 6, pt. 1, p. 42; Emma L. Howard, *Alabama Narratives*, vol. 6, pt. 1, p. 212; Dellie Lewis, *Alabama Narratives*, vol. 6, pt. 1, p. 212; Cornelia Robinson, *Alabama Narratives*, vol. 6, pt. 1, p. 332; Mary Veals, *South Carolina Narratives*, vol. 3, pt. 4, p. 167; Eliza Evans, *Oklahoma Narratives*, vol. 7, pt. 1, p. 95 (Alabama slave); Liza Jones, *Texas Narratives*, vol. 4, pt. 2, p. 244; Alice Houston, *Texas Narratives*, vol. 4, pt. 2, p. 161; Caroline Ates, *Georgia Narratives*, supp. ser. 1, vol. 3, pt. 1, p. 24; Susannah Wyman, *Georgia Narratives*, vol. 13, pt. 4, p. 315.

24. Caroline Ates, *Georgia Narratives*, supp. ser. 1, vol. 3, pt. 1, p. 25; Berry Smith (male), *Mississippi Narratives*, ser. 1, vol. 10, pt. 5, p. 1983 (on being taught to pick cotton by his mother); Fannie Moore, *North Carolina Narratives*, vol. 15, pt. 2, p. 129; Davis, *Cotton Kingdom*, p. 52. On children's working under the direction of their mothers, see Jim Allen, *Mississippi Narratives*, ser. 1, vol. 6, pt. 1, p. 54; Grammaw, *Georgia Narratives*, supp. ser. 1, vol. 4, pt. 2, p. 572; Nicholas Bryor Massenburg Books, 21 Sept. 1836, SHC. On trash gangs, see Annie Stephenson, *North Carolina Narratives*, vol. 15, pt. 2, p. 313; Elsie Moreland, *Georgia Narratives*, supp. ser. 1, vol. 4, pt. 2, p. 454; Ida Adkins, *North Carolina Narratives*, vol. 14, pt. 1, p. 9; Annie Huff, *Georgia Narratives*, vol. 12, pt. 2, p. 233. See also Matilda, *Georgia Narratives*, vol. 13, pt. 4, p. 217; Rosina Hoard, *Texas Narratives*, vol. 4, pt. 2, p. 142; Mary Johnson, *South Carolina Narratives*, vol. 3, pt. 3, p. 56; Ellen Resnick, *South Carolina Narratives*, vol. 3, pt. 4, p. 9; Chana Littlejohn, *North Carolina Narratives*, vol. 15, pt. 2, p. 57; Botkin, *Lay My Burden Down*.

25. Betty Brown, *Arkansas Narratives*, vol. 11, pt. 8, p. 52; Eliza Holman, *Texas Narratives*, vol. 4, pt. 2, p. 148; Mary Island, *Arkansas Narratives*, vol. 9, pt. 3, p. 389.

26. Margaret Thornton, *North Carolina Narratives*, vol. 15, pt. 2, p. 353; Amos Gadsden, *South Carolina Narratives*, vol. 2, pt. 2, p. 91; Maggie Black, *South Carolina Narratives*, vol. 2, pt. 1, p. 57; Liza Strickland, *Mississippi Narratives*, supp. ser.

1, vol. 10, pt. 5, pp. 2065–66; Amanda McDaniel, *Georgia Narratives*, vol. 13, pt. 3, p. 72.

27. Lucy McCullough, *Georgia Narratives*, vol. 13, pt. 3, pp. 67–68.

28. On attempted poisonings, see Mary (Jeffreys) Bethell Diary, 24 Jan. 1853, SHC; chap. 6 below.

29. Bremer, *Homes of the New World*, 2:280; Olmsted, *Journey in the Back Country*, p. 153; Sophie D. Belle, *Arkansas Narratives*, vol. 8, pt. 2, p. 137; Mandy Morrow, *Texas Narratives*, vol. 5, pt. 3, p. 139. See also Fannie Fulcher, *Georgia Narratives*, supp. ser. 1, vol. 3, pt. 1, p. 250; Liza Jones, *Texas Narratives*, vol. 4, pt. 2, p. 242; Milton Hammond, *Georgia Narratives*, vol. 12, pt. 2, p. 92; Botkin, *Lay My Burden Down*, p. 79.

30. Julia Glover, *Georgia Narratives*, supp. ser. 1, vol. 3, pt. 1, pp. 263–64; Julia Larken, *Georgia Narratives*, vol. 13, pt. 3, p. 37; Cicely Cawthon, *Georgia Narratives*, supp. ser. 1, vol. 3, pt. 1, p. 179. See also William McWhorter, *Georgia Narratives*, vol. 13, pt. 3, p. 94; Jane Bradley, *South Carolina Narratives*, vol. 2, pt. 1, p. 74; Molly Ammonds, *Alabama Narratives*, vol. 6, pt. 1, p. 9; Sara Colquit, *Alabama Narratives*, vol. 6, pt. 1, p. 83; Silvia King, *Texas Narratives*, vol. 4, pt. 2, p. 292. For a slaveholding woman's recollection of the kitchen during her youth, see Wade, "Recollections," pp. 9–10, UTLA.

31. Smedes, *Southern Planter*, pp. 150–51.

32. Caroline Ates, *Georgia Narratives*, supp. ser. 1, vol. 3, pt. 1, p. 24; Molly Ammonds, *Alabama Narratives*, vol. 6, pt. 1, pp. 9–11; Mandy Morrow, *Texas Narratives*, vol. 5, pt. 3, p. 139; Sophie D. Belle, *Arkansas Narratives*, vol. 8, pt. 1, p. 137; Julia Banks, *Texas Narratives*, vol. 4, pt. 1, p. 95; Fannie Cawthon Coleman, *Georgia Narratives*, supp. ser. 1, vol. 3, pt. 1, p. 212; Pauline Grice, *Texas Narratives*, vol. 4, pt. 2, p. 98. On cooking, see Genovese, *Roll, Jordan, Roll*, pp. 535–49. For a comparative view of diet, see Handler and Corruccini, "Plantation Slave Life in Barbados." On gardens, see Julia Larken, *Georgia Narratives*, vol. 13, pt. 3, p. 35.

33. Ellen Betts, *Texas Narratives*, vol. 4, pt. 1, pp. 75–76; "Ma" Eppes, *Alabama Narratives*, vol. 6, pt. 1, p. 120; Sarah Louise Augustus, *North Carolina Narratives*, vol. 14, pt. 1, p. 54.

34. Broidrick, "Recollection of Thirty Years Ago," LSU. See also Parkhurst, "Role of the Black Mammy"; Harper, "Black Aristocrats"; White, *Ar'n't I a Woman?*, pp. 27–51.

35. Laura S. Tibbetts to Mrs. Sophie Tibbetts, 23 Jan. 1853, John C. Tibbetts Correspondence, LSU; Yetman, *Life under the "Peculiar Institution,"* pp. 119–20 (Lindsey Faucette). On wetnurses, see Sarah Louise Augustus, *North Carolina Narratives*, vol. 14, pt. 1, p. 54; Mattie Logan, *Oklahoma Narratives*, vol. 7, pt. 1, p. 187 (Mississippi slave); Clayton Holbert, *Kansas Narratives*, vol. 16, pt. 1, p. 3; John F. Van Hook, *Georgia Narratives*, vol. 13, pt. 4, pp. 74–75; Millie Barber, *South Carolina Narratives*, vol. 2, pt. 1. p. 39; Mary Kincheon Edwards, *Texas Narratives*, vol. 4, pt. 2, p. 15. Mrs. John Wade adds what is admittedly a postbellum remembrance, but probably true in its basic facts: "I had a black mammy, a very black one, and from her dark breast drew my infant sustenance, and smiled up into her face, I have no doubt, with as much satisfied pleasure as that of my own fair, sweet, mother and perhaps imbibed from her milk a better understanding and good and kindly feeling for character" ("Recollections," p. 5, UTLA).

36. Works Progress Administration, *Negro in Virginia*, p. 45; Thomas Bayne,

"Autobiographical Sketch," Bayne and Gayle Family Papers, SHC; Broidrick, "Recollection of Thirty Years Ago," LSU. See also Puckett, *Folk Beliefs of the Southern Negro*, p. 365; Mary E. Bateman Diary, 22 Mar. 1856 and passim, SHC; Du Bois, *Gift of Black Folk*, p. 144.

37. Jones, *Ladies of Richmond*, p. 89.

38. Fisk University, *Unwritten History of Slavery*, pp. 95, 151; M. D. Cooper to William Cooper, 22 Nov. 1842, Cooper Papers, TSLA; Liza Strickland, *Mississippi Narratives*, supp. ser. 1, vol. 10, pt. 5, p. 2065.

39. Fisk University, *Unwritten History of Slavery*, p. 7.

40. Wiltse, *John C. Calhoun: Nullifier*, p. 116. See also Harper, "Black Aristocrats."

41. Mary Jones to Mary Sharpe Jones, 22 Dec. 1856, in Myers, *Children of Pride*, p. 278.

42. Hannah Plummer, *North Carolina Narratives*, vol. 15, pt. 2, p. 178.

43. For aggregate figures, see Tryon, *Household Manufactures*. We lack thorough studies of yeoman women, although Stephanie McCurry's dissertation-in-progress on the South Carolina lowcountry yeomanry will vastly expand our knowledge. My description of the lives of yeoman women derives from general reading in the plantation sources, former slave narratives, and bits and pieces in the secondary literature. See, e.g., Drake, *Pioneer Life*. In making these tentative remarks, I am deeply indebted to long conversations with Stephanie McCurry. See McCurry, "In Defense of Their World."

44. Mary Lindsay, *Oklahoma Narratives*, vol. 7, pt. 1, p. 178; Fisk University, *Unwritten History of Slavery*, pp. 95, 134.

45. Susan McIntosh, *Georgia Narratives*, vol. 13, pt. 3, p. 80. See also Queen Elizabeth Bunts, *Georgia Narratives*, supp. ser. 1, vol. 3, pt. 1, p. 119. On washing, see Hannah Plummer, *North Carolina Narratives*, vol. 15, pt. 2, pp. 178–79; Jefferson Franklin Henry, *Georgia Narratives*, vol. 12, pt. 2, pp. 184–85; Adeline Grey, *South Carolina Narratives*, vol. 2, pt. 2, p. 206; Amos Gadsden, *South Carolina Narratives*, vol. 2, pt. 2, p. 91; Mary Frances Webb, *Oklahoma Narratives*, vol. 7, pt. 1, pp. 314–15; Charity Anderson, *Alabama Narratives*, vol. 6, pt. 1, p. 13; Julia Stubbs, *Mississippi Narratives*, supp. ser. 1, vol. 10, pt. 5, p. 2069; Georgina Gibbs, *Virginia Narratives*, vol. 16, pt. 5, p. 15. See also Betty Cofer, *North Carolina Narratives*, vol. 14, pt. 1, p. 169; Gracie Gibson, *South Carolina Narratives*, vol. 2, pt. 2, p. 113; Willis Dukes, *Florida Narratives*, vol. 17, p. 121; Duncan Gaines, *Florida Narratives*, vol. 17, pp. 134–35; Martha R. Jackson Diary, 28 Aug. 1833, SHC. See also Anna Matilda Page King to Thomas Butler King, 11, 12 Aug. 1842, Thomas Butler King Papers, SHC. Mary Fraser's daughter wrote to her mother that she would be obliged "to take boys and girls out of the fields to mind children" (17 July 1832, Mary DeSaussure Fraser Papers, DU). See also James Cornelius, who reported that his mother worked in the big house and the field (*Mississippi Narratives*, vol. 7, pt. 2, p. 26); Flanders, "Two Plantations and a County," p. 10.

46. Sally Brown, *Georgia Narratives*, supp. ser. 1, vol. 3, pt. 1, pp. 94–108.

47. Ibid., pp. 97–98.

48. Solomon Caldwell, *South Carolina Narratives*, vol. 2, pt. 1, p. 171; R. S. Taylor, *North Carolina Narratives*, vol. 15, pt. 2, p. 337; Bob Mobley, *Georgia Narratives*, supp. ser. 1, vol. 4, pt. 2, p. 449; Fannie Moore, *North Carolina Narratives*, vol. 15, pt. 2, p. 134; Gus Feaster, *South Carolina Narratives*, vol. 2, pt. 2, p. 55; Sarah

Ford, *Texas Narratives*, vol. 4, pt. 2, p. 42; Mary Kindred, *Texas Narratives*, vol. 4, pt. 2, p. 285; Lina Anne Pendergrass, *South Carolina Narratives*, vol. 3, pt. 3, p. 249; Davis, *Plantation Life*, pp. 433, 440. On slave medicine, see also Savitt, *Medicine and Slavery*, pp. 171–84; Genovese, *Roll, Jordan, Roll*, pp. 224–29; Levine, *Black Culture*, pp. 64–66; White, *Ar'n't I a Woman?*, pp. 115–16.

49. Sally Brown, *Georgia Narratives*, supp. ser. 1, vol. 3, pt. 1, pp. 94–108.

50. For a somewhat different discussion of the same patterns, see White, *Ar'n't I a Woman?*.

51. Sellers, *Slavery in Alabama*, p. 66; Olmsted, "The Southerners at Home, No. 1," in *Papers*, 2:310.

52. Lila Nichols, *North Carolina Narratives*, vol. 15, pt. 2, p. 149; Liddie Aiken, *Arkansas Narratives*, vol. 8, pt. 1, p. 19; William Brown, *Arkansas Narratives*, vol. 8, pt. 1, p. 317; Chana Littlejohn, *North Carolina Narratives*, vol. 15, pt. 2, p. 57; Henry James Trentham, *North Carolina Narratives*, vol. 15, pt. 2, p. 364; Henrietta McCullers, *North Carolina Narratives*, vol. 15, pt. 2, p. 73; Fisk University, *Unwritten History of Slavery*, p. 103. On women plow hands, see Phillips and Glunt, *Florida Plantation Records*, pp. 33, 515; Greene, *Diary of Landon Carter*, 2:683 (15 May 1772); John Walker Diary, 5 Mar. 1834, SHC; Olmsted, *Papers*, 2:310; Olmsted, *Journey in the Back Country*, p. 81; Everard Green Baker Diary, 31 July 1856, SHC; Easterby, *South Carolina Rice Plantation*, p. 290; Sydnor, *Gentleman of the Old Natchez Region*, p. 113; Sellers, *Slavery in Alabama*, p. 66.

53. Nicholas Bryor Massenburg Books, 1834–39, SHC. See Sally Brown, *Georgia Narratives*, supp. ser. 1, vol. 3, p. 97; Mary Frances Webb, *Oklahoma Narratives*, vol. 7, pt. 1, p. 314; Henrietta McCullers, *North Carolina Narratives*, vol. 15, pt. 2, p. 74; Lila Nichols, *North Carolina Narratives*, vol 15, pt. 2, p. 149; James Bertrand, *Arkansas Narratives*, vol. 8, pt. 1, p. 157. On the seasonality of agricultural labor, see Seaborn Hawks Plantation Book, 1854–62, GDAH; Cody, "Slave Demography and Family Formation."

54. Nicholas Bryor Massenburg Books, 1834–39, SHC. On the African origins of men's basket weaving, see Smith, *Slavery and Rice Culture*, p. 179.

55. James Hervey Greenlee Diary, 1848–53 passim, SHC.

56. Joyner, *Down by the Riverside*, p. 45; Easterby, *South Carolina Rice Plantation*, pp. 271–73; Phillips and Glunt, *Florida Plantation Records*, pp. 209–338; Davis, *Plantation Life*; Phillips, *Plantation and Frontier Documents*, 1:213–14; Josephine Bacchus, *South Carolina Narratives*, vol. 2, pt. 1, p. 23.

57. Franklin Hudson Diaries, 2 Mar. 1854, 28 Mar. 1855, LSU; "Record Book, 1859–1866," LeBlanc Family Papers, LSU; H. M. Seale Diary, 7 Mar. 1857, LSU; James Monette Day Book and Diary, LSU; Riley, "Diary of a Mississippi Planter," pp. 343–44. See also Bayside Plantation Records, 6, 27 Sept. 1861, SHC; William Ethelbert Ervin Book, 2 Jan. 1839, 19 July 1841, 7 Aug. 1844, 13, 29 Jan. 1846, 2 Sept. 1847, 18 Jan. 1850, SHC; James Hervey Greenlee Diary, 1850–51, SHC; Samuel Andrew Agnew Diary, 18 Mar. 1865, SHC; Moody, "Slavery on Louisiana Sugar Plantations"; Clifton, *Life and Labor on Argyle Island*, p. 142; Northup, *Twelve Years a Slave*, pp. 155–56; Joyner, *Down by the Riverside*, pp. 45, 74–75; Easterby, *South Carolina Rice Plantation*, p. 101.

58. Gus Feaster, *South Carolina Narratives*, vol. 2, pt. 2, p. 50; Mary Frances Webb, *Oklahoma Narratives*, vol. 7, pt. 1, p. 314; Callie Donalson, *Arkansas Narratives*, vol. 8, pt. 2, p. 166; Sally Brown, *Georgia Narratives*, supp. ser. 1, vol. 3, pt. 1,

p. 97. See also Jane Hollins, *South Carolina Narratives*, vol. 2, pt. 2, p. 292; Mary Lindsay, *Oklahoma Narratives*, vol. 7, pt. 1, p. 178; Julia E. Haney, *Arkansas Narratives*, vol. 9, pt. 3, p. 151; Sarah Wilson, *Oklahoma Narratives*, vol. 7, pt. 1, p. 249; James Turner McLean, *North Carolina Narratives*, vol. 15, pt. 2, p. 83; Elsie Moreland, *Georgia Narratives*, supp. ser. 1, vol. 4. pt. 2, p. 454; Ann E. Wise to Henry A. Wise, 14 Dec. [1834], in Torrence, "Letters of Mrs. Ann (Jennings) Wise to Her Husband," pp. 497–99.

59. James Bertrand, *Arkansas Narratives*, vol. 8, pt. 1, p. 157. Henry James Trentham, *North Carolina Narratives*, vol. 15, pt. 2, p. 364; William Brown, *Arkansas Narratives*, vol. 8, pt. 1, p. 317; Liddie Aiken, *Arkansas Narratives*, vol. 8, pt. 1, p. 19; Lila Nichols, *North Carolina Narratives*, vol. 15, pt. 2, p. 149; Aunt Ferebe Rogers, *Georgia Narratives*, vol. 13, pt. 3, p. 210; Mary Kincheon Edwards, *Texas Narratives*, vol. 4, pt. 2, p. 16. On women cotton pickers and superior field hands, see also Sydnor, *Slavery in Mississippi*, pp. 96–97; Bonner, "Plantation Experiences of a New York Woman"; Edmund Ruffin, Jr., Plantation Diary, 6 Mar. 1857, SHC.

60. George Washington Browning, *Georgia Narratives*, supp. ser. 1, vol. 3, pt. 1, pp. 113–14; Fannie Moore, *North Carolina Narratives*, vol. 15, pt. 2, p. 129; Betty Brown, *Arkansas Narratives*, vol. 11, pt. 8, p. 52; Queen Elizabeth Bunts, *Georgia Narratives*, supp. ser. 1, vol. 3, pt. 1, p. 126; Hannah Plummer, *North Carolina Narratives*, vol. 15, pt. 2, p. 179; Billie Smith, *Mississippi Narratives*, supp. ser. 1, vol. 10, pt. 5, p. 1989. See also Betty Powers, *Texas Narratives*, vol. 5, pt. 3, p. 191; Gus Feaster, *South Carolina Narratives*, vol. 2, pt. 2, p. 66; Gracie Gibson, *South Carolina Narratives*, vol. 2, pt. 2, p. 114; Matilda McKinney, *Georgia Narratives*, vol. 13, pt. 3, pp. 88–89; Margaret Hughes, *South Carolina Narratives*, vol. 2, pt. 2, p. 327; Jefferson Franklin Henry, *Georgia Narratives*, vol. 12, pt. 2, p. 184; Works Progress Administration, *Negro in Virginia*, p. 65.

61. Bob Mobley, *Georgia Narratives*, supp. ser. 1, vol. 4, pt. 2, p. 450; Oliver Blanchard, *Texas Narratives*, vol. 4, pt. 1, p. 90; Ed McCree, *Georgia Narratives*, vol. 13, pt. 3, p. 62; Georgina Gibbs, *Virginia Narratives*, vol. 16, pt. 5, p. 15.

62. Martha King, *Oklahoma Narratives*, vol. 7, pt. 1, p. 170; Julia Stubbs, *Mississippi Narratives*, supp. ser. 1, vol. 10, pt. 5, p. 2069; Betty Brown, *Arkansas Narratives*, vol. 11, pt. 8, p. 52.

63. In the absence of detailed studies, it remains difficult to determine the actual extent of household textile production. During the late antebellum period, cheap cloth was easily available and many planters purchased it for slave clothes. Possibly some of the former slaves' recollections of textile production reflect the conditions of the war years rather than the antebellum period proper, when there may have been less weaving than the narratives suggest. Nonetheless, farm and plantation books from the antebellum period confirm that weaving was a regular activity on at least some plantations, and spinning and sewing on most if not all. Furthermore, for weaving to have resurfaced so quickly after the outbreak of war, some slave women must have known how to weave. And there is some evidence that, at least on some plantations, slave men and boys wore homespun (McDaniel, *Hearth and Home*, p. 114). Perhaps some of the weaving done during the antebellum period was for the slaves' fancy clothes and for sheets and other household textiles. My thinking on this matter has been sharpened by conversations and debates with Allan Kulikoff. See Annie Row, *Texas Narratives*, vol. 5, pt. 3, p. 259; Betty Cofer, *North Carolina Narratives*, vol. 14, pt. 1, pp. 168–70; Billie Smith, *Mississippi Narra-*

tives, supp. ser. 1, vol. 10, pt. 5, p. 1989; Anna Mitchel, *North Carolina Narratives,* vol. 15, pt. 2, pp. 114–15; Rebecca Jane Grant, *South Carolina Narratives,* vol. 2, pt. 2, p. 183; Hannah Plummer, *North Carolina Narratives,* vol. 15, pt. 2, pp. 178–79.

64. Fannie Cawthon Coleman, *Georgia Narratives,* supp. ser. 1, vol. 3, pt. 1, p. 212; Phoebe Banks, *Oklahoma Narratives,* vol. 7, pt. 1, p. 8; Laura Caldwell, *South Carolina Narratives,* vol. 2, pt. 1, p. 169; Willis Easter, *Texas Narratives,* vol. 4, pt. 2, p. 1; Silvia King, *Texas Narratives,* vol. 4, pt. 2, p. 292.

65. Susan Snow, *Mississippi Narratives,* supp. ser. 1, vol. 10, pt. 5, p. 2006; Gracie Gibson, *South Carolina Narratives,* vol. 2, pt. 2, p. 114; Charlie Grant, *South Carolina Narratives,* vol. 2, pt. 2, p. 172; Martha Everette, *Georgia Narratives,* supp. ser. 1, vol. 3, pt. 1, p. 240; Betty Cofer, *North Carolina Narratives,* vol. 14, pt. 1, p. 170; Alice Houston, *Texas Narratives,* vol. 4, pt. 2, p. 160; Lidia Jones, *Arkansas Narratives,* vol. 9, pt. 4, p. 151; Queen Elizabeth Bunts, *Georgia Narratives,* supp. ser. 1, vol. 3, pt. 1, pp. 126–27; Priscilla Gibson, *Texas Narratives,* vol. 4, pt. 2, p. 67; Orelia Alexie Franks, *Texas Narratives,* vol. 4, pt. 2, p. 61; Willis Easter, *Texas Narratives,* vol. 4, pt. 2, p. 1; Phoebe Henderson, *Texas Narratives,* vol. 4, pt. 2, p. 136; Josephine Bristow, *South Carolina Narratives,* vol. 2, pt. 1, p. 100; Barney Alford, *Mississippi Narratives,* supp. ser. 1, vol. 6, pt. 1, p. 36; Charles Anderson, *Arkansas Narratives,* vol. 8, pt. 1, p. 46; Maggie Black, *South Carolina Narratives,* vol. 2, pt. 1, p. 58; Betty Abernathy, *Arkansas Narratives,* vol. 11, pt. 8, p. 6; Silvia King, *Texas Narratives,* vol. 4, pt. 2, p. 292.

66. Ida Adkins, *North Carolina Narratives,* vol. 14, pt. 1, p. 9; Maggie Black, *South Carolina Narratives,* vol. 2, pt. 1, p. 58; Josephine Bristow, *South Carolina Narratives,* vol. 2, pt. 1, p. 100; Charles Anderson, *Arkansas Narratives,* vol. 8, pt. 1, p. 46; Queen Elizabeth Bunts, *Georgia Narratives,* supp. ser. 1, vol. 3, pt. 1, p. 119; Betty Abernathy, *Arkansas Narratives,* vol. 11, pt. 8, p. 6. See also Isaiah Green, *Georgia Narratives,* vol. 12, pt. 2, p. 51.

67. Barney Alford, *Mississippi Narratives,* supp. ser. 1, vol. 6, p. 36; Josephine Bristow, *South Carolina Narratives,* vol. 2, pt. 1, p. 100; Charles Anderson, *Arkansas Narratives,* vol. 8, pt. 1, p. 46; Willis Easter, *Texas Narratives,* vol. 4, pt. 2, p. 1; Orelia Alexie Franks, *Texas Narratives,* vol. 4, pt. 2, p. 61; Priscilla Gibson, *Texas Narratives,* vol. 4, pt. 2, p. 67; Anna Mitchel, *North Carolina Narratives,* vol. 15, pt. 2, pp. 114–15. See also Alice Houston, *Texas Narratives,* vol. 4, pt. 2, p. 160.

68. Sarah Graves, *Missouri Narratives,* vol. 11, pt. 8, pp. 130–31; Aunt Sarah Waggoner, *Missouri Narratives,* vol. 11, pt. 8, pp. 359–60; Annie Mae Weathers, *Arkansas Narratives,* vol. 11, pt. 7, p. 72; Alice Battle, *Georgia Narratives,* supp. ser. 1, vol. 3, pt. 1, pp. 42–43.

69. Lidia Jones, *Arkansas Narratives,* vol. 9, pt. 4, p. 151.

70. Works Progress Administration, *Negro in Virginia,* p. 72; Bonner, "Plantation Experiences of a New York Woman"; Mary Childs, *Georgia Narratives,* vol. 3, pt. 1, p. 201.

71. Martineau, *Society in America,* 1:301–2; Ed McCree, *Georgia Narratives,* vol. 13, pt. 3, p. 63. On gossip, see also Lyell, *Second Visit,* 1:264; White, *Ar'n't I a Woman?,* p. 123.

72. Mary Frances Webb, *Oklahoma Narratives,* vol. 7, pt. 1, pp. 314–15; Gracie Gibson, *South Carolina Narratives,* vol. 2, pt. 2, pp. 113–14; Julia E. Haney, *Arkansas Narratives,* vol. 9, pt. 3, p. 151; Hannah Hancock, *Arkansas Narratives,* vol. 9, pt. 3, pp. 142–43; Hammett Dell, *Arkansas Narratives,* vol. 8, pt. 2, p. 138; Davis,

Cotton Kingdom, pp. 67–68. See also Della Fountain, *Oklahoma Narratives*, vol. 7, pt. 1, p. 102; Willis Dukes, *Florida Narratives*, vol. 17, p. 121; Duncan Gaines, *Florida Narratives*, vol. 17, pp. 134–35; Mandy Morrow, *Texas Narratives*, vol. 5, pt. 3, p. 139.

73. John Durant Ashmore Book, p. 72, SHC; Yetman, *Life under the "Peculiar Institution"*; Sam Kilgore, *Texas Narratives*, vol. 4, pt. 2, p. 256; Lucy McCullough, *Georgia Narratives*, vol. 13, pt. 3, pp. 66–70.

74. H. C., "On the Management of Negroes"; Susan Snow, *Mississippi Narratives*, vol. 7, pt. 2, pp. 136, 139–40.

75. Leonard Franklin, *Arkansas Narratives*, vol. 8, pt. 2, p. 366.

76. Josie Jordan, *Oklahoma Narratives*, vol. 7, pt. 1, p. 160 (Tennessee slave); Aunt Margaret Bryant, *South Carolina Narratives*, vol. 2, pt. 1, p. 147; Solomon Oliver, *Oklahoma Narratives*, vol. 7, pt. 1, p. 234 (Mississippi slave).

77. David Gavin Diary, 9 Nov. 1855, SHC; Catterall, *Judicial Cases*, 2:85–86. See also Davidson, "Record of Inquisitions," 31 Dec. 1833, DU.

78. Easterly, *South Carolina Rice Plantation*, p. 2.

79. Analiza Foster, *North Carolina Narratives*, vol. 14, pt. 1, pp. 312–13.

80. Drew, *The Refugee*, p. 71. On drivers, see DeBurg, *Slave Drivers*; Genovese, *Roll, Jordan, Roll*, pp. 365–88; Williams, *Narrative of James Williams*; Owens, *This Species of Property*, pp. 121–35.

Chapter 4

1. Quoted in Simpson, *Good Southerner*, p. 11.

2. Eugene D. Genovese and I will discuss these institutions in depth in our forthcoming book, *The Mind of the Master Class* (title tentative). On women's church networks, see Friedman, *Enclosed Garden*. On networks of female friendships, see, e.g., Susan Davis (Nye) Hutchinson Diary, 13 June 1832, 28, 30 July, 3, 14, 26 Oct. 1837, SHC; Fannie Page Hume Diary, 28 June 1860, SHC; "Autobiography," Lucy Walton Muse Fletcher Journal, 1841 ff., DU; Pleasants, "Letters of Molly and Hetty Tilghman." See also Kincheloe, "Transcending Role Restrictions"; Johnson, "Recreational and Cultural Activities."

3. For a taste of the religious defense of gender conventions, see Jones, *Glory of Woman*; Smythe, *Mary, Not a Perpetual Virgin*. See also Rivers, *Elements of Moral Philosophy*, esp. pp. 329–81.

4. Meta (Morris) Grimball Journal, 2 Sept. 1862, SHC; Mitchell, *Gone with the Wind*.

5. Mrs. Isaac Hilliard Diary, 20 Jan. 1850, LSU; Mary Jones to Mary S. Mallard, 26 June 1857, in Myers, *Children of Pride*, p. 339.

6. "Influence of Slavery on the Condition of the Female Sex," in Dew, *Review of the Debates*, pp. 35–38 (citations pp. 36, 37, 35); these ideas were developed in "Professor Dew on Slavery," in Dew, *Pro-Slavery Argument*, pp. 336–42. See also Dew's "Dissertation on the Characteristic Differences between the Sexes," in which he discusses the differences between women and men in civilized society. For an example of the Scottish Historical School, see Robertson, *Works*, esp. *Reign of the Emperor Charles V* and *History of America*. For the proslavery argument, see William Sumner Jenkins (*Pro-Slavery Thought*) and Drew Gilpin Faust (*Ideology of*

Slavery), although neither addresses the relation between women's position and slavery. See also Tucker, *Series of Lectures on the Science of Government*, p. 296 (on women's need for protection); Fletcher, *Studies on Slavery*, p. 407 (on inequality in heaven). See also Ross, *Slavery Ordained of God*.

7. Harper, *Memoir on Slavery*, pp. 3, 4, 6, 7.

8. Fitzhugh, *Sociology for the South*, pp. 247, 213–15. On women's duty, see "She Hath Done What She Could." For a contrary view of the effect of slavery on southern white women, see Bourne, *Slavery Illustrated*. Also see Just, "Freedom, Slavery, and the Female Psyche."

9. Wyatt-Brown, *Southern Honor*; Greenberg, *Masters and Statesmen*; Stowe, *Intimacy and Power*; Meta (Morris) Grimball Journal, 19 Aug. 1862, SHC; Tucker, *Series of Lectures on the Science of Government*, pp. 62, 198–99.

10. Wyatt-Brown, *Southern Honor*, pp. 329–61; Breen, "Horses and Gentlemen"; Hackney, "Southern Violence"; Bruce, *Violence and Culture*. See also Susan Davis (Nye) Hutchinson Diary, 15, 16 Feb. 1838, SHC; Gay, "Tangled Skein of Romanticism"; Rainard, "Gentlemanly Ideal." For a recollection of the time "'when knighthood was in flower'" on a "big pioneer Texas plantation" and "lavishly scattered its seed over our beautiful Southland," see Wade, "Recollections," UTLA.

11. Davis, *Plantation Life*, p. 370.

12. Chief Justice Pearson, as quoted in Turrentine, *Romance of Education*, p. 27. See also Miles, *Women "Nobly Planned"*; O'Neall, *Address on Female Education*; chap. 1 above. Bertram Wyatt-Brown (*Southern Honor*) does not accord as much importance to slavery as to a system of class relations, but he does emphasize the identification of white southern men across class lines.

13. See esp. Johnson, "Planters and Patriarchy"; Smith-Rosenberg, "Sex as Symbol." Carroll Smith-Rosenberg does not explicitly address southern models of masculinity, but she does discuss the Davy Crockett figure as a model that embodied a certain amount of violence or lawlessness, especially on the frontier. On the southern yeomanry, see Wyatt-Brown, *Southern Honor*; esp., Hahn, *Roots of Southern Populism*; Fox-Genovese and Genovese, *Fruits of Merchant Capital*, chap. 9 ("Yeomen Farmers in a Slaveholders' Democracy").

14. Buckingham, *Slave States*, 2:29–30.

15. On northern women, see, among others, Kerber, *Women of the Republic*; Cott, *Bonds of Womanhood*; Ryan, *Empire of the Mother*; Jensen, *Loosening the Bonds*. And on southern women, see Smith, *Inside the Great House*; Lewis, *Pursuit of Happiness*. For southern adaptations of the bourgeois discourse of womanhood, see, e.g., Dew, "Dissertation on the Characteristic Differences between the Sexes." For a contemporary view of the difference between northern and southern women, see Shippee, *Bishop Whipple's Southern Diary*, pp. 114–15.

16. Among many contemporary portraits of the southern lady, see Charles Colcock Jones, Jr., to Rev. and Mrs. Charles Colcock Jones, 9 Sept. 1851, in Myers, *Children of Pride*, p. 226; Le Conte, "Female Education"; Stephens, *Joseph Le Conte*, p. 65; Andrews, *Reminiscences*, p. 12; Mary Telfair to Mary Few, 4 Aug. [n.d.], William Few Collection, GDAH. For a view of the southern lady that emphasizes the link between her position and the social relations of slave society, see Bartlett and Cambor, "History and Psychodynamics." See also Stowe, *Intimacy and Power*; Scott, *Southern Lady*; Clinton, *Plantation Mistress* and "Caught in the

Web of the Big House"; Grantham, "History, Mythology, and the Southern Lady"; Seidel, "Southern Belle as an Antebellum Ideal"; Hagler, "Ideal Woman in the Antebellum South"; Pope, "Preparation for Pedestals," pp. 157–73; Thomas, "Diary of Anna Hasell Thomas," pp. 128–29, 141. Thomas Dew ("Dissertation on the Characteristic Differences between the Sexes") insists especially on women's honor, which he identifies with their sexual purity.

17. Wyatt-Brown, *Southern Honor*, p. 270. On southern women's standing at law, see also Boatwright, "Political and Civil Status of Women"; Lebsock, *Free Women of Petersburg* and "Radical Reconstruction"; Censer, "'Smiling through Her Tears'"; Van Ness, "On Untieing the Knot"; McDonnell, "Desertion, Divorce, and Class Struggle"; Gundersen and Gampel, "Married Women's Legal Status"; Salmon, *Women and the Law of Property*, pp. 655–85, and "Debtor's Wife." On the North, see Rabkin, *Fathers to Daughters*; Basch, *In the Eyes of the Law* and "Invisible Women"; Salmon, *Women and the Law of Property*. For a frank discussion of the property rights of a married woman, see Iverson L. Brookes to John Wood, 19 June 1857, and Iverson L. Brookes, "Letter of Advice to Wood and Wife," 20 Mar. 1857, Iverson L. Brookes Papers, SCL.

18. Natalie de Delage Sumter Diary, SCL; Keziah Goodwyn Hopkins Brevard Diary, SCL. See also Weiner, "Plantation Mistress/Female Slave"; Smith, *Philosophy and Practice of Slavery*, pp. 284–85. Catherine Clinton (*Plantation Mistress*) finds that 25 percent of the women she has studied did manage plantations on their own. I cannot pretend to scientific precision on the matter, which in any event requires systematic study, but I do suspect that the difference in our readings depends primarily on the relative importance we ascribe to the assistance of men (kin, overseers, drivers, factors, etc.) and, above all, to the importance we ascribe to knowledge of their existence as confirmation of the mistress's authority in the eyes of the slaves. In other words, at this stage in precise knowledge, both of our arguments are impressionistic.

19. Faust, *James Henry Hammond*, pp. 58–65; Bleser, *Hammonds of Redcliffe*; Thomas Butler King Papers (e.g., Thomas Butler King to Anna Matilda King, 10, 16 Dec. 1842, Anna Matilda King to Thomas Butler King, 9 Sept., 12, 15, 19 Dec. 1853, 28 Aug., 7 Sept. 1854, 17 Feb., 23 Apr. 1855, George C. Dunham to Anna Matilda King, 23, 28 June, 14 Aug. 1841), SHC; Mary E. Bateman Diary, SHC (on her cousin Margaret Campbell). See also Phillips, *Correspondence of Toombs, Stephens, and Cobb*, p. 80, n. 1. Bern Keating reports that in 1860 Mrs. Mary Evans, with 170 cultivated acres, produced the highest yield per acre in the county and that Miss Fanny Smith ran a plantation of 1,600 cleared acres—one of the biggest and best harvests of the year (*Washington County, Mississippi*).

20. David Outlaw to Emily Outlaw, 18, 15, 13 Dec. 1849, David Outlaw Papers, SHC.

21. Eliza[beth] Quitman to John A. Quitman, 15 Nov. 1842, John A. Quitman to Eliza Quitman, 18 Nov. 1842, Quitman Family Papers, SHC.

22. Wiltse, *John C. Calhoun: Nationalist*, p. 343; Bassett, *Southern Plantation Overseer*, pp. 174, 181, 207, 210–11; John Grimball to Meta (Morris) Grimball, 27 Apr. 1852, Grimball Family Papers, SHC; Rhea, *Hugh Swinton Legaré*, p. 59; Webb, *Mistress of Evergreen*. See also Craven, *Rachel of old Louisiana*; W. H. Quince to Mrs. R. Quince, 6, 30 Nov. 1861; John Quitman to Eliza[beth] Quitman, 5 June 1834, Quitman Family Papers, SHC.

23. Mooney, *Slavery in Tennessee*, pp. 10–11; Mary E. Bateman Diary, SHC; Wiley, *Southern Negroes*, pp. 50–51, 65; Keziah Goodwyn Hopkins Brevard Diary, 7, 8 Feb. 1861, SCL. See also Sarah A. (Haynsworth) Gayle Journal, SHC; Sarah Haynsworth Gayle Diary, HSC.

24. Smith, *Philosophy and Practice of Slavery*, pp. 284–85; H. C., "On the Management of Negroes," 175; Olmsted, *Journey in the Back Country*, p. 215; Easterby, *South Carolina Rice Plantation*, pp. 85, 89, 122; Kibler, *Benjamin F. Perry*, p. 185; Webb, *Mistress of Evergreen*; and esp. Mohr, *On the Threshold of Freedom*, pp. 221–25.

25. Georgia King to Thomas Butler King, 22 Feb. 1850, Thomas Butler King to Anna Matilda King, 29 Apr. 1857, Thomas Butler King Papers, SHC.

26. Sarah A. (Haynsworth) Gayle Journal, SHC; Lucy Walton Muse Fletcher Journal, 26 Feb. 1857, DU; Kate S. Carney Diary, 24, 27 June, 3 Aug. 1859, SHC; Mary Eliza (Eve) Carmichael Diary, 24 Feb. 1838, SHC.

27. Mary ["Mollie"] Jane Allen Mitchell to her Sister Mag [Margaret] Stevens Browne, 12 Oct. 1853, William Phineas Browne Collection, ADAH. See also E. A. Estes to Harriett Sarah Estes, 30 May 1847, Iverson L. Brookes Papers, SCL. Even Martha Foster, who was living away from home as a teacher and who chose her own husband, was not free to travel alone and could only visit her family when an acceptable escort was available (Martha Foster Crawford Diary, DU).

28. Mary E. Bateman Diary, 31 July 1856, SHC; John C. Brown, *South Carolina Narratives*, vol. 2, pt. 1, pp. 127–30; Millie Markham, *North Carolina Narratives*, vol. 15, pt. 2, pp. 106–8; John Hamilton Cornish Diary, 1 Oct. 1840, 8 June 1841, SHC. See also Censer, *North Carolina Planters*; Francis McMillan Carmack Diary, SHC; William Scott, *North Carolina Narratives*, vol. 15, pt. 2; Laura Hare, *Arkansas Narratives*, vol. 9, pt. 3, pp. 190–92; Clinton, *Plantation Mistress*, chap. 5, and "Caught in the Web of the Big House." On wartime conditions, see De Leon, *Four Years* and *Belles, Beaux, and Brains*. For a comparative perspective, see Martinez-Alier, *Marriage, Class, and Colour*.

29. Lucy Walton Muse Fletcher Journal, June 1841, Winter 1843, DU; H., "Misfortune and Genius"; Meta (Morris) Grimball Journal, 4 Aug. 1863, SHC; Rutledge, "Four Letters." See also Stowe, "Not-So-Cloistered Academy"; Seidel, "Southern Belle"; Olmsted, *Journey in the Back Country*, p. 134. Thomas Dew ("Dissertation on the Characteristic Distinctions between the Sexes") devoted a long passage to belles, whose excesses he deplored.

30. Lavinia Campbell to Henry Campbell, 20 Jan. 1833, Campbell Family Papers, DU. See also Lizzie [?] to Virginia Brookes, 21 Apr. 1848, n.d., and Emma [?] to Virginia Brookes, 9 Aug. 1852, Iverson L. Brookes Papers, SCL; Martha Foster Crawford Diary, DU.

31. Meta (Morris) Grimball Journal, 30 Sept. 1862, SHC.

32. *MCCW*, pp. 604–5. For a more conventional account of travel, see Laurens, "Journal of a Visit to Greenville."

33. Juliana Margaret Conner Diary, 13 June, 7 July 1827, SHC.

34. Kate S. Carney Diary, 10 Apr., 27 June 1859, 3 Mar. 186[1], SHC; M. Cain to Minerva R. Cain, 14 Apr. 1833, Todd Robinson Caldwell Papers, SHC.

35. Anna Matilda Page King to Lord King, 10 Mar. 1851, Thomas Butler King Papers, SHC; William Osborne Gregory to Martha Gregory, 6 Feb. 1825, Robert A. Jackson Papers, SHC. See also E. A. Estes to Harriett Sarah Estes, 30 May 1849, Iverson L. Brookes Papers, SCL.

36. David Outlaw to Emily Outlaw, 1, 9 May 1850, David Outlaw Papers, SHC.

37. Sarah Guignard to James S. Guignard, 31 Jan. 1829, in Childs, *Planters and Business Men*, p. 21. See also Olmsted, *Journey in the Back Country*, pp. 165–66.

38. Emily Caroline Douglas, "Autobiography" (written in 1904, but probably based on diary of 1855–68), Emily Caroline Douglas Papers, LSU. See also Harriett Sarah Estes to her mother, 22 Sept. [1847 or 1849], and E. A. Estes to Harriett Sarah Estes, 4 Nov. 1849, Iverson L. Brookes Papers, SCL.

39. Ella Gertrude Clanton Thomas Diary, 28, 30 Sept., 1 Oct. 1848, Apr. 1852, DU. See also Pope, "Preparation for Pedestals," p. 178; Henrietta Maria Tilghman to Polly Pearce, 28 Apr. [1783 or 1784], and Molly Tilghman to Polly Pearce, 29 Jan. [1789], in Pleasants, "Letters of Molly and Hetty Tilghman," pp. 27–29, 231–35; Mary Clay to "Dearest Nancy," 10 Nov. 1782, Mary Clay Letter, SHC.

40. *MBC*, p. 65; Octavia LeVert Journal, 18 Jan. 1851, ADAH; Lucy Walton Muse Fletcher Journal, [n.d.] 1841, DU; Juliana Margaret Conner Diary, 24, 21 June 1827, SHC. See also James M. Nicholson to Rebecca Lloyd, 3 Feb. 1837, in Shippen, "Mrs. B. I. Cohen's Fancy Dress Party"; Ann Calvert Stuart to Elizabeth Lee, 19 Oct. 1806, in Montague, "Cornelia Lee's Wedding"; Montague, "Letters Home." For a scathing critique of rural dress, see E. Thomas to Mariah Louisa Smith, 20 Mar. 1853, Aaron Smith Family Papers, GDAH.

41. Lucy Walton Muse Fletcher Journal, [n.d.] 1841, DU; Sue Battle to "Dear Sister," 10 Mar. 1839, Clement Claiborne Clay Family Papers, DU. See also Boyd, *Alabama in the Fifties*, p. 112; Susan Davis (Nye) Hutchinson Diary, 12 Apr., 2 July 1815, SHC; Laurens, "Journal of a Visit to Greenville." For views of society on the frontier, see Franklin, "Memoirs of Mrs. Annie P. Harris"; Graham, "Texas Memoirs"; Harris, "Reminiscences."

42. Mary Hamilton Campbell to David Campbell, 1 Dec. 1822, Mary Hamilton Campbell Letterbook, DU.

43. Bleser and Heath, "Impact of the Civil War on a Southern Marriage," esp. pp. 202–3; *MCCW*, p. 32 (19 Mar. 1861); Susan Davis (Nye) Hutchinson Diary, 29 June 1815, SHC. See also Meta (Morris) Grimball Journal, 24 Aug. 1861, SHC.

44. Sarah A. (Haynsworth) Gayle Journal, 18 Apr. 1833, 31 June, 11 Oct. 1832, SHC.

45. Louise Taylor Pharr Book, 1830, Louise Taylor Pharr Manuscripts, LSU; *MCCW*, p. 40 (31 Mar. 1861); Amos Lincoln, *Texas Narratives*, vol. 5, pt. 3, p. 18; Sellers, *Slavery in Alabama*, p. 46; Keziah Goodwyn Hopkins Brevard Diary, 13 Feb. 1861, SCL. See also Wade, "Recollections," p. 22, UTLA. Mrs. Wade's grandfather purchased "beautiful bandana handkerchiefs," that were "to twist into turbans for the women and girls, for no female servant about the house must be without her 'head-rag' as she termed it and it must be snowy white or a beautiful bandana."

46. Smedes, *Southern Planter*, p. 34; Gus Feaster, *South Carolina Narratives*, vol. 2, pt. 2, p. 61. See also Works Progress Administration, *Negro in Virginia*, p. 73; Genovese, *Roll, Jordan, Roll*, pp. 550–61.

47. Andrews, *South since the War*, p. 187; O'Neall, *Negro Law of South Carolina*. See also Litwack, *Been in the Storm*, pp. 6, 116, 245, 315. On antebellum Charleston, see Johnson and Roark, *No Chariot Let Down* and *Black Masters*.

48. *MCCW*, p. 69 (4 June 1861).

49. Susan Cornwall Book, 31 Jan. 1861, SHC.

50. Buckingham, *Slave States*, 1:75, 122–24, 2:562–63. On the social whirl of the springs, see Renier, *Springs of Virginia*, pp. 55–56, 149; MacCorkle, *White Sulphur Springs*.

51. Anderson, *Brokenburn*, p. 239. See also Smedes, *Southern Planter*, p. 99; Trollope, *Domestic Manners*, p. 241; Royall, *Sketches of History*, pp. 56–57; Olmsted, *Journey in the Back Country*, pp. 140, 231; Clay-Clopton, *Belle of the Fifties*, pp. 90, 225; Andrews, *War-Time Journal*, p. 111; Bryant, "Role and Status of the Female Yeomanry"; McCurry, "'Their Ways Are Not Our Ways.'"

52. Eliza Carolina (Burgwin) Clitherall Books, Book 7, SHC.

53. Ibid., Book 6; Butler King to Thomas Butler King, 6 Mar. 1854, Thomas Butler King Papers, SHC. On the attitudes of gentlemen who did not expect the yeomen they patronized to treat them as equals, see also C., "Servility."

54. Kate S. Carney Diary, 23, 27 July 1859, SHC.

55. Meta (Morris) Grimball Journal, 23 July 1862, SHC; Joseph W. Jackson to Martha Jackson, 17 May 1829, Jackson and Prince Family Papers, SHC.

56. Anna Matilda Page King to Thomas Butler King, 16, 20 Jan. 1855, Thomas Butler King Papers, SHC; Meta (Morris) Grimball Journal, 29 Nov. 1861, SHC; Anna Matilda Page King to Thomas Butler King, 14 May 1855, Thomas Butler King Papers, SHC. See also Mary Eliza (Eve) Carmichael Diary, 16 Mar. 1838, SHC; Susan Davis (Nye) Hutchinson Diary, 1 July 1815, 2 Oct. 1831, SHC.

57. Lucilla Agnes (Gamble) McCorkle Diary, Mon. after 4th Sabbath of Nov. 1848, SHC.

58. Butler King to Anna Matilda Page King, 23 Apr. 1849, Thomas Butler King Papers, SHC.

59. Ibid., 14 May 1849; Butler King to Georgia King, 20 May 1849, Thomas Butler King Papers, SHC.

60. Martha Jackson to Henry Jackson, Jr., 14 Jan. 1835, Jackson and Prince Family Papers, SHC; Juliana Margaret Conner Diary, 13 Oct. 1827, SHC.

61. Sarah A. (Haynsworth) Gayle Journal, Feb. 1835 [after the 6th, but date unclear because of cut pages], SHC.

62. Ibid., 16 Nov. 1832.

63. Meta (Morris) Grimball Journal, 13 Feb. 1863, 22 May 1864, SHC.

64. Ibid., 5, 30 Sept. 1862.

65. Ibid., 5 Sept. 1862, 14 Apr. 1861.

66. Lucy Walton Muse Fletcher Journal, Summer 1842, DU. See also Fannie Page Hume Diary, 28 Dec. 1860, SHC.

67. Mary Steele Ferrand Henderson Journal, 20, 13 Aug. 1855, SHC. Here, and in what follows, I am not suggesting that attitudes of condescension did not prevail in the North as well. Christine Stansell shows that an upper-class concern with dependency and deference informed charity in New York (*City of Women*, pp. 30–37). But the charities she is discussing were informed by bourgeois attitudes and grounded in bourgeois institutions—frequently administered by men. It is possible that something resembling the southern patterns persisted in, say, the Hudson River Valley, or that wealthy New York women called upon working-class women, but it seems unlikely that they participated in the kinds of hierarchical rural and village networks that prevailed in the South.

68. Susan Davis (Nye) Hutchinson Diary, 19 June 1839, 22 July 1815, SHC; Kate S. Carney Diary, 30 July, 19, 21 Apr. 1859, 17 Apr. 1861, 21, 29 Jan. 1861, SHC.

69. Friedman, *Enclosed Garden*; Mathews, *Religion in the Old South*. Anne Loveland (*Southern Evangelicals*) and E. Brooks Holifield (*Gentlemen Theologians*) do not address women per se, but both are excellent on religion and attitudes toward social order. See also Bruce, *And They All Sang Hallelujah*; Baker, *Southern Baptist Convention*. On the difference between northern and southern attitudes, see Taylor, *Ante-bellum South Carolina*, pp. 59–73, esp. p. 71. For northern women, see Welter, *Dimity Convictions*; Cott, "Young Women in the Second Great Awakening"; Ryan, "Women's Awakening"; Martha Tomhave Blauvelt, "Women and Revivalism," in Ruether and Keller, *Women and Religion in America*, 1:1–45 (which does pay some attention to southern women). For examples of southern women's charitable organizations in an urban setting, see Ladies Benevolent Society, *Constitution*; Ladies' Benevolent Society of Charleston, *Constitution and Regulations*; Ladies' Auxiliary Christian Association, *First Annual Report*; Middleton, *Sketch of the Ladies Benevolent Society*; and Winsborough, *Woman's Auxiliary*.

70. For a thoughtful first attempt to assess the changes, see Mathews, *Religion in the Old South* and *Slavery and Methodism*.

71. Cary, *Letters on Female Character*, pp. 18–19.

72. Lewis, *Pursuit of Happiness*.

73. Eliza Carolina (Burgwin) Clitherall Books, Book 6, SHC; Mary (Jeffreys) Bethell Diary, 16 Sept. 1863, SHC. See also Anna Matilda Page King to Thomas Butler King, 20 Mar. 1850, Thomas Butler King Papers, SHC.

74. Mary (Jeffreys) Bethell Diary, 29 July 1863, 10 Mar. 1862, SHC.

75. Susan Davis (Nye) Hutchinson Diary, 22 July 1815, SHC.

76. Ibid., 2 Oct. 1831; Kate S. Carney Diary, 4 Mar., 21 Apr. 1859, SHC; Meta (Morris) Grimball Journal, 28 Nov. 1862, SHC; Eliza Carolina (Burgwin) Clitherall Books, Book 7, SHC; Sarah A. (Haynsworth) Gayle Journal, 29 Apr. 1833, SHC. See also Mahala (Eggleston) Roach Diary, 9 Nov. 1853, SHC.

77. Eliza Carolina (Burgwin) Clitherall Books, Books 5, 8, SHC. On southern women's charitable organizations, see Mary Telfair to Mary Few, 5 Feb. [n.d.], William Few Collection, GDAH; Pinckney, *Centennial Pamphlet*; Lebsock, *Free Women of Petersburg*, pp. 195–236.

78. Anne Firor Scott argues that many women found the double sexual standards that governed social life difficult to accept and had premarital and extramarital sexual affairs (*Southern Lady*, pp. 54–55). No doubt many communities had a scandal or two, but it remains to be established empirically that such attitudes and behavior existed on a significant scale outside New Orleans and perhaps Charleston—and even there doubts may be entertained about more than occasional transgressions of social norms by the women of the elite. See also Clinton, "Caught in the Web of the Big House." Thomas Dew, in "Dissertation on the Characteristic Distinctions between the Sexes," discusses the conventions of chastity.

79. Walter Reid Memorandum, Taylor Beatty Books, SHC; Bryan, *Mary Austin Holley*, p. 14. On seduction, see also Tucker, *Series of Lectures on the Science of Government*, p. 65n.

80. Lucy Walton Muse Fletcher Journal, Summer 1849, DU.

81. Julia A. Gilmer Diary, 1859 [prob. Feb.], SHC.

82. David Outlaw to Emily Outlaw, 26 Sept. 1850, 17 Dec. 1848, 9 Dec. 1849, 11 June 1850, David Outlaw Papers, SHC.

83. Thomas Butler King Papers, SHC. Steven Stowe also discusses the Kings' marriage (*Intimacy and Power*).

84. Anna Matilda Page King to Lord King, 28 Sept. 1848, Thomas Butler King Papers, SHC; Faust, *James Henry Hammond*, pp. 314–17. See also Meta (Morris) Grimball Journal, 22 May 1864, SHC.

85. Anna Matilda Page King to Thomas Butler King, 20 June 1849, Thomas Butler King Papers, SHC.

86. Lucilla Agnes (Gamble) McCorkle Diary, 4th Sabbath Nov. 1847, 2d Sabbath Nov. 1848, 1st Sabbath Dec. 1850, SHC.

87. Susan Davis (Nye) Hutchinson Diary, 19, 23 Oct. 1826, 11 Dec. 1827, 19 Jan. 1828, 3, 5 Jan., 8, 19 Sept. 1829, SHC.

88. Ibid., 9 Jan. 1830, 2 Sept., 21 Oct., 27 July, 8 Aug. 1831.

89. See, among many, David Outlaw to Emily Outlaw, 16 Dec. 1848, 9 Feb. 1849, David Outlaw Papers, SHC; Anna Matilda Page King to Thomas Butler King, 26 June 1849, Thomas Butler King Papers, SHC; John A. Quitman to Eliza Quitman, 8, 10 Apr. 1836, Quitman Family Papers, SHC; Robert Allston to "My Dear Adele," 7 May 1854, Allston Family Papers, SCL.

90. Hopkins, "The Windhover: To Christ Our Lord," in *Poems*, p. 69.

91. Proust, *A la recherche du temps perdu*.

Chapter 5

1. In the category of writings, I am including diaries, journals, correspondence, novels, poetry, drama, and occasional pieces. On the value of various writings according to date, see Carol Bleser ("Southern Wives and Slavery"), with whom I agree and to whom I am very much indebted, here and elsewhere, for discussions of these matters. For the details of McCord's life, see Fraser, "Louisa C. McCord"; Thorp, *Female Persuasion*, pp. 178–214; Smythe, *For Old Lang Syne*. Among Louisa McCord's many published works, see those listed in the bibliography below.

2. Hentz, *Planter's Northern Bride*; Gilman, *Recollections of a Southern Matron*. Cf. Stowe, *Uncle Tom's Cabin*; Fern, *Ruth Hall*; Warner, *Wide, Wide World*. On northern domestic fiction, see esp. Tompkins, *Sensational Designs*; Davidson, *Revolution and the Word*; Kelley, *Private Woman, Public Stage*; Douglas, *Feminization of American Culture*; Papashvily, *All the Happy Endings*. On proslavery fiction, see Tandy, "Pro-Slavery Propaganda." We do not have a full study of antebellum southern women's fiction, but see Jones, *Tomorrow Is Another Day*; Gwin, *Black and White Women*; Meriwether, *South Carolina Women Writers*; *MBC*. Southern women writers who deserve more attention include Susan Petigru King and, especially, Augusta Evans.

3. Quoted from Caroline Gilman's autobiographical sketch, in Forrest, *Women of the South*, p. 53.

4. Moragne, *Neglected Thread*, pp. xxvii–xxviii, 109; Frances Moore (Webb) Bumpas Diary, 30 Sept. 1854, SHC. See also Martha Foster Crawford Diary, 5 Oct. 1850, DU.

5. See, e.g., Kelley, *Private Woman, Public Stage*; Conrad, *Perish the Thought*; Baym, *Woman's Fiction*; Papashvily, *All the Happy Endings*; Brown, *Sentimental*

Novel in America; Kolodny, *Land Before Her*; Homans, *Bearing the Word*; Showalter, *Literature of Their Own*. For a selection of women's writings with which the southern audience was familiar, see Forrest, *Women of the South*; Hart, *Female Prose Writers*. See also various critical notices in the *Southern Quarterly Review*, esp. L., "Female Prose Writers"; "Miss Sedgwick's Letters from Abroad"; "Miss Lee's Social Evenings"; "Mrs. Dana's Letters"; "Biographies of Good Wives"; "Memoir of the Life of Anne Boleyn"; "Annals of the Queens of Spain"; "Lady Wortley's Travels"; "Ellet's Women of the Revolution"; J. S. T., "Ida Norman."

6. Sarah Rootes Jackson Diary, 7 Mar., 4 June 1835, SHC; Sarah A. (Haynsworth) Gayle Journal, 10 Mar. 1834, SHC; Susan Davis (Nye) Hutchinson Diary, 13 Jan. 1829, SHC. See also Martha R. Jackson Diary, 11, 14 Nov. 1833, SHC; Whitman, "Private Journal of Mary Ann Owen Simms."

7. Kate S. Carney Diary, [n.d.] Jan., 10 May, 29 Mar. 1859, 3 Feb. 1875, SHC.

8. Bonner, *Journal of a Milledgeville Girl*, pp. 28–29; Elizabeth Ruffin Diary, 5 Mar. 1827, SHC.

9. Ella Gertrude Clanton Thomas Diary, 30 Sept. 1848, 29 Sept. 1849, 17, 19 May, 20 June, 9 July 1852, DU.

10. Charlotte Beatty Diary, [n.d.] 1843; 20, 21 Jan. 1845, SHC.

11. Mary Eliza (Eve) Carmichael Diary, 18 Apr. 1839, 6 May 1843, SHC; Frances Webb (Moore) Bumpas Diary, 12 Mar. 1842, SHC. See also Martha Foster Crawford Diary, 5, 14, 25, 29 Sept., 17 Oct. 1850, DU; Helmreich, "Prayer for the Spirit of Acceptance"; Robertson, "Diary of Dolly Lunt Burge," esp. 44:213, 216–19, 325, 333 (13, 26, 27, 28 Feb., 4 Mar., 16 Apr. 1848, 19 Feb. 1849), 46:67 (29 Sept. 1867).

12. Lucilla Agnes (Gamble) McCorkle Diary, 24 [4th Sabbath] Jan. 1847, Mon. morning after the 1st Sabbath Apr. 1847, 6 June [1st Sabbath] 1847, SHC.

13. Anne Turberville (Beale) Davis Journal, SHC; Lucilla Agnes (Gamble) McCorkle Diary, 2d Sabbath Apr. 1850, 1st Sabbath May 1850, SHC. See also Sarah Wadley's summary of a sermon she had heard by Dr. William Leord, pastor of the Episcopal church at Vicksburg, Miss., 26 Feb. 1860, in the Sarah Lois Wadley Diary, SHC; William Hollinshead to Mary Fraser, 24 Oct. 1797, M. Desaussure to Mary Fraser, 9 Apr. 1796, Mary Finley to Mary Fraser, 31 Oct. 1816, Mary DeSaussure Fraser Papers, DU; Scott, *Southern Lady*, pp. 10–11, and *Making the Invisible Woman Visible*, pp. 175–211.

14. On Louisa McCord's life, see Fraser, "Louisa C. McCord"; Thorp, *Female Persuasion*, pp. 179–214; Smythe, "Recollections of Louisa McCord," and correspondence between Louisa McCord Smythe and Jessie Melville Fraser, Dulles-Cheves-Lovell-McCord Family Papers, SCHS. Smythe informed Fraser that her use of Louisa C. McCord was incorrect, because Louisa Cheves had adopted the legal name Louisa S. Cheves before her marriage and kept the "S." after it for legal reasons, even though she would have preferred to use Cheves as a middle name. For a personal account of a young woman's schooling in Philadelphia—where Louisa McCord and her sister also attended school, four decades earlier—see Kate S. Carney Diary, SHC. For the copybook kept by Anna Winship while she was a student at Wesleyan College from 1848 to 1851, see Winship-Flournoy Papers, AHS; Nannie E. Cross Compositions, 1856, Cross Family Papers, Mullins Library, University of Arkansas. For Mary Chesnut's experience at Mme Talvande's in Charleston, see *MBC*. We lack adequate studies of the education of slaveholding women, but see, e.g., Blandin, *History of Higher Education of Women*; Knight,

Documentary History of Education; Woody, *History of Women's Education*. For a close look at a leading southern academy for women, see Griffin, *Less Time for Meddling*; Wenhold, "Salem Boarding School." The archives of Salem College contain invaluable information on students, curricula, and academy life.

15. Fraser, "Louisa C. McCord."

16. Margaret Thorp refers to the letter from the mother, but does not indicate its location (*Female Persuasion*, p. 190). On Louisa Cheves's inheritance of Lang Syne, see Louisa Smythe to Miss Fraser, 5 May 1920, Dulles-Cheves-Lovell-McCord Family Papers, SCHS.

17. Louisa Cheves to Langdon Cheves, 7 Oct. 1839, Cheves Family Papers, SCL.

18. Fragmentary notes in Louisa S. McCord's hand, in the Dulles-Cheves-Lovell-McCord Family Papers, SCHS. The notes, which have a slightly obsessive quality, would appear to be those which Louisa McCord drafted to prepare her heated response to Benjamin F. Perry's sketch of her father in *Reminiscences of Public Men*, pp. 83–87. Perry's portrait was gracious enough but did not begin to satisfy McCord's very high opinion of her father. See McCord, "Langdon Cheves."

19. McCord, *My Dreams*.

20. Kate S. Carney Diary, 27 July 1859, SHC; Elizabeth Ruffin Diary, 26, 29 Feb. 1827, SHC. For a lively discussion of the advantages of "Single Blessedness," see Mary Telfair to Mary Few, 28 Oct., 26 Nov. 1814, 17 Jan. [n.d.], 19 Oct. [n.d.], 6 Apr. 1825, 2 Dec. 1829, William Few Collection, GDAH.

21. Elizabeth Ruffin Diary, 11 Feb. 1827, SHC.

22. Sarah A. (Haynsworth) Gayle Journal, Friday [n.d.], June 1833, SHC (on her own premature aging); Hajnal, "European Marriage Patterns"; Boucher, "Wealthy Planter Families," p. 42; Clinton, *Plantation Mistress*.

23. McCord, *Caius Gracchus*.

24. McCord, "Woman and Her Needs," p. 272.

25. In addition to the references in note 14, above, see Stowe, "Not-So-Cloistered Academy"; Clinton, "Equally Their Due"; Salley et al., *Life at St. Mary's*; Mary Boykin Chesnut, "A Boarding School Fifty Years Ago," Williams-Chesnut-Manning Papers, SCL; Barbour, "College Education for Women in Georgia"; Green, "Higher Education of Women in the South"; Orr, *History of Education in Georgia*, pp. 42–45; Gilman, "Studies of Rebecca and Catherine Edwards"; "Catalogues," EU; Pierce, "Georgia Female College"; Jones, "Manner of Educating Females"; D., "Laws of Life"; "Education"; White, *Portal of Wonderland*, pp. 40–45. For one young woman's letters home from school, see Holman, "Charleston in the Summer of 1841." See also Censer, *North Carolina Planters*; Lewis, *Pursuit of Happiness*. Eugene Genovese and I will discuss female education more fully in our forthcoming book, *Mind of the Master Class* (title tentative).

26. Johnson, *Address*, pp. 11, 12–13, 18, 23, 28. Such addresses were legion and were frequently delivered by prominent political leaders. See, e.g., Miles, *Women "Nobly Planned"*; O'Neall, *Address on Female Education*; Chandler, *Address on Female Education*; Pierce, "Georgia Female College"; Lipscomb, *Relations of the Anglo-Saxon Race to Christian Womanhood*.

27. Johnson, *Address*, pp. 14–15.

28. Ibid., pp. 24–25.

29. Ibid., p. 20; Sarah Rootes Jackson Diary, 12 Jan., 3 June 1835, SHC; Caroline Lee (Whiting) Hentz Diary, 3 Apr. 1836, SHC; Mary Eliza (Eve) Carmichael

Diary, 28 Sept. 1837, SHC; Kate S. Carney Diary, 2, 19, 20 Jan., 19 Feb., 16, 17, 24 Apr. 1861, SHC; Elizabeth Ruffin Diary, 27 Feb., 2 Mar. 1827, SHC.

30. Mary Hamilton Campbell to David Campbell, 29 Jan. 1822, Mary Hamilton Campbell Letterbook, DU; Mary Hamilton Campbell to David Campbell, 14 Dec. 1822, Campbell Family Papers, DU. See also Martha R. Jackson Diary, 20 Dec. 1833, SHC.

31. Fannie Page Hume Diary, 11, 18, 23 Nov. 1860, SHC; Eliza Carolina (Burgwin) Clitherall Books, 21 May 1856, SHC; Susan Davis (Nye) Hutchinson Diary, 25 Feb. 1833, SHC; Elizabeth Ruffin Diary, 9 Feb. 1827, SHC.

32. Elizabeth Ruffin Diary, 10, 15 Feb., 8 Mar. 1827, SHC.

33. On the Reverend Dr. Charles Deems, see Turrentine, *Romance of Education*, p. 59. On family reading, see, e.g., Geo. D. Martin to Susan Henry, 29 Apr. 1854, Gustavus Adolphus Henry Papers, SHC; Louisa Quitman to John A. Quitman, [?] Feb. 1847, Quitman Family Papers, SHC; James Hervey Greenlee Diary, 27 Jan., 17 Mar. 1850, SHC; William Hooper Haigh Diary, 15 May 1844, William Hooper Haigh Papers, SHC; Francis McMillan Carmack Diary, 30 Nov. 1853, SHC. On little Miss Palmer, see Johnson, *Benjamin Morgan Palmer*, pp. 38–39.

34. Fannie Page Hume Diary, 18 Feb., 4, 5 Sept. 1861, 2, 4, 6 Jan., 24 Nov., 4 July, 20 Mar. 1860, SHC; Mahala (Eggleston) Roach Diary, 3 Feb. 1853, SHC.

35. Fannie Page Hume Diary, 13, 19, 21 Nov. 1860, SHC; Ella Gertrude Clanton Thomas Diary, 28 Sept., 2, 8 Oct. 1848, DU; David Outlaw to Emily Outlaw, 10 May 1850, David Outlaw Papers, SHC; Josey to Fuddy King, 14 Mar. 1859, Thomas Butler King Papers, SHC; Reavis, "Accounts of the Henderson Post Office," 1849, 1850, 1854, 1855, DU. See also Kate S. Carney Diary, 2 Feb. 1859, SHC; Hoole, "Gilmans and the Southern Rose"; Cardwell, "Quiver and the Floral Wreath."

36. Fannie Page Hume Diary, 18 Jan., 30 Nov. 1860, 1, 5 Jan., 6 Feb. 1861, SHC. See also the letters of Mary Telfair to Mary Few, William Few Collection, GDAH; Louisa Quitman to John A. Quitman, 14 May 1842, Quitman Family Papers, SHC; and Natalie de Delage Sumter Diary, 1, 3 July 1840, SCL.

37. Eliza Carolina (Burgwin) Clitherall Books, 1 Dec. 1859, 23 Mar., 7 June, 22 Oct., 8 June 1860, SHC.

38. Elizabeth Ruffin Diary, 11, 13 Feb. 1827, SHC; Lucilla Agnes (Gamble) McCorkle Diary, 2d Sabbath Jan. 1847, Mon. night after 4th Sabbath Mar. 1847, 28 Oct. [4th Sabbath] 1847, SHC. John Bunyan's *Pilgrim's Progress* and *Holy War* were also favorites of the mother of the prominent William Harris Hardy of Alabama (see Hardy and Hardy, *No Compromise with Principle*, p. 28).

39. Lucy Walton Muse Fletcher Journal, 1840–41, Summer 1842, Summer 1843, Summer 1844, DU.

40. The one yeoman woman's diary I know of is that of Mary Davis Brown of South Carolina, although Miss Abby, who kept a diary for the last year of the war in upcountry Georgia, probably participated in a culture very similar to that of the wealthier yeomanry. On yeoman women, see McCurry, "'Their Ways Are Not Our Ways'" and esp. "In Defense of Their World." See also Spufford, *Small Books and Pleasant Histories*.

41. Kate S. Carney Diary, 16, 17 Mar. 1859, SHC; Charlotte Beatty Diary, 30 Dec. 1843, SHC; Susan Davis (Nye) Hutchinson Diary, 15 July 1838, 12 May 1839, SHC; Lucy Walton Muse Fletcher Journal, Sabbath Notebook for 1841, DU; Elizabeth

Ruffin Diary, 18 Feb. 1827, SHC; Susan Davis (Nye) Hutchinson Diary, 3 Oct. 1831, 9 Dec. 1832, SHC; Anne Turberville (Beale) Davis Journal, 11 Nov. 1838, SHC; Sarah Eve Adams Diary, 5, 19 Dec. 1813, DU; Susan Davis (Nye) Hutchinson Diary, 11, 13, 16 Feb. 1827, SHC; Eliza Carolina (Burgwin) Clitherall Books, 9 May 1853, SHC; Fannie Page Hume Diary, 3 Feb. 1861, 12 Feb., 19 Aug. 1860, SHC; Natalie de Delage Sumter Diary, 1, 3 July, 1, 18 Dec. 1840, SCL. See also Gillespie, "Modesty Canonized" and "'Clear Leadings of Providence.'"

42. Fannie Page Hume Diary, 16 Jan., 5, 6, 7 Feb. 1860, SHC.

43. Fraser, "Louisa C. McCord."

44. Not many of the women whose papers I have read complained directly about violence to themselves, but many included reports of the cruelty of other women's husbands. For one woman who complained about her own husband, see Susan Davis (Nye) Hutchinson Diary, SHC. For other views of slaveholders' marriages, see esp. Bleser, *Hammonds of Redcliffe*, "Perrys of Greenville," and "Southern Wives and Slavery"; Stowe, *Intimacy and Power*. See also Rosengarten, *Tombee*; Myers, *Children of Pride*; Crabtree and Patton, *Journal of a Secesh Lady*; Campbell Family Papers, DU; Meta (Morris) Grimball Journal, SHC; Grimball Family Papers, SHC; Thomas Butler King Papers, SHC; Mary Eliza (Eve) Carmichael Diary, SHC; John Houston Bills Papers, SHC; Mahala (Eggleston) Roach Diary, SHC; Elizabeth Blanks Papers, DU; Jackson and Prince Family Papers, SHC; Iverson Brookes Family Papers, DU; Sarah Eve Adams Diary, DU; "A Freedmen's Bureau Superintendent of Marriages to the Freedmen's Bureau Agent at Alexandria, Virginia, Freedmen's Village, Va., June 1st 1866," in Berlin et al., *The Black Military Experience*, pp. 672–73.

45. McCord, *My Dreams*, pp. 185–89, 160–61.

46. Most commonly, those who claimed to reject the married state were adolescents. See, e.g. Kate S. Carney Diary, SHC; Elizabeth Ruffin Diary, SHC; Mary Telfair to Mary Few, 28 Oct., 26 Nov. 1814, 17 Jan. [n.d.], William Few Collection, GDAH. Mary Bateman, in her diary, did not claim to reject marriage, although she did record brushing off her family's teasing about the interest of prospective suitors. She remained single.

47. See prologue, above; Anna Matilda Page King to Thomas Butler King, 11 Apr. 1850, Thomas Butler King Papers, SHC; Meta (Morris) Grimball Journal, 10 Mar. 1863, SHC. See also Sarah Clinton Southall Diary, 7 June 1855, LSU; Frances Moore (Webb) Bumpas Diary, 30 Dec. 1842, SHC; Hartridge, *Letters of Robert Mackay*.

48. Mahala (Eggleston) Roach Diary, 26 Nov. 1853, SHC; Henry Jackson to Martha Jackson, 28 May 1829, Jackson and Prince Family Papers, SHC; Everard Green Baker Diary, 12 July 1849, SHC. See also Simpson, *Good Southerner*, p. 70 (on the quality of the marriage of Sarah and Henry Wise).

49. John Hamilton Cornish Diary, 13 Feb. 1864, SHC; Lucilla Agnes (Gamble) McCorkle Diary, 3 Jan. [1st Sabbath] 1847, SHC; Mary Hamilton Kendall to Lydia Hamilton, 5 Aug. 1854, and Mary Hamilton Kendall to Abigail Hamilton, 1 Sept. 1854, Hamilton/Kendall Family Letters, GDAH; letter addressed to "My Dear Adele," 7 May 1854, Allston Family Papers, SCL. On women's feelings for "my" church, see Mary Eliza (Eve) Carmichael Diary, 27 Sept. 1826 [*sic*, but the date should be 1840], SHC. Meta Morris Grimball, among many, expressed special pleasure when her daughters joined her church (Meta [Morris] Grimball Journal,

SHC). See, e.g., Mary (Jeffreys) Bethell Diary, 25 Sept 1864, SHC; Julia A. Gilmer Diary, [prob. Feb. or Mar.] 1859, SHC. See also Andrews, *Miscellanies.*

50. Caroline Lee (Whiting) Hentz Diary, 7 June 1836, SHC; Unsigned memo on Louisa McCord, in Dulles-Cheves-Lovell-McCord Family Papers, SCHS (prob. by Louisa Smythe); Smythe, "Recollections of Louisa McCord," SCHS.

51. Smythe, "Recollections of Louisa McCord," SCHS; Louisa S. McCord to Mary Middleton, 17 July 1852, Middleton Family Papers, SCHS.

52. Smythe, "Recollections of Louisa McCord," SCHS.

53. Louisa S. McCord to Mary Middleton, 21 June, 17 July 1852, Middleton Family Papers, SCHS.

54. Sally Baxter to George Baxter, 15 Apr. 1855, in Hampton, *Divided Heart*, pp. 20–23. See also McCord, "Uncle Tom's Cabin"; Hall, "Yankee Tutor"; "Stowe's Key to Uncle Tom's Cabin"; and, of course, Stowe, *Uncle Tom's Cabin.*

55. Fraser, "Louisa C. McCord," pp. 34–35; *MCCW*, pp. 372, 374, 377, 386, 394, 402, 414, 628, 675–76.

56. McCord, *Caius Gracchus*, dedication. See Kuhn, *Mother's Role in Childhood Education*; Sklar, *Catharine Beecher*; Ryan, *Empire of the Mother*; Strickland, *Victorian Domesticity*. For southern women's private writings about their feelings as mothers, see, e.g., Sarah A. (Haynsworth) Gayle Journal, SHC; Eliza Carolina (Burgwin) Clitherall Books, SHC; Frances Moore (Webb) Bumpas Diary, SHC; Mary (Jeffreys) Bethell Diary, SHC; Meta (Morris) Grimball Journal, SHC; Anna Matilda Page King Correspondence, Thomas Butler King Papers, SHC; Sarah Lois Wadley Diary, SHC; Mahala (Eggleston) Roach Diary, SHC; Ella Gertrude Clanton Thomas Diary, DU; Virginia Campbell Shelton Correspondence, Campbell Family Papers, DU; Mary DeSaussure Fraser Papers, DU; Lucy Walton Muse Fletcher Journal, DU; Susan Davis (Nye) Hutchinson Diary, SHC. See also McMillen, "Mothers' Sacred Duty."

57. Mahala (Eggleston) Roach Diary, 14 Nov. 1853, SHC; Charlotte Beatty Diary, 23 Feb. 1843, SHC; Mary (Jeffreys) Bethell Diary, 6 Jan. 1858, 13 Aug. 1860, SHC; Mary Eliza (Eve) Carmichael Diary, SHC; Meta (Morris) Grimball Journal, SHC; Thomas Butler King Papers, SHC. See also F. Henry Quitman to Eliza Quitman, 30 Sept. 1850, Quitman Family Papers, SHC; Susan Morcock to William Morcock, 24 Feb. 1854, Morcock/Baldy/Smith/Williams Family Papers, GDAH.

58. Anne Turberville (Beale) Davis Journal, 19 May 1839, SHC; Frances Moore (Webb) Bumpas Diary, 6 Feb. 1844, SHC; Lucilla Agnes (Gamble) McCorkle Diary, 27 Dec. [4th Sabbath] 1846, SHC; Mary (Jeffreys) Bethell Diary, introductory autobiography, 12 Dec. 1853, 6 June 1855, 9 Dec. 1857, 10 Feb. 1862, SHC; Mary Steele Ferrand Henderson Journal, 15 Aug. 1855, SHC. See also Susan Davis (Nye) Hutchinson Diary, 19 Oct. 1831, 16 Feb. 1832, SHC; Mary Hamilton Kendall to Lydia Hamilton, 26 June 1853, Hamilton/Kendall Family Letters, GDAH.

59. Susan Davis (Nye) Hutchinson Diary, 26 Aug. 1827, SHC; Lucilla Agnes (Gamble) McCorkle Diary, 27 Dec. [4th Sabbath] 1846, SHC.

60. Mary (Jeffreys) Bethell Diary, introductory autobiography, SHC; Mary Steele Ferrand Henderson Journal, 1855 passim, esp. Oct., SHC; Thomas Butler King Papers, SHC; Robertson, "Diary of Dolly Lunt Burge," 9, 21 Apr. 1848.

61. Mary (Jeffreys) Bethell Diary, 12 Jan. 1858, SHC; Frances Moore (Webb) Bumpas Diary, 24 Apr. 1845, SHC; Mahala (Eggleston) Roach Diary, 28, 29 Mar., 28 Apr., 24 June 1853, SHC. See also Mary Hamilton Kendall to Lydia Hamilton, 5

Aug. 1854, Hamilton/Kendall Family Letters, GDAH; Deas, "Eleanor Parke Lewis to Mrs. C. C. Pinckney." For an unmarried woman's thoughts on childrearing, see Mary Telfair to Mary Few, 29 June [n.d.], 25 [n.d.], William Few Collection, GDAH.

62. Elizabeth Eve's Book, 1803, Carmichael Family Books, SHC.

63. Mahala (Eggleston) Roach Diary, 16, 27 Jan., 29 Mar., 6, 13, 18 June 1853, SHC; Frances Moore (Webb) Bumpas Diary, 24 Apr., 11, 15 June 1845, SHC.

64. Susan Davis (Nye) Hutchinson Diary, 14 June 1827, SHC. For mothers' feelings for their sons, see, among many, Meta (Morris) Grimball Journal, 30 July, 2 Sept., 1 Oct. 1864, SHC. For mothers' feelings for their daughters, see, among many, Mary (Jeffreys) Bethell Diary, SHC; Eliza Carolina (Burgwin) Clitherall Books, SHC. For women's feelings for their own mothers, see, among many, Samuel Andrew Agnew Diary, 11 July 1854, SHC; Mahala (Eggleston) Roach Diary, 14 June 1853, SHC; Meta (Morris) Grimball Journal, SHC; Julia A. Gilmer Diary, Sept. 1861, SHC. For a young man's perspective, see DeWitt, "Education of Humanity," Marcus B. DeWitt Papers, SHC.

65. Ryan, *Empire of the Mother.*

66. Bastiat, *Sophisms of the Protective Policy*; McCord, "Justice and Fraternity" and "Right to Labor."

67. Eugene Genovese and I have discussed Louisa McCord's political economy elsewhere; here I shall only evoke its essential features as they bear upon her general views on the twin social questions of gender and slavery. Genovese and Fox-Genovese, "Slavery, Economic Development, and the Law."

68. See chap. 1 above. See also Hughes, *Treatise on Sociology*; Lyman, *Selected Writings of Henry Hughes*; Kaufman, *Capitalism, Slavery, and Republican Values*; Genovese and Fox-Genovese, "Slavery, Economic Development, and the Law."

69. Fee, "Science and the Woman Problem."

70. E.g., McCord, "Enfranchisement of Woman," p. 325.

71. McCord, "Woman and Her Needs," p. 282, and "Enfranchisement of Woman," p. 234. See also Genovese and Fox-Genovese, "Religious Ideals of Southern Slave Society"; Fox-Genovese and Genovese, "Old South Considered as a Religious Society."

72. McCord, "Woman and Her Needs," p. 278. In fact, she hedged on the question, sometimes claiming that at least some women (she had to take account of herself) were as intelligent as men, sometimes suggesting that there might be innate differences for which discrepancies in education could not account. See also A. G. M., "Condition of Woman"; "Women Physiologically Considered"; and "Men and Women of the Eighteenth Century."

73. McCord, "Enfranchisement of Woman," pp. 322, 330.

74. Ibid., 324–25, 332, 334; McCord, "Woman and Her Needs," p. 275.

75. McCord, "Woman and Her Needs," p. 268, and "Enfranchisement of Woman," p. 326.

76. McCord, "Woman and Her Needs," p. 289.

77. On Beecher, see Sklar, *Catharine Beecher*, pp. 244–57, esp. 246–47.

78. For a sample of Louisa McCord's views on slavery and the races, see "Negro and White Slavery" and "Diversity of the Races." See also Nott, "Dr. Nott's Reply to 'C'"; J. T., "Negro Mania"; "North and the South"; Baldwin, *Dominion*; C. M. T., "Diversity and Origins"; E. H. B., "Political Philosophy of South Caro-

lina"; N., "State of Georgia"; R., "Agricultural Prospects"; Beta, "Cartwright on Negroes"; E. M. S., "Emancipation in the British West Indies"; N. B. P., "Treatment of Slaves"; "Is Southern Civilization Worth Preserving?"; "Prospects before Us." On the developing views of James Henley Thornwell, see Palmer, *Life and Letters*.

79. McCord, *Caius Gracchus*, act 5, sc. 1. On the mother of the Gracchi, see Wiltse, *John C. Calhoun: Nullifier*, p. 70. The *Ladies Magazine*, the first Georgia publication for women, proclaimed in its announcement that mothers were the key educators and cited Cornelia and her jewels—her sons (Savannah, Ga., 1819). See Fleming, *Early Georgia Magazines*, p. 14.

80. McCord, *Caius Gracchus*, act 5, sc. 1.

81. See Hayne's "Speech on Mr. Foote's Resolution," 21 Jan. 1830, as quoted, with approbation, in Washington, "Social System of Virginia"; Tucker, *Series of Lectures on the Science of Government*, p. 371; Perry, *Writings*, 2:59.

Chapter 6

1. See, among many, Genovese, *Roll, Jordan, Roll*, esp. pp. 494–501; Blassingame, *Slave Community*, pp. 3–48; Owens, *This Species of Property*, pp. 136–81; Levine, *Black Culture*, pp. 3–81; Gutman, *Black Family*, pp. 340–43. For work on slave women in particular, see White, *Ar'n't I a Woman?* and "Female Slaves"; and, for the attempt to establish an appropriate Pan-African context, Steady, *Black Woman Cross-Culturally*.

2. White, "Female Slaves," pp. 248–61, and "Ain't I a Woman?" The mammy figured widely in the diaries, journals, and letters of southern women. Meta Morris Grimball and Louisa McCord had mammies for their children; Eliza Clitherall had a mammy for her daughter; Mrs. John A. Wade remembered having had a mammy as a child; even such a redoubtable opponent of slavery as Mary Minor Blackford had her Mamm' Peggy. For references to mammies and nurses, see chaps. 2, 3, 4, and 5 above.

3. On "Jezebel" and "Mammy," see White, *Ar'n't I a Woman?*, pp. 27–51. Also see Foster, "Changing Concepts of the Black Woman"; Parkhurst, "Role of the Black Mammy."

4. The best-known passage is cited in chap. 1 above. The text is reprinted in Loewenberg and Bogin, *Black Women in Nineteenth-Century American Life*, pp. 235–36. The original was privately printed in Boston in 1854. See also Gilbert, *Sojourner Truth's Narrative*.

5. See chap. 1 above, and also Fox-Genovese, "Antebellum Southern Households." See also White, "Female Slaves" and *Ar'n't I a Woman?*, pp. 62–90; Hine and Wittenstein, "Female Slave Resistance"; Davis, "Reflections on the Black Woman's Role."

6. Davis, *Plantation Life*, pp. 49, 50; Lizzie Barker, *North Carolina Narratives*, vol. 14, pt. 1, p. 67; Victoria Adams, *South Carolina Narratives*, vol. 2, pt. 1, p. 10. Throughout his diary, Bennet H. Barrow regularly refers to the work done by his hands as if they were assigned tasks and worked in groups by gender—e.g., "women spinning." On the gender division of labor among slaves, see chap. 3 above.

7. Mary Boykin Chesnut and other women of the slaveholding class could be vehement on the ubiquity and destructiveness of white men's exploitation of slave women. But the most direct expression of a slave woman's own refusal to accept such domination can be found in *ILSG*.

8. Kolchin, *Unfree Labor*, pp. 195–240, and "Reevaluating the Antebellum Slave Community"; Genovese, *Roll, Jordan, Roll*, pp. 7–25, 73–75, 133–49; Levine, *Black Culture*, pp. 3–5, 133–35; Stuckey, *Slave Culture*, chap. 1, and "Through the Prism of Folklore."

9. Genovese, *World the Slaveholders Made*; Tannenbaum, *Slave and Citizen*; Mintz, *Caribbean Transformations* and "Economic Role and Cultural Tradition"; Gonzalez, *Black Carib Household Structure*, pp. 50–54; Clarke, *My Mother Who Fathered Me*; Justus, "Women's Role in West Indian Society"; Moses, "Female Status."

10. Stone, *Family, Sex, and Marriage*; Trumbach, *Rise of the Egalitarian Family*; Flandrin, *Families in Former Times*; Fox-Genovese and Genovese, *Fruits of Merchant Capital*, pp. 90–135, 299–336.

11. For an excellent discussion of the ways in which conquerors can manipulate and refashion a conquered people's sense of the relations between women and men, see Silverblatt, *Moon, Sun, and Witches*. See also Mullin, "Women, and the Comparative Study of American Negro Slavery."

12. Berlin et al., *The Black Military Experience*, p. 672.

13. Ibid.; Litwack, *Been in the Storm So Long*, pp. 245–47; Gutman, *Black Family*, pp. 165–68; Jones, *Labor of Love*, pp. 11–78; Drago, "Black Household"; Frankel, "Workers, Wives, and Mothers"; Horton, "Freedom's Yoke"; Franklin, *Free Negro in North Carolina*; Johnson and Roark, *Black Masters*, pp. 209–70; Brooks, "Women's Movement in the Black Church"; Frazier, *Black Bourgeoisie*.

14. White, *Ar'n't I a Woman?*, pp. 119–41; Hopkins, *Economic History of West Africa*.

15. Hopkins, *Economic History of West Africa*, pp. 18–27.

16. Brooks, "*Signares* of Saint-Louis and Goree"; Robertson, "Ga Women and Socioeconomic Change"; Mullings, "Women and Economic Change in Africa"; Gessain, "Coniagui Women"; Dupire, "Position of Women in a Pastoral Society"; Lebeuf, "Role of Women in the Political Organization of African Societies"; Boserup, *Woman's Role in Economic Development*; Hopkins, *Economic History of West Africa*, p. 21; Bay, "Servitude and Worldly Success."

17. For a view of African women as the independent representatives of a distinct woman's sphere, see Van Allen, " 'Aba Riots' or Igbo 'Women's War'?" and " 'Sitting on a Man.' " On women and the slave trade, see MacCormack, "Slaves, Slave Owners, and Slave Dealers"; Brooks, "Nhara of the Guinea-Bissau Region"; Mouser, "Women Slavers of Guinea-Conakry." On the significance of the persistence of African gender and property relations for women's identity in the Caribbean, see Moses, "Female Status." For a perceptive general discussion of women in African society, see Bozzoli, "Marxism, Feminism, and South Africa." On women in peasant societies, see Segalen, *Mari et femme*; Bennett, *Women in the Medieval English Countryside*; Fox-Genovese, "Women and Work."

18. Meillassoux, "Female Slavery." See also Davis, *Problem of Slavery in Western Culture*, esp. pp. 58–61, and *Problem of Slavery in the Age of Revolution*, esp. pp. 39–49.

19. Meillassoux, "Female Slavery"; Elkins, *Slavery*; Patterson, *Slavery and Social Death*, esp. pp. 38–45.

20. Harding, *There Is a River*, pp. 3–23 passim.; Mannix and Cowley, *Black Cargoes*, pp. 104–30; Davidson, *African Slave Trade*; Greene, "Mutiny on Slave Ships"; Wax, "Negro Resistance"; Klein, "African Women in the Atlantic Slave Trade." Donnan, *Documents Illustrative of the Slave Trade*, includes many references to women's activities on the middle passage.

21. Lee, "Problem of the Slave Community"; Wood, *Black Majority*, pp. 131–66; Morgan, *American Slavery, American Freedom*, esp. pp. 295–337; Bruce, *Economic History of Virginia*, 2:57–130; McGowan, "Creation of a Slave Society"; Holmes, "Abortive Slave Revolt at Pointe Coupee"; Dorman, "Persistent Spectre"; Kulikoff, *Tobacco and Slaves*, esp. pp. 317–80.

22. For the debate over the formation of the slave community, see Kulikoff, *Tobacco and Slaves*, "Origins of Afro-American Society," "A 'Prolifick' People," and "Beginnings of the Afro-American Family"; Lee, "Problem of the Slave Community"; Cody, "Slave Demography and Family Formation." On gender, see Norton, "Gender and Defamation"; Gundersen, "Double Bonds." On maroon societies, see Price, *Maroon Societies*; Genovese, *From Rebellion to Revolution*; Aptheker, *American Negro Slave Revolts*, "Additional Data on American Maroons," "Maroons within the Present Limits of the United States," and *To Be Free*, pp. 11–30. For a comparative perspective, see, e.g., Debien, "Marronage aux Antilles"; Kopytoff, "Jamaican Maroon Political Organization" and "Early Political Development of Jamaican Maroon Societies"; Sheridan, "Jamaican Slave Insurrection Scare"; Patterson, "Slavery and Slave Revolts." On the relations of slaves with poor whites and Indians, see Wood, *Black Majority*, pp. 40–42, 48, 54–55, 115–18; McGowan, "Creation of a Slave Society"; Klein, "Ordering the Back Country" and *Unification of a Slave State*; Brown, *South Carolina Regulators*. For specific examples of women's leadership in eighteenth-century revolts, see Harding, *There Is a River*, p. 39; Catterall, *Judicial Cases*, 3:424. See also Wood, *Black Majority* (on cases of arson, poisoning, etc.); Mullin, *Flight and Rebellion* (on runaways and, esp. p. 40, on the ratio of women to men); Meaders, "South Carolina Fugitives"; Johnson, "Runaway Slaves and the Slave Communities"; Phillips, *Plantation and Frontier Documents*, 2:90, 93; Gregory, "Black Women in Pre-Federal America." Benjamin Quarles includes passing references to women but focuses on black men's participation in the war (*Negro in the American Revolution*, e.g., pp. 27, 120–21).

23. Harding, *There Is a River*, pp. 39, 61; Catterall, *Judicial Cases*, 3:424; Wood, "'Until You Are Dead, Dead, Dead.'" See also Wood, *Black Majority*, p. 292, and "'The Dream Deferred'"; Aptheker, *American Negro Slave Revolts*, pp. 189–90, 242, 281, 90–91.

24. Wood, *Black Majority*, p. 241; Mullin, *Flight and Rebellion*, p. 40; Wood, "Some Aspects of Female Slave Resistance." In addition, see Meaders, "South Carolina Fugitives"; Windley, *Runaway Slave Advertisements*.

25. Phillips, *Plantation and Frontier Documents*, 2:90, 93; Gregory, "Black Women in Pre-Federal America." Betty Wood ("Some Aspects of Female Slave Resistance") finds that women constituted 24 percent of all runaways during the Revolutionary period.

26. Wood, *Black Majority*, pp. 324–25.

27. Harding, *There Is a River*, p. 35. Vincent Harding, like Herbert Aptheker

(*American Negro Slave Revolts*) and Peter Wood (*Black Majority*), does not make a point of women's absence from these military bands, but the evidence of all three clearly indicates that women did not participate in them. But, as Aptheker and Harding show, women clearly did participate in other kinds of collective risings. See also Horsmanden, *New York Conspiracy*. On women's political roles in Africa, see Aidoo, "Asante Queen Mothers in Government and Politics"; Broadhead, "Slave Wives, Free Sisters"; Lebeuf, "Role of Women in the Political Organization of African Societies"; Obbo, *African Women*, pp. 39–50; Davidson, *Black Mother*, e.g., 151–52, and *History of West Africa*; Lovejoy, *Transformations in Slavery*, esp. pp. 66–87, 108–28. A variety of recent works point to African traditions of gender-based associations. On women's relation to warfare in Europe, see Hacker, "Women and Military Institutions." See also Kuyk, "African Derivation of Black Fraternal Orders"; Jules-Rosette, "Women in Indigenous African Cults and Churches" (which focuses on the recent past and the contemporary period).

28. Phillips, *Plantation and Frontier Documents*, 2:118–19. See also chap. 3 above; Davis, *Plantation Life*; Phillips, *Plantation and Frontier Documents*, 1:213–14; Nicholas Bryor Massenburg Books, SHC.

29. Morgan, "Black Life." See Pope-Hennesey, *Sins of the Fathers*, p. 65; Levine, *Black Culture*, pp. 64–66; references to the narratives in chap. 3 above, on women's transmission of knowledge of herbs.

30. Wood, *Black Majority*, pp. 290, 292; Cooper and McCord, *Statutes at Large of South Carolina*, 7:422–23. See also Hawes, "Minute Book," pp. 251–53; Pope-Hennesey, *Sins of the Fathers*, p. 227; Brackett, *Negro in Maryland*, pp. 132–33; Aptheker, *American Negro Slave Revolts*, pp. 143–44, 198; Henry, *Police Control*.

31. Phillips, *Plantation and Frontier Documents*, 2:113. The citation is from the "Memorial of the Citizens of Charleston to the Senate and House of Representatives of the State of South Carolina [Charleston 1822]."

32. Aptheker, *American Negro Slave Revolts*, pp. 293–324; Harding, *There Is a River*. See also, among many, Wade, "Vesey Plot"; Starobin, "Denmark Vesey's Slave Conspiracy"; Freehling, *Prelude to Civil War*, pp. 53–60; *An Account of the Late Intended Insurrection*; Carroll, *Slave Insurrections*, pp. 83–117; Lofton, *Insurrection in South Carolina*; Duff and Mitchell, *Nat Turner Rebellion*; Foner, *Nat Turner*; Morris, "Panic and Reprisal"; Oates, *Fires of Jubilee*; Higginson, *Black Rebellion*. For contemporaneous testimony, see Killens, *Trial Record of Denmark Vesey*; Tragle, *Southampton Slave Revolts*. The records of the Gabriel Prosser revolt have recently become available at the University of Virginia. On Afro-American slave revolts in the southern colonies and states, see, among many, Aptheker, *American Negro Slave Revolts*; Harding, *There Is a River*; Genovese, *From Rebellion to Revolution* and *Roll, Jordan, Roll*, pp. 587–660; Wish, "American Slave Insurrections"; Blassingame, *Slave Community*, pp. 192–222; Levine, *Black Culture*, pp. 75–77; Owens, *This Species of Property*, pp. 70–105; Rawick, *From Sundown to Sunup*, pp. 95–121. For a recent overview and a good bibliography, see Boles, *Black Southerners*, pp. 140–81. For the pioneering work of Carter G. Woodson and his colleagues at the *Journal of Negro History*, see Goggin, "Carter G. Woodson."

33. For a recent summary of views on Nanny, see Mathurin, *Rebel Woman*; Tuelon, "Nanny—Maroon Chieftainess"; Williams, *Maroons of Jamaica*, pp. 379–480. It should be noted that Nanny may not have been a real woman, but rather a persona created to protect the identities of male rebel leaders. For a similar phe-

nomenon in Great Britain, see Williams, *Rebecca Riots*; for an overview of women's roles in social protest in early modern Europe, see Thomis and Grimmet, *Women in Protest*, esp. pp. 138–46. On the Igbo "Women's War," see Van Allen, "'Aba Riots' or Igbo 'Women's War'?" and "'Sitting on a Man.'" See also Hufton, "Women in Revolution" and "Women and the Family Economy." See also Johnson, "Old Wine in New Bottles." The literature on African women in the seventeenth and eighteenth centuries remains sparse, but for illuminating discussions of the gender relations of modern Africa, see the essays in Hafkin and Bay, *Women in Africa*; Paulme, *Women of Tropical Africa*; Leith-Ross, *African Women*; Obbo, *African Women*; Steady, *Black Woman Cross-Culturally*, esp. the section on Africa; Robertson and Klein, *Women and Slavery in Africa*. For a pioneering statement of the cultural manifestations of gender relations, see Davis, *Society and Culture*, pp. 124–51. For the persistence of African patterns in the Caribbean, see Mintz and Hall, "Origins of the Jamaican Internal Marketing System."

34. The most recent and most fully developed version of this position is found in White, *Ar'n't I a Woman?*, pp. 76–84. See also Davis, "Reflections on the Black Woman's Role"; Jones, "'My Mother Was Much of a Woman'"; Drago, "Militancy and Black Women"; and Steady, "Black Woman Cross-Culturally."

35. Ida Henry, *Oklahoma Narratives*, vol. 7, pt. 1, p. 135; Douglas Dorsey, *Florida Narratives*, vol. 17, pp. 94–95; Hannah Plummer, *North Carolina Narratives*, vol. 15, pt. 2, pp. 178–82. See also Ella Johnson, *Georgia Narratives*, supp. ser. 1, vol. 4, pt. 2, p. 347.

36. Tempe Pitts, *North Carolina Narratives*, vol. 15, pt. 2, pp. 174–76; Anonymous, *Tennessee Narratives*, vol. 18, p. 134; Leigh, *Ten Years*. See also Dennett, *South as It Is*, esp. pp. 175–77.

37. Lou Smith, *Oklahoma Narratives*, vol. 7, pt. 1, p. 301; Easter Wells, *Oklahoma Narratives*, vol. 7, pt. 1, p. 317.

38. Harriet Robinson, *Oklahoma Narratives*, vol. 7, pt. 1, p. 271; Dave Lawson, *North Carolina Narratives*, vol. 15, pt. 2, p. 45; Josie Jordan, *Oklahoma Narratives*, vol. 7, pt. 1, p. 161; Fanny Cannady, *North Carolina Narratives*, vol. 14, pt. 1, p. 160. See also Brackett, *Negro in Maryland*, p. 133.

39. Susan Shaw, *Mississippi Narratives*, supp. ser. 1, vol. 10, pt. 5, pp. 2003–4; Lila Nichols, *North Carolina Narratives*, vol. 15, pt. 2, p. 149; Eliza Washington, *Arkansas Narratives*, vol. 11, pt. 7, p. 54.

40. Drew, *Refugee*, p. 156; Ellen Cragin, *Arkansas Narratives*, vol. 8, pt. 2, p. 42.

41. Mary Armstrong, *Texas Narratives*, vol. 4, pt. 1, pp. 25–26; Rachel O'Connor to A. T. Conrad, 26 May 1836, Weeks Papers, LSU; Olmsted, *Journey in the Seaboard Slave States*, p. 194. See also DuBois, *Biography of the Slav Who Whipt Her Mistres*.

42. E.g., Morris Hillyer, *Oklahoma Narratives*, vol. 7, pt. 1, p. 138; Lizzie Barnett, *Arkansas Narratives*, vol. 8, pt. 2, p. 113. On the general phenomenon, see Bauer and Bauer, "Day to Day Resistance."

43. Fannie Dorum, *Arkansas Narratives*, vol. 8, pt. 2, p. 181. See also Sophie Word, *Kentucky Narratives*, vol. 16, pt. 2, p. 67; Rachel Fairley, *Arkansas Narratives*, vol. 8, pt. 2, p. 258; Mary (Jeffreys) Bethell Diary, 22 June 1862, SHC. On slaves' attitudes toward theft, see Genovese, *Roll, Jordan, Roll*, pp. 599–612.

44. Catterall, *Judicial Cases*, 2:241–42; Eliza L. Magruder Diary, 26 July 1857, LSU; Smiley, *Lion of White Hall*, p. 71; Manigault Plantation Record Book, 22

Mar. 1867, Manigault Papers, DU; *PMC*, p. 394 (15 Mar. 1864); Lila Nichols, *North Carolina Narratives*, vol. 15, pt. 2, p. 148. On poisoning, see also Jake McCleod, *South Carolina Narratives*, vol. 3, pt. 3, p. 158; Scarborough, *Overseer*, p. 172; Phillips, "Slave Crime in Virginia," p. 338; Francis Terry Leak Diary, 31 July 1852, Francis Terry Leak Books, SHC.

45. Bassett, *Southern Plantation Overseer*; Scarborough, *Overseer*, pp. 97–101. See also Lucindy Allison, *Arkansas Narratives*, vol. 8, pt. 1, p. 42; Katherine Clay, *Arkansas Narratives*, vol. 8, pt. 2, p. 13.

46. Lily Perry, *North Carolina Narratives*, vol. 15, pt. 2, p. 163; Martha Bradley, *Alabama Narratives*, vol. 6, pt. 1, p. 46; Waters Brooks, *Arkansas Narratives*, vol. 8, pt. 1, p. 255. On the organization of field slaves by gender, see chap. 3 above; Davis, *Plantation Life* (refers throughout to "women" doing thus and so—frequently, but by no means exclusively, spinning); "Extracts from the journal of the manager of Belmead Plantation, Powhatan County, Virginia, 1854," in Phillips, *Plantation and Frontier Documents*, e.g., 1:211–14 ("Women cleaning water furrows," "Women open water furrow," "Ben and Women grubbing the Land too hard frozen to plough"); Joyner, *Down by the Riverside*, esp. pp. 61–63. The same tendency to speak of work as being segregated by gender appears in innumerable manuscript sources, e.g., Nicholas Bryor Massenburg Books, SHC. On women's work experience, see also White, *Ar'n't I a Woman?*.

47. Irene Coates, *Florida Narratives*, vol. 17, p. 76.

48. Ruben Laird, *Mississippi Narratives*, supp. ser. 1, vol. 8, pt. 3, p. 1299; Josie Jordan, *Oklahoma Narratives*, vol. 7, pt. 1, pp. 160–61.

49. Chana Littlejohn, *North Carolina Narratives*, vol. 15, pt. 2, p. 57; Catterall, *Judicial Cases*, 2:206–7. On women's networks, see also White, *Ar'n't I a Woman?*, pp. 119–41, and esp. "Female Slaves."

50. Fannie Alexander, *Arkansas Narratives*, vol. 8, pt. 1, p. 30; Annie Coley, *Mississippi Narratives*, vol. 7, pt. 2, pp. 441–42.

51. Douglass, *Narrative*; Northup, *Twelve Years a Slave*; Craft and Craft, "Running a Thousand Miles for Freedom"; Brown, *Slave Life in Georgia*; Henson, *Autobiography*.

52. Joe Rollins, *Mississippi Narratives*, supp. ser. 1, vol. 9, pt. 4, p. 1892; Celestia Avery, *Georgia Narratives*, vol. 12, pt. 1, p. 23; Mattie Fannen, *Arkansas Narratives*, vol. 8, pt. 2, p. 265; Julia Green, *Arkansas Narratives*, vol. 9, pt. 3, p. 65; Sarah Wells, *Arkansas Narratives*, vol. 11, pt. 7, p. 90; Martha Jackson, *Alabama Narratives*, vol. 6, pt. 1, p. 220.

53. Evie Harris, *Mississippi Narratives*, supp. ser. 1, vol. 8, pt. 3, p. 988; L. B. Barnes, *Oklahoma Narratives*, supp. ser. 1, vol. 12, pt. 1, p. 38; Clayborn Gaitling, *Florida Narratives*, vol. 17, p. 141. See also Granny Cain, *South Carolina Narratives*, vol. 1, pt. 1, p. 166.

54. Hamp Kennedy, *Mississippi Narratives*, supp. ser. 1, vol. 8, pt. 3, p. 1270; Rulen Fox, *Mississippi Narratives*, supp. ser. 1, vol. 7, pt. 2, p. 777; John Elliott, *Arkansas Narratives*, vol. 8, pt. 2, p. 236; Nancy Thomas, *Texas Narratives*, supp. ser. 2, vol. 9, pt. 8, p. 3810. See also Sally Brown, *Georgia Narratives*, supp. ser. 1, vol. 3, pt. 1, p. 102; Cicely Cawthon, *Georgia Narratives*, supp. ser. 1, vol. 3, pt. 1, p. 189.

55. Campbell, "Work, Pregnancy, and Infant Mortality."

56. Anna Baker, *Mississippi Narratives*, vol. 7, pt. 2, p. 13.

57. Lou Smith, *Oklahoma Narratives*, vol. 7, pt. 1, p. 302; Celia Robinson, *North Carolina Narratives*, vol. 15, pt. 2, pp. 217–19; Mary (Jeffreys) Bethell Diary, 6 June 1860, SHC; Hine and Wittenstein, "Female Slave Resistance"; Johnson, "Smothered Slave Infants."

58. If the court records and slaveholders' papers abound with references to slave women's killing—or "smothering"—their infants, recent work on Sudden Infant Death Syndrome (SIDS) and work loads suggests that not all infant slave deaths should be attributed to killing. See Steckel, "Miscegenation and the American Slave Schedules"; Campbell, "Work, Pregnancy, and Infant Mortality"; Hine and Wittenstein, "Female Slave Resistance"; Johnson, "Smothered Slave Infants," pp. 510–15. Michael Johnson has clearly established the importance of SIDS as a cause of slave infant deaths, but some sources also suggest that at least some slave women did commit infanticide, by smothering as well as other methods (Bauer and Bauer, "Day to Day Resistance"). Angela Davis ("Reflections on the Black Women's Role") and Bell Hooks (*Ain't I a Woman?*) emphasize the sexual exploitation of slave women, but they do not discuss its relation to slave women's resistance. See also Catterall, *Judicial Cases*, 1:84; White, "Ain't I a Woman?" and "Female Slaves." In *Beloved*, Toni Morrison offers a powerful picture of the possible psychological dynamics of the consequences of slavery for slave women's attitudes.

59. Lt. L. Bost, *North Carolina Narratives*, vol. 14, pt. 1, p. 142; Martha R. Jackson Diary, 22 July 1834, SHC; Gutman, *Black Family*, pp. 185–229; Cody, "Naming, Kinship, and Estate Dispersal" and "There Was No 'Absalom' on the Ball Plantations"; Wood, *Black Majority*, pp. 181–85; Joyner, *Down by the Riverside*, pp. 217–22; Genovese, *Roll, Jordan, Roll*, pp. 443–50.

60. Eliza Washington, *Arkansas Narratives*, vol. 11, pt. 7, p. 54.

61. Anonymous, *Georgia Narratives*, vol. 13, pt. 4, p. 295; Annie Young, *Oklahoma Narratives*, vol. 7, pt. 1, p. 362. See also Celia Robinson, *North Carolina Narratives*, vol. 15, pt. 2, pp. 217–19; Simuel Riddick, *North Carolina Narratives*, vol. 15, pt. 2, p. 208; Jacob Manson, *North Carolina Narratives*, vol. 15, pt. 2, p. 97; Lizzie Williams, *North Carolina Narratives*, vol. 15, p. 2, p. 396; Hattie Rogers, *North Carolina Narratives*, vol. 15, pt. 2, pp. 227–31; Solomon Oliver, *Oklahoma Narratives*, vol. 7, pt. 1, p. 233; Lucretia Alexander, *Arkansas Narratives*, vol. 8, pt. 1, pp. 35–36.

62. Supreme Court of Alabama, *Toulmin* v. *Chadwick*, 1861, quoted in Sellers, *Slavery in Alabama*, p. 226; Davidson, "Record of Inquisitions," 31 Dec. 1833, DU. On the law of slavery, see, e.g., O'Neall, *Negro Law of South Carolina*; Cobb, *Inquiry into the Law of Negro Slavery*; Genovese, *Roll, Jordan, Roll*, pp. 25–49; Tushnet, *American Law of Slavery*, esp. pp. 158–69.

63. Annie Tate, *North Carolina Narratives*, vol. 15, pt. 2, p. 333; Lily Perry, *North Carolina Narratives*, vol. 15, pt. 2, pp. 163–66; Sallie Carder, *Oklahoma Narratives*, supp. ser. 1, vol. 12, pt. 1, pp. 97–98; biographical sketch of H. C. Anderson by his granddaughter, Mrs. Rundle Smith, Harrod C. Anderson Papers, LSU.

64. For examples, see Catterall, *Judicial Cases*, 3:86, 89–90, 160, 210, 594; Davis, *Plantation Life*, pp. 85, 98, 125, 139, 183, 202, 324, 357, 435. See also Sidney D. Bumpas Journal, 19 May 1843, SHC; McDonnell, "Slave against Slave."

65. McDonnell, "Slave against Slave."

66. See, e.g., Sobel, *Trabelin' On*; Raboteau, *Slave Religion*; Genovese, *Roll, Jordan, Roll*; Touchstone, "Planters and Slave Religion."

67. Fannie Moore, *North Carolina Narratives*, vol. 15, pt. 2, p. 130.

68. Nancy Rogers Bean, *Oklahoma Narratives*, vol. 7, pt. 1, p. 13; T. W. Cotton, *Arkansas Narratives*, vol. 8, pt. 2, p. 40; Charlotte Foster, *South Carolina Narratives*, vol. 2, pt. 2, p. 81.

69. Richard Mocks, *Maryland Narratives*, vol. 16, pt. 3, p. 53.

70. Lee Guidon, *Arkansas Narratives*, vol. 9, pt. 3, p. 121; Catterall, *Judicial Cases*, 1:84. See also Susan Davis (Nye) Hutchinson Diary, 29 Sept., 12 Nov. 1829, SHC; Mrs. Isaac Hilliard Diary, 19 June 1850, LSU.

71. E.g., White, "Ain't I a Woman?"; Lebsock, "Free Black Women." Most comparisons between the experience of black and white women concern the postbellum period, e.g., Neverdon-Morton, "Black Woman's Struggle for Equality"; Terborg-Penn, "Discrimination against Afro-American Women." Filomina Chioma Steady (*Black Woman Cross-Culturally*) provides a comparative perspective on the experiences of African and Afro-American women, but not on the role of women in revolts in the different New World societies. Richard Price (*Maroon Societies*) provides information on women in different maroon societies. See also Berkin and Lovett, *Women, War, and Revolution*; Urdang, *Fighting Two Colonialisms*; Minces, "Women in Algeria"; Phillip, "Feminism and Nationalist Politics"; and Philipp, "Women and Revolution in Iran."

72. Fanon, "Algeria Unveiled," in *Dying Colonialism*, pp. 35–68.

73. Harding, *There Is a River*, p. 55 and throughout; Genovese, *Roll, Jordan, Roll*, pp. 232–55; Sobel, *Trabelin' On*, pp. 33–34.

74. Albert J. Raboteau, in *Slave Religion*, minimizes the role of women, but see his references on pp. 79 and 238. On associations, see Kuyk, "African Derivation of Black Fraternal Orders"; Jules-Rosette, "Women in Indigenous African Cults and Churches" (which focuses on the recent past and the contemporary period). See also White, "Female Slaves."

75. Daniel Goddard, *South Carolina Narratives*, vol. 2, pt. 2, p. 150; Maria Tilden Thompson, *Texas Narratives*, supp. ser. 2, vol. 9, pt. 8, p. 3859; Elizabeth Russell, *Indiana Narratives*, supp. ser. 1, vol. 5, p. 180.

76. Thus we cannot assume that slave women's participation in revolts derived directly from a specific African heritage. For slave women in the Caribbean, see Bush, "Towards Emancipation" and " 'Family Tree Is Not Cut' "; Terborg-Penn, "Black Women in Resistance." For the discrete patterns of slave women's resistance in the United States, see Obitko, " 'Custodians of a House of Resistance' "; Fox-Genovese, "Strategies and Forms of Resistance."

77. Catterall, *Judicial Cases*, 2:57.

Chapter 7

1. Among the many discussions of this internal contradiction, see esp. Davis, *Problem of Slavery in the Age of Revolution*; Morgan, *American Slavery, American Freedom*. On the revolutionary tradition and republican motherhood, see Kerber, *Women of the Republic*; Norton, *Liberty's Daughters*; Lewis, "Republican Wife";

Bloch, "Gendered Meanings of Virtue"; Gundersen, "Independence, Citizenship, and the American Revolution." On women's appropriation of revolutionary rhetoric, see Dublin, *Women at Work*, pp. 93, 98–99. On the problem of women and individualism, see Kerber, "Can a Woman Be an Individual?"; Fox-Genovese, "Female Self in the Age of Bourgeois Individualism." On the seventeenth-century discussions, see Locke, *Two Treatises on Government*; Ezell, *Patriarch's Wife*; Fox-Genovese, "Property and Patriarchy."

2. Kerber, *Women of the Republic*; Cott, *Bonds of Womanhood*; Basch, "Equity vs. Equality"; Meckel, "Educating a Ministry"; Bloch, "American Feminine Ideals in Transition" and "Untangling the Roots of Modern Sex Roles"; Fox-Genovese, "Women, Affirmative Action, and the Myth of Individualism."

3. See, e.g., Basch, *In the Eyes of the Law*; Hersh, *Slavery of Sex*; DuBois, *Feminism and Suffrage*; Melder, *Beginnings of Sisterhood*; Griffith, *In Her Own Right*; Jensen, *Loosening the Bonds*. Even Lowell mill workers borrowed from this discourse (see Dublin, *Women at Work*).

4. See Davis, *Problem of Slavery in the Age of Revolution* and *Slavery and Human Progress*. See also Kerber, "Can a Woman Be an Individual?"; Fox-Genovese, "Women, Affirmative Action, and the Myth of Individualism" and "Female Self in the Age of Bourgeois Individualism"; Bloch, "Gendered Meanings of Virtue."

5. "Is Southern Civilization Worth Preserving?," p. 224.

6. For a good example, see Hentz, *Planter's Northern Bride*.

7. Fitzhugh, *Cannibals All!* and *Sociology for the South*; Genovese, *World the Slaveholders Made*, pt. 2 passim.

8. Porcher, "Southern and Northern Civilization Contrasted," p. 101. See also *MCCW*; *PMC*; *MBC*; Wall, "Letters of Mary Boykin Chesnut." Miss Abby, who began her diary on 1 January 1864, was an ardent Union sympathizer who deplored the abuses of the Confederate government and longed for the restoration of legitimate government, for the triumph of "truth" over "treason." Living near Atlanta, she knew many men who had deserted the Confederate army because their wives and children were without food. She deeply mistrusted the blacks and spoke neither of feminism nor abolitionism. See Miss Abby Diary, University of Georgia Library, Athens, Ga.; and, on the defections of the upcountry yeomanry, Robinson, "Day of Jubilo," pp. 522–80, and "Beyond the Realm of Social Consensus."

9. Faust, "Real Mary Chesnut."

10. *MBC*, pp. 12–17 (quote p. 15).

11. Ibid., pp. 18–25 (quote p. 18).

12. Ibid., pp. 25–42 (quote p. 29). For Mary Chesnut's own recollections, see Mary Boykin Chesnut, "A Boarding School Fifty Years Ago," Williams-Chesnut-Manning Papers, SCL; and the fictionalized but essentially autobiographical account, "Two Years—or the Way We Lived Then," which comprises part 3 of Muhlenfeld, "Mary Boykin Chesnut." For the letters of another young woman who attended Mme Talvande's, see Holman, "Charleston in the Summer of 1841." For a sensitive picture of young women's schooling in Charleston, see Stowe, "City, Country, and the Feminine Voice"; and, for a contemporaneous, fictional picture, see Hentz, *Eoline*.

13. *MBC*, pp. 43–49.

14. Ibid., pp. 47–59. The reference to James Chesnut's politics is taken from a private memoir by Mary Chesnut, quoted in *MBC*, p. 59.

15. *MBC*. See also, e.g., *MCCW*, p. 32 (19 Mar. 1861). For a contemporaneous picture of Washington political society, see Pryor, *Reminiscences of Peace and War*, pp. 3–92.

16. *PMC*, pp. 124, 130, 146 (13, 19, 29 Aug. 1861).

17. *MBC*, pp. 100–102, 129–30, 145–49.

18. *MCCW*, p. 23 (11 Mar. 1861).

19. Mary Boykin Chesnut to James Chesnut, Jr., 28 May 1850, Williams-Chesnut-Manning Papers, SCL, published in Wall, "Letters of Mary Boykin Chesnut."

20. *PMC*, p. 4 (18 Feb. 1861).

21. On Webster's dramatic speech in favor of the Compromise of 1850, see Nevins, *Ordeal of the Union*, pp. 286–91.

22. Thanks to the monumental efforts of C. Vann Woodward and Elisabeth Muhlenfeld, we now have a clear picture of the successive versions of the diary, including Mary Chesnut's substantial revisions of the manuscript and the various published forms. See *MCCW* and *PMC*.

23. I take great comfort that Carol Bleser, with her vast knowledge of the subject, has independently arrived at the same conclusion ("Southern Wives and Slavery"). See Avary, *Virginia Girl*, p. 1. See also, e.g., Anderson, *Brokenburn*, p. 13, in which Kate Stone opens her diary with a mention of her brother's departure: "He is wild to be off to Virginia."

24. *MCCW*, p. 15 (4 Mar. 1861).

25. *PMC*, p. 21 (4 Mar. 1861).

26. Ibid., pp. 20–21 (4 Mar. 1861).

27. *MCCW*, p. 15 (4 Mar. 1861).

28. Ibid., pp. 29, 31 (18 Mar. 1861). Cf. *PMC*, p. 42 (18 Mar. 1861).

29. *MCCW*, pp. 28, 31 (18 Mar. 1861). Cf. *PMC*, pp. 42–43 (18 Mar. 1861).

30. *PMC*, pp. 41, 44–45 (17, 21 Mar. 1861). Cf. *MCCW*, pp. 32–33 (19 Mar. 1861).

31. *MCCW*, p. 172 (29 Aug. 1861).

32. *PMC*, p. 145 (29 Aug. 1861).

33. Ibid.

34. *MCCW*, p. 32 (19 Mar. 1861).

35. *PMC*, p. 74 (30–31 May 1861); *MCCW*, p. 65 (27 May 1863).

36. She reports having taken opium on the same day of her entry on the "monstrous system" (*MCCW*, p. 29 [18 Mar. 1861]).

37. *PMC*, p. 207 (26 Nov. 1861); *MCCW*, p. 245 (27 Nov. 1861). Charles William Holbrook, a recent graduate of Williams College in Massachusetts who was serving as a tutor for the children of the Galloway brothers in North Carolina, reported that when Mr. Galloway first took up *Uncle Tom's Cabin* he admired it. The next day he wrote: "Mr. Galloway says he will burn 'Uncle Tom's Cabin.' He has changed his mind on it. Mrs. G. thinks Mrs. Stowe is worse than Legree!" (Hall, "Yankee Tutor in the South," p. 90 [15, 16 Oct. 1852]). See also "Stowe's Key to Uncle Tom's Cabin," esp. p. 249.

38. *MCCW*, p. 245 (27 Nov. 1861).

39. Ibid., pp. 246 (27 Nov. 1861), 428 (23 Sept. 1863); Hentz, *Planter's Northern Bride*. See also Genovese and Fox-Genovese, "Slavery, Economic Development, and the Law"; Fox-Genovese, "Slavery as the Solution to the Social Question"; Genovese, "Ordinary Slaveholders' Response."

40. *MCCW*, pp. 307–8 (13 Mar. 1862).

41. Ibid., pp. 715 (16 Feb. 1865), 127 (3 Aug. 1861), 59 (9 May 1861).

42. Ibid., pp. 307–8 (13 Mar. 1862), 381 (12 June 1862), 606 (8 May 1864).

43. McCord, "Uncle Tom's Cabin," pp. 83, 87–88, 90. For evidence that the more princely slave traders could achieve respectability and marry into the planter class, see Bancroft, *Slave Trading*; Stephenson, *Isaac Franklin*.

44. McCord, "Uncle Tom's Cabin," pp. 100, 101, 104.

45. Ibid., pp. 96, 90.

46. See, e.g., Hersh, *Slavery of Sex*; Hentz, *Planter's Northern Bride*; and, for a clerical view, Brownlow, *Ought American Slavery to Be Perpetuated*, pp. 160–69. Chesnut's one reference to Martineau can be found in a letter of 12 September 1886 to Sister [Virginia Caroline Tunstall] Clay: "Did you ever read Miss Martineau—well my heart Dr. Barrick says is identically effected like hers—think of my ever lasting ill luck Miss Martineau—old Ham[l]et's heart & not her head——" (Clement Claiborne Clay Family Papers, DU, published in Wall, "Letters of Mary Boykin Chesnut"). On Fuller, see *MCCW*, p. 43 (7 Apr. 1861).

47. *MCCW*, p. 168 (27 Aug. 1861). This passage does not figure at all in the original diary.

48. Ibid., pp. 168–70 (27 Aug. 1861).

49. Ibid., p. 170 (27 Aug. 1861).

50. *PMC*, p. 73 (26–28 May 1861); *MCCW*, p. 65 (27 May 1861). *Say and Seal* was published in 1860 under the pseudonyms "Elizabeth Wetherrell" and "Amy Lothrop," but it was written by Anna Bartlett Warner and Susan Bogert Warner. On domestic fiction, see Davidson, *Revolution and the Word*; Kelley, *Private Woman, Public Stage*; Tompkins, *Sensational Designs*; Papashvily, *All the Happy Endings*.

51. For a good introduction to the religious and legal plans for the reformation of slavery before and during the war, see Wiley, "Movement to Humanize." Well before the war, prominent southerners were calling for such sweeping reforms as the legalization of slave marriages, repeal of the laws against slave literacy, and stern punishment of cruel masters. Ministers like James Henley Thornwell, George Foster Pierce, and C. C. Jones and lawyers and jurists like T. R. R. Cobb and John Belton O'Neall led the way, although they and other such reformers firmly defended slavery as a system and insisted that its safety required an end to its "evils" and "abuses." See, e.g., Jones, *Religious Instruction of Negroes*. Miss Abby railed at the Confederate clergy's defense of the Cause: "I became only more & more embittered, by hearing from the pulpit such vile aspersions continually cast upon the government [by which she meant Washington]—such prayers for its destruction—such assertions that our 'cause is just, and a just God will crown it with success'" (Miss Abby Diary, 14 Feb. 1864, University of Georgia Library, Athens, Ga.). On Thornwell, see Farmer, *Metaphysical Confederacy*, and Palmer, *Life and Letters*. See also Smyth, *Sin and the Curse*, for the view that the Union was the true source of disunion.

52. Anna Matilda Page King to Thomas Butler King, 8 June 1849, and Georgia King to Fuddy King, 11 Nov. 1860, Thomas Butler King Papers, SHC. For another defense of southern institutions by a young woman, see Herd, "Sue Sparks Keitt." See also Stowe, *Intimacy and Power*, pp. 224–49 (for a discussion of the Kings' marriage); Bleser, "Southern Wives and Slavery."

53. Keziah Goodwyn Hopkins Brevard Diary, SCL.

54. Meriwether, *Recollections*; Blackford, *Mine Eyes Have Seen the Glory*; Clarence Mohr suggests that some Georgia women had moral qualms about slavery (*On the Threshold of Freedom*, pp. 264–68).

55. Ella Gertrude Clanton Thomas Diary, 11 Apr. 1855, DU. Mary Elizabeth Massey, in "Making of a Feminist," discusses Ella Gertrude Clanton Thomas's entire career. With great respect for her scholarship and insights, I see a sharper break than she does in Thomas's views. Thomas's postwar feminism seems to me to have constituted a long advance over her basically conventional antebellum social views.

56. Ella Gertrude Clanton Thomas Diary, 20 May 1855, 17 Apr. 1856, DU.

57. Ibid., 17, 20 Apr., 26 June 1856.

58. Ibid., 18 Aug. 1856, 16 Sept. 1857. See also Gaskell, *Ruth*.

59. Ibid., 8 Feb. 1858.

60. Susan Becton to Jane, 14 Dec. 1862, Susan Becton Letter, John Hall Private Collection, Columbia, S.C.

61. Ella Gertrude Clanton Thomas Diary, 15 July 1861, DU.

62. Crabtree and Patton, *Journal of a Secesh Lady*, p. 1 ([n.d.] 1860).

63. *MCCW*, p. 3 (18 Feb. 1861); *PMC*, p. 3 (18 Feb. 1861). Conecuh is the Alabama county in which her brother lived; Ems is her nickname for her mother, who lived with him.

Epilogue

1. Jean Fagan Yellin has authenticated the narrative, recovered extensive evidence of Jacobs's life, and published a superb edition of the narrative. Her edition, abbreviated here as *ILSG*, contains a fine introduction and rich documentation, including a selection of relevant correspondence. See also the correspondence between Harriet Jacobs and Amy Post, Post Family Papers, University of Rochester Library, Rochester, N.Y. In addition, see Yellin, "Written By Herself" and "Texts and Contexts"; and, for the context of Jacobs's experience in North Carolina, Franklin, *From Slavery to Freedom* and *Free Negro in North Carolina*. For Jacobs's writing in the context of that of other Afro-American women, see, e.g., Sterling, *We Are Your Sisters*; Andrews, *Sisters of the Spirit*; Wilson, *Our Nig*; Stewart, *Productions of Mrs. Maria Stewart*. Of the 130 extant narratives, only 16 were written by women, and most of them by free northern women. See the bibliography in Davis and Gates, *Slave's Narrative*, pp. 319–30. *Autobiography of a Female Slave* was written by Mattie Griffiths, a white southern woman. For an illuminating discussion of antebellum Afro-American women's autobiographical writings as the origin of a distinct Afro-American women's fictional tradition, see McCaskill, "'Eternity for Telling.'"

2. Douglass, *Narrative*. See also Douglass, *Life and Times* and *My Bondage and My Freedom*; Martin, *Mind of Frederick Douglass*. There is an extensive and growing literature on slave narratives and on Afro-American autobiography. See, e.g., Davis and Gates, *Slave's Narrative*; Sekora and Turner, *Art of Slave Narrative*; Stepto, *From Behind the Veil*; Starling, *Slave Narrative*; Baker, *Journey Back*.

3. *ILSG*, p. 16. On Afro-American women's autobiographical writings in this

perspective, see Fox-Genovese, "To Write Myself" and, for a development of the argument, "My Statue, My Self." On problems of readership, see, e.g., Tompkins, *Reader-Response Criticism*. On the reception of *Uncle Tom's Cabin* and larger problems of the community of readers, see Tompkins, *Sensational Designs*.

4. There are strong echoes of Samuel Richardson's *Pamela* in *Incidents*. Jacobs, who read widely, may well have read the novel, but if not, she had surely read much of the fiction that was influenced by it. See Smith-Rosenberg, "Misprisioning Pamela." On domestic fiction, women's culture, and slavery, see esp. Brown, "Getting in the Kitchen with Dinah"; Douglas, *Feminization of American Culture* and introduction to Stowe, *Uncle Tom's Cabin*; Tompkins, *Sensational Designs*.

5. *ILSG*, pp. 3–4. Throughout I will distinguish between Harriet Jacobs and Linda Brent. Even if the fictional name represented only an attempt at disguise, so that Jacobs could simply be substituted for Brent, the problems of the relation between author and textual self-representation that surround any autobiographical writing would persist. For my views on the problem and references to relevant literature, see Fox-Genovese, *Autobiography of Du Pont de Nemours*, intro. Beyond those basic problems, I see more reason than Jean Yellin does to credit Jacobs with self-conscious craft, and even artifice, in her representation of herself.

6. *ILSG*, p. 9. Hereafter, pages will be cited parenthetically in the text.

7. Gloria Watkins [Bell Hooks], to whom I am indebted for conversations on these and related matters, would argue that the silence at the center of the narrative veils Linda Brent's rape by her master. For a thoughtful discussion of the theme of sexual purity that differs somewhat from my own, see Taves, "Spiritual Purity and Sexual Shame."

Bibliography

Manuscript Sources

Athens, Georgia
Hargrett Rare Book and Manuscript Library, University of Georgia
　Miss Abby Diary

Atlanta, Georgia
Atlanta Historical Society
　Winship-Flournoy Family Papers
Georgia Department of Archives and History
　Iraminta Antoinette Alexander Papers
　William Few Collection
　Hamilton/Kendall Family Letters
　Seaborn Hawks Plantation Book
　Ann Matilda Page King Plantation Record Book
　Morcock/Baldy/Smith/Williams Family Papers
　Ogletree Family Papers
　Mary Elizabeth (Lizzie) Osborn (Ozburn) Family Papers
　Aaron Smith Family Papers
Robert W. Woodruff Library, Emory University
　"Catalogues." (Select List of College Catalogs)

Auburn, Alabama
Auburn University Archives
　Tait Collection

Austin, Texas
Eugene C. Barker Texas History Center, University of Texas
　Wade, Mrs. John W. "Recollections of an Octogenarian"

Baltimore, Maryland
Maryland Historical Society
　Hollyday Family Papers

Baton Rouge, Louisiana
Louisiana and Lower Mississippi Valley Collections, Louisiana State University
Library
    Harrod C. Anderson Papers
    H. M. Beale Diary
    Broidrick, Annie Laurie. "A Recollection of Thirty Years Ago"
    Emily Caroline Douglas Papers
    Farrar Family Papers
    Mrs. Isaac Hilliard Diary
    Franklin Hudson Diaries, John H. Randolph Papers
    LeBlanc Family Papers
    Eliza L. Magruder Diary
    Eliza Ann Marsh Diary
    James Monette Day Book and Diary
    Louise Taylor Pharr Manuscripts, Pharr Family Papers
        Watts, Amelia Thompson. "A Summer on a Louisiana Cotton Plantation in
            1832"
    Pugh Plantation Diary
    H. M. Seale Diary
    Sarah Clinton Southall Diary
    John C. Tibbetts Correspondence
    Samuel Walker Diary
    Weeks Family Papers

Chapel Hill, North Carolina
Southern Historical Collection, University of North Carolina Library
    Samuel Andrew Agnew Diary
    James W. Albright Books
    John Durant Ashmore Book
    Everard Green Baker Diary
    Mary E. Bateman Diary
    Bayne and Gayle Family Papers
        Sarah A. (Haynsworth) Gayle Journal
    Bayside Plantation Records
    Beale and Davis Family Papers
        Anne Turberville (Beale) Davis Journal
    Taylor Beatty Books
        Charlotte Beatty Diary
        Walter Reid Memorandum
    Mary (Jeffreys) Bethell Diary
    John Houston Bills Papers
    Bumpas Family Papers
        Frances Moore (Webb) Bumpas Diary
        Sidney D. Bumpas Journal
    Todd Robinson Caldwell Papers
    Francis McMillan Carmack Diary
    Carmichael Family Books
        Mary Eliza (Eve) Carmichael Diary

Kate S. Carney Diary
Mary Clay Letter
Eliza Carolina (Burgwin) Clitherall Books
Elizabeth Collier Diary
Juliana Margaret Conner Diary
John Hamilton Cornish Papers
   John Hamilton Cornish Diary
Susan Cornwall Book
Craft, Fort, and Thorne Family Papers
   Henry Craft Diary
Marcus B. DeWitt Papers
William Ethelbert Ervin Book
David Gavin Diary
Gayle and Crawford Family Papers
Julia A. Gilmer Diary
James Hervey Greenlee Diary
Grimball Family Papers
   J. B. Grimball Diary
   Meta (Morris) Grimball Journal
William Hooper Haigh Papers
John Steele Henderson Papers
   Mary Steele Ferrand Henderson Journal
Gustavus Adolphus Henry Papers
Hentz Family Papers
   Caroline Lee (Whiting) Hentz Diary
Fannie Page Hume Diary
Susan Davis (Nye) Hutchinson Diary
Robert A. Jackson Papers
Jackson and Prince Family Papers
   Martha R. Jackson Diary
   Sarah Rootes Jackson Diary
Thomas Butler King Papers
Joshua Lawrence Papers
Francis Terry Leak Books
Lenoir Family Letters
William Parsons McCorkle Papers
   Lucilla Agnes (Gamble) McCorkle Diary
Nicholas Bryor Massenburg Books
David Outlaw Papers
Quitman Family Papers
Roach and Eggleston Family Papers
   Mahala (Eggleston) Roach Diary
Ruffin, Roulhac, and Hamilton Papers
   Edmund Ruffin, Jr., Plantation Diary
   Elizabeth Ruffin Diary
Sarah Lois Wadley Diary
John Walker Diary
Walton Family Papers

Charleston, South Carolina
South Carolina Historical Society Library
   Charleston Ladies Benevolent Society. Manuscript Collection
   Langdon I. Cheves Papers
   Dulles-Cheves-Lovell-McCord Family Papers
      Smythe, Louisa McCord. "Recollections of Louisa McCord"
   Middleton Family Papers
   West Manuscripts

Columbia, South Carolina
South Caroliniana Library, University of South Carolina
   Allston Family Papers
   Keziah Goodwyn Hopkins Brevard Diary
   Iverson L. Brookes Papers
   Mary Davis Brown Diary
   Cheves Family Papers
   Natalie de DeLage Sumter Diary
   Williams-Chesnut-Manning Papers
John Hall, Private Collection
   Susan Becton Letter

Durham, North Carolina
Manuscript Department, William R. Perkins Library, Duke University
   Sarah Eve Adams Diary
   Eleanor J. W. Baker Journal
   Elizabeth Blanks Papers
   Iverson Brookes Family Papers
   Campbell Family Papers
      David Campbell's Private Journal
      Mary Hamilton Campbell Letterbook
   Clement Claiborne Clay Family Papers
   Davidson, James. "Record of Inquisitions Taken by James Davidson, Coroner
      of the Town of Petersburg, Petersburg, Va., Commencing 16 September 1825"
   Lucy Walton Muse Fletcher Journal
   Martha Foster Crawford Diary
   Mary DeSaussure Fraser Papers
   Manigault Papers
   Reavis, William W. "Accounts of the Henderson Post Office, Vance County,
      N.C.," 1849, 1850, 1854, 1855
   Ella Gertrude Clanton Thomas Diary
   Henry Watson Family Papers

Fayetteville, Arkansas
David W. Mullins Library, University of Arkansas
   Nannie E. Cross Compositions, Cross Family Papers

Jackson, Mississippi
Mississippi Department of Archives and History
  Samuel Hairston Diary

Montgomery, Alabama
Alabama State Department of Archives and History
  William Phineas Browne Collection
  Gayle Family Papers
    "Sarah Haynsworth Gayle and Her Journal"
  Jefferson Franklin Jackson Papers
    Mrs. (Eleanor) Jefferson Franklin Jackson Diary.
  Octavia LeVert Journal

Nashville, Tennessee
Tennessee State Library and Archives
  Carson Family Papers
  Cooper Papers
  Joel B. Fort Diary
  [Walton, Emily Donelson]. "Autobiography of E.D.W." Lawrence Family
    Papers

New Orleans, Louisiana
Manuscripts, Rare Books, and University Archives, Howard-Tilton Memorial
Library, Tulane University
  R. R. Barrow Family Papers

Richmond, Virginia
Virginia Historical Society
  McKean Letterbook

Rochester, New York
Department of Rare Books and Special Collections, Rush Rhees Library,
University of Rochester
  Post Family Papers

Rocky Mount, North Carolina
Private possession of Kate (W. B.) Harrison
  Manly, Louise. "Early Life and Marriage of Charlotte Elizabeth (Whitfield)
    Manly"

University, Alabama
William Stanley Hoole Special Collections, Amelia Gayle Gorgas Library,
University of Alabama
  Gayle and Gorgas Family Papers
    Sarah Ann Haynsworth Gayle Diary

Washington, D.C.
Library of Congress
    Carter G. Woodson Papers

Winston-Salem, North Carolina
North Carolina Baptist Historical Collection, Wake Forest University Library
    Fannie Exile Scudder Heck Papers
Siewers Room, Dale H. Gramley Library, Salem College

Published Sources

A. G. M. "The Condition of Woman." *Southern Quarterly Review* 10 (July 1846): 148–73.
Aidoo, Agnes Akosua. "Asante Queen Mothers in Government and Politics in the Nineteenth Century." In *Black Woman Cross-Culturally*, edited by Filomina Chioma Steady, 65–77. Cambridge, Mass., 1981.
Albert, Peter Joseph. "The Protean Institution: The Geography, Economy, and Ideology of Slavery in Post-Revolutionary Virginia." Ph.D. diss., University of Maryland, 1976.
Albion, Robert Greenlagh. *The Rise of the Port of New York (1815–1860)*. New York, 1939.
Alcott, Louisa May. *Work: A Story of Experience*. Edited by Sarah Elbert. 1873. Reprint. New York, 1980.
Allen, Lee N. "The Woman Suffrage Movement in Alabama, 1910–1920." *Alabama Review* 11, no. 2 (April 1958): 83–99.
Allen, Madeline May. "An Historical Study of Moravian Education in North Carolina: The Evolution and Practice of the Moravian Concept of Education as It Applied to Women." Ph.D. diss., Florida State University, 1971.
Allman, John M., III. "Yeoman Regions in the Antebellum Deep South: Settlement and Economy in Northern Alabama, 1815–1860." Ph.D. diss., University of Maryland, 1979.
Allmendinger, David F., Jr. "Mount Holyoke Students Encounter the Need for Life-Planning, 1837–1850." *History of Education Quarterly* 19, no. 1 (Spring 1979): 24–46.
An Account of the Late Intended Insurrection among a Portion of the Blacks of this City. Published by the authority of the Corporation of Charleston. Charleston, S.C., 1822.
Anderson, John Q., ed. *Brokenburn: The Journal of Kate Stone, 1861–1868*. Baton Rouge, La., 1955.
Anderson, Michael. *Family Structure in Nineteenth-Century Lancashire*. Cambridge, Eng., 1971.
Anderson, Ralph V., and Robert E. Gallman. "Slaves as Fixed Capital: Slave Labor and Economic Development." *Journal of American History* 44 (1977): 24–46.
Andreano, Ralph, ed. *New Views on American Economic Development: A Selective Anthology of Recent Work*. Cambridge, Mass., 1965.

Andrew, J. O. *Miscellanies: Comprising Letters, Essays, and Addresses to Which Is Added a Biographical Sketch of Mrs. Ann Amelia Andrew*. Louisville, Ky., 1854.

Andrews, Eliza Frances. *The War-Time Journal of a Georgia Girl, 1864–1865*. New York, 1908.

Andrews, Evangeline Walker, ed. *Journal of a Lady of Quality: Being the Narrative of a Journey from Scotland to the West Indies, North Carolina, and Portugal, in the Years 1774 to 1776*. New Haven, Conn., 1923.

Andrews, Garnett. *Reminiscences of an Old Georgia Lawyer*. Atlanta, 1870.

Andrews, Sidney. *The South since the War*. 1866. Reprint. New York, 1969.

Andrews, William L., ed. *Sisters of the Spirit: Three Black Women's Autobiographies of the Nineteenth Century*. Bloomington, Ind., 1986.

Andriot, John L., comp. and ed. *Population Abstracts of the United States*. Rev. and enl. ed. 2 vols. McLean, Va., 1983.

"Annals of the Queens of Spain." *Southern Quarterly Review* 19 (January 1851): 273–74.

Anthony, Carl. "The Big House and the Slave Quarters. Part I. Prelude to New World Architecture." *Landscape* 20 (Spring 1976): 8–19.

_____. "The Big House and the Slave Quarters. Part II. African Contributions to the New World." *Landscape* 21 (Autumn 1976): 9–15.

Aptheker, Herbert. "Additional Data on American Maroons." *Journal of Negro History* 32 (October 1947): 452–60.

_____. *American Negro Slave Revolts*. New York, 1943.

_____. *Essays in the History of the American Negro*. New York, 1945.

_____. "Maroons within the Present Limits of the United States." In *Maroon Societies: Rebel Slave Communities in the Americas*, edited by Richard Price, 151–67. Garden City, N.Y., 1973.

_____. *To Be Free: Studies in American Negro History*. New York, 1948.

Arendale, Marirose. "Tennessee and Women's Rights." *Tennessee Historical Quarterly* 39 (1980): 62–78.

Ashworth, William. *The Genesis of Modern British Town Planning: A Study in Economic and Social History of the Nineteenth and Twentieth Centuries*. London, 1954.

Aston, Trevor H., ed. *Crisis in Europe, 1560–1660*. Garden City, N.Y., 1967.

Aston, Trevor H., and C. H. E. Philpin, eds. *The Brenner Debate: Agrarian Class Structure and Economic Development in Pre-Industrial Europe*. New York, 1985.

Atkinson, Maxine P., and Jacqueline Boles. "The Shaky Pedestal: Southern Ladies Yesterday and Today." *Southern Studies* 24, no. 4 (Winter 1985): 398–406.

Avary, Myrta Lockett, ed. *A Virginia Girl in the Civil War, 1861–1865*. New York, 1903.

Awe, Bolanle. "The Iyalode in the Traditional Yoruba Political System." In *Sexual Stratification: A Cross-Cultural View*, edited by Alice Schlegel. New York, 1977.

Bailey, David Thomas. "A Divided Prism: Two Sources of Black Testimony on Slavery." *Journal of Southern History* 46, no. 3 (August 1980): 381–404.

_____. *Shadow on the Church: Southwestern Evangelical Religion and the Issue of Slavery, 1783–1860*. Ithaca, N.Y., 1985.

Bailey, Fred A. "Tennessee's Antebellum Society from the Bottom Up." *Journal of Southern Studies* 22 (Fall 1983): 260–73.

Bailey, Hugh C., and William Dale Pratt II. "Missus Alone in de 'Big House.'" *Alabama Review* 8, no. 1 (January 1955): 43–54.

Bailyn, Bernard. *New England Merchants in the Seventeenth Century.* Cambridge, Mass., 1955.

Bairoch, Paul. *Révolution industrielle et sous-développement.* 4th ed. Paris and La Haye, 1974.

Baker, Houston A. *The Journey Back: Issues in Black Literature and Criticism.* Chicago, 1980.

Baker, Jean H. *Affairs of Party: The Political Culture of Northern Democrats in the Mid-Nineteenth Century.* Ithaca, N.Y., 1983.

Baker, Robert A. *The Southern Baptist Convention and Its People, 1607–1972.* Nashville, Tenn., 1974.

Baldwin, Samuel Davies. *Dominion, or, the Unity of the Human Race.* Nashville, Tenn., 1858.

Bancroft, Frederick. *Slave Trading in the Old South.* New York, 1931.

Bancroft, George. *History of the United States, from the Discovery of the American Continent.* 10 vols. Boston, 1846-75.

Barbour, Joan Elizabeth. "College Education for Women in Georgia before the Civil War." Honors thesis, Emory University, 1972.

Barron, Hal S. *Those Who Stayed Behind: Rural Society in Nineteenth-Century New England.* Cambridge, Eng., 1984.

Bartlett, Irving H., and C. Glenn Cambor. "The History and Psychodynamics of Southern Womanhood." *Women's Studies* 2 (1974): 9–24.

Basch, Norma. "Equity vs. Equality: Emerging Concepts of Women's Political Status in the Age of Jackson." *Journal of the Early Republic* 3, no. 3 (Fall 1983): 297–318.

_____. *In the Eyes of the Law: Women, Marriage, and Property in Nineteenth-Century New York.* Ithaca, N.Y., 1982.

_____. "Invisible Women: The Legal Fiction of Marital Unity in Nineteenth-Century America." *Feminist Studies* 5 (Summer 1979): 346–66.

Bassett, John Spencer. *Slavery and Servitude in the Colony of North Carolina.* Baltimore, Md., 1899.

_____. *The Southern Plantation Overseer as Revealed in His Letters.* Northampton, Mass., 1925.

Bassett, John Spencer, and Sidney Bradshaw Fay, eds. *The Westover Journal of John A. Selden, Esqr.* Northampton, Mass., 1921.

Bastiat, Frederic. *Sophisms of the Protective Policy.* Translated by Mrs. D. J. McCord. New York, 1848.

Bateman, Fred, and Thomas Weiss. "Comparative Regional Development in Antebellum Manufacturing." *Journal of Economic History* 35, no. 1 (March 1975): 182–208.

_____. *A Deplorable Scarcity: The Failure of Industrialization in the Slave Economy.* Chapel Hill, N.C., 1981.

_____. "Manufacturing in the Antebellum South." *Research in Economic History* 1 (1976): 1–44.

Bauer, Raymond A., and Alice H. Bauer. "Day to Day Resistance to Slavery." *Journal of Negro History* 27 (October 1942): 388–419.

Baugh, Daniel A., ed. *Aristocratic Government and Society in Eighteenth-Century England: The Foundations of Stability.* New York, 1974.

Bay, Edna G. "Servitude and Worldly Success in the Palace of Dahomey." In

Women and Slavery in Africa, edited by Claire C. Robertson and Martin A. Klein, 340–67. Madison, Wis., 1984.

Baym, Nina. *Woman's Fiction: A Guide to Novels by and about Women in America, 1820–1870.* Ithaca, N.Y., 1978.

Bean, Richard N., and Robert P. Thomas. "The Adoption of Slave Labor in British America." In *The Uncommon Market: Essays in the Economic History of the Atlantic Slave Trade,* edited by Henry A. Gemery and Jan S. Hogendorn, 377–98. New York, 1979.

Beaty, Rives Lang, ed. "Recollections of Harriet DuBose Kershaw Lang." *South Carolina Historical Magazine* 59 (1958): 159–70, 195–205.

Beck, Lois, and Nikki Keddie, eds., *Women in the Muslim World.* Cambridge, Mass., 1978.

Beecher, Catharine E. *A Treatise on Domestic Economy.* 1841. Reprint. New York, 1977.

Beecher, Catharine E., and Harriet Beecher Stowe. *The American Woman's Home: Or, Principles of Domestic Science.* 1869. Reprint. New York, 1971.

Beeman, Richard. *The Evolution of the Southern Backcountry: A Case Study of Lunenburg County, Virginia, 1746–1832.* Philadelphia, 1984.

Beeman, Richard R., and Rhys Isaac. "Cultural Conflict and Social Change in the Revolutionary South: Lunenburg County, Virginia." *Journal of Southern History* 46, no. 4 (November 1980): 525–50.

Bell, Malcolm, Jr., *Major Butler's Legacy: Five Generations of a Slaveholding Family.* Athens, Ga., 1987.

Bellows, Barbara. "'Insanity Is the Disease of Civilization': The Founding of the South Carolina Lunatic Asylum." *South Carolina Historical Magazine* 82, no. 3 (July 1981): 263–72.

Bender, Donald R. "A Refinement of the Concept of Household: Families, Co-residence and Domestic Functions." *American Anthropologist* 69, no. 5 (October 1967): 493–504.

Bender, Thomas. *Community and Social Change in America.* New Brunswick, N.J., 1978.

Bennett, Judith. *Women in the Medieval English Countryside: Gender and Household in Brigstock before the Plague.* New York, 1987.

Benstock, Shari, ed. *Feminist Issues in Literary Scholarship.* Bloomington, Ind., 1987.

———. *The Private Self: Theory and Practice of Women's Autobiographical Writings.* Chapel Hill, N.C., 1988.

Berg, Barbara J. *The Remembered Gate: Origins of American Feminism; the Woman and the City, 1800–1860.* New York, 1978.

Berkeley, Kathleen C. "'Colored Ladies also Contributed': Black Women's Activities from Benevolence to Social Welfare, 1866–1896." In *The Web of Southern Social Relations: Women, Family, and Education,* edited by Walter J. Fraser, Jr., R. Frank Saunders, Jr., and Jon L. Wakelyn, 181–203. Athens, Ga., 1985.

Berkin, Carol R., and Clara Lovett, eds. *Women, War, and Revolution.* New York, 1980.

Berkin, Carol R., and Mary Beth Norton, eds. *Women of America: A History.* Boston, 1979.

Berkner, Lutz Karl. "The Use and Misuse of Census Data for the Historical

Analysis of Family Structure." *Journal of Interdisciplinary History* 5, no. 4 (Spring 1975): 721–38.

Berlin, Ira. *Slaves without Masters: The Free Negro in the Antebellum South.* New York, 1976.

_____. "The Slave Trade and the Development of Afro-American Society in English Mainland North America, 1619–1775." *Southern Studies* 20, no. 2 (Summer 1981): 122–36.

_____. "Time, Space, and the Evolution of Afro-American Society in British Mainland North America." *American Historical Review* 85, no. 1 (February 1980): 44–78.

Berlin, Ira, and Herbert G. Gutman. "Natives and Immigrants, Free Men and Slaves: Urban Workingmen in the Antebellum American South." *American Historical Review* 88, no. 5 (December 1983): 1175–1200.

Berlin, Ira, and Ronald Hoffman, eds. *Slavery and Freedom in the Age of the American Revolution.* Charlottesville, Va., 1983.

Berlin, Ira, Joseph P. Reidy, and Leslie S. Rowland, eds. *The Black Military Experience.* Series 2 of *Freedom: A Documentary History of Emancipation, 1861–1867.* New York, 1982.

Bernard, Jessie. "George Tucker: Liberal Southern Social Scientist." *Social Forces* 25, nos. 2, 4 (December 1946, May 1947): 131–45, 406–46.

Bernard, Richard M., and Maris A. Vinovskis. "The Female School Teacher in Ante-Bellum Massachusetts." *Journal of Social History* 10 (March 1977): 332–39.

Berry, Brian J. L., and Allan R. Pred. *Central Place Studies: A Bibliography of Theory and Applications.* Philadelphia, 1961.

Beta. "Cartwright on Negroes." *Southern Quarterly Review* 22 (July 1852): 49–63.

Bidwell, Percy W. "The Agricultural Revolution in New England." *American Historical Review* 26, no. 4 (July 1921): 683–702.

"Biographies of Good Wives." *Southern Quarterly Review* 9 (April 1846): 539.

Bishir, Catherine W. "Black Builders in Antebellum North Carolina." *North Carolina Historical Review* 61, no. 4 (October 1984): 423–61.

Blackford, L. Minor. *Mine Eyes Have Seen the Glory.* Cambridge, Mass., 1954.

Blackwelder, Julia Kirk. *Women of the Depression: Caste and Culture in San Antonio, 1929–1939.* College Station, Tex., 1984.

Blair, Karen J. *The Clubwoman as Feminist: True Womanhood Redefined, 1868–1914.* New York, 1980.

Blandin, Mrs. I. M. E. *History of Higher Education of Women in the South prior to 1860.* 1909. Reprint. Washington, D.C., n.d.

Blassingame, John W. *The Slave Community: Plantation Life in the Antebellum South.* Rev. and enl. ed. New York, 1979.

_____. *Slave Testimony: Two Centuries of Letters, Speeches, Interviews, and Autobiographies.* Baton Rouge, La., 1977.

_____. "Using the Testimony of Ex-Slaves: Approaches and Problems." *Journal of Southern History* 41, no. 4 (November 1975): 473–92.

Bleser, Carol K. "The Perrys of Greenville: A Nineteenth-Century Marriage." In *The Web of Southern Social Relations: Women, Family, and Education,* edited by Walter J. Fraser, Jr., R. Frank Saunders, Jr., and Jon L. Wakelyn, 72–89. Athens, Ga., 1985.

_____. "Southern Wives and Slavery." Paper presented at the annual meeting of the Organization of American Historians, New York, N.Y., 12 April 1986.

_____, ed. *The Hammonds of Redcliffe*. New York, 1981.

Bleser, Carol K., and Frederick M. Heath. "The Impact of the Civil War on a Southern Marriage: Clement and Virginia Tunstall Clay of Alabama." *Civil War History* 30 (September 1984): 197–220.

Blight, David W. "Perceptions of Intransigence and the Rise of Antislavery Thought, 1816–1830." *Journal of the Early Republic* 3, no. 1 (Spring 1983): 139–63.

Bloch, Ruth H. "American Feminine Ideals in Transition: The Role of the Moral Mother, 1785–1815." *Feminist Studies* 4, no. 2 (June 1978): 100–126.

_____. "The Gendered Meanings of Virtue in Revolutionary America." *Signs* 13, no. 1 (Autumn 1987): 37–58.

_____. "Untangling the Roots of Modern Sex Roles: A Survey of Four Centuries of Change." *Signs* 4, no. 2 (Winter 1978): 237–52.

Boatright, Eleanor M. "The Political and Civil Status of Women in Georgia: 1783–1860." *Georgia Historical Quarterly* 25, no. 4 (December 1941): 301–24.

Boggs, Marion Alexander, ed. *The Alexander Letters, 1787–1900*. Savannah, Ga., 1910.

Bois, Guy. *Crise du féodalisme: Économie rurale et démographie en Normandie orientale du début du 14e siècle au milieu du 16e siècle*. Paris, 1976.

Boles, John B. *Black Southerners, 1619–1869*. Lexington, Ky., 1984.

_____. *The Great Revival, 1787–1805: The Origins of the Southern Evangelical Mind*. Lexington, Ky., 1972.

_____. *Religion in Antebellum Kentucky*. Lexington, Ky., 1976.

Boles, John B., and Evelyn Thomas Nolen, eds. *Interpreting Southern History: Historiographical Essays in Honor of Sanford W. Higginbotham*. Baton Rouge, La., 1987.

Bonner, James C. "Journal of a Mission to Georgia in 1827." *Georgia Historical Quarterly* 44 (March 1960): 74–85.

_____. *Milledgeville, Georgia's Antebellum Capital*. Athens, Ga., 1978.

_____. "Plantation Experiences of a New York Woman." *North Carolina Historical Review* 33, nos. 2, 3 (July, October 1956): 384–412, 529–46.

_____, ed. *The Journal of a Milledgeville Girl, 1861–1867*. Athens, Ga., 1964.

Bonomi, Patricia U., and Peter R. Eisenstadt. "Church Adherence in the Eighteenth-Century British American Colonies." *William and Mary Quarterly*, 3d ser., vol. 39, no. 2 (August 1982): 245–86.

Bontemps, Arna, ed. *Great Slave Narratives*. Boston, 1969.

Bordin, Ruth. *Women and Temperance: The Quest for Power and Liberty, 1873–1900*. Philadelphia, 1981.

Boserup, Ester. *Women's Role in Economic Development*. London, 1970.

Botkin, Benjamin A., ed. *Lay My Burden Down: A Folk History of Slavery*. Chicago, 1945.

Boucher, Ann Williams. "Wealthy Planter Families in Nineteenth-Century Alabama." Ph.D. diss., University of Connecticut, 1978.

Bourne, George. *Slavery Illustrated in its Effects upon Woman and Domestic Society*. Boston, 1837.

Bowen, Peter. "Agricultural Prices, Farm Profits, and Rents." In *The Agrarian*

History of England and Wales, edited by Joan Thirsk, 4:593–695. Cambridge, Eng., 1967.

Bowie, Lucy Leigh. "Madame Greland's French School." *Maryland Historical Magazine* 39, no. 2 (June 1944): 141–48.

Boyd, Minnie C. *Alabama in the Fifties: A Social Study*. New York, 1931.

Boylan, Anne M. "Evangelical Womanhood in the Nineteenth Century." *Feminist Studies* 4 (1978): 62–80.

Bozzoli, Belinda. "Marxism, Feminism, and South Africa." *Journal of South African Studies* 9, no. 2 (Spring 1983): 139–71.

Bracey, John, August Meier, and Elliott Rudwick, eds. *American Slavery: The Question of Resistance*. Belmont, Calif., 1971.

Brackett, Jeffrey R. *The Negro in Maryland: A Study of the Institution of Slavery*. Baltimore, Md., 1889.

Bradford, M. E. *A Better Guide Than Reason: Studies in the American Revolution*. La Salle, Ill., 1979.

———. *A Worthy Company: Brief Lives of the Framers of the United States Constitution*. Marlborough, N.H., 1982.

Braudel, Fernand. *Afterthoughts on Material Civilization and Capitalism*. Translated by Patricia M. Ranum. Baltimore, Md., 1977.

———. *Capitalism and Material Life, 1400–1800*. Translated by Sian Reynolds. 2 vols. London, 1981–84.

Breen, Timothy H. "Horses and Gentlemen: The Cultural Significance of Gambling among the Gentry of Virginia." *William and Mary Quarterly*, 3d ser., vol. 34, no. 2 (April 1977): 239–57.

Breen, Timothy H., and Stephen Innes. *"Myne Owne Ground": Race and Freedom on Virginia's Eastern Shore, 1640–1676*. New York, 1980.

Bremer, Frederika. *The Homes of the New World: Impressions of America*. Translated by Mary Howitt. 2 vols. New York, 1853.

Brenner, Robert. "Agrarian Class Structure and Economic Development in Pre-Industrial Europe." *Past and Present*, no. 70 (February 1976): 30–75.

———. "Agrarian Class Structure and Economic Development in Pre-Industrial Europe: The Agrarian Roots of European Capitalism." *Past and Present*, no. 97 (November 1982): 16–113.

———. "The Origins of Capitalist Development: A Critique of Neo-Smithian Marxism." *New Left Review*, no. 104 (July/August 1977): 25–92.

———. "The Social Basis of Economic Development." In *Analytical Marxism: An Anthology*, edited by John Roemer, 23–53. Cambridge, Eng., 1986.

Bridenbaugh, Carl. *Vexed and Troubled Englishmen, 1590–1642*. New York, 1968.

Briggs, Asa. *The Making of Modern England, 1783–1867: The Age of Improvement*. 1959. Reprint. New York, 1960.

———. *Victorian Cities*. London, 1963.

Broadhead, Susan Herlin. "Slave Wives, Free Sisters: Bakongo Women and Slavery c. 1700–1850." In *Women and Slavery in Africa*, edited by Claire C. Robertson and Martin A. Klein, 160–81. Madison, Wis., 1984.

Brooks, Evelyn. "The Women's Movement in the Black Church, 1880–1920." Ph.D. diss., University of Rochester, 1984.

Brooks, George E., Jr. "A Nhara of the Guinea-Bissau Region: Mae Aurelia

Correia." In *Women and Slavery in Africa*, edited by Claire C. Robertson and Martin A. Klein, 295–319. Madison, Wis., 1984.

_____. "The *Signares* of Saint-Louis and Goree: Women Entrepreneurs in Eighteenth Century Senegal." In *Women in Africa*, edited by Nancy J. Hafkin and Edna G. Bay, 19–44. Stanford, Calif., 1976.

Brown, David. *The Planter: Or, Thirteen Years in the South, by a Northern Man.* 1853. Reprint. Upper Saddle River, N.J., 1970.

Brown, Dorothy M. *Setting a Course: American Women in the 1920s.* Boston, 1987.

Brown, Gillian. "Getting in the Kitchen with Dinah: Domestic Politics in Uncle Tom's Cabin." *American Quarterly* 36, no. 4 (Fall 1984): 503–23.

Brown, Herbert Ross. *The Sentimental Novel in America, 1789–1860.* Durham, N.C., 1940.

Brown, John. *Slave Life in Georgia: A Narrative of the Life, Sufferings, and Escape of John Brown, a Fugitive Slave.* Edited by F. N. Boney. Savannah, Ga., 1972.

Brown, Judith K. "An Anthropological Perspective on Sex Roles and Subsistence." In *Sex Differences: Social and Biological Perspectives*, edited by Michael S. Teitelbaum, 122–37. Garden City, N.Y., 1976.

Brown, Richard Maxwell. *The South Carolina Regulators.* Cambridge, Mass., 1963.

Browne, Gary Lawson. *Baltimore in the Nation, 1789–1861.* Chapel Hill, N.C., 1980.

Brownell, Blaine A. "Urbanization in the South: A Unique Experience?" *Mississippi Quarterly* 26, no. 2 (Spring 1973): 105–20.

Brownell, Blaine A., and David R. Goldfield, eds. *The City in Southern History: The Growth of Urban Civilization in the South.* Port Washington, N.Y., 1977.

Brownlow, W. G. *Ought American Slavery to Be Perpetuated: A Debate between Reverend W. G. Brownlow and Reverend A. Pryne Held at Philadelphia, September 1858.* 1858. Reprint. Miami, 1969.

Bruce, Dickson D., Jr. *And They All Sang Hallelujah: Plain Folk Camp-Meeting Religion, 1800–1845.* Knoxville, Tenn., 1974.

_____. "Religion, Society, and Culture in the Old South: A Comparative View." *American Quarterly* 26, no. 4 (1974): 399–416.

_____. *Violence and Culture in the Antebellum South.* Austin, Tex., 1979.

Bruce, H. C. *The New Man. Twenty-Nine Years a Slave. Twenty-Nine Years a Free Man.* 1895. Reprint. New York, 1969.

Bruce, Philip Alexander. *Economic History of Virginia in the Seventeenth Century: An Inquiry into the Material Condition of the People Based upon Original and Contemporaneous Records.* 2 vols. 1895. Reprint. New York, 1935.

Bryan, J. P., ed. *Mary Austin Holley: The Texas Diary, 1835–1838.* Austin, Tex., 1965.

Bryant, Keith L., Jr. "The Role and Status of the Female Yeomanry in the Antebellum South: The Literary View." *Southern Quarterly* 18 (Winter 1979/80): 73–88.

Buck, Paul H. "The Poor Whites of the Antebellum South." *American Historical Review* 31, no. 1 (October 1925): 41–54.

Buckingham, J. S. *The Slave States of America.* 2 vols. 1842. Reprint. New York, 1968.

Burke, Emily. *Reminiscences of Georgia.* Oberlin, Ohio, 1850.

Burnham, Dorothy. "The Life of the Afro-American Woman in Slavery." *International Journal of Women's Studies* 1 (July/August 1978): 363–77.

Burstyn, Joan N. *Victorian Education and the Ideal of Womanhood.* London, 1980.

Burton, Orville Vernon. "Anatomy of an Antebellum Rural Free Black Community: Social Structure and Social Interaction in Edgefield District, South Carolina, 1850–1860." *Southern Studies* 21, no. 3 (Fall 1982): 294–325.

_____. *In My Father's House Are Many Mansions: Family and Community in Edgefield, South Carolina.* Chapel Hill, N.C., 1985.

Burton, Orville Vernon, and Robert C. McMath, Jr., eds. *Class, Conflict, and Consensus: Antebellum Southern Community Studies.* Westport, Conn., 1982.

Bush, Barbara. "Defiance or Submission? The Role of Slave Women in Slave Resistance in the British Caribbean." *Immigrants and Minorities* 1 (1982): 16–38.

_____. "'The Family Tree Is Not Cut': Women and Cultural Resistance in Slave Family Life in the British Caribbean." In *In Resistance: Studies in African, Caribbean, and Afro-American History*, edited by Gary Y. Okihiro, 117–32. Amherst, Mass., 1986.

_____. "Towards Emancipation: Slave Women and Resistance to Coercive Labour Regimes in the British West Indian Colonies, 1790–1838." *Slavery and Abolition* 5, no. 3 (December 1984): 222–43.

Butler, Mrs. F. A., ed. *Frances Webb Bumpas: Autobiography and Journal.* Nashville, Tenn., 1899.

Butler, Lindley S., and Alan D. Watson, eds. *The North Carolina Experience: An Interpretive and Documentary History.* Chapel Hill, N.C., 1984.

C. "Servility." *Southern Literary Messenger* 1, no. 1 (August 1834): 6.

C. M. T. "The Diversity and Origins of the Human Races." *Southern Quarterly Review* 20 (October 1851): 458–80.

Campbell, John. "Work, Pregnancy, and Infant Mortality among Southern Slaves." *Journal of Interdisciplinary History* 14, no. 4 (Spring 1984): 793–812.

Cantor, Milton, and Bruce Laurie, eds., *Class, Sex, and the Woman Worker.* Westport, Conn., 1977.

Capers, Gerald M., Jr. *The Biography of a River Town: Memphis, Its Heroic Age.* Chapel Hill, N.C., 1939.

Cardwell, Guy A. "The Quiver and the Floral Wreath: Two Rare Charleston Periodicals." *North Carolina Historical Review* 16, no. 4 (October 1939): 418–27.

Carr, Lois G., and Russell R. Menard. "Immigration and Opportunity: The Freedman in Early Colonial Maryland." In *The Chesapeake in the Seventeenth Century: Essays on Anglo-American Society*, edited by Thad W. Tate and David L. Ammerman, 206–42. Chapel Hill, N.C., 1979.

Carrigan, Jo Ann. "Nineteenth-Century Rural Self-Sufficiency: A Planter's and Housewife's 'Do-it-Yourself' Encyclopedia." *Arkansas Historical Quarterly* 21, no. 2 (Summer 1962): 132–45.

Carroll, Joseph Cephas. *Slave Insurrections in the United States, 1800–1865.* 1938. Reprint. New York, 1968.

Carroll, Patrick J. "Mandinga: The Evolution of a Mexican Runaway Slave Community, 1735–1827." *Comparative Studies in Society and History* 19, no. 4 (October 1977): 488–505.

Carus-Wilson, E. M., ed. *Essays in Economic History.* 3 vols. London, 1962.

Cary, Virginia. *Letters on Female Character: Addressed to a Young Lady on the Death of Her Mother.* Hartford, Conn., 1831.

Cash, Wilbur J. *The Mind of the South.* New York, 1941.

Catterall, Helen T., ed. *Judicial Cases Concerning American Slavery and the Negro.* 5 vols. Washington, D.C., 1936.

Censer, Jane Turner. *North Carolina Planters and Their Children, 1800–1860.* Baton Rouge, La., 1984.

_____. "'Smiling through Her Tears': Ante-Bellum Southern Women and Divorce." *American Journal of Legal History* 25, no. 1 (January 1982): 114–34.

Chafe, William Henry. *The American Woman: Her Changing Social, Economic, and Political Roles, 1920–1970.* New York, 1972.

Chambers-Schiller, Lee Virginia. *Liberty a Better Husband: Single Women in America: The Generations of 1780–1849.* New Haven, 1984.

Chandler, Daniel. *An Address on Female Education, Delivered before the Demosthenian and Phi Kappa Societies, on the Day after Commencement, in the University of Georgia.* Washington, Ga., 1835.

Charleston Ladies' Auxilliary Christian Association. *First Annual Report of the Ladies Auxilliary Christian Association of Charleston, S.C., Presented May 8, 1858.* Charleston, 1858.

Chartres, J. A. "The Marketing of Agricultural Produce." In *The Agrarian History of England and Wales,* edited by Joan Thirsk, 5 (pt. 2): 406–502. Cambridge, Eng., 1984.

Chatman, Seymour, ed. *Literary Style: A Symposium.* New York, 1974.

Chayanov, A. V. *The Theory of the Peasant Economy.* Edited by Daniel Thorner, Basile Kerblay, and R. E. F. Smith. Homewood, Ill., 1966.

Cheatham, Edgar Jones. "Washington County, Mississippi: Its Antebellum Generation." M.A. thesis, Tulane University, 1950.

Cheever, George B. *The Guilt of Slavery and the Crime of Slaveholding Demonstrated from the Hebrew and Greek Scriptures.* Boston, 1860.

Chesnut, Mary Boykin. *Two Years—or, the Way We Lived Then.* In "Mary Boykin Chesnut: The Writer and Her Work," by Elisabeth S. Muhlenfeld. Ph.D diss., University of South Carolina, 1978.

Childs, Arney R., ed. *Planters and Business Men: The Guignard Family of South Carolina, 1795–1930.* Columbia, S.C., 1957.

Childs, St. Julien R., ed. "A Letter Written in 1771 by Mary Stafford to Her Kinswoman in England." *South Carolina Historical Magazine* 81, no. 1 (1980): 1–7.

Christaller, Walter. *Central Places in Southern Germany.* Translated by Carlisle W. Baskin. 1933. Reprint. Englewood Cliffs, N.J., 1966.

Clark, Alice. *The Working Life of Women in the Seventeenth Century.* 1919. Reprint. London, 1968.

Clark, Blanche Henry. *The Tennessee Yeomen, 1840–1860.* 1942. Reprint. New York, 1971.

Clark, Christopher Frederic. "The Household Economy, Market Exchange, and the Rise of Capitalism in the Connecticut Valley, 1800–1860." *Journal of Social History* 13, no. 2 (Winter 1979): 169–90.

_____. "Households, Market, and Capital: The Process of Economic Change in the Connecticut Valley of Massachusetts, 1800–1860." Ph.D. diss., Harvard University, 1982.

Clark, John G. *New Orleans, 1718–1812: An Economic History.* Baton Rouge, La., 1970.

Clark, Peter, ed. *The Early Modern Town: A Reader.* London, 1976.

Clark, Peter, and Paul Slack. *English Towns in Transition, 1500–1700.* London, 1976.

Clarke, Edith. *My Mother Who Fathered Me: A Study of the Family in Three Selected Communities in Jamaica.* London, 1957.

Clay-Clopton, Virginia. *A Belle of the Fifties: Memoirs of Mrs. Clay of Alabama, Covering Social and Political Life in Washington and the South, 1853–66.* Edited by Ada Sterling. New York, 1905.

Clemens, Paul G. E. *The Atlantic Economy and Colonial Maryland's Eastern Shore: From Tobacco to Grain.* Ithaca, N.Y., 1980.

———. "The Rise of Liverpool, 1665–1750." *Economic History Review,* 2d ser., vol. 29, no. 2 (May 1976): 211–35.

Clifton, James M., ed. *Life and Labor on Argyle Island: Letters and Documents of a Savannah River Plantation, 1833–1867.* Savannah, Ga., 1978.

Clinton, Catherine. "Caught in the Web of the Big House: Women and Slavery." In *The Web of Southern Social Relations: Women, Family, and Education,* edited by Walter J. Fraser, Jr., R. Frank Saunders, Jr., and Jon L. Wakelyn, 19–34. Athens, Ga., 1985.

———. "Equally Their Due: The Education of the Planter Daughter in the Early Republic." *Journal of the Early Republic* 2, no. 1 (Spring 1982): 39–60.

———. *The Plantation Mistress: Woman's World in the Old South.* New York, 1982.

Clowse, Converse D. *Economic Beginnings in Colonial South Carolina, 1670–1730.* Columbia, S.C., 1971.

Coats, Alfred W., and Ross M. Robertson, eds. *Essays in American Economic History.* London, 1969.

Cobb, Thomas R. R. *An Inquiry into the Law of Negro Slavery in the United States of America.* 1858. Reprint. New York, 1968.

Cochran, Thomas C. "The Business Revolution." *American Historical Review* 79, no. 5 (December 1974): 1449–66.

Coclanis, Peter A. "Economy and Society in the Early Modern South: Charleston and the Evolution of the South Carolina Low Country." Ph.D. diss., Columbia University, 1984.

Cody, Cheryll Ann. "Naming, Kinship, and Estate Dispersal: Notes on Slave Family Life on a South Carolina Plantation, 1786 to 1833." *William and Mary Quarterly,* 3d ser., vol. 39, no. 1 (January 1982): 192–211.

———. "Slave Demography and Family Formation: A Community Study of the Ball Family Plantations, 1720–1896." Ph.D. diss., University of Minnesota, 1982.

———. "There Was No 'Absalom' on the Ball Plantations: Slave-Naming Patterns in the South Carolina Low Country, 1720–1865." *American Historical Review* 92, no. 3 (June 1987): 563–96.

Cole, Johnetta B., ed. *Anthropology for the Eighties: Introductory Readings.* New York, 1982.

Confino, Michael. *Systèmes agraires et progrès agricole: L'assolement triennal en Russie aux XVIII–XIX siècles.* Paris, 1969.

Conner, Paul. "Patriarchy: Old World and New." *American Quarterly* 17, no. 1 (1965): 48–62.

Conrad, Susan Phinney. *Perish the Thought: Intellectual Women in Romantic America, 1830–1860.* New York, 1976.

Cook, Mrs. Henry Lowell. "'Maids for Wives.'" *Virginia Magazine of History and Biography* 50, no. 4 (October 1942): 300–20; 51, no. 1 (January 1943): 71–86.

Cooper, Thomas, ed. *Institutes of Justinian*. New York, 1841.

Cooper, Thomas, and David J. McCord, eds. *The Statutes at Large of South Carolina*, 10 vols. Columbia, S.C., 1836–41.

Cornelius, Janet. "Slave Marriages in a Georgia Congregation." In *Class, Conflict, and Consensus: Antebellum Southern Communities*, edited by Orville Vernon Burton and Robert C. McMath, Jr., 128–45. Westport, Conn., 1982.

Cott, Nancy F. *The Bonds of Womanhood: "Woman's Sphere" in New England, 1780–1835*. New Haven, Conn., 1977.

———. "Young Women in the Second Great Awakening in New England." *Feminist Studies* 3, no. 1/2 (Fall 1975): 15–29.

Cott, Nancy F., and Elizabeth Pleck, eds. *A Heritage of Her Own: Toward a New Social History of American Women*. New York, 1979.

Coulter, E. Merton. "The Ante-Bellum Academy Movement in Georgia." *Georgia Historical Quarterly* 5, no. 4 (December 1921): 11–42.

———. *Old Petersburg and the Broad River Valley of Georgia: Their Rise and Decline*. Athens, Ga., 1965.

Cowden, Gerald Steffens. "Spared by Lightning: The Story of Lucy (Harrison) Randolph Necks." *Virginia Magazine of History and Biography* 89 (1981): 294–307.

Cowing, Cedric B. "Sex and Preaching in the Great Awakening." *American Quarterly* 20, no. 3 (Fall 1968): 624–44.

Crabtree, Beth G., and James W. Patton, eds. *The Journal of a Secesh Lady: The Diary of Catherine Ann Devereux Edmonston, 1860–1866*. Raleigh, N.C., 1979.

Craft, William, and Ellen Craft. "Running a Thousand Miles for Freedom: Or, the Escape of William and Ellen Craft from Slavery." In *Great Slave Narratives*, edited by Arna Bontemps, 269–331. Boston, 1969.

Craven, Avery O. *Rachel of Old Louisiana*. Baton Rouge, La., 1975.

Craven, Wesley Frank. *White, Red, and Black: The Seventeenth-Century Virginian*. Charlottesville, Va., 1971.

Cross, Whitney. *The Burned-Over District: The Social and Intellectual History of Enthusiastic Religion in Western New York, 1800–1850*. New York, 1965.

Crow, Jeffrey J., and Larry E. Tise, eds. *The Southern Experience in the American Revolution*. Chapel Hill, N.C., 1978.

Crowley, John E. "The Importance of Kinship: Testamentary Evidence from South Carolina." *Journal of Interdisciplinary History* 16, no. 4 (Spring 1986): 559–77.

Crowther, Simeon J. "Urban Growth in the Mid-Atlantic States, 1785–1850." *Journal of Economic History* 36, no. 3 (September 1976): 624–44.

Curry, Leonard P. *The Free Black in Urban America, 1800–1850: The Shadow of the Dream*. Chicago, 1981.

———. "Urbanization and Urbanism in the Old South: A Comparative View." *Journal of Southern History* 40, no. 1 (February 1974): 43–60.

Curtin, Philip. *The Atlantic Slave Trade: A Census*. Madison, Wis., 1969.

D. "Laws of Life." *Southern Quarterly Review* 22 (October 1852): 478–89.

Dabney, Robert L. *Defence of Virginia [and through Her, of the South] in Recent and Pending Contests against the Sectional Party.* 1867. Reprint. New York, 1969.

Dabney, Virginius. *Richmond: The Story of a Southern City.* Garden City, N.Y., 1976.

Dale, Robert Brent. *Sketch of St. James Parish.* New York, 1874.

Dandamaev, Muhammad A. *Slavery in Babylonia: From Nabopolassar to Alexander the Great (626–331 B.C.).* Rev. ed. Translated by Victoria A. Powell. Edited by Marvin A. Powell and David B. Weisberg. DeKalb, Ill., 1984.

Daniel, W. Harrison. "Virginia Baptists and the Negro in the Early Republic." *Virginia Magazine of History and Biography* 80, no. 1 (January 1972): 60–69.

Dannenbaum, Jed. "The Origins of Temperance Activism and Militancy among American Women." *Journal of Social History* 15, no. 2 (Winter 1981): 235–52.

Davidoff, Leonore. *The Best Circles: Society, Etiquette and the Season.* London, 1973.

Davidoff, Leonore, and Catherine Hall. *Family Fortunes: Men and Women of the English Middle Class, 1780–1850.* London, 1987.

Davidson, Basil. *Black Mother: The Years of the African Slave Trade.* Boston, 1961.

————. *A History of West Africa to the Nineteenth Century.* Garden City, N.Y., 1966.

Davidson, Cathy. *Revolution and the Word: The Rise of the Novel in America.* New York, 1986.

Davies, Margery W. *Woman's Place Is at the Typewriter: Office Work and Office Workers, 1870–1930.* Philadelphia, 1982.

Davis, Angela Y. "Reflections on the Black Woman's Role in the Community of Slaves." *The Black Scholar* 3 (December 1971): 3–15.

————. *Women, Race, and Class.* New York, 1981.

Davis, Charles S. *The Cotton Kingdom in Alabama.* Montgomery, Ala., 1939.

Davis, Charles T., and Henry Louis Gates, Jr., eds. *The Slave's Narrative.* New York, 1985.

Davis, David Brion. *The Problem of Slavery in the Age of Revolution, 1770–1823.* Ithaca, N.Y., 1975.

————. *The Problem of Slavery in Western Culture.* Ithaca, N.Y., 1966.

————. *Slavery and Human Progress.* New York, 1984.

————. "Slavery and the Post-World War II Historians." *Daedalus* 103, no. 2 (Spring 1974): 1–16.

Davis, Edwin Adams, ed. *Plantation Life in the Florida Parishes of Louisiana, 1836–1846: As Reflected in the Diary of Bennet H. Barrow.* New York, 1943.

Davis, Esther S. [Reynolds]. *Memories of Mulberry.* Camden, S.C., 1975.

Davis, James E. *Frontier America, 1800–1840: A Comparative Demographic Analysis of the Settlement Process.* Glendale, Calif., 1977.

Davis, Lance E., Richard A. Easterlin, William N. Parker, Dorothy S. Brady, Albert Fishlow, Robert E. Gallman, Stanley Lebergott, Robert E. Lipsey, Douglass C. North, Nathan Rosenberg, Eugene Smolensky, and Peter Temin. *American Economic Growth: An Economist's History of the United States.* New York, 1972.

Davis, Natalie Zemon. *Society and Culture in Early Modern France.* Stanford, Calif., 1975.

Dawson, Sarah Morgan. *A Confederate Girl's Diary.* Edited by James I. Robertson, Jr. Westport, Conn., 1972.

Deas, Alston, ed. "Eleanor Parke Lewis to Mrs. C. C. Pinckney." *South Carolina Historical Magazine* 63 (1962): 12–17.

Debien, Gabriel. "Le marronage aux Antilles Françaises au XVIIIe siècle." *Caribbean Studies* 6, no. 3 (October 1966): 3–43.

De Bow, J. D. B. *Statistical View of the United States.* Washington, D.C., 1854.

DeBurg, William. *The Slave Drivers: Black Agricultural Labor Supervisors in the Antebellum South.* Westport, Conn., 1979.

DeButts, Mary Custis Lee, ed. *Growing Up in the 1850s: The Journal of Agnes Lee.* Chapel Hill, N.C., 1984.

Deen, James W., Jr. "Patterns of Testation: Four Tidewater Counties in Colonial Virginia." *American Journal of Legal History* 16 (April 1972): 154–76.

Degler, Carl N. *At Odds: Women and the Family in America from the Revolution to the Present.* New York, 1980.

De Leon, Thomas Cooper. *Belles, Beaux, and Brains of the 60's.* New York, 1909.

———. *Four Years in Rebel Capitals: An Inside View of Life in the Southern Confederacy, from Birth to Death.* Mobile, Ala., 1890.

Della, M. Ray, Jr. "An Analysis of Baltimore's Population in the 1850's." *Maryland Historical Magazine* 68, no. 1 (Spring 1973): 20–35.

Demos, John. *A Little Commonwealth: Family Life in Plymouth Colony.* New York, 1970.

Dennett, John Richard. *The South as It Is, 1865–1866.* Edited by Henry M. Christman. New York, 1967.

De Pauw, Linda Grant. "Women and the Law: The Colonial Period." *Human Rights* 6, no. 2 (Winter 1977): 107–13.

Deutrich, Mabel E., and Virginia C. Purdy, eds. *Clio Was a Woman: Studies in the History of American Women.* Washington, D.C., 1980.

DeVries, Jan. *European Urbanization, 1500–1800.* Cambridge, Mass., 1984.

Dew, Thomas Roderick. "Dissertation on the Characteristic Differences between the Sexes, and on the Position and Influence of Woman in Society." *Southern Literary Messenger* 1, nos. 11, 12 (July, August 1835): 621–32, 672–91.

———. *Pro-Slavery Argument.* Philadelphia, 1853.

———. *Review of the Debate in the Virginia Legislature of 1831 and 1832.* 1832. Reprint. Westport, Conn., 1970.

Deweese, Charles W. "Deaconesses in Baptist History: A Preliminary Study." *Baptist History and Heritage* 12, no. 1 (January 1977): 52–57.

Dickinson, Robert E. *The West European City: A Geographical Interpretation.* London, 1951.

Dictionary of American Biography. 20 vols. New York, 1928–36.

Diggs, Irene. "Dubois and Women: A Short Story of Black Women, 1910–1934." *A Current Bibliography on African Affairs* 7, no. 3 (Summer 1974): 260–303.

Dill, Bonnie Thornton. "The Dialectics of Black Womanhood." *Signs* 4, no. 3 (Spring 1978): 543–55.

Diner, Hasia R. *Erin's Daughters in America: Irish Immigrant Women in the Nineteenth Century.* Baltimore, Md., 1983.

Dobb, Maurice. *Studies in the Development of Capitalism.* New York, 1947.

Donnan, Elizabeth, ed. *Documents Illustrative of the Slave Trade to America.* 4 vols. 1935. Reprint. New York, 1965.

Dorman, James H. "The Persistent Spectre: Slave Rebellion in Territorial Louisiana." *Louisiana History* 18 (Fall 1977): 389–404.

Dorsett, Lyle W., and Arthur H. Shaffer. "Was the Antebellum South Antiurban? A Suggestion." *Journal of Southern History* 38, no. 1 (February 1972): 93–100.

Douglas, Ann. *The Feminization of American Culture*. New York, 1977.

Douglass, Frederick. *Life and Times of Frederick Douglass: Written by Himself*. 1892. Reprint. New York, 1962.

———. *My Bondage and My Freedom*. New York, 1866.

———. *Narrative of the Life of Frederick Douglass, an American Slave, Written by Himself*. 1845. Reprint. New York, 1968.

Dow, Peggy. *Vicissitudes: Or, the Journey of Life*. Philadelphia, 1816.

Drago, Edmund L. "The Black Household in Dougherty County, Georgia, 1870–1900." *Journal of Southwest Georgia History* 1 (Fall 1983): 38–48.

———. "Militancy and Black Women in Reconstruction Georgia." *Journal of American Culture* 1, no. 4 (Winter 1978): 838–44.

Drake, Daniel. *Pioneer Life in Kentucky, 1785–1800*. Edited by Emmet Field Horine. 1870. Reprint. New York, 1948.

Drew, Benjamin. *The Refugee: Or a North-Side View of Slavery*. Edited by Tilden G. Edelstein. Reading, Mass., 1969.

Dublin, Thomas. *Women at Work: The Transformation of Work and Community in Lowell, Massachusetts, 1826–1860*. New York, 1979.

DuBois, Ellen Carol. *Feminism and Suffrage: The Emergence of an Independent Women's Movement in America, 1848–1869*. Ithaca, N.Y. 1978.

———. "Working Women, Class Relations, and Suffrage Militance: Harriot Stanton Blatch and the New York Woman Suffrage Movement, 1894–1909." *Journal of American History* 74, no. 1 (June 1987): 34–58.

———, ed. *Elizabeth Cady Stanton, Susan B. Anthony: Correspondence, Writings, Speeches*. New York, 1981.

DuBois, Ellen Carol, Mari Jo Buhle, Temma Kaplan, Gerda Lerner, and Carroll Smith-Rosenberg. "Politics and Culture in Women's History: A Symposium." *Feminist Studies* 6, no. 1 (Spring 1980): 26–44.

DuBois, Silvia. *A Biography of the Slav Who Whipt Her Mistres and Gand Her Fredom*. Edited by C. W. Larison. Ringos, N.J., 1883.

Du Bois, W. E. B. *Darkwater: Voices from the Veil*. 1921. Reprint. Millwood, N.Y., 1975.

———. *The Gift of Black Folk*. Millwood, N.Y., 1975.

Dudden, Faye E. *Serving Women: Household Service in Nineteenth-Century America*. Middletown, Conn., 1983.

Duff, John B., and Peter M. Mitchell, eds. *The Nat Turner Rebellion: The Historical Event and the Modern Controversy*. New York, 1971.

Dunn, Richard S. *Sugar and Slaves: The Rise of the Planter Class in the English West Indies, 1624–1713*. New York, 1972.

———. "A Tale of Two Plantations: Slave Life at Mesopotamia in Jamaica and Mount Airy in Virginia, 1799 to 1828." *William and Mary Quarterly*, 3d ser., vol. 34, no. 1 (January 1977): 32–65.

Dupire, Marguerite. "The Position of Women in a Pastoral Society (The Fulani WoDaaBa, Nomads of the Niger)." In *Women of Tropical Africa*, edited by Denise Paulme, 47–96. Berkeley, Calif., 1973.

DuPlessis, Robert S., and Martha C. Howell. "Reconsidering the Early Modern

Urban Economy: The Cases of Leiden and Lille." *Past and Present*, no. 94 (February 1982): 49–84.

Durham, Walter T. "Tennessee Countess." *Tennessee Historical Quarterly* 39 (1939): 323–40.

Dusinberre, William. "The Aftermath of Slavery." *History* 68, no. 222 (February 1983): 64–79.

Dye, Nancy Schrom. *As Equals and as Sisters: Feminism, the Labor Movement, and the Women's Trade Union League of New York*. Columbia, Mo., 1980.

E. H. B. "Political Philosophy of South Carolina." *Southern Quarterly Review* 23 (January 1853): 120–40.

E. M. S. "Emancipation in the British West Indies." *Southern Quarterly Review* 23 (April 1853): 422–54.

Earle, Carville. *The Evolution of a Tidewater Settlement System: All Hallow's Parish, Maryland, 1650–1793*. Chicago, 1975.

Earle, Carville, and Ronald Hoffman. "The Foundations of the Modern Economy: Agriculture and the Costs of Labor in the United States and England, 1800–60." *American Historical Review* 85, no. 5 (December 1980): 1055–94.

––––––. "Staple Crops and Urban Development in the Eighteenth-Century South." *Perspectives in American History* 10 (1976): 7–78.

Easterby, J. H., ed. *The South Carolina Rice Plantation as Revealed in the Papers of R. W. Allston*. Chicago, 1945.

––––––. "South Carolina through New England Eyes: Almira Coffin's Visit to the Low Country in 1851." *South Carolina Historical Magazine* 45 (1944): 127–36.

Easterlin, Richard A. "Farm Production and Income in Old and New Areas at Mid-Century." In *Essays in Nineteenth Century Economic History: The Old Northwest*, edited by David C. Klingaman and Richard K. Vedder, 77–117. Athens, Ohio, 1975.

Eastman, Mrs. Mary H. *Aunt Phyllis's Cabin: Or, Southern Life as It Is*. 1852. Reprint. New York, 1968.

Eaton, Clement J. *The Freedom-of-Thought Struggle in the Old South*. Rev. ed. New York, 1964.

––––––. *The Growth of Southern Civilization, 1790–1860*. New York, 1961.

––––––. *The Mind of the Old South*. Baton Rouge, La., 1964.

––––––. "Mob Violence in the Old South." *Mississippi Valley Historical Review* 29 (December 1942): 351–70.

"Education." *Southern Quarterly Review* 1 (April 1842): 317–29.

Eisenstein, Sarah. *Give Us Bread but Give Us Roses: Working Women's Consciousness in the United States, 1890 to the First World War*. London, 1983.

Elkins, Stanley. *Slavery: A Problem in American Life*. Chicago, 1959.

"Ellet's Women of the Revolution." *Southern Quarterly Review* 17 (July 1850): 315–54.

Engerman, Stanley L., and Eugene D. Genovese, eds. *Race and Slavery in the Western Hemisphere; Quantitative Studies*. Princeton, N.J., 1975.

English, Elizabeth D., ed. "House Furnishings of the 1830's as Described in the Letters of Martha Keziah Peay." *South Carolina Historical Magazine* 43 (1942): 69–87.

Epstein, Barbara Leslie. *The Politics of Domesticity: Women, Evangelism, and Tem-*

perance in Nineteenth-Century America. Middletown, Conn., 1981.

Ernst, Joseph A., and J. Roy Merrens. "'Camden's Turrets Pierce the Skies!': The Urban Process in the Southern Colonies during the Eighteenth Century." *William and Mary Quarterly*, 3d ser., vol. 30, no. 4 (October 1973): 549–74.

Erwin, John Seymour, ed. *Like Some Green Laurel: Letters of Margaret Johnson Erwin, 1821–1863*. Baton Rouge, La., 1981.

Escott, Paul D. *Slavery Remembered: A Record of Twentieth-Century Slave Narratives*. Chapel Hill, N.C., 1979.

Evans, Augusta Jane. *Beulah*. 1859. Reprint. New York, 1898.

Everitt, Alan. "Farm Labourers." In *The Agrarian History of England and Wales*, edited by Joan Thirsk, 5:396–465. Cambridge, Eng., 1967.

_____. "The Marketing of Agricultural Produce." In *The Agrarian History of England and Wales*, edited by Joan Thirsk, 4:446–92. Cambridge, Eng., 1967.

Ezell, Margaret J. M. *The Patriarch's Wife: Literary Evidence and the History of the Family*. Chapel Hill, N.C., 1987.

Fanon, Frantz. *A Dying Colonialism*. Translated by Haakon Chewalie. New York, 1965.

Faragher, John Mack. "History from the Inside Out: Writing the History of Women in Rural America." *American Quarterly* 33 (1981): 537–57.

_____. "Open-Country Community: Sugar Creek, Illinois, 1820–1850." In *The Countryside in the Age of Capitalist Transformation: Essays in the Social History of Rural America*, edited by Steven Hahn and Jonathan Prude, 233–58. Chapel Hill, N.C., 1985.

_____. *Sugar Creek: Life on the Illinois Prairie*. New Haven, Conn., 1986.

_____. *Women and Men on the Overland Trail*. New Haven, Conn., 1979.

Farmer, James Oscar, Jr. *The Metaphysical Confederacy: James Henley Thornwell and the Synthesis of Southern Values*. Macon, Ga., 1986.

Farnham-Pope, Christie. "Preparation for Pedestals: North Carolina Antebellum Female Seminaries." Ph.D. diss., University of Chicago, 1977.

Faust, Drew Gilpin. "Culture, Conflict, and Community: The Meaning of Power on an Ante-Bellum Plantation." *Journal of Social History* 14, no. 1 (Fall 1980): 83–98.

_____. "In Search of the Real Mary Chesnut." *Reviews in American History* 10, no. 1 (March 1982): 54–59.

_____. *James Henry Hammond and the Old South: A Design for Mastery*. Baton Rouge, La., 1982.

_____, ed. *Ideology of Slavery: Proslavery Thought in the Antebellum South, 1830–1860*. Baton Rouge, La., 1981.

Featherstonhaugh, G. W. *Excursion through the Slave States*. 1844. Reprint. New York, 1968.

Fee, Elizabeth. "Science and the Woman Problem: Historical Perspectives." In *Sex Differences: Social and Biological Perspectives*, edited by Michael S. Teitelbaum, 175–223. Garden City, N.Y., 1976.

Felton, Rebecca Latimer. *Country Life in Georgia in the Days of My Youth*. 1919. Reprint. New York, 1980.

Ferleger, Louis. "Self-Sufficiency and Rural Life on Southern Farms." *Agricultural History* 58, no. 3 (July 1984): 314–29.

_____. *Tools and Time: Southern Farmers after Reconstruction* (title tentative). Forthcoming.

Fern, Fanny. *Ruth Hall and Other Writings.* Edited by Joyce W. Warren. New Brunswick, N.J., 1986.

Fidler, William Perry. *Augusta Evans Wilson, 1835–1909: A Biography.* University, Ala., 1951.

Fields, Barbara Jeanne. *Slavery and Freedom on the Middle Ground: Maryland during the Nineteenth Century.* New Haven, Conn., 1985.

Filler, Louis, ed. *An Ohio Schoolmistress: The Memoirs of Irene Hardy.* Kent, Ohio, 1980.

Finch, Marianne. *An Englishwoman's Experience in America.* 1853. Reprint. New York, 1969.

Finkelman, Paul. "Exploring Southern Legal History." *North Carolina Law Review* 114, no. 1 (November 1985): 77–116.

Finley, M. I. *Ancient Slavery and Modern Ideology.* New York, 1980.

Fishburne, Anne Sinkler. *Belvidere: A Plantation Memory.* Columbia, S.C., 1949.

Fishlow, Albert. *American Railroads and the Transformation of the Ante-Bellum Economy.* Cambridge, Mass., 1965.

_____. "Antebellum Interregional Trade Reconsidered." In *New Views on American Economic Development: A Selective Anthology of Recent Work,* edited by Ralph Andreano, 187–200. Cambridge, Mass., 1965.

Fisk University. *God Struck Me Dead: Religious Conversion Experiences and Autobiographies of Ex-Slaves.* Edited by Clifton H. Johnson. 1945. Reprint. Philadelphia, 1969.

_____. *Unwritten History of Slavery: Autobiographical Accounts of Negro Ex-Slaves.* 1945. Reprint. Washington, D.C., 1968.

Fitzgerald, Ruth Coder. *A Different Story: A History of Fredericksburg, Stafford, and Spotsylvania, Virginia.* Greensboro, N.C., 1979.

Fitzhugh, George. *Cannibals All!* Edited by C. Vann Woodward. Cambridge, Mass., 1960.

_____. "The Impending Fate of the Country." *DeBow's Review* 11 (December 1866): 560–71.

_____. "The Revolutions of 1776 and 1861 Contrasted." *Southern Literary Messenger* 35 (November/December 1863): 718–26.

_____. *Sociology for the South, or the Failure of Free Society.* 1854. Reprint. New York, 1965.

Flanders, Ralph B. "Two Plantations and a County of Ante-Bellum Georgia." *Georgia Historical Quarterly* 12 (March 1928): 1–37.

Flandrin, Jean-Louis. *Families in Former Times: Kinship, Household, and Sexuality.* Translated by Richard Southern. Cambridge, Eng., 1979.

Fleisig, Heywood. "Slavery, the Supply of Agricultural Labor, and the Industrialization of the South." *Journal of Economic History* 36, no. 3 (September 1976): 572–97.

Fleming, Bertram Holland. *Early Georgia Magazines: Literary Periodicals to 1865.* Athens, Ga., 1944.

Fletcher, John. *Studies on Slavery, in Easy Lessons.* 1852. Reprint. Miami, 1965.

Flexner, Eleanor. *Century of Struggle: The Women's Rights Movement in the United*

States. Rev. ed. Cambridge, Mass., 1975.

Foby. "The Management of Servants." *Southern Cultivator* 11 (August 1853): 227.

Fogel, Robert W. *Without Consent or Contract: The Rise and Fall of American Slavery*. New York, 1988.

Fogel, Robert W., and Stanley L. Engerman. *Time on the Cross: The Economics of American Negro Slavery*. 2 vols. Boston, Mass., 1974.

_____, eds. *The Reinterpretation of American History*. New York, 1971.

Foner, Eric. *Free Soil, Free Labor, Free Men: The Ideology of the Republican Party before the Civil War*. New York, 1970.

_____. *Tom Paine and Revolutionary America*. New York, 1976.

_____, ed. *Nat Turner*. Englewood Cliffs, N.J., 1971.

Ford, Franklin L. *Strasbourg in Transition, 1648–1789*. Cambridge, Mass., 1958.

Ford, Lacy K., Jr. "Social Origins of a New South Carolina: The Upcountry in the Nineteenth Century." Ph.D. diss., University of South Carolina, 1983.

Forrest, Mary. *Women of the South Distinguished in Literature*. New York, 1861.

Fortes, Meyer, and E. E. Evans-Pritchard, eds. *African Political Systems*. London, 1940.

Foster, Frances S. "Changing Concepts of the Black Woman." *Journal of Black Studies* 3, no. 4 (June 1973): 433–54.

_____. "Ultimate Victims: Black Women in Slave Narratives." *Journal of American Culture* 1, no. 4 (Winter 1978): 845–63.

Foust, James D. *The Yeoman Farmer and Westward Expansion of U.S. Cotton Production*. New York, 1975.

Fox, Edward W. *History in Geographic Perspective: The Other France*. New York, 1971.

Fox-Genovese, Elizabeth. "Antebellum Southern Households: A New Perspective on a Familiar Question." *Review* 7, no. 2 (Fall 1983): 215–53.

_____. "Culture and Consciousness in the Intellectual History of European Women." *Signs* 12, no. 3 (Spring 1987): 529–47.

_____. "The Female Self in the Age of Bourgeois Individualism." Presented as the Joanne Goodman Lectures, University of Western Ontario, October 1987.

_____. "Gender, Class, and Power: Some Theoretical Considerations." *The History Teacher* 15, no. 2 (February 1982): 255–76.

_____. Introduction to *French Women and the Age of Enlightenment*, edited by Samia I. Spencer, 1–29. Bloomington, Ind., 1984.

_____. "The Many Faces of Moral Economy: A Contribution to a Debate." *Past and Present*, no. 58 (February 1973): 161–68.

_____. "My Statue, My Self: Autobiographical Writings of Afro-American Women." In *The Private Self: Theory and Practice of Women's Autobiographical Writings*, edited by Shari Benstock. Chapel Hill, N.C., 1988.

_____. "The Personal Is Not Political Enough." *Marxist Perspectives* 2, no. 4 (Winter 1979/80): 94–113.

_____. "Placing Women's History in History." *New Left Review*, no. 133 (May/June 1982): 5–29.

_____. "Property and Patriarchy in Classical Bourgeois Political Theory." *Radical History Review* 4 (Spring/Summer 1977): 36–59.

_____. "Slavery as the Solution to the Social Question." Paper presented at the Southern Historical Association Meeting, New Orleans, La., 1987.

_____. "Strategies and Forms of Resistance: Focus on Slave Women in the United States." In *In Resistance: Studies in African, Caribbean, and Afro-American History*, edited by Gary Y. Okihiro, 143–65. Amherst, Mass., 1986.

_____. "To Write Myself: The Autobiographies of Afro-American Women." In *Feminist Issues in Literary Scholarship*, edited by Shari Benstock, 161–80. Bloomington, Ind., 1987.

_____. "Women, Affirmative Action, and the Myth of Individualism." *George Washington Law Review* 54, no. 2/3 (January/March 1986): 338–74.

_____. "Women and the Enlightenment." In *Becoming Visible: Women in European History*, edited by Renate Bridenthal, Claudia Koonz, and Susan Stuard, 251–77. Boston, 1987.

_____. "Women and Work." In *French Women and the Age of Enlightenment*, edited by Samia I. Spencer, 111–27. Bloomington, Ind., 1984.

_____, trans. and ed. *The Autobiography of Du Pont de Nemours*. Wilmington, Del., 1984.

Fox-Genovese, Elizabeth, and Eugene D. Genovese. "The Divine Sanction of Social Order: Religious Foundations of the Southern Slaveholders' World View." *Journal of the American Academy of Religion* 55, no. 2 (June 1987): 201–23.

_____. *Fruits of Merchant Capital: Slavery and Bourgeois Property in the Rise and Expansion of Capitalism*. New York, 1983.

_____. *The Mind of the Master Class: The Life and Thought of Southern Slaveholders* (title tentative). Forthcoming.

Frankel, Noralee. "Workers, Wives, and Mothers: Black Women in Mississippi, 1860–1879." Ph.D. diss., George Washington University, 1982.

Franklin, Ethel Mary, ed. "Memoirs of Mrs. Annie P. Harris." *Southwestern Historical Quarterly* 40, no. 3 (January 1937): 231–46.

Franklin, John Hope. *The Free Negro in North Carolina, 1790–1860*. Chapel Hill, N.C., 1943.

_____. *From Slavery to Freedom: A History of Negro Americans*. 5th ed. New York, 1980.

_____. "Negro Episcopalians in Ante Bellum North Carolina." *Historical Magazine of the Protestant Episcopal Church* 13 (1944): 216–34.

Fraser, Jessie Melville. "Louisa C. McCord." M.A. thesis, University of South Carolina, 1919.

Fraser, John. *America and the Patterns of Chivalry*. Cambridge, Eng., 1972.

Fraser, Walter J., Jr., R. Frank Saunders, Jr., and Jon L. Wakelyn, eds. *The Web of Southern Social Relations: Women, Family, and Education*. Athens, Ga., 1985.

Frazier, E. Franklin. *Black Bourgeoisie*. Glencoe, Ill., 1957.

_____. *The Negro Family in the United States*. 1948. Reprint. Chicago, 1966.

Freedman, Estelle. *Their Sisters' Keepers: Women's Prison Reform in America, 1830–1930*. Ann Arbor, Mich., 1981.

Freehling, William. *Prelude to Civil War: The Nullification Controversy in South Carolina, 1816–1836*. New York, 1966.

Frey, Sylvia R. "'Bitter Fruit from the Sweet Stem of Liberty': Georgia Slavery and the American Revolution." Paper presented at the annual meeting of the American Historical Association, New York, N.Y., December 1985.

Friedl, Ernestine. "The Position of Women: Appearance and Reality." *Anthropological Quarterly* 40, no. 3 (July 1967): 97–108.

Friedman, Jean E. *The Enclosed Garden: Women and Community in the Evangelical South, 1830–1900.* Chapel Hill, N.C., 1985.

Friedmann, Harriet. "Household Production and the National Economy: Concepts for the Analysis of Agrarian Formations." *Journal of Peasant Studies* 7, no. 2 (January 1980): 158–84.

Gaines, Francis Pendleton. *The Southern Plantation: A Study in the Development and the Accuracy of a Tradition.* New York, 1925.

Galenson, David W., and Russell R. Menard. "Approaches to the Analysis of Economic Growth in Colonial British America." *Historical Methods* 13, no. 1 (Winter 1980): 3–18.

Gallman, Robert E. "Slavery and Southern Economic Growth." *Southern Economic Journal* 45, no. 4 (April 1979): 1007–22.

Gaskell, Elizabeth. *Ruth.* Boston, 1853.

Gaspar, David Barry. *Bondmen and Rebels: A Study of Master-Slave Relations in Antigua, with Implications for Colonial British America.* Baltimore, Md., 1985.

———. "Slave Women and Resistance in the Caribbean: Antigua, 1623–1763." Paper presented at the annual meeting of the Southern Historical Association, Houston, Tex., November 1985.

Gaston, Kay Baker. "The Remarkable Harriet Whiteside." *Tennessee Historical Quarterly* 40, no. 4 (Winter 1981): 333–47.

Gay, Dorothy Ann. "The Tangled Skein of Romanticism and Violence in the Old South: The Southern Response to Abolitionism and Feminism, 1830–1861." Ph.D. diss., University of North Carolina, 1975.

Geggus, David. "The Enigma of Jamaica in the 1790s: New Light on the Causes of Slave Rebellions." *William and Mary Quarterly,* 3d ser., vol. 44, no. 2 (April 1987): 274–99.

Gehrke, William Herman. "Negro Slavery among the Germans in North Carolina." *North Carolina Historical Review* 14, no. 4 (October 1937): 307–24.

Genovese, Eugene D. *From Rebellion to Revolution: Afro-American Slave Revolts in the Making of the Modern World.* Baton Rouge, La., 1979.

———. *In Red and Black: Marxian Explorations in Southern and Afro-American History.* 2d ed. Knoxville, Tenn., 1984.

———. "Ordinary Slaveholders' Response to Slavery as the Solution to the Social Question." Paper presented at the Southern Historical Association Meeting, New Orleans, La., 1987.

———. *The Political Economy of Slavery: Studies in the Economy and Society of the Slave South.* New York, 1965.

———. *Roll, Jordan, Roll: The World the Slaves Made.* New York, 1975.

———. "The Significance of the Slave Plantation for Southern Economic Development." *Journal of Southern History* 28, no. 4 (November 1962): 422–37.

———. *The World the Slaveholders Made: Two Essays in Interpretation.* New York, 1969.

Genovese, Eugene D., and Elizabeth Fox-Genovese. "The Religious Ideals of Southern Slave Society." *Georgia Historical Quarterly* 70, no. 1 (Spring 1986): 1–16.

———. "Slavery, Economic Development, and the Law: The Dilemma of the Southern Political Economists, 1800–1860." *Washington and Lee Law Review* 41, no. 1 (Winter 1984): 1–29.

George, C. H. "The Origins of Capitalism: A Marxist Epitome and a Critique of Immanuel Wallerstein's Modern World-System." *Marxist Perspectives* 3, no. 2 (Summer 1980): 70–100.

George, Margaret. "From 'Goodwife' to 'Mistress': The Transformation of the Female in Bourgeois Culture." *Science and Society* 37, no. 2 (Summer 1973): 153–77.

Gessain, Monique. "Coniagui Women (Guinea)." In *Women of Tropical Africa*, edited by Denise Paulme, 17–46. Berkeley, Calif., 1973.

Giddings, Paula. *When and Where I Enter: The Impact of Black Women on Race and Sex in America*. New York, 1984.

Gilbert, Olive, ed. *Sojourner Truth's Narrative and Book of Life*. Battle Creek, Mich., 1878.

Gilchrist, David, ed. *The Growth of Seaport Cities 1790–1825*. Charlottesville, Va., 1967.

Gillespie, Joanna Bowen. "'The Clear Leadings of Providence': Pious Memoirs and the Problems of Self-Realization for Women in the Early Nineteenth Century." *Journal of the Early Republic* 5, no. 2 (Summer 1985): 197–221.

———. "Modesty Canonized: Female Saints in Antebellum Methodist Sunday School Literature." *Historical Reflections/Reflexions Historiques* 10, no. 2 (Summer 1983): 195–219.

Gilley, B. H. "Kate Gordon and Louisiana Woman Suffrage." *Louisiana History* 24, no. 3 (Summer 1983): 289–306.

Gilman, Caroline. *Recollections of a Southern Matron*. New York, 1838.

Gilman, S. "Studies of Rebecca and Catherine Edwards for the Year 1841." *South Carolina Historical Magazine* 55 (1954): 127–28.

Gilmore, Al-Tony, ed. *Revisiting Blassingame's "The Slave Community": The Scholars Respond*. Westport, Conn., 1978.

Glass, D. V., and D. E. C. Eversley, eds. *Population in History: Essays in Historical Demography*. London, 1965.

Gleig, George Robert. *The History of the Bible*. New York, 1842.

Glover, Cato D. *The Stray and the Strange from "Mulberry": Camden, S.C.* N.p., 1972.

Goggin, Jacqueline. "Carter G. Woodson and the Movement to Promote Black History." Ph.D. diss., University of Rochester, 1984.

Goheen, Peter G. "Industrialization and the Growth of Cities in Nineteenth-Century America." *American Studies* 14, no. 1 (Spring 1973): 49–65.

Goldfield, David R. "Pursuing the American Urban Dream: Cities in the Old South." In *The City in Southern History: The Growth of Urban Civilization in the South*, edited by Blaine A. Brownell and David R. Goldfield, 52–91. Port Washington, N.Y., 1977.

———. *Urban Growth in the Age of Sectionalism: Virginia, 1847–1861*. Baton Rouge, La., 1977.

Goldin, Claudia. "The Economic Status of Women in the Early Republic: Quantitative Evidence." *Journal of Interdisciplinary History* 16, no. 3 (Winter 1986): 375–404.

———. "A Model to Explain the Relative Decline of Slavery: Empirical Results." In *Race and Slavery in the Western Hemisphere: Quantitative Studies*, edited by Stanley L. Engerman and Eugene D. Genovese, 427–50. Princeton, N.J., 1975.

————. *Urban Slavery in the American South*. Chicago, 1976.

Goldin, Claudia, and Kenneth Sokoloff. "Women, Children, and Industrialization in the Early Republic: Evidence from the Manufacturing Censuses." *Journal of Economic History* 42, no. 4 (December 1982): 741–74.

Gonzalez, Nancie L. Solien. *Black Carib Household Structure: A Study of Migration and Modernization*. Seattle, Wash., 1969.

Goodson, Martha Graham. "The Slave Narrative Collection: A Tool for Reconstructing Afro-American Women's History." *Western Journal of Black Studies* 3, no. 26 (1976): 116–22.

Gordon, Ann D. "The Young Ladies Academy of Philadelphia." In *Women of America: A History*, edited by Carol R. Berkin and Mary Beth Norton, 68–91. Boston, 1979.

Gordon, Asa H. *Sketches of Negro Life and History in South Carolina*. 1929. 2d ed. Columbia, S.C., 1971.

Gorgas, Amelia Gayle, ed. *Extracts from the Journal of Sarah Haynesworth Gayle*. New Rochelle, N.Y., 1895.

Graham, Philip, ed. "Texas Memoirs of Amelia E. Barr." *Southwestern Historical Quarterly* 69, no. 4 (1963): 473–515.

Grantham, Dewey W. "History, Mythology, and the Southern Lady." *Southern Literary Journal* 3 (Spring 1971): 98–108.

Gray, Lewis Cecil. *History of Agriculture in the Southern United States to 1860*. 2 vols. 1933. Reprint. Gloucester, Mass., 1958.

Gray, Virginia Gearhart. "Activities of Southern Women: 1840–1860." *South Atlantic Quarterly* 27, no. 3 (July 1928): 264–79.

Green, Elizabeth Alden. *Mary Lyon and Mount Holyoke: Opening the Gates*. Hanover, N.H., 1979.

Green, Fletcher M. *Democracy in the Old South and Other Essays*. Edited by J. Isaac Copeland. Nashville, Tenn., 1969.

————. "Higher Education of Women in the South prior to 1860." In *Democracy in the Old South and Other Essays*, 199–219.

Greenberg, Kenneth S. *Masters and Statesmen: The Political Culture of American Slavery*. Baltimore, Md., 1985.

Greene, Jack P., ed. *The Diary of Landon Carter of Sabine Hall*. 2 vols. Charlottesville, Va., 1965.

Greene, Jack P., and J. R. Pole, eds. *Colonial British America: Essays in the New History of the Early Modern Period*. Baltimore, Md., 1984.

Greene, John C. "The American Debate on the Negro's Place in Nature, 1780–1815." *Journal of the History of Ideas* 15, no. 3 (June 1954): 384–96.

Greene, Lorenzo. "Mutiny on Slave Ships." *Phylon* 5 (January 1944): 346–54.

Gregory, Chester W. "Black Women in Pre-Federal America." In *Clio Was a Woman: Studies in the History of American Women*, edited by Mabel E. Deutrich and Virginia C. Purdy, 53–72. Washington, D.C., 1980.

Greven, Philip J., Jr. *Four Generations: Population, Land, and Family in Colonial Andover, Massachusetts*. Ithaca, N.Y., 1970.

————. *The Protestant Temperament: Patterns of Child-Rearing, Religious Experience, and the Self in Early America*. New York, 1977.

Griffin, Frances. *Less Time for Meddling: A History of Salem Academy and College, 1772–1866*. Winston-Salem, N.C., 1979.

Griffith, Elizabeth. *In Her Own Right: The Life of Elizabeth Cady Stanton.* New York, 1984.

Griffiths, Mattie. *Autobiography of a Female Slave.* 1857. Reprint. Miami, 1969.

Grimké, Angelina. *An Appeal to the Christian Women of the South.* New York, 1836.

Groene, Bertram H. *Ante-Bellum Tallahassee.* Tallahassee, Fla., 1971.

Grund, Francis J. *The Americans in Their Moral, Social, and Political Relations.* Edited by Robert F. Berkhofer, Jr. New York, 1968.

Gullickson, Gay L. *Spinners and Weavers of Auffay: Rural Industry and the Sexual Division of Labor in a French Village, 1750–1850.* New York, 1986.

Gundersen, Joan R. "The Double Bonds of Race and Sex: Black and White Women in a Colonial Virginia Parish." *Journal of Southern History* 52, no. 3 (August 1986): 351–72.

———. "Independence, Citizenship, and the American Revolution." *Signs* 13, no. 1 (Autumn 1987): 59–77.

———. "The Non-Institutional Church: The Religious Role of Women in Eighteenth-Century Virginia." *Historical Magazine of the Protestant Episcopal Church* 51, no. 4 (December 1982): 347–57.

Gundersen, Joan R., and Gwen Victor Gampel. "Married Women's Legal Status in Eighteenth-Century New York and Virginia." *William and Mary Quarterly,* 3d ser., vol. 39, no. 1 (January 1982): 114–34.

Gunderson, Gerald. "Slavery." In *Encyclopedia of American Economic History,* edited by Glen Porter, 552–61. New York, 1980.

Gutman, Herbert G. *The Black Family in Slavery and Freedom, 1750–1925.* New York, 1976.

Gwin, Minrose C. *Black and White Women of the Old South: The Peculiar Sisterhood in American Literature.* Knoxville, Tenn., 1985.

H. "Misfortune and Genius: A Tale Founded on Fact." *Southern Literary Messenger* 1, no. 2 (October 1834): 36–39.

H. C. "On the Management of Negroes." *Southern Agriculturalist* 7 (July 1834): 368.

Hacker, Barton C. "Women and Military Institutions in Early Modern Europe: A Reconnaissance." *Signs* 6, no. 4 (Summer 1981): 643–71.

Hackney, Sheldon. "Southern Violence." *American Historical Review* 74, no. 3 (February 1969): 906–25.

Hafkin, Nancy J., and Edna G. Bay, eds. *Women in Africa: Studies in Social and Economic Change.* Stanford, Calif., 1976.

Hagler, D. Harland. "The Ideal Woman in the Antebellum South: Lady or Farmwife?" *Journal of Southern History* 46, no. 3 (August 1980): 405–18.

Hahn, Steven. *The Roots of Southern Populism: Yeoman Farmers and the Transformation of the Georgia Upcountry, 1850–1890.* New York, 1983.

———. "The 'Unmaking' of the Southern Yeomanry: The Transformation of the Georgia Upcountry, 1860–1890." In *The Countryside in the Age of Capitalist Transformation: Essays in the Social History of Rural America,* edited by Steven Hahn and Jonathan Prude, 179–203. Chapel Hill, N.C., 1985.

Hahn, Steven, and Jonathan Prude, eds. *The Countryside in the Age of Capitalist Transformation: Essays in the Social History of Rural America.* Chapel Hill, N.C., 1985.

Hajnal, J. "European Marriage Patterns in Perspective." In *Population in History:*

Essays in Historical Demography, edited by D. V. Glass and D. E. C. Eversley, 101–43. London, 1965.

Hall, Catherine. "The Early Formation of Victorian Domestic Ideology." In *Fit Work For Women*, edited by Sandra Burman, 15–32. London, 1979.

Hall, D. D. "A Yankee Tutor in the South." *New England Quarterly* 33 (March 1960): 82–91.

Hall, Jacquelyn Dowd. *Revolt against Chivalry: Jessie Daniel Ames and the Women's Campaign against Lynching*. New York, 1979.

Hampton, Ann Fripp, ed. *A Divided Heart: Letters of Sally Baxter Hampton, 1853–1862*. Spartanburg, S.C., 1980.

Handler, Jerome S., and Robert S. Corruccini. "Plantation Slave Life in Barbados: A Physical Anthropological Analysis." *Journal of Interdisciplinary History* 14 (Summer 1983): 65–90.

Harding, Vincent. *There Is a River: The Black Struggle for Freedom in America*. New York, 1981.

Hardy, William Harris, and Toney A. Hardy. *No Compromise with Principles: Autobiography and Biography of William Harris Hardy*. New York, 1946.

Harley, Sharon, and Rosalind Terborg-Penn, eds. *The Afro-American Woman: Struggles and Images*. Port Washington, N.Y., 1978.

Harper, C. W. "Black Aristocrats: Domestic Servants on the Antebellum Plantation." *Phylon* 46, no. 2 (June 1985): 123–35.

Harper, Cecil, Jr. "Slavery without Cotton: Hunt County, Texas, 1846–1864." *Southwestern Historical Quarterly* 88, no. 4 (April 1985): 387–405.

Harper, William. *Memoir on Slavery, Read before the Society for the Advancement of Learning at Its Annual Meeting in Columbia, 1837*. Charleston, S.C., 1838.

Harris, Mrs. Dilue. "The Reminiscences of Mrs. Dilue Harris." *Texas Historical Association Quarterly* 4, nos. 1, 3 (1900, 1901): 85–127, 155–89; 7, no. 3 (1904): 214–22.

Harris, J. R., ed. *Liverpool and Merseyside: Essays in the Economic and Social History of the Port and Its Hinterland*. London, 1969.

Harris, J. William. *Plain Folk and Gentry in a Slave Society: White Liberty and Black Slavery in Augusta's Hinterlands*. Middletown, Conn., 1985.

Harris, Olivia. "Households and Their Boundaries." *History Workshop*, no. 13 (Spring 1982): 143–52.

Hart, Francis R. "Notes for an Anatomy of Modern Autobiography." *New Literary History* 1, no. 3 (Spring 1970): 485–511.

Hart, John S. *The Female Prose Writers of America*. Philadelphia, 1852.

Hartman, Susan M. *The Home Front and Beyond: American Women in the 1940s*. Boston, 1982.

Hartridge, Walter Charlton, ed. *The Letters of Robert Mackay to His Wife, Written from Ports in America and England, 1795–1816*. Athens, Ga., 1949.

Hartwell, R. M. *The Industrial Revolution and Economic Growth*. London, 1971.

Hartz, Louis. *The Liberal Tradition in America: An Interpretation of American Political Thought since the Revolution*. New York, 1955.

Harvey, David. *Consciousness and the Urban Experience: Studies in the History and Theory of Capitalist Urbanization*. Baltimore, Md., 1985.

———. *The Urbanization of Capital: Studies in the History and Theory of Capitalist Urbanization*. Baltimore, Md., 1985.

Hawes, Lilla Mills, ed. "Minute Book, Savannah Board of Police, 1779." *Georgia Historical Quarterly* 45, no. 3 (1961): 245–57.

Hawks, Joanne V., and Sheila L. Skemp, eds. *Sex, Race, and the Role of Women in the South*. Jackson, Miss., 1983.

Hays, Florence. *Daughters of Dorcas: The Story of the Work of Women for Home Missions since 1802*. New York, 1952.

Heck, Fannie S. *In Royal Service: The Mission Work of Southern Baptist Women*. Richmond, Va., 1913.

Heffernan, William. "The Slave Trade and Abolition in Travel Literature." *Journal of the History of Ideas* 34, no. 2 (April/June 1973): 185–208.

Heller, Thomas C., Morton Sosna, and David E. Wellberg, with Arnold I. Davidson, Ann Swidler, and Ian Watt, eds. *Reconstructing Individualism: Autonomy, Individuality, and the Self in Western Thought*. Palo Alto, Calif., 1986.

Helmreich, Jonathan E. "A Prayer for the Spirit of Acceptance: The Journal of Martha Wayles Robertson." *Historical Magazine of the Protestant Episcopal Church* 46 (December 1977): 397–408.

Henretta, James A. "Families and Farms: *Mentalité* in Pre-Industrial America." *William and Mary Quarterly*, 3d ser., vol. 35, no. 1 (January 1978): 3–32.

Henry, H. M. *Police Control of the Slave in South Carolina*. 1914. Reprint. New York, 1968.

Henson, Josiah. *An Autobiography of the Reverend Josiah Henson*. 1881. Reprint. Reading, Mass., 1969.

Hentz, Mrs. Caroline Lee. *Eoline, or Magnolia Vale*. Philadelphia, 1852.

———. *The Planter's Northern Bride*. 1854. Reprint. Chapel Hill, N.C., 1970.

Herd, Elmer Don, Jr., ed. "Sue Sparks Keitt to a Northern Friend, March 4, 1861." *South Carolina Historical Magazine* 62 (1961): 82–87.

Hersh, Blanche Glassman. *The Slavery of Sex: Feminist-Abolitionists in America*. Urbana, Ill., 1978.

Herskovits, Melville J. "A Note on 'Woman Marriage' in Dahomey." *Africa* 10, no. 3 (July 1937): 335–41.

Hewitt, Nancy A. "Feminist Friends: Agrarian Quakers and the Emergence of Woman's Rights in America." *Feminist Studies* 12, no. 1 (Spring 1986): 27–50.

———. *Women's Activism and Social Change: Rochester, New York, 1822–1872*. Ithaca, N.Y., 1984.

Heyward, Duncan Clinch. *Seed from Madagascar*. Chapel Hill, N.C., 1937.

Higginson, Thomas Wentworth. *Black Rebellion*. Edited by James McPherson. New York, 1969.

Hilliard, Sam Bowers. *Hog Meat and Hoe Cake: Food Supply in the Old South, 1840–1860*. Carbondale, Ill., 1972.

Hilton, Rodney, ed. *The Transition from Feudalism to Capitalism*. London, 1976.

Hindess, Barry, and Paul Q. Hirst. *Pre-Capitalist Modes of Production*. London, 1975.

Hine, Darlene C. "Female Slave Resistance: The Economics of Sex." *Western Journal of Black Studies* 3, no. 2 (1979): 123–27.

Hine, Darlene C., and Kate Wittenstein. "Female Slave Resistance: The Economics of Sex." In *Black Woman Cross-Culturally*, edited by Filomina Chioma Steady, 289–99. Cambridge, Mass., 1981.

Hobsbawn, Eric. "The General Crisis of the European Economy in the Seventeenth Century." *Past and Present*, nos. 5, 6 (May, November 1954): 33–53, 44–65.

Hodge, Charles. "The Bible Argument on Slavery." In *Cotton Is King, and Proslavery Arguments*, edited by E. N. Elliott, 841–77. 1860. Reprint. New York, 1969.

Hoffman, Ronald, Thad W. Tate, and Peter J. Albert, eds. *An Uncivil War: The Southern Backcountry during the American Revolution*. Charlottesville, Va., 1985.

Hohenberg, Paul M., and Lynn Hollen Lees. *The Making of Urban Europe, 1000–1950*. Cambridge, Mass., 1985.

Holbrook, Abigail Curlee. "A Glimpse of Life on Antebellum Slave Plantations in Texas." *Southwestern Historical Quarterly* 76, no. 4 (April 1973): 361–83.

Holder, Edward M. "Social Life of the Early Moravians in North Carolina." *North Carolina Historical Review* 11, no. 3 (July 1934): 167–84.

Holifield, E. Brooks. *The Gentlemen Theologians: American Theology in Southern Culture, 1795–1860*. Durham, N.C., 1978.

Holman, Harriet R., ed. "Charleston in the Summer of 1841: The Letters of Harriott Horry Rutledge." *South Carolina Historical and Genealogical Magazine* 46 (1945): 1–14.

Holmes, Alester G., and George R. Sherrill. *Thomas Green Clemson: His Life and Work*. Richmond, Va., 1937.

Holmes, Jack D. L. "The Abortive Slave Revolt at Pointe Coupe, Louisiana, 1795." *Louisiana History* 11 (Fall 1970): 341–62.

Homans, Margaret. *Bearing the Word: Language and Female Experience in Nineteenth-Century Women's Writing*. Chicago, 1986.

Hooks, Bell. *Ain't I a Woman?: Black Women and Feminism*. Boston, 1981.

Hoole, William Stanley. "The Gilmans and the Southern Rose." *North Carolina Historical Review* 11 (1934): 116–28.

Hopkins, A. G. *An Economic History of West Africa*. New York, 1973.

Hopkins, Gerard Manley. *The Poems of Gerard Manley Hopkins*. Edited by W. H. Gardner and N. H. MacKenzie. New York, 1970.

[Hopley, Catherine Cooper]. *Life in the South from the Commencement of the War, by a Blockaded British Subject*. 2 vols. 1863. Reprint. New York, 1971.

Horowitz, Morton J. *The Transformation of American Law, 1780–1860*. Cambridge, Mass., 1977.

Horsmanden, Daniel. *The New York Conspiracy*. Edited by Thomas J. Davis. Boston, 1971.

Horton, James Oliver. "Freedom's Yoke: Gender Conventions among Antebellum Free Blacks." *Feminist Studies* 12, no. 1 (Spring 1986): 51–76.

Horton, James Oliver, and Lois E. Horton. *Black Bostonians: Family Life and Community Struggle in the Antebellum North*. New York, 1979.

House, Albert Virgil, ed. *Planter Management and Capitalism in Ante-Bellum Georgia: The Journal of Hugh Fraser Grant, Ricegrower*. New York, 1954.

Howarth, William L. "Some Principles of Autobiography." *New Literary History* 5 (1973/74): 363–81.

Howell, Martha C. *Women, Production, and Patriarchy in Late Medieval Cities*. Chicago, 1986.

Hoyt, William D., Jr., ed. "The Calvert-Stier Correspondence: Letters from

America to the Low Countries, 1797–1828." *Maryland Historical Magazine* 38, nos. 2, 3, 4 (June, September, December 1943): 123–40, 261–72, 337–44.

———. "Self-Portrait: Eliza Custis, 1808." *Virginia Magazine of History and Biography* 53, no. 2 (1945): 89–100.

Hubka, Thomas C. *Big House, Little House, Back House, Barn: The Connected Farm Buildings of New England*. Hanover, N.H., 1984.

Huetz de Lemps, Christian. *Géographie du commerce de Bordeaux à la fin du règne de Louis XIV*. Paris and La Haye, 1975.

Hufton, Olwen. "Women and the Family Economy in Eighteenth-Century France." *French Historical Studies* 9 (1975): 1–22.

———. "Women in Revolution, 1789–1796." *Past and Present*, no. 53 (1971): 90–108.

Hughes, Henry. *Treatise on Sociology, Theoretical and Practical*. 1854. Reprint. New York, 1968.

Hull, Augustus Longstreet. *Annals of Athens, Georgia, 1801–1901*. Athens, Ga., 1906.

Hunter, Frances L. "Slave Society on the Southern Plantation." *The Journal of Negro History* 7 (January 1922): 1–10.

Ingraham, Joseph Holt. *The South-West. By a Yankee*. 2 vols. 1835. Reprint. New York, 1966.

———, ed. *The Sunny South: Or, the Southerner at Home, Embracing the Five Years' Experience of a Northern Governess in the Land of Sugar and Cotton*. 1860. Reprint. New York, 1968.

Isaac, Rhys. *The Transformation of Virginia, 1740–1790*. Chapel Hill, N.C., 1982.

"Is Southern Society Worth Preserving?" *Southern Quarterly Review* 19 (January 1851): 189–225.

J. S. T. "Ida Norman." *Southern Quarterly Review* 13 (April 1848): 331–46.

J. T. "Negro Mania." *Southern Quarterly Review* 21 (January 1852): 153–75.

Jackson, Luther P. "Manumission in Certain Virginia Cities." *Journal of Negro History* 15 (1930): 278–314.

Jacob, Kathryn Allamong. "The Woman's Lot in Baltimore Town, 1729–97." *Maryland Historical Magazine* 71 (Fall 1975): 287–95.

Jacobs, Harriet A. *Incidents in the Life of a Slave Girl: Written by Herself*. Edited by Jean Fagan Yellin. Cambridge, Mass., 1987.

James, D. Clayton. *Antebellum Natchez*. Baton Rouge, La., 1968.

James, Janet Wilson, ed. *Women in American Religion*. Philadelphia, 1980.

Jameson, Anna Brownell (Murphy). *Diary of an Ennuyee*. Boston, 1875.

———. *Sacred and Legendary Art*. London, 1850.

———. *Visits and Sketches at Home and Abroad*. 2 vols. New York, 1834.

Janiewski, Dolores E. *Sisterhood Denied: Race, Gender, and Class in a New South Community*. Philadelphia, 1985.

Jeffrey, Julie Roy. *Frontier Women: The Trans-Mississippi West, 1840–1880*. New York, 1979.

Jenkins, William Sumner. *Pro-Slavery Thought in the Old South*. Chapel Hill, N.C., 1935.

Jenkins, William Thomas. "Antebellum Macon and Bibb County, Georgia." Ph.D. diss., University of Georgia, 1966.

Jensen, Joan. *Loosening the Bonds: Mid-Atlantic Farm Women, 1750–1850*. New Haven, Conn., 1986.

Jenson, Carol Elizabeth. "The Equity Jurisdiction and Married Women's Property in Ante-Bellum America: A Revisionist View." *International Journal of Women's Studies* 2, no. 2 (March/April 1979): 144–54.

John, A. J. "Aspects of English Economic Growth in the First Half of the Eighteenth Century." In *Essays in Economic History*, edited by E. M. Carus-Wilson, 2:360–73. London, 1962.

Johnson, Guion Griffis. *Ante-Bellum North Carolina: A Social History*. Chapel Hill, N.C., 1937.

_____. "Recreational and Cultural Activities in the Ante-Bellum Towns of North Carolina." *North Carolina Historical Review* 6 (1929): 17–37.

Johnson, H[ershel]. V. *Address by the Hon. H. V. Johnson, at the Commencement Exercises of the Wesleyan Female College, Macon, Georgia, on the 14th of July, 1853*. Macon, Ga., 1853.

Johnson, James Hugo. "The Participation of White Men in Virginia Negro Insurrections." *Journal of Negro History* 16 (1931): 158–67.

Johnson, Mary Durham. "Old Wine in New Bottles: The Institutional Changes for Women of the People during the French Revolution." In *Women, War, and Revolution*, edited by Carol Berkin and Clara Lovett, 107–43. New York, 1980.

Johnson, Michael P. "Planters and Patriarchy: Charleston, 1800–1860." *Journal of Southern History* 46, no. 1 (February 1980): 45–72.

_____. "Runaway Slaves and the Slave Communities in South Carolina, 1799 to 1830." *William and Mary Quarterly*, 3d ser., vol. 38, no. 3 (July 1981): 418–41.

_____. "Smothered Slave Infants: Were Slave Mothers at Fault?" *Journal of Southern History* 47 (November 1981): 493–520.

_____. *Toward a Patriarchal Republic: The Secession of Georgia*. Baton Rouge, La., 1977.

_____. "Work, Culture, and the Slave Community: Slave Occupations in the Cotton Belt in 1860." *Labor History* 27, no. 3 (Summer 1986): 325–55.

Johnson, Michael P., and James L. Roark. *Black Masters: A Free Family of Color in the Old South*. New York, 1984.

_____. "'A Middle Ground': Free Mulattoes and the Friendly Moralist Society of Antebellum Charleston." *Southern Studies* 21, no. 3 (Fall 1982): 246–65.

_____, eds. *No Chariot Let Down: Charleston's Free People of Color on the Eve of the Civil War*. Chapel Hill, N.C., 1984.

Johnson, Paul E. *A Shopkeeper's Millennium: Society and Revivals in Rochester, New York, 1815–1837*. New York, 1978.

Johnson, Thomas Cary. *The Life and Letters of Benjamin Morgan Palmer*. Richmond, Va., 1908.

Johnston, James Hugo. *Race Relations in Virginia and Miscegenation in the South, 1776–1860*. Amherst, Mass., 1970.

Johnston, Mary Tabb, with Elizabeth Johnston Lipscomb. *Amelia Gayle Gorgas: A Biography*. University, Ala., 1978.

Jones, Anne Goodwyn. *Tomorrow Is Another Day: The Woman Writer in the South, 1859–1936*. Baton Rouge, La., 1981.

Jones, Charles Colcock. *The Glory of Woman Is the Fear of the Lord*. Philadelphia, 1847.

_____. *The Religious Instruction of the Negroes in the United States*. Savannah, Ga., 1842.

Jones, Mrs. Delia. "The Manner of Educating Females." *North Carolina Journal of Education* 2, no. 8 (August 1859): 227–37.

Jones, F. D., and W. H. Mills, eds. *History of the Presbyterian Church in South Carolina since 1850*. Columbia, S.C., 1926.

Jones, Jacqueline. *Labor of Love, Labor of Sorrow: Black Women, Work, and the Family from Slavery to the Present*. New York, 1985.

_____. " 'My Mother Was Much of a Woman': Black Women, Work, and the Family under Slavery." *Feminist Studies* 8, no. 2 (Summer 1982): 235–70.

Jones, Katharine M. *Ladies of Richmond; Confederate Capital*. Indianapolis, Ind., 1962.

Jordan, Paula S., with Kathy W. Manning. *Women of Guilford County, North Carolina: A Study of Women's Contributions, 1740–1979*. Greensboro, N.C., 1979.

Jordan, Terry G. "The Imprint of the Upper and Lower South on Mid-Nineteenth Century Texas." *Annals of the Association of American Geographers* 57, no. 4 (December 1967): 667–90.

Jordan, Weymouth T. *Antebellum Alabama, Town and Country*. Tallahassee, Fla., 1957.

_____. *Hugh Davis and His Alabama Plantation*. University, Ala., 1948.

Jordan, Winthrop D. "American Chiaroscuro: The Status and Definition of Mulattoes in the British Colonies." *William and Mary Quarterly*, 3d ser., vol. 19, no. 2 (April 1962): 183–200.

Joyner, Charles. *Down by the Riverside: A South Carolina Slave Community*. Urbana, Ill., 1984.

Jules-Rosette, Benetta. "Women in Indigenous African Cults and Churches." In *Black Woman Cross-Culturally*, edited by Filomina Chioma Steady, 185–207. Cambridge, Mass., 1981.

Just, Roger. "Freedom, Slavery, and the Female Psyche." *History of Political Thought* 6, no. 1/2 (1985): 169–88.

Justus, Joyce Bennett. "Women's Role in West Indian Society." In *Black Woman Cross-Culturally*, edited by Filomina Chioma Steady, 431–50. Cambridge, Mass., 1981.

Kaestle, Carl F., and Maris A. Vinovskis. *Education and Social Change in Nineteenth Century Massachusetts*. Cambridge, Eng., 1980.

Kaplan, Temma. "Female Consciousness and Collective Action: The Case of Barcelona, 1910–1918." *Signs* 7 (Spring 1982): 545–66.

Katz, Esther, and Anita Rapone, eds. *Women's Experience in America: An Historical Anthology*. New Brunswick, N.J., 1980.

Katzman, David M. *Seven Days a Week: Women and Domestic Service in Industrializing America*. New York, 1978.

Kaufman, Allen. *Capitalism, Slavery, and Republican Values: Antebellum Political Economists, 1819–1848*. Austin, Tex., 1982.

Kaufman, Polly Welts. *Women Teachers on the Frontier*. New Haven, Conn., 1984.

Kearney, Belle. *A Slaveholder's Daughter*. 1900. Reprint. New York, 1969.

Keating, Bern. *A History of Washington County, Mississippi*. Greenville, Miss., 1976.

Keckley, Elizabeth. *Behind the Scenes: Or Thirty Years a Slave and Four Years in the White House*. New York, 1868.

Keller, Rosemary Skinner, Louise L. Queen, and Hilah F. Thomas, eds. *Women in New Worlds: Historical Perspectives on the Wesleyan Tradition*. 2 vols. Nashville, Tenn., 1981–82.

Kelley, Mary. *Private Woman, Public Stage: Literary Domesticity in Nineteenth-Century America*. New York, 1984.

Kemble, Frances Anne. *Journal of a Residence on a Georgian Plantation in 1838–1839*. Edited by John A. Scott. Athens, Ga., 1984.

Kemp, Kathryn W. "Jean and Kate Gordon: New Orleans Social Reformers, 1898–1933." *Louisiana History* 24, no. 4 (1983): 389–401.

Kennedy, Hugh. "From Polis to Madina: Urban Change in Late Antique and Early Islamic Syria." *Past and Present*, no. 106 (February 1985): 3–27.

Kennedy, Susan Estabrook. *If All We Did Was to Weep at Home: A History of White Working Class Women in America*. Bloomington, Ind., 1979.

Kenny, Courtney Stanhope. *The History of the Law of England as to the Effects of Marriage on Property and on the Wife's Legal Capacity*. London, 1879.

Kerber, Linda K. "Can a Woman Be an Individual? Women and Individualism in American History." Patton Lecture, 1987.

———. "Daughters of Columbia: Educating Women for the Republic, 1787–1805." In *The Hofstader Aegis: A Memorial*, edited by Stanley Elkins and Eric McKitrick, 36–59. New York, 1974.

———. *Women of the Republic: Intellect and Ideology in Revolutionary America*. Chapel Hill, N.C., 1980.

Kerridge, Eric. *The Agricultural Revolution*. London, 1967.

Kessler-Harris, Alice. *Out to Work: A History of Wage-Earning Women in the United States*. New York, 1982.

———. *Women Have Always Worked: A Historical Overview*. Old Westbury, N.Y., 1981.

Kibler, Lillian Adele. *Benjamin F. Perry: South Carolina Unionist*. Durham, N.C., 1946.

Killens, John Oliver, ed. *The Trial Record of Denmark Vesey*. Boston, 1970.

Killion, Ronald, and Charles Waller, eds. *Slavery Time When I Was Chillun down on Marster's Plantation*. Savannah, Ga., 1973.

Kilson, Marion D. de B. "Towards Freedom: An Analysis of Slave Revolts in the United States." *Phylon* 25, no. 2 (Summer 1964): 175–87.

Kincheloe, Joe L., Jr. "Transcending Role Restrictions: Women at Camp Meetings and Political Rallies." *Tennessee Historical Quarterly* 40 (Summer 1981): 158–69.

King, C. Richard, ed. *Victorian Lady on the Texas Frontier: The Journal of Ann Raney Coleman*. Norman, Okla., 1971.

King, Spencer Bidwell, Jr., ed. *Ebb Tide: As Seen through the Diary of Josephine Clay Habersham, 1863*. Athens, Ga., 1958.

Kingsley, Charles. *Two Years Ago*. Boston, 1857.

Klapisch-Zuber, Christiane. *Women, Family, and Ritual in Renaissance Italy*. Translated by Lydia Cochrane. Chicago, 1985.

Klein, Ethel. *Gender Politics: From Consciousness to Mass Politics*. Cambridge, Mass., 1984.

Klein, Herbert S. "African Women in the Atlantic Slave Trade." In *Women and*

Slavery in Africa, edited by Claire C. Robertson and Martin A. Klein, 29–38. Madison, Wis., 1984.

Klein, Herbert S., and Stanley L. Engerman. "The Demographic Study of the American Slave Population: With Particular Attention Given the Comparison between the United States and the British West Indies." Paper presented at the International Colloquium on Historical Demography, Montreal, 8–10 October 1975.

————. "Fertility Differentials between Slaves in the United States and the British West Indies: A Note on Lactation Practices and Their Possible Implications." *William and Mary Quarterly*, 3d ser., vol. 35, no. 2 (April 1978): 357–74.

Klein, Rachel N. "Frontier Planters and the American Revolution: The South Carolina Backcountry, 1775–1782." In *An Uncivil War: The Southern Backcountry during the American Revolution*, edited by Ronald Hoffman, Thad W. Tate, and Peter J. Albert, 37–69. Charlottesville, Va., 1985.

————. "Ordering the Back Country: The South Carolina Regulation." *William and Mary Quarterly*, 3d ser., vol. 38, no. 4 (October 1981): 661–80.

————. *The Unification of a Slave State: The Rise of the Planters in the South Carolina Backcountry, 1760–1808*. Chapel Hill, N.C., forthcoming.

Klingaman, David C., and Richard K. Vedder, eds. *Essays in Nineteenth Century Economic History: The Old Northwest*. Athens, Ohio, 1975.

Kloppenberg, James T. "The Virtues of Liberalism: Christianity, Republicanism, and Ethics in Early American Political Discourse." *Journal of American History* 74, no. 1 (June 1987): 9–33.

Knight, Edgar W. *A Documentary History of Education in the South before 1860*. 5 vols. Chapel Hill, N.C., 1949.

Kolchin, Peter. "Reevaluating the Antebellum Slave Community: A Comparative Perspective." *Journal of American History* 70, no. 3 (December 1983): 579–601.

————. *Unfree Labor: American Slavery and Russian Serfdom*. Cambridge, Mass., 1987.

Kolodny, Annette. *The Land Before Her: Fantasy and Experience of the American Frontiers, 1630–1860*. Chapel Hill, 1984.

Kopytoff, Barbara. "The Early Political Development of Jamaican Maroon Societies." *William and Mary Quarterly* 3d ser., vol. 35, no. 2 (April 1978): 287–307.

————. "Jamaican Maroon Political Organization: The Effects of the Treaties." *Social and Economic Studies* 25 (June 1976): 87–105.

Kopytoff, Igor. "Slavery." *Annual Review of Anthropology* 2 (1982): 207–30.

Kousser, J. Morgan, and James McPherson, eds. *Region, Race, and Reconstruction: Essays in Honor of C. Vann Woodward*. New York, 1982.

Krech, Shepard, III. "Black Family Organization in the Nineteenth Century: An Ethnological Perspective." *Journal of Interdisciplinary History* 12 (Winter 1982): 429–52.

Krige, Eileen Jensen. "Woman-Marriage, with Special Reference to the Lovedu— Its Significance for the Definition of Marriage." *Africa* 44, no. 1 (January 1974): 11–37.

Kuhn, Anne L. *The Mother's Role in Childhood Education: New England Concepts, 1830–1860*. New Haven, Conn., 1947.

Kula, Witold. *An Economic Theory of the Feudal System: Towards a Model of the Pol-*

ish Economy, 1500–1800. Translated by Lawrence Garner. London, 1976.

————. "Secteurs et régions arriérés dans l'économie du capitalisme naissant." *Studi Storici* 1, no. 3 (April/June 1960): 569–85.

Kulikoff, Allan. "The American Yeoman Classes." Paper delivered at the annual meeting of the American Historical Association, New York, December 1985.

————. "The Beginnings of the Afro-American Family in Maryland." In *Law, Society, and Politics in Early Maryland,* edited by Aubrey C. Land, Lois Green Carr, and Edward C. Papenfuse, 171–96. Baltimore, Md., 1977.

————. "The Colonial Chesapeake: Seedbed of Antebellum Southern Culture." *Journal of Southern History* 45, no. 4 (November 1979): 513–40.

————. "The Origins of Afro-American Society in Tidewater Maryland and Virginia, 1700 to 1790." *William and Mary Quarterly,* 3d ser., vol. 35, no. 2 (April 1978): 226–59.

————. "A 'Prolifick' People: Black Population Growth in the Chesapeake Colonies, 1700–1790." *Southern Studies* 16, no. 4 (Winter 1977): 391–428.

————. *The Rise and Destruction of the American Yeoman Classes* (title tentative). Forthcoming.

————. *Tobacco and Slaves: The Development of Southern Cultures in the Chesapeake, 1680–1800.* Chapel Hill, N.C., 1986.

Kuyk, Betty M. "The African Derivation of Black Fraternal Orders in the United States." *Comparative Studies in Society and History* 25, no. 4 (October 1983): 559–92.

Kuznesof, Elizabeth Anne. "Household Composition and Headship as Related to Changes in Mode of Production: Sao Paulo, 1765 to 1836." *Comparative Studies in Society and History* 22, no. 1 (January 1980): 78–108.

L. "Female Prose Writers of America." *Southern Quarterly Review* 21 (January 1852): 114–21.

Labbe, Dolores Egger. "Women in Early Nineteenth-Century Louisiana." Ph.D. diss., University of Delaware, 1975.

Ladies' Auxiliary Christian Association of Charleston, S.C. *First Annual Report.* Charleston, S.C., 1858.

Ladies Benevolent Society. *Constitution.* Charleston, S.C., 1814.

Ladies' Benevolent Society of Charleston. *Constitution and Regulations for the Visiting Committee.* Charleston, S.C., 1852.

"Lady Wortley's Travels in America." *Southern Quarterly Review* 21 (January 1852): 232.

Lampard, Eric E. "The Evolving System of Cities in the United States: Urbanization and Economic Development." In *Issues in Urban Economics,* edited by Harvey S. Perloff and Lowdon Wingo, 81–139. Baltimore, Md., 1968.

Land, Aubrey C. "Economic Base and Social Structure: The Northern Chesapeake in the Eighteenth Century." *Journal of Economic History* 25 (1967): 639–54.

————. "Economic Behavior in a Planting Society: The Eighteenth-Century Chesapeake." *Journal of Southern History* 33 (1967): 469–85.

————. "The Tobacco Staple and the Planter's Problems: Technology, Labor, and Crops." *Agricultural History* 43 (1969): 69–81.

Land, Aubrey C., Lois G. Carr, and Edward C. Papenfuse, eds. *Law, Society, and Politics in Early Maryland.* Baltimore, Md., 1977.

Landes, David. *The Unbound Prometheus: Technological Change and Industrial De-*

velopment in Western Europe from 1750 to the Present. Cambridge, Eng., 1969.

Landrum, Grace Warren. "Notes on the Reading of the Old South." *American Literature* 3 (1931): 60–71.

———. "Sir Walter Scott and His Literary Rivals in the Old South." *American Literature* 2 (November 1930): 256–76.

Lara, Oruno D. "Resistance to Slavery: From Africa to Black America." In *Comparative Perspectives on Slavery in New World Plantation Societies*, edited by Vera Rubin and Arthur Tuden, 464–80. New York, 1977.

Laslett, Peter, ed., with Richard Wall. *Household and Family in Past Time: Comparative Studies in the Size and Structure of the Domestic Group over the Last Three Centuries in England, France, Serbia, Japan, and Colonial North America, with Further Materials from Western Europe*. Cambridge, Eng., 1972.

Laurens, Caroline Olivia. "Journal of a Visit to Greenville from Charleston in the Summer of 1825." *South Carolina Historical Magazine* 72, nos. 3, 4 (July, October 1971): 164–73, 220–33.

Lebeuf, Annie M. D. "The Role of Women in the Political Organization of African Societies." In *Women of Tropical Africa*, edited by Denise Paulme, 93–119. Berkeley, Calif., 1973.

Lebsock, Suzanne, "Free Black Women and the Question of Matriarchy: Petersburg, Virginia, 1784–1820." *Feminist Studies* 8, no. 2 (Summer 1982): 271–92.

———. *The Free Women of Petersburg: Status and Culture in a Southern Town, 1784–1860*. New York, 1984.

———. "Radical Reconstruction and the Property Rights of Southern Women." *Journal of Southern History* 42 (May 1977): 195–216.

Le Conte, Joseph. "Female Education." *Southern Presbyterian Review* 13 (April 1861): 60-91.

Lee, Jean Butenhoff. "The Problem of Slave Community in the Eighteenth-Century Chesapeake." *William and Mary Quarterly*, 3d ser., vol. 43, no. 3 (July 1986): 333–61.

Lees, Andrew, and Lynn Lees, eds. *The Urbanization of European Society in the Nineteenth Century*. Lexington, Mass., 1976.

Lehning, James R. *The Peasants of Marlhes: Economic Development and Family Organization in Nineteenth-Century France*. Chapel Hill, N.C., 1980.

Leigh, Mrs. Frances B. *Ten Years on a Georgia Plantation since the War*. 1883. Reprint. New York, 1969.

Leigh, John T. "Report." *DeBow's Review* 7 (November 1849): 380–81.

Leith-Ross, Sylvia. *African Women: A Study of the Ibo of Nigeria*. London, 1939.

Leland, Isabella Middleton, ed. "Middleton Correspondence, 1861–1865." *South Carolina Historical Magazine* 63 (1962): 33–41, 61–70, 164–74, 204–10; 64 (1963): 28–38, 95–104, 158–68, 212–19; 65 (1964): 33–44, 98–109.

Leloudis, James L., II. "Subversion of the Feminine Ideal: The *Southern Lady's Companion* and White Male Morality in the Antebellum South, 1847–1854." In *Women in New Worlds*, edited by Rosemary Skinner Keller, Louise L. Queen, and Hilah F. Thomas, 2:60–75. Nashville, Tenn., 1982.

Lemons, J. Stanley. *The Woman Citizen: Social Feminism in the 1920s*. Urbana, Ill., 1973.

Lerner, Gerda, ed. *Black Women in White America: A Documentary History*. New York, 1972.

———. "The Lady and the Mill Girl: Changes in the Status of Women in the Age of Jackson, 1800–1840." *Midcontinent American Studies Journal* 10 (Spring 1969): 5–14.

———. *The Majority Finds Its Past: Placing Women in History.* New York, 1979.

Leslie, Kent Anderson. "A Myth of the Southern Lady: Antebellum Proslavery Rhetoric and the Proper Place of Woman." *Sociological Spectrum* 6 (1986): 31–49.

Levine, David. *Family Formation in an Age of Nascent Capitalism.* New York, 1977.

———, ed. *Proletarianization and Family History.* Orlando, Fla., 1984.

Levine, Lawrence. *Black Culture and Black Consciousness: Afro-American Folk Thought from Slavery to Freedom.* New York, 1977.

Levy, Barry. "'Tender Plants': Quaker Farmers and Children in the Delaware Valley, 1681–1735." *Journal of Family History* 3, no. 2 (Summer 1978): 116–35.

Lewis, Jan. "Domestic Tranquility and the Management of Emotion among the Gentry of Pre-Revolutionary Virginia." *William and Mary Quarterly*, 3d ser., vol. 39, no. 1 (January 1982): 134–49.

———. *The Pursuit of Happiness: Family and Values in Jefferson's Virginia.* New York, 1983.

———. "The Republican Wife: Virtue and Seduction in the Early Republic." *William and Mary Quarterly*, 3d ser., vol. 44, no. 4 (October 1987): 689–721.

Lewis, Ronald L. *Coal, Iron, and Slaves: Industrial Slavery in Maryland and Virginia, 1715–1865.* Westport, Conn., 1979.

Linden, Fabian. "Economic Democracy in the Slave South: An Appraisal of Some Recent Views." *Journal of Negro History* 31 (April 1946): 140–89.

Lindstrom, Diane. *Economic Development in the Philadelphia Region, 1810–1850.* New York, 1978.

Lines, Amelia Akehurst. *To Raise Myself a Little: The Diaries and Letters of Jennie, a Georgia Teacher, 1851–1886.* Edited by Thomas Dyer. Athens, Ga., 1982.

Lipscomb, A. A. *The Relations of the Anglo-Saxon Race to Christian Womanhood: An Address Delivered before the Wesleyan Female College, at Macon, Ga., July 11, 1860.* Macon, Ga., 1860.

Littlefield, Daniel C. *Rice and Slaves: Ethnicity and the Slave Trade in Colonial South Carolina.* Baton Rouge, La., 1981.

Litwack, Leon. *Been in the Storm So Long: The Aftermath of Slavery.* New York, 1979.

Locke, John. *Two Treatises on Government.* Edited by Peter Laslett. Cambridge, Eng., 1970.

Lockridge, Kenneth A. *A New England Town: The First Hundred Years, Dedham, Massachusetts, 1636–1736.* New York, 1970.

Loewenberg, Bert James, and Ruth Bogin, eds. *Black Women in Nineteenth-Century American Life: Their Words, Their Thoughts, Their Feelings.* University Park, Pa., 1976.

Lofton, John. *Insurrection in South Carolina: The Turbulent World of Denmark Vesey.* Yellow Springs, Ohio, 1964.

Lounsbury, Richard. "*Ludibria Rerum Mortalium*: Charlestonian Intellectuals and Their Classics." In *Intellectual Life in Antebellum Charleston*, edited by Michael O'Brien and David Moltke-Hansen, 325–69. Knoxville, Tenn., 1986.

Lovejoy, Paul. *Transformations in Slavery: A History of Slavery in Africa.* Cambridge, Eng., 1983.

Loveland, Anne C. *Southern Evangelicals and the Social Order, 1800–1860*. Baton Rouge, La., 1980.

Lovell, Caroline Couper. *The Golden Isles of Georgia*. Boston, 1933.

Lumpkin, Katherine DuPre. *The Making of a Southerner*. Westport, Conn., 1971.

Lumpkin, William L. "The Role of Women in Eighteenth-Century Virginia Baptist Life." *Baptist History and Heritage* 8 (1973): 158–67.

Lyell, Sir Charles. *A Second Visit to the United States of North America*. 2 vols. New York, 1849.

Lyman, Stanford M., ed. *Selected Writings of Henry Hughes*. Jackson, Miss., 1985.

McAdoo, Harriette Pipes, ed. *Black Families*. Beverly Hills, Calif., 1981.

McBeth, Harry Leon. "The Role of Women in Southern Baptist History." *Baptist History and Heritage* 8, no. 3 (July 1973): 158–67.

McCarthy, Kathleen D. *Noblesse Oblige: Charity and Cultural Philanthropy in Chicago, 1849–1929*. Chicago, 1982.

McCaskill, Barbara. "'Eternity for Telling': Topological Traditions in Afro-American Women's Literature." Ph.D. diss., Emory University, 1988.

McCollen, Robert. *Slavery and Jeffersonian Virginia*. 2d ed. Urbana, Ill., 1973.

McCord, Louisa S. [L. S. M.] *Caius Gracchus: A Tragedy*. New York, 1851.

———. "Carey on the Slave Trade." *Southern Quarterly Review* 25 (January 1854): 115–84.

———. "Diversity of the Races: Its Bearing upon Negro Slavery." *Southern Quarterly Review* 19 (April 1851): 392–419.

———. "Enfranchisement of Women." *Southern Quarterly Review* 21 (April 1852): 322–41.

———. "Justice and Fraternity." *Southern Quarterly Review* 15 (July 1849): 356–74.

———. "Langdon Cheves: Review of 'Reminiscences of Public Men.'" *XIX Century* 2, no. 5 (April 1870): 885–88.

———. *My Dreams*. Philadelphia, 1848.

———. "Negro and White Slavery—Wherein Do They Differ?" *Southern Quarterly Review* 20 (July 1851): 118–32.

———. "The Right to Labor." *Southern Quarterly Review* 16 (October 1849): 138–60.

———. "Uncle Tom's Cabin." *Southern Quarterly Review* 23 (January 1853): 81–120.

———. "Woman and Her Needs." *DeBow's Review* 13 (September 1852): 272.

MacCorkle, William Alexander. *White Sulphur Springs: The Traditions, History, and Social Life of the Greenbrier White Sulphur Springs*. New York, 1916.

MacCormack, Carol P. "Slaves, Slave Owners, and Slave Dealers: Sherbro Coast and Hinterland." In *Women and Slavery in Africa*, edited by Claire C. Robertson and Martin A. Klein, 271–94. Madison, Wis., 1984.

McCurry, Stephanie. "In Defense of Their World: Class, Gender, and the Yeomanry of the South Carolina Lowcountry, 1820–1861." Ph.D. diss., State University of New York, Binghamton, in progress.

———. "'Their Ways Are Not Our Ways': Elite Perceptions of Yeomen Women." Paper presented at the annual meeting of the Southern Historical Association, Houston, Tex., November 1985.

McCusker, John J., and Russell R. Menard. *The Economy of British America, 1607–1789: Needs and Opportunities for Study*. Chapel Hill, N.C., 1985.

McDaniel, George W. *Hearth and Home: Preserving a People's Culture*. Philadelphia, 1982.

McDannell, Coleen. *The Christian Home in Victorian America, 1840–1900*. Bloomington, Ind., 1986.

McDonald, Forrest, and Ellen S. McDonald. "The Ethnic Origins of the American People, 1790." *William and Mary Quarterly*, 3d ser., vol. 37, no. 2 (April 1980): 177–99.

McDonald, Forrest, and Grady McWhiney. "The Antebellum Southern Herdsman: A Reinterpretation." *Journal of Southern History* 41 (May 1975): 147–66.

————. "The South from Self-Sufficiency to Peonage: An Interpretation." *American Historical Review* 85 (December 1980): 1095–1118.

McDonnell, Lawrence T. "Desertion, Divorce, and Class Struggle: Contradictions of Patriarchy in Antebellum South Carolina." Paper presented at the annual meeting of the Southern Historical Association, Houston, Tex., November 1985.

————. "Slave against Slave: Dynamics of Violence within the American Slave Community." Paper presented at the annual meeting of the American Historical Association, San Francisco, December 1983.

McGowan, James Thomas. "Creation of a Slave Society: Louisiana Plantations in the Eighteenth Century." Ph.D. diss., University of Rochester, 1976.

Mackay, Alex. *The Western World: Or, Travels in the United States in 1846–47*. 3 vols. 1849. Reprint. New York, 1968.

McKelvey, Blake. *Rochester the Flower City: 1855–1890*. Cambridge, Mass. 1949.

————. *Rochester the Water-Power City: 1812–1854*. Cambridge, Mass., 1945.

Maclean, Ian. *The Renaissance Notion of Women: A Study in the Fortunes of Scholasticism and Medical Science in European Intellectual Life*. Cambridge, Eng., 1980.

MacLeod, Duncan J. *Slavery, Race, and the American Revolution*. Cambridge, Eng., 1974.

McLoughlin, William G., and Winthrop D. Jordan. "Baptists Face the Barbarities of Slavery." *Journal of Southern History* 29 (1963): 495–501.

McMillen, Sally Gregory. "Mothers' Sacred Duty: Breast-feeding Patterns among Middle- and Upper-class Women in the Antebellum South." *Journal of Southern History* 51, no. 3 (August 1985): 333–56.

————. "Women's Sacred Occupation: Pregnancy, Childbirth, and Early Infant Rearing in the Antebellum South." Ph.D. diss., Duke University, 1985.

MacPherson, C. B. *The Political Theory of Possessive Individualism: Hobbes to Locke*. Oxford, 1962.

McReynolds, James Michael. "Family Life in a Borderland Community: Nacogdoches, Texas, 1779–1861." Ph.D. diss., Texas Tech University, 1978.

Magdol, Edward, and Jon L. Wakelyn, eds. *The Southern Common People: Studies in Nineteenth-Century Social History*. Westport, Conn., 1980.

Main, Gloria L. *Tobacco Colony: Life in Early Maryland, 1650–1720*. Princeton, N.J., 1982.

Malone, Ann Patton. "The Nineteenth Century Slave Family in Rural Louisiana: Its Household and Community Structure." Ph.D. diss., Tulane University, 1985.

Mandle, Jay R. *The Roots of Black Poverty: The Southern Plantation Economy after the Civil War*. Durham, N.C., 1978.

Mannix, Daniel P., and Malcolm Cowley. *Black Cargoes: A History of the Atlantic*

Slave Trade. New York, 1962.

"Marengo Planter." *American Cotton Planter* 2 (September 1854): 279–80.

Marszalek, John F., ed. *The Diary of Miss Emma Holmes*. Baton Rouge, La., 1979.

Martin, Josephine Bacon, ed. *Life on a Liberty County Plantation: The Journal of Cornelia Jones Pond*. Darien, Ga., 1974.

Martin, Waldo E., Jr. *The Mind of Frederick Douglass*. Chapel Hill, N.C., 1984.

Martineau, Harriet. *Retrospect of Western Travel*. 3 vols. 1838. Reprint. New York, 1969.

———. *Society in America*. 2 vols. New York, 1837.

———. *Views of Slavery and Emancipation*. New York, 1837.

Martinez-Alier, Verena. *Marriage, Class, and Colour in Nineteenth-Century Cuba: A Study of Racial Attitudes and Sexual Values in a Slave Society*. Cambridge, Eng., 1974.

Massey, Mary Elizabeth. *Bonnet Brigades*. New York, 1966.

———. "The Making of a Feminist." *Journal of Southern History* 39, no. 1 (February 1973): 3–22.

Mathews, Donald G. *Religion in the Old South*. Chicago, 1977.

———. *Slavery and Methodism: A Chapter in American Morality, 1780–1845*. Princeton, N.J., 1965.

Mathis, Ray. *John Horry Dent : South Carolina Aristocrat on the Alabama Frontier*. University, Ala., 1979.

Mathurin, Lucille. *The Rebel Woman in the British West Indies during Slavery*. Kingston, Jamaica, 1975.

Mattaiason, Carolyn J., ed. *Many Sisters: Women in Cross-Cultural Perspective*. New York, 1974.

Matthews, Jean. "Race, Sex, and the Dimensions of Liberty in Antebellum America." *Journal of the Early Republic* 6, no. 3 (Fall 1986): 275–91.

May, Allen Madeline. "An Historical Study of Moravian Education in North Carolina: The Evolution and Practice of the Moravian Concept of Education as It Applied to Women." Ph.D. diss., Florida State University, 1971.

May, Robert E. *John A. Quitman: Old South Crusader*. Baton Rouge, La., 1985.

Meaders, Daniel E. "South Carolina Fugitives as Viewed through Local Colonial Newspapers, with Emphasis on Runaway Notices, 1732–1801." *Journal of Negro History* 60 (April 1975): 288–319.

Meckel, Richard A. "Educating a Ministry of Mothers: Evangelical Maternal Associations, 1815–1860." *Journal of the Early Republic* 2, no. 4 (Winter 1982): 403–23.

Medick, Hans. "The Proto-Industrial Family Economy: The Structural Function of Household and Family during the Transition from Peasant Society to Industrial Capitalism." *Social History* 1, no. 3 (October 1976): 291–315.

Meillassoux, Claude. "Female Slavery." In *Women and Slavery in Africa*, edited by Claire C. Robertson and Martin A. Klein, 49–66. Madison, Wis., 1984.

Melder, Keith E. *Beginnings of Sisterhood: The American Woman's Rights Movement*. New York, 1978.

———. "Ladies Bountiful: Organized Women's Benevolence in Early Nineteenth-Century America." *New York History* 55 (July 1974): 231–54.

"Memoir of the Life of Anne Boleyn." *Southern Quarterly Review* 18 (November 1850): 536.

"Men and Women of the Eighteenth Century." *Southern Quarterly Review* 22 (July 1852): 63–77.

Menard, Russell R. "Economy and Society in Early Colonial Maryland." Ph.D. diss., University of Iowa, 1975.

————. "From Servants to Slaves: The Transformation of the Chesapeake Labor System." *Southern Studies* 16 (Winter 1977): 122–36.

————. "Immigrants and Their Increase: The Process of Population Growth in Early Colonial Maryland." In *Law, Society, and Politics in Early Maryland*, edited by Aubrey C. Land et al., 88–105. Baltimore, Md., 1977.

————. "Population, Economy, and Society in Seventeenth-Century Maryland." *Maryland Historical Magazine* 79, no. 1 (Spring 1984): 71–92.

————. "The Tobacco Industry in the Chesapeake Colonies, 1617–1730: An Interpretation." *Research in Economic History* 5 (1980): 109–77.

————. "Why African Slavery? Free Land, Plantation Agriculture, and the Supply of Labor in the Growth of British-American Slave Societies." Paper delivered at the Conference on New World Slavery, Rutgers University at Newark, May 1980.

Mendenhall, Marjorie Stratford. "Southern Women of a 'Lost Generation.'" *South Atlantic Quarterly* 33, no. 4 (October 1934): 334–53.

Mendras, Henri. *Sociétés paysannes: Éléments pour une théorie de la paysannerie.* Paris, 1976.

Meriwether, Elizabeth Avery. *Recollections of Ninety-two Years, 1824–1916.* Nashville, Tenn., 1958.

Meriwether, James B., ed. *South Carolina Women Writers: Proceedings of the Reynolds Conference, University of South Carolina, October 24–25, 1975.* Columbia, S.C., 1979.

Meriwether, Robert W. "Galloway College: The Early Years, 1889–1907." *Arkansas Historical Quarterly* 40, no. 4 (Winter 1981): 291–337.

Merrick, Caroline E. *Old Times in Dixie Land: A Southern Matron's Memories.* New York, 1901.

Merrill, Michael. "Cash Is Good to Eat: Self-Sufficiency and Exchange in the Rural Economy of the United States." *Radical History Review* 4, no. 1 (Winter 1977): 42–71.

Merrington, John. "Town and Country in the Transition to Capitalism." *New Left Review*, no. 93 (September/October 1975): 71–92.

Meyers, Rose. *A History of Baton Rouge, 1699–1812.* Baton Rouge, La., 1976.

Middleton, Alicia Hopton, ed. *Life in Carolina and New England during the Nineteenth Century as Illustrated by Reminiscences and Letters of the Middleton Family of Charleston.* Bristol, R.I., 1929.

Middleton, Margaret Simons. *A Sketch of the Ladies Benevolent Society.* Charleston, S.C., n.d.

Miles, Edwin A. "The Mississippi Slave Insurrection Scare of 1835." *Journal of Negro History* 42 (1957): 48–60.

Miles, William Porcher. *Women "Nobly Planned": How to Educate Our Girls: An Address Delivered by the Honorable William Porcher Miles, President of the Agricultural College of South Carolina, before the Young Ladies of the Yorkville Female College.* N.p., n.d.

Miller, John Chester. *The Wolf by the Ears: Thomas Jefferson and Slavery*. New York, 1977.

Mills, Gary. "Coincoin: An Eighteenth-Century 'Liberated Woman.'" *Journal of Southern History* 42 (May 1976): 205–22.

Minces, Juliette. "Women in Algeria." In *Women in the Muslim World*, edited by Lois Beck and Nikki Keddie, 159–71. Cambridge, Mass., 1981.

Mintz, Sidney W. *Caribbean Transformations*. Chicago, 1974.

———. "Economic Role and Cultural Tradition." In *Black Woman Cross-Culturally*, edited by Filomina Chioma Steady, 515–34. Cambridge, Mass., 1981.

Mintz, Sidney W., and Richard Price. *An Anthropological Approach to the Afro-American Past: A Caribbean Perspective*. Philadelphia, 1976.

"Miss Lee's Social Evenings." *Southern Quarterly Review* 2 (October 1842): 531–32.

"Miss Sedgwick's Letters From Abroad." *Southern Quarterly Review* 1 (January 1842): 173–85.

"Mrs. Dana's Letters." *Southern Quarterly Review* 8 (October 1845): 524–25.

Mitchell, Margaret. *Gone with the Wind*. New York, 1936.

Mitterauer, Michael, and Reinhard Sieder. *The European Family: Patriarchy to Partnership from the Middle Ages to the Present*. Translated by Karla Oosterveen and Manfred Horzinger. Chicago, 1982.

Mohr, Clarence C. *On the Threshold of Freedom: Masters and Slaves in Civil War Georgia*. Athens, Ga., 1986.

Moltke-Hansen, David. "The Expansion of Intellectual Life: A Prospectus." In *Intellectual Life in Antebellum Charleston*, edited by Michael O'Brien and David Moltke-Hansen, 3–46. Knoxville, Tenn., 1986.

———. "Why History Mattered: The Background of Ann Pamela Cunningham's Interest in the Preservation of Mount Vernon." *Furman Studies*, n.s. 26 (December 1980): 34–42.

Montague, Ludwell Lee, ed. "Cornelia Lee's Wedding as Reported in a Letter from Ann Calvert Stuart to Mrs. Elizabeth Lee, October 19, 1806." *Virginia Magazine of History and Biography* 80, no. 4 (October 1972): 453–60.

———. "Letters Home to Maine from Virginia, 1841–1859." *Virginia Magazine of History and Biography* 79, no. 4 (October 1971): 436–61.

"Montgomery Mail." *Southern Cultivator* 14 (June 1856): 192.

Moody, V. Alton. "Slavery on Louisiana Sugar Plantations." *Louisiana Historical Quarterly* 7, no. 2 (April 1924): 190–301.

Mooney, Chase C. *Slavery in Tennessee*. Bloomington, Ind., 1957.

Moragne, Mary E. *The Neglected Thread: A Journal from the Calhoun Community, 1836–1842*. Edited by Delle Mullen Craven. Columbia, S.C., 1951.

Morgan, Edmund S. *American Slavery, American Freedom: The Ordeal of Colonial Virginia*. New York, 1975.

———. *Virginians at Home: Family Life in the Eighteenth Century*. Williamsburg, Va., 1952.

Morgan, Philip D. "Black Life in Eighteenth-Century Charleston." *Perspectives in American History*, n.s. 1 (1984): 187–232.

———. "Black Society in the Lowcountry, 1760–1810." In *Slavery and Freedom in the Age of the American Revolution*, edited by Ira Berlin and Ronald Hoffman, 83–141. Charlottesville, Va., 1983.

_____. "Development of Slave Culture in Eighteenth-Century Plantation America." Ph.D. diss., University of London, 1977.

Morrill, Lily Logan, ed. *My Confederate Girlhood: The Memoirs of Kate Virginia Cox Logan.* 1932. Reprint. New York, 1980.

Morris, Charles Edward. "Panic and Reprisal: Reaction in North Carolina to the Nat Turner Insurrection, 1831." *North Carolina Historical Review* 62, no. 1 (1985): 29–52.

Morrison, Toni. *Beloved.* New York, 1987.

Morrissey, Marietta. "Women's Work, Family Formation, and Reproduction among Caribbean Slaves." *Review* 9, no. 3 (Winter 1986): 339–68.

Moses, Yolanda T. "Female Status, the Family, and Male Dominance in a West Indian Community." In *Black Woman Cross-Culturally,* edited by Filomina Chioma Steady, 499–513. Cambridge, Mass., 1981.

Mouser, Bruce L. "Women Slavers of Guinea-Conakry." In *Women and Slavery in Africa,* edited by Claire C. Robertson and Martin A. Klein, 320–39. Madison, Wis., 1984.

Muhlenfeld, Elisabeth. *Mary Boykin Chesnut: A Biography.* Baton Rouge, La., 1981.

Mullin, Gerald W. *Flight and Rebellion: Slave Resistance in Eighteenth-Century Virginia.* New York, 1972.

Mullin, Michael. "British Caribbean and North American Slaves in an Era of War and Revolution, 1775–1807." In *The Southern Experience in the American Revolution,* edited by Jeffrey J. Crow and Larry E. Tise, 235–67. Chapel Hill, N.C., 1978.

_____. "Jamaican Maroon Women and the Cultural Dimension of American Negro Slavery." Paper presented at the Twelfth Meeting of the Association of Caribbean Historians, University of the West Indies, St. Augustine, Trinidad, April 1980.

_____. "Women, and the Comparative Study of American Negro Slavery." *Slavery and Abolition* 6, no. 1 (May 1985): 25–58.

Mullings, Leith. "Women and Economic Change in Africa." In *Women in Africa: Studies in Social and Economic Change,* edited by Nancy J. Hafkin and Edna G. Bay, 239–64. Stanford, Calif., 1976.

Mumford, Lewis. *The City in History: Its Origins, Its Transformations, and Its Prospects.* New York, 1961.

Murchie, Miriam [Mullikin]. " 'Copperhead? I Thank You for It!': A Contemporary Response to *The Planter's Northern Bride.*" M.A. thesis, University of North Carolina, 1973.

Murray, Amelia M. *Letters from the United States, Cuba, and Canada.* 1856. Reprint. New York, 1969.

Murray, Elizabeth Reid. *Wake: Capital County of North Carolina.* Vol. 1, *Prehistory through Centennial.* Raleigh, N.C., 1983.

Mutch, Robert E. "Yeoman and Merchant in Pre-Industrial America: Eighteenth-Century Massachusetts as a Case Study." *Societas* 7, no. 4 (Autumn 1977): 279–302.

Myers, Robert Manson, ed. *The Children of Pride: A True Story of Georgia and the Civil War.* New Haven, Conn., 1972.

_____. *A Georgian at Princeton.* New Haven, Conn., 1972.

Myres, Sandra L. *Westering Women and the Frontier Experience, 1800–1915.* Albuquerque, N.M., 1982.

N. "The State of Georgia—Its Duties and Its Destiny." *Southern Quarterly Review* 8 (October 1845): 421–80.

N. B. P. "The Treatment of Slaves in the South." *Southern Quarterly Review* 21 (January 1852): 209–20.

Nash, Gary B. *The Urban Crucible: Social Change, Political Consciousness, and the Origins of the American Revolution.* Cambridge, Mass., 1979.

Nelson, Margaret K. "Vermont Female Schoolteachers in the Nineteenth Century." *Vermont History* 49, no. 1 (Winter 1981): 5–30.

Nesbitt, Martha C. "To Fairfield with Love: A Rural Maryland House and Household." *Maryland Historical Magazine* 70, no. 1 (Spring 1975): 68–89.

Netting, Robert M. "Marital Relations in the Jos Plateau of Nigeria—Women's Weapons: The Politics of Domesticity among the Kofyar." *American Anthropologist* 71, no. 6 (December 1969): 1037–46.

Neverdon-Morton, Cynthia. "The Black Woman's Struggle for Equality in the South, 1895–1925." In *The Afro-American Woman: Struggles and Images,* edited by Sharon Harley and Rosalind Terborg-Penn, 43–57. Port Washington, N.Y., 1978.

Nevins, Allan. *Ordeal of the Union: Fruits of Manifest Destiny, 1847–52.* New York, 1947.

Newman, Debra L. "Black Women in the Era of the American Revolution in Pennsylvania." *Journal of Negro History* 61, no. 3 (July 1976): 276–89.

Nielsen, George R., ed. "Lydia Ann McHenry and Revolutionary Texas." *Southwestern Historical Quarterly* 74, no. 3 (1971): 393–408.

Nisbet, Robert A. *The Sociological Tradition.* New York, 1966.

Noble, Jeanne. *Beautiful, Also, Are the Souls of My Black Sisters: A History of the Black Woman in America.* Englewood Cliffs, N.J., 1978.

Nobles, Gregory H. "Commerce and Community: A Case Study of the Rural Broommaking Business in Antebellum Massachusetts." *Journal of the Early Republic* 4, no. 3 (Fall 1984): 287–308.

North, Douglass C. *The Economic Growth of the United States, 1790–1860.* Englewood Cliffs, N.J., 1961.

"The North and the South." *De Bow's Review* 7 (1849): 304–16.

Northup, Solomon. *Twelve Years a Slave.* Edited by Philip S. Foner. 1854. Reprint. New York, 1970.

Norton, Anne. *Alternative Americas: A Reading of Antebellum American Culture.* Chicago, 1986.

Norton, Mary Beth. "The Evolution of White Women's Experience in Early America." *American Historical Review* 89, no. 3 (June 1984): 593–619.

———. "Gender and Defamation in Seventeenth-Century Maryland." *William and Mary Quarterly,* 3d ser., vol. 44, no. 1 (January 1987): 3–39.

———. *Liberty's Daughters: The Revolutionary Experience of American Women, 1750–1800.* Boston, 1980.

Nott, Doctor. "Dr. Nott's Reply to 'C.'" *Southern Quarterly Review* 8 (July 1845): 148–90.

Nuermberger, Ruth Ketring. *The Clays of Alabama: A Planter-Lawyer-Politician Family.* Lexington, Ky., 1958.

Oakes, James. "The Politics of Economic Development in the Antebellum South." *Journal of Interdisciplinary History* 15, no. 2 (Autumn 1984): 305–16.

———. *The Ruling Race: A History of American Slaveholders.* New York, 1982.

Oates, Stephen B. *The Fires of Jubilee: Nat Turner's Fierce Rebellion.* New York, 1975.

Obbo, Christine. *African Women: Their Struggle for Economic Independence.* London, 1980.

Obitko, Mary Ellen. "'Custodians of a House of Resistance': Black Women Respond to Slavery." In *Women and Men: The Consequences of Power,* edited by Dana V. Hiller and Robin Ann Sheets, 256–69. Cincinnati, Ohio, 1979.

O'Brien, Michael. *All Clever Men Who Make Their Way: Critical Discourse in the Old South.* Columbia, Mo., 1985.

O'Brien, Michael, and David Moltke-Hansen, eds., *Intellectual Life in Antebellum Charleston.* Knoxville, Tenn., 1986.

Ohmann, Carol. "The Autobiography of Malcolm X: A Revolutionary Use of the Franklin Tradition." *American Quarterly* 22 (Summer 1970): 131–49.

Okihiro, Gary Y., ed. *In Resistance: Studies in African, Caribbean, and Afro-American History.* Amherst, Mass., 1986.

Olmsted, Frederick Law. *A Journey in the Back Country, 1853–1854.* Edited by Clement Eaton. 1860. Reprint. New York, 1970.

———. *A Journey in the Seaboard Slave States, with Remarks on Their Economy.* 1856. Reprint. New York, 1968.

———. *A Journey through Texas, or, a Saddle-Trip on the South-Western Frontier.* 1857. Reprint. Austin, Tex., 1978.

———. *The Papers of Frederick Law Olmsted.* Vol. 2, *Slavery and the South, 1852–1857.* Edited by Charles E. Beveridge and Charles Capen McLaughlin. Baltimore, Md., 1981.

O'Neall, John Belton. *An Address on Female Education: Delivered at the Request of the Trustees of the Johnson Female Seminary.* Anderson, S.C., 1849.

———. *The Negro Law of South Carolina.* Columbia, S.C., 1848.

"On the Management of Negroes." *American Cotton Planter and Soil of the South,* n.s. 2 (January 1858): 21.

Orr, Dorothy. *History of Education in Georgia.* Chapel Hill, N.C., 1950.

Osgood, John. *A Letter of Prudent Advice.* Savannah, Ga., 1774.

Ostrogorski, M. *The Rights of Women: A Comparative Study in History and Legislation.* London, 1893.

Otto, John Solomon. "A New Look at Slave Life." *Natural History* 88, no. 1 (January 1979): 8–30.

Owen, Thomas McAdory. *History of Alabama and Dictionary of Alabama Biography.* 4 vols. Chicago, 1921.

Owens, Leslie Howard. *This Species of Property: Slave Life and Culture in the Old South.* New York, 1976.

Owsley, Frank L. *Plain Folk of the Old South.* Baton Rouge, La., 1949.

Painter, Diane Holland. "The Black Woman in American Society." *Current History* 70 (May 1976): 224–34.

Palmer, B. M., ed. *The Life and Letters of James Henley Thornwell.* Richmond, Va., 1875.

Palmer, Bryan D. "Social Formation and Class Formation in North America,

1800–1900." In *Proletarianization and Family History*, edited by David Levine, 229–309. New York, 1984.

Papashvily, Helen Waite. *All the Happy Endings: A Study of the Domestic Novel in America, the Women Who Wrote It, the Women Who Read It, in the Nineteenth Century*. New York, 1956.

Pariset, François-Georges, ed. *Bordeaux au XVIIIe siècle*. Bordeaux, 1968.

Parker, William N. "The Slave Plantation in American Agriculture." In *Essays in American Economic History*, edited by Ross M. Robertson, 131–39. London, 1969.

———. "Slavery and Southern Economic Development: An Hypothesis and Some Evidence." *Agricultural History* 44, no. 1 (January 1970): 115–25.

Parkhurst, Jessie W. "The Role of the Black Mammy in the Plantation Household." *Journal of Negro History* 23, no. 3 (July 1938): 349–69.

Parks, Edd Winfield. *Ante-Bellum Southern Literary Critics*. Athens, Ga., 1962.

Patterson, Orlando. "Slavery." *Annual Review of Anthropology* 3 (1977): 407–49.

———. "Slavery and Slave Revolts: A Socio-Historical Analysis of the First Maroon War, 1655–1740." *Social and Economic Studies* 19, no. 3 (September 1970): 289–325.

———. *Slavery and Social Death: A Comparative Study*. Cambridge, Mass., 1982.

Paulme, Denise, ed. *Women of Tropical Africa*. Translated by H. M. Wright. Berkeley, Calif., 1973.

Peniston, Gregory S. "The Slave Builder-Artisan." *Western Journal of Black Studies* 2, no. 4 (1978): 284–95.

Perkins, Linda M. "The Black Female Missionary Educator during and after the Civil War." *Black Women's Educational Policy and Research Network Newsletter* 1, no. 5 (March/April 1982): 6–9.

Perry, Benjamin F. *The Writings of Benjamin F. Perry*. Vol. 2, *Reminiscences of Public Men*. Edited by Stephen Meats and Edwin T. Arnold. 1889. Reprint. Spartanburg, S.C., 1980.

Phifer, Edward W. "Slavery in Microcosm: Burke County, North Carolina." *Journal of Southern History* 28 (1962): 137–60.

Philipp, Mangol Bayat. "Women and Revolution in Iran, 1905–1911." In *Women in the Muslim World*, edited by Lois Beck and Nikki Keddie, 295–308. Cambridge, Mass., 1978.

Phillip, Thomas. "Feminism and Nationalist Politics in Egypt." In *Women in the Muslim World*, edited by Lois Beck and Nikki Keddie, 277–94. Cambridge, Mass., 1978.

Phillips, Ulrich Bonnell. *American Negro Slavery: A Survey of the Supply, Employment, and Control of Negro Labor as Determined by the Plantation Regime*. Edited by Eugene D. Genovese. Baton Rouge, La., 1966.

———. *A History of Transportation in the Eastern Cotton Belt to 1860*. 1908. Reprint. New York, 1968.

———. *Life and Labor in the Old South*. Boston, 1929.

———. "Slave Crime in Virginia." *American Historical Review* 20 (January 1915): 336–40.

———. *The Slave Economy of the Old South: Selected Essays in Economic and Social History*. Edited by Eugene D. Genovese. Baton Rouge, La., 1968.

———, ed. *The Correspondence of Robert Toombs, Alexander H. Stephens, and How-*

ell Cobb. Washington, D.C., 1913.

————. *Plantation and Frontier Documents, 1649–1863.* 2 vols. Cleveland, Ohio, 1909.

Phillips, Ulrich B., and James David Glunt, eds. *Florida Plantation Records from the Papers of George Noble Jones.* St. Louis, Mo., 1927.

Pierce, George F. "The Georgia Female College—Its Origin, Plan, and Prospects." *Wesleyan Quarterly Review* 1, no. 2 (May 1964): 93–108.

Pike, Burton. "Time in Autobiography." *Comparative Literature* 28 (1976): 326–42.

Pinckney, Elise. *Centennial Pamphlet of the Ladies Benevolent Society.* Charleston, S.C., 1913.

————, ed. *The Letterbook of Eliza Lucas Pinckney, 1739–1762.* Chapel Hill, N.C., 1972.

————. "Letters of Eliza Lucas Pinckney." *South Carolina Historical Magazine* 76 (1975): 143–70.

Pirenne, Henri. *Medieval Cities: Their Origins and the Revival of Trade.* Translated by Frank D. Halsey. Princeton, N.J., 1925.

Planck, Ulrich. *Der bäuerliche Familienbetrieb zwischen Patriarchat und Partnerschaft.* Stuttgart, 1964.

Plant, Raymond. *Community and Ideology: An Essay in Applied Social Philosophy.* London, 1974.

Pleasants, J. Hall, ed., "Letters of Molly and Hetty Tilghman: Eighteenth Century Gossip of Two Maryland Girls." *Maryland Historical Magazine* 21, nos. 1, 2, 3 (March, June, September 1926): 20–39, 123–49, 219–41.

Pope-Hennessy, James. *Sins of the Fathers: A Study of the Atlantic Slave Traders, 1441–1807.* New York, 1968.

Pope-Hennessy, Una, ed. *The Aristocratic Journey: Being the Outspoken Letters of Mrs. Basil Hall, Written during a Fourteen Months' Sojourn in America, 1827–1828.* New York, 1931.

Porcher, Frederick. "Southern and Northern Civilization Contrasted." *Russell's Magazine* 1, no. 2 (May 1857): 97–107.

Porter, Glen, ed. *Encyclopedia of American Economic History.* New York, 1980.

Porterfield, Amanda. *Feminine Spirituality in America: From Sarah Edwards to Martha Graham.* Philadelphia, 1980.

Powdermaker, Hortense. *After Freedom: A Cultural Study in the Deep South.* 1939. Reprint. New York, 1969.

Pred, Allan R. *Urban Growth and City-Systems in the United States, 1840–1860.* Cambridge, Mass., 1980.

————. *Urban Growth and the Circulation of Information: The United States System of Cities, 1790–1840.* Cambridge, Mass., 1973.

Prescott, William Hickling. *History of the Conquest of Mexico.* 3 vols. New York, 1843.

————. *History of the Reign of Ferdinand and Isabella.* 2 vols. New York, 1837.

Price, Jacob M. "Economic Function and the Growth of American Port Towns in the Eighteenth Century." *Perspectives in American History* 8 (1974): 123–86.

————. *France and the Chesapeake: A History of the French Tobacco Monopoly, 1674–1791, and of its Relationship to the British and American Tobacco Trades.* Ann Arbor, Mich., 1973.

————. "One Family's Empire: The Russell-Lee-Clerk Connection in Maryland,

Britain, and India, 1707–1857." *Maryland Historical Magazine* 72, no. 2 (Summer 1977): 165–225.

_____. "The Rise of Glasgow in the Chesapeake Tobacco Trade, 1707–1775." *William and Mary Quarterly*, 3d ser., vol. 2, no. 2 (April 1954): 179–99.

Price, Jacob M., and Paul G. E. Clemens. "A Revolution of Scale in Overseas Trade: British Firms in the Chesapeake Trade, 1675–1775." *Journal of Economic History* 47, no. 1 (March 1987): 1–43.

Price, Richard, ed. *Maroon Societies: Rebel Slave Communities in the Americas.* Garden City, N.Y., 1973.

Pringle, Elizabeth W. Allston. *Chronicles of Chicora Wood.* Boston, 1940.

Prior, Mary Barbot, ed. "Letters of Martha Logan to John Bartram, 1760–1763." *South Carolina Historical Magazine* 59 (1958): 38–46.

"The Prospects before Us." *Southern Quarterly Review* 19 (April 1851): 533–41.

Proust, Marcel. *A la recherche du temps perdu.* 3 vols. Paris, 1913–27.

Prude, Jonathan. *The Coming of Industrial Order: Town and Factory Life in Rural Massachusetts, 1810–1860.* Cambridge, Eng., 1983.

Pryor, Mrs. Roger A. *Reminiscences of Peace and War.* 1904. Reprint, rev. and enl. ed. New York, 1905.

Puckett, Newbell N. *Folk Beliefs of the Southern Negro.* 1926. Reprint. New York, 1968.

Pugh, Evelyn L. "Women and Slavery: Julia Gardiner Tyler and the Duchess of Sutherland." *Virginia Magazine of History and Biography* 88, no. 2 (April 1980): 186–202.

Quarles, Benjamin. *The Negro in the American Revolution.* Chapel Hill, N.C., 1961.

_____. "The Revolutionary War as a Black Declaration of Independence." In *An Uncivil War: The Southern Backcountry during the American Revolution*, edited by Ronald Hoffman, Thad W. Tate, and Peter J. Albert, 283–301. Charlottesville, Va., 1985.

Quattlebaum, Isabel. "Twelve Women in the First Days of the Confederacy." *Civil War History* 7 (December 1961): 370–85.

R. "The Agricultural Prospects of South Carolina: Her Resources and Her True Policy." *Southern Quarterly Review* 8 (July 1845): 118–47.

Rabkin, Peggy A. *Fathers to Daughters: The Legal Foundations of Female Emancipation.* Westport, Conn., 1980.

_____. "The Origins of Law Reform: The Social Significance of the Nineteenth-Century Codification Movement and Its Contribution to the Passage of Early Married Women's Property Acts." *Buffalo Law Review* 24, no. 3 (Spring 1975): 683–760.

Raboteau, Albert J. *Slave Religion: The "Invisible Institution" in the Antebellum South.* New York, 1978.

Radford, John P. "Race, Residence, and Ideology: Charleston, South Carolina, in the Mid-Nineteenth Century." *Journal of Historical Geography* 2, no. 4 (1976): 329–46.

Radway, Janice A. *Reading the Romance: Women, Patriarchy, and Popular Literature.* Chapel Hill, N.C., 1984.

Rainard, R. Lyn. "The Gentlemanly Ideal in the South, 1660–1860: An Overview." *Southern Studies* 25, no. 3 (Fall 1986): 295–304.

Rattray, R. S. *Ashanti Law and Constitution.* Oxford, 1929.

Ravenel, C. P. "The Ladies' Benevolent Society." In *Yearbook City of Charleston, So. Ca., 1896*, 418–21. Charleston, S.C., 1896.

Rawick, George P. *From Sundown to Sunup: The Making of the Black Community.* Vol. 1 of *The American Slave: A Composite Autobiography.* Westport, Conn., 1972.

————, ed. *The American Slave: A Composite Autobiography.* 19 vols. Contributions in Afro-American and African Studies, no. 11. Westport, Conn., 1972.

————. *The American Slave: A Composite Autobiography. Supplement.* 12 vols. Westport, Conn., 1977.

Renier, Perceval. *The Springs of Virginia: Life, Love, and Death at the Waters, 1775–1900.* Chapel Hill, N.C., 1941.

Renza, Louis A. "The Veto of the Imagination: A Theory of Autobiography." *New Literary History* 9 (1977): 1–26.

Reynolds, Thomas Caute. "Testaments Under the Civil Law Adverse to the Rights of Heirs: Manumission of Slaves." *DeBow's Review* 3 (1847): 547–53.

Rhea, Linda. *Hugh Swinton Legaré, a Charleston Intellectual.* Chapel Hill, N.C., 1934.

Richards, Caroline Cowles. *Village Life in America, 1852–1872, Including the Period of the American Civil War as Told in the Diary of a School-Girl.* New York, 1912.

Riley, B. F. *A History of the Baptists in the Southern States East of the Mississippi.* Philadelphia, 1898.

Riley, Franklin L., ed. "Diary of a Mississippi Planter, January 1, 1840, to April 1863." *Publications of the Mississippi Historical Society* 10 (1909): 305–481.

Riley, Glenda. *Frontierswomen: The Iowa Experience.* Ames, Iowa, 1981.

Rivers, Larry. "'Dignity and Importance': Slavery in Jefferson County, Florida, 1827 to 1860." *Florida Historical Quarterly* 61 (April 1983): 404–30.

Rivers, R. H. *Elements of Moral Philosophy.* Nashville, Tenn., 1859.

Robertson, Claire C. "Ga Women and Socioeconomic Change in Accra, Ghana." In *Women in Africa: Studies in Social and Economic Change*, edited by Nancy J. Hafkin and Edna G. Bay, 111–33. Stanford, Calif., 1976.

Robertson, Claire C., and Martin A. Klein, eds. *Women and Slavery in Africa.* Madison, Wis., 1984.

Robertson, James I., Jr., ed. "The Diary of Dolly Lunt Burge." *Georgia Historical Quarterly* 44, nos. 2–4 (1960): 220–29, 321–37, 434–55; 45, nos. 1–4 (1961): 57–72, 155–70, 257–86, 367–84; 46, no. 1 (1962): 59–78.

Robertson, Mary D., ed. *Lucy Breckinridge of Grove Hill: The Journal of a Virginia Girl, 1862–1864.* Kent, Ohio, 1979.

Robertson, William. *Works.* 8 vols. Oxford, 1825.

Robinson, Armstead Louis. "Beyond the Realm of Social Consensus: New Meanings of Reconstruction for American History." *Journal of American History* 68, no. 2 (September 1981): 276–97.

————. "Day of Jubilo: Civil War and the Demise of Slavery in the Mississippi Valley, 1861–1865." Ph.D. diss., University of Rochester, 1976.

Robson, David W. "'An Important Question Answered': William Graham's Defense of Slavery in Post-Revolutionary Virginia." *William and Mary Quarterly*, 3d ser., vol. 37, no. 4 (October 1980): 644–52.

Rodney, Walter. "Upper Guinea and the Significance of the Origins of Africans

Enslaved in the New World." *Journal of Negro History* 54, no. 4 (October 1969): 327–45.

Rogers, Daniel T. *The Work Ethic in Industrial America.* Chicago, 1974.

Rogers, George C., Jr. *Charleston in the Age of the Pinckneys.* 1969. Reprint. Columbia, S.C., 1980.

————. *Evolution of a Federalist: William Loughton Smith of Charleston (1758–1812).* Columbia, S.C., 1962.

Rogers, Susan Carol. "Woman's Place: A Critical Review of Anthropological Theory." *Comparative Studies in Society and History* 20, no. 1 (January 1978): 123–62.

Romaine, William. *Treatises upon the Life, Walk, and Triumph of Faith.* Hartford, Conn., 1831.

Roos, Rosalie. *Travels in America, 1851–1855.* Edited by Carl Anderson. Carbondale, Ill., 1982.

Rosaldo, M. Z. "The Use and Abuse of Anthropology: Reflections on Feminism and Cross-Cultural Understanding." *Signs* 5, no. 3 (Spring 1980): 389–417.

Rose, Willie Lee. *Rehearsal for Reconstruction: The Port Royal Experiment.* Indianapolis, Ind., 1964.

Rosenbloom, Nancy Jean. "Cincinnati's Common Schools: The Politics of Reform, 1829–1853." Ph.D. diss., University of Rochester, 1981.

Rosengarten, Theodore. *Tombee: Portrait of a Cotton Planter with the Journal of Thomas B. Chaplin (1822–1890).* New York, 1986.

Ross, Frances Mitchell, ed. " 'A Tie between Us That Time Cannot Sever': The Latta Family Letters, 1855–1872." *Arkansas Historical Quarterly* 40, no. 1 (1981): 31–78.

Ross, Frederick A. *Slavery Ordained of God.* 1857. Reprint. Miami, Fla., 1969.

Rothenberg, Winifred B. "The Emergence of a Capital Market in Rural Massachusetts, 1730–1838." *Journal of Economic History* 45, no. 4 (December 1985): 781–808.

————. "The Market and Massachusetts Farmers, 1750–1855." *Journal of Economic History* 41, no. 2 (June 1981): 283–314.

Rothman, David J. *The Discovery of the Asylum: Social Order and Disorder in the New Republic.* Boston, 1971.

Rothstein, Morton. "The Antebellum South as a Dual Economy: A Tentative Hypothesis." *Agricultural History* 41, no. 4 (October 1967): 373–82.

Roupnel, Gaston. *La ville et la campagne au XVIIe siècle: Étude sur les populations du pays dijonnais.* 1922. Reprint. Paris, 1955.

Royall, Anne Newport. *Letters from Alabama, 1817–1822.* Edited by Lucille Griffith. University, Ala., 1969.

————. *Sketches of History, Life, and Manners in the United States, by a Traveller.* New York, 1970.

Ruether, Rosemary Radford, and Rosemary Skinner Keller, eds. *Women and Religion in America: A Documentary History.* Vol. 1, *The Nineteenth Century.* Vol. 2, *The Colonial and Revolutionary Periods.* San Francisco, 1981, 1983.

Ruoff, John C. "Frivolity to Consumption: Or, Southern Womanhood in Antebellum Literature." *Civil War History* 18 (September 1972): 213–29.

Russel, Robert R. "The Effects of Slavery upon Nonslaveholders in the Ante

Bellum South." *Agricultural History* 15, no. 2 (April 1941): 112–26.

Russo, David J. *Families and Communities: A New View of American History.* Nashville, Tenn., 1974.

Rutledge, Anna Wells, ed. "Four Letters of the Early Nineteenth Century." *South Carolina Historical Magazine* 43 (1942): 50–56.

Rutman, Darret B., and Anita H. Rutman. *A Place in Time: Middlesex County, Virginia, 1650–1750.* 2 vols. New York, 1984.

Ryan, Mary P. *Cradle of the Middle Class: The Family in Oneida County, New York, 1790–1865.* Cambridge, Eng., 1981.

———. *The Empire of the Mother: American Writing about Domesticity, 1830–1860.* New York, 1982.

———. "The Power of Women's Networks: A Case Study of Female Moral Reform in Antebellum America." *Feminist Studies* 5, no. 1 (Spring 1979): 66–85.

———. "A Women's Awakening: Evangelical Religion and the Families of Utica, New York, 1800–1840." *American Quarterly* 30 (1978): 602–23.

S. C. *The Old Pine Farm: Or, the Southern Side.* Nashville, Tenn., 1860.

Salley, Katherine Batts, Katharine Drane Perry, Emilie Smedes Holmes, Alice Dugger Grimes, Nell Battle Lewis, Jane Toy Coolidge, and Anna Brooke Allan, eds. *Life at St. Mary's.* Chapel Hill, N.C., 1942.

Salmon, Marylynn. "The Debtor's Wife: A Case Study in Eighteenth-Century Southern Paternalism." Paper presented at the annual meeting of the Southern Historical Association, Memphis, Tenn., November 1982.

———. "Life, Liberty, and Dower: The Legal Status of Women after the American Revolution." In *Women, War, and Revolution*, edited by Carol Berkin and Clara Lovett, 85–106. New York, 1980.

———. "Women and Property in South Carolina: The Evidence from Marriage Settlements, 1730 to 1830." *William and Mary Quarterly*, 3d ser., vol. 39, no. 4 (October 1982): 655–85.

———. *Women and the Law of Property in Early America.* Chapel Hill, N.C., 1986.

Sanders, Charles Richard. *The Cameron Plantation in Central North Carolina, 1776–1973.* Durham, N.C., 1974.

Savitt, Todd L. *Medicine and Slavery: The Diseases and Health Care of Blacks in Antebellum Virginia.* Urbana, Ill., 1978.

Scarborough, William Kauffman. *The Overseer: Plantation Management in the Old South.* Baton Rouge, La., 1966.

Schlegel, Alice, ed. *Sexual Stratification: A Cross-Cultural View.* New York, 1977.

Schlesinger, Arthur Meier. "The Rôle of Women in American History." In *New Viewpoints in American History*, 126–59. New York, 1925.

Schlissel, Lillian. *Women's Diaries of the Westward Journey.* New York, 1982.

Schmidt, Frederika Teute, and Barbara Ripel Wilhelm, eds. "Early Proslavery Petitions in Virginia." *William and Mary Quarterly*, 3d ser., vol. 30, no. 1 (January 1973): 133–46.

Schnell, J. Christopher, and Patrick E. McLear. "Why the Cities Grew: A Historiographical Essay on Western Urban Growth, 1850–1880." *Bulletin of the Missouri Historical Society* 28, no. 3 (April 1972): 162–77.

Schoolcraft, Mrs. Henry Rowe. *Plantation Life: The Narratives of Mrs. Henry Rowe Schoolcraft.* 1852–60. Reprint. New York, 1969.

Schweninger, Loren. "A Slave Family in the Ante-Bellum South." *Journal of Negro*

History 60 (January 1975): 29–44.

Scott, Anne Firor. *Making the Invisible Woman Visible*. Urbana, Ill., 1984.

———. *The Southern Lady from Pedestal to Politics, 1830–1930*. Chicago, 1970.

———. "Women's Perspective on the Patriarchy." *Journal of American History* 61 (June 1974): 52–64.

Scott, Joan W. "Gender: A Useful Category of Historical Analysis." *American Historical Review* 91, no. 5 (December 1986): 1053–75.

Scott, John Anthony. "Segregation: A Fundamental Aspect of Southern Race Relations, 1800–1860." *Journal of the Early Republic* 4, no. 4 (Winter 1984): 421–41.

Segalen, Martine. *Mari et femme dans la société paysanne*. Paris, 1980.

Seidel, Kathryn L. "The Southern Belle as an Antebellum Ideal." *Southern Quarterly* 15 (July 1977): 387–401.

Sekora, John, and Darwin T. Turner. *The Art of Slave Narrative: Original Essays in Criticism and Theory*. Macomb, Ill., 1982.

Sellers, James B. *Slavery in Alabama*. 2d ed. University, Ala., 1950.

Shafer, Robert S. "White Persons Held to Racial Slavery in Antebellum Arkansas." *Arkansas Historical Quarterly* 44, no. 2 (1985): 134–55.

Shaffer, Arthur H. "Between Two Worlds: David Ramsay and the Politics of Slavery." *Journal of Southern History* 50, no. 2 (May 1984): 175–96.

Shalhope, Robert E. "Republicanism and Early American Historiography." *William and Mary Quarterly*, 3d ser., vol. 39, no. 2 (April 1982): 334–56.

Shammas, Carole. "Black Women's Work and the Evolution of Plantation Society in Virginia." *Labor History* 26 (Winter 1985): 5–28.

———. "How Self-Sufficient Was Early America?" *Journal of Interdisciplinary History* 13, no. 2 (Autumn 1982): 247–72.

———. "The World Women Knew: Women Workers in the North of England during the Late Seventeenth Century." In *The World of William Penn*, edited by Richard S. Dunn and Mary Maples Dunn, 99–115. Philadelphia, 1986.

Shanin, Theodor. "The Nature and Logic of the Peasant Economy I: A Generalization." *Journal of Peasant Studies* 1, no. 1 (October 1973): 63–80.

Shapiro, Stephen A. "The Dark Continent of Literature: Autobiography." *Comparative Literature Studies* 5 (December 1968): 421–54.

Sharpless, John B. "The Economic Structure of Port Cities in the Mid-Nineteenth Century, Boston and Liverpool, 1840–1860." *Journal of Historical Geography* 2, no. 2 (April 1976): 131–43.

"She Hath Done What She Could," or the Duty and Responsibility of Woman: A Sermon, Preached in the Chapel of St. Mary's School, by the Rector, and Printed for the Pupils at Their Request. Raleigh, N.C., 1851.

Shepherd, James F., and Gary M. Walton. *Shipping, Maritime Trade, and the Economic Development of Colonial North America*. Cambridge, Eng., 1972.

Sheppard, Francis. *London, 1808–1870: The Infernal Wen*. Berkeley, 1971.

Sheridan, Richard B. "The Jamaican Slave Insurrection Scare of 1776 and the American Revolution." *Journal of Negro History* 61, no. 3 (July 1976): 290–309.

Shiels, Richard D. "The Feminization of American Congregationalism: 1730–1835." *American Quarterly* 33, no. 1 (Spring 1981): 46–62.

Shippee, Lester B., ed. *Bishop Whipple's Southern Diary, 1843–1844*. New York, 1968.

Shippen, Rebecca Lloyd Post, ed. "Mrs. B. I. Cohen's Fancy Dress Party, Thursday, February 2, 1837." *Maryland Historical Magazine* 14 (1919): 348–58.

Shore, Laurence. *Southern Capitalists: The Ideological Leadership of an Elite, 1832–1885*. Chapel Hill, N.C., 1986.

Showalter, Elaine. *A Literature of Their Own: British Women Novelists from Brontë to Lessing*. Princeton, N.J., 1977.

Shryock, R. H. "The Early Industrial Revolution in the Empire State." *Georgia Historical Quarterly* 11, no. 2 (June 1927): 109–28.

Sides, Sudie Duncan. "Southern Women and Slavery." *History Today* 20 (January 1970): 54–60.

———. "Women and Slaves: An Interpretation Based on the Writings of Southern Women." Ph.D. diss., University of North Carolina, 1969.

Silverblatt, Irene. *Moon, Sun, and Witches: Gender Ideologies and Class in Inca and Colonial Peru*. Princeton, N.J., 1987.

Simler, Lucy. "Tenancy in Colonial Pennsylvania: The Case of Chester County." *William and Mary Quarterly*, 3d ser., vol. 43, no. 4 (October 1986): 542–69.

Simpson, Craig. *A Good Southerner: The Life of Henry A. Wise of Virginia*. Chapel Hill, N.C., 1985.

Simpson, Lewis P. *The Brazen Face of History: Studies in the Literary Consciousness in America*. Baton Rouge, La., 1980.

———. *The Dispossessed Garden: Pastoral and History in Southern Literature*. Athens, Ga., 1975.

Sims-Wood, Janet. *The Progress of Afro-American Women: A Bibliography*. Westport, Conn., 1980.

Singleton, Theresa Ann. "The Archaeology of Afro-American Slavery in Coastal Georgia: A Regional Perception of Slave Household and Community Patterns." Ph.D. diss., University of Florida, 1980.

Sioussat, Anna. "Colonial Women of Maryland." *Maryland Historical Magazine* 2 (1907): 214–26.

Sirmans, M. Eugene. *Colonial South Carolina: A Political History, 1663–1763*. Chapel Hill, N.C., 1966.

Sitterson, J. Carlyle. "The McCollams: A Planter Family of the Old and New South." *Journal of Southern History* 6, no. 3 (August 1940): 347–67.

Sizer, Sandra S. *Gospel Hymns and Social Religion: The Rhetoric of Nineteenth-Century Revivalism*. Philadelphia, 1978.

Sklar, Kathryn Kish. *Catharine Beecher: A Study in American Domesticity*. New Haven, Conn., 1973.

———. "Hull House in the 1890s: A Community of Women Reformers." *Signs* 10, no. 4 (Summer 1985): 658–77.

Smallwood, James. "Emancipation and the Black Family: A Case Study in Texas." *Social Science Quarterly* 47, no. 4 (March 1977): 849–57.

Smedes, Susan Dabney. *A Southern Planter*. London, 1889.

Smedley, Audrey. "Women of Udu: Survival in a Harsh Land." In *Many Sisters: Women in Cross-Cultural Perspective*, edited by Carolyn J. Mattaiasson, 205–28. New York, 1974.

Smelser, Neil. *Social Change in the Industrial Revolution: An Application of Theory to the British Cotton Industry*. London, 1959.

Smiley, David L. *Lion of White Hall: The Life of Cassius M. Clay*. Madison, Wis., 1962.

Smith, Alfred Glaze, Jr. *Economic Readjustment of an Old Cotton State: South Carolina, 1820–1860*. Columbia, S.C., 1958.

Smith, Daniel Blake. *Inside the Great House: Planter Family Life in Eighteenth-Century Chesapeake Society*. Ithaca, N.Y., 1980.

Smith, Daniel Scott. "Family Limitation, Sexual Control, and Domestic Feminism in Victorian America." *Feminist Studies* 1 (Winter/Spring 1973): 40–57.

Smith, James Morton, ed. *Seventeenth-Century America: Essays in Colonial History*. Chapel Hill, N.C., 1959.

Smith, Julia Floyd. *Slavery and Plantation Growth in Antebellum Florida, 1821–1860*. Gainesville, Fla., 1973.

_____. *Slavery and Rice Culture in Low Country Georgia, 1750–1860*. Knoxville, Tenn., 1985.

Smith, Timothy L. *Revivalism and Social Reform: American Protestantism on the Eve of the Civil War*. 2d ed. Baltimore, Md., 1980.

Smith, William A. *Lectures on the Philosophy and Practice of Slavery*. 1856. Reprint. Nashville, Tenn., 1969.

Smith-Rosenberg, Carroll. "Beauty, the Beast, and the Militant Woman: A Case Study in Sex Roles and Social Stress in Jacksonian America." *American Quarterly* 23 (1971): 562–84.

_____. *Disorderly Conduct: Visions of Gender in Victorian America*. New York, 1985.

_____. "Misprisioning Pamela: Representations of Gender and Class in Nineteenth-Century America." *Michigan Quarterly Review* 26, no. 1 (Winter 1987): 9–28.

_____. *Religion and the Rise of the American City: The New York City Mission Movement, 1812–1870*. Ithaca, N.Y., 1970.

_____. "Sex as Symbol in Victorian Purity: An Ethnological Analysis of Jacksonian America." In *Turning Points: Historical and Sociological Essays on the Family*, edited by John Demos and Sandra Spence Boocock, S212–47. Chicago, 1978.

Smolensky, Eugene, and Donald Ratajczak. "The Conception of Cities." *Explorations in Entrepreneurial History*, 2d ser., vol. 2 (Winter 1965): 90–131.

Smyth, Thomas. *Mary Not a Perpetual Virgin, nor the Mother of God: But Only a Sinner Saved by Grace*. Charleston, S.C., 1846.

_____. *The Sin and the Curse: Or, the Union, the True Source of Disunion, and Our Duty in the Present Crisis*. Charleston, S.C., 1860.

Smythe, Louisa McCord. *For Old Lang Syne. Collected for My Children*. Charleston, S.C., 1900.

Sobel, Mechal. *Trabelin' On: The Slave Journey to an Afro-Baptist Faith*. Westport, Conn., 1979.

_____. *The World They Made Together: Black and White Values in Eighteenth-Century Virginia*. Princeton, N.J., 1987.

Sokoloff, Kenneth Lee. "Industrialization and the Growth of the Manufacturing Sector in the Northeast, 1820–1850." Ph.D. diss., Harvard University, 1982.

Spencer, Samia, ed. *French Women and the Age of Enlightenment*. Bloomington, Ind., 1984.

Speth, Linda. "More Than Her 'Thirds': Wives and Widows in Colonial Virginia." In *Women, Family, and Community in Colonial America: Two Perspectives,* by Linda E. Speth and Alison Duncan Hirsch, 5–41. New York, 1982.

Spruill, Julia Cherry. *Women's Life and Work in the Southern Colonies*. 2d ed. New York, 1972.

Spufford, Margaret. *Small Books and Pleasant Histories: Popular Fiction and Its Readers in Seventeenth-Century England*. Athens, Ga., 1981.

Stampp, Kenneth M. "An Analysis of T. R. Dew's *Review of the Debates in the Virginia Legislature*." *Journal of Negro History* 27, no. 4 (October 1942): 380–87.

————. *The Peculiar Institution: Slavery in the Antebellum South*. New York, 1956.

Stansell, Christine. *City of Women: Sex and Class in New York, 1789–1860*. New York, 1986.

Starling, Marion Wilson. *The Slave Narrative: Its Place in American History*. Boston, 1981.

Starobin, Robert S. "Denmark Vesey's Slave Conspiracy of 1822: A Study in Rebellion and Repression." In *American Slavery: The Question of Resistance*, edited by John Bracey, August Meier, and Elliott Rudwick, 142–58. Belmont, Calif., 1971.

————. *Industrial Slavery in the Old South*. New York, 1970.

Stavinsky, Leonard Price. "Industrialism in Ante Bellum Charleston." *Journal of Negro History* 36, no. 3 (July 1951): 302–22.

Steady, Filomina Chioma, ed. *The Black Woman Cross-Culturally*. Cambridge, Mass., 1981.

————. "The Black Woman Cross-Culturally: An Overview." In *The Black Woman Cross-Culturally*, edited by Filomina Chioma Steady, 7–41. Cambridge, Mass., 1981.

Steckel, Richard H. "Miscegenation and the American Slave Schedules." *Journal of Interdisciplinary History* 11, no. 2 (Autumn 1980): 251–63.

Stephens, Lester D. *Joseph Le Conte, Gentle Prophet of Evolution*. Baton Rouge, La., 1982.

Stephenson, Wendell Holmes. *Isaac Franklin: Slave Trader and Planter of the Old South: With Plantation Records*. Baton Rouge, La., 1938.

Stepto, Robert B. *From Behind the Veil: A Study of the Afro-American Narrative*. Urbana, Ill., 1979.

Sterkx, H. E. *Partners in Rebellion: Alabama Women in the Civil War*. Rutherford, N.J., 1970.

Sterling, Dorothy, ed. *We Are Your Sisters: Black Women in the Nineteenth Century*. New York, 1984.

Stewart, James Brewer. "'A Great Talking and Eating Machine': Patriarchy, Mobilization, and the Dynamics of Nullification in South Carolina." *Civil War History* 27 (September 1981): 197–220.

Stewart, Maria. *Productions of Mrs. Maria W. Stewart*. New York, 1835.

Stewart, Peter C. "Railroads and Urban Rivalries in Antebellum Eastern Virginia." *Virginia Magazine of History and Biography* 81, no. 1 (January 1973): 3–22.

Stigler, George. "The Division of Labor Is Limited by the Extent of the Market." *Journal of Political Economy* 59, no. 3 (June 1951): 185–93.

Stirling, James. *Letters from the Slave States*. 1857. Reprint. New York, 1969.

Stiverson, Gregory A. *Poverty in a Land of Plenty: Tenancy in Eighteenth-Century Maryland*. Baltimore, Md., 1977.

Stone, Albert E. "Identity and Art in Frederick Douglass' Narrative." *CLA Journal* 17 (1973): 192–213.

Stone, Lawrence. *The Family, Sex, and Marriage in England, 1500–1800.* New York, 1977.

Stowe, Harriet Beecher. *Uncle Tom's Cabin.* Edited by Ann Douglas. 1852. Reprint. New York, 1981.

Stowe, Steven M. "City, Country, and the Feminine Voice." In *Intellectual Life in Antebellum Charleston,* edited by Michael O'Brien and David Moltke-Hansen, 295–325. Knoxville, Tenn., 1986.

———. *Intimacy and Power in the Old South: Ritual in the Lives of the Planters.* Baltimore, Md., 1987.

———. "The Not-So-Cloistered Academy: Elite Women's Education and Family Feeling in the Old South." In *The Web of Southern Social Relations: Women, Family, and Education,* edited by Walter J. Fraser, Jr., R. Frank Saunders, Jr., and Jon L. Wakelyn, 90–106. Athens, Ga., 1985.

"Stowe's Key to Uncle Tom's Cabin." *Southern Quarterly Review* 24 (July 1853): 214–54.

Strasser, Susan. *Never Done: A History of American Housework.* New York, 1982.

Stratton, Joanna L. *Pioneer Women: Voices from the Kansas Frontier.* New York, 1981.

Strickland, Charles. *Victorian Domesticity: Families in the Life and Art of Louisa May Alcott.* University, Ala., 1985.

Stuckey, Sterling. *Slave Culture: Nationalist Theory and the Foundations of Black America.* New York, 1987.

———. "Through the Prism of Folklore: The Black Ethos of Slavery." *Massachusetts Review* 9, no. 3 (Summer 1968): 417–37.

Sudarkasa, Niara. "African and Afro-American Family Organization." In *Anthropology for the Eighties: Introductory Readings,* edited by Johnetta B. Cole, 132–60. New York, 1982.

———. "Interpreting the African Heritage in Afro-American Family Organization." In *Black Families,* edited by Harriette Pipes McAdoo, 37–53. Beverly Hills, Calif., 1981.

———. "'The Status of Women' in Indigenous African Societies." *Feminist Studies* 12, no. 1 (Spring 1986): 91–104.

Sutherland, Daniel E. *Americans and Their Servants: Domestic Service in the United States from 1800 to 1920.* Baton Rouge, La., 1981.

Swados, Felice. "Negro Health on the Ante Bellum Plantations." *Bulletin of the History of Medicine* 10 (1941): 460–72.

Sweet, Leonard I. *The Minister's Wife: Her Role in Nineteenth-Century Evangelicalism.* Philadelphia, 1982.

Sydnor, Charles S. *A Gentleman of the Old Natchez Region: Benjamin L. C. Wailes.* Durham, N.C., 1938.

———. *Slavery in Mississippi.* 1933. Reprint. Gloucester, Mass., 1965.

Syrett, Harold C., ed. *The Papers of Alexander Hamilton.* 26 vols. New York, 1961–79.

Tait, David. "The Family, Household, and Minor Lineage of the Konkomba." *Africa* 26, no. 3 (July 1956): 219–49.

Takaki, Ronald T. *A Proslavery Crusade: The Agitation to Reopen the African Slave Trade.* New York, 1971.

Tandy, Jeanette Reid. "Pro-Slavery Propaganda in American Fiction of the Fifties." *South Atlantic Quarterly* 21 (January 1922): 41–50.

Tannenbaum, Frank. *Slave and Citizen: The Negro in the Americas.* New York, 1946.

Tate, Thad W., and David L. Ammerman, eds. *The Chesapeake in the Seventeenth Century: Essays on Anglo-American Society.* Chapel Hill, N.C., 1979.

Taves, Ann. "Spiritual Purity and Sexual Shame: Religious Themes in the Writings of Harriet Jacobs." *Church History* 56, no. 1 (March 1987): 59–72.

Tax, Meredith. *The Rising of the Women: Feminist Solidarity and Class Conflict, 1880–1917.* New York, 1980.

Taylor, A. Elizabeth. "Revival and Development of the Woman Suffrage Movement in Georgia." *Georgia Historical Quarterly* 42 (December 1974): 339–54.

Taylor, George Rogers. *The Transportation Revolution, 1815–1860.* New York, 1951.

Taylor, Joe Gray. *Negro Slavery in Louisiana.* Baton Rouge, La., 1963.

Taylor, Rosser H. *Ante-bellum South Carolina: A Social and Cultural History.* Chapel Hill, N.C., 1942.

Taylor, William R. *Cavalier and Yankee: The Old South and American National Character.* New York, 1961.

Teitelbaum, Michael S., ed. *Sex Differences: Social and Biological Perspectives.* Garden City, N.Y., 1976.

Tentler, Leslie Woodcock. *Wage-Earning Women: Industrial Work and Family Life in the United States, 1900–1930.* New York, 1979.

Terborg-Penn, Rosalyn. "Black Women in Resistance: A Cross-Cultural Perspective." In *In Resistance: Studies in African, Caribbean, and Afro-American History*, edited by Gary Y. Okihiro, 188–209. Amherst, Mass., 1986.

———. "Discrimination against Afro-American Women in the Woman's Movement, 1830–1920." In *The Afro-American Woman: Struggles and Images*, edited by Sharon Harley and Rosalyn Terborg-Penn, 28–42. Port Washington, N.Y., 1978.

Terhune, Mary V. H. *Marion Harland's Autobiography.* 1910. Reprint. New York, 1980.

Thirsk, Joan, ed. *The Agrarian History of England and Wales.* Vol. 4, *1500–1640*; vol 5, *1640–1750*. Cambridge, Eng., 1967, 1985.

Thomas, Charles E. "The Diary of Anna Hasell Thomas." *South Carolina Historical Magazine* 74 (1973): 128–43.

Thomis, Malcom I., and Jennifer Grimmet. *Women in Protest.* New York, 1983.

Thompson, Ernest Trice. *Presbyterians in the South.* 3 vols. Richmond, Va., 1963–73.

Thornton, J. Mills, III. *Politics and Power in a Slave Society: Alabama, 1800–1860.* Baton Rouge, La., 1978.

Thorp, Margaret Farrand. *Female Persuasion: Six Strong-Minded Women.* New Haven, Conn., 1949.

Tise, Larry E. *Proslavery: A History of the Defense of Slavery in America, 1701–1840.* Athens, Ga., 1987.

Tompkins, Jane P. *Reader-Response Criticism: From Formalism to Post-Structuralism.* Baltimore, Md., 1980.

_____. *Sensational Designs: The Cultural Work of American Fiction, 1790–1860*. New York, 1985.

Tönnies, Frederic. *Gemeinschaft und Gesellschaft, Grundbegriffe der Reinen-Soziologie*. 8th ed. Leipzig, 1935.

Torrence, Clayton, ed. "Letters of Mrs. Ann (Jennings) Wise to Her Husband, Henry A. Wise." *Virginia Magazine of History and Biography* 58, no. 4 (October 1950): 492–515.

_____. "A Virginia Lady of Quality and Her Possessions." *Virginia Magazine of History and Biography* 56, no. 1 (January 1948): 42–56.

Touchstone, Donald Blake. "Planters and Slave Religion in the Deep South." Ph.D. diss., Tulane University, 1973.

Tragle, Henry Irving, comp. *The Southampton Slave Revolts of 1831: A Compilation of Source Material*. Amherst, Mass., 1971.

Treckel, Paula Ann. "English Women on Seventeenth Century American Frontiers." Ph.D. diss., Syracuse University, 1978.

_____. "Women in Early Virginia." Paper presented at the Citadel Conference on the History of the South, Charleston, S.C., 1987.

Trollope, Frances. *Domestic Manners of the Americans*. 1832. Reprint. Gloucester, Mass., 1974.

Truedly, Mary Bosworth. "The 'Benevolent Fair': A Study of Charitable Organization among American Women in the First Third of the Nineteenth Century." *Social Service Review* 14 (September 1940): 509–22.

Trumbach, Randolph. *The Rise of the Egalitarian Family: Aristocratic Kinship and Domestic Relations in Eighteenth-Century England*. New York, 1978.

Tryon, Rolla Milton. *Household Manufactures in the United States, 1640–1860*. 1917. Reprint. New York, 1966.

Tucker, George. *Progress of the United States in Population and Wealth in Fifty Years, as Exhibited by the Decennial Census from 1790 to 1840*. 1855. Reprint. New York, 1964.

Tucker, N. Beverley. *A Series of Lectures on the Science of Government, Intended to Prepare the Student for the Study of the Constitution of the United States*. Philadelphia, 1845.

Tuelon, Alan. "Nanny—Maroon Chieftainess." *Caribbean Quarterly* 19 (December 1973): 20–27.

Turner, Charles W., ed. *An Old Field School Teacher's Diary*. Verona, Va., 1975.

Turner, Frederick Jackson. *The United States, 1830–1850: The Nation and Its Sections*. New York, 1935.

Turrentine, Samuel Bryant. *A Romance of Education: A Narrative Including Recollections and Other Facts Connected with Greensboro College*. Greensboro, N.C., 1946.

Tushnet, Mark V. *The American Law of Slavery, 1810–1860: Considerations of Humanity and Interest*. Princeton, N.J., 1981.

Twelve Southerners. *I'll Take My Stand: The South and the Agrarian Tradition*. New York, 1930.

Tyrrell, Ian R. "Women and Temperance in Antebellum America, 1830–1860." *Civil War History* 28, no. 2 (June 1982): 128–52.

Uchendu, Victor C. "Concubinage among Ngwa Igbo of Southern Nigeria." *Africa* 30, no. 2 (April 1965): 187–97.

Ulmer, Barbara. "Benevolence in Colonial Charleston." In *Proceedings of the South Carolina Historical Association*, edited by William S. Brockington, Jr., and W. Calvin Smith, 1–12. Columbia, S.C., 1980.

Ulrich, Laurel Thatcher. *Good Wives: Image and Reality in the Lives of Women in Northern New England, 1650–1750*. New York, 1982.

United States. Bureau of the Census. *Historical Statistics of the United States, Colonial Times to 1970, Bicentennial Edition*. Washington, D.C., 1975.

————. *1980 Census of Population*. Vol. 1, *Characteristics of the Population*. Washington, D.C., 1983.

Urdang, Stephanie. *Fighting Two Colonialisms: Women in Guinea-Bissau*. New York, 1979.

Usner, Daniel H., Jr., "The Frontier Exchange Economy of the Lower Mississippi Valley in the Eighteenth Century." *William and Mary Quarterly*, 3d ser., vol. 44, no. 2 (April 1987): 165–92.

Van Allen, Judith. "'Aba Riots' or Igbo 'Women's War'? Ideology, Stratification, and the Invisibility of Women." In *Women in Africa: Studies in Social and Economic Change*, edited by Nancy J. Hafkin and Edna G. Bay, 59–85. Stanford, Calif., 1976.

————. "'Sitting on a Man': Colonialism and the Lost Political Institutions of Igbo Women." *Canadian Journal of African Studies* 6, no. 2 (1972): 165–81.

Van Deburg, William L. *The Slave Drivers: Black Agricultural Labor Supervisors in the Antebellum South*. Westport, Conn., 1979.

Van Ness, James S. "On Untieing the Knot: The Maryland Legislature and Divorce Petitions." *Maryland Historical Magazine* 67, no. 2 (Summer 1942): 171–75.

Van Zandt, A. B. *"The Elect Lady," a Memoir of Mrs. Susan Catherine Bott of Petersburg, Va.* Philadelphia, 1857.

Verlinden, Charles. *The Beginnings of Modern Colonization*. Translated by Yvonne Freccero. Ithaca, N.Y., 1970.

Ver Steeg, Clarence L. *Origins of a Southern Mosaic: Studies of Early Carolina and Georgia*. Athens, Ga., 1975.

Vigier, François. *Change and Apathy: Liverpool and Manchester during the Industrial Revolution*. Cambridge, Mass., 1970.

Vinovskis, Maris A. *The Origins of Public High Schools: A Reexamination of the Beverly School Controversy*. Madison, Wis., 1985.

W. "Mrs. Dana's Letters." *Southern Quarterly Review* 11 (January 1847): 168–98.

Wade, John Donald. *Augustus Baldwin Longstreet: A Study of the Development of Culture in the South*. New York, 1924.

Wade, Richard C. *Slavery in the Cities: The South, 1820–1860*. New York, 1964.

————. *The Urban Frontier: The Rise of Western Cities, 1790–1830*. Cambridge, Mass., 1959.

————. "The Vesey Plot: A Reconsideration." *Journal of Southern History* 30 (May 1964): 143–61.

Wade-Gayles, Gloria. "Black Women Journalists in the South, 1880–1905: An Approach to the Study of Black Women's History." *Callaloo* 4 (February/October 1981): 138–52.

Wall, Allie Patricia. "The Letters of Mary Boykin Chesnut." M.A. thesis, University of South Carolina, 1977.

Wallace, Anthony F. C. *Rockdale: The Growth of an American Village in the Early Industrial Revolution.* New York, 1978.

Wallenstein, Peter. *From Slave South to New South: Public Policy in Nineteenth-Century Georgia.* Chapel Hill, N.C., 1987.

Wallerstein, Immanuel. *The Modern World System.* 2 vols. New York, 1974–80.

Walters, Ronald G. *American Reformers 1815–1860.* New York, 1978.

————. "The Erotic South: Civilization and Sexuality in American Abolitionism." *American Quarterly* 25, no. 2 (May 1973): 177–201.

Wandersee, Winifred. *Women's Work and Family Values, 1920–1940.* Cambridge, Mass., 1981.

Ward, David. "The Early Victorian City in England and America: On the Parallel Development of an Urban Image." In *European Settlement and Development in North America: Essays on Geographical Change in Honour and Memory of Andrew Hill Clark,* edited by James R. Gibson, 170–89. Toronto, 1978.

Ward, James. A. "A New Look at Antebellum Southern Railroad Development." *Journal of Southern History* 39, no. 3 (August 1973): 409–20.

Ware, Susan. *Beyond Suffrage: Women in the New Deal.* Cambridge, Mass., 1981.

Warner, Susan. *The Wide, Wide World.* 1850. Reprint. New York, 1987.

Washington, Henry Augustine. "The Social System of Virginia." In *All Clever Men Who Make Their Way: Critical Discourse in the Old South,* edited by Michael O'Brien, 228–62. Fayetteville, Ark., 1982.

Waters, John J. "Patrimony, Succession, and Social Stability: Guilford, Connecticut in the Eighteenth Century." *Perspectives in American History* 10 (1976): 131–60.

————. "The Traditional World of the New England Peasants: A View from Seventeenth-Century Barnstable." *The New England Historical and Genealogical Register* 130, no. 1 (January 1976): 3–21.

Watson, Alan D. "Women in Colonial North Carolina: Overlooked and Underestimated." *North Carolina Historical Review* 58 (Winter 1981): 1–22.

Watts, Steven. "Masks, Morals, and the Market: American Literature and Early Capitalist Culture, 1790–1820." *Journal of the Early Republic* 6, no. 2 (Summer 1986): 127–49.

Wax, Darold D. "Negro Resistance to the Early American Slave Trade." *Journal of Negro History* 51 (January 1966): 1–15.

Weaver, Herbert. *Mississippi Farmers, 1850–1860.* Nashville, Tenn., 1945.

Weaver, Richard M. *The Southern Tradition at Bay: A History of Postbellum Thought.* Edited by George Core and M. E. Bradford. New Rochelle, N.Y., 1968.

Webb, Allie Bayne Windham, ed. *Mistress of Evergreen Plantation: Rachel O'Connor's Legacy of Letters, 1823–1845.* Albany, N.Y., 1983.

Weber, Adna Ferrin. *The Growth of Cities in the Nineteenth Century: A Study in Statistics.* New York, 1899.

Webre, Stephen. "The Problem of Indian Slavery in Spanish Louisiana, 1769–1803." *Louisiana History* 25, no. 2 (1984): 117–35.

"Wedding Menu, 1856." *South Carolina Historical Magazine* 64 (1963): 202.

Weiman, David F. "Farmers and the Market in Antebellum America: A View from the Georgia Upcountry." *Journal of Economic History* 47, no. 3 (September 1987): 627–47.

———. "Petty Commodity Production in the Cotton South: Upcountry Farmers in the Georgia Cotton Economy, 1840 to 1880." Ph.D. diss., Stanford University, 1984.

———. "Slavery, Plantation Settlement, and Regional Development in the Antebellum Cotton South." Paper delivered at the annual meeting of the Economic History Association, New York, September 1985.

Weiner, Marli Frances. "Plantation Mistress/Female Slave: Gender, Race, and South Carolina Women, 1830–1880." Ph.D. diss., University of Rochester, 1985.

Weir, Robert M. *Colonial South Carolina: A History*. Millwood, N.Y., 1983.

Weld, Theodore. *American Slavery as It Is: Testimony of a Thousand Witnesses*. New York, 1839.

———. *The Bible against Slavery: Or, an Inquiry into the Genius of the Mosaic System and the Teachings of the Old Testament on the Subject of Human Rights*. 1864. Reprint. Detroit, 1970.

Wellman, Judith. "Women and Radical Reform in Antebellum Upstate New York: A Profile of Grassroots Female Abolitionists." In *Clio Was a Woman: Studies in the History of American Women*, edited by Mabel E. Deutrich and Virginia C. Purdy, 113–27. Washington, D.C., 1980.

Welter, Barbara. "The Cult of True Womanhood: 1800–1860." *American Quarterly* 18 (1966): 151–74.

———. *Dimity Convictions: The American Woman in the Nineteenth Century*. Athens, Ohio, 1976.

Wenhold, Lucy Leinbach. "The Salem Boarding School between 1802 and 1822." *North Carolina Historical Review* 27, no. 1 (January 1950): 32–45.

Wertenbaker, Thomas J. *Norfolk: Historic Southern Port*. 2d ed. Edited by Marvin W. Schlegel. Durham, N.C., 1962.

Wertheimer, Barbara Mayer. *We Were There: The Story of Working Women in America*. New York, 1977.

Westbury, Susan. "Slaves of Colonial Virginia: Where They Came From." *William and Mary Quarterly*, 3d ser., vol. 42, no. 2 (April 1985): 228–37.

Wheaton, Henry. *Some Account of the Life, Writings, and Speeches of William Pinkney*. Baltimore, Md., 1826.

White, Deborah Gray. "Ain't I a Woman? Female Slaves in the Antebellum South." Ph.D. diss., University of Illinois at Chicago, 1979.

———. *Ar'n't I a Woman? Female Slaves in the Plantation South*. New York, 1985.

———. "Female Slaves: Sex Roles and Status in the Antebellum Plantation South." *Journal of Family History* 8, no. 3 (Fall 1983): 248–61.

White, Mary Culler. *The Portal of Wonderland: The Life-Story of Alice Culler Cobb*. New York, 1925.

Whitman, Clifford Dale, ed. "Private Journal of Mary Ann Owen Sims." *Arkansas Historical Quarterly* 35, nos. 2, 3 (Summer, Fall 1976): 142–87, 261–91.

Whyte, Martin K. *The Status of Women in Preindustrial Societies*. Princeton, N.J., 1978.

Wiener, Jonathan M. "Female Planters and Planters' Wives in Civil War and Reconstruction Alabama, 1850–1870." *Alabama Review* 30, no. 2 (April 1977): 135–49.

Wilentz, Sean. *Chants Democratic: New York City and the Rise of the American Working Class, 1788–1850*. New York, 1984.

Wiley, Bell Irvin. "The Movement to Humanize the Institution of Slavery during the Confederacy." *Emory University Quarterly* 5 (December 1949): 207–20.
———. *Southern Negroes, 1861–1866.* 1938. Reprint. New Haven, Conn., 1965.
Willan, T. S. *Elizabethan Manchester.* Manchester, Eng., 1980.
Williams, David. *The Rebecca Riots: A Study in Agrarian Discontent.* Cardiff, Wales, 1955.
Williams, James. *Narrative of James Williams, an American Slave, Who Was for Several Years a Driver on a Cotton Plantation in Alabama.* Philadelphia, 1969.
Williams, Joseph J. *The Maroons of Jamaica.* Anthropological Series of the Boston College Graduate School, vol. 3, no. 4. Chesnut Hill, Mass., 1938.
Williams, Raymond. *The Country and the City.* New York, 1973.
Williamson, Jeffrey G. "Urbanization in the American Northeast, 1820–1870." In *The Reinterpretation of American History,* edited by Robert W. Fogel and Stanley L. Engerman, 426–36. New York, 1971.
Williamson, Jeffrey G., and Joseph A. Swanson. "The Growth of Cities in the American Northeast, 1820–1870." *Explorations in Entrepreneurial History,* 2d ser., vol. 4, no. 1, suppl. (1966): 3–101.
Wilson, Charles Reagan. *Baptized in Blood: The Religion of the Lost Cause, 1865–1920.* Athens, Ga., 1980.
Wilson, Harriet E. *Our Nig: Or, Sketches from the Life of a Free Black.* Edited by Henry Louis Gates, Jr. New York, 1983.
Wilson, Joan Hoff. "The Illusion of Change: Women and the American Revolution." In *The American Revolution: Explorations in the History of American Radicalism,* edited by Alfred F. Young, 383–445. DeKalb, Ill., 1976.
Wilson, W. Emerson, ed. *Plantation Life at Rose Hill: The Diaries of Martha Ogle Forman, 1814–1845.* Wilmington, Del., 1976.
Wiltse, Charles M. *John C. Calhoun: Nationalist, 1782–1822.* Indianapolis, Ind., 1944.
———. *John C. Calhoun: Nullifier, 1829–1839.* Indianapolis, Ind., 1949.
Windley, Lathan A. "Flight and Rebellion: A Case of Hyperbolic Exaggeration." *Negro History Bulletin* 41, no. 5 (1978): 895.
———. *Runaway Slave Advertisements: A Documentary History from the 1730s to 1790.* 4 vols. Westport, Conn., 1983.
Winsborough, Hallie Paxson. *The Woman's Auxiliary Presbyterian Church, U.S.: A Brief History of Its Background, Organization, and Development.* Richmond, Va., n.d.
Wirth, John D., and Robert L. Jones, eds. *Manchester and Sao Paulo: Problems of Rapid Urban Growth.* Stanford, Calif., 1978.
Wish, Harvey. "American Slave Insurrections before 1861." *Journal of Negro History* 22 (July 1937): 299–320.
Wolfe, Margaret Ripley. "The Southern Lady: Long Suffering Counterpart of the Good Ole' Boy." *Journal of Popular Culture* 11, no. 1 (Summer 1977): 18–27.
"Women Physiologically Considered." *Southern Quarterly Review* 2 (October 1842): 279–311.
Wood, Betty. *Slavery in Colonial Georgia, 1730–1775.* Athens, Ga., 1984.
———. "Some Aspects of Female Slave Resistance to Chattel Slavery in the Georgia Low Country, 1736–1815." Paper delivered at the annual meeting of the Society for the History of the Early Republic, Knoxville, Tenn., July 1986.

_____. "'Until You Are Dead, Dead, Dead': The Judicial Treatment of Slaves in Eighteenth-Century Georgia." Paper presented at the annual meeting of the Georgia Association of Historians, Milledgeville, Ga., April 1987.

Wood, Peter H. *Black Majority: Negroes in Colonial South Carolina from 1670 through the Stono Rebellion*. New York, 1974.

_____. "'The Dream Deferred': Black Freedom Struggles on the Eve of White Independence." In *In Resistance: Studies in African, Caribbean, and Afro-American History*, edited by Gary Y. Okihiro, 166–87. Amherst, Mass., 1986.

_____. "'Taking Care of Business' in Revolutionary South Carolina: Republicanism and the Slave Society." In *The Southern Experience in the American Revolution*, edited by Jeffrey J. Crow and Larry E. Tise, 268–93. Chapel Hill, N.C., 1978.

Woodman, Harold D. "Economic History and Economic Theory: The New Economic History in America." *Journal of Interdisciplinary History* 3, no. 2 (August 1972): 323–50.

_____. *King Cotton and His Retainers: Financing and Marketing the Cotton Crop of the South, 1800–1925*. Lexington, Ky., 1968.

Woodward, C. Vann. "History from Slave Sources." *American Historical Review* 79, no. 2 (April 1974): 470–81.

_____, ed. *Mary Chesnut's Civil War*. New Haven, Conn., 1981.

Woodward, C. Vann, and Elisabeth Muhlenfeld, eds. *The Private Mary Chesnut: The Unpublished Civil War Diaries*. New York, 1984.

Woody, Thomas. *A History of Women's Education in the United States*. 2 vols. 1909. Reprint. New York, 1966.

Works Progress Administration. *The Negro in Virginia*. 1940. Reprint. New York, 1969.

Wright, Mrs. D. Giraud. *A Southern Girl in '61: The War-Time Memories of a Confederate Senator's Daughter*. New York, 1905.

Wright, Gavin. "Agriculture in the South." In *Encyclopedia of American Economic History*, edited by Glen Porter, 371–85. New York, 1980.

_____. *Old South, New South: Revolutions in the Southern Economy since the Civil War*. New York, 1986.

_____. *The Political Economy of the Cotton South: Households, Markets, and Wealth in the Nineteenth Century*. New York, 1978.

Wrigley, E. A. "A Simple Model of London's Importance in Changing English Society and Economy, 1650–1770." In *Aristocratic Government and Society in Eighteenth Century England: The Foundations of Stability*, edited by Daniel A. Baugh, 62–95. New York, 1974.

Wyatt-Brown, Bertram. "The Ideal Typology and Antebellum Southern History: A Testing of a New Hypothesis." *Societas* 5 (1975): 1–29.

_____. *Southern Honor: Ethics and Behavior in the Old South*. New York, 1982.

Yans-McLaughlin, Virginia. *Family and Community: Italian Immigrants in Buffalo, 1880–1930*. Ithaca, N.Y., 1977.

Yellin, Jean Fagan. "Texts and Contexts of Harriet Jacobs' *Incidents in the Life of a Slave Girl: Written by Herself*." In *The Slave's Narrative*, edited by Charles T. Davis and Henry Louis Gates, Jr., 262–82. New York, 1985.

_____. "Written by Herself: Harriet Jacobs' Slave Narrative." *American Literature* 53, no. 3 (November 1981): 479–86.

Yerby, William E. W., and Mabel Yerby Lawson. *History of Greensboro, Alabama, from Its Earliest Settlement.* Northport, Ala., 1963.

Yetman, Norman R. "The Background of the Slave Narrative Collection." *American Quarterly* 19, no. 3 (Fall 1967): 534–53.

_____, ed. *Life under the "Peculiar Institution": Selections from the Slave Narrative Collection.* New York, 1970.

Zuckerman, Michael. *Peaceable Kingdoms: New England Towns in the Eighteenth Century.* New York, 1970.

_____. "William Byrd's Family." *Perspectives in American History* 12 (1979): 255–311.

Index